THE COMPLETE
MAISKY
DIARIES

VOLUME 1

THE RISE OF HITLER AND
THE GATHERING CLOUDS OF WAR
1932–1938

EDITED BY GABRIEL GORODETSKY

Translated by Tatiana Sorokina and Oliver Ready

Yale UNIVERSITY PRESS
NEW HAVEN AND LONDON

Published with the permission of the Scheffer-Voskressenski family—Ivan Maisky's heirs. Photographs from Agniya Maisky's album are published with the permission of the Voskressenski family, owners of the copyright and Ivan Maisky's heirs.

Yale University Press books may be purchased in quantity for educational, business, or promotional use. For information, please e-mail sales.press@yale.edu (U.S. office) or sales@yaleup.co.uk (U.K. office).

Set in Minion Pro and ITC Stone Sans type by Newgen.
Printed in the United States of America.

Library of Congress Control Number: 2017942542
ISBN 978-0-300-11782-0 (hardcover : alk. paper)

A catalogue record for this book is available from the British Library.

This paper meets the requirements of ANSI/NISO Z39.48-1992 (Permanence of Paper).

10 9 8 7 6 5 4 3 2 1

Annals of Communism

Each volume in the series Annals of Communism will publish selected and previously inaccessible documents from former Soviet state and party archives in a narrative that develops a particular topic in the history of Soviet and international communism. Separate English and Russian editions will be prepared. Russian and Western scholars work together to prepare the documents for each volume. Documents are chosen not for their support of any single interpretation but for their particular historical importance or their general value in deepening understanding and facilitating discussion. The volumes are designed to be useful to students, scholars, and interested general readers.

Yale University Press gratefully acknowledges the financial support given for this publication by the John M. Olin Foundation, the Lynde and Harry Bradley Foundation, the Historical Research Foundation, Roger Milliken, the Rosentiel Foundation, Lloyd H. Smith, Keith Young, the William H. Donner Foundation, Joseph W. Donner, Jeremiah Milbank, the David Woods Kemper Memorial Foundation, and the Smith Richardson Foundation.

Contents

Acknowledgements

This diary is published with the permission of the Scheffer-Voskressenski family – Ivan Maisky's heirs. I am most grateful for their cooperation and assistance in its preparation. I should also like to thank the Russian Foreign Ministry, the custodians of the Maisky diaries, for allowing me access to the original diaries, and for their help with archival sources and photographs. Particular thanks are due to Tel Aviv University for the generous grant towards the costs of the translation of the diary into English.

Few publishers today would enthusiastically embrace a project which involves the publication of three large volumes of a heavily annotated diary. I am therefore indebted to Jonathan Brent, former director of the 'Annals of Communism Series' at Yale University Press, for recognizing the tremendous significance of the diary and for commissioning its publication. My friends, Paul Kennedy and Niall Ferguson, spared no effort in making sure the rare document saw the light of day. I am particularly grateful to John Donatich, the director of YUP, for his continued faith in the project and unstinting support. Jaya Chatterjee, my editor at the press, efficiently and in masterly fashion oversaw the production of the very complex three-volume edition.

This is the fruit of more than fifteen years of extensive research. I was most fortunate to profit from a series of generous fellowships at the Institute for Advanced Study at Princeton, the Institute for Advanced Study at Freiburg and the Rockefeller Research Center at Bellagio. They provided most conducive conditions for pursuing my work and fertile ground for testing and sharing my ideas with leading fellow historians. The lion's share of my work, however, was done under the auspices of All Souls College, Oxford. It was Isaiah Berlin, a legendary fellow of the college, who first introduced me to Oxford in 1969 and encouraged me to write my dissertation there, and the circle was miraculously completed when I was first offered a visiting fellowship at the college in 2006 and then subsequently elected as a fellow. I can hardly find the proper words to describe the friendships I have forged at All Souls, and the challenging yet congenial environment I have encountered at the college – undoubtedly a guardian of scholarship in its purest form. Sir John Vickers, warden of the college, and the former warden John Davis made me feel at home and spared no effort in providing me with the utmost assistance and encouragement.

I was extremely fortunate to have Tatiana Sorokina and Oliver Ready as translators of the diary. Their combined efforts have produced a meticulous and elegant translation that is convincingly idiomatic, yet faithful to Maisky's unique literary prose. I was equally fortunate to have Clive Liddiard as my copyeditor. His succinct yet wise and punctilious interventions improved the text considerably, as did his command of the Russian language and familiarity with Slavic and East European cultures.

The staffs of the National Archives in London and Washington, as well as those of the State Archives in Moscow, were most responsive to my queries and helpful in producing relevant material for my research. Likewise, I am grateful to the dedicated archivists of the scores of collections of private papers which I consulted. They were all most responsive and enthusiastic about the diary and did their utmost to supplement it with precious material.

Special appreciation is due to Hillel Adler, who initially helped me set up a most sophisticated database which allowed us to tame and master a voluminous body of archival sources. Dr Ruth Brown was as helpful in assisting me to set up the glossary of more than a thousand people mentioned in the diary. Dr James Womack produced some exquisite translations from the Russian of various letters in Maisky's private archives.

Finally, Ruth Herz, my wife, friend and companion, would be the first to admit that rather than a burden in our life, the years spent with Maisky represented a fascinating joint journey.

The quintessential Maisky – putting pen to paper.

Introduction

The unique and fascinating diary of Ivan Mikhailovich Maisky, Soviet ambassador to London from 1932 to 1943, is one of the few diaries kept by a Soviet dignitary in the 1930s and during the Second World War.[1] Stalin discouraged his entourage from putting pen to paper, and would not allow notes to be taken during meetings at the Kremlin. Keeping a diary, we are reminded, was 'a risky undertaking when people scared to death were burning papers and archives. Diaries were particularly vulnerable, sought after by the police when they searched the dwellings of suspected "enemies of the people".'[2] Indeed, Maisky's journals were eventually seized by the Ministry for State Security, together with his vast personal archive, following his arrest in February 1953 (two weeks before Stalin's death) on accusations of spying for Britain.[3] Pardoned in 1955, Maisky led a protracted – yet ultimately futile – campaign to retrieve them. His pleas were turned down by the Ministry for Foreign Affairs on the grounds that the diary 'contained various official materials'. He was given only one year of limited access to it while he wrote his memoirs, but was denied access to any other archival sources.[4] The diary remained inaccessible to researchers for decades.

Serendipity often lies at the heart of scholarly discoveries. In 1993, under the aegis of both the Israeli and the Soviet foreign ministries, I launched a research project which culminated in the joint official publication of documents on Israeli–Soviet relations. It is hard to describe my excitement when, while seeking information on Maisky's involvement in the Soviet decision to support the partition plan for Palestine in 1947, the archivist at the Russian Foreign Ministry emerged from the stacks with Maisky's voluminous diary for the eventful year of 1941. No personal document of such breadth, value and size had before emerged from the Soviet archives to throw fresh light on the Second World War and its origins. Flipping through the volume, I was struck by its immediacy and frankness, by Maisky's astute and penetrating insights, and by his superb prose. It emerged that the diary comprises over half a million words, minutely and candidly depicting the observations, activities and conversations of the ubiquitous Soviet ambassador in London. Maisky typed his daily impressions in the evening, though there are also handwritten entries (remarkably, some of which are missing from the Russian edition) which were often written away from the scrutinizing 'oeil de Moscou' within his office at the embassy. Examples of this are the report of his conversation with Eden on 10 June 1941, concerning rumours of a possible German offensive against Russia, and his appraisal of a possible Anglo-German agreement in the wake of the flight of Rudolf Hess, Hitler's deputy, to Scotland in May 1941.

Appreciative of the distinctive value of the diary, Yale University Press generously agreed to publish the entire diary, with my extensive commentary, in three volumes. An abridged version has already appeared, containing about 25 per cent of the original diary, but stripped of the vast referential apparatus which is available here. Only a couple of entries, which were repetitive or technical in nature, have been excluded. Any abridgements are indicated by an initial space followed by ellipsis and a subsequent space. Wherever Maisky himself uses ellipsis, there is no initial space. When Maisky employs a word (or phrase) in English, that word appears in *italics* (editorial conventions also dictate that italics are used for such things as the names of newspapers or ships); whenever Maisky underlines a phrase for emphasis, an <u>underscore</u> is used here. The process of having the diaries declassified and then published in Russia (a legal prerequisite for any publication of such documents in the West) was long and arduous. The editorial work on the Russian edition was shared between the Institute of General History of the Russian Academy of Sciences, under the guidance of its director Alexander Oganovich Chubarian, and Vitaly Yurevich Afiani, director of the Archives of the Russian Academy of Sciences, which houses Maisky's vast personal archives. I am much indebted to both for their cooperation. Their competent edition nonetheless conveys a strong official aplomb and tends to uphold the traditional Russian historiography of the events leading up to the Second World War, as if oblivious to the now freshly available Soviet archival sources, not to mention the vast Western archival sources and research literature.

The commentary and annotations in the present volume bear no resemblance to those in the Russian edition. The obvious temptation was to reduce any editorial intervention to the minimum and allow Maisky to tell his own tale. However, a detailed contextual commentary seemed indispensable, considering the ruthless conditions under which Maisky kept his diary – forcing him to leave many blank spots in the otherwise rich and informative account – when the storm battered the gates of his own embassy. Fearful and concerned that the diary might be confiscated and denied to future generations, Maisky in fact kept at least three copies of it. The atmosphere turned so oppressive that, shortly before accompanying Eden to Moscow in December 1941, he sent one copy of the earlier part of the diary to Stalin, in what appears to have been an attempt to forestall possible arrest.[5] The commentary is therefore by no means confined to the common practice of providing the reader with the basic auxiliary tools. The editorial work inevitably required a reconstruction of the gaps and missing dimensions in the diary, as well as unfolding its historical context. This called for thorough archival research of both Russian and Western archives. Maisky's entries were juxtaposed with the voluminous correspondence in his private archives (which I unearthed in Moscow), as well as with the telegrams he sent to the Soviet Foreign Ministry (Narkomindel), and the reports by his interlocutors of their meetings. I was also privileged to gain access to Maisky's personal photo albums: some of the images (many of which reflect the events described in the diary) are reproduced here. They often convey what thousands of words fail to do. I am most grateful to Dr Alexei D. Voskressenski, Maisky's great-nephew and heir, for allowing me to share with readers Maisky's incredibly personal, and at times intimate, gaze.

The publication of Maisky's diary conforms to the new approach in Russian history, which focuses on 'Soviet subjectivity' in the Stalin era.[6] This diary, however, is not the typical Soviet diary, a vehicle to 'self-perfection', which was encouraged by the regime as a means of political education and transformation. It is a personal diary, which would have been classified by the Soviet authorities as 'inherently bourgeois', revolving as it does largely around the theme of the self, rather than being a self-critical effort to become a good communist. It is a testament to the pivotal role which personal friendships, conflicts and rivalries played in early Soviet politics, transcending controversies over policy and ideology. It confirms that Soviet society and politics cannot be appropriately described without resorting to the human factor which exposes the unknown personal bonds. While Maisky's commitment to communism is manifestly proclaimed, he is fully immersed in the tradition of diary writing among the Western 'bourgeois' intelligentsia. In fact, regardless of the obvious cultural differences, it resembles Pepys's diary in its astute observation of the British political and social scene, spiced with anecdotes and gossip. Like Churchill, Maisky surprisingly hails the role of 'great men' in history. He further acknowledges the uniqueness of events, rather than following the Marxist interpretation, which subsumes the individual into larger social patterns. Most telling is the recurrent noncommittal statement in the diary: 'let us wait and see' – a powerful recognition of the dynamics of history, which is occasionally punctured by a determinist view of the inevitable success of the socialist revolutionary movement, though the timing and nature of the revolution always remain very distant and vague. Far from dismissing 'the "personal contribution" to the great general cause', Maisky openly argued in a letter to Georgii Chicherin, the commissar for foreign affairs, that one could 'scarcely deny that "personality" plays or can play a certain role in history. At times, even not a minor one.' It was 'enough to remember,' he reminded him 'what Ilich[7] meant for our revolution'.[8] He had little doubt as to his own central role in shaping history. Describing a crucial meeting with Churchill in September 1941, when the fate of Moscow hung in the air, he wrote:

> I left home a quarter of an hour before the appointed time. The moon shone brightly. Fantastically shaped clouds raced from west to east. When they blotted the moon and their edges were touched with red and black, the whole picture appeared gloomy and ominous. As if the world was on the eve of its destruction. I drove along the familiar streets and thought: 'A few more minutes, and an important, perhaps decisive historical moment, fraught with the gravest consequences, will be upon us. Will I rise to the occasion? Do I possess sufficient strength, energy, cunning, agility and wit to play my role with maximum success for the USSR and for all mankind?'

The diary spans a dramatic and crucial epoch and covers a vast spectrum of topics. It was manifestly written with an eye to posterity and awareness of Maisky's own central role in the process.[9] Maisky found himself at the forefront of events, which he believed (far earlier than others) were likely to drag Europe into a world war. He dwells on the shift in Soviet foreign policy in the early thirties and on the motives for joining the League of Nations and for adherence to 'collective security'. It was Maisky who first alerted Moscow to the danger of appeasement. He fervently attempted to harmonize Soviet and British interests. His task, however, became increasingly difficult when Chamberlain arrived as prime minister in 1937 and pursued his 'appeasement' policy, against the backdrop of the ferocious purges raging in Moscow. The voluminous entries for 1938 provide

1. Forging the Grand Alliance. Maisky clinking vodka glasses with Churchill.

an insight into the events leading up to the Munich Conference and their devastating repercussions for collective security, as well as for the personal and political fate of both Maisky and Maksim Litvinov, the Soviet commissar for foreign affairs. The diary for 1939 unveils the tremendous psychological pressure under which Maisky acted in his desperate attempts to hasten the conclusion of a tripartite agreement between the Soviet Union, Great Britain and France, intended to forestall a Soviet drift towards isolation. It reveals how often he found himself at odds with his own government, culminating in a stormy meeting at the Kremlin on 21 April, at which both he and Litvinov were harshly criticized and which led to the dismissal of the latter two weeks later. The diary further exposes the confusion which engulfed Soviet diplomats in the wake of the Ribbentrop–Molotov Pact and bears witness to Britain's transition from peace to war.

Just as gripping is Maisky's description, as an informed outsider, of London during the Blitz, and of his frequent intimate meetings with Churchill and Eden. The significance of his war reminiscences can hardly be overstated. While it was the practice of the foreign secretary to keep a record of his meetings with ambassadors, this did not apply to the prime ministers. Consequently, no records are to be found in the British archives of the many crucial conversations held between Maisky and Churchill before and during the Second World War. The only records preserved for posterity are therefore Maisky's detailed and immediate accounts in his diary and his more succinct telegrams to the Foreign Ministry. The diary thus becomes an indispensable source, replacing the retrospective accounts – tendentious and incomplete – which have served historians so far. It would hardly be an exaggeration to suggest that the diary rewrites some history which we thought we knew. The unprecedented and extraordinary relations Maisky forged with the British leaders are well reflected in a farewell letter that the ambassador wrote to Churchill after his recall:

> Looking back now on these eleven years, I can say without hesitation that from a personal and political point of view my associations with you, extending over such a long time, have been the highlight of my Ambassadorship here ... I greatly enjoyed all our meetings and talks, irrespective of whether you were in or out of office, as I always felt that I was dealing with one of the most remarkable Englishmen of our time.

To this, Churchill replied:

> Your ambassadorship here has indeed covered a decisive period in the history of our two countries and of the whole world. I look back upon it with many pleasant recollections of our meetings both official and private ... I look forward to seeing you myself in the not too distant future, and to renewing the personal friendship which we have already built up.[10]

The leitmotif interwoven with Maisky's principal historical narrative is his personal struggle for physical survival during the ferocious purges, at the end of which only he and his friend, the feminist Aleksandra Kollontay, Soviet ambassador in Stockholm, remained at their posts in Europe.[11] Throughout his ambassadorship, Maisky had to walk a tightrope: being frank in his conversations with his British interlocutors and yet careful not to antagonize the Kremlin. The inner tensions are evident throughout the diary. Fearing that relations between the two countries were poisoned by mutual suspicion, and aware of his own precarious position, Maisky often withheld vital information from the Kremlin. A striking example was the suppression of information concerning Churchill's admission in 1943 that he could not even undertake to launch a cross-channel attack in 1944.[12]

The intertwined narratives are highlighted by penetrating – at times amusing – observations and anecdotes on British society, politicians, royalty, writers and artists which enliven the historical narrative. Maisky's penchant for writing prose and poetry betrayed a compulsive urge for self-expression. The result is a hybrid of literature and history. 'I had had literary inclinations since childhood,' he reminisces:

> As a boy I was fond of keeping a diary and corresponding with relations and friends ... As far back as I remember, I was always composing or describing something – a forest after rain, an ambulance station, a trip to Chernoluchye, a pine wood not far from Omsk, and so on. Having grown up a little, I tried my powers in diaries, school essays and articles on current topics.

In later years, Maisky would confess to his close friend, the Fabian Beatrice Webb, who also entertained literary aspirations, that 'he dislikes the profession of diplomacy; he and his wife would have been far happier in the academic or professional world; in

2. A page from Maisky's earlier diaries, following his arrest and exile in 1906.

the lecture room, library or laboratory'.[13] Indeed, when he was incarcerated at the age of 70, he wrote a compelling novel *Close and Far Away*.

Maisky was further blessed with an extraordinary memory which, enhanced by penetrating psychological insight, powerful observation and insatiable curiosity, turned him into one of the most astute witnesses of the dramatic events and personalities of the 1930s. 'Long diplomatic practice,' he explained,

> had trained my memory to act as a sort of photographic plate, which could without difficulty take up all the characteristics of the people I met. Their appearance, words, gestures and intonations were rapidly recorded on this plate, building up into sharply defined, detailed images. Often I would reach a mental conclusion about a person – positive or negative, with or without qualifications – on the spot, straight after our first acquaintance.[14]

'You used to look down upon us from the Gallery in Parliament,' recalled Harold Nicolson – author, diplomat and diarist – in a letter to Maisky, 'with benevolent interest rather like a biologist examines the habits of newts in a tank.'[15]

Having spent two years in London in exile during the First World War, followed by two years as chargé d'affaires at the embassy in the 1920s and 11 years as ambassador, his circle of acquaintances was vast. The very intimacy Maisky enjoyed with the top echelons of British politicians and officials, as well as with intellectuals and artists, gave him a perfect vantage point. Records of his conversations cover *inter alia* five British prime ministers – Lloyd George, Ramsay MacDonald, Stanley Baldwin, Neville Chamberlain and Winston Churchill – as well as King George V, Edward VIII and an impressive array of prominent figures such as Anthony Eden, Lord Halifax, Lord Beaverbrook, Lord Simon, Lady Nancy Astor, Samuel John Hoare, Herbert Morrison, Clement Attlee, Sidney and Beatrice Webb, Hugh Dalton, Stafford Cripps, John Maynard Keynes, John Strachey, Robert Vansittart, Joe Kennedy, Harry Hopkins, Jan Christian Smuts, Jan Masaryk, Bernard Shaw and H.G. Wells, to name just a few.

For non-experts, with limited access to the rich and fascinating documents published by the Russians on the events leading up to the war, the diary provides a rare glimpse into the inner state of the Soviet mind: its entries question many of the prevailing, often tendentious, interpretations of both Russian and Western historiography. For experts, it supplements the documents published in the *Dokumenty vneshnei politiki* by providing a colourful and candid description of Maisky's interlocutors, disclosing his own emotional, ideological and political thoughts, which are missing from the official documents. Moreover, it is stunning to discover the extent to which politicians and officials such as Beaverbrook, Lloyd George, Eden and Vansittart spoke candidly and openly with the Soviet ambassador – at times with more sympathy for the Soviet cause than has been conceived so far. It was one thing to hear from Beatrice Webb 'that in her opinion the capitalist system has only 20–30 years left to live', but quite another to learn from Brendan Bracken, Churchill's confidant, that he was 'unsure about capitalism's future ... arguing that the world is heading for the triumph of socialism, even if not exactly the socialism we have in the Soviet Union'.[16] In one of their intimate fireside talks, Eden reacted to Maisky's passing remark that capitalism was 'a spent force', thus:

> Yes, you are right. The capitalist system in its present form has had its day. What will replace it? I can't say exactly, but it will certainly be a different system. State capitalism? Semi-socialism? Three-quarter socialism? Complete socialism? I don't know. Maybe it will be a particularly pure British form of 'Conservative socialism'.[17]

The plethora of memoirs and diaries of Western politicians that revolve around the Second World War is striking in comparison with the dearth on the Soviet side. The only significant memoirs to have emerged from Russia were those written by the military in the 1960s. The generals were allowed to shift the blame for the unpreparedness of the Red Army in June 1941 onto Stalin as part of the de-Stalinization process. Because of the paucity of personal recollections, Maisky's series of memoirs[18] (quoting selectively from his diary) turned out to be an indispensable source for historians in reconstructing Soviet policy. Compelling as they are, the memoirs, written with hindsight at the height of the Cold War, are contentious and misleading. That is why his extemporary and spontaneous diary assumes tremendous historical significance. The memoirs present Soviet foreign policy as morally and politically righteous, glossing over issues of contention. The memoirs have therefore often led historians up a blind alley and should indeed be reconsidered now that the full diary, which conveys the immediate and far less biased impressions, is available for inspection.

The discrepancy between the memoirs and the diary is hardly surprising. Throughout his professional life, Maisky paid a heavy price for siding with the Mensheviks during the revolution. By the late 1940s, his star was already on the wane. An early sign of his eclipse was the criticism of a booklet by Boris Shtein (Soviet ambassador in Italy during the 1930s) on the origins of the Second World War, in the Communist Party journal *Bolshevik*. The criticism of Shtein's 'objective approach' spill over onto Maisky, who had reviewed the book favourably.[19] At the height of the anti-Jewish frenzy following the Doctors' Plot of 1952, Maisky was arrested and charged with espionage, treason and involvement in Zionist conspiracy. Although Stalin's death two weeks later, in March 1953, spared his life, his incarceration was extended by two more years for alleged association with Stalin's former henchman, L.P. Beria. Beria, who apparently wished to see Maisky installed as foreign minister in 1953, assigned him to coordinate intelligence activities in Britain at the Ministry of Home Security. In July 1953, however, Beria himself was arrested and soon afterwards executed. Maisky's alleged association with Beria and his imprisonment seemed to reinforce the memory of his never-forgotten past association with the Mensheviks.

As soon as Stalin died, Maisky hastened to address Georgii Malenkov, the newly elected chairman of the Council of Ministers, from his prison cell. He proposed to atone for his past mistakes by assisting in setting up a group of young, capable Soviet historians who would 'specialize in combating the bourgeois falsification of contemporary history. The practicalities of this could be later discussed, in case it was found possible to save my life.'[20] In 1955, at the age of 72, frail and sick after two and a half years of humiliation and imprisonment, Maisky faced a long and frantic struggle to reinstate his party membership and his position at the Academy of Sciences, and above all to secure full rehabilitation.[21] Hardly out of prison, Maisky complained to Nikita Khrushchev that he was being 'ostracized', and vowed to do 'his utmost for the benefit of the party' by 'effectively serving the Soviet State as an academic-historian'. He proposed to engage in research into the historiography of the Second World War which would 'critically evaluate the literature published in the West'.[22] Likewise he expressed to Voroshilov, chairman of the Presidium of the Supreme Soviet, the 'most ardent desire ... to best serve the Soviet State' in the remaining years of his life by becoming the '*in-house historian of the USSR's foreign policy* ... unmasking the most eminent bourgeois falsifiers of contemporary history, particularly of the period of the Second World War'.[23]

Appearing before the powerful Control Committee of the Party in spring 1957, Maisky restated his fundamental objective of 'unmasking the anti-Soviet falsifications of the Second World War history which currently are literally flooding the book markets of the capitalist world'.[24] In July 1958, he again offered his services to Khrushchev in unveiling 'the truth'. He even promised to submit his memoirs for Party approval, as he was 'more than prepared to introduce whatever changes were necessary'.[25] Even posthumously, when the Soviet Academy of Sciences honoured the centenary of Maisky's birth in 1984 with a symposium and a book devoted to his life and work, his memoirs were hailed, *inter alia*, as 'a weapon in the struggle against the reactionary historiography'.[26] The historical value of the memoirs was further compromised by the severe censorship they were subjected to in the first place. His servility became even more pronounced when he was forced to remove criticism of Stalin from the final Russian edition of his memoirs in 1971.[27]

The history of Maisky's long ambassadorship in London is indeed breath-taking. Early in the nineteenth century the British diplomat Stratford Canning predicted that public opinion might turn out to be 'a power more tremendous than was perhaps ever yet brought into action in the history of mankind'. His French colleague, Jules Cambon, an experienced diplomat, suggested that in getting to know a country fully, an ambassador should not confine himself to ministerial contacts, and on occasion might find that 'even the friendship of women of high social standing would be of great value to him'. But it was really Maisky who heralded a revolutionary style of diplomacy, which at the time irritated many of his interlocutors, but which has since been so much in vogue. He certainly was the first ambassador to systematically manipulate and mould public opinion, mostly through the press. A guest at the embassy recalled seeing Maisky's first secretary in the corridor 'lecturing to Cummings, the political editor of *News Chronicle*, that his writings on the Finnish war had been "grossly exaggerated"'.[28] A superb 'public relations' man at a time when the concept hardly existed, Maisky did not shy away from aligning himself with opposition groups, backbenchers, newspaper editors, trade unionists, writers, artists and intellectuals. 'I have never known a representative of a foreign power,' recalled John Rothenstein, the director of the Tate Gallery, 'who spoke so disarmingly, as though his listener had his entire confidence, or who took so much trouble to make the policy, or the ostensible policy, of his Government understood by the politically insignificant. And unlike most of his Soviet colleagues he seemed very ready to form private friendships.'[29]

Iverach McDonald, the young foreign correspondent of *The Times*, left a captivating recollection of Maisky's *modus operandi*:

Most British officials were scandalised at the way Maisky would sail along, when it suited him, unhampered by normal diplomatic conventions ... He would never hesitate, by means of timely and artful disclosures, to give his hearers ammunition which they could use against Chamberlain, John Simon, and the others. His luncheon parties could be formal and orthodox, or they could be like meetings of opposition cliques ... Whenever I went to see him at his embassy in Millionaires' Row, he seemed to have all the time in the world to talk to a young man. In a flattering way he would unplug his telephone as a sign we were not to be disturbed. Or he would take me down to the end of the garden, with Kensington Gardens just over the hedge, where we could walk and talk with all the benefits of warm sunshine and complete privacy.[30]

Maisky cultivated a significant segment of the British press with consummate skill. He read the whole British press, practically without exception, daily and weekly. His 'grasp of day-by-day changes in thought and emotion and his genial but unruffled contemplation of the whole war in all its details,' remarked an American journalist, rendered him 'one of the most thoroughly competent observers' in London.[31] What an ambassador has to aim at, Maisky told his friend Beatrice Webb, 'is intimate relations with all the live-wires in the country to which he is accredited – among all parties or circles of influential opinion, instead of shutting himself up with the other diplomatists and the inner governing circle – whether royal or otherwise'. Naturally he was first and foremost his own government's agent, but when he spoke in his quiet, often humorous,

3. Maisky inseparable from the newspapers.

way he always gave the impression of 'speaking as an individual rather than a mere record of his master's voice'. He used to boast that he could place a letter in *The Times* whenever he chose to.[32]

Courting the press magnate Lord Beaverbrook certainly paid off. His *Daily Express* hailed the rise of Stalin as a defender of Soviet national interests rather than of the idea of world revolution. In autumn 1936, Beaverbrook reminded Maisky of his newspapers' 'friendly attitude' towards Stalin and promised that 'nothing shall be done or said by any newspaper controlled by me which is likely to disturb your tenure of office'.[33] In 1939, Beaverbrook strongly recommended that Maisky arrange for a young journalist from the *Sunday Express* to go to Russia. The journalist, he wrote to the ambassador, 'follows in his Master's footsteps in all his political opinions. Of course, it is commonly said that the Master follows after Maisky.' Eventually Beaverbrook became the champion of a second front in 1942.[34]

Persuasion was often rewarded by boons. 'I venture to keep my promise to you,' Maisky wrote to Beaverbrook, 'and hope you will find to your liking the sample of Russian vodka I am sending. My wife told you, I believe, something of the Russian liqueur called "Zapenkanka", and she is enclosing a sample of that which she hopes you will enjoy.'[35] William Camrose, editor of the conservative *Daily Telegraph*, clearly appreciated the ambassador's yearly supply of Russian caviar for Christmas:

My dear ambassador
    No gift could have come more appropriately or welcome than did the delightful cases of caviar which I received last night.
    If nothing else good ever came out of Russia, caviar alone has been a great gift to civilisation!... Very many thanks for your kind thought.[36]

4. Maisky entertaining high society at his residence in London.

As did Vernon Bartlett, diplomatic correspondent of *News Chronicle*:

> My dear Ambassador,
>   I only returned to London yesterday from a short holiday and found your very kind gift awaiting me. May I thank you most sincerely. My passion for caviar is enormous and ought not to be encouraged in this way.[37]

At the Foreign Office, they were extremely frustrated by the fact that 'no restrictions were placed on [Maisky] to prevent him doing pretty well anything he likes', and that he had and was making 'very plentiful use of free access to all Cabinet Ministers and others'.[38] And yet Alexander Cadogan, the permanent undersecretary of state, reluctantly admitted that 'It has not yet been possible to detect any personal weakness of M. Maisky that would be gratified by a present from the Secretary of State or Prime Minister.'[39] And none of the official remonstrations proved effective. Faced with harsh criticism for feeding the press with vital details from the secret negotiations of the Non-Intervention Committee during the Spanish Civil War, Maisky commented in the diary: 'I remained utterly calm as if the noises had nothing to do with me whatever.' At the time, his tactics were resented as mischievous and a gross breach of diplomatic practice. And yet today, looking back, they hardly seem so outrageous.[40]

His ideological predilections drove Maisky to seek particularly close contacts with the City, which he assumed controlled British politics. As soon as he landed in London, he asked his old friend, H.G. Wells to organize an 'informal meeting with a "few intelligent bankers" ... so that there may be an opportunity for a proper talk'. Wells complied. 'We

5. Dining with industrialists in Birmingham.

have done nothing,' he urged Brendan Bracken, 'to gratify Maisky's morbid craving to smack Bankers on their backs and call them by their Christian names.'[41] Francis Williams, editor of the *Daily Herald*, recalls how he was caught off guard during a *tête-à-tête* delicious luncheon at the embassy by 'a very agreeable and civilized conversation' on the London theatre and literature. However, as soon as the 'English-seeming butler' had withdrawn, leaving them to coffee and brandy, Maisky spoke of his esteem for Williams' City column. Williams confesses to having felt 'a little uncomfortable' when, after discovering the extent of German dealings in the City, Maisky went on to interrogate him about the general outlook of the City and the influence it exercised on the British government. It dawned on him, as he later admitted, 'that in the most delicate possible way the extent of my "reliability" from the Russian point of view was being probed'. In parting, Maisky expressed the hope that he could lunch with the journalist in the future, and did not shrink from making the following proposal:

> I suppose you would not contemplate sending me written reports from time to time on City institutions and affairs in the City? I would find it very interesting if you could. There must be much that you do not find it possible to print. It would be most valuable and we (the 'we' was stressed ever so slightly) would be most grateful.

This was supplemented every Christmas by a jar of caviar and a bottle of vodka with the ambassador's personal compliments. Indeed, the grey zone between being recruited and retaining a professional integrity was manifestly crossed by many of the leading publicists and journalists, if not politicians, as the diary clearly reveals.[42]

Then, as now, the legacy of preconceived ideas about Russia and its people – the most lethal feature of relations between Britain and Russia since the eighteenth century – rendered Maisky's position in London particularly precarious. The severe hurdles which he had to face in accomplishing his mission reflected the long legacy of mistrust and suspicion characterizing Anglo-Russian relations. Ever since Russia's emergence as a major power in the eighteenth century, the Western world has found it difficult to accept it as an integral part of Europe. This rebuff, embedded in a deep-rooted Russophobic tradition, was now heightened by the Bolshevik Revolution. In 1839, Marquis de Custine, whose entire family had been sent to the guillotine, sought comfort in Russia, the bastion of monarchical rule in Europe. He came back appalled, warning his readers that the Russians were 'Chinese masquerading as Europeans'. Two centuries later, Churchill referred to the Soviet Union as 'a riddle wrapped in a mystery inside an enigma'. The continuity in the Western perception of Russia was likewise conspicuous in his choice of the 'iron curtain', a mere paraphrase of the 'cordon sanitaire', with which Lord Curzon had hoped to isolate Western civilization from the Bolshevik 'epidemic' in the wake of the revolution. Nor have the Russians been immune to xenophobia, or clear about their own identity and destiny. The debate, in various shapes and forms, has accompanied each twist in Russian history. From the early 1830s, the Russian intelligentsia pursued a fierce debate between the Westerners and the Slavophiles over the road which Russia should follow to surmount her political, social and economic backwardness. The revolution further demonized the Western bourgeoisie. Seen from both the Western and the Russian sides, vindictiveness and resentment gave birth to preconceived ideas and mutual suspicion, which in turn shaped policies and were the main contributors to the calamitous events described in Maisky's diary.

Although Maisky was universally acclaimed as perhaps the most outstanding and informed ambassador to the Court of St James's, he was met with suspicion bordering on hostility. He was little helped by the wide popularity he enjoyed among the people, which became a source of 'irritation and contempt' in the higher echelons, where he was often referred to as 'that little Tartar Jew'.[43] Even friends could not refrain from alluding to his 'subfallstaffian figure'. 'He sits there in his ugly Victorian study,' flowed the venomous ink of Harold Nicolson in his diary, 'like a little gnome in an arm-chair, twiddling his thumbs, twinkling his eyes and giving the impression that his feet do not reach the floor.'[44] The ambivalence was perhaps best encapsulated in General Edward Spears' observation of Maisky: 'sturdily built, obviously very strong and clever, a typical Tartar and no doubt basically cruel as are the people of his race' – oblivious to the fact that Maisky's roots (at least on his father's side) were Jewish-Polish from the Russian pale of settlement.[45] Beatrice Webb, who was particularly close to Maisky, wondered

> what the aristocratic Eden, the fascist charmer Grandi, the Nazi bounder Von Ribbentrop feel towards the stocky, ugly Jew-tartar Soviet emissary, who compares more to a shrewd business man negotiating in a world market than to a professional diplomatist manoeuvring among the governments of the world. Half the government and half the Foreign Office regard him as enemy No. 1.,

whilst the others glance nervously towards him as a possible ally in saving the British Empire from the militant envy of Germany and Italy.[46]

A graphic description of such perceptions appears in Harold Nicolson's impressions of a lunch hosted by Maisky at the Soviet embassy:

> The door was opened by a gentleman in a soft collar and a stubby yellow moustache. I was ushered into a room of unexampled horror where I was greeted with effusion by Mr Maisky ... We stood in this grim ante-room while we were given corked sherry, during which time the man with a yellow moustache and a moujik's unappetizing daughter carried tableware and bananas into the room beyond.
>
> We then went into luncheon, which was held in a winter-garden, more wintery than gardeny. We began with caviar, which was all to the good. We then had a little wet dead trout. We then had what in nursing-homes is called 'fruit jelly' ... During the whole meal, I felt that there was something terribly familiar about it all. It was certainly not the Russia of my memory. And then suddenly I realized it was the East. They were playing at being Europeans ... They have gone oriental.[47]

The condescending attitude was widely shared. The director of the Tate Gallery remembered a similar event when

> ... my own glass was filled and refilled so often by a member of the Embassy staff that I so far momentarily forgot the importance of the occasion as to say to him that there was something funny about the insignia of the Hammer and Sickle, which one was accustomed to see chalked upon factory walls and in public lavatories, being engraved with such elegance on such magnificent table silver. This diplomat, who had not neglected his own glass, oblivious of the impertinence of my words, gave me a mournful stare, and indicating with his thumb the insignia on the handle of a fork said thickly, 'It used to be birds' – an allusion to the eagles of Imperial Russia.[48]

However, to others, such as the Labourite Herbert Morrison, Maisky appeared to be 'a cogent talker' who could 'argue reasonably and vividly, but with an almost Western objectivity which made discussion with him, in contrast with the case of most communists, stimulating and useful'.[49] Likewise Rab Butler (then undersecretary of state for foreign affairs) recognized that Maisky was 'certainly the most pertinacious' of all foreign representatives in London. Bernard Pares, the doyen of the British historians of Russia, marvelled at Maisky who had 'never given [him] any forecast which did not prove true'.[50] Finally, Bruce Lockhart, an old hand at Russian affairs, conceded that Maisky 'certainly knew his England thoroughly, indeed too thoroughly for some people. But when I said goodbye, I thought that we might wait long before we were sent as good a Russian ambassador.'[51]

Unlike the reserved and harsh demeanour which characterized the later 'Stalinist school of diplomacy', Maisky and Agniya worked as a team and did their utmost to

6. Agniya Maisky, the ever-charming hostess.

7. Reverent Agniya – the genuine Bolshevik – unveils a plaque at a house in London where Lenin lived.

influence British public opinion by a display of sheer friendliness. Conservatives were just as welcome at their luncheon parties as Labourites. When Maisky arrived in London, he asked Bruce Lockhart to introduce him to the London society. Lockhart expressed surprise, suggesting that Maisky surely knew the British socialists better than he did. 'Yes,' replied Maisky, 'but I want to meet more of the people who are running this country.' At first Maisky's receptions were 'filled with Leftists dressed in queer clothes … gradually the guests had progressed from red ties to stiff shirts and evening dress, until one evening H.G. Wells who had come to a large party in an ordinary day suit found himself the only person so dressed'.[52] Indeed Maisky lost few of his British friends even in the most difficult period, during the Soviet–German pact and the Soviet–Finnish war. Louis Fischer, the well-informed international journalist, commented on how Maisky 'diligently and with infinite care … cultivated numerous important individuals in British political life', while 'his attractive wife added to his popularity in high society'.[53] Agniya was omnipresent in his life, and on the rare occasion when she indulged herself with a shopping expedition, staying longer in Paris en route from a League of Nations meeting in Geneva, he would seem to lose his bearings. 'My dearest Turchik,' he wrote to her on one such occasion,

> I am bored to death. It's not just that I am alone, completely alone within the four walls of this flat, but also that up to yesterday I didn't even go down to the street … I'm reading a lot, listening to the radio and to records. Marusiya is feeding me well enough and the domestic side of things is in general 'all right' … Can't wait to see you again soon. I kiss my dear sweet Turchik hard, and wait for her impatiently. Mikhailichi.[54]

The image they projected was of 'strongly contrasting temperaments: she was gay, confident and an uncompromising revolutionary, he was quiet, with an occasional air of apprehension, and, though a loyal and devoted ambassador, rather liberal in his outlook'.[55] Like her husband, Agniya seems to have been lured by the comfort and the glittering facet of life in London. Herbert Morrison observed that she 'enjoyed her stay in London, for she admired the Londoners and liked their ways. I remember at a reception at the Soviet Embassy obliging her as best I could when she begged me to teach her the Lambeth Walk.[56] She always remembered it.'[57] A woman of 'conventional charm and good manners, pretty' and 'attractively dressed', she was criticized in parliament for 'spending 1,500 guineas on a mink coat' while the Russian armies were 'being battered by the Germans' and money was being raised by her in the factories for the Red Cross.[58] In the late 1920s, Narkomindel had set up a sartorial and dressmaking establishment to produce garments for the wives, as well as for the diplomats themselves. They were, observed Beatrice Webb (who was attracted by high couture), 'carefully designed according to the fashions prevalent at the courts or capitals concerned. Which accounts for the elegance of Madame Maisky and Madame Litvinoff, much commented on in the fashion papers.' This was not the case with the ambassador, whose 'stocky figure', she observed, was often dressed 'in a holiday attire, loose light garments of the most unconventional cut and colour'. Far more ideologically militant than her husband, Agniya could at times be pugnacious and allow her emotions to run wild. At a reception at Buckingham Palace she came across one of the Russian empress's ladies in waiting wearing a medallion with the tsarina's portrait. It was rumoured that she 'spat on the picture'.[59]

It is most amazing to glean from Maisky's diary how much room for manoeuvre was left for ambassadors, even under Stalin's most ruthless authoritarian regime. Many of his initiatives were adopted as policy, at times even against the prevailing views held in the

Kremlin – the most striking examples being his unstinting support for the negotiation of a triple alliance with the West in early 1939 and the campaign for the second front in 1941–43. To get his way, Maisky often had to attribute his own ideas to his interlocutors, although the archives show that it was he who had initiated them. I have drawn the reader's attention to a handful of such instances in my commentary. A typical example would be Maisky's attempts to discourage Stalin from moving towards isolation and Nazi Germany following the exasperating experience of the Munich Agreement. He was not as successful in his attempts to halt Stalin and Litvinov from retreating from Spain. In the diary entry of 1 October 1938, he describes the advice he had given the government to adhere to collective security by citing a conversation with Lloyd George (well manipulated by him) who apparently exclaimed: 'Just don't leave Spain, whatever you do!', further urging that 'isolationism would be a bad policy for the USSR'.[60] It was Maisky who early on warned of the impact the purges were having on British public opinion, proposing that justice should be seen to be done through public trials. Later he went on to warn Moscow of the dire impact of the purges of the military on the prospects for concluding a triple alliance.[61] He also engineered Eden's ground-breaking trip to Moscow and his meeting with Stalin in 1935, preferring him to Lord Simon, the then foreign secretary.[62] As early as the end of 1937, Maisky advised Stalin how to address the appeasers: 'Let "Western democracies" reveal their hand in the matter of the aggressors. What is the point of us pulling the chestnuts out of the fire for them? To fight <u>together</u> – by all means; to serve as cannon fodder for them – never!' Stalin indeed repeated the ambassador's words almost verbatim in his famous speech of March 1939.[63] During his heyday in London, after the German attack on Russia, it was Maisky who forged the alliance when paralysis struck the Kremlin, prompting Churchill's famous speech and paving the way

8. English tea in the embassy's conservatory.

for the visit of Harry Hopkins, Roosevelt's right-hand adviser, to Moscow in July 1941, as well as for Eden's trip that December, and Churchill's first visit to Moscow in August 1943.

* * *

Attached to the original text there were numerous relevant press clippings, occasional correspondence and copies of some of the telegrams exchanged between Churchill and Stalin during the war. As most of those sources are easily available in print, they have been largely excluded from the present collection. On a few occasions, the long reports of conversations in the diary served Maisky as the basis for his official reports, some of which have previously been published, but only in Russian compilations.

The introductory biographical notes about individuals appear on first mention. In most cases, the reference is to the position held by the individual during the period covered by the diary. To help the reader grasp the impact of the purges on the diplomatic corps, an attempt has been made to trace the fate of those at the London embassy and among the old cadre of Narkomindel who were purged during the repression.

I have broadly followed the transliteration guidelines of the Library of Congress, with various simplifications. The two most important exceptions are: 'ю' is rendered throughout the diary as 'yu' (not 'iu'), and 'я' as 'ya' (not 'ia'). To remain faithful to the conventions of the time, the endings of proper names in 'ий' are transcribed throughout as 'y', not 'ii' (Maisky, Trotsky, etc.). Chinese transliteration follows pinyin; names that are perhaps better known in some other transliteration system are also given in the biographical notes. Strictly speaking, until 1946 the title of the Soviet foreign minister was people's commissar for foreign affairs, while that of Soviet ambassadors was *polpred*. I have employed mostly the Western terms, which were used indiscriminately, even by the ambassadors themselves at the time.

The Making of a Soviet Diplomat

Ivan Mikhailovich Lyakhovetsky was born on 7 January 1884 in the ancient Russian town of Kirillov, near Nizhny-Novgorod, in the comfortable environment of a nobleman's castle, where his father was a tutor to the son of the family. Maisky (Man of May), was a *nom de plume* he assumed in 1909 while in exile in Germany. His childhood was spent in Siberia, in Omsk, where his father, having studied medicine in St Petersburg, served as a medical officer.[1] His father was of Jewish Polish descent, a fact which Maisky preferred to conceal. In his enchanting childhood memoirs he went a long way to stress the atheist atmosphere at home, but made the point that 'officially, of course, we were considered to be Orthodox ... as a schoolboy I was obliged to learn the catechism in class, to attend Vespers on Saturdays and Mass on Sundays, and to go to confession without fail before Easter'. Maisky, though, would find it difficult to shake off the 'Jewish image'. Both in England and in the Soviet Union he was often perceived to be Jewish. The nephew of the famous Russian historian, Evgeny Tarle, recalled that his aunt, who 'had a nose for Jews who'd been promoted at the time of the proletarian revolution', confided in him that she thought 'Maisky wasn't really called Maisky, let alone "Ivan Mikhailovich": "Isaak Moiseevich", more likely'. Victor Gollancz, the Jewish leftist publisher, remembered Maisky telling 'wonderful Jewish stories, which he called Armenian, and loved listening to mine, which he called Armenian too'.[2]

His father's 'secret love' and the 'mainspring of his soul' was the 'passion for science'. He served as a formidable role model for Maisky and as a source of inspiration for an insatiable intellectual aptitude and curiosity, professional dedication and unbridled ambition. His father's rigidity and somewhat reserved nature were cushioned by Maisky's mother, Nadezhda Ivanovna (née Davydova), who was a village teacher with a strong literary and artistic proclivity. In his memoirs, Maisky depicts her fondly as being 'of a choleric temperament – lively, inconsistent, quick-tempered and talkative ... She had something unique in herself, a kind of charm, which attracted people to her and easily made her the centre of attention.'

Maisky was exposed to literature from an early age. The packed bookshelves at home housed beautifully bound collected works of Shakespeare, Byron and Schiller, as well as the writing of the more radical intelligentsia such as Nekrasov, Dobrolyubov, Herzen and Pisarev. Maisky was well aware of the debate raging at the time on the purpose of literature and art, and on realism and aestheticism. Though claiming in later years, for obvious reasons, to have sided with the 'utilitarians', the young Ivan uncritically devoured 'stacks of books and periodicals'. He was particularly captivated by Heine, his

9. Jan Lyakhovetsky (Maisky) with his younger sister.

lifetime compass and companion, whose portrait was to hang over his desk. Barely sixteen years of age, he expressed this admiration in a letter to Elizaveta, his confidante cousin:

> I have never seen a finer face than Heine's. Every day I discover more and more excellence in Heine and I am convinced that his perpetually satirical, perpetually sceptical Aristophanes of the nineteenth century is one of the greatest geniuses and judges of the human soul in general, and of the people of our times in particular. Heine is humanity. He personifies it to perfection as nobody else has done. In him is reflected all the good and bad in humanity, the wide and motley panorama of the human marketplace, all its suffering and sorrow, all its anger and indignation.[3]

The literary atmosphere at home refined Maisky's acute powers of observation, which were enhanced by his rich imagination and his curiosity. It helped forge his complex personality, which, while romantic and artistic, was also governed by a belief in 'reason, science, knowledge, and the right of man to be master of life on earth'.[4] The novels opened a window on Europe and awakened in Maisky a longing for travel and an interest in geography which would gradually shape his cosmopolitan outlook once in exile. That particular inquisitiveness was enriched by exposure to the bustling life of Omsk's port, where Maisky spent any free moment he had strolling about the wharves and by the steamers, 'looking at everything, listening and nosing about ... I listened to the stories of the pilots and sailors about their work and adventures and about the distant towns and places they visited.'[5]

In reconstructing a revolutionary past, Maisky would later identify a rebellious streak in the family – a dissident member of the clergy who went off the rails and joined certain revolutionary circles in the mid-nineteenth century. Likewise he would claim that his own parents sympathized with the Populist movement, that his mother had even 'gone down to the people', and that his father had come into conflict with the authorities at the hospital he worked in over his failure to prevent the young medical cadets from expressing revolutionary ideas in 1905. He makes much of the special relationship he cultivated with his artist uncle, M.M. Chemodanov, who worked as a *zemstvo* doctor in a remote village and was mildly involved in revolutionary activities. However, at its core, Maisky's background and education were typical of the professional middle class, devoid of any political awareness.[6]

Having graduated from the local gymnasium (grammar school) at the age of 17 with a gold medal, Maisky enrolled at St Petersburg University, where he read history and philology. His literary talents were noticed around that time, when his first poem, 'I Wish to Be a Great Thunderstorm', was published in *Siberian Life* under the pseudonym 'New Man'. His university education at St Petersburg, however, came to an abrupt and premature end when he was arrested and charged with revolutionary agitation.[7] He was put under police surveillance in Omsk, where he joined the Menshevik wing of the Russian Social Democratic Movement. In 1906 he was detained once again for taking an active part in the 1905 revolution, and was sentenced to exile in Tobolsk, where he produced a manuscript inspired by Sidney and Beatrice Webb and their *History of Trade Unionism*. Maisky had stumbled upon this by sheer chance when he was a student in St Petersburg. He would later confess to the Webbs that it 'greatly contributed to my political education and to a certain extent helped me to find the path which I followed in my subsequent life'. 'Never indeed,' he wrote to his cousin in 1901, 'have I read any novel with such a thrill as the Webbs' book! How feeble, miserable and nonsensical all

10. A model pupil in the gymnasium (front row, fifth from the right).

C. Reisener ST.PÉTERSBOURG.

11. The breeding of a revolutionary: Maisky as a student at St Petersburg University.

my former literary enthusiasms seem to me!'[8] The evolutionary Fabian stream, with its strong social-humanist bent, suited Maisky's temperament and served him as a political beam of light. Its residue was always close to the surface, even when he had to break with his Menshevik past and display loyalty to Bolshevism. Once in England, he cultivated intimate relations with the Webbs which lasted until their death, as is well attested in both his and Beatrice Webb's diaries.

Maisky's sentence was eventually commuted to exile abroad. In his memoirs, written under the cloud of the purges in the wake of the Ribbentrop–Molotov Pact (when his stock was low in Moscow), Maisky claims that his desire to emigrate was driven by a wish to study 'socialism and the European workers' movement'. However, the attraction of exile seems to have been more profound, revealing a cosmopolitan streak and a prodigious curiosity which can be traced back to his childhood, when he used to accompany his father – who believed that 'nothing develops a child so much as travel and getting to know new places, new people, new races and customs' – on his distant missions across Siberia. When the family moved to St Petersburg for a year, we find the nine-year-old Ivan still fascinated, 'standing a long while on the granite quays of the Neva, watching the complicated manoeuvres of the Finnish boats, the loading of foreign ships, the tiny Finnish steamers darting briskly in all directions like dark blue beetles'. His exile further enhanced an enduring admiration for European (particularly German) culture, as he openly confessed in a letter to his mother: 'I am still extremely happy with being abroad. I feel that I am growing quickly and powerfully here, in mind and in spirit. And, in fact, I'm almost grateful to the circumstances which have forced me to quit Russian soil.'[9] 'I like travel,' he confessed to Bernard Shaw years later, 'and I have travelled much over Europe and Asia … When I see people boarding a train, a ship or a plane, I feel a sort of romantic glow.'[10]

After a brief stay in Switzerland, Maisky settled in Munich, then the hub for Russian immigrants and artists, notably Kandinsky and his circle. Though associated with the Russian revolutionary movement, Maisky was as much involved in the activities of the German Social Democratic Party and the trade unions. He obtained his Master's degree in economics at Munich University, and was well on with his doctoral dissertation when the gathering clouds of war led to an unanticipated and fateful new emigration – to London. The nomadic life suited his nature:

> After Germany, it'll be very good to get acquainted with life and people in the United Kingdom, and ultimately I don't mind where I live: Munich or London. On the way to England I'll stop off for a week in Paris, to have a look at the city … And then I'll head on from there to the British capital. I go to new countries with great interest and great expectations; we'll see whether the latter come true. Ultimately, I think the main charm in life is a constant change of impressions, and nothing aids that so much as travel, rapid movement from one place to another.[11]

However, Maisky's first encounter with London in November 1912, rather belied his later fascination with England. His Russian upbringing and life in the German socialist milieu did not predispose him to the kind of blind admiration for British liberalism that seized many of the romantic exiles of the nineteenth century. London, he felt, 'swallowed and suffocated' him. He did not know the language and felt lost in that 'giant stone ocean'.[12] Indeed, those early gloomy impressions are evident in a letter to his mother:

> Of course, I find London very interesting – from the political and socio-economic points of view – and I'm not at all sorry that I'm spending the current winter here. But I wouldn't want to stop in these parts too long. Just the thought of getting stuck here permanently brings on a freezing ennui. No, I definitely don't like London! It's huge, dark, dirty, uncomfortable, with boring rows of identical little houses, permanently shrouded in fog … You don't see the sun here for weeks, and that's terribly depressing. I now understand why spleen is called the English disease, and I also understand why Heine so disliked the country of the proud Britons. 'The ocean would have swallowed England long ago,' he once commented, 'if it weren't afraid of an upset stomach.' And he wasn't far wrong: to digest a 'nut' like England wouldn't be that easy.[13]

And yet the years in London and his friendship with Georgii Vasilevich Chicherin and Maksim Maksimovich Litvinov (who, for two decades, as commissars for foreign affairs, were to steer Soviet foreign policy) were to have a profound impact on Maisky's later career. The three were brought together by Litvinov's future wife, Ivy, who was born in London, the product of an implausible union between a Jewish intellectual and an Indian army colonel's daughter. A non-conformist writer and rebel, she found solace from her despised employment (with an insurance firm) at the Golders Green home of her aunt and uncle, the Eders, who were left-wing thinkers. They held lively intellectual soirées, with revolutionaries, Freudians, Fabians and literary figures such as Bernard Shaw and H.G. Wells.[14] It was at the Eders' house that Maisky, a frequent visitor, cemented his friendship with Litvinov and Chicherin.[15]

The three lived just around the corner from each other, first in Golders Green and then in Hampstead Heath, amidst a thriving colony of political exiles who found a bond with one another, regardless of the schism within the Russian socialist movement. Chicherin, whose aristocratic family could trace its origins and name to an Italian courtier who had settled in Russia at the time of Tsar Ivan III, had worked in the archives of the tsarist foreign minister. He was something of a polymath, endowed with an encyclopaedic memory. A renaissance man, well versed in literature and culture, he was also a fine pianist and the author of a highly acclaimed book on Mozart's operas. He cut an eccentric and ascetic figure in London, leading a rather bohemian life. The conscience-stricken Chicherin had initially been a disciple of Tolstoy, before he joined the Russian revolutionary movement in exile, leaning towards Menshevism. This short-lived deviation did not deter Lenin from later appointing him commissar for foreign affairs. His signature would adorn the Brest-Litovsk and Rapallo agreements, the pillars of Soviet diplomacy.

Litvinov, who had an obscure Jewish background and did not entertain any intellectual pretensions, was later to be meticulous in his work in Narkomindel (the Soviet Foreign Ministry), fastidiously observing the rules and etiquette of diplomatic work, and almost dismissive of the ideological constraints imposed on him. Surprisingly, despite his conspicuous personal contempt for Chicherin, the two were able to work together harmoniously for almost a decade.

By the time they met in England, Litvinov, who was only eight years older than Maisky, had already gained a reputation as a seasoned revolutionary. It was therefore only natural for him to become Maisky's mentor, introducing him to the country, its political institutions, its culture and a wide circle of people. What most endeared Litvinov to Maisky was his strong character, as well as his ability to grasp the essentials of a question without getting bogged down in the details, and his penchant for irony.

The outbreak of the First World War, however, brought an estrangement between the two which was to mar their future working relationship. While Litvinov adopted Lenin's position and was in favour of militant defeatism, Maisky sided with the Menshevik's internationalist pacifist position, which sought an end to the war. For a while, Maisky even displayed great interest in the then all-encompassing popular ideas of the 'Middle Europe' movement, propagated by F. Neumann, which tried to merge the two most powerful waves of German history – the national-bourgeois wave and the socially oriented proletarian. It further sought to synthesize the precepts of Christianity with German idealism, humanism with class solidarity, and democracy.[16] Maisky's ingrained pragmatism and humanistic outlook, further enhanced by his English experience, came to the fore as the First World War dragged on. He was particularly obsessed with the fate of Western civilization and the European intelligentsia, who were being slaughtered in great numbers on the front line, and wanted humanism to be placed before any party considerations. 'You see,' he responded to a rebuke from Julius Martov, the Menshevik leader,

12. Ivy and Maksim Litvinov sipping tea with Ivan and Agniya at the Soviet embassy, 1935.

the longer the war drags on, the more a very serious danger appears before the belligerent nations: an enormous number of intellectuals – writers, artists, scholars, engineers, etc. – will die on the battlefields. The countries are exhausting their spiritual aristocracy, without which, whatever you say, no mental, social or political progress is possible … Of course, any losses are difficult to bear: losses of peasants, losses of workers, etc.; but I still think that losses among the intelligentsia are, in relative terms, the hardest, because they are the most difficult to make good. The intelligentsia is a fruit that grows slowly, and it might need a whole generation before the depletion in its ranks caused by the war is even partly put right.

That's why I think that a period has now begun when nations, for their own self-preservation, will have to protect intellectuals the way they protect, for instance, skilled mechanics, chemists, trained armaments workers, etc.[17]

Although Maisky is at pains to demonstrate in his diary (and even more so in his autobiography) the kinship and warmth that characterized his relations with Litvinov – a presentation that has led historians to pair the two – at times that relationship was troubled. Their temperaments were hardly compatible, and Litvinov did not shy away from rebuking Maisky, criticizing his essays on foreign affairs; on several occasions he even complained about him to Stalin.[18] It was typical of Litvinov to keep people at arm's length, though much of this was a deep-seated disdain for the cosmopolitan intellectuals. 'Litvinov had no friends,' recalled Gustav Hilger, a veteran and well-informed counsellor at the German embassy in Moscow. 'There was one member of the *kollegia* of the Foreign Commissariat with whom I had established a relationship of mutual confidence. I asked him once how he got along with Litvinov, and received the significant answer "You don't *get along* with Litvinov; you only work with him – if you have no other choice."'[19]

Moreover, Litvinov detested those diplomats (and Maisky was certainly one of them) who sought the limelight. 'Dignity', it was said of him, 'came natural to him ... Flattery and bootlicking were entirely foreign. Nor could he bear these traits in others.'[20] And yet they shared a common view of the international scene in the 1930s, and Litvinov did not shy away from supporting Maisky and even shielding him from the repressions which engulfed the ministry in 1938.[21] Maisky was to continue to cultivate the special relationship which had been forged in exile. Congratulating Litvinov on his negotiations in Washington, which would lead in 1934 to American recognition of the Soviet Union, Maisky wrote: 'Perhaps it's because you and I are joined by a 20-year acquaintance and by the years of emigration we shared in London that I always follow your work and your speeches on the Soviet and international arena with a very special interest and an emotion of an almost personal character ... Our long acquaintance gives me the right to tell you frankly things which, in other circumstances, could only seem out of place.'[22]

Maisky's relations with Aleksandra M. Kollontay, the flamboyant and militant feminist and a future Soviet ambassador to Norway and then Sweden, at whose house he first met Litvinov, were entirely different. With her he maintained a warm personal friendship throughout his life. 'I find it interesting to be with Maisky,' Kollontay noted in her diary, 'because we don't only talk business. He is a lively man with eyes, mind and feelings open to perception of life in all its manifestations and in all fields. He isn't a boring, narrow-minded person who doesn't step beyond current business and issues.'[23]

Shortly after the February revolution of 1917, which brought down the tsarist regime, Maisky returned to Russia and was asked by Aleksandr Kerensky to join the Provisional Government as the deputy minister of labour. His politics were fast veering to the right of the Menshevik Party. In the wake of the dissolution of the Constituent Assembly by the Bolsheviks, in January 1918, and the outbreak of the Civil War, Maisky failed to convince the Mensheviks to support the Samara-based Committee for the Re-convocation of the Assembly (*Komuch*) in its struggle against the Bolsheviks. His appeal to them was in keeping with his belief – a legacy of his European social-democratic experience – that staying neutral in the Civil War was 'contrary to human nature and logic', and that the *Komuch* government, composed of refugees from the Assembly, was a 'democratic counter-revolution'. Acting on his personal convictions, Maisky defied the party, and in July 1918 crossed the front line to join the forlorn *Komuch* government as its minister for labour. He thus emerged as the champion of the sole armed socialist insurgence against Bolshevism.[24] This was a move that would haunt him for the rest of his life and would lead to an ignominious repentance, which was dismissed by the Mensheviks as 'memoirs of a renegade'. The 'newly baptized' convert was duly expelled from Menshevik ranks and admitted to his adopted church, branded with the eternal mark of Cain.[25]

When the White Admiral Kolchak seized control of the rebel government in 1919, persecuting the socialists, Maisky had to flee again, this time to Mongolia. His year in Mongolia, spent 'crossing Genghis Khan's former homeland on horseback and camelback ... among the deserted mountains and steppes, far from the political struggle, the heated public atmosphere, the influence of party traditions and prejudices', made him reflect on the nature of the revolution – and on his own personal future.[26]

Maisky's earlier timid and procrastinating attempts in summer 1919 to break with the past and make it up with the Bolsheviks – undertaken at a time when their fate was still hanging in the balance – were regarded as inadequate contrition.[27] A year later he wrote to People's Commissar for Education A.V. Lunacharsky, whom he had befriended during his years in exile:

> I now see that the Mensheviks were virtuous but talentless pupils of the past, timid imitators of long-outlived models, thinking in old clichés and formulae from books, without that precious feel for life, feel for the epoch ... The Bolsheviks, on the other hand, excelled in boldness and originality, felt no particular piety towards the behests of the past or towards dogmatic incantations. They were flexible, practical and decisive ... they spoke a new word in the field of revolutionary creativity, they created new forms of state, of economic life, and of social relations ... which others lacked the boldness to realize.[28]

Throughout his life, and particularly during the dark days of the 'great terror', Maisky's earlier association with the Mensheviks, and particularly the role he played in the Civil War (something that was meticulously glossed over in his memoirs and writings), cast a huge shadow over his career and credibility in Moscow. The constructed narrative of his conversion to Bolshevism that he sent to Lunacharsky – atonement for his failure to recognize the Bolshevik Revolution as a legitimate socialist one – concealed the torment of soul-searching which the transition involved and which was never to be fully resolved.

Maisky's inner conflict was reflected in *The Peaks* (*Vershiny*), a four-act drama in verse which revealed the everlasting romantic nature of his thinking, deeply immersed as it was in the nineteenth-century universal humanist tradition of the Russian intelligentsia and coloured by utopian visions. The distinctive codex of the intelligentsia was the formation of a Russian intellectual, independent of his class origin. The title page of *The Peaks* bore an epigraph from Maisky's favourite poet, Heinrich Heine, in German with a Russian translation: 'We want to create the kingdom of heaven here, on earth!' Its theme was 'humanity's endless movement towards the glittering peaks of knowledge and freedom, which were visible and beautiful, but which could never be reached, because the movement was endless'. The extent to which Maisky genuinely repented and fully identified with the Bolsheviks (as he manifestly claimed to do in the first volume of his memoirs, written in dire circumstances in 1939–40) is hard to ascertain. In a self-reflective mood, Maisky related with empathy to Chicherin's account of his conversion to Bolshevism which seemed to be a mirror image of how he felt:

> 'Although I was once a Menshevik our ways have parted. The war has taught me a lot and now all my sympathies are on the side of the Russian Jacobins.' He hesitated for a moment and then added: 'I mean the Bolsheviks.' I cannot be certain that at the time of this conversation Georgii Vasilevich was a convinced Bolshevik.[29]

13. Maisky visiting his Fabian socialist idol and intimate friend Beatrice Webb at her countryside home.

Later on, in her diary, Beatrice Webb, one of Maisky's few trusted and intimate friends, painted a succinct and precise picture of Maisky's intellectual and political character:

> Certainly Maisky is one of the most open minded of Marxists, and is fully aware of the misfits in Marxian terminology – scholastic and dogmatic. But then he has lived abroad among infidels and philistines and his mind has been perhaps slightly contaminated by the foreign sophistical agnostic outlook on the closed universe of the Moscow Marxians.[30]

Concerned with the 'earthly punishments' awaiting him in Moscow for his 'political sins', Maisky hoped to secure through Lunacharsky an amnesty for his past and a guarantee of safe passage as surety 'against arrest, search, conscription, etc., on the road'. Lunacharsky passed on *The Peaks* and the covering letter to Lenin, recommending rehabilitation and even admittance to the Bolshevik Party. The Politburo approved, though in guarded terms, suggesting that Maisky's expertise in economics should 'first be used in the provinces'. He was accordingly instructed to proceed to Omsk, where he eventually established the first Siberian State Plan (*Gosplan*). Meanwhile his repentance was published in *Pravda*.[31]

Maisky's ambitions, however, were intellectual rather than political. They led him at the first possible opportunity to Moscow, where he immediately established contact with Chicherin and Litvinov – 'for old times' sake', as he later recalled,[32] but clearly in the hope of enhancing his credibility, which had been shattered by his association with the Mensheviks.[33] He grudgingly accepted a proposal to become head of the press department of the People's Commissariat for Foreign Affairs (*Narkomindel*), regarding the position as merely a springboard to greater things. At the ministry he met Agniya

Aleksandrovna Skipina, a strong-willed socialist activist, who was to become his third wife (a brief earlier marriage had produced a daughter, who went to live with her mother in St Petersburg and with whom Maisky, who had no further children, maintained sporadic contact; he had also had a short marriage of convenience to help a Russian stranded in London).

Hardly had he settled in his new post than Maisky quarrelled with Lev Karakhan,[34] Chicherin's protégé, seeking his dismissal. Having failed to achieve his goal, he did succeed in steering Molotov, then the organizational secretary of the party's Central Committee, to send him to Petrograd, where he briefly acted as the deputy editor of *Petrogradskaya Pravda*. This interlude as second fiddle ended in harsh discord with the chief editor, who, as Maisky complained to Molotov, had 'taken care to make it impossible for [him] to work at the paper'. A brief spell as editor of the social and literary journal *Zvezvda* (*The Star*) came to a similar end in early 1925, following a squabble within the editorial board. On the whole, life in Leningrad did not agree with Maisky (or, more likely, with his young wife). He felt, as he explained to Molotov, like an 'outsider … a second-class citizen'. In the relatively calm days of the New Economic Policy (NEP), Maisky could still comfortably manoeuvre his career, informing Molotov that he was 'seriously contemplating returning' to work in Narkomindel.[35]

Maisky's first steps in his Bolshevik career revealed an inflated self-esteem, marked by a sense of intellectual superiority and a stubbornness which did not endear him to his colleagues and superiors and often set him on a collision course with them. Although the survival instinct somewhat suppressed those traits during the oppressive 1930s, they would nonetheless keep resurfacing throughout his ambassadorship in London, particularly in his encounters with British officials.

Back in Moscow, Maisky's fraternal relations with Litvinov, who was gradually taking over from Chicherin as the strong man in Narkomindel, proved propitious. In 1925 he was appointed counsellor at the Soviet embassy in London, a position which he clearly cherished. As he wrote to his mother, he and his wife Agniya:

> have taken a small house where no one else lives, we have a maid and we look after our own household … Agniya is learning singing and English and she's starting to chatter a little in English. Our house is in one of the best London suburbs, next to the botanical garden, the air is beautiful, but it's just a shame we don't get more chance to enjoy it.[36]

But his stay in London was again marred by poor relations with his superiors at the embassy. Maisky opted to go back to Moscow, but within a year was persuaded by Litvinov to return to the embassy. Those were turbulent years in Anglo-Soviet relations, following the 'Zinoviev letter' affair of 1924 and the 'Russian gold' contribution to the miners during the General Strike of 1926. There was a fear in Moscow of a rupture in relations, and perhaps even of renewed military intervention. Matters were further exacerbated by the premature death of Leonid Krasin, the Soviet ambassador in London. As one of the few revolutionaries fluent in English and well versed in British affairs, Maisky found his services required. It is rarely recognized that, with no ambassador in London, as counsellor Maisky actually functioned as the *de facto polpred*. 'In the old days,' he boasted in a letter to his father, 'a counsellor would have figured very high on the "table of ranks". Nowadays, the table of ranks has lost any significance for us; however, I can assure you that the work of a counsellor in a place like London is highly interesting and important ... London today is the powerful centre of world politics which can only be compared to Moscow.'[37] His enforced departure from England, following the severance of diplomatic relations in May 1927, left Maisky, as he confided to C.P. Scott, the pro-Russian editor of the *Manchester Guardian*, with 'a feeling very much akin to personal grief'. His years in exile in London and the experience in the embassy had led him 'to understand and respect British culture, which, although so unlike Russian Culture, contains much which is both valuable and great'.[38]

After six weeks of rest and treatment 'on doctors' orders' at the Kislovodsk sanatorium in the Caucasus, Maisky was appointed counsellor at the Soviet embassy in Tokyo, where he spent the next two years. For a while, the appointment suited him well. 'I arrived in Tokyo at the end of October,' he wrote to H.G. Wells, 'and at the present time look around with the greatest possible interest studying this most extraordinary country, which some twenty years ago gave you a good deal of inspiration to write "Modern Utopia".' Writing to the left-wing publicist Henry Brailsford, Maisky hailed Japan as a 'unique country ... combining in some extraordinary manner Oriental Mediaeval with the most modern Americanism ... Add to this beauty of Nature, "Eigentumlichkeit" of people, of habits and customs ... No wonder that so far I had no reasons to complain that our Foreign Office has sent me to this country.'[39]

Always indignant when placed in a subordinate position, Maisky was glad to see the Soviet ambassador transferred to Paris, as this put him (temporarily at least) in charge of the embassy. His experience in Japan helped shape his views on diplomacy, and particularly the belief that diplomats should be fully immersed in the culture and language of the country they were posted to.[40] As a way of introducing the Russian

14. Apprenticeship at the Tokyo embassy.

public to Japanese culture, he organized an extensive visit by the leading Kabuki theatre to Russia, which encountered resistance within Japanese conservative circles. Indeed, during the troupe's first performance back in Japan, following its triumphant tour of Russia, hired thugs released 'live snakes under chairs all around the hall, just before it began. During the show, the snakes began hissing and crawling amidst the audience. A fearful panic broke out. Men snarled, women shrieked, children cried, the curtain had to be lowered and the performance was interrupted.'[41]

Several months later, once again in a subordinate position far from Moscow and Europe, and on the fringes of diplomacy, Maisky was feeling depressed. Moreover, as would be manifested time and again, he was easily led by the whims of his wife, who, he confided to a friend, was 'feeling herself insignificant: primarily unemployed'.[42] The embassy had become a hotbed of intrigue and calumny. Agniya and the wife of the trade representative were 'at daggers drawn' as to who should be the 'First Lady' at state functions. This antagonism between the two, which led to a flurry of correspondence between the embassy and Narkomindel, was not settled in Agniya's favour, and split the Russian colony into factions.[43] Barely a year into his mission, Maisky complained to Chicherin that living in Japan was 'generally dull and wearisome: there is little political work (not enough for two), and any even slightly important question is dealt with in Moscow'. By now, however, Chicherin was ravaged by severe diabetes and was losing his grip on Narkomindel.[44]

Maisky therefore turned to Litvinov with an explicit demand for a prompt transfer, motivated by the Ménière's disease which had troubled his wife since their sojourn in London and which, he claimed, had got worse in Tokyo, leaving her deaf in one ear. He further complained about the havoc which the weather in Tokyo was playing with his own health. Though it was up to the Collegium of Narkomindel to decide on his future appointment, Maisky did not fight shy of stating his own preference for spending a year or two in Moscow (though he was quick to add that he had 'no objection whatsoever to returning to the West'). Litvinov responded favourably, proposing an ambassadorial role in Kovno, which he presented as the fourth most important post after Berlin, Paris and Warsaw. He was, however, also prepared to discuss alternatives if the offer did not appeal to Maisky. It is remarkable that, at the turn of the decade, it was still possible for a Soviet diplomat to dictate his own terms of employment.

It was with great relief that Maisky received the news of the Politburo's decision to withdraw him from Tokyo in January 1929. 'Your attitude,' he wrote to Litvinov in his now familiar supercilious yet cunning way, 'inevitably invigorates my "Narkomindel patriotism" and wish to work in this environment.'[45] On 4 April he was assigned to Narkomindel's press department, but within a week the decision was taken to appoint him as minister plenipotentiary to Helsinki, where he spent the next three years. His stay there culminated in the successful conclusion of the Helsinki Agreement on non-aggression in 1932.[46] Though a weighty post, even Helsinki was far from attractive to Maisky, who clearly aspired to a much more prestigious and challenging position in Central or Western Europe. 'The Russophobia and Sovietophobia here,' he lamented to H.G. Wells, 'are supreme. It is a sort of a general delirium's attack.' For the moment, however, he tried to maintain 'a cheerful and a good fighting spirit'.[47]

Service in London clearly continued to attract Maisky. Even after his expulsion from England in 1927, he had remained attuned to the British political scene. He was thoroughly briefed by Brailsford, H.G. Wells and others about the prospects of the 1929 general election, which could signal the resumption of diplomatic relations – if not indeed his return to London. Those hopes, however, were dashed after the elections, when Ramsay MacDonald's foreign secretary, Arthur Henderson, made the re-establishment of relations with the Soviet Union conditional on a settlement of tsarist debts. MacDonald, so Maisky learned from his sources in London, 'whether by accident or design, tumbled right into the Tory trap, and repeated his old declaration about the identity of the Soviet Government with the Komintern [sic]'. The three months he spent in Moscow before taking up his post in Helsinki convinced Maisky that, despite the critical domestic situation, the Soviet government was 'at present not at all in the mood to pay that exorbitant price'.[48] His main thrust, therefore, was now directed towards Central Europe.

Maisky's prospects of advancement brightened when Litvinov replaced the ailing Chicherin as commissar for foreign affairs in July 1930. Maisky was quick off the mark in congratulating Litvinov, though in a somewhat condescending way, reminiscing about their shared dreams and hopes while in exile in London, and the endless evenings spent together discussing world affairs in a 'murky, sooty flat at 72 Oakley Square'. This was only a prelude to repeated requests for a transfer from Helsinki, a 'small political nowhereville … and a very dull one', hardly a place where 'an active and energetic polpred can remain for long'. Maisky again tried to dictate his own terms, this time by setting the beginning of the year as the deadline for his transfer – even to the extent of apparently being prepared to forsake his position at Narkomindel. 'My intention to seriously commit myself to a long-term diplomatic work, of which I wrote to you a few years ago from London, has not weakened in the intervening years but rather intensified,' he informed Litvinov, 'so that I should be reluctant to leave Narkomindel. Of course, if any concrete prospects for transfer do turn up, I would ask you first to consult with me.'[49]

By now Stalin's firm grip on the commissariat was restricting Litvinov's room for manoeuvre. Neither Maisky's personal pleading, while on vacation in Moscow at the start of 1931, nor a later appeal, again harping on Agniya's failing health (which he claimed could only be treated in Vienna), seemed to move an increasingly disgruntled Litvinov. 'As you ought to know,' he reminded Maisky, 'this issue is not decided by me alone, but by other authorities who are least of all inclined to take account of personal considerations.'[50] Little deterred, Maisky went on pushing forward his own plan, alas in vain: 'Are you certain that working in Vienna would condemn me to diplomatic passivity? Is it really impossible to work on Hungary and the Balkans from Vienna? Won't it be possible to make Vienna our immediate link in dealings with the League of Nations, etc.?'[51]

In the absence of any response, Maisky confined himself to heaping praise on Litvinov, while vigilantly awaiting new opportunities: 'I have no affairs for you today, I just wanted to congratulate you even at a distance on your recent successes in Geneva … The diplomats here are also showing a heightened interest in your personality, and talk quite often of your Geneva successes.'[52]

Resigned to a prolonged stay in Helsinki, Maisky was dumbfounded when the unexpected news of his appointment as plenipotentiary to London was conveyed to him by telephone on 3 September 1932. When, a month or so earlier, the Maiskys had visited Kollontay in Stockholm and candidly confided in her, the appointment to the United Kingdom was certainly not on the cards. 'After a minor post as plenipotentiary to Finland,' an amazed Kollontay commented in her diary, 'suddenly London and at such a troublesome period.'[53] Many diplomats were shocked by his appointment, remembering his dubious past in the Samara government during the Civil War. The decision was obviously made in great haste and reflected a change in the orientation of Soviet foreign policy. Litvinov had succeeded in convincing Stalin that Maisky's familiarity with England – and particularly his ability to communicate and engage people in conversation – was vital. Stalin saw in it 'some sort of an experiment'.[54] Within two days, Litvinov sought an *agrément* for Maisky. The feeble excuses he offered for Ambassador Sokolnikov's abrupt withdrawal were the latter's desire 'to assume work in the Soviet Union' and 'the London climate which does not suit him'. As Maisky's name did not appear on the Home Office's 'black list' of Soviet diplomats who were engaged in subversive activities during the crisis of 1927,[55] the Foreign Office grudgingly agreed that there was 'nothing in M. Maisky's record that would make him persona non grata to H.M.G.'. The more so as his record in Finland was 'not too bad'.[56]

The appointment, perfectly tailored to Maisky's temperament and ambitions, was perceived by him as recognition of his talents and status, placing him as a lead actor at the front of the stage. 'London,' he wrote to his father, 'is a world centre. The other world centre is Moscow. I have to work at the intersection of these two world systems, so it's no surprise that all my time and energy goes on dealing with the many problems that arise from the simultaneous existence of the Soviet and capitalist worlds.'[57] To Whitehall, the appointment of Maisky signalled the Soviet Union's wish to shake off its revolutionary image in Britain by adopting a pragmatic and gradualist course towards socialism. Sokolnikov was evidently ill-suited to the position. Like Maisky, he was the son of a Jewish doctor in the provinces. He had signed the Brest-Litovsk peace agreement with Germany in 1918 and excelled as a minister of finance during NEP. However, his association in 1924 with the 'new opposition' of Kamenev and Zinoviev, who were calling for the removal of Stalin as general secretary of the party, led to his exile as ambassador to London in 1929–32. As long as relations with Britain remained on a low flame, Sokolnikov could be safely kept in England. However, his isolation clearly took its toll and undermined his ability to act in the quickly changing circumstances which now rendered relations with Britain vital to Russian national interests. His English was poor, and even the benevolent Beatrice Webb found him 'studious and ascetic – a veritable puritan – non smoker, did not drink his wine … with a naive faith in communism as the last word of science'. He spent most of his leisure time in the British Museum reading room. He was, she thought, 'a strange member of the diplomatic circle … a nonentity'.

Maisky, on the other hand, was chosen by Litvinov precisely because of his engaging personality. When Sir Esmond Ovey, the British ambassador in Moscow, met Maisky for the first time, he found him 'affable and talkative … a much better "mixer" than his predecessor'. Mentioning those qualities to Litvinov drew an immediate response: 'That is why I appointed him!'[58] In Stockholm, Kollontay attributed his appointment to the growing fear in Moscow that the deteriorating relations might again, as in 1927, lead to their severance. The fact that she had been inundated by telegrams from Litvinov, seeking any possible piece of information about British politics, implied that the ambassador in London was no longer trusted.

15. Maisky trying hard to become a Bolshevik.

The timing of the appointment was propitious, as Stalin's desire to remove Sokolnikov from his post coincided with Litvinov's wish to shift his diplomatic efforts from Berlin to London and to break through the wall of Conservative hostility. Maisky's success in concluding a non-aggression pact with Finland and his constant lobbying surely played their part, the more so as Litvinov was apprised of his wide range of acquaintances in England, his command of the language and his familiarity with the country.[59] Sokolnikov's outspoken militancy, observed Beatrice Webb after first meeting Maisky, was replaced by 'a more accomplished diplomat and less ardent Communist'. Indeed, Maisky's Menshevik past did not go unnoticed in the Foreign Office, and nor did the circumstances which led to his admittance 'to the Bolshevik fold' only after he had made 'a formal recantation'. Soviet communism, as Maisky confided to Beatrice Webb, was 'in the making'. He brushed off the 'fanatical metaphysics' (a substitute term for 'ideology') and the repressions as an inevitable transition stage. He believed in 'the *new civilisation*' established in the Soviet Union as a '*next* step' in human progress, but not the 'final one', without being 'fanatical'.[60] The human race, he told Webb, would 'go on marching to ever increasing knowledge, love and beauty'. He indulged in utopian dreams about a time when the individual would 'be absorbed in the pursuit of the interests of the whole community. Through the advance of knowledge man would conquer this planet and then he would proceed to conquer Venus!'[61]

Likewise, when it was still relatively safe to express views freely, Maisky wrote to Bernard Shaw that he did not regard the Soviet Union under Stalin to be the ultimate socialist achievement. Confronted by Shaw with a biting critic of the 1936 constitution, Maisky recalled that it was a 'Constitution for the Soviet Union in the present stage of its struggle towards the Communist society' – 'the socialist stage'. Playing with the Webbs the 'dangerous game' of what would happen 'after the disappearance of Stalin', Maisky dismissed the idea that he would be replaced by another 'idolized' leader. An idol leader would be 'dispensed with and a completely free communist democracy established'.[62]

On 5 September 1932, Maisky was informed by Litvinov that he had 'carried the decision on [his] appointment with the *instantsiya* [Stalin], so it only needs to be passed by the Central Executive Committee, which will be done upon receiving the *agrément*'. Maisky, who had already agreed to give up his summer vacation, was encouraged to proceed to Moscow for a week of briefing before being whisked off to London. The instructions he received, Litvinov assured him, were not a reflection of his 'own personal views, but the directives of our higher authorities'.[63] Maisky was made privy to the apprehension in the Kremlin that Weimar Germany was on its 'last legs' and that Hitler's imminent seizure of power was bound to introduce chaos on the international scene and threaten peace, which was indispensable for the domestic, economic and political transformation of the Soviet Union. Litvinov had already commented with irony that it was hardly possible to make five-year plans in international politics. The advance of Nazism therefore required a dramatic volte-face in relations with Great Britain, hitherto considered to be the spearhead in the crusade against the Russian Revolution. Foreign policy, unlike domestic politics, had become largely reactive, flexing according to shifting challenges.[64]

The harsh reality dictated a shift from attempts to mobilize socialist solidarity and support for the Russian Revolution among Labour circles to courting the Conservatives, who were, as Litvinov never tired of stressing, 'the real bosses in Britain!'[65] Within days, Maisky returned to Litvinov with a working plan which would characterize his unconventional diplomacy, particularly his recourse to the press and to personal diplomacy, aimed at 'extending as widely as possible the series of visits which diplomatic etiquette imposes on a newly appointed Ambassador, and in doing so to include not only the narrow circle of persons connected with the Foreign Office but also a number of members of the Government, prominent politicians, people of the City and representatives of the cultural world'.[66]

Working with the Conservatives was particularly challenging, heightening the ingrained tension which characterized the work of Soviet diplomats. While in Helsinki, Maisky had already been grappling with the nature of a revolutionary diplomacy. He had sought guidance from Brailsford: 'Do you know of any work describing diplomatic activities/diplomatic relations, position of revolutionary diplomats at foreign courts and governments, etc. of English, American (1776) and French (1789) revolutions? Do not you know perhaps some interesting memoirs of such revolutionary diplomats?' He was still preoccupied with the subject in 1933, trying to find out, as he confided to Beatrice Webb, 'how the revolutionary diplomats were received and how they behaved'.[67] The dilemma for the often ostracized Bolshevik diplomat, allured by the charm of the bourgeoisie, was how to adopt a conformist manner and way of life and to fraternize (if not identify) with the 'enemy', while keeping the revolutionary zeal and ethos alive. This became particularly testing after the diplomatic setbacks inflicted on the Russians in 1927, a consequence of their involvement in the 1926 General Strike, which resulted in the collapse of the 'united front' tactics, deprived Soviet ambassadors of the cushion of Labour support and threw them into the Conservative lion's den. This dichotomy haunted Maisky throughout his long diplomatic career, and he had only a modicum of success in coping with it. Considering his Menshevik and 'counter-revolutionary' past, he was particularly susceptible to accusations of betrayal, which he fervently tried to wave away. When an article in *Pravda* spelled out the problem, Maisky was quick to exonerate himself in a long letter, implying his full awareness of the problem:

> Among the people we have working abroad there is a constant internal struggle between two elements: the healthy revolutionary and proletarian element, which can give a true assessment of 'protocol', and a more sickly, opportunist element, comparatively easily subjected to the influence of the bourgeois surroundings … The struggle between these two elements follows the rule that 'now one, now the other is driven to one side'. In particular, there is a danger that the supporters of 'protocol' might gain a certain advantage … It would be very important if you would continue not to forget our 'abroad' and from time to time to publicize questions of the life of Soviet diplomacy outside the USSR. That would be a strong support for those elements among our overseas workers who consider 'protocol' merely a necessary evil and who therefore try to reduce all bourgeois conventionalities to the absolutely necessary minimum. For I myself have heard more than once how in doubtful cases, where it was unclear where exactly the unavoidable minimum lay, Soviet diplomats have said 'Better too much than not enough', 'You don't spoil the gruel with butter', etc.[68]

Similar pangs of conscience were expressed in Maisky's personal letter to Chicherin, congratulating him on ten years at the helm of Narkomindel:

> You were faced with a very difficult task: to create a completely new type of foreign minister … That task was far harder than creating, say, a new type

16. The alluring bourgeois environment at the embassy.

17. Ballet for the young: the *vie quotidienne* for the children of the embassy staff.

of finance minister or a new type of agriculture minister, because by the nature of your work you have always had to tread the fine line that divides us from the bourgeois world. You had a devilishly difficult position.[69]

Discomfort with the diplomatic role, if not feelings of guilt, continued to obsess Maisky, who was always eager to vindicate his position. In a letter to Litvinov congratulating him on his appointment as commissar for foreign affairs, he wrote:

Do you remember, Maksim Maksimovich, how in summer 1913, when you were secretary to the Herzen Circle and I was travelling from London to Germany, you were the initiator of a 'farewell luncheon' for me which took place in the company of a number of comrades at the Communist Club in Charlotte Street? Well, it seems that it was then that we started to learn 'diplomatic etiquette'![70]

And yet, it is most telling that Maisky preferred to be known in Britain (and indeed signed his letters) as Jean – the French variant of John, or the Polish Jan, as he was named by his father in his youth – rather than the archetypical Russian rendition of Ivan.

The dichotomy rendered Soviet diplomats particularly vulnerable to accusations of counter-revolutionary deviation. Surprisingly, during the purges only a few prominent diplomats defected while serving abroad. It has been suggested that the main reason for the paucity of defections, especially at the peak of the purges, was the stringent regime of prohibitive measures followed by the People's Commissariat for Internal Affairs (NKVD).[71] It seems, however, that the reason why defection was not a viable option for most diplomats had more to do with their commitment to and affinity with both the regime and the country. They were engaged, as is attested by Maisky's diary, in a continuous self-searching process, seeking to successfully resist the seductive 'devil', while genuinely believing that those recalled and tried had betrayed the revolution. Maisky was alarmed by each case of deviation, defection or purge of a diplomat, even if he was only remotely associated with the person involved: he was always keen to prove that he had no connection, and consistently asserted his allegiance to the revolution. He was shattered by the early defection, in 1929, of Grigorii Besedovsky, the acting ambassador in Paris. In self-defence, Maisky hastened to reprimand Narkomindel for its failure to detect obvious early signals from Paris. At the same time, he advocated harsh measures, including 'the purge of overseas workers'. 'When will it happen, and in what forms?' he probed Litvinov. In a follow-up letter, he expressed the view that the Soviet Union was going through a critical stage in its development, when various 'unreliable, narrow-minded, careerist elements which have hung on to the party should depart from us with or without scandals. Not only abroad, but also in the USSR.' He was even going to suggest pre-emptive steps, which, he wrote to Litvinov, 'were better discussed in person than put in writing'. At the turn of the decade, with Stalin not yet quite firmly in the saddle, 'purges' – unlike the repressions which came in their wake – were embedded in the revolutionary culture.[72]

Prelude

27 October 1937[i]

The first five-year plan of my ambassadorship in England has come to an end!
I vividly remember 27 October 1932.

My appointment as ambassador in London came as a complete surprise to
me. True, I had read in the *Manchester Guardian* in Helsingfors [i.e. Helsinki]
that Sokolnikov[i] would soon be leaving and I had often wondered who might
succeed him. But, running through the candidates in my mind, I for some
reason never considered myself. I felt I was as yet 'unworthy' of such a lofty and
responsible post. Yes, rumours had reached me that NKID[2] considered me one
of the most successful ambassadors and that I would probably be transferred
soon from Finland to some other place (this, at least, is what First Secretary
Pozdnyakov told me in August 1932, when he returned from his holidays in
Moscow), but my imagination stretched no further than Prague or Warsaw.

Then suddenly, on 3 September, I received a notification from M.M.
[Litvinov][ii] that I had been appointed ambassador to Britain. I could hardly
believe my eyes. The telegram arrived early in the morning. I went to the
bedroom, where Agniya[iii] was still sleeping, woke her up and said: 'I have some
important news.'

---

[i] Grigorii Yakovlevich Sokolnikov (Grish Yankelevich Brilliant) was, like Maisky, the son of a
Jewish doctor in the provinces. He was a signatory of the Brest-Litovsk peace agreement with
Germany in 1918 and excelled as a minister of finance during the New Economic Policy (NEP),
a post he lost after demanding the removal of Stalin from the position of general secretary
and criticizing collectivization. He was ambassador in London, 1929–32, and deputy people's
commissar for foreign affairs, 1933–34. Arrested in 1936, he was convicted of Trotskyite activities
and sentenced to ten years' imprisonment, but on Beria's orders was murdered by prison inmates
in 1939.
[ii] Maksim Maksimovich Litvinov (Meir Moiseevich Vallakh), member of the Russian Social
Democratic Party from 1898; Soviet diplomatic representative in London, 1917–18, and in the
USA, 1918; deputy to the people's commissar for foreign affairs, 1921–30; people's commissar for
foreign affairs, 1930–39; Soviet representative at the League of Nations, 1934–38; deputy minister
for foreign affairs, 1941–46; ambassador to the USA, 1941–43 (frequently referred to as M.M. in
the diary).
[iii] Agniya Aleksandrovna Maiskaya (*née* Skipina), wife of I.M. Maisky (frequently referred to as A.
or A.A. in the diary).

'What? What has happened?' she asked, immediately worried. 'It's about N., isn't it?'

We were having great difficulties at the time with one of our staff, and I was expecting a decision any minute from Moscow.

'Forget N.!' I exclaimed. 'This is a lot more serious.'

I told Agniya about my new appointment. She was no less astonished than me. There, in the bedroom, we began to discuss the new situation from every possible angle and to draft our plans for the immediate future.

I was greatly touched by the trust that M.M. and the 'high instance' [Stalin][i] had shown in me and I expressed my feelings in a return telegram. The news of my transfer to London astounded our Helsingfors colony, especially the trade representative, the late Stokovsky. They congratulated me, shook my hand, and wished me every success and happiness. We took several photographs of the whole colony and in various groups. The colony gave us a warm send-off.

I dropped in at the Foreign Ministry a few days later and told Yrjö-Koskinen,[ii] then minister of foreign affairs, that I was leaving Finland for good.

'How do you mean, for good?' Koskinen asked in bewilderment. 'What are you going to do now?'

'My government has appointed me ambassador to London.'

'To London?'

Koskinen's slow Finnish mind just couldn't take in the meaning of my words. So I explained to him in detail that I had been appointed ambassador to Britain, that my work in Helsingfors would naturally come to an end, and that I would soon be leaving Finland forever. I uttered a few polite words of satisfaction concerning my three and a half years in Helsingfors and expressed my pleasure at working with him for a year and a half. Only then did it dawn on Koskinen what had happened. He was silent for a moment, then said: 'I would express my deep regret at losing you, were I not aware of how great a promotion this is for you. Let me therefore congratulate you.'

Then the wait began for the British *agrément*. London did not hurry to reply: nearly three weeks passed before a response finally arrived from England.

M.M. wrote to say that I must be in London by the second half of October at the latest and suggested, therefore, that I immediately take a month's leave.

---

[i] Iosif Vissarionovich Stalin (Dzhugashvili), general secretary of the Central Committee of the Communist Party of the Soviet Union (CPSU) from April 1922 and member of its Politburo (Presidium) 1919–53; concurrently chairman of the USSR Council of People's Commissars from May 1941. During the Great Patriotic War, served as people's commissar for defence, supreme commander-in-chief, marshal of the Soviet Union in 1943, and generalissimo of the Soviet Union in 1945.
[ii] Aarno Armas Sakari Yrjö-Koskinen, foreign minister of Finland, 1931–32; ambassador to the USSR, 1930–39.

But I was finishing my editing of the second edition of *Contemporary Mongolia*[3] and I understood that I would have no time in England for literary activity, especially in the first six months, so I declined a holiday in order to stay in Finland to complete the work (unfortunately, the second edition of my book on Mongolia has still not appeared for various reasons).

The Finns were surprised and upset that I was leaving. True, I'd had my share of fights with them. In the very last weeks before leaving Helsingfors, I'd bloodied their nose once again following the absurd behaviour of a police officer in Salla, who thought it would be a good idea to arrest both me and my car (in truth, he hadn't known who was in the car) just because I'd overtaken him. Nonetheless, the Finns sensed that rather than desiring to aggravate our relations, I was working to improve them. Besides, it flattered them that I was interested in Finland, her people, history and art... In a word, the Finns were upset. They arranged a 'friendly send-off', at which Koskinen's wife (he was in Geneva) had a few too many. The Finnish journalists, for whom I arranged a farewell reception, showered me with compliments. I left Helsingfors on 2 October and, after a short stop in Leningrad, finally arrived in Moscow.

I have vague memories of my stay in Moscow. We spent a fortnight in the capital and we were always in a hurry. I had several meetings with M.M., and familiarized myself with the materials. Before leaving, I visited V.M. [Molotov][i] He gave me the following instruction: 'Develop as many contacts as possible, in all strata and circles! Be *au fait* with everything that happens in England and keep us informed.'

I followed this advice during my work in London. And, I may say, not without success.

I left for my new post in London on 20 October or thereabouts. I travelled with the late Dovgalevsky[ii] and his N.P. They were returning to Paris after their holidays. I spoke a lot with G.S[okolnikov]. He gave me a detailed account, among other things, of his talks with Henderson[iii] on the resumption of Anglo-Soviet relations. We made a stop in Berlin. Dovgalevsky left for Paris the same day, while Agniya and I spent about two days in Berlin. We also stopped for a few days in Paris, where Agniya stocked up on essentials – when a woman

[i] Vyacheslav Mikhailovich Molotov (Skryabin), member of the Politburo, 1926–52; chairman of the USSR Council of People's Commissars, 1930–57; people's commissar for foreign affairs, 1939–49 and 1953–56.

[ii] Valerian Savelevich Dovgalevsky, Soviet ambassador in Sweden, 1924–27; in Japan, March–October 1927, and in France, 1927–34. Signed the protocol restoring Anglo-Soviet relations in 1929.

[iii] Arthur Henderson, general secretary of the Labour Party, 1911–34; led the government mission to Russia in 1917; secretary of state for foreign affairs, 1929–31; president of the Geneva Disarmament Conference, 1932–33; Nobel Prize for Peace in 1934.

18. A victorious return to London.

decides to replenish her wardrobe, it always takes a good deal of time. In fairness, though, Agniya is a rather modest person in this respect.

We left Paris for London on the morning of the 27th. I had phoned London beforehand to ask Kagan[i] to meet me in Dover. Our journey between the two Western capitals passed without incident.[4] The sea was fairly calm. On the way from Dover to London, Kagan briefed me on matters at hand. Nearly the whole colony was waiting for us at the station in London: some 300 people. Monck[ii] was also there, representing the Foreign Office. There was an awful commotion on the platform. Our comrades crowded around us, cheering loudly, and there was a terrible crush. Newspaper photographers unleashed their own bombardment. Poor Monck was pushed far aside. I managed to find him and say a few polite words. Monck had not changed one bit: he was just as I'd found him seven years ago when I paid him my first visit in 1925 after being appointed counsellor.

Led by a few gallant policemen, we inched along the platform to the exit, surrounded by a noisy crowd of comrades. A moment later and we were in a

---

[i] Sergei Borisovich (Samuil Bentsionovich) Kagan was first secretary at the Soviet embassy in London in 1932–35, but on Maisky's recommendation was raised to the rank of counsellor, 1935–36, and served as his right-hand man. Banished from Narkomindel in 1939 and employed as a financial worker in the party's municipal committee in Moscow.

[ii] John B. Monck, vice-marshal of the diplomatic corps, 1936–45.

stylish embassy car, speeding along familiar London streets towards our 'home' at 13 Kensington Palace Gardens, W8…

We slowly ascend the stone steps to the entrance hall… We climb to the first floor… Open our apartment doors, marked 'Private'… Walk around the rooms… Look out the windows…

A new home, a new country, a new job. Five years have passed since then. What years they were! A thought runs through my mind, like lightning: 'How much time have I to spend here? What will I see? What will I live through? And what will the future bring me?…'

[Visibly beguiled by the lofty position he now assumed, Maisky left a marvellous description in his memoirs of the presentation of his credentials:

At half past ten two State coaches, mounted on the long soft springs of olden days, and each drawn by two horses, arrived at the Embassy. On the box of each coach sat a majestic coachman in a long, dark coat and cape. On his head was a shining silk hat with cockade, on his hands white gloves and he held the reins and a whip on a long handle. The box was so high that the coachman projected from it like a statue from a plinth. At the back, on a footrest, also lifted higher than the roof of the coach, stood two grooms, likewise in livery. The whole picture was redolent of bygone days and the memories of knightly tourneys. From the first coach stepped a high Foreign Office official who graciously bowed and said that he had been instructed to accompany me from the Embassy to the Palace. He was dressed in the ceremonial gold-embroidered uniform of his office. I was in evening dress, complete with patent leather shoes, black overcoat and silk hat. How different I looked in such attire from the émigré who twenty years before had stood on Folkestone quay!

As we began to go down together from the porch, photographers came running up from all sides and the cameras clicked merrily. The neighbours gathered at entrances to the Embassy grounds and gazed curiously at the unusual ceremony. A groom lowered the folding steps and my companion hastened to make me comfortable in the soft leather seat before taking his place at my side. The second coach was occupied by my 'suite' – the Embassy secretaries whom diplomatic etiquette required to accompany me in my attendance on the King. The cortege started off, and everywhere as we passed through the streets and parks we were a centre of public interest. Pedestrians stopped and closely followed us with their eyes… At last our coach arrived at the gates of Buckingham Palace.[5]

After his return to Russia, Maisky recalled in his diary, on 18 November 1943, the first visit he paid to the prime minister, Ramsay MacDonald,[i] following his appointment.

---

[i] James Ramsay MacDonald, prime minister of the first and second Labour governments of 1924 and 1929–31; prime minister of the National Government, 1931–35; lord president of the council, 1935–37.

During the First World War, Maisky had been 'particularly close' to MacDonald in their unorthodox opposition to the war. MacDonald welcomed the Russian Revolution, expecting it to 'free mankind from the horrors and sufferings of war'. He 'walked in daze' and kept repeating to Maisky: '*Ex Oriente lux.*' Bidding farewell to Maisky, who was hastily leaving for Russia, MacDonald, who 'fell into a solemn, sentimental mood', said: 'If only the Provisional Government would send you back to England as ambassador!... You and me... How much we would achieve here...' Fifteen years later, Maisky was received by MacDonald at 10, Downing Street:

It was a murky November morning. Heavy grey clouds moved slowly across the sky. The light drizzle was typical for autumn in London. Perhaps it was this coldness and dullness in the general atmosphere that lent the beginning of my conversation with MacDonald a strictly official and dispassionate character.

We sat at the long, green table used for Cabinet meetings. Later this room and this table would become quite familiar to me. I grew accustomed to them as one grows accustomed to an office which one frequents to settle matters large and small. I would see MacDonald, Baldwin,[i] Chamberlain[ii] and Churchill[iii] sitting here in the prime minister's armchair. More than once would I find myself in this room, talking, arguing, becoming agitated, experiencing disappointment or joy. Here is where I would spend a lot of nerves and blood... But on that murky November morning all this was still in a future which I could not foresee.

... I looked at MacDonald and thought: Is this the same MacDonald or not? His appearance had not changed much: true, his hair had turned grey and wrinkles had begun to appear, but he held himself upright as before and spoke just as confidently and clearly.

We conversed for about half an hour. He began to thaw towards the end of our conversation, his voice sounding softer and friendlier. He looked at me attentively and said: 'You've changed a lot since the days of Howitt Street.'

'Hardly surprising!' I replied. 'The years pass and we're not getting any younger. Compliments aside, though, I must say that you've hardly aged.'

This remark evidently pleased MacDonald.

'Do you remember,' I continued, 'how you once expressed the hope that I would come to London as ambassador of the Provisional Government?'

'But of course I remember!' MacDonald responded.

'Well, your wish has come true, but with two adjustments. First, I have come not in 1917 but in 1932. I'm 15 years late. Second, I have come as ambassador of the permanent, not provisional, government of Russia.'

MacDonald looked at me suspiciously and asked:

---

[i] Stanley Baldwin (1st Earl Baldwin of Bewdley), British prime minister, 1923–24, 1924–29 and 1935–37.

[ii] Arthur Neville Chamberlain, chancellor of the exchequer, 1923–24 and 1931–37; minister of health, 1923, 1924–29 and August–November 1931; prime minister and first lord of the Treasury, 1937–40.

[iii] Sir Winston Leonard Spencer Churchill, Conservative MP for Epping, 1924–31 and 1939–45; chancellor of the exchequer, 1924–29; the 'wilderness years', 1929–39; first lord of the Admiralty, 1939–40; prime minister, 1940–45 and 1951–55.

'Are you a Bolshevik?'

'Naturally,' I answered.

'But you were a Menshevik in those times.'

'That's right,' I responded, 'the revolution has taught me a thing or two.'

MacDonald shrugged his shoulders.

I waited for a second and said in measured tones, casting a somewhat ironical glance at the prime minister: 'And in those times you were the leader of the Independent Labour Party…'

MacDonald frowned and his face clouded. Then he rose from his armchair, letting me understand that the audience was over. With a dissatisfied grunt, he added: 'Everyone learns in his own way.'

I bowed and left.]

19. Presentation of credentials at the Court of St James's in London.

1934

[Maisky arrived in London with Anglo-Soviet relations at rock bottom, following the arrest in Moscow in July 1933 of six British engineers from the Metro-Vickers firm, charged with wrecking and espionage. Ever since diplomatic relations between the Soviet Union and Great Britain were established in 1921, they had been dominated by mutual suspicion, fuelled by preconceived ideas on both sides. The Foreign Office and the Conservative governments had found it hard to conceive of normal relations with a state that professed subversive revolutionary aspirations. Relations were therefore characterized by major diplomatic crises followed by emotional outbursts of anti-Bolshevism.[1] Maisky had experienced this hostility during the General Strike of 1926, and a year later, when he was forced to leave Britain following the severance of diplomatic relations. The most memorable episode in which he was personally involved during those years took place at Stratford-upon-Avon. He had been invited by mistake to the Shakespeare birthday celebrations in April 1926, and various clumsy attempts were made by the Foreign Office to dissuade him from attending. Once there, he made a cultured little speech about Shakespeare's popularity in Russia, after which his hosts, highly embarrassed by his presence, whisked him away in a car to a remote railway station, where he was put on the London train.[2]

The Metro-Vickers trial marked the high-point of an economic and diplomatic running battle, which had been inflamed by the Labour government's conclusion in 1930 of an Anglo-Soviet trade agreement, the terms of which appeared to be detrimental to the British. The new National Government, effectively a Tory one, which came to power in 1931, employed piecemeal retaliatory action to no avail. In summer 1932, measures were introduced to curtail British imports of grain and timber from Russia – a particularly devastating measure for the Russians, considering the disastrous economic consequences of the failed forced collectivization. Those measures partly reflected the wishful thinking that the strain of the famine, economic hardship and political struggle at the Kremlin might hasten the collapse of the Soviet regime. The Russians were reluctantly forced into negotiations for a new, more equitable trade agreement; but the talks stalled following the conviction of the British engineers. The denunciation of the treaty by Lord Simon,[i] the foreign secretary, coincided with the Soviet decision to send Maisky to London. It somewhat dampened the enthusiasm with which he embarked on his mission. Litvinov even forbade Maisky from issuing a friendly press

---

[i] John Allsebrook Simon (1st Viscount Simon), secretary of state for foreign affairs, 1931–35; home secretary, 1935–37; chancellor of the exchequer, 1937–40; lord chancellor, 1940–45.

release, which the two had carefully drafted earlier. During his first visit to Whitehall, shortly after arriving in London, he was cold-shouldered by Simon.[3] Maisky felt, as he told Beatrice Webb,[i] that he was subjected to particularly rude treatment at the hands of the government. He cited a case when 'Simon and some six Foreign Office officials had accepted the invitation to their reception ... not *one* had come and no kind of excuses had been sent – which, as he observed, was not "good manners".'[4]

The Metro-Vickers case was exploited by Stalin in the domestic sphere to tighten his grip on the OGPU (the Soviet security forces), which were accused of mishandling the affair and undermining Soviet international standing.[5] With Hitler now firmly ensconced in power and unwilling to rekindle the Rapallo spirit, conditions seemed conducive for improving relations with Britain. Litvinov's presence at the World Economic Conference in London, in June 1933, led to a meeting with Simon and to the lifting of all punitive economic measures imposed on Russia, while the imprisoned British engineers were released. Fresh negotiations on a trade agreement were promptly resumed and a new agreement was signed on 16 February 1934, paving the way for Russia to join the League of Nations later that year.[6]

Sent by Litvinov to woo the ruling class in Britain, Maisky was particularly pleased, as the agreement appeared to be the first 'formal recognition of the Soviet Union by the Conservative Party ... a victory of common sense and political realism'.[7] 'The USSR,' wrote Maisky to H.G. Wells,[ii] an acquaintance from his days in exile in London, 'begins to exercise a greater influence than before on the shaping of world affairs.'[8]

In going about his ambassadorial duties in London, Maisky studiously followed the lead of Litvinov, who had spotted the Nazi threat as early as 1931. However, it took Litvinov almost a year to convince Stalin that Hitler's rise to power had meant that 'ultimately war in Europe was inevitable'.[9] Following consultations at Narkomindel in July 1933, Kollontay[iii] grumbled: 'For now we are striving to maintain the appearance of normal relations with Germany. Not enough attacks from our side.' She admitted, though, that the rapprochement between Germany and Poland was most disturbing and was leading the Soviet Union to conclude pacts of friendship with the Little Entente

---

[i] Beatrice Webb, born in 1858 to wealthy and progressively minded businessman Richard Potter, Webb devoted herself to philanthropy in the early 1880s, working first for the Charity Organisation Society among London's poor. She met Sidney Webb in 1890 through George Bernard Shaw, their mutual acquaintance at the Fabian Society. Although Sidney's radical Liberal background and the anti-democratic Toryism of Beatrice's family seemed incompatible, they married in 1892 and their partnership made a significant contribution to the establishment of socialism in Britain. The Webbs believed that the First World War had undermined capitalism and when, in the early 1930s, Sidney retired from public life, the pair promoted Soviet communism, touring Soviet Russia in 1932 and gathering material for their last major work, *Soviet Communism: A new civilisation?*

[ii] Herbert George Wells, a science fiction writer and popularizer of history, Wells, who had close and warm relations with Maisky, was sympathetic to the socialist idea, but became increasingly critical of Stalin in the 1930s.

[iii] Aleksandra Mikhailovna Kollontay (*née* Domontovich) was born into a wealthy family. The daughter of a colonel on the tsarist general staff, she turned out to be an eminent pioneer of women's equality. She was critical of the bourgeois liberal feminist movement, though in retrospect was perceived to be one of its prophets. A militant revolutionary, she was first a member of the Mensheviks, but sided with Lenin and the Bolsheviks at the outbreak of the First World War. In 1917, she became people's commissar for social welfare, but her political career was nipped in the bud due to her association with the Workers' Opposition. She was then sidelined in ambassadorial posts in Norway, 1923–26 and 1927–30, Mexico, 1926–27 and Sweden, 1930–45. She was recalled to a non-active role as a counsellor at the Soviet Ministry of Foreign Affairs, 1945–52.

and, of course, with France.[10] The formal shift in Soviet foreign policy from an isolationist militant 'class against class' position toward a system of collective security in Europe and in the Far East occurred in December 1933. It was a response to an initiative by French Foreign Minister Paul-Boncour,[i] who sought to enhance a non-aggression treaty signed with Moscow in 1932 with a bilateral mutual assistance pact. It was he who urged the USSR to join the League of Nations. Litvinov acquiesced, but pressed for the conclusion of a regional pact of mutual defence within the framework of the League of Nations. He wished to see the Soviet Union, Belgium, France, Czechoslovakia, Poland, Finland and the Baltic States included in what the Russians termed 'Eastern Locarno'. The objective of the Eastern Pact was to extend the Locarno Agreement of 1926, which had provided guarantees to the countries of Western Europe but left the borders in the east vulnerable.[11] Like Churchill, Louis Barthou,[ii] who became foreign minister of France in February 1934, had been a fierce enemy of the Bolshevik Revolution. However, now that the Nazis were firmly in power, he became an ardent supporter of an alliance with the USSR. In Geneva, he wasted little time in producing, together with Litvinov, a draft agreement for an Eastern Pact in June 1934. His efforts to enlist British support were cut short when he was killed in Marseilles by a Croatian terrorist, together with King Alexander of Yugoslavia.[iii]

Simon's support for the Eastern Pact had more to do with relations in western than in eastern Europe.[12] Traumatized by the 'old diplomacy' of alliances, generally held to be the major contributor to the outbreak of the First World War, Simon believed that the pact, with Germany's participation, might break the deadlock and lead to a reconciliation between France and Germany over the issue of German rearmament. He further feared that driving a wedge between France and Russia might encourage the Germans to seek a revival of the Rapallo spirit. Litvinov was only too happy to embrace the British idea of replacing France with Germany in the Eastern Pact, which would then be tied to the Locarno Agreement of 1926. Eastern Locarno, Maisky assured Robert Vansittart,[iv] the influential permanent undersecretary of state, was in no way 'intended to encircle Germany'.[13]

Vansittart's drift towards the Soviet Union has been the subject of various interpretations. It is all too simple to present him as a blinkered thinker, driven only by an irrepressible Germanophobia. Vansittart was a product of the 'Edwardian' old school of diplomacy. He rejected the practices of Simon, Eden[v] and Neville Chamberlain of espousing bilateral agreements with rivals as the best means of preserving peace and stability – practices which eventually led to appeasement.[14] His own strategic vision, following Hitler's rise to power, rested on the premise that Britain could preserve a

---

[i] Augustin Alfred Josef Paul-Boncour, French premier, 1932–33; minister of foreign affairs, 1932–34, 1936 and 1938; French permanent delegate to the League of Nations, 1932–36.

[ii] Jean Louis Barthou, French foreign minister, 1934. Visited London on 9–10 July.

[iii] King Alexander I of Yugoslavia, 1921, assassinated in 1934.

[iv] Robert Gilbert Vansittart (1st Baron Vansittart), principal private secretary to Lord Curzon, 1920–24, and to successive prime ministers, 1928–30; permanent undersecretary of state for foreign affairs, 1930–38; chief diplomatic adviser to the foreign secretary, 1938–41 (often referred to as V. in the diary).

[v] Anthony Robert Eden (1st earl of Avon), Conservative MP for Warwick and Leamington, 1923–57; undersecretary of state for foreign affairs, 1931–34; lord privy seal, 1934–35; minister for League of Nations affairs in 1935; foreign secretary, 1935–38, 1940–45 and 1951–55; secretary of state for dominion affairs, 1939–40; secretary of state for war in 1940.

local balance of power in both Europe and the Far East by allying itself with the Soviet Union, which could place a check on both Japanese and German expansion. A critic of emotional politics, he did not allow his abhorrence of communism to sway him from playing the vital Russian card in the power game.[15] He thus gravitated towards European security based on the pre-1914 entente of Britain, France and Russia. Like many of his colleagues at the Foreign Office, he found Simon most unsuited to his position. Cadogan,[i] who represented the United Kingdom in Geneva (and who was to replace Vansittart under Chamberlain), delivered a devastating judgement on him:

> I have heard it said by those who knew him better perhaps than I did that Sir John Simon's highest ambition for a number of years was to become one day Foreign Secretary. I do not know how much truth there was in that – whether he actually confessed to his intimates that he harboured such a design, or whether he ever made any definite move to win such a prize. If any true friend of his was the recipient of such a confidence he should have urged John to forget it.[16]

Consequently, Vansittart and Maisky assumed the Cassandra role, resolutely giving voice to premonitions about Hitler's intentions. The Vansittarts first encountered Maisky and his wife at a reception at Buckingham Palace in 1933. Lady Vansittart was appalled at the way the ambassador and his wife were snubbed by society. When a peeress seated next to Agniya Maisky hitched up her skirt and stalked away, Lady Vansittart felt moved to sit down beside Agniya and strike up an animated conversation. The couples were to end up meeting frequently, as Maisky and Vansittart not only shared a political outlook, but also went on to forge a literary and cultural bond based on a common admiration of Heine, Lermontov and Kant. While Maisky recited Horace's 'Tenth Ode', Vansittart would retort with snippets from Voltaire. Their conversation would drift to de Basil's Ballets Russes at Covent Garden or to the new production of Bernard Shaw's *Saint Joan* at the Russian embassy. However, what really drew them close was the clairvoyant conviction that Nazi Germany posed a formidable menace to Britain and the Soviet Union.[17] Both also shared a belief in the importance of personal relationship in diplomacy.[18] This was manifested in Vansittart's practice, well recorded throughout Maisky's diary, of leaking information as a means of exerting public pressure – a method which Maisky soon mastered to perfection. 'Curious,' observed Dalton,[ii] 'how these two very dissimilar witnesses corroborate each other's evidence on many points.'[19] Chamberlain's rise to power, however, led to Vansittart's 'promotion' to the specially created new post of 'chief diplomatic adviser' at the beginning of 1938, effectively removing him from the process of policy-making and depriving Maisky, at a crucial moment, of an important ally within the Foreign Office.

Their first meeting of consequence took place during a lunch given by Vansittart in Maisky's honour on 21 June 1934, which was also attended by Simon. Referring to the secretary of state, Lady Vansittart whispered into Maisky's ear: 'I suppose it's my neighbour on the left who is making difficulties?... why should you not have a frank talk about this with Van?' Her indiscreet intervention led to a series of meetings on 3, 12 and

---

[i] Alexander Cadogan, permanent undersecretary for foreign affairs, 1938–46.
[ii] Hugh Dalton, chairman of the National Executive of the Labour Party, 1936–37; minister of economic warfare, 1940–42; president of the Board of Trade, 1942–45; made a life peer, 1960.

18 July (described in the diary), heralding a long-lasting association which introduced a thaw in Anglo-Soviet relations, and in turn helped Litvinov push through the collective security line in Moscow.[20]]

12 July

Vansittart asked me over to brief me about the results of Barthou's visit.[21] The British are very pleased with its outcome. The British government has promised to support the Eastern Pact scheme, as well as the project for a supplementary Franco-Soviet guarantee pact, but under the crucial condition that Germany be allowed to participate in the pact on an equal footing with France and the USSR. Simon will speak to this effect in the House tomorrow. The British ambassadors in Berlin and Warsaw have been instructed to advise ('in a friendly manner') participation in the Eastern Pact, while the British ambassador in Rome has been instructed to ask the Italian government to support the British move.

I expressed satisfaction with Vansittart's report and promised to inform the Soviet government of the British desire to draw Germany into the guarantee pact. I then asked whether Simon intended to make any statement on the Far Eastern issue in his speech tomorrow.

Vansittart was somewhat embarrassed: he did not know for sure, but he would see the foreign secretary in half an hour and discuss the issue with him. Barthou, it turns out, has also asked the British government to define its Far Eastern position.

18 July

I informed Vansittart today that the Soviet government is ready to admit Germany as an equal member to the Franco-Soviet guarantee pact. Vansittart was very pleased and promised to take measures to secure wide coverage in the press. It would be good if the Soviet government also made its decision public. Germany's sole objection to the Eastern Pact has now been removed. If Germany, nonetheless, once again declines the proposal, she will have only herself to blame when other countries become suspicious of her intentions.

I inquired about the reception of the British démarches in Berlin and Warsaw, of which Vansittart informed me on 12 July.

V. replied that Neurath's[i] attitude was cold and hostile, and Beck's[ii] – chilly. Both, however, had promised 'to study the issue'. So far there has been no response from them.

---

[i] Konstantin von Neurath, German ambassador in London, 1930–32; foreign minister, 1932–38; Reich protector of Bohemia and Moravia, 1939–41.
[ii] Józef Beck, Polish foreign minister and representative at the League of Nations, 1932–39.

V. then impressed on me once again the British government's desire to improve Anglo-Soviet relations. 'A certain improvement is already apparent,' said Vansittart, 'but I can see no reason why this process should not go significantly further.' The USSR is concerned about Britain's attitude to Germany and Japan, but Simon defined the British government's position towards the former country in the House on 13 July (I nodded and said that his speech went down well in our country).[22] At the earliest suitable opportunity, Simon or another leading Cabinet member will publicly define Britain's attitude to Japan and emphasize that the British government is interested in securing peace in the Far East no less than in Europe. This should satisfy the Soviet government.

V., however, has a complaint of his own to make concerning the conduct of the Soviet press, which not infrequently accuses Britain of setting Japan and Germany against the USSR. The tone of the Soviet press hampers the improvement of relations, and he would very much like my help in altering it. The point is not that the Soviet press should stop criticizing Britain, or that the British press should stop criticizing the USSR. That, of course, is impossible. But it is desirable to avoid direct accusations that Britain is preparing for war against the USSR, which only serve the cause of elements hostile to Anglo-Soviet *rapprochement* in the press and in parliament ('all the more so as such suspicions are absolutely unfounded').

I replied that although I could fully sympathize with V.'s feelings and intentions, I could hardly agree with his criticisms of the conduct of our press. The press only reflects attitudes prevalent in wide circles of the Soviet population. Why are these attitudes so hostile towards Britain? The question hardly calls for lengthy explanations. The nineteenth century has undoubtedly left a burdensome legacy, while the Soviet period has been characterized by Britain's unceasing struggle against the young workers' and peasants' state. Is it surprising that the Soviet masses have grown to regard Great Britain as their enemy? I am delighted that a turn for the better seems to be emerging in Anglo-Soviet relations. But even I only learnt about it from V. a mere fortnight ago. A considerable period of time will be needed to change the mind-sets of the Soviet masses, even if the turn, which I have just mentioned, is reinforced and persists. But, for now, no miracles can be expected either from the Soviet masses or the Soviet press.

V. agreed, but he asked my assistance in accelerating the process of re-educating Soviet public opinion, without which it would be difficult to establish amicable relations between our countries.

9 August

I called on Vansittart to say goodbye before leaving for my holidays, and he used my visit for a serious political talk.

First of all, V. announced that in reply to our démarche of 3 August (made by Kagan during my visit to Scotland), the British government would willingly support the USSR's admission to the League of Nations and approve the League of Nations' invitation.[23] V. does not anticipate any complications, since Great Britain, France and Italy are unanimous on this matter. Who might object? I mentioned Switzerland. V. gestured disdainfully. I named Poland. V. remarked that Poland would not risk openly opposing the admittance of the USSR, but she might wish to trade her agreement for a permanent place on the Council. France must lean on Poland beforehand. Britain could also help if it came to it.

'So,' V. continued, 'we shall soon be members of the same "club" (V. meant the League of Nations). I am very pleased. At the present time I fail to see a single major international problem that could seriously divide Britain and the USSR. The very course of events and the logic of things are pushing our countries towards each other, both in Europe and in the Far East. We take the same line on where the threat to the world is coming from – so our views on how to parry the danger should also concur in many respects. Our serious and frank discussions (particularly the first one, on 3 July) have greatly contributed to the elucidation of our reciprocal positions and to the growth of mutual understanding. But this is only the beginning. The fact that the British government has supported the Eastern Pact and is now ready to support the entry of the USSR to the League of Nations is the best proof of a serious shift in Anglo-Soviet relations.'

I replied that the Soviet government shares the sincere wish to improve relations between our countries and welcomes both my talks with V. and the parliamentary debates of 13 June, but – allow me to speak openly – it is not yet certain that the shift in Anglo-Soviet relations, which has certainly been apparent over the last two months, will be fully sustained.

'During your holidays,' said V., 'you will, of course, see Mr Litvinov. Tell him, please, that in order to improve our relations it would be desirable to avoid all vexatious incidents. Take, for example, the Metro-Vickers case or the dispute over Lena Goldfields.[24] These cases may not be that crucial *per se*, but the danger lies in arousing passions among the English masses that it would be better not to inflame. It is also important that the press of both countries should act with discretion. Now that Britain and the USSR are becoming members of the same "club", it would be strange if we began to accuse each other of cheating or of pointing guns at one another under the table.[25] Anything that might paint our relations in a bad light in the eyes of the world is to be avoided. It would, by contrast, be extremely helpful to emphasize everything that unites us.'

I concurred with these wishes, but I added that if V. had cause for complaint against the Soviet press (despite its marked change of tone since the debates of 13 July), then I, too, had grievances against the English press. How, for instance, should one understand the campaign concerning the non-existent 'hunger' in the USSR conducted by *The Times* and the *Daily Express*?[26] My words need not be interpreted as a formal protest, but doesn't V. see that such statements in the press hardly contribute to an improvement in the mood of Anglo-Soviet relations?

V. admitted that the English press was also not beyond reproach, but he complained that it was impossible for the F[oreign]O[ffice] to exert a particularly active influence. A few days ago, for instance, Hoesch[i] (the German ambassador) called on him to protest about Low's[ii] caricature in the *Evening Standard* of 1 August. V. informed the paper about Hoesch's protest. The result? Beaverbrook's[iii] press merely used the occasion for renewed attacks on Hitler.

In conclusion, I asked V. what he knew about the Eastern Pact. V. said that Germany and Poland were maintaining silence. This cannot last for long. Both governments have had enough time to 'study' the issue of the pact. A direct answer must now be demanded of them. If a response is not forthcoming, France and the USSR must act. It would be dangerous to delay the signing of the pact. In general, Hitler's position has become more and more enigmatic of late. Following the death of Hindenburg,[iv] he has become Germany's true master. What does he want? War or peace? Austria ought to be the touchstone. Time will tell. So far, Hitler has stuck to the recipe of *Alice's Adventures in Wonderland*: 'Jam tomorrow and jam yesterday – but never jam today.' That's just how Hitler is with peace. He always promises peace tomorrow, but not today.

We parted warmly and arranged to meet two months later, upon my return to London.

[A keen traveller, Maisky left England for an absorbing three-month journey through the much-admired cradle of Western civilization – Italy, Greece and Constantinople – before returning to the Soviet Union. Little did he know that this would be his last opportunity to travel freely in Europe before the dark clouds of repression engulfed Russia.[27] In future, he would only be able to indulge his passion by stealing precious moments in Paris or Switzerland on his way to the League of Nations in Geneva, or in

---

[i] Leopold von Hoesch, German ambassador to France, 1924–32, and to Great Britain, 1932–36.
[ii] David Low, British political cartoonist and caricaturist in *The Star*, 1919–27, *Evening Standard*, 1927–50, *Daily Herald*, 1950–53 and *Manchester Guardian* from 1953.
[iii] William Maxwell Aitken (1st Baron Beaverbrook), Canadian-born British politician, financier and newspaper proprietor; publisher of the *Daily Express* group of newspapers from 1916; founder of the *Sunday Express* in 1918 and proprietor of the London *Evening Standard* from 1923; Conservative MP, 1910–49; minister for aircraft production, 1940–41; minister of supply, 1941–42; minister of war production and lord privy seal, 1943–45.
[iv] Paul Ludwig von Hindenburg, field marshal during the First World War, 1916–18; president of the Weimar Republic of Germany, 1925–34.

Stockholm en route to Moscow. Back home, balancing his act, Maisky spent some six weeks extensively touring the Ukraine and the south of Russia 'studying conditions on the spot, both on the collective farms and in the countryside, as well as machine tractor stations', forming a vivid picture of what was happening in Russia.[28]

While on his travels, Maisky sought (but in vain) a meeting with Litvinov, who was undergoing a spa cure in Europe. Maisky's continued efforts, either through flattery or by exploiting his friendship with Litvinov, to obtain preferential treatment, and perhaps a more pronounced role in the formulation of foreign policy, went unheeded. Earlier, in May, he had begged Litvinov, who was in Geneva 'but a stone's throw away from me', to allow him to come over for a day and discuss with him acute issues which could not be put in writing. Litvinov was clearly irritated: 'Almost all our plenipotentiaries in Europe address similar requests to me. You must agree that Geneva is the last place it would be convenient to hold a congress of Soviet plenipotentiaries.' If indeed serious matters arose, Maisky was encouraged to convey them to Litvinov either *en clair* in a letter or in a coded telegram via Moscow.[29] Maisky's further reproaches directed at the elusive Litvinov for his tendency 'not to inform the plenipotentiaries about your movements across Europe', evoked a sharp response that there was no need for Maisky 'to spend money and time' on visiting him.[30] However, shortly before his return to London, Maisky did have two days of intensive talks with Stalin and Litvinov on the future course of Soviet foreign policy, prompted primarily by rumours of an impending Anglo-Japanese rapprochement, rather than by any imminent fear of Germany.[31] As important for the future of his mission was the impression he gained at the Kremlin that Stalin 'had now established very nearly the same mental superiority over his colleagues as Lenin once enjoyed'.[32]

Back in London, Maisky hastened to lunch with the Conservative MP Robert Boothby,[i] who was close to Eden and Churchill, and fervently tried to convince him that the Soviet Union had abandoned its dynamic revolutionary drive. Boothby had pressed the government in parliament to write off the tsarist debts and seek a rapprochement with Russia as 'the best guarantee for world peace'.[33] Maisky conveyed Stalin's own evaluation that British and Soviet interests no longer overlapped, and that the Soviet long-term designs were 'to consolidate their position in what was after all one-sixth of the globe, and in this respect they would have more than enough on their hands for the next twenty years', rather than contest 'Britain's wish to preserve her existing Empire'. 'Stalin's policy,' he hammered on, was '100% one of internal development and consolidation, and not designed to overthrow any foreign government. This indeed was the issue which divided Stalin from Trotsky[ii] and ultimately drove the latter from power.' Peace on the international front had therefore become indispensable for a successful construction of socialism and for raising the standard of life within the Soviet Union;

---

[i] Robert John Graham Boothby (Baron Boothby), Conservative MP, 1924–58; parliamentary private secretary to the chancellor of the exchequer, 1926–29; together with Churchill in the wilderness throughout the 1930s, sharing his anti-appeasement efforts; parliamentary secretary, Ministry of Food, 1940–41.

[ii] Leon Trotsky (Lev Davidovich Bronshtein), second only to Lenin in his stature as a revolutionary in 1917, he went on to become the first commissar for foreign affairs, 1917–18, followed by a career as the commissar for military and navy affairs, before being chased out of politics, and of Russia, by Stalin in 1927. The most severe critic of Stalinism, he was assassinated in Mexico in 1940, where he had sought refuge.

subsequently, he went on, 'other countries – especially Great Britain – might well be able to adapt themselves to the economic requirements of the modern age without any revolutionary upheavals. Marx himself had believed this to be possible.' Far from aspiring to a revolution, he concluded, Stalin had expressed the fear that war might be 'the end of civilization as we knew it'.

Maisky was faithfully following instructions from Moscow, which is obvious from his detailed conversation with Simon on 9 November. But mutual suspicion remained the main obstacle to any breakthrough. Maisky's admissions were dismissed in the Foreign Office. They showed 'the length to which [the Soviet government] was prepared to go to secure favour here … it was more likely to have been dictated by expediency than by conviction'.[34] However, the fear that the Russians and the Germans might close ranks, rekindling the Rapallo spirit, encouraged the British government to respond favourably to the Soviet overtures. Moreover, the Soviet desire for closer relations provided an opportunity to 'press them for a settlement of the various outstanding [economic] questions'.[35]]

30 October

Yesterday, on the eve of the opening of parliament, the National Labour Party[36] held an important lunch which was attended by nearly the entire Cabinet, with MacDonald, Baldwin and Simon delivering major speeches. Their gist was that we are living, as before, in very threatening times and that 'the National Government' ought to remain in place. Baldwin even made it clear that a return to the traditional policy of single-party Cabinets was hardly to be expected in the near future. Simon plunged into philosophy: the post-war situation, it turns out, has demanded everywhere an extraordinary concentration of national forces. On the continent, this concentration takes the form of one-man dictatorships of various peoples, while in 'democratic England' it issues in a 'National Government'. Evidently, yesterday's lunch supplied the decision-making circles of the ruling classes with their guidelines, slogans and platform for the coming winter and perhaps even beyond.

31 October

I was told the other day that when the prime minister appears on the newsreel, the audience laughs.

MacDonald's personal authority seems to be at a very low ebb.

1 November

I am increasingly convinced that despite everything, Baldwin is still the real leader of the Conservative Party and, consequently, the leader of England and the British Empire. But he is no ordinary leader. H. Macmillan[i] (Conservative) once told me that Baldwin 'is our Kutuzov' (he meant the Kutuzov of L. Tolstoy's *War and Peace*).

[In what today would be a routine practice, but was in the 1930s quite uncommon, Maisky diligently cultivated relations with the proprietors and editors of leading newspapers, particularly the more Conservative ones. His intensive correspondence with Garvin,[ii] the editor of the *Observer*, is a striking example. Maisky would brief Garvin, sometimes in a subtle way and sometimes quite bluntly, about issues which he deemed of sufficient importance to be raised in the paper. Shortly after his return from vacation in Europe, his new initiatives now endorsed by Stalin and Litvinov, he hastily approached Garvin: 'There is so much to talk about concerning the international situation that one has the desire to discuss many topical questions with a well-informed student of international affairs.' He would raise a trivial matter, such as a request for Garvin to put him up for membership of the London Library, *en passant* giving him marks for a recent editorial in which Garvin had put the case for peace 'very ably and convincingly', while congratulating him on 'the magnificent service [he had] done to the cause of peace'. Maisky also did not hesitate to reproach Garvin for a leader which, he feared, was likely to encourage those influential circles in Britain seeking appeasement with Germany and which could create the wrong impression in Germany that Britain was leaving Eastern Europe out in the cold. He was then quick off the mark to congratulate Garvin on a corrective article which appeared the following week in the *Observer*, further briefing him on topics which he expected Garvin to raise in a second instalment. 'The attitude of the British press to this question,' he reassured Garvin, 'is very important and that is why I feel that "Face to Face" was doubly welcome and timely.'[37]]

4 November

In today's *Observer* Garvin sharply attacks Japan's demand for naval parity with Britain and the USA. Seen from the perspective of British imperialism, there is much truth in his arguments. Garvin draws the following conclusion: if an agreement between Japan, the USA and Britain proves impossible, then an agreement must be sought between the USA and Britain (against Japan). Garvin also chivvies the Americans into building grand sea and air fleets. Once again, from the point of view of British imperialism, Garvin's conclusions are perfectly sensible.

The same issue of the *Observer* carries news from Calcutta that Gandhi,[iii] tired and disillusioned, is retiring, and that the Indian Congress, which now

---

[i] Harold Maurice Macmillan (1st earl of Stockton), Conservative MP, 1924–29 and 1931–64; parliamentary secretary to the Ministry of Supply, 1940–42; undersecretary of state for the colonies, 1942–45.
[ii] James Louis Garvin, founder and editor of the *Observer*, 1908–42.
[iii] Mohandas Karamchand Gandhi, leader of the Indian nationalist movement against British rule. Maisky's evaluation of Gandhi reflects the official Soviet critical view of Gandhi, whose ideology of non-violent resistance was identified with the interests of the national bourgeoisie.

consists almost exclusively of highly pragmatic political dealers, is ready to reconcile itself to the reform of the Indian Constitution being prepared by the British and to take full advantage of the positions and cosy jobs that it will make available. Gandhi's 'impractical idealism' merely inhibits these dealers. That's why they are glad to see him bowing out...

One should, of course, treat the *Observer*'s report with the utmost caution. Its British-imperialist tendencies are inescapable. Nonetheless, there can be no doubt that Gandhi's political role is played out. The manual spinning loom has been cruelly defeated by the modern mechanical spindle. British imperialism has once again won out over homespun Indian nationalism, skilfully taking it apart by the tactics of 'carrot and stick'. How long for? Only the future will tell. Yet one thing is clear: when Indian nationalism recovers its strength to fight anew for the independence of the country, it will no longer do so under the banner of Gandhi. An entire historical epoch in the development of the Indian national idea has come to an end. A new epoch is beginning, but it is still in its infancy...

Gandhi! I have Fülöp-Miller's book *Lenin und Gandhi*, published in Vienna in 1927. The author sketches the two leaders with considerable talent, juxtaposing them as the two equal 'peaks' of our time. Seven years ago this comparison seemed absurd only to communists, and perhaps to a few of the more perspicacious representatives of the European bourgeoisie. But now? Who, even among the ranks of bourgeois intellectuals, would dare equate Lenin[i] and Gandhi? Today, any man, even an enemy, can see that Lenin is an historical Mont Blanc, who will forever remain a radiant guiding peak in the thousand-year evolution of humanity, while Gandhi is just a cardboard mountain who shone with a dubious light for some ten years before rapidly disintegrating, to be forgotten just a few years later in the dustbin of history. This is how time and events separate authentically precious metal from its cheap imitation.

5 November

Thank heavens! Yesterday, in Moscow, an agreement was signed between Glavkontsesskom (Comrade Trifonov)[ii] and Lena Goldfields (Marshall)[iii] to annul an old dispute that dated back to 1930. When I think of the bother this case has given me! All this time it has been a thorn in the side of Anglo-Soviet relations! A major impediment to the improvement of these relations has been

---

[i] Vladimir Ilich Lenin (Ulyanov), founder of the Russian Communist Party (Bolsheviks), leader of the Bolshevik Revolution, 1917, and chairman of the Council of People's Commissars, 1917–24.
[ii] Valentin Andreevich Trifonov, chairman of the Central Concession Committee of the Soviet government, 1930–37.
[iii] The representative of the stockholders of Lena Goldfields.

removed; the path for further steps toward *rapprochement* (insofar as this is possible) has been cleared…

6 November

Surits[i] is down on his luck. Hitler kept him waiting for a fortnight without setting a date for the presentation of his credentials, while the secret police arrested a number of German communists who worked at the embassy right after his arrival in Berlin. The arrests were made on 20–21 October. When I arrived in Berlin on 22 October, on my way back from Moscow to London, there was no one to meet me at the station: the embassy chauffeur had been arrested. Bessonov[ii] (councillor) sent a protest to the German Foreign Ministry the same day, but to no avail. It seems that Hitler was highly annoyed with Surits for excessively delaying his departure from Moscow, in the face of Germany's insistent requests.

7 November

We celebrated the seventeenth anniversary of the October Revolution at the embassy last night. I gave a talk. Afterwards there were refreshments, followed by singing and dancing. People were in unusually high spirits. Partly, perhaps, because we were served only champagne and not vodka. It all ended at about 4 a.m.

9 November

Today I had a long meeting with Simon. Referring to M.M. [Litvinov], I formulated my question in the following way: We welcome the initial improvement in Anglo-Soviet relations, we desire further progress in this direction and see no objective causes that could impede this course of events. For: (1) The two sides have no designs on the territorial integrity of one another (the tsarist government may have coveted India, but the Soviet government pursues no such ambitions; the problem for Great Britain at the current time is not to acquire new lands but to preserve those it already has); (2) They are not competing on the global market; (3) They have no serious disagreements

---

[i] Yakov Zakharovich Surits, like Maisky, joined the revolutionary movement in 1902. He was arrested and exiled first to Tobolsk and eventually to Berlin, where he studied political science. Recruited to NKID in 1918, he served as Soviet ambassador to Turkey, 1923–34, to Germany, 1934–37, and to France, 1937–40. Declared *persona non grata* by the French in March 1940, he was recalled to Moscow and consigned to the backstage of diplomacy until his retirement in 1948.
[ii] Sergei Alekseevich Bessonov, counsellor at the Soviet embassy in Berlin, 1933–35; subsequently provisional acting head of the second western department of NKID.

over any of the major international issues of our time (*Europe*: both sides want to preserve peace and to prevent Germany from violating it; the *Middle East*:[38] both sides are interested in maintaining the independence of Turkey, Persia and Afghanistan; the Soviet government has no claims on Constantinople and the Straits; the *Far East*: both sides are interested in preserving peace and the integrity of China, and in preventing Japan from breaking the peace; (4) Both sides have excellent reasons to desire peace – the USSR because it is engaged in socialist construction and has no incentives for war: its domestic market is huge, it has every raw material except rubber on its territory, and it has no investments abroad; and Great Britain because any war in which it gets involved would threaten the integrity of the Empire. This, of course, is just a rough, schematic summary of my thoughts. Why, then, should we not try to improve relations further between the USSR and Great Britain? Why not take advantage of the chance that has come our way?

My words clearly made a great impression on S. He stated categorically that the British government has no designs on Soviet territory, that the government has never supported advocates of the theory that Great Britain would profit from a *nice little war* in the Far East between the USSR and Japan, and that it seeks the possibility of an improvement in relations with the USSR (he mentioned the signing of a trade treaty, and the British government's attitude to the Eastern Pact and to the USSR's entry into the League of Nations). At the same time, he made it clear that *rapprochement* with the USSR should not advance to the detriment of Britain's relations with any other third power (he obviously had Japan, and perhaps Germany, in mind) and, just as unexpectedly, he raised the 'propaganda' issue, which, he thought, might prove a serious obstacle to better relations.[39] I smiled in response to this last point and said that 'propaganda' (whatever each side thinks of it) has played a negligible role in Anglo-Soviet relations recently, and that it would be simply ridiculous if our *rapprochement*, dictated by an array of very serious considerations and a mutual desire to preserve peace, should stumble on this tiny stone. In conclusion, S. said: 'The issues you have raised are so important to the future of Anglo-Soviet relations that I consider it essential to inform Cabinet of our talk. We will then have another conversation on this issue.'

Then I made representation on the anti-Soviet statements made by Lord Hailsham[i] (war minister) in the House of Lords on 31 October and by Duff Cooper[ii] (secretary to the Treasury) at the women's Conservative conference in

---

[i] Douglas Hogg (1st Viscount Hailsham), lord chancellor, 1928–29 and 1935–38; secretary of state for war, 1931–35.

[ii] Duff Alfred Cooper (1st Viscount Norwich of Aldwick), financial secretary to the Treasury, 1934–35; secretary of state for war, 1935–37; first lord of the Admiralty, 1937–38; minister of information, 1940–41; chancellor of the duchy of Lancaster, 1941–43.

Nottingham on 26 September. S. was most displeased by this, but in the end he was obliged to declare that he accepted my representation as a hint about things that should not occur.

In conclusion, I requested an explanation from S. regarding Lord Barnby's[i] mission to Manzhouguo and Japan, and also regarding rumours about the flotation of a Japanese loan in London, adding that any financial aid to Japan would mean promoting the cause of war. S. replied that Barnby's mission was of a strictly commercial nature, that its members' statements were the opinions of private individuals, and that the British government had nothing to do with the mission, did not associate with it, and should not be held responsible for it. S. said he knew nothing about the loan, but he promised to investigate and to inform me about it at our next meeting.

Today's talk with S. may prove to be a soap-bubble, or it may become an important historical event. Everything depends on the Cabinet's judgement.

I'm sitting at my typewriter, wondering which of the alternatives will materialize?

Let's wait and see.

10 November

Last night I attended the lord mayor's[ii] annual dinner. November 9th is a great day in the life of the City. Lord mayors have been inaugurated on this day since time immemorial (they are elected every year from a list of the so-called aldermen of the City). The *Lord Mayor Show*, a medieval ceremony, proceeds along the streets of the town and in the evening a sumptuous banquet is held at the Guildhall for London notables, attended by some 500–600 guests. Heads of mission are also included in the list of guests, but… first, they are invited without their wives (though the English notables come with their ladies) and, secondly, not all heads receive this honour – only the ambassadors and the two most senior heads of mission.

The evening ceremony is most curious. The newly elected lord mayor and his wife – the present lord mayor is a widower and he was therefore accompanied by his daughter – stand on a small dais at the far end of the long hall of the Guildhall's library. A beautiful dark-red carpet, along which the newly arrived guests proceed, stretches from the hall's entrance to the dais. A herald clad in Tudor dress loudly announces the name of each guest. The guest should walk

---

[i] Francis Vernon (2nd Baron Barnby) was a Conservative MP, 1918–22, president of the Federation of British Industries, 1925–26 and director of Lloyds Bank. The report of the large fact-finding mission he led to Japan and Manzhouguo (where the Japanese had set up a puppet government after seizing the region in 1932) was tantamount to recognition of their rule and was published in December 1934.
[ii] Sir Stephen Henry Molyneux Killik, lord mayor of London, 1934–35.

the length of the carpet at a stately pace, step onto the dais and shake hands with the lord mayor and his wife. Then he moves away to the right or to the left of the host, depending on his position and rank. Gradually, large crowds of guests gather on either side of the carpet, scrutinizing each new arrival. According to the custom, outstanding guests are greeted with applause. The volume of applause varies sharply in proportion to the guest's status and popularity. Once the last guests have arrived, the ceremonial procession is formed. Trumpeters lead the way in medieval dress, followed by the City marshal and the lord mayor's confessor. Then comes the mace-bearer on the left, followed by the lord mayor, wearing a hat and a robe with a long train; then the prime minister (MacDonald) with the sword-bearer on the right and behind them the prime minister's wife (on this occasion his daughter Ishbel[i]) and the lord mayor's wife. They are followed by twenty so-called maids of honour, of which this time only four were female (the wife of the outgoing lord mayor and three other ladies of the highest society); the rest were ambassadors and envoys. The maids of honour follow in pairs after the head of the procession (my companion was the Italian ambassador Grandi[ii]). Then come: the archbishop of Canterbury,[iii] the lord chancellor,[iv] the lord president of the council (Baldwin) and his wife, the bishop of London,[v] various ministers (War Minister Hailsham, Simon, Aviation Minister Londonderry,[vi] Secretary of State for Scotland Collins) and their wives, the high commissioners of India, Canada, Australia and Ireland, along with General Smuts[vii] from South Africa, six leading judicial dignitaries, the sheriffs with their wives, and two more prominent notables (Sir [Frank] Bowater[viii] and Viscount Wakefield[ix]) and wives. The recorder of London rounds off the procession. The entire procession passes slowly through the Guildhall's picture gallery and moves around the banquet hall before its members finally take their places at the dinner table. The 'feast' then gets under way, beginning with the obligatory turtle soup, which I seem to find quite indigestible…

Music of different nations is played during the meal (Tchaikovsky, among others); alcoholic drinks are served and toasts made: to the king and the royal

---

[i] Ishbel MacDonald, inn proprietor and daughter of former Prime Minister Ramsay MacDonald. See diary entry for 27 November 1938.

[ii] Dino Grandi, Italian minister of foreign affairs, 1929–32; ambassador to Great Britain, 1932–39; minister of justice, 1939–43.

[iii] William Cosmo Gordon Lang, archbishop of Canterbury, 1928–42.

[iv] Viscount John Sankey, lord chancellor, 1929–35.

[v] Arthur Foley Winnington Ingram, bishop of London, 1901–39.

[vi] Charles Vane-Tempest-Stewart (7th marquess of Londonderry), Conservative MP, 1906–15; secretary of state for air, 1931–35; leader of the House of Lords and lord privy seal, 1935.

[vii] Jan Christian Smuts, field marshal, prime minister, foreign minister and defence minister of the Union of South Africa, 1939–48.

[viii] Sir Frank Henry Bowater, sheriff of London, 1929–30; member of London County Council, 1934–37; lord mayor of London, 1938–39.

[ix] Charles Cheers Wakefield (1st Viscount Wakefield), lord mayor of London, 1915–16.

family, to the foreign ambassadors and envoys, to the government, to the army, to the navy, etc. The prime minister usually delivers a major political speech (though no longer than 30 to 40 minutes). By 11 p.m. the evening draws to a close and the guests make their way home. Those who wish to may stay a bit longer and dance to the orchestra in the library – but few tend to do so...

On the whole, the scene impresses one with the vividness of its colours and its medieval solemnity. No wonder: the programme and the banquet menu bear on their cover an engraving of the Charter of King John of 9 May 1215 that asserted the liberties of the City of London and granted the barons the right annually to elect their mayor, who should be loyal to the king, modest and fit to rule the city, and who should be presented to the king, or to his supreme judge in the king's absence, immediately upon election.

* * *

There were some interesting moments at yesterday's banquet.

I attended the lord mayor's dinner for the first time two years ago, directly after my appointment as ambassador. Anglo-Soviet relations were strained; the Conservatives were still obsessed with the idea of breaking relations with the USSR; the old trade agreement of 1930 had just been renounced. It so happened that I had to walk the red carpet in the Guildhall library straight after the Japanese ambassador Matsudaira.[i] He was received warmly with long and cordial applause. I was met with icy silence. Not a single clap echoed in the enormous hall as I made my way from the entrance to the lord mayor.[40] The splendid crowd, closely packed on both sides of the carpet, followed me with their curious and hostile gazes. Pointing at me with their lorgnettes, fashionably attired ladies whispered to each other venomously and laughed. What were my feelings at that moment? They were mixed, but two predominated: profound vexation at this motley, gold-spangled throng, which so vividly embodied the old world of dying capitalism; and joyous pride in our revolution, the USSR and the Communist Party, which embodied no less vividly the rising epoch of socialism. Two worlds, two epochs met in this long hall decorated with carved wood, on the knife-edge of the narrow red carpet; and it was not without inner satisfaction that I observed the sharp repulsion between the positive and negative electric charges of our era. In my thoughts I addressed the crowd that surrounded me: 'Aha! You are afraid of me and hate me, you take me for a bandit who has suddenly burst in on your holy of holies, on your life's feast; you passionately want to set your dogs and guards on me, to throw me out of this dazzling hall into the dark and damp of the November night – but *you cannot do this*! I am here in the name of the great revolution, I was sent here by the

---

[i] Tsuneo Matsudaira, Japanese ambassador in London, 1929–36.

Soviet government and the Communist Party of the USSR, and you, despite all your enmity, are *obliged* to receive me. Your lord mayor, gritting his teeth, *has to* make a pleasant face and shake my hand as a friend! Therein is the sign of *our force and of our future triumph* the world over!'⁴¹

That's how it was two years ago. Last year I didn't have to attend as I was on leave in Moscow. And now? As chance would have it, this time, too, I followed Matsudaira onto the red carpet. How did the crowd respond? Once again, Matsudaira was greeted with applause, but sporadic and short, not loud and generous. I was greeted in a similar manner – with sporadic, short claps. The conclusion is clear: in the last two years Japan's stock has fallen significantly on the British political market (because of dumping and the aggression in East Asia), while Soviet stock has risen considerably (thanks to our stupendously growing might and to the success of our policy of peace). In the last two years, the great shift of historical forces that began in October 1917 has made a great stride forward, and this was reflected yesterday at the lord mayor's banquet...

I met the famous General Smuts at the banquet. We were introduced by the American ambassador, Bingham.ⁱ Smuts immediately showed a great deal of friendliness towards me, even warmth. He literally 'buttonholed' me and started talking about the USSR. I was not a little surprised to discover that he was very familiar with events in our country, and that his attitude to us was far from hostile. He developed at length the thought that although we may have made many mistakes, and continued to make them, we were nevertheless building a new world. 'The old Russia, which appeared to be dying and falling apart,' he said, 'was suddenly revived and rejuvenated. That impetus will carry you through for at least one hundred years.' Smuts has a very pessimistic view of international affairs, especially in Europe. 'Squabbles and rows' within the European family of nations upset him all the more because of the new and very dangerous threat looming on the historical horizon – the 'yellow peril'. Japan sets the tone and China, sooner or later, will follow. In general, 'Asia is stirring', and if Europe fails to come to its senses and sort out its domestic affairs, the yellow race will defeat the white one. Smuts is very concerned by Japan's aggression and is highly critical of it.

See how much confusion can reign in a single head – a far from stupid head, but bourgeois!...

* * *

When, in search of my seat, I found myself two chairs away from my destination, I was suddenly struck by the sound of Russian speech. I raised my head and saw the following scene. On the other side of the table, directly opposite my seat,

---

ⁱ Robert Worth Bingham, US ambassador to London, 1933–37.

a tall grey-haired lady wearing a grey-blue silk dress and a yellowish brocade cloak was in quite a state and making gestures. Her face was quite pleasant, but now it was all blotched with red. Two young people hung about her, quite at a loss: a young girl in green and a respectable grey-headed gentleman wearing a velvet suit with a star on his breast. I heard the woman saying hysterically in Russian: 'I cannot sit here! I just can't!'

The respectable gentleman whispered something into the grey woman's ear in an attempt to calm her down, but without success. 'I won't sit here! I'm leaving!' the obstinate lady continued to yell.

The green girl rearranged the sets on the table and moved the lady two chairs away from me. The lady calmed down a touch, but she flared up again when she saw me on the point of taking my seat and shouted, her face aflame: 'Blood on your hands!'

I cast an ironic glance at the agitated lady and started talking calmly to my neighbour. The lady flopped into her seat and angrily shifted a vase so that I could not see her behind the flowers.

In the course of conversation I asked my neighbour, who turned out to be the wife of the senior alderman Twyfold, for the surname of the woman who had just made a scene.

'Oh,' she said. 'That's Lady Kynaston Studd. Her husband Sir Kynaston Studd[i] (the gentleman in a velvet suit) was an alderman. He served as lord mayor for a year, then retired. He is rich, and she is a Russian princess. They married during the war.'

Then my neighbour added with a meaningful intonation: 'Lady Studd is a charming woman, but she is somewhat highly strung.'

What delicacy of expression! How very English! The husband of the Russian princess, evidently taken aback by his wife's behaviour, took pains to be especially nice to me (once again, in the English fashion) and even toasted my health. Meanwhile, his stubborn wife, a little flushed with wine, seemed to have 'tempered justice with mercy'. She pushed aside the vase that separated us and started to scrutinize me with unconcealed insolence...

My neighbour, the wife of the senior alderman, was saying: 'I'm from Australia, but my husband is English. I've only been in London for a while and it still doesn't quite feel like home.'

'How long have you been living in London?' I asked for the sake of saying something.

'Twenty-four years,' she answered calmly.

I was stunned.

---

[i] Sir John Edward Kynaston Studd, senior sheriff of London, 1922–23; alderman of the City of London, 1923–42; lord mayor of London, 1928–29.

That's English stability for you!

* * *

MacDonald delivered a half-hour speech at the banquet, devoted to the situation at home and abroad. He welcomed, among other things, the USSR's entry to the League of Nations, reproached Germany for its tendency to self-isolation, and made an emotional appeal for the preservation of peace the world over.

12 November

I met Jennie Lee[i] and her husband, the Labour MP Aneurin Bevan,[ii] at Naomi Mitchison's[iii] literary soirée. They were in a foul mood. Jenny was particularly displeased. She is thought to be so far left as to be all but a communist, but now she is utterly depressed: the working masses have moved left, but they don't even listen to the 'left'. They believe in Labour, pin great hopes on a third Labour Cabinet which could rely on its own majority, and surrender all their sympathies and votes to Labour. The left, according to Jenny, is out of a job.

'It's all right for you in Russia,' she finally said. 'You've already entered the formative stage of socialism, you can work. But what about us?... I'd like to fall asleep now and wake up when it's easier to serve the cause.'

How do you like that?! Of course we're happy in the Soviet Union. We really are building socialism. But think what this happiness has cost us! If we had whined like Jennie at difficult moments, what would have remained of us? What would have happened to the revolution?...

I also saw Pritt[iv] (a prominent left-minded Labour lawyer) at the party. He was in low spirits as well. He spoke of the 'catastrophe' of the Socialist League[42] and of Morrison's[v] domination in the Labour Party.

15 November

Today I attended the dinner given by the ancient guild, The Worshipful Company of Stationers and Newspaper Makers (already 600 years old).

---

[i] Baroness Janet (Jennie) Lee of Asheridge.

[ii] Aneurin Bevan, Labour MP, 1929–60.

[iii] Naomi Mitchison, Scottish social activist and author of more than 70 books for adults and children.

[iv] Denis Nowell Pritt, Labour MP, 1935–50, president of the British Society for Cultural Relations with the USSR, 1933–69; expelled from the Labour Party in 1940 for supporting the USSR's war against Finland. On his close relations with Maisky, see *VSD*, pp. 211–14.

[v] Herbert Stanley Morrison (Baron Morrison of Lambeth), Labour MP, leader of the London County Council, 1934–40, minister of supply, 1940; home secretary and minister of home security, 1940–45; member of the War Cabinet, 1942–45.

I had expected the dinner to be accompanied by some very old customs, but I was disappointed. It was a dinner like all the others, right down to the inescapable turtle soup, and only the painted arched windows of the dining hall suggested the past. I tell a lie: there was also 'The loving cup', but I had seen that already at the lord mayor's banquets. The guests, though – they really did bring the odd whiff of medieval times. To my right sat Lord Marshall[i] (a big publisher and a former lord mayor of London), who proudly declared that he had been in the guild for 55 years!

'Is membership hereditary?' I asked in some perplexity.

'No,' answered Lord Marshall, 'it is not. I joined the guild as soon as I became an apprentice in my profession.'

It turned out that my neighbour was already 70. To my left sat Lord Wakefield, a major oil industrialist, prominent philanthropist and London alderman. He's also about 70 years old (a schoolmate of Marshall's!). This venerable notable of the British Empire told me that about 30 years ago (a truly English time span!) he had planned a visit to St Petersburg and had even booked the tickets when suddenly, at the last moment, he received a telegram, claiming 'plague in Russia'. Naturally, he decided not to travel. Perhaps now was the time to go?... I seconded his intention.

'Tell me,' he continued, wiping his brow and appearing to remember something. 'You seem to have a man... Lenin... Is he really terribly clever?'

'I can assure you he was,' I answered, smiling, 'but unfortunately he died back in 1924.'

'Died?' Wakefield sounded disappointed. 'Really?... I wasn't aware of that.'

See how well the cream of the English bourgeoisie is informed about Soviet affairs!

Truly it smacks of the Middle Ages!...

* * *

Since last year, the chairman (or Master) of the guild has been the prince of Wales.[ii] Our 'friend' the archbishop of Canterbury made a witty toast in honour of the prince (the archbishop, it must be said, is an outstanding dinner speaker), and the prince responded in the customary manner. Then everybody moved to the smoking room. Here the prince, who considered it his duty as host to exchange a couple of niceties with every diplomat present, quite unexpectedly engaged me in a long and inappropriately serious conversation. First, he asked me whether I have to deliver many speeches. When I complimented him on his speech he, somewhat embarrassed, started talking about the best English

---

[i] Horace Brooks Marshall (1st Baron Marshall of Chipstead), lord mayor of London, 1918–19.
[ii] Prince of Wales, 1911–36; King Edward VIII of Great Britain, January 1936, becoming Prince Edward, duke of Windsor, after abdicating from the throne in December 1936.

orators, past and present. He named the late Lord Birkenhead,[i] General Smuts and Lloyd George,[ii] but not MacDonald. He said of the premier, with a slight grimace: 'You know, he is not exactly...' Then he told me that only today he had attended an exhibition of machine-tools and had been delighted to learn that the USSR was a very loyal consumer of British machinery. I confirmed this and cited a few figures. He asked me about our process of reconstruction and the successes of the five-year plan, and remarked that he hoped for a further increase in Soviet orders placed in Britain. I responded with a smile: 'Agreed, but give us appropriate conditions of credit.' The prince made a gesture as if to say, 'That is not really my business.' He then moved on to international politics, speaking at length about the threat of war and the complicated international situation, before finally concluding: no one wants war – not England, not France ('she only stands to lose by war!') and not even Germany. I expressed my doubts as to the peaceful intentions of the latter, as well as of Japan. The prince did not object, but he began to argue emphatically that England strives only for peace, and that militarist ideas are alien to the spirit of the British nation. 'When I have to say some parting words to a regiment or battalion headed to China or any other place in Asia,' the prince continued, 'I always tell them: I hope you will never need to use your weapons.' He then praised the British soldiers and sailors, describing them as nice lads, amiable gentlemen, etc. For my part, I stated that Soviet foreign policy was a policy of peace, and that I was glad to hear from the prince of Wales that Great Britain seeks the same aim. This pleased the prince, who repeated that nobody really wanted war and that the forces of peace were far more numerous and mightier than the forces of war. I remarked, however, that the forces of war were much better organized, especially arms manufacturers, so the threat of war was very serious indeed. The prince agreed and added musingly: 'You mention arms manufacturers... True, they do well out of war, but they could do no worse in peace time. Take the plan to build floating aerodromes in the Atlantic to facilitate the movement by air of passengers and mail between Europe and America. Wouldn't that be

---

[i] Frederick Edwin Smith (1st earl of Birkenhead), a scholar in Oxford, later Conservative MP; secretary of state for India, 1924–28.

[ii] David Lloyd George, Liberal MP for Caernarvon, 1890–1945; prime minister of Great Britain, 1916–22; leader of the Liberal Party, 1926–31. When Hitler came to power, he advocated frontier concessions over the Saar, Danzig, Polish corridor and the Rhineland. He even visited Hitler at Berchtesgaden, describing him as the 'George Washington of Germany'. In the wake of the Munich Agreement, he recognized the case of the Sudeten Germans but pressed for the end of appeasement and the launching of a vigorous policy of rearmament. He championed an alliance with the Soviet Union. Hindsight tends to overlook his powerful position well into the war; his speech in the Commons on 8 May 1940 was a major contributory factor in Chamberlain's downfall and Churchill's rise to power. He declined offers to join Churchill's War Cabinet and the ambassadorship in Washington. On the 50th anniversary of his entry into parliament, Maisky, who had cultivated particularly close relations with him, sent him an exhilarated letter thanking him for their conversations 'which will undoubtedly for ever remain in my memory as events of outstanding interest and pleasure'; RAN f.1702 op.4 d.994 ll.11–13, 12 April 1940.

good *business* for metallurgical companies? You could find many other similar opportunities.' I entirely agreed with him and added that the forces of peace must be also well organized in order to combat effectively the forces of war. The states that oppose war must cooperate in safeguarding peace. The prince agreed with me. Towards the end of our conversation he inquired about my past, so I described my career in diplomacy. He then asked: 'Where did you learn English?' I answered that for five years, between 1912 and 1917, I had lived in England as a political émigré. The prince laughed and exclaimed: 'And now you are the ambassador! It's a sign of the times. We are living in an astonishing epoch!'[43]

Our chat lasted for 10–15 minutes. The prince and I stood in the centre of the smoking-room, while a crowd of shocked diplomats and some two hundred British notables, headed by the archbishop of Canterbury, stood around us, exchanging glances and whispers. The Turkish ambassador, Fethi Bey,[i] tried several times to enter the conversation, but without success. The prince spoke to me the entire time. It was clearly done for show, and quite intentionally so. Not for nothing was the prince's secretary, Sir Godfrey Thomas,[ii] also present at the dinner, where Lord Marshall had said to me with particular emphasis: 'There is the power behind the throne.'

Quite clearly, the ruling elite wished to make a public demonstration of the improvement in Anglo-Soviet relations. Fine. But I have heard not a squeak from Simon in response to our talk of 9 November. Let's be cautious in our evaluations and vigilant in registering the symptoms.[44]

16 November

I visited Eden on returning from holiday. I hadn't meant to discuss serious matters, but our conversation seemed to veer of its own accord towards current political issues. The most important:

(1) Eden said, word for word: 'At the present moment, no conflicts exist between Great Britain and the USSR anywhere in the world. On the contrary, they have one common and highly important interest – the preservation of peace. You need peace to complete your great experiment, and need it for the development and flourishing of trade. This creates favourable conditions for improving Anglo-Soviet relations.' Eden knows about my talk with Simon on 9 November. Boothby had also informed him about his talk with me on 6 November.

(2) Eden was very glad to learn that we had not abandoned our efforts to conclude the Eastern Pact. He stated that he would discuss this issue with

---

[i] Ali Fethi Bey (subsequently Fethi Okyar), Turkish ambassador in London 1934–39.
[ii] Sir Godfrey John Vignoles Thomas, private secretary to the prince of Wales, 1919–36.

Beck in Geneva (Eden leaves for Geneva tomorrow to attend the session of the Council of the League of Nations).

(3) The talks between Eden and Ribbentrop[i] bore an entirely frivolous character. Eden is very sceptical about the likelihood of Germany's imminent return to the League of Nations. It is possible that Hitler himself does not want war, but everything that is now taking place in Germany clearly points towards it. That's why Germany is the main potential seat of war at the present time.

(4) The British government does not want to get involved in intense debates on disarmament and other international issues until the Saar question is fully resolved, so it is prepared to support Henderson's suggestion to adopt his memorandum promptly (to draw up a disarmament convention relating to issues of secondary importance on which agreement is possible) and to leave the rest to the conference chairman and the [International] bureau.

Eden invited me to drop in when he returns from Geneva.[45]

17 November

The Chinese envoy Guo Taiqi[ii] came by. We had a long talk about current political issues. G.'s mood was not the best. He told me bluntly: 'It's all right for you: the USSR is a mighty power, and England has to take you seriously. Not so with China. Each time Chinese and Japanese interests clash, England invariably sacrifices our interests for those of Japan.'

At the moment G. views England's behaviour with great suspicion. He has been informed that Simon and Matsudaira are conducting secret political talks concerning the settlement of their mutual conflicts in the Far East. Naturally, both England and Japan expect this to happen at the expense of China. G. tried to find out what I knew about this issue.

G. also said, in reply to my query, that Sir Frederick,[iii] head of British customs in China, had been exploring the possibility in London of raising a loan to China for internal reconstruction (roads, harbours, etc.), but had not met with a sufficient response. In the first place, English banks are extremely reluctant today to invest money abroad. Secondly, the only form in which they can conceive of such a loan is an international consortium with the participation of Japan, but this does not suit the Chinese, who fear that the forming of a consortium would immediately raise the issue of old Chinese debts, in particular the 'Nishihara loans'[46] granted by Japan. That may indeed be true.

---

[i] Joachim von Ribbentrop, German ambassador to Great Britain, 1936–38; foreign minister, 1938–45.
[ii] Guo Taiqi, Chinese ambassador to London, 1932–41; Chinese delegate to the League of Nations, 1934–38; minister of foreign affairs, April–December 1941.
[iii] Sir Frederick William Maze, inspector-general of Chinese Maritime Customs, 1929–43.

In any case, G.'s information about the Chinese loan should be treated with a certain degree of caution, since he is an interested party.

18 November

Today's *Observer* features a very interesting article, 'Crisis in the Pacific', by Lord Lothian.[i] Concern over the future of British interests in the Far East seems to be growing. More far-sighted British politicians have already started looking for ways out of the situation that is developing – mainly, by promoting Anglo-American *rapprochement*. Well, from the point of view of our – Soviet – interests, this is not damaging. On the contrary, it could even be beneficial, since Anglo-American *rapprochement* isolates Japan.

23 November

'*Functions*' linked to the royal wedding have begun.[47] Today our doyen, the Brazilian de Oliveira,[ii] held a reception for the diplomatic corps 'to meet the Duke of Kent[iii] and Princess Marina'.[iv] At around 6 p.m., all the Heads of Mission gathered in the doyen's relatively small residence, accompanied by their wives. Only the Americans were missing, along with the ambassadors of Czechoslovakia and Afghanistan. These last two were away, but I can't explain the absence of the Americans. The happy couple arrived at 6.30, accompanied by the parents of the bride. Excitement was growing in the hall. Silence, snatched whispers, ladies casting curious glances… Eventually the guests appeared, preceded by the doyen and his wife. Marina looked charming to me, much better than she did in the newspapers: a blonde with luxurious hair, a rosy complexion, bright eyes. Thin and refined. One diplomat later told me that her photographers should have been shot for ruining Marina. Right he was! The duke of Kent isn't bad either: tall, slender, with quite a pleasant face. He stoops a little and seems to be very shy. In any case, he is the most handsome of the king's sons. On the whole, seen from the physical and physiological point of view, they make a nice couple. The bride's parents – Prince Nicholas of Greece[v] and his wife (a Russian princess, I believe) – resemble provincial landowners of middling means…

The doyen made a short welcome speech in English and presented the bride and groom with a large silver tureen and two silver salad bowls on behalf of the

---

[i] Philip Henry Kerr (11th marquess of Lothian), Lloyd George's private secretary, 1916–21; chancellor of the duchy of Lancaster, 1931–32; ambassador to the USA, 1939–40.
[ii] Raul Regis de Oliveira, Brazilian ambassador in London, 1925–40; doyen of the diplomatic corps, 1933–40, succeeded by Maisky.
[iii] Prince George Edward, duke of Kent, fourth son of George V.
[iv] Princess Marina, duchess of Kent, wife of Prince George, duke of Kent.
[v] Prince Nicholas of Greece, father of Princess Marina who in 1934 married the duke of Kent.

entire diplomatic corps. (Today, I received a letter from the doyen, notifying me that the cost of the present was 300 pounds, of which my share is 6). The facsimile signatures of all the heads of mission who contributed to the gift are engraved on the inside of the tureen, and my name is among the first. It immediately catches the eye when one looks inside. Won't that be fun for Marina! It may spoil her appetite, I'm afraid. But there's nothing to be done: such are the contradictions of our times. Grin and bear it. Moreover, I shall be attending Marina's wedding. Responding to the doyen, the duke mumbled a few embarrassed words of gratitude, after which he and the princess went closer to inspect the silverware. Then the doyen and his wife started introducing all the members of the diplomatic corps to the duke and Marina, and also to Marina's parents. It was all quite badly organized. There was even a minor commotion at the beginning. As a result, Agniya and I, having greeted the bride and groom, failed to exchange greetings with the bride's parents. Some ladies did not understand that they should curtsey, as etiquette demands. Some had their trains trodden on, or their feet. In the end, though, everybody was introduced. I watched Marina attentively: when the doyen announced my title, her bright eyes suddenly became as tense and cold as steel, yet she remained utterly composed. But when we moved away, Marina cast furtive, searching glances at A. and myself…

The doyen and his wife obviously thought they were in seventh heaven. Mrs de Oliveira's secretary told our Finimor afterwards, when Finimor came to make some inquiries: 'Her Excellency is so very happy to have received this rare honour – to participate in a royal wedding, to the greater splendour and glory of the royal family…'

Yes, 'to the greater splendour and glory…' Hm!

When the first excitement subsided and the guests of honour entered into lively conversation with the more sociable members of the diplomatic corps, the room filled once again with the hum of idle chatter. The gathering divided into groups. I found myself in a corner talking to the new Norwegian envoy, Colban.[i] He arrived in London only recently, after representing his country for ten years at the League of Nations and four in Paris. Thin, with a slight limp, he gives the impression of a thoughtful, intelligent man. Our conversation developed as follows:

I: Our doyen's daughter is a beauty, isn't she? (she was passing us at that moment).

Colban: Oh, yes, she is charming… And this dazzling society supplies such a fine frame for her beauty!

---

[i] Erik Andreas Colban, Norwegian ambassador in France, 1930–34, and in London, 1934–46.

I: Do you think so? But this dazzling society also represents a great danger to such a young girl.

C.: (interpreting my words in his own way): You may be right. Just think: this beautiful young girl will marry a man with neither the means nor the status to mingle in such fine society. She will be unsatisfied and will consider herself unhappy.

I: It's quite possible. But I'm thinking of another thing. What will happen to this pretty girl, pampered with a refined upbringing, unfit for any of life's struggles, in another 10, 15, or 25 years?

C. gives me a perplexed and somewhat frightened look.

I: Well, yes – there are plenty of reasons to believe that many of those who are now at the top will find themselves at the bottom over the next 25 years...

C.: (with bated breath): So you think it will take another 25 years?!...

I: (smiling): I can't vouch for an exact period, but even assuming it to be 25 years, what will happen to this beautiful girl by that time? In what conditions will she see out her life?

C.: (after pausing for thought): I fear that 25 is too many. Take Central Europe, the Balkans, or some eastern countries... They won't stay the way they are for another 25 years. They are sure to be transformed much earlier... In a peaceful way, perhaps... But more likely through violence.

I: I won't argue with you on that. But am I not right, then, to be sceptical about the future of this pretty girl?

C.: You are certainly right. I have a daughter who is 15 years old, and I try my best to isolate her as best I can from diplomatic society. Most of all, I would like to keep her at home, in Norway... The atmosphere there is quite different... In Norway, I believe that the inevitable transformation will occur peacefully.

I: (to myself): Every bourgeois tends to claim that revolution is inevitable in all countries but his own. Well, if it makes them feel better...

Quite an indicative conversation, isn't it? And isn't it indicative that the conversation took place during an official function intended 'for the greater splendour and glory' of the British royal family?

A sign of the times, the prince of Wales should have said.

* * *

This conversation reminds me of another, comparable episode. At a dinner party in Finland, three years or so ago, I was sitting next to the wife of the Polish envoy, Charwat.[i] We spoke of various things and finally came to her children

---

[i] Franciszek Charwat, Polish ambassador in Finland, 1928–35.

(a boy and a girl, aged 6 and 8). I asked Mrs Charwat what careers she was preparing her children for. My interlocutor, a clever and educated woman with a PhD from some university, at first talked at great length about her hopes and expectations for her children, but then she suddenly broke off and said with great emotion: 'Here I am speaking to you of my plans and calculations, but what's the use? Life is so difficult and unstable nowadays, and the future is so dark and uncertain, that you don't even want to think about it. I've got through my life one way or another, but what's in store for my children? I don't know.'

She paused and added gloomily: 'When I think of my children's future, sometimes I don't know whether I should rejoice that I have them, or be sorry.'

The shadow of the future clouds the face of the present like the London fog. The more thoughtful representatives of the bourgeoisie feel this and understand it.

24 November

I had the following conversation with the Swedish envoy Palmstierna[i] at breakfast.

Palmstierna: You, of course, do not believe in God?

I: No, I do not.

P.: And you, of course, are a materialist?

I: Absolutely correct – I'm a dialectical materialist.

P.: Well, just wait till you reach my age.

I: And what then?

P.: I, too, was a materialist in my youth. I read much and even wrote on the subject. I also used to say that matter is the basis of all things, that economics determines the relationships between people and states... But now I've come to a different conclusion. The longer I live the keener I feel that there is a god who rules the world and that the ideal is more important than the material. You're surprised, I imagine? Perhaps you think me an eccentric? Never mind, just reach my age – you'll see!

P.: When I was the minister of foreign affairs in 1919 and 1920, I often had to deal with the difficulties of the Russian Revolution, at least insofar as it concerned Sweden. In that period I met Mr Krasin,[ii] whom I consider to this day a great, honest and sincere man. Mrs Krasin published a nasty book about

---

[i] Baron Erik Kule Palmstierna, Swedish foreign minister, March–October 1920; ambassador in London, 1920–37.

[ii] Leonid Borisovich Krasin, Soviet commissar for foreign trade from 1920; trade representative in Great Britain 1921–23; Soviet ambassador in France, 1924–25, in Great Britain, 1925–26; died in post. Signed the trade agreement with Great Britain in March 1921, which led to the establishment of *de facto* relations between the two countries.

her husband after his death. She didn't understand the first thing about her husband… So, do you know what I did at that time in order to understand and imagine the Russian Revolution better? I read Carlyle's[i] two volumes on the French Revolution.

I: And did that help?

P.: Oh, yes, greatly. I developed a better understanding of the spirit, mechanics, and prospects of the Russian Revolution.

25 November

For the last three days, there has been noise and confusion on the political stock exchange of Europe. Archimbaud,[ii] a Radical deputy, speaking on the defence budget in the French National Assembly on 22 November, said among other things that a military defence alliance exists between France and the USSR. This immediately caused uproar in all the European capitals. The Parisian minister of foreign affairs [Laval][iii] came out with a *démenti*, albeit a rather evasive one. M.M., who is presently in Geneva, rather cunningly told the journalists: it is up to Laval, not me, to correct Archimbaud. Yesterday Archimbaud himself offered some explanations to the press regarding his statement at the Assembly. Formally denying the existence of an alliance, he at the same time created the impression that it could be concluded at any moment. Allegedly, the ground for such an alliance has been thoroughly prepared. Here in England the press made a sensation out of Archimbaud's statement, and I had to calm things down a bit.

What's it all about? My explanation goes as follows. The Radicals, who suspect Laval is striving to cut a deal with Germany, want to thwart his schemes. Moreover, they want to frighten Poland, to whom the French have today dispatched a note concerning the Eastern Pact: refuse your consent and there will be a Franco-Soviet alliance.

27 November

The second 'function' concerning the royal wedding!

A grand evening reception in honour of Marina at Buckingham Palace. More than 800 guests, including all heads of mission. On top of that, a whole 'brigade' of royalties – the entire royal family (the king[iv] and queen,[v] the prince of Wales,

---

[i] Thomas Carlyle, Scottish author and historian (1795–1881).
[ii] Léon Archimbaud, Radical Party Deputy of Drôme, 1919–40.
[iii] Pierre Laval, prime minister of France, 1931–32, 1935–36, 1940 and 1942–44; foreign minister, 1934–36.
[iv] King George V of Great Britain, 1910–36.
[v] Victoria Mary, queen consort of King George V, 1910–36.

the duke of York[i] and his wife, the duke of Kent, the younger son John, the so-called 'princess royal', i.e. the king's daughter, together with her husband; only the duke of Gloucester[ii] was absent – he's currently in Australia), as well as the king of Denmark[iii] and his wife, the king of Norway[iv] and his wife, Prince Regent Paul of Yugoslavia,[v] Princess Juliana of Holland[vi] (the heiress), and so on. There was also a great quantity of grand princes of various nationalities, including Kirill Vladimirovich Romanov[vii] ('Emperor of All Russia'!) accompanied by his wife and daughter Kira,[viii] who was one of the eight bridesmaids. Add to that an endless number of princesses (Greek, Yugoslav, and others)…

The procedure: all the ambassadors and envoys of the countries whose heads were present at the wedding formed a semicircle according to seniority in the round hall of the palace, while the remaining envoys and chargés d'affaires were put in the adjoining long hall. Representatives of the English nobility and the upper bourgeoisie were gathered in groups in the other rooms. A long and dazzling cavalcade of royalties emerged from the corner room adjacent to the round hall. First, the British king and queen passed along a line of ambassadors and wives, shaking hands with all of them and exchanging a few pleasantries with some chosen guests. Among the latter were our doyen (by virtue of his rank) and Matsudaira (the English are scared of the Japanese!). The royal couple passed from the round hall to the adjoining room, where the envoys were, but they did not pause there before individual diplomats, confining themselves to general bows to the right and to the left. Foreign royal couples (Danish, Norwegian, etc.) followed their example, as did members of the British royal family. They all shook hands with us and smiled politely… Actually, that's not quite true: there were exceptions. Marina's mother demonstratively walked past Agniya and me without greeting us. Well, we'll get by in this world without her handshakes! Two or three wizened old witches, ugly as sin, came out of the corner room and hesitated, whispering secretively and glancing in our direction, before deciding to proceed directly to the envoys' room, bypassing the line of ambassadors. The Soviet ambassador had given them a fright! There were also some ladies and gentlemen decorated with ribbons and diadems, who stumbled at the sight of me and immediately backed off every which way. That

---

[i] Prince Albert, later King George VI.
[ii] Prince Henry William, duke of Gloucester, third son of King George V.
[iii] King Christian X of Denmark, 1912–47.
[iv] King Haakon VII of Norway (born Christian Frederik), 1905–57.
[v] Prince Paul of Yugoslavia, prince regent of Yugoslavia, 1934–41; deposed in a coup d'état after he signed the agreement on Yugoslavia's access to the Axis in March 1941.
[vi] Princess Juliana van Oranje-Nassau; queen of the Netherlands, 1948–80.
[vii] Kirill Vladimirovich Romanov, Russian grand duke; assumed the titular Emperor and Autocrat of All the Russias, 1924–38, being next in line to the throne following the murder of the tsar's family.
[viii] Grand Duchess Kira Kirillovna, second daughter of Grand Duke Kirill Vladimirovich of Russia.

must have been Kirill and his retinue. On the whole, my presence at the royal reception was an unpleasant disappointment for a certain group of guests. The Lithuanian (Balutis)[i] told me that, standing in the envoys' room, he'd overheard a conversation in Russian: 'Look, there's Maisky over there,' said a grey-haired gentleman with a long moustache, pointing at me from a distance.

His neighbour, a younger gentleman, glanced in my direction and uttered angrily: 'Now there's a son of a bitch!'

He said this with great feeling and irritation... Indeed, the passions engendered by our revolution have not yet cooled. Their echoes resound even in the halls of Buckingham Palace.

Leaving the diplomatic corps behind, the long line of royalties sailed off down the halls and enfilades of the palace, greeting everyone and gracing the chosen few with some conversation. Meanwhile, the ambassadors began to talk to one another.

'What happens next?' Agniya asked a Spanish lady, who scoffed and replied sarcastically: 'Next? The usual *merry-go-round*.'

Dino Grandi, the Italian, declared defiantly: 'I'm off to bed!'

He really did disappear early, at the first opportunity.

The Bulgarian (Khadzhi-Mishiyev) assumed an elegiac tone and began to philosophize: 'What splendour! What riches! We haven't had such an extravagant gathering of royalties for many years! Yet there's a whiff of the past about it all...'

'Don't you think,' I responded, 'that the British court is the last splendid court left in Europe? It's an interesting historical relic that has survived to this day thanks to an array of specific circumstances.'

'You are quite right,' the Bulgarian replied. 'Here, in London, we have probably the last major royal court, which traces its line back to Charles I and Louis XIV.'

* * *

I witnessed a curious scene at the end of the reception.

The king approached Baldwin and began to speak to him. I don't know what they were talking about, since I was standing too far away, but I couldn't help observing them. The king – short, balding, frail, his arms almost straight down by his sides – moved his lips slowly and, bending slightly forward, gazed ingratiatingly at the Conservative leader. Baldwin – solidly built with a paunch, red hair and a confident grinning face – was leaning back arrogantly and listening to the king in a calm and somewhat majestic manner. First he

---

[i] Bronius Kazys Balutis, Lithuanian ambassador in Washington, 1928–33, and in London from 1934.

stood akimbo, then he unceremoniously scratched the back of his head, before finally folding his arms across his fat chest. The king just talked on and on... Observing the scene, one was apt to ask: 'Which of the two is the master?' It certainly didn't seem to be the king.

* * *

Lady Astor[i] caught hold of me. Clad in a fine green velvet dress, as buoyant and ardently vigorous as ever, she made a very favourable impression against the general background of laxity and degeneration.

'I've just had a real fight with Kira!' she exclaimed with great enthusiasm.

'Over what?' I inquired.

'Well, naturally, over the USSR! I was trying to prove to her that she is wrong and that you, *bloody Bolsheviks*, are good people.'

'I can imagine the impression that made on Kira!' I chuckled.

'Don't laugh!' Lady Astor flared up. Whereupon, she took me by the arm and dragged me after her, saying: 'Come on, I'll introduce you to Kira. She wants to see you!'...

It was with some difficulty that I succeeded in extracting myself and vanishing in the crowd.

What a crazy woman!

[Maisky's memoirs, and particularly their Russian edition, geared as they were towards vindicating Soviet policies on the eve of the war, present a sinister and often factually inaccurate portrait of Lady Astor. They also conceal how intriguing he found the strikingly glamorous and witty American, who in 1919 was the first woman to enter parliament – a Conservative MP who championed the Soviet cause, following a tour of Russia and a meeting with Stalin at the Kremlin in 1931. Maisky was clearly attracted, though not beguiled, by the 'small, thin, elegant lady with the slightly whipped dark hair, a minute expressive face and lively crafty eyes' which rendered her the 'absolute embodiment of eternal restlessness'. In retrospect, he would rue his overestimation of the power exerted by Lady Astor, wrongly assuming that close relations with her would 'open to him the doors of other Conservative citadels'. In fact, he never ceased to seek her company. He remained a frequent visitor to her Versailles-modelled mansion at Cliveden, Buckinghamshire, even after 1937, when it became a Mecca for appeasers such as Chamberlain, Halifax, Hoare and others, who spent long weekends there. He was observed playing 'absurd games' at her instigation after dinner. 'Who, for example, would ever expect to see Ivan Maisky ... and four or five members of the British Government playing musical chairs?' recalled Vernon Bartlett,[ii] the journalist-

---

[i] Lady Nancy Astor, Conservative MP for Plymouth, 1919–45, and the first woman to sit in the House of Commons. An unconventional politician, she accompanied Bernard Shaw on a tour of the Soviet Union and met Stalin, but diverted her sympathies to Hitler when she established the 'Cliveden Set', a spearhead in the appeasement of Nazism.

[ii] Vernon Bartlett, a leftist anti-appeaser correspondent of the *News Chronicle*.

turned-politician.[48] Maisky's vision, coloured by cultural ideological predilections, led him to attach undue significance to those weekends, during which, he believed, crucial decisions were reached by the prime minister.[49]

Relations between Maisky and Lady Astor, though often contentious, remained courteous and correct right up until his departure from England. Their intimate correspondence suggests, though, that the relationship was also mutually beneficial. There were only a few people whom Maisky would address as he did her – 'My dear Lady Astor' – or whose company he would seek thus: 'It is a long, long time since my wife and I saw you last and it would be so nice if you could lunch with us one day … We shall be so glad to hear that you can come on one of these days.'[50] Even after the Munich Agreement was signed, Maisky continued to court Lady Astor, though by then he would be mostly interested in gleaning from her the 'secrets' of Cliveden.[51] Indeed, *Time* magazine reported from London in 1939 that 'The Soviet Ambassador Ivan Maisky even had lunch at the London house of Lady Astor, hostess of the famed appeasement-favoring Cliveden Set.'[52] Years later, Lady Astor would vividly recall the presence of Maisky at Cliveden, 'because he made such a terrific noise eating his food'.[53] Maisky did not even flinch from participating in her infamous 'musical chairs', though when the German ambassador was present at one such event he did not fulfil the hopes of those present 'of seeing those two scrabbling for the last chair'.[54] The relationship was as beneficial for Lady Astor herself. As soon as Maisky left the room, following a lunch given by her in his honour shortly after Germany's invasion of Czechoslovakia, the hostess told the other guests: 'Of course I hate the Russians, but I've got to be nice to that little man because he may become our ally in the war.'[55] After the German attack on Russia, Lady Astor wrote to Bernard Shaw[i] (with whom she enjoyed a close relationship, regardless of the fact that they were poles apart politically) that she was 'on the most cordial terms with the Maiskys'.[56]]

28 November

Between 3 and 5 p.m. Agniya and I were at St James's Palace, at a specially arranged viewing of the wedding gifts presented to the Duke of Kent and Marina. A great mass of people. An incredible crush and confusion. There were so many presents that when we entered the hall with the tables, chairs, beds and others gifts presented to the bride and groom, you might have thought you were in a furniture store. The greatest attention was lavished on the items of jewellery, especially the three diamond diadems given to Marina by her fiancé, her father and the British queen. The diadems were kept under glass, and the wives of the ambassadors and British notables were simply dying of envy and rapture. Out of all the books presented to the duke and Marina, it was a thick

---

[i] George Bernard Shaw, Irish playwright, dramatist, critic and socialist; member of the Executive Committee of the Fabian Society, 1885–1911; journalist and art critic to *Pall Mall Gazette*, 1885–88, *The Star*, 1888–90, *The World*, 1890–94, *Saturday Review*, 1895–98; winner of the Nobel Prize for Literature in 1925. Continued to write plays throughout the 1930s, including *On the Rocks* (1933), *The Millionairess* (1934), *Geneva* (1936) and *In Good King Charles's Golden Days* (1939). A close friend of the Maiskys.

leather-bound volume entitled *Russian Imperial Dinner Service* that caught my eye.

As we travelled from the embassy to the palace, a heavy black fog started descending quickly on London. It was a remarkable scene: in one direction the sky was already black and impenetrable, in the other it still glowed with rapidly fading lights of pink and straw-like complexion. There was something menacing and tragic in this rare combination of colours. As if some mighty natural calamity were taking place or drawing near, like the destruction of Pompeii or the great earthquake of 1923 in Japan…

29 November

The royal wedding finally took place today. From first light, and even from the previous night, London seemed to be overflowing its banks. Up to half a million people descended on the capital from all over the country. Many foreigners arrived from the continent. The streets along which the wedding procession would pass were filled to bursting by an immense crowd that had gathered on the previous evening to occupy the best places. Typically, the crowd consisted almost entirely of women. I, at least, noticed barely a single man on my way from the embassy to Westminster Abbey. Some newspapers also noted this (the *Manchester Guardian* for one). Large platforms were erected at various points along the procession, with seats being sold for between one and ten guineas. The city, particularly its central part, was decked out gaudily with flags, festoons and banners showing portraits of the bridegroom and the bride; and in the evening, the town was lavishly illuminated. The full works, in other words. The wedding was turned into a real national event.

This is evidence of two things. First, the utter shallowness and political backwardness of the average Englishman, including hundreds of thousands of workmen. Second, the extraordinary deftness of the English bourgeois elite, which has managed to exploit these features of the hoi polloi to superb effect, in order to inflame dynastic sentiments on the one hand, and to give an artificial boost to industry and trade on the other (hotels, restaurants, tailors, milliners, jewellers and so on – all made a good *Geschäft* out of the wedding). At the same time, this display of solid 'national unity' before the world (Labour leaders were also in attendance, among them Lansbury,[i] Henderson, Attlee,[ii] Morgan Jones[iii]) can do no harm at all to the interests of British diplomacy…

---

[i] George Lansbury, leader of the Labour Party, 1931–35.
[ii] Clement Richard Attlee (1st Earl Attlee), deputy leader of the Labour Party in the House of Commons, 1931–35; Labour Party leader, 1935–55; lord privy seal, 1940–42; deputy prime minister and secretary of state for dominion affairs, 1942–43; lord president of the council, 1943–45; prime minister, 1945–51.
[iii] Morgan Jones, trade union leader, 1931–38.

On this occasion I was obliged to attend the wedding ceremony itself, in Westminster Abbey. That's what Moscow decided. It was the first time I had attended a church service since leaving school, 33 years ago! That's quite a stretch.

The diplomatic corps sat to the right of the entrance, and members of the government on the left. Simon was my partner on the opposite side. MacDonald zealously chanted psalms during the service, Baldwin yawned wearily, while Elliot[i] simply dozed. Churchill looked deeply moved and at one point even seemed to wipe his eyes with a handkerchief. Henderson sang 'God Save the King' with an extraordinary display of energy. All the royalties gathered to the right and left of the pulpit, and the remaining space was crammed with representatives of the aristocracy and *big business*. A choir clad in white occupied the special seats upstairs, where the organ droned away, filling the high vaults of the cathedral with the sounds of Bach, Handel and Elgar.

My appearance in the church caused an exchange of glances and whispers among diplomats and members of the government. So far, though, the newspapers have made no great fuss about it. The *Segodnya* of 19 November and *Poslednie Novosti* of 21 November informed readers of the 'forthcoming "meeting" between [Grand Duke] Kirill Vladimirovich and Ambassador Maisky' at the royal reception, but they didn't speculate about my possible presence in the abbey. The Whites evidently can't have expected me to go to church...

My neighbour, a Nepalese minister [General Bahadur S.J.B. Rana],[ii] was very striking: on his head he wore a gold hat sprinkled with big diamonds and rubies, and topped by a huge 'cock's tail'. The general effect was rather amusing; but at that moment the Nepalese envoy was undoubtedly carrying tens of thousands of pounds on his head.

1 December

A terrible disaster! Comrade Kirov[iii] has been killed in the Smolny in Leningrad. Who killed him? With what motives? Who sent him?... As yet, I know nothing. Fleet Street is thick with rumours and alternative versions. Some say that the assassin was an engineer with a grudge against Kirov. Others (the *Daily Express*)

---

[i] Walter Elliot, Conservative MP, 1924–45; minister of agriculture, 1932–36, secretary of state for Scotland, 1936–38; minister of health, 1938–40; director of public relations, War Office, 1941–42.
[ii] Minister General Bahadur S.J.B. Rana, first Nepalese ambassador in London, 1934–36. He went on to become director of the Nepal Bank and later headed the Nepalese contingent in India in the Second World War. He was president of the 1947 Constitutional Reform Committee and eastern commanding general until 1951, which put him two places below the maharaja; the Rana prime minister and effective ruler of the country. He vanished from public life after the end of the Rana regime. I am indebted to Prof. David Gellner of All Souls College, Oxford, for the information. See a diary entry on the ambassador on 5 June 1935.
[iii] Sergei Mironovich Kirov (Kostrikov), first secretary of the Leningrad Regional Committee of the CPSU, 1926–34, member of the party's Politburo from 1930.

suggest that Alfred Rosenberg,[i] Hitler's aide-de-camp, had a hand in it. I know only one thing for sure: the obituary signed by Stalin, Molotov, Voroshilov[ii] and others (I caught it on the radio) states that 'the assassin was dispatched by class enemies'.[57]

We got news of the assassination at around 9 p.m. By 11.30 p.m. the Ozerskys,[iii] Alperovich, and Kagan had all gathered in my office. We all felt like being together, seeking sympathy in the collective and an outlet for our agitation. We talked, exchanging thoughts, suppositions and conjectures. We sent the following telegram to Moscow:

> To Stalin and Molotov, Moscow. Profoundly shocked at the news of the tragic death of Comrade Kirov, who has perished at the hands of a class enemy, we mourn the heavy loss together with the whole Soviet country. The death of Comrade Kirov, who always set an example of selfless devotion to the cause of the working class and the Soviet state, will only make us – together with all workers, peasants, and public servants in the Soviet Union – close ranks ever more tightly around the Central Committee of the Party, its leader Comrade Stalin, and the Soviet government, in the name of the great struggle for the building of socialism and the creation of a classless society. On behalf of the Soviet community in London, Maisky and Ozersky.

It's simply horrid! An entirely unexpected break in the path of development which our country has been following for the past year. The sooner I find out all the details, the easier it will be to judge the significance of this tragic event in the Smolny.

5 December

Baldwin won a brilliant victory yesterday. A conference of the Council of the Conservative Party (attended by 1,500 to 1,600 members) was convened specially to discuss the Indian reform.[58] Baldwin defended the Joint Select Committee Report that guarantees a degree of self-rule to the provinces and establishes a limited central government on the basis of a federation of

---

[i] Alfred Rosenberg, editor of the Nazi Party newspaper *Völkischer Beobachter*; minister for eastern occupied territories, 1941–44.
[ii] Kliment Efremovich Voroshilov, people's commissar for defence, 1934–40; marshal of the Soviet Union from 1935; commander-in-chief of the Soviet forces in the war against Finland, 1939–40; deputy chairman of the USSR Council of People's Commissars, 1940–45; commander-in-chief of the north-west armies and of the Leningrad front, 1941.
[iii] Aleksandr Vladimirovich Ozersky, head of the Soviet trade mission in Great Britain, 1931–37. Recalled to Moscow, arrested and executed. Rehabilitated posthumously.

provinces and princes. The opposition, headed by Churchill, Lord Salisbury,[i] Page Croft[ii] and others, argued that the new constitution meant abandoning the fundamental positions of British imperialism in India and agreed only to an acknowledgement of the self-government of the provinces. Once, the opposition was very strong and many believed that Baldwin's position as party leader was teetering. Yesterday, Baldwin's authority was strengthened as never before. The result of the vote was 1,102 for the government and 390 against, with a few abstentions.

Baldwin delivered a very interesting speech. It resounded with the voice of the ages and of the experience in power accumulated over centuries by the British bourgeoisie. One felt that, making this speech, Baldwin saw before him the American War of Independence, the Indian Uprising of 1857, the South African war, Ireland's struggle for autonomy and much else besides. He spoke as a true leader and yet again confirmed my long-held conviction that he is the real master of the Conservative Party and, consequently, of Great Britain and the British Empire.

There is a remarkable passage in Baldwin's speech:

I spoke of the preservation of the Empire. It is for that very preservation that I have come largely to the conclusion to which I have come. You must remember that in many parts of the Empire there is sympathy with the ideals of India. You can gather that from General Smuts' speech last time he was in England. As I said early during these discussions, I say again to you now. It is my considered judgement in all the changes and chances of this wide world today that you have a good chance of keeping the whole of that sub-continent, of India in the Empire for ever. You have a chance and a good chance, but I say to you deliberately, it is my firm conviction that if you refuse her this opportunity, if you refuse it to her, you will infallibly lose India whatever you do before two generations are passed. That to my mind is the choice. Believing that, I can do no other than give you the advice I do.[59]

To be sure, Baldwin miscalculated here. He measures the pace of our time by the speed of the tortoise. Just think, he gives England another half-century of rule in India even if the anticipated reform is rejected. Isn't he a little too sure of himself? In my view, England may receive a suspension of ten to fifteen years provided the reform is carried through, but without the reform it won't even last that long…

---

[i] James Edward Hubert Gascoyne-Cecil (4th marquess of Salisbury), Conservative undersecretary of state for foreign affairs, 1900–03; lord privy seal, 1903–14 and 1924–29.
[ii] Henry Page Croft (1st Baron Croft), Conservative MP, 1910–40; undersecretary of state for war, 1940–45.

Be that as it may, Baldwin's victory yesterday has strengthened the government considerably. Now, if nothing out of the ordinary happens, the present government will see out its term, i.e. about a year or a year and a half.

6 December

Today the urn with Comrade Kirov's ashes was immured in the Kremlin wall on Red Square. Hundreds of thousands of people were present, along with troops, members of the Central Committee and the government…

Here, in London, we also remembered our departed leader. The embassy flag flew at half-mast. Our entire Soviet community gathered in the embassy. The hall was decorated with greenery and flowers. A bust of Lenin and portraits of Stalin and Kirov were placed near and along the walls. I made a brief speech in memory of the deceased. Lazyan[i] (from the trade mission) shared with us his reminiscences of Kirov. We sang a funeral march to piano accompaniment. Then we parted, in a quiet and pensive mood…

I simply cannot come to terms with this awful tragedy. Only six weeks ago I was sitting in Kirov's office, deep in discussion with him about the international situation, and in particular Anglo-Soviet relations. Kirov had an excellent understanding of foreign affairs. His opinions were usually simple in form, but profound and vivid in substance. He viewed the British Conservatives as an extremely serious enemy. I remember visiting him in Leningrad on my way to Helsinki in the autumn of 1931, after the elections in Britain had handed the Conservatives a landslide victory. When our conversation touched on the elections, Kirov exclaimed: 'To win such a victory while fully retaining one's self-control – it's the highest manifestation of the art of governance! Only yesterday was there a mutiny in the navy (he meant Invergordon).[60] What would Mussolini[ii] have done after such a triumph? He would have crushed the mutineers into smithereens; he would have shot hundreds of sailors… And what did the Conservatives do? They kept their heads; they were not intoxicated by success. They won a tremendous victory and said to the mutineers: let's forget the past! Yes, these people know how to rule. They need to be taken seriously.'

Kirov's voice expressed deep loathing, mixed with deep respect.

During our last meeting Kirov welcomed the prospects of improvement in Anglo-Soviet relations that I had laid out to him. He believed that the British card was worth a high price, and promised to apply himself to the placement of big orders in Great Britain. He never had to!

---

[i] I. Lazyan, a protegé of Mikoyan in the London trade mission.
[ii] Benito Mussolini, Italian fascist dictator and prime minister of Italy, 1922–43.

The assassination of Kirov comes at a very bad time for us politically. It runs counter to the general course of our internal and external development. It is impossible that it derived from some serious processes occurring in the depths of the Soviet system. Rather, it smacks of the dregs of the past, still not entirely expunged. But which?!…

In any case, the assassination will have some repercussions for us in Europe. Not major complications, perhaps, but complications nevertheless. Time will tell.

11 December

There was a reception for journalists in the embassy on the occasion of the arrival of Comrade Doletsky[i] (head of TASS) in London en route from Moscow to the USA. About a hundred people were present. Sir Arthur Willert,[ii] head of the Foreign Office press bureau, visited the embassy for the first time. In general, it went off well. Today's *Star* carries a semi-humorous account of the reception:

> I attended a party at the Soviet Embassy in Kensington Palace gardens given in honour of I. Doletsky, the head of the Russian news agency, Tass, which is responsible for issuing such news as is allowed to leave the USSR.
>
> My experience of Soviet hospitality was just a little disappointing in that it was the same as any other such social function, with one or two slight differences.
>
> The cloak-room attendant was smoking a cigarette, but I was bowed into the presence of the Ambassador by immaculate white-waist-coated waiters. The first man I spoke to looked a commissar from top to toe, in democratic clothes and the wildest of hair. He replied to my polite conversation in the broadest of North Country accents.
>
> Tea, too, came not from samovars, but from silver urns supplied by the Mayfair Catering Company, and one was offered Indian or China, but no Russian variety. The whisky was Irish, and the only really Russian things were vodka, which I thought had been abolished, and the cigarettes, those three-quarter cardboard tubes from which if one is not careful one suddenly draws a shower of sparks into one's mouth.

---

[i] Yakov Genrikhovich Doletsky (Fenigstein), director of the TASS agency, 1921–37. Purged in 1937.
[ii] Sir Arthur Willert, British delegate to the Geneva Disarmament Conference, 1932–34, and to the League of Nations, 1929–34; resigned from the Foreign Office, 1935.

Doletsky seemed pleased, but who knows for sure? After all, wasn't he telling anyone who would listen that he had been received better than M.M. [Litvinov] and MacDonald in the USA? He also hinted quite transparently that when M.M. visited America last year, he 'muddled things up a bit' and that if he, Doletsky, had been sent there instead of M.M., things would have turned out much better. Given such a degree of self-love, our modest reception might have struck D. as unworthy of his rank and status.

13 December

At M.M. [Litvinov]'s instruction, I acquainted Vansittart with the Franco-Soviet Protocol of 5 December.[61] V. was obviously flattered by our attention and confirmed once again that the British government remains in favour of the Eastern Pact, as it was in the summer.

Then we turned to more general questions. We hadn't seen each other since 9 August, i.e. more than four months: I was on leave for more than two months and when I returned, V. had taken his leave. Today was our first opportunity to meet.

We spoke about the current status of Anglo-Soviet relations. We both acknowledged their significant improvement over the past six months. V. remarked that he thought 'our summer conversations were a turning point in Anglo-Soviet relations'. I told him that Comrade Litvinov was also pleased with our talks and that he had asked me to convey his feelings to V. Then V. expressed his satisfaction at the successful elimination of the Lena Goldfields problem – a thorn removed from our flesh. Now we could think of the next steps towards the further improvement of our relations.

I supported V. and proposed, as a sort of 'prelude', that we run our eyes over the map of the world, to see if we could find a single region where the interests of Britain and the USSR might clash. V. willingly agreed and we began.

I: First of all, the USSR bears no aggressive intentions towards the British Empire. That tsarist fantasy of a campaign against India has been dismissed out of hand by the Soviet government.

V.: We believe that. On my part, I can guarantee that Great Britain nurtures no aggressive designs against the USSR. Geography has taken care of the fact that there can be no mutual suspicion of territorial aggression between the two partners.

I: We have established, then, that neither side has reason to fear an attack by the other. This is a very important condition for the improvement of Anglo-Soviet relations.

V.: And what is the current state of your relations with Japan and Germany?

I: Our relations with these two countries are characterized precisely by the presence of strong suspicions that they have aggressive aspirations regarding our territory.

V.: Yes, I receive almost daily reports concerning Germany's aggressive plans towards the Ukraine. However, you are not alone in being threatened by the Germans. They speak constantly about expansion in all directions – whether to the east, the south, the west, Africa, and so on. Germany is a highly unsettled place today. One can expect all sorts of surprises from there.

I: But let's return to Anglo-Soviet relations. Apart from the absence of suspicions of territorial aggression, a further highly positive aspect in this area is the fact that Britain and the USSR are not competitors on the world market.

V.: You are absolutely right, and this is a great boon for the development of good relations between our countries. Trade competition always has an unfavourable effect on relations between countries.

I: And sometimes leads even to war.

V.: Yes, even to war, however sad that may be.

I: Now, let us switch to Europe. Our Soviet interest in this part of the world is the following: to maintain peace and to prevent Germany, by all means available to us, from violating peace. What is your British interest?

V.: Our British interest is absolutely identical to yours: to maintain peace and to prevent Germany, by all means available to us, from violating peace.

I: Very good. Our goals coincide fully. Of course, there may be discrepancies in the methods and means of achieving the common goal, but even if such differences were to surface in the future they would nevertheless be of secondary importance.

V.: That's right. But at the present time there are no disagreements between us even on issues of methods and means. You hold the Eastern Pact to be an instrument of peace – we support it as well. We are also as one now on the question of the League of Nations.

I: Let us turn to the Middle East. Our Soviet interest in this once highly explosive region is as follows: to uphold the independence of Turkey, Persia and Afghanistan and to maintain friendly political and economic relations with them. The USSR, unlike tsarist Russia, has no claims on Constantinople and the Straits. We may say, to paraphrase Bismarck's[i] famous aphorism, that Constantinople and the Straits are not worth the bones of a single Red Army soldier. Our principled position also precludes us from seizing foreign lands. What is your British interest in the Middle East?

V.: The same as yours. We likewise strive to uphold the independence of the said states, to nurture friendly relations with them, and also to raise their

---

[i] Otto von Bismarck, German chancellor, 1871–90.

cultural and economic level, since this is important for our trade. We set due store by the USSR's rejection of any claims on Constantinople, but, after all, you have such excellent relations with Turkey.

I: Finally, the Far East. Our Soviet interest in East Asia consists of the following: peace, the integrity and independence of China, open doors, and the prevention of any Japanese aggression with the help of all means accessible to us. In what does your British interest in the Far East consist?

V.: The same: peace, open doors, and maintaining the status quo in terms of the balance of power. (It struck me that he did not mention the integrity and independence of China while listing the main elements of the British interest in the Far East, though this might have been a chance omission.)

I: I'm glad to hear it. But do all in England think so? I know that there is a group in the Conservative camp which is of the opinion that 'a nice little war between the USSR and Japan' would be very beneficial to British interests in the Pacific.

V.: Only a madman could desire a Japanese–Soviet war. It would lead inevitably to world war. The people holding such views are a negligible group without weight in British politics.

I: There is another group, which believes that England has three alternatives: (1) building a powerful navy so that she can defend her interests against Japan independently and effectively; (2) forming an Anglo-American entente; (3) forming an Anglo-Japanese entente or even an alliance on the basis of a China divided into spheres of influence (the north for Japan, and the centre and south for England). The first alternative is unachievable for financial reasons, the second because of the isolationist tendencies of the USA. So only the third alternative remains – that of an Anglo-Japanese entente.

V.: I agree that the first two alternatives should be excluded. About the Americans now. They are grossly mistaken to think that geography insures them against all international troubles. Nonetheless, this conviction is widespread among them and perhaps the experience of an entire generation will be needed for the Americans to be cured of their isolationism. As for an Anglo-Japanese entente, it is as unrealistic as the Anglo-American version. First (even if we leave aside the issue of our virtue), Japan would not agree to a partition. It is clearly set on seizing all East Asia for itself. Second, I very much doubt that one could come to terms with the Japanese on such a complicated and delicate matter as the division of China into spheres of influence. It is hard enough to agree on far simpler matters with the Japanese, such as the restriction of fleets. And you want us to reach agreement on the partition of a country of 400 million.

I: But if the third alternative is also to be discounted, then what does the policy of Great Britain in the Far East consist of?

V.: Caution, and again caution!

I: If you say so, although I do not entirely understand what concrete forms this political line could assume. In any case, our comparison of the interests of the two countries – the USSR and Great Britain – seems to suggest that they do not clash anywhere, including the Far East.

V.: Yes, if we ran our eyes over the entire map of the world, we would find no point at which they conflict. Moreover, the USSR and England have one shared and very important interest: the preservation of peace. This is a good foundation for achieving *rapprochement* between our two countries.

I expressed satisfaction with the results of our analysis and added that I had talked to Simon on the same subject some five weeks ago. Simon wanted to acquaint the Cabinet with the substance of our conversation. V. raised his eyebrows in astonishment. No, he knows nothing about Simon's démarche. But he will seek clarification…

I told V. not to worry himself, but decided for myself that Simon, in his usual two-faced way, had obviously not done what he promised.

At that moment V.'s secretary entered the room and whispered something in his ear. V. excused himself, on account of some urgent business, but he asked me to come and see him in a few days' time to conclude our interesting discussion.

16 December

Garvin told me today:

There are only two genuine world powers on earth: Great Britain and the USSR. One fact of tremendous importance is often underestimated in England: our interests extend over all Europe and Asia from the Atlantic to the Pacific. Your interests also extend over all Europe and Asia from the Atlantic to the Pacific. This creates a commonality of interests between Great Britain and the USSR. I don't see a single point on earth, and I don't know a single international problem, where our interests might collide. On the contrary, we share one all-consuming and all-embracing interest: <u>peace</u>. Since our aspirations coincide on this fundamental issue, there is no basis for poor, nor even merely average relations between the two countries. Rather, every prerequisite exists for profoundly amicable relations. Above all, I am concerned about the Far East. The next five years will be a decisive period in the history of the white race: either it will be able to repel the attack of Japan, which has to be viewed as the vanguard of the yellow race, or it is doomed to perish. Anglo-American friendship could greatly strengthen the position of the white race.

Anglo-American-Soviet friendship would secure its future forever. Besides, a tripartite friendship of this sort would guarantee peace in Europe and the Pacific. This is where we must look for humanity's escape from its current difficulties! In January, after the resumption of the political season, I shall write an article on this subject for the *Observer*.

Garvin struck the table firmly with his fist and exclaimed: 'We shall not just write about it, we shall do it!'

When I was getting into the car, Garvin repeated with great enthusiasm: 'We shall do it!'

We'll see. Garvin is very unstable in his moods. I'll refrain from any conclusions until the article appears (if it ever does).

17 December

I invited the Coles[i] over today and had a serious talk with them about the *Declaration of the 43*.[62] As I had assumed, the declaration was indeed their doing. During their conversation with me, both were highly agitated, now turning pale, now turning red. Mrs Cole's hands even trembled nervously.[63]

I gave my guests a stern ticking-off. I told them that over the last three or four months the Soviet authorities had established the existence of a large terrorist conspiracy against our Party leaders, beginning with Comrade Stalin. It is being organized and financed by the German 'Nazis'. Its agents are Russian White Guards and all those dissatisfied little groups which exist inside the USSR. The White Guards secretly cross the border in Poland, Latvia and Finland with the assistance of the authorities of the listed countries and, once in the USSR, enter into contact with conspirators of Soviet citizenship. Recent months have seen a series of attempts on the lives of Comrades Stalin, Voroshilov, Molotov, Postyshev,[ii] Balitsky,[iii] and others. Fortunately, such attempts have as yet proved unsuccessful, thanks to the vigilance of the NKVD. The plotters got lucky with Kirov. The death of Kirov was striking proof of the gravity of the terrorist threat. In such a situation, the Soviet government had no choice but to take tough measures against the plotters – not only those who were guilty of Kirov's death, but all those arrested at various times and in various places in recent months in connection with terrorism. We couldn't try the terrorists publicly

---

[i] G.D.H. Cole, fellow of Magdalen College, Oxford, 1912–19, of University College, 1925–44 and Chichele Professor of Social and Political Theory and fellow of All Souls, Oxford, 1944–57; chairman of the Fabian Society (1939–46 and 1948–50) and its president, 1952–57.
[ii] Pavel Petrovich Postyshev, member of the Central Committee of the Communist Party of Ukraine, 1925–37.
[iii] Vsevolod Apollonovich Balitsky, people's commissar for home affairs in Ukraine, 1924–30 and 1934–37.

without risking serious complications with Germany and other states, who would undoubtedly have been implicated in this case. We haven't forgotten the Metro-Vickers affair. We have only just witnessed a conflict between Hungary and Yugoslavia as a result of the protection extended by the Hungarian government to the terrorists who assassinated King Alexander and Barthou. Our policy is a policy of peace. We do not want to jeopardize peace on account of the machinations of terrorists who are in the pocket of the Nazis. Hence the necessity and legitimacy of the 'secret trials'. By killing our leaders and creating the impression that the Soviet regime is weak and barely able to contain the indignation of the masses, the Nazis aim to prevent, or at least to hamper, the rapid normalization of relations between the USSR and Western states, and in particular the process of *rapprochement* between the USSR and France. It is, of course, a desperate resort, but the situation of the German Nazis is indeed desperate. They are attempting, in other words, to obstruct the consolidation of peace and to assist the unleashing of war. The Soviet government would have failed in its duties before the peoples of the USSR and before the workers of the world had it not taken severe measures against the warmongers. It is a hard and unpleasant thing to shoot 80–100 people, but it is still better than to risk the lives of millions of workers and peasants on the battlefield. Moreover, one should never forget the words of Mirabeau,[i] who said, some 140 years ago, that revolution cannot be made with lavender oil.

The Coles did not object. To put it bluntly, they had no case to argue. They just asked me questions and confided their doubts and bewilderment. They were particularly troubled by the question: what were these executions? A return to the 'red terror' of the past or an isolated exceptional act of passing significance? I reassured them, saying that the 'new course' launched this spring is not being revised. The 'new course' continues. The measures taken against the terrorists represented an exceptional event brought about by exceptional circumstances. With the passing of these circumstances, the measures which they had begotten would also fall into disuse.

By the end of our conversation the Coles had cheered up. They promised to inform all the signatories of the *Declaration of the 43* about the content of our talk.

18 December

Today, Vansittart and I concluded the conversation begun on 13 December.

V. began by expressing his satisfaction with the result of our joint 'survey' of Anglo-Soviet relations. I also expressed my satisfaction, but added that

---

[i] Comte de Mirabeau, prominent figure in the period of the French Revolution, favouring a constitutional monarchy.

rapprochement between the USSR and Great Britain remained a very tender and delicate flower that required much attention and care to grow normally and develop. Then, to illustrate the difficulties that stand in the way of a genuine improvement of relations between our countries, I presented a series of facts that may be placed under two headings: 'Suspicions' and 'Discrimination'.

Suspicions. What really lay behind Lord Barnby's mission to Manchuria? Is there any basis to the rumours that a Japanese loan is being prepared on the London market? V. hastened to reply that Barnby's mission had been organized by the Federation of British Industries and was of a purely commercial nature. English industrialists want to find out whether they can make some money in Manchuria, and no more. The mission pursues no political ends. The FO had nothing to do with the sending of the mission and can express no solidarity whatsoever with the 'absurd' speeches made by some members of the mission in Tokyo. As for any plans for a Japanese loan, V. knew nothing about it (I added here that in our conversation of 9 November, Simon had promised to clarify the matter, but had not as yet replied), but he will make the necessary inquiries and inform me. In conclusion, V. remarked that the Soviet government is too suspicious and that if it took a more straightforward approach to various matters, it would get on better with other powers. I objected that the 17-year history of the USSR had, regrettably, given us good reason to be suspicious.

Discrimination. Why are two absolutely absurd and tasteless films of anti-Soviet persuasion, *Fugitives* and *Forbidden Territory*, being shown freely in London? I'm sure that the British censors would have taken a different line had the matter concerned Germany, France or Italy. Another point: why was the entire diplomatic corps invited to the official reception arranged by the aviation minister, Londonderry, on 19 November, on the eve of the parliamentary session, bar me? I'm not inclined to attach excessive importance to the above-mentioned facts (they are in themselves rather trivial), but it is significant that these facts are typical of the 'discrimination' towards the USSR which is so widespread in England. This sort of 'discrimination' poisons the atmosphere of Anglo-Soviet relations every day and every hour. It should be done with if we are really serious about improving these relations.

V.'s countenance changed somewhat, particularly when I mentioned London-derry's reception. He wrote something in his notebook and announced that he would take the appropriate measures. He promised to acquaint himself with the content of the films I had named and to try to do something to prevent similar incidents in the future; but he warned that this was a tall order in the English context.

We then addressed the question: what next? 'The current phase of Anglo-Soviet relations,' I said, 'brings the following picture to mind: after a long spell of stormy days, calm weather has finally arrived. It's a bit foggy. A bit chilly. The sky is overcast. The sun is not yet in sight. It is, of course, a great step forwards when compared with what went before…'

'But it's not enough, you wish to say,' V. exclaimed with a laugh. 'One needs a bit of sun, a bit of warmth…'

'And why not?' I replied.

'I couldn't agree with you more,' said V.

So we began to discuss practical steps for achieving a better atmosphere in Anglo-Soviet relations. We agreed that the FO should exert whatever influence it can on the tone of *The Times* and other conservative papers in respect to the USSR; that it was most desirable that Cabinet members should speak in and outside parliament about the advisability of better relations between the two countries; and that it was especially important that the British government should make a clear and categorical statement in favour of maintaining peace in the Far East. Already in the summer, V. had assured me that Simon would make such a statement at the earliest opportunity, but the promise remained unfulfilled. V. made yet another note and said that he would do everything in his power to implement the steps that we had outlined.

At the very end of our conversation, we turned to the possibility of British ministers and major public figures paying visits to the USSR. 'Why,' I asked, 'do high-ranking Englishmen travel easily and freely over the entire world, with the exception of the USSR? Is this not also a form of entrenched "discrimination"? Yet their visits could contribute greatly to the demolition of the Chinese wall that has arisen between our countries since the revolution.'

V. tried to defend British ministers by referring to their extremely busy schedules. 'I hardly ever leave London,' he noted, by way of a telling argument. 'I've only been to America once, when I visited Hoover[i] with MacDonald in 1929.'

I smiled and remarked half-jokingly: 'But you spent your holidays in Italy! Why not spend them in the Caucasus?'

V. laughed in some embarrassment and added that he still hoped to visit the Caucasus one day. Many years ago, before the war, he had spent a week there on his way back from Persia to London. The Caucasus produced an indelible impression on him. He saw no reason why, given the right circumstances, he shouldn't make another visit to that truly fascinating land.[64]

19 December

The newspapers can't stop writing about the Franco-Soviet alliance. On its front page, under the banner headline 'The Conditions of the Franco-Russian Pact',

---

[i] Herbert Hoover, president of the United States, 1929–33.

the *Star* has published the stunning news that an agreement on the pact was finally reached on 10 December, that the alliance has been drawn up for five years with the option of a further five-year prolongation, and that it is clearly directed against Germany and Japan. According to the *Star*'s sources, the alliance is of a defensive nature and stipulates cooperation between the staffs of the two countries, full cooperation in the air, the exchange of military missions, the immediate provision of the Soviet army with 400 French tanks, etc. In the event of a Japanese–Soviet war, France undertakes to supply ammunition and other war matériel to the USSR to a value of 4 million francs; and in the event of a Franco-German, war the USSR undertakes to supply grain to France to a similar sum. The pact does not stipulate direct mutual military assistance. This shocking sensation is seasoned with portraits of Laval and M.M. [Litvinov].

Newspapers and agencies immediately inundated the embassy with questions. The telephone rang off the hook. We had to issue a flat denial.

Where did the *Star* get this nonsense? Who thought it up?

In any case, the issue of a Franco-Soviet alliance appears to be very much in the air. Not without reason, perhaps. But the *Star*'s scoop is most premature. It might never become reality.

I received a visit from F.W. Pethick-Lawrence,[i] a former member of the Labour government and current president of the Dimitrov Committee.[65] He spoke in the name of his committee and in the spirit of the *Declaration of the 43*. I replied in the spirit of my conversation with the Coles. In the end the old man calmed down and cheered up.

20 December

JEWS WHO MARRY ARYANS
   Streicher[ii] Demands Death
MUNICH, DECEMBER 19

'The marriage of a Jew to a non-Jewish woman must be punished with death', said Herr Julius Streicher, the Governor of Silesia, when he addressed 3,000 lawyers and judges of North Bavaria at a Nazi Bar Association meeting in Munich. And the words were greeted with cheers.

'The blood corpuscles of a Jew,' he added, 'are completely different from those of a Nordic. A non-Jewish girl is lost forever to her own people the moment she marries a Jew.'

---

[i] Frederick William Pethick-Lawrence (1st Baron Pethick-Lawrence), Labour MP, 1923–31 and 1935–45.
[ii] Julius Streicher, founder and editor of the anti-Semitic weekly newspaper *Der Stürmer*.

'Children resulting from such a marriage can only be characterised as bastards who are doomed to lead our people further into decadence and destruction.' – Reuter

The *Manchester Guardian*, 20 Dec. 1934

Utter idiots! And blood-thirsty beasts to boot. The day of reckoning will come, and Hitler will pay for the suffering of millions.[66]

The kafuffle over the shootings does not abate. Barely have I liquidated the protests of the 'left' Labourites than the right appears on the horizon. It is mostly the work of Citrine.[i] Today, the *Daily Herald* published an indignant editorial.[67]

24 December

The White émigrés are clearly in great disarray. The Mensheviks, headed by Dan[ii] and Abramovich,[iii] have taken an 'awfully leftist' stand. They back the idea of a united front against fascism and speak out not only against intervention, but even about defending the USSR in the event of an attack by a capitalist state. Dan had been expecting an amnesty, before 7 November, and had already packed his suitcases for Moscow... The Milyukovites from *Poslednie Novosti* are against intervention, against Japan, and against Germany. Early in the year Milyukov[iv] delivered a report on 'Russia and Europe' at the Royal Institute of International Affairs in London, declaring that, were he to be serving as Russian Minister of Foreign Affairs, he would pursue exactly the same policy as Litvinov!... And now the monarchists from *Vozrozhdenie* are seeking points of contact with the 'new Russia' under the banner of zoological nationalism...

And all this is because the Soviet order has proved so secure, strong and rapid in its development! People do not judge victors; they seek to make their peace with them.

27 December

Vansittart unexpectedly asked me over, at the height of the Christmas season. I felt somewhat anxious on my way to the FO. In fact, however, there was no cause for concern. This became clear at the very beginning of our conversation.

---

[i] Walter McLennan Citrine, secretary of the General Council of the TUC, 1926–46; director of the *Daily Herald*, 1929–46. Opposed the alliance between the Soviet and British trade unions in 1925–27.

[ii] Fedor Ilich Dan (Gurvich), leader of the Menshevik Party from 1905, exiled in 1922.

[iii] Rafail Abramovich, a Menshevik activist.

[iv] Pavel Nikolaevich Milyukov, liberal historian; founder and leader of the Constitutional Democratic (Kadet) Party, 1905–17, and foreign minister in the Provisional Government in the wake of the February 1917 revolution. Emigrated to the United States once the Bolsheviks seized power.

On 17 December I attended a lunch that Boothby had arranged for me in parliament. Among those present were Burgin,[i] junior minister for trade, and Hudson,[ii] the junior minister of labour. We had an open, *gloves off*, discussion of the issues of the day. Burgin, and especially Hudson, defended the idea of an Anglo-Japanese alliance and the division of China into spheres of influence. I argued with them. Boothby told V. about the lunch. V. got very worked up and decided to see me right away.

V. was really very annoyed with Burgin and Hudson. They were 'foolish people' who hadn't a clue about foreign policy. Their views do not in any way reflect those of the British government on the issue of the Far East. V. would like to affirm once again, and quite categorically, that the British government desires peace in the Far East and does not intend to renew the Anglo-Japanese alliance. He now considers it more desirable than ever that an authoritative Cabinet member should make a speech in parliament clearly setting out the British government's policy in the Far East. He will speak to Baldwin on this matter and hopes that such a declaration will be made when the Houses reopen at the end of January.

I thanked V. for his explanation and endorsed his idea of a public statement by Baldwin or Simon defining the British line in the Far East. This would assist greatly in clearing the air in Anglo-Soviet relations.

V. further informed me that he had given a lot of thought to our last conversations and had arrived at the conclusion that ministerial visits to the USSR would be one of the best ways of improving relations between our countries. Why shouldn't Walter Elliot, for one, make a trip to the USSR? For him, as minister of agriculture, the USSR ought to be of considerable interest. And why shouldn't some other members of government also pay visits to the USSR? As a last resort, if none of the Cabinet members are currently available to travel, he is ready to suggest himself in their place, although a visit by a politician and Cabinet member would of course have greater significance. These words do not reflect the decision of some government agency; rather, he was just thinking out loud.

I replied that I wholly endorsed V.'s 'thoughts' and that I would deem it useful if they took the form of concrete decisions in the nearest future. These English visits might be official, semi-official or even private, depending on the circumstances. The details can be agreed on in each individual case.

---

[i] Edward Leslie Burgin, Liberal MP, 1929–45; parliamentary secretary, Board of Trade, 1932–37; minister of transport, 1937–39; minister of supply, 1939–40.
[ii] Robert Spear Hudson (1st Viscount Hudson), parliamentary secretary to the Ministry of Labour, 1931–35; minister of pensions, 1935–36; secretary in the Department of Overseas Trade, 1937–40; privy counsellor, 1938.

V. agreed with me fully and added that if he himself were to go, he would prefer the form of a private or semi-official visit, since he is no orator, and official visits always involve a great deal of '*speech making*'. Then I showed him the interview given by Neurath to the Berlin correspondent of *Messaggero*, where he stated that 'if the Eastern Pact means the perpetuation of the present territorial and political situation in Eastern Europe, then Germany will never join it'. V., who had not seen the interview, became very agitated and, upon reading the statement, exclaimed: 'This is the crux. It's very serious.'

I steered the conversation to the Pact of the Four proposed by Neurath to counterbalance the Eastern Pact, and declared plainly that the Pact of the Four is absolutely unacceptable to us in any form (e.g. as a pact of five or six powers), for it will only undermine the authority of the League of Nations. V. promised to inform the Cabinet of our attitude to the Pact.[68]

When I was about to leave, V. took a very intimate and friendly tone and informed me, 'in absolute confidence', that if Soviet 'interference' in England's domestic affairs were to continue, all our efforts to improve Anglo-Soviet relations would go to rack and ruin. V. has had reason to convince himself of this 'interference' only recently. I asked him what exactly he meant, but he refused to tell me the facts known to him and merely asked me to bear in mind that he had taken the liberty of raising this subject as a 'friend' and advocate of Anglo-Soviet *rapprochement*.[69]

31 December

Another year has ended, and I stand on the threshold of a new year! Involuntarily, my gaze is cast back over the twelve months that have passed…

Politically and economically speaking, this last year has been a success for us, although it was darkened at its end by the death of Kirov. We have grown stronger, grown up, and begun to play a major global role. Our trajectory has risen steeply all the time. In particular, the past year has marked a turning point in Anglo-Soviet relations: the signing of the trade treaty, my summer talks with Vansittart, the British government's declaration in favour of the Eastern Pact, the astonishing debates in parliament on 13 July, during which Churchill and Austen Chamberlain[i] declared themselves 'friends' of the Soviet Union and insisted on its admittance to the League of Nations – all this marks the onset of a new phase in relations between the USSR and Great Britain. Not that the English lords have suddenly developed an affection for us, the unwashed Bolsheviks – no, this is not the case and never will be. It's just that the moment arrived

---

[i] Joseph Austen Chamberlain, Conservative MP, 1892–1937; elder half-brother of Neville Chamberlain; secretary of state for foreign affairs, 1924–29; architect of the Locarno Agreement, for which he received the Nobel Peace Prize, 1925.

20. Touring Scotland.

when the skill at 'facing the facts' (whether pleasant or unpleasant) which is so characteristic of British politicians finally overcame their enmity towards us on grounds of class and politics. We have now become such a major and stable international force that, willy-nilly, even the most incorrigible Conservative beasts can ignore us no longer and are forced to 'acknowledge' our existence and, as inveterate political operators, to derive from us whatever profit they can. Well, let them try – it's their right. But we are not sheep ourselves, to be shorn by anyone who wishes it. We'll see 'who beats whom'. In any case, the new tactics of the British bourgeoisie will force them to draw in their claws for a while, or at least to hide them better. Excellent. For now, this is in our interests. A new *round* in the history of Anglo-Soviet relations is beginning – we shall try to play it better...

How has the year been for me personally? I mull it over, recollect, sort out facts and dates. Agniya and I are both quite well. Feka[i] stayed with us in London for a month and we went on a very pleasant tour together of England and Scotland (Stratford-upon-Avon, Birmingham, Manchester, the English lakes, Glasgow, Edinburgh, the Scottish lakes, Newcastle, Sheffield, Nottingham). The trip took about a week (the end of July to early August). Alksnis,[ii] Tupolev,[iii]

[i] Feoktista (Feka) Poludova, Agniya's sister. Her husband Poludov signed the 'platform of 10' letter against Stalin, was arrested and shot while she was banished to the gulag for eight years.
[ii] Yakov Ivanovich Alksnis, commander of the Red Army air force, 1926–37; deputy people's commissar for defence with responsibility for aviation in 1937.
[iii] Andrei Nikolaevich Tupolev, eminent Soviet aircraft designer of 50 original aircraft and over 100 modifications of military bombers and civilian airliners, including the world's first supersonic passenger plane. A victim of the repression in 1937.

Molokov,[i] Levanevsky[ii] and a host of other pilots and engineers came to London in late June for the air show in Hendon. We struck up friendships with Alksnis and Tupolev. Then we went on a two-and-a-half-month vacation to the USSR, both ways via Berlin. We were in Moscow, Leningrad (just me, Agniya didn't travel), Kislovodsk, Sochi, Sukhumi, Gagra and Novy Afon. We put on some weight and blew out the cobwebs. I left the spa weighing 69 kilos. In the Caucasus, we became close friends with L. Polonsky.[iii] And that, I think, is about it. Not all that much and not all that interesting. Pale when compared with those truly major events which 1934 witnessed in the political, social and economic life of the USSR. And rather pale when compared with events in the sphere of Anglo-Soviet relations. But why pale? It's how it should be: for communists, the personal must dissolve in the general, or, at the very least, retreat far into the background.[70]

The whole colony gathered in the embassy to celebrate the New Year. I had to say a few words, as usual. Then we drank, sang and danced. I must confess, though, that I was not in a particularly good mood. It had been ruined by my afternoon meeting with the Labour deputation on 31 December. This had left an unpleasant, bitter aftertaste. But I'll write about the Labour deputation another time, all the more so as the incident is not yet over.

Labour protest against death sentences in the USSR[71]

The Labourites behaved fairly decently towards us until mid-December. True, none of them offered condolences upon Kirov's death either personally or officially, but nor did any make official or semi-official protests against the execution of the terrorists. The *Daily Herald* also observed the rules of propriety. Telegrams from Moscow and all other types of information were quite tolerable. There was not a single editorial devoted to the executions.

In mid-December, however, the situation changed. First, on the evening of 15 December I received the *Declaration of the 43*, about which I telegraphed in due course. On the 17th, I invited the Coles, who initiated the Declaration, for a lengthy discussion. Comrades Kagan and Astakhov[iv] took part in the conversation. As a result, the Coles agreed that they had made a mistake by

---

[i] Vasilii Sergeevich Molokov, distinguished Soviet air commander.
[ii] Sigizmund Aleksandrovich Levanevsky, pilot; awarded the Hero of the Soviet Union in 1934.
[iii] Lev Polonsky and Elizaveta Polonskaya. Of Jewish–Russian background, Elizaveta studied medicine in the Sorbonne but became a popular writer after the revolution. In 1934 she published *People of the Soviet Working Days*, a volume of essays.
[iv] Georgii Aleksandrovich Astakhov, counsellor at the Soviet embassy in London, 1934–35; chief of the press department of NKID, 1936–37; counsellor and temporary Soviet chargé d'affaires in Germany, 1937–39. Regarded as a Litvinov disciple, he was banished from the Foreign Ministry in 1939, accused of treason and sent to a labour camp, where he died in 1942.

issuing the Declaration without clarifying the facts with me beforehand. They also made the promise (which they upheld) to inform all who signed the *Declaration of the 43* about the content of our conversation. On 18 December I met Pethick-Lawrence, former member of the Labour government and president of the Dimitrov Committee, who played a significant role before, during and after the Leipzig trial. At Dimitrov's request, the committee continued functioning after his liberation and was engaged, in the main, with offering assistance to victims of fascist terror in Germany, Austria, the Balkans and elsewhere. Pethick-Lawrence expounded more or less the same thoughts as the *Declaration of the 43*. With him, too, I had a very long conversation, at the end of which he recognized the rightness of our position and promised to exert influence on the committee's members in this regard. The statement of the 43 and the Dimitrov Committee reflected the attitudes of Labour's left wing. The pronouncements were made in a cordial tone and bore an unofficial manner. Nothing appeared in the press. But although the group of 43 seemed to be friendly, it nevertheless composed its declaration without attempting to contact me and learn the true facts.

On 20 December, the *Daily Herald* published a thunderous editorial about the executions in the USSR. Late that evening, I received a letter signed by Henderson and Citrine which set out the content of the resolution passed earlier in the day by the National Joint Council (representing the General Council of the Trades Union Congress, the Executive Committee of the Labour Party, and the Executive Committee of the Parliamentary Labour Party). The letter asked me to name a date when I could receive a special Labour deputation to discuss the matter. The next morning, 21 December, the resolution of the National Joint Council appeared in all the London papers. It should be emphasized that none of the members of the National Joint Council had deemed it necessary to see me or any other member of the embassy before passing the resolution, in order to establish the true facts concerning the executions in the USSR. On the contrary, it is absolutely clear from the information at my disposal that Citrine, the main instigator of the National Joint Council's anti-Soviet statement, had a conscious desire to prevent such a meeting. Citrine feared that if a meeting took place, it would become impossible to pass the anti-Soviet resolution. For this reason, discussion of the resolution was not even on the agenda of the Council's meeting of 20 December. The Council members did not know in advance that this issue would be discussed. It was raised at the very end of the session under 'Miscellaneous' by Conley, last year's president of the General Council of the Trades Union Congress. There is no doubt, however, that Conley's speech had been prepared in advance by Citrine. Having contacted Moscow, I replied to the deputation on 24 December, agreeing to a meeting. As it was Christmas Eve, and all the Labourites were leaving London, I offered two dates: 28 or 31 December. Even the 28th was too early for them, so they came on 31 December.

It was an impressive deputation. Ten people came: Kean[i] (president of the General Council), Citrine (secretary of the General Council), and Hicks,[ii] Pugh[iii] and Bolton[iv] from the Trades Union Congress; representing Labour were Lansbury (chairman of the parliamentary faction), Clynes[v] (former home secretary in the Labour Cabinet), Adamson[vi] (vice-chairman of the Executive Committee of the Labour Party), Lathan,[vii] and Middleton[viii] (secretary of the Labour Party). Our side was represented by myself, Comrade Kagan and Comrade Astakhov. Thus, nearly an entire parliament was assembled in my office.

The first to take the floor was Kean, president of the Trades Union Congress, who presented the delegation to me in a brief and official manner. The next and most important speaker was Citrine. His speech boiled down to the following. First, on behalf of the National Joint Council, he extended sympathy to the Soviet government for its great loss and expressed indignation towards those guilty of Kirov's death. There followed a solemn declaration to the effect that the British Labour movement has always condemned struggle by terrorist means. Furthermore, Citrine assured us that interference in the internal affairs of the USSR was entirely alien to the deputation, as to the whole British Labour movement. On the contrary, the British Labour movement regards the USSR with great sympathy, as it had shown so clearly at the very beginning of the Russian Revolution and during the Soviet–Polish war. The British Labour movement understands the difficulties facing the USSR on internal and external fronts and therefore always tries, if at all possible, to refrain from public criticism of the Soviet government's actions. But in this case the National Joint Council found itself forced to make an open statement.

The USSR is the only socialist state in the world. Although socialism was implemented there in a way which seemed incorrect to the British Labour movement – there should be no illusions about that – Labour considers our

[i] William Kean, president of the General Council of the TUC, 1934–35.

[ii] George Ernest Hicks, a trade unionist and Labour MP, 1931–50; TUC leader involved in the formation of the Anglo-Russian Joint Advisory Committee, 1925–27.

[iii] Sir Arthur Pugh, secretary of the Iron and Steel Trades Confederation, 1917–37; chairman of both the TUC General Council and the Special Industrial Committee during the 1926 general strike.

[iv] W.J. Bolton, clerk, who during 40 years with the TUC became head of its international department.

[v] John Robert Clynes, deputy leader of the Labour Party, 1919 and 1922–31; lord privy seal, January–October 1924; home secretary, 1929–31.

[vi] William Adamson, Labour MP, 1910–31; secretary of state for Scotland, January–November 1924 and 1929–31.

[vii] George Lathan, president of the National Federation of Professional Workers, 1921–37; member of Advisory Committee in the International Labour Office (Geneva), 1923–37.

[viii] James Smith Middleton, secretary of the Labour Party, 1934–44.

ultimate goals to be identical. Socialism was currently taking its exam in Russia, so to speak, and the British Labour movement has a stake in its success. They, the Labourites, would like the Soviet state to be a model in all respects, so that the superiority of the socialist system over the capitalist one might be obvious every step of the way. Meanwhile, the events of the past weeks have caused great damage to the prestige of the Soviet government and to the prestige of the socialist state. Even in the most backward bourgeois states, murderers are tried in public courts, with the observance of every procedural formality. Even in Hitler's Germany, Dimitrov was tried publicly, which made it possible to save his life. In the USSR, on the contrary, terrorists are tried secretly. The general public knows nothing about the circumstances of the case and the reasons for the verdict. It merely learns from the newspapers that so-and-so and so-and-so have been shot, accused of planning terrorist acts. These judicial methods make a painful impression in England, and in particular on the English working masses. All are agreed that such methods of administering justice should have no place in a socialist state.[72]

Extraordinary measures were all the less excusable given the strength and might of the Soviet government, which has no reason to fear a serious threat from counter-revolutionaries or terrorists. Guided by such considerations, the National Joint Council had found it expedient to send a special deputation to me in order to convey the feelings aroused in the British Labour movement by the recent executions and to ask me to bring it to the notice of the Soviet government.

Citrine said all this smoothly, ingratiatingly, with unctuous courtesy and a velvety voice, presenting himself as the Soviet Union's most devoted friend. But throughout the speech, the cordial façade could not conceal a deep-seated hostility to the USSR.

Lansbury took the floor after Citrine. He first pointed out that the recent executions had put the Labour Party in an awkward position in parliament. His party always protested against such acts, wherever they took place: in India, Germany, Spain, the Balkans or South America. Often, the Conservatives would report: 'Don't try to pull the wool over our eyes. Things are much worse in your beloved Russia.' Lansbury and the whole Labour Party had always rejected such accusations indignantly. But now they had been driven into a corner and had to agree. He could no longer see how Labour could protest against cruelty in a capitalist country after the executions in the Soviet Union.

The Labour Party was often asked from many sides to make statements of protest, but now it would have to refrain from doing so. For Lansbury personally, the recent events in the USSR have been a terrible blow. He had sympathized with the Russian liberation movement throughout his life and had actively supported Russian revolutionaries. L. recalled a list of famous individuals from the old revolutionary movement in Russia whom he had known and helped in the past. He'd been in the USSR in 1920. The times were terribly hard and the Russian people suffered enormously. Hunger and terror reigned in the country. It was most unpleasant, but Lansbury did not consider it possible then to condemn the Soviet government. He'd had a firm belief that some new system would gradually emerge from the chaos of 15 years ago, and that a strong government based on the principles of freedom and democracy would be formed. He had nearly lost this hope. The USSR has existed for 17 years, but its dictatorial methods of government, crossing over at times into open terror, have persisted in full force. The Soviet government evinces a cynical disregard for world public opinion. L. was more convinced than ever that a strong system could not be built on the basis of terrorism. Russia can survive by terrorist methods of government no better than Germany. This has to change. He was disheartened to see what was going on in the USSR, because Russia, as Citrine had said, embodies the ideas and ideals to which the British Labour movement aspires. Russia is the star of the future, but today the star has been darkened by the shadow of the bloody executions.

Unlike Citrine, Lansbury spoke with great candour and emotion. He often stumbled as he looked for the right words, he gesticulated, his voice sometimes trembled, and his big grey head shook nervously.

Clynes was the third speaker. He spoke calmly and briefly. Clynes said that if the USSR were to be waging a war against an external enemy, all the Labourites would understand it and would not condemn the Soviet government's actions. But the USSR was not at war, peace reigned on its borders, and in such a situation Labour could not understand the need for so many executions. Such actions merely strengthened the forces of capitalism in other countries. Besides, executions by shooting were a very dangerous thing.

He recalled the shooting of a dozen Irish revolutionaries by English soldiers during the war in 1916, after the national uprising in Dublin had been suppressed. Those shootings completely spoiled Anglo-Irish relations and resulted in an Irish national front more united than ever before in the history of Ireland. The memory of the bloodshed will long remain an obstacle to the establishing of friendly relations between the Irish and English peoples. He, Clynes, hated to say all this in connection with the recent events in the USSR because he, like the previous speakers, thought that the USSR was the main guardian of the idea of socialism, and that the executions had cast a shadow on the name of this guardian.

Since nobody else wished to speak, it was now my turn to reply. I began by sweeping aside any disputes on abstract issues of principle. The speakers had touched upon such subjects, but I was not going to follow the same path. It had to be realized that we and Labour were embracing different worldviews and different political philosophies. It would be useless to argue about, say, the merits of proletarian dictatorship or bourgeois democracy, since both we and they have definite and entrenched opinions on this topic. We would never be able to convince one another of our arguments. A theoretical discussion of general problems was therefore a waste of time, even though I would have had plenty to say in reply to the previous speakers' arguments had I so wished. I preferred to limit myself to a discussion of this particular case. First of all, I felt obliged to say that it was most regrettable that the National Joint Council had not had genuine information about what had happened in the USSR when it passed its resolution on 20 December. None of the Council members had bothered to see me in advance to clarify the matter (although many Council members knew me personally). Making its decision, the National Joint Council must have been under the sway of the tendentious reports published by the bourgeois press, with their hostility to the USSR. In other words, they had only listened to one side and had not wished to listen to the other. Did this comply with the English principle of *fair play*?

Citrine stirred at this point and interceded irritably: 'We used not only the bourgeois English press, but also the Soviet press. Here are relevant translations from *Pravda* and *Izvestiya*.' Citrine pointed to a thick dossier lying on the table in front of him. It was clear that the Congress secretary had arrived for the meeting fully armed.

I replied that a reference to *Pravda* and *Izvestiya* made no odds in this case. We, too, do not publish everything in our newspapers out of various considerations (to do with foreign policy in particular). Members of the Council could have learned much from a private talk with me that they would not have found on the pages of the Soviet press. But it seemed superfluous to insist on this point, so I turned directly to the issue of the executions. As the National Joint Council had passed a quite official resolution on the events in the USSR, I also found it necessary to give a quite official reply.

I then read the following statement (the text is attached).[73] Having read the statement, I handed out copies that had been made beforehand to the members of the deputation and added: 'The National Joint Council made its resolution public. I hope my reply will be published too – for the sake of *fair play*.'

My statement made a very powerful impression. All members of the deputation hastened to reread my text, their faces showing considerable agitation. Then I read translated excerpts from the White Guard newspaper *Za Rossiyu*, which had called openly last November for the murder of Soviet leaders, Comrade Kirov in particular. The citations produced a devastating effect. 'But we didn't know that!' Hicks cried out. I replied: 'Precisely. That is why I regret that the Council members did not talk to me before passing the resolution.' Citrine was also flustered and began to put down the paper's name, issue number, place of publication, etc. Then he said: 'The statement we have just heard does not answer many of the questions we posed. It's not the kind of answer we expected. Besides, we must protest strongly against the accusation that the British Labour movement encourages terrorists or sympathizes with them in one way or another. The injustice of this accusation is shown by the very first part of the resolution passed on 20 December, where the National Joint Council expresses deep indignation at the assassination of Kirov and great sympathy [with the Soviet Union] for its great loss.'

I replied that I simply couldn't agree with Citrine's arguments. My statement was precisely a reply to the main thrust of the Labour démarche. As regards Labour's cordial response to the events in the USSR, I had doubts there too. When was Kirov assassinated? On 1 December. When did the Labourites deem it appropriate to express their sympathy? On 20 December. Why didn't they show any signs of life for three weeks after the assassination? How to explain that even in the resolution of 20 December they, having expressed their sympathy in the first paragraph, actually annul the purport of this gesture in the second paragraph by expressing indignation at the executions?

'There is a simple and exhaustive answer to this,' Citrine put in. 'The British Labour movement is built on the principles of democracy. The National Joint Council alone had the right to extend sympathy to the Soviet government on behalf of the Labour movement. The first session of the Council after Kirov's assassination was held on 20 December.'

I replied that Citrine's answer did not satisfy me. First, I doubted that the secretaries of the Trades Union Congress and the Labour Party could not, at their own discretion, send a message of sympathy themselves on such an exceptional occasion. Second, let us assume that, according to the constitution, they could not present official condolences on behalf of the British Labour movement before 20 December. But, being friends of the USSR, could they not do so personally? For instance, could not Citrine, who has been on friendly terms with us for over ten years, call me by telephone or write a message of condolence immediately after the assassination of Kirov? Could not other leaders of the Labour movement, who had been saying that they were friends of the USSR all those years, do the same?

Silence fell. The members of the deputation exchanged glances and didn't know what to say. Lansbury, with his usual candour, finally exclaimed in desperation: 'It simply didn't occur to me! I didn't even know who Kirov was. I hadn't imagined that he occupied a top post in the USSR... I'm very sorry that I didn't think of sending condolences to you. But you shouldn't question our friendly sentiments towards the USSR because of that. We sympathize with the USSR very much, we wish you every happiness in building socialism. We have always defended you against the attacks of the capitalist world and will continue to do so. We hate terrorists and abhor the assassination of Kirov – and you accuse us of sympathizing with terrorists. It's impossible.'

Lansbury's utterance prompted the members of the deputation to speak again. Citrine, Hicks, Lathan, Middleton and others vied with one another in expressing their displeasure at the final phrase of my statement. Citrine produced, among other things, a translation of the decree of 1 December concerning the expedition of court proceedings for terrorist cases and, citing it, began to claim that the decree essentially abolished justice in the USSR.

Comrade Kagan intervened and explained to Citrine calmly but effectively that the decree was issued as a normal edict by normal legislative organs of the USSR, that it was a 'lawful law', like any other decision of the Central Executive Committee, that the expedition of court proceedings for terrorist cases derived from the urgent need to protect the USSR, and that if Citrine had deemed it necessary to see the Soviet ambassador before passing the resolution of 20 December he would have heard a lot of things which might have convinced him of the necessity of the severe measures taken by the Soviet government.

Citrine retorted in an offended tone that the executive bodies of the British Labour movement often have to take a stand regarding the actions of foreign governments. If the National Joint Council sent its secretaries to foreign embassies for explanations on every occasion, it would never adopt a single resolution. It would always be waiting for replies.

Comrade Kagan objected that, considering the particular friendly relations that existed and continue to exist between the British Labour movement and the USSR, about which members of the deputation had just spoken with such fervour, we had the right to expect that the National Joint Council would not lump the Soviet embassy in London in one category with the embassies of capitalist countries. Are Citrine's personal and political relations with the German or Polish ambassador really as amicable as those with the Soviet ambassador? Wouldn't it have been natural, then, for the National Joint Council to consult the Soviet ambassador to find out what was actually happening in the USSR before discussing the resolution?

I sided with Comrade Kagan and added that the Council's conduct had been an unpleasant surprise in several respects. First, Citrine stressed in his speech that Labour understands and appreciates the difficult situation facing the Soviet government. Until recently, I had also assumed this to be so. But the resolution of 20 December convinced me that I was mistaken. Most likely, Labour does not quite understand our difficulties. The measures the Soviet government had to take after the assassination of Comrade Kirov were the measures necessary for the USSR to protect itself against the intrigues of international counter-revolution. True, those were rigorous measures, but as Mirabeau said, revolution cannot be made with lavender oil. If Labour really appreciated our difficulties, it would not protest against the shooting of terrorists. Second, I was struck in a most disagreeable way not just by the fact of the resolution being adopted, but also by the manner in which this was done. The session of the National Joint Council on 20 December raised the question of the events in the USSR. Not one member of the Council made an attempt to see me earlier in order to learn from a primary source what was really happening in my country. The Council derived all its information from the bourgeois press and obviously deemed this sufficient. Then the resolution was adopted, where the wicked words of the second part obliterated the good words of the first. The resolution was delivered to me late in the evening of the 20th, and the next morning I read it in the papers. After the resolution was published, I was asked to receive a deputation – what for? To express official protest? If you now claim so ardently to be friends of the USSR, why didn't you act in a friendly manner a fortnight ago? I believe that, given the circumstances, your first duty was to find out the facts of the matter. All the more so as the matter in hand concerned a country for which you express such friendly feelings. Citrine or somebody else could have come to me and asked: Tell me, what does it mean? I would have given him exhaustive information. He might have disagreed with me – that would be up to him – but at least his behaviour would have been correct and cordial. What actually happened represents the complete negation of amicable relations.

Silence fell again. The members of the deputation were obviously embarrassed. Once again Lansbury was the first to speak: 'Let's assume we made a mistake by not talking to you first. But does this give sufficient grounds to accuse us of the absence of friendly feelings? Does it give you the right to suspect us of sympathy with the terrorists?'

Other members of the deputation also became excited and began to justify their conduct. Hicks, sitting closer to me, muttered under his breath: 'It's true. We acted stupidly.' Middleton tried to justify the Council's behaviour by remarking that at least ten hours passed from the time I received the resolution to the time of its publication (from the evening of the 20th to the morning of the 21st). I objected: 'The letter attached to the resolution did not mention that you were going to publish it. I had no idea you were going to do so. What is the significance of the fact that the resolution was formally delivered to me several hours before it appeared in the papers? Besides, what could be done at 11 p.m.?'

Once the members of the deputation had finished pouring out their feelings, insisting all over again that they sympathized with the USSR and hated terrorists deeply, the fount of their eloquence ran dry. We (i.e. myself, Kagan and Astakhov) did not speak either.

Complete silence reigned in the room for a few moments.

The Labourites seemed not to know what to do. At last Middleton said hesitantly: 'So, you are going to leave your statement as it is?'

I confirmed I was. Then Lansbury suddenly got to his feet and, jabbing his finger at the final phrase, cried out indignantly: 'No, if this is published, it will spell the end! It will mean a split between the British Labour movement and the Soviet government. We shall not be able to work together afterwards. If the statement is published, I doubt I will even be able to maintain personal relations with you, however well I think of you.'

Other members of the deputation sided with Lansbury. I replied: 'I fail to see the grounds for such a conclusion. We've disagreed on this particular matter, but that doesn't mean that we can't and shouldn't work together on other issues.'

But Lansbury would not calm down. He objected in a trembling voice: 'No, things are much more serious. We haven't just disagreed on this particular matter – that's only half the problem. But you tell us in your statement: you are babblers and hypocrites. If you hold such a view of us, what kind of collaboration can there be? What kind of relations, even personal relations, can there be between us?'

The other members of the deputation nodded their heads approvingly.

Desiring to allay the conflict somewhat, I objected that we should not view our disagreement on this matter in such tragic terms and, what is more important, we should not generalize. I certainly did not wish to suggest with my statement that all Labourites were hypocrites and windbags. I could well understand that, in adopting the resolution, they were guided subjectively by the best intentions, sympathy with the USSR and hatred for terrorists. But the objective significance of their behaviour – even if this occurred against their will and conscious intentions – was undoubtedly harmful. And that is what the final phrase of my statement was driving at.

Lansbury would not give in. He waved his hands indignantly and exclaimed: 'No, you think of us as hypocrites and babblers.'

Again I emphasized that although we disagree on the matter of executing the terrorists, we should not forget that we can and must have a common line. In particular, we have a great common goal – the preservation of peace. Hence, disagreement on this particular matter should not preclude our further cooperation. On the contrary, we must cooperate in all matters relating to the preservation of peace and the improvement of Anglo-Soviet relations.

Lansbury muttered something in reply that could be understood roughly as follows: 'I still doubt that further cooperation is possible.' Everyone felt that the conversation had come to an end. The Labourites rose, but hesitated to leave. Lansbury suggested that we should at least avoid arguments in the press. The deputation would publish a communiqué about their visit. He would like the text to be agreed between us. I answered that I could not take responsibility for a communiqué issued by the National Joint Council. The only thing I could do was to look it through and say whether I would have to issue a reply in the press. In addition, I insisted that the full text of my statement should be published together with the communiqué. Lansbury did not object. We agreed that Citrine and Middleton would write the communiqué and show it to me.

As we parted, Lansbury said bitterly: 'I deeply regret what has happened. I never thought I would live through such a moment in the 76th year of my life.'

Citrine and Middleton wanted to come and show me their communiqué the next morning, 1 January. However, I had to wait for a reply from Moscow, so I dodged the meeting under the pretext of the New Year and asked them to come on the 2nd. By then I had received the necessary instructions from the Ministry of Foreign Affairs.

On the morning of the 2nd, I received Citrine, Middleton and Bolton (head of the international department of the General Council of the Trades Union Congress). At first, their mood was sour and confused. To judge by the information at my disposal, the deputation had returned home in a very distressed state of mind after talking to me. The rebuff with which they had been met had affected them greatly. Disagreements had begun among the members of the deputation. Middleton, who had disapproved of the move initiated by Citrine from the very beginning, now said openly that the National Joint Council had acted foolishly, that its behaviour towards me had been tactless, that condolences should have been sent right after Kirov's death, and that they should have talked to me in private before undertaking any steps. Some other members of the deputation, Hicks and Lansbury in particular, were of the same opinion. Generally, the Labourites felt they had fallen into a swamp and needed to find a way out of the situation.

Citrine and Middleton showed me the draft communiqué. It contained my statement, but was otherwise highly unpleasant in tone and content. I said that this communiqué might force me to resort to a public dispute with Labour. Comrade Kagan, who was present at our meeting, drew the attention of Citrine and Middleton to some especially odious passages in the communiqué. The two secretaries then opened a heated and lengthy debate with us. It was clear that the communiqué was merely a pretext and that in fact they wished to discuss with me again the issues they had raised and to find out whether a compromise could be achieved in order to avoid open conflict between the USSR and the Labour movement. Our discussion, which was of a confidential nature and embraced the whole range of questions relating to the assassination of Kirov, lasted nearly two hours.

In the course of the discussion, I explained to Citrine and Middleton the inner and outer workings of the assassination of Kirov and the reasons why the

21. Agniya in the sanatorium in Sochi.

22. An obligatory visit to a kolkhoz near Sochi.

Soviet government had acted the way it had. My words made a great impression on them. Even Citrine finally recognized that it was hard to argue with the actions of the Soviet government; yet still he would not abandon his 'fetish' of a public trial. Middleton was considerably more obliging on this point, as on all others. To make a concession to the Labourites, and wishing to keep good relations with the Trades Union Congress and Labour, I agreed to remove the last phrase from my statement, which accused them of sympathizing with the actions of the terrorists. Citrine and Middleton sighed with obvious relief and quickly agreed to an amicable arrangement. They compiled a new text of the communiqué right away, which was published in the press on 3 January. The new text was much better than the first. At any rate, there was no need for me to make any polemical replies in the press. (Naturally, as had been agreed with Lansbury, the Labourites alone were responsible for the communiqué.)

Citrine and Middleton assured me that as soon as the communiqué appeared in the press the next morning, the National Joint Council would consider the incident closed and would not return to it again.

1935

8 January

A fire at the embassy.

Tonight, at about 11 p.m., smoke suddenly appeared from under the floor near the fireplace in my study. There was a general agitation, the alarm was sounded, and when we raised the floorboards we found a flame in the wall near the flue. We doused the fire as best we could, but some smoke persisted all the same, albeit less than before. We spent a lot of time trying to locate the cause, but in the end I decided to call the fire brigade. Five lads arrived in copper helmets. They smashed apart the floorboards, fireplace and wall and found that a thick wooden joist adjoining the main flue under the floor was on fire. The firemen thought that the joist had probably been burning for several weeks or even months, but because there was no airflow the flame had remained low, smouldering away and charring the girder. Perhaps that was so, but that was no help to me. The fire was put out, the girder amputated, and at around 4 a.m. the firemen left, leaving the room in a terrible mess. Now we shall have to see to it that the flue, the wall and the beam are properly repaired.

What a nuisance! And what an absurd structure: a wooden joist lying right on the flue. Previously the flue had been clogged up, there had been little draught and the beam had caused no harm. Last autumn we had the flue cleaned, the draught increased, the flame began penetrating the places it was not supposed to through cracks in the flue, and finally the beam caught fire. How idiotic! Experts say that this system was widely employed about a hundred years ago, in the first half of the nineteenth century. So our embassy must be at least a hundred years old.

9 January

Mikhail Botvinnik[i] left today. He had come here to attend an international chess tournament in Hastings. He spent about a fortnight in England, played nine

---

[i] Mikhail Moiseevich Botvinnik, Russian chess grandmaster, world champion 1948–57, 1958–60 and 1961–63.

games and finished fifth. He was somewhat disappointed with the result, but he took it fairly well. All things considered, the result was not bad at all. Botvinnik is still very young – just 23. He's been playing for 11 years. In Hastings, Botvinnik had to compete with the great champions of the world, such as Capablanca, Euwe, Flohr and others. What's more, English food proved a terrible trial for him, and he had to play at an unfamiliar time – in the mornings. Add to that the inescapable effect of the climate. Given all these conditions, which must influence the state of any player, it should be said that Botvinnik coped with his task if not brilliantly, then at least perfectly well. His time is sure to come. But it is important that our top players should start arriving at international tournaments not at the last moment, but at least a week in advance, in order to get used to their surroundings. Lasker,[i] whom Botvinnik met in London, is of the same opinion. I have written about this to N.V. Krylenko.[ii]

Botvinnik makes an excellent impression: modest, thoughtful, deep and unusually observant. He noticed more things in the two days he spent in London than many of our comrades have over the course of many years' work. Belongs to the Komsomol.

Botvinnik was accompanied by his coach S.O. Vainshtein[iii] (himself an average chess player) – his minder, patron and the editor of a chess newspaper. Incidentally, I learned from Vainshtein that the chess capital of the Soviet Union is Leningrad, not Moscow. Or is Vainshtein simply in the grip of Leningrad jingoism?

15 January

I have just returned from the first lunch of the Contact Circle, organized by the Russian–British chamber of commerce. The Contact Circle's purpose is to let English and Soviet economists meet in an informal setting and to give them the chance to get to know one another better. It will arrange lunches once a month, charging two shillings and sixpence per person. Not a bad idea. The first lunch was today, and I was asked to say a few words and give my blessing. I did so. The other speakers were Mather[iv] (president of the chamber), Maginness[v] (vice-chairman), Ozersky and someone else. After the lunch, the Russian–British chamber held its annual meeting, at which Ozersky presented a report.

---

[i] Emanuel Lasker, prominent German chess player, world champion, 1894–1920.
[ii] Nikolai Vasilevich Krylenko, people's commissar for justice of the Russian Federation, 1931–36, and of the USSR, 1936–38, during the height of the repression campaign. He fell victim to the purges in 1938, when he was sentenced to death by a kangaroo court in just 20 minutes.
[iii] Samuil Osipovich Vainshtein, head of the All-Russian Chess Union.
[iv] Loris Emerson Mather.
[v] Sir Greville Simpson Maginness.

18 January

Mikhail Sholokhov[i] has left. He spent about a fortnight in London with his wife. They lived in the embassy. I arranged two receptions for him: one for journalists who interviewed Sholokhov (the interview was poorly covered in the press) and the other for writers. In addition, the SCR [Society for Cultural Relations with the USSR] held a grand evening soirée attended by some 400 guests. It was a brilliant success. Professor Abercrombie[ii] presided, Sholokhov and I gave speeches. Sir William Rothenstein,[iii] director of the Royal Academy of Arts in London, made the closing speech. The literary, academic and artistic worlds were well represented (among the guests were Keynes[iv] and his wife[v]). There were also many journalists, but once again the press failed to cover the evening. Sholokhov gave a very vivid and interesting speech.

He spoke about the new Russian writers and readers, the readers' keen interest in writers, the thousands of letters of advice and criticism he receives from readers all over the country, the readers' conferences at which he has to 'answer' for his work, the huge reserve of writing talent among the 2 million correspondents in industry and agriculture, and many things besides. The audience listened to Sholokhov with bated breath, often interrupting his speech with applause. Sholokhov spoke in Russian, of course, and his interpreter (a good one) was Stevens, who translated the first volume of *The Quiet Don*, published recently by Putnam. I devoted my speech to old and new Russian literature (before and after the revolution), stressing in particular that our classic literature was for the most part a literature of 'weak people' and pessimism, whereas the new Soviet literature is a literature of 'strong people' and healthy optimism. My speech was a great success too, and Putnam asked for the text so that he could publish it in the *Contemporary Review*.

I liked Sholokhov very much. He is young (29) and full of *joie de vivre*. An ardent hunter and angler. Despite his fame, he has not been spoiled. He is modest and straightforward. Will this last? We'll see. He has a very good wife – intelligent, positive, pleasant. This is a great boon for him. A wife like her will keep him away from the many follies that our young writers are so prone to. Sholokhov has a very charming appearance: a well-proportioned blue-eyed

---

[i] Mikhail Aleksandrovich Sholokhov, winner of the Nobel Prize for Literature in 1965, author of *And Quiet Flows the Don*, *Virgin Soil Upturned* and *They Fought for their Country*.
[ii] Lascelles Abercrombie, British poet and critic, professor of English Literature at the University of London, 1929–35, and reader in English at the University of Oxford, 1935–38.
[iii] William Rothenstein, principal of the Royal College of Art, 1920–35; trustee of the Tate Gallery, 1927–33; director of the Tate Gallery, 1938–64.
[iv] John Maynard Keynes (Baron Keynes of Tilton), British economist, author of *The General Theory of Employment, Interest and Money* (1936) and editor of the *Economic Journal*, 1911–44. An agnostic and liberal, he deplored Marxism, which he argued rested on erroneous economic premises. If one needed religion, it could hardly be found 'in the turbid rubbish of the red bookshop'.
[v] The Russian ballerina Lidiya Lopukhova of the Ballets Russes.

blond of medium height, with delicate features, a shock of curly hair over a large, open forehead and a pipe permanently stuck in his teeth. Just as you would imagine a poet. What a shame he saw so little of England. He spent most of his time meeting literary people, attending parties and shopping (he had a lot of money – the fee he received for the publication of *The Quiet Don* abroad).

25 January

From London, where he had arrived via Sweden and Denmark, Sholokhov travelled to Paris, from where he was to return home, to the Soviet Union. Sholokhov stayed in Paris for just two days. He had an unpleasant incident there. He was supposed to leave Paris at 11 p.m. Everything was ready: the tickets were in his pocket, his bulky luggage (eight suitcases!) had been sent to the railway station, and the Sholokhovs were just about to get in the taxi, when Sholokhov suddenly realized that his passport had disappeared. They ransacked their pockets and searched the room, but the passport was nowhere to be found. They hastily sent a man to the railway station to see to it that their luggage should be kept back. In complete desperation they delayed their departure, wondering in vain where their passport might be. Then it suddenly turned up – at the bottom of a suitcase, stuffed in with collars, ladies' stockings and gloves.

Yesterday I gave a lecture on planning in the USSR at Cambridge. The lecture was arranged by the Marshall Society. Marshall's[i] widow is still alive. She is 80, rides a bicycle, and works diligently every day in the library bequeathed by her husband to Cambridge University and managed to all intents and purposes by the Marshall Society. This curious old lady sat in the first row at my lecture and took notes all the time. Agniya, who came to Cambridge with me and was introduced to Mrs Marshall, was congratulated by her on my success. That's how robust people are in England!

My lecture really was a great success. I structured it as follows: history of Soviet planning, methods of planning, planning apparatus, results of planning (basically, the most important achievements of the five-year plans). The meeting was held in the Arts School. The main lecture hall, which can hold 500 students, was packed to the rafters, with people sitting on windowsills and the bare floor or perching on pillars and various platforms located in the hall. The audience consisted mostly of students, with a smattering of teachers and professors. I couldn't help recalling our student gatherings of years ago. I was greeted with loud applause. During the lecture, which lasted for about an hour, the audience

---

[i] Sir Alfred Marshall, after whom the Cambridge Marshall Society was named in 1927 to promote discussion of economics.

23. Maisky tries his hand at punting in the land of the 'Cambridge Five'.

was intently silent. Many took notes. When it was all over, there was a storm of applause and prolonged stamping. The lecture was itself often interrupted by applause (in response to citations from Lenin, a statement that the world crisis stopped at the borders of the USSR, etc.). Then I was bombarded with questions, some of which were intended to trip me up; but there were not many of those. Most were to the point. My every successful riposte was met by generous clapping. On the whole, the friendliness of the audience was beyond doubt.

After the lecture we had tea at Trinity College, in David Layton's flat (David is the son of Sir Walter Layton,[i] the editor of *The Economist*), and chatted indefatigably about a great variety of topics. There were about 15 people, smoking, making a racket, knocking over cups – i.e. behaving just as one would expect at a noisy student gathering. My general impression is that young people in Cambridge are at the crossroads. They have serious qualms about the past, and they are seeking something new to meet the demands of the present. It is a condition full of promise and danger: who will catch the mood of the young? The right or the left? Fascists or communists? For the present, the fascists have the better chances, and that is where the main danger lies.[i] It was past 11 p.m. when we left Cambridge. White (our driver) lost his way, so we reached home at around three in the morning.

26 January

Today's *Times* carries an editorial dealing with the forthcoming visit to London of the French premier and foreign minister, Laval. The article ends in characteristic fashion:

---

[i] Sir Walter Layton, editor of the *Economist*, 1922–38; director-general of programmes, Ministry of Supply, 1940–42.

German equality within a system of security is a principle that has been accepted by all. The moment has come for an act of trust and boldness and for removing the restrictions upon the German, Austrian, Hungarian and Bulgarian governments in regard to armaments in exchange for a general system of limitation. The restrictions imposed by the peace treaties were not meant to be permanently unilateral, and until equality is practically recognized no stable international system is likely to be established.

So *The Times* (which very often reflects MacDonald's views most fully) quite openly proposes lifting all military restrictions on Germany, Austria, Hungary and Bulgaria, in exchange for a convention on arms limitation. There is not a single word about a security system, or about the Eastern Pact. In all probability, the British government will try to persuade the French to satisfy themselves with the convention and not to insist too zealously on the Eastern Pact. One should be on the alert!

28 January

This was truly remarkable!

Today Ozersky and I had lunch with Pease,[i] president of Lloyd's Bank, in the bank's very building – an unheard-of event in the entire 15-year history of Anglo-Soviet relations. Whatever one may say, it's a sign of the times!

This is how it happened. During the first lunch arranged by the Contact Circle, about which I wrote a few days ago, a junior director of Lloyds Bank named Parks came up to me and congratulated me on the successful beginning of a good endeavour. I thanked Parks and started teasing him, saying that English bankers are the most conservative in the world, that they always lag behind the course of events by at least a quarter of a century, and that they still fancy a Bolshevik to be a fierce chap clad in a leather jacket, loaded with cartridge belts, rifles and hand grenades – the image that frightened children and adults alike in the first years of the revolution. Parks was visibly nettled. He grew angry, blushed and assured me that my opinion of bankers was excessively low and that he would prove this to me in practice. Two days later I received a letter from Pease inviting me to lunch on the 28th or 30th of January. I chose the first date and requested that Ozersky, too, should be invited. Pease had no objection. So, today we lunched with the head of one of the Big Five. The entire top rung was present: Pease himself; his two deputies, Beane and Abel; four

---

[i] John William Beaumont Pease (1st Baron Wardington), British banker, chairman of Lloyds Bank, 1922–45, and chairman of the Bank of London and South America, 1922–47.

junior directors including Parks; Lord Luke,[i] member of the board and head of the famous Bovril company; and a few others. Of course, we talked during and after lunch. Ozersky and I had agreed beforehand not to talk shop at this first lunch, so the conversations were of a more general nature. But they were some conversations!

After Pease and Abel had pumped out of me all that I was ready to tell them about the scope of our gold mining (they were particularly interested in this matter), they passed to the principles of our foreign trade. Are we for autarky? I said, 'No!' and spelt out the reasons for this and the conditions on which we are ready to trade with the rest of the world. Pease liked my answer and observed thoughtfully: 'Well, that's quite correct and comforting to hear.' Aren't we planning to resort to dumping? They, the English, have been supplying textile and other machinery to Japan for half a century, and now Japan is ousting Great Britain from the market with the same equipment. Couldn't something similar happen with the USSR? I again answered, 'No!' and again tried to explain why not. In doing so I had to touch upon the basic principles of socialist economics. What followed defies description. The eyes of Sheathe, Abel, Beane and Luke, widened in amazement. They could not believe their ears. And why not! The walls of this magnificent 'temple of Mammon' had never heard such blasphemy. My interlocutors, who had imbibed the categories of capitalist economics with their mother's milk, simply could not accommodate in their minds the basic concepts of socialism. Pease, for example, asked: tell me then, what would happen in a developed socialist society, where goods would not be bought and sold but distributed free of charge, if somebody suddenly felt the urge to accumulate commodities in excess of his needs? What then? What if everybody suddenly wanted a car? Or felt like owning a private aeroplane? Or started demanding their personal yacht? And when I gave the most elementary answers to these infantile questions, the Lloyd's Bank bosses gasped and let their jaws drop, as if they had heard some stupendous revelation. But I don't think they really believed me. They probably thought: 'He's a fibber, that Bolshevik.' They can think what they want. But they didn't get the better of me. My mind was cast back thirty years, when I was doing propaganda work among the most backward workers. The same questions, the same doubts, the same disbelief. Yet my partners today were the most brilliant representatives of the financial capital of the world, and in a country like England!

That's what it means to live and work at the junction of the socialist and capitalist worlds. The long coexistence of these two worlds in the confines of our planet often gives rise to scenes and situations bursting with inner contradictions.

---

[i] George Lawson Johnston Luke (1st Baron Luke).

1 February

Today all the English papers published the following telegram from America:

RUSSIAN DEBTS TO USA.
   FAILURE OF NEGOTIATIONS
   WASHINGTON, Jan. 31. – Mr. Cordell Hull,[i] the Secretary of State, after a brief conversation with M. Troyanovsky,[ii] the Soviet Ambassador, to-day, announced that in view of the present attitude of the Soviet Government he could not encourage the hope that any agreement on the problem of Russian debts was now possible... – *Reuter*
   The Times, 1 Feb. 1935

How vexing! Troyanovsky's trip to Moscow last October 'to report to the government' was surely a mistake. It only succeeded in raising American hopes, when no solution to the difficulties was foreseeable. And now, with Troyanovsky declaring on his return that he has brought nothing new, a natural reaction has set in. I envy neither Troyanovsky nor Boev,[iii] especially Boev: what will he do and how will he trade after such a falling out? This American incident is sure to reverberate everywhere, England included.

4 February

I learned the following details about the meeting between the English and French ministers.[2]

   MacDonald and Simon have always been advocates of Hitler, especially MacDonald. Baldwin and Eden cautiously supported the French. Vansittart stressed the particular importance of Italy's participation in all European combinations. MacDonald made every effort to convince the French of the unfeasibility of the Eastern Pact ('Germany doesn't want it, and it is impossible to impose anything on Germany'), recommending that they should not insist on it, but limit themselves to the organization of Western security, leaving Eastern Europe to follow the natural course of events.

---

[i] Cordell Hull, member of the Tennessee House of Representatives, 1893–97; judge of the Fifth Judicial District, 1903–07; Democratic member of congress, 1907–21 and 1923–31, and of the Senate, 1931–33; US secretary of state, 1933–44.
[ii] Aleksandr Antonovich Troyanovsky, Soviet ambassador to Japan, 1927–33, and to the USA, 1933–38. Demoted to teach at the diplomatic academy of Narkomindel after his recall, and employed in the Soviet Information Bureau from 1941.
[iii] Ivan V. Boev, deputy people's commissar of foreign trade, 1932–33; member and then chairman of the Soviet AMTORG Trading Corporation in Washington, 1934–47.

MacDonald and Simon encountered stiff opposition from the French. True, Flandin[i] kept silent for the most part, but Laval spoke at great length. He said he was bound by promises to Litvinov and the Little Entente[3] (a typical argument: it is his promise that matters, not his personal conviction!) and he had to insist on including the Eastern Pact of mutual assistance in the communiqué. The English agreed, but MacDonald ensured the addition of the words 'freely concluded' (the pact, that is). Then Laval extracted a promise from the English that, if necessary, they would support the Eastern Pact with diplomatic démarches in Berlin and Warsaw. The French also suggested that an air convention based on mutual assistance should be concluded by the Locarno powers. The British government willingly accepted the proposal (with the exception of Cunliffe-Lister,[ii] the minister for colonial affairs). The French tried to establish priorities in dealing with the issues listed in the communiqué, and favoured the advancing of the Eastern Pact. The English resisted, but a compromise was finally achieved: all problems included in the communiqué were to be resolved 'concurrently'. However, this method lacks all clarity. Germany is not present in Geneva, but where outside Geneva could one find a suitable venue for holding such complicated negotiations with the participation of so many powers? The English seem to be willing to play the part of honest broker in negotiations between Germany and other states, but the French don't like the idea at all. We'll see.

The French are terribly annoyed with Poland. In his talk with the publisher of the *Daily Telegraph*, Flandin used the following expression: 'I don't give a damn about Poland'. Laval made a similar comment in private talks.

So the communiqué of 3 February represents a compromise between the English and French points of view, but the English are clearly still hoping to water it down to mean no more than the organization of 'western security'. Very typically, today's press barely mentions the Eastern Pact (not a single reference in *The Times*). Instead, attention is principally focused on the 'air convention' between the Locarno powers.

6 February

Masaryk[iii] (the Czech envoy) informed me today that yesterday he had a frank talk with Vansittart. M. didn't hide his concern about the meeting of English

---

[i] Pierre Étienne Flandin, prime minister of France, 1934–35.
[ii] Phillip Cunliffe-Lister (1st earl of Swinton), Conservative president of the Board of Trade, 1922–29 and 1931; secretary of state for the colonies, 1931–35; secretary of state for air, 1935–38.
[iii] Jan Garrigue Masaryk, Czechoslovak ambassador to Great Britain, 1925–38; minister of foreign affairs of the Czechoslovak government in exile in London, 1940–45 and deputy prime minister, 1941–45.

and French ministers and the communiqué of 3 February. But V. assured him that Czechoslovakia had no reason to be afraid for her future. He said that England was extremely interested in Czechoslovakia's integrity and welfare. V. is rather sceptical about the upcoming talks with Germany and hardly expects a positive outcome. Yet such a step should be taken, if only for the sake of enlightening British public opinion. M. said that Beneš[i] spoke to Laval today on the telephone from Prague and was assured that the Little Entente had nothing to be afraid of: France would continue to adhere to its commitments.

I found out from a reliable journalistic source that Hoesch (the German ambassador) has advised Hitler, with Simon's consent, that in his reply to the joint English and French proposal he should place the issue of the Eastern Pact at the bottom of the negotiations agenda. Should agreement be reached on all preceding items, the Eastern Pact could easily be 'buried in the sand'. A crafty move! But will Hitler be smart enough to follow his ambassador's advice?[4]

10 February

MacDonald and Simon, supported by *The Times*, *Daily Mail* and some other papers, are pursuing a systematic campaign to muzzle the Eastern Pact and divert attention entirely onto questions of 'western security'. In other words, they are telling Hitler: 'Leave France and England alone and, by way of compensation, do whatever you like in Eastern Europe.' I am of the impression that Baldwin, Eden and Vansittart are aware of the impossibility and perils of a policy of aiding and abetting, yet for the time being they are giving MD and S. *carte-blanche*.

Only for the time being? Possibly: many symptoms suggest that a full consensus in Cabinet on issues of European security is lacking. Perhaps Baldwin is waiting for a more appropriate moment to interfere. But for how long will the current situation continue?...

Our Soviet activity is now an important factor on the international scene. I think that the time has come to clarify our Soviet attitude to the communiqué of 3 February.[5] To date we have merely maintained a dissatisfied silence. On 19 February I will be delivering a lecture on Soviet planning at the London conference of the League of Nations Union. The talk was agreed upon two months or so ago, but why not take advantage of the occasion for a serious statement about the problems of European security? I'll ask M.M. [Litvinov].

---

[i] Edvard Beneš, Czechoslovakia's representative at the Paris Peace Conference, 1919–20; foreign minister of Czechoslovakia, 1918–35; president of the Czechoslovak Republic, 1935–38 and 1946–48; president-in-exile of the Provisional Czechoslovak government in London, 1940–45.

12 February

Litvinov agrees. He also thinks it appropriate to say a few *plain words* on current issues. He suggests that I should focus attention on the thesis that 'the world is indivisible' (there can be no 'western security' without 'eastern security'), and that the problem of security cannot be resolved through the efforts of great powers alone (the Pact of the Four!), but only through the collective efforts of big states and small states. As for the fact that disarmament is impossible in the absence of 'eastern security', that is best left unmentioned for the time being.

Now I'll set to work on the text of my speech.

14 February

Yesterday Vansittart invited me over to the Foreign Office. Until now I did not want to initiate such a meeting. V. had a long conversation with me, the primary aim of which was to reassure the Soviet government and dispel our fears concerning the communiqué of 3 February. The principal points of our talk can be summed up as follows:

(1) V. is very sceptical about the prospects of talks with Germany. In his opinion Hitler will probably approve the air convention, may swallow the Rome agreements, but will never accept the Eastern Pact, the disarmament convention, or agree to return to the League of Nations.

(2) The programme set forth in the communiqué of 3 February is a single package that cannot be split up as the Germans would like. However, when I asked what position the British government would take if Hitler were to accept all the items of the communiqué bar the Eastern Pact, V., somewhat embarrassed, said that in such a case the British government would have to consult with the French government, then added that a solution might have to be found through a modification of the character of the pact. However, V. hastened to assure me of the British government's continued support of the Eastern Pact of mutual assistance. I dropped a hint that a fresh public statement in support of the Eastern Pact from the British government might be desirable, but V. avoided giving a straightforward promise.

(3) V. was viciously critical of Lothian for his articles in *The Times* of 30 and 31 January, and of the position taken by the newspaper's editors on the German issue. It runs entirely counter to that of the Foreign Office. V. ridiculed the stupidity of those who think it would be in England's interests for Germany to be given a free hand in the east. He asks us to be realistic about these things and not to get worked up without good reason. The forthcoming talks between England and France present no danger whatsoever either to Franco-Soviet

rapprochement or to the further improvement of Anglo-Soviet relations. The fundamental fact, which no conference or diplomatic document can eradicate, is the existence in the centre of Europe of a country, Germany, which is rapidly building up its arms and 'whose true intentions are not known to anyone in any detail'. This situation is inevitably pushing the countries surrounding Germany towards *rapprochement*. With certain modifications, the situation that prevailed prior to 1914 is being repeated.

(4) V. expressed his regret concerning the personal attacks against Ovey[i] contained in Molotov's speech at the 7th Congress of the Soviets. What was the point of them? Why stir up old, half-dead passions? We should be thinking now not of the past, but of the future, and specifically of the further improvement of Anglo-Soviet relations, for which we currently have all the requisite premises. I gave V. the necessary explanations.

(5) Vansittart was very glad to hear from me that Moscow would welcome a private visit by him and Elliot to the USSR. He said he would now set about organizing this in a more concrete fashion; moreover, he named Eden as another possible candidate. Initially, V. (as if 'thinking aloud') named Simon. I naturally gave my approval, albeit with little enthusiasm. Then V. exclaimed: 'No, you know what I think – Eden will be a better choice. He is accustomed to visiting foreign countries and he knows Mr Litvinov personally...' I seconded Eden's candidature heartily.[6]

15 February

The long-awaited German reply to the joint Anglo-French proposal of 3 February has arrived at last. It disappointed even Vansittart's modest expectations. Hitler consented only to the air convention, which he wants to detach entirely from the context of the London programme. The rest is of no concern to him. He offers not the slightest hope of consent even in regard to the Rome agreements. The Eastern Pact, disarmament, and a return to the League of Nations are all taboo...

Very good! Hitler's reply clarifies the situation greatly. It's a real blow for the advocates of 'western security'. The wily advice of Simon and Hoesch proved unacceptable to the German dictator. We can't be too sorry about that.

20 February

Yesterday I delivered my lecture at the League of Nations Union. I informed the London papers beforehand that I was planning to make an important political

---

[i] Esmond Ovey, British ambassador to the USSR, 1929–33.

statement.[7] As a result, the hall at the School of Economics was chock-full (some 600 people came), and correspondents from every newspaper and agency sat at the press desk, with many foreigners among them. Lady Astor presided. Lord Passfield (Sidney Webb)[i] and Jarvie,[ii] a banker, also spoke on planning in the USSR. The audience listened to my lecture with bated breath, although I was speaking (or rather reading) for about an hour. The mood in the auditorium could be described as one of strained sympathy. The lecture was interrupted by applause at many points, as when I said that there was no unemployment in the USSR and that women enjoyed equal rights, or when I described the peace policy pursued by the Soviet government. The final part of the lecture, dealing with the communiqué of 3 February, attracted particular attention. Excerpts from it were broadcast last night on the radio. The presidium of the conference thanked me for choosing the platform of the League of Nations Union to make a political statement of major importance. Today all organs of the press gave a detailed account of the lecture, and some featured it in their editorials. Excellent! We've fired the first shot at MacDonald and Simon. The bullet seems to have hit the target. But we cannot rest on our laurels.

21 February

The second shot followed sooner than I had even imagined.

Early on the morning of 20 February I received from Moscow our evaluation of the London communiqué, with the request to hand the text over to Simon today. M.M. [Litvinov] had a talk with Alphand[iii] in Moscow, after which Alphand approached his government asking whether he should obtain the response to the communiqué of 3 February from the Soviet government. Paris and London consulted between themselves, and finally Alphand and Chilston[iv] approached M.M. on behalf of their governments on 19 February with the official request that he state his views about the Anglo-French agreement of 3 February. M.M. wrote up a response on the same day to be presented the following day, 20 February, by me to Simon and by Potemkin[v] to Laval. I called Simon immediately and arranged to meet him at 4 p.m. This was clearly a

---

[i] Sidney James Webb, a Fabian; served as president of the Board of Trade in the first Labour government, 1924, and in the House of Lords as secretary of state for the colonies, 1929–31.
[ii] J. Gibson Jarvie, chairman of the United Dominions Trust, hailed Stalin's five-year plan in a major speech in Glasgow in 1932 which was then often quoted by Stalin, who omitted Jarvie's qualifying comment that although Russia was claiming 'to be a Communist State, nevertheless that country to-day was, unquestionably, practising state capitalism' (*The Times*, 21 October 1932).
[iii] Charles Alphand, French ambassador to Moscow, 1933–36.
[iv] Aretas Akers-Douglas (2nd Viscount Chilston), British ambassador in Moscow, 1933–38.
[v] Vladimir Petrovich Potemkin, a pedagogue, embarked on a career devising a revolutionary curriculum for schools in the People's Commissariat for Education of the RSFSR. Success in political agitation during the Civil War led to a diplomatic career. He was Soviet ambassador in Italy, 1932–34, and in France, 1934–37, and deputy people's commissar for foreign affairs, 1937–

burning issue in Moscow, because Gershelman[i] telephoned me from the NKID at about 2 p.m. and inquired when I was likely to see the foreign secretary. We agreed that after my meeting with Simon I would tell Gershelman about it over the telephone.

Simon received me in the Houses of Parliament. Eden was present throughout the meeting, but he spoke little. Simon began with my speech at the League of Nations Union, complimented me and asked me to explain various points. Then I read our evaluation of the communiqué aloud and put the document on the foreign secretary's desk. S. began speaking about the evaluation and expressed his satisfaction with the Soviet government's positive attitude towards the communiqué of 3 February. It will greatly facilitate its implementation, he said. I reminded him that our positive attitude derived from an acknowledgement of the integrity and indivisibility of the whole London programme. S. replied that it could not be otherwise. The British government views the London programme precisely as a single package, and Germany's attempt to tear out individual aspects of the programme was doomed to failure. The British government also continues to support the Eastern Pact… I put before S. the question I had put before Vansittart a few days earlier, namely, what would the British government do should Germany accept all the points of the London programme bar the Eastern Pact? My question embarrassed my interlocutor and he began talking through his hat using high-flown but incoherent phrases. What they seemed to amount to was this: if Germany were to resist our demand, the pact would be 'castrated' – instead of mutual assistance, we would have a straightforward pact of non-aggression.

I began objecting fiercely; I confess that I did not mince my words. I stated that mutual military assistance is the heart of the pact, that we could make no concessions on this point, and that without an Eastern Pact of mutual assistance there will also be neither disarmament nor European security, even in its limited Western form.

S. was clearly concerned. Massaging the bridge of his nose, he asked cynically: what are you ready to propose to buy Germany's consent to the Eastern Pact? I replied that the guarantee of security which Germany would receive along with the other powers if the pact were concluded would be sufficient reward. S. raised his eyes to the ceiling and shrugged his shoulders in a rather ambiguous manner.

I left with the very definite impression that Simon had finally understood that the attempt to exclude the USSR from the resolution of the issue of

40. Survived Litvinov's demise in 1939, but a year later was removed from office and entrusted with the revival of the traditional Russian national-cultural values in Soviet schools.
[i] E.E. Gershelman, principal secretary of the NKID; relieved of his post in 1937.

'European appeasement' had failed. If anything is to be achieved in this area, the USSR needs to be brought in on equal terms with the other great powers.

Excellent! Even those members of the British government most hostile to us have taken on board M.M.'s motto: 'the world is one'. This is a step forward. And here's the proof: today's *Times* and *Daily Telegraph* carry articles of obvious provenance suggesting that the idea has arisen in government circles that a British minister should travel to Moscow. The Foreign Office reacts quickly.[8]

22 February

M.M. [Litvinov] informs me that the lecture on the British constitution which Simon is to read in Paris on 26 February will be used for a meeting between the British and French governments on the line they should take in connection with the German response to the proposals of 3 February. Roughly the following steps are envisaged: the British government will be authorized to negotiate with the German government, for which S. will go to Berlin (he is very keen on doing so), while the French government will be authorized to demand a final response from Germany on the Eastern Pact. The British government, by all appearances, is thinking of focusing attention primarily on the air convention.

A wealth of facts and communications suggests that S. is maintaining his anti-Soviet line and wants to come to an agreement with Germany at all costs, even if it means giving her a free hand in the east. But he won't succeed. We won't allow it.

28 February

I've been in a very difficult situation this past week.

I never had the slightest doubt that the reports in *The Times* and the *Daily Telegraph* about a British minister visiting Moscow were the work of the Foreign Office and of Vansittart in particular. Over the course of the following week, the press persistently and systematically inflated this topic in every way possible. Not by accident, of course. Leeper[i] (head of the FO press department) told Maiorsky[ii] bluntly that he was guiding the press in this direction. When Simon lunched with us, he asked Agniya about the best routes to Moscow, letting it be understood that he was planning a visit to the USSR. Elliot, whom I met at Lady Astor's party, told me that the British government was discussing the question of sending a 'senior minister' to Moscow. Vansittart told me, at

---

[i] Reginald Allen ('Rex') Leeper, press department of the Foreign Office, 1933–40.
[ii] N. Maiorsky, TASS correspondent in London.

about the time I was presenting Putna[i] to him, that although the Foreign Office had nothing to do with the press campaign concerning a minister's visit, the idea itself deserved a very good hearing. In a word, it was absolutely clear that the British government, having realized that it would be impossible to cobble together 'European security' without us, had decided that it could at least turn a profit from engaging the USSR in the organization of security – in particular, by playing the role of 'honest broker' (a role the English have always enjoyed) in seeking a compromise between Berlin and Moscow on the question of the Eastern Pact. Election considerations also played their part here – after all, polling day is not far off. It was crystal clear, then, that the British government really wanted to send a minister to Moscow, but hesitated to raise the matter officially, fearing an affront from our side. We should have made an encouraging gesture, if only through the Soviet press...

But our people in Moscow wouldn't yield. To my first request about the line I should adhere to, which I sent right after the first communications appeared in the press, I received the reply that newspaper reports lack authority, that I should remain calm, and that I was to inform Moscow if the Foreign Office approached me. Initially, it seems, the NKID even had the impression that Simon's visit to Moscow would serve to camouflage his visit to Warsaw (it was said in the press that the British minister would go to Warsaw from Berlin and then on to Moscow). I objected, referring to the material at my disposal, and asked whether the Soviet press could show, albeit cautiously, that it was well disposed to Simon's visit. But the NKID would not agree even to this, citing doubts about whether Simon really did want to go. Nevertheless, by 26 February I did manage to secure permission to at least encourage the idea for Simon's visit in the event of the Foreign Office, or circles close to it, approaching me on the subject. That day Collier[ii] met Kagan at a reception and told him that the British government had decided the previous day to send Simon to Berlin and that during the same meeting the Cabinet members had exchanged views on the desirability of Simon's visit to Moscow. In essence, nearly all were in favour of the visit, but on condition that the Soviet government sent an invitation. On 25 February, responding to a question in the House of Commons, Simon said that the government was considering the issue of his visit to Moscow. I appealed to M.M. again and today I at last received the instruction to tell Vansittart that I was authorized to extend an official invitation to Simon just as soon as the British government had definitively resolved the question of an English minister's visit

---

[i] Vitovt Kazimirovich Putna, who distinguished himself in the Civil War, sided with Trotsky's opposition in 1923. Between 1927 and 1931 he was Soviet military attaché in three countries – Japan, Finland and Germany; and then in Great Britain, 1934–36. Recalled from London and arrested in summer 1936, tortured and sentenced to death. Maisky was forced to denounce him in Moscow in 1938. Rehabilitated posthumously in 1957.
[ii] Laurence Collier, head of the northern department of the British Foreign Office, 1934–42.

to the USSR. But the NKID wants to see Simon and nobody else… Hm! Surely, considerations of prestige are playing their part here: if Simon is going to Berlin, then it is he who must also go to Moscow. Clear enough. But still, I would not make such an ultimatum about Simon. Actually, Eden would probably be more advantageous. Be that as it may, today came as a great relief…

1 March (1)

Lloyd George's family and nearly his whole 'party' had lunch with us yesterday: the old man himself, his wife, Gwilym[i] and Megan.[ii] Also present were Steel-Maitland[iii] (a prominent Conservative), Jarvie, a banker, the 'independent' Labourite Josiah Wedgwood[iv] and others.

I couldn't help but admire Lloyd George. He is 72 and still bursts with life. He looked magnificent after his recent vacation: a strong, tanned, fresh face under a shock of bright white hair. The old man was in a cheerful mood. He didn't drink wine at table, but he enjoyed the vodka and drank one or two more portions after the first.

L-G said that he is not greatly interested in the German question at the moment. The fears aroused by German belligerence are highly exaggerated. Germany needs at least ten more years to restore her military, economic and financial might. Until then Europe can sleep easily.

L-G is far more concerned about matters in the Far East. The Pacific is the most important problem of world politics in our age; all European issues are secondary in comparison. What is going on in the Far East? Japan, through the widespread use of carrot and stick, is clearly bent on establishing a powerful 'yellow' empire on the Asian continent. If Japan succeeds in subjugating China, Europe and America will be facing a gigantic bloc of yellow nations numbering no fewer than 500 million people. What then?…

How to fight the yellow menace? According to L-G there is one way only: close cooperation in the Pacific between England, America and the USSR. L-G inquired: what is our opinion on the matter.

I replied that the Soviet policy was and remains a policy of peace and collective security.

'What does that mean exactly?' L-G exclaimed. 'Does it mean that you, having dug your trench, will say good riddance to the rest of the world?'

---

[i] Gwilym Lloyd George, Lloyd George's son; Liberal MP and parliamentary secretary at the Board of Trade.
[ii] Megan Lloyd George, Lloyd George's daughter; Liberal MP, 1929–51, and Labour MP, 1957–66.
[iii] Arthur Steel-Maitland (1st Baronet Steel-Maitland), Conservative politician who served in Lloyd George's wartime coalition government.
[iv] Josiah Clement Wedgwood (1st Baron Wedgwood), Labour MP, 1919–42; sought to become ambassador to Moscow in 1940, but Churchill opted for Stafford Cripps.

I replied that the USSR does not take an isolationist stance. We advocate collective security everywhere, including the Pacific. And what position does England take on the matter? I don't remember hearing a word about the present Cabinet's readiness to cooperate with the USSR either in Europe or in the Pacific.

L-G flared up and unleashed a torrent of criticism in the direction of the government. He was in his element here and he castigated the government venomously, calling them dunderheads devoid of the slightest imagination, with no policy worth the name. MacDonald and Chamberlain were singled out for particular abuse.

1 March (2)

I visited Vansittart yesterday[9] and told him about Moscow's attitude to Simon's visit. V. was glad and only felt sorry that they had not made the move earlier. He had worked on the visit intensively during the past week, but the lack of response from the Soviet side somewhat weakened his position, all the more so as there are those in the Cabinet who oppose the visit (according to my information, these are the war minister, Lord Hailsham, and the minister for Indian affairs, Hoare[i]). Now V. can expedite the matter. The Cabinet will make a decision in three or four days' time. Simon's visit to Berlin has been approved only in theory; the dates and further itinerary have not yet been set. The Polish government has sent an unofficial invitation to visit Warsaw, but the official invitation has yet to arrive. V. was not quite sure who would go to Moscow – Simon or Eden, but I emphasized that we were expecting Simon.

Corbin[ii] (the French ambassador) called on me yesterday, stressing at great length that there was no time to waste: we must take advantage of the favourable change in the British mood to organize a British minister's visit to Moscow. C. was unhappy that we had not issued the formal invitation right after our note (our appraisal of the communiqué of 3 February) and my speech to the League of Nations Union – the two crucial factors in changing the mood of the British ruling circles. I objected that, in my view, nothing at all had been lost as a result of our 'delay'. I told him about my conversation with Vansittart two hours earlier. C. calmed down and left. It would seem that he visited me on instructions from Paris.

---

[i] Samuel John Hoare (1st Viscount Templewood), Conservative, minister for Indian affairs, 1931–35; secretary of state for foreign affairs, 1935; first lord of the Admiralty, 1936–37; secretary of state for home affairs, 1937–39; lord privy seal, 1939–40; secretary of state for air, 1940; ambassador to Spain on special mission, 1940–44.

[ii] Andre Charles Corbin, French ambassador in Great Britain, 1933–40.

2 March

One must give Hitler his due – his energy is inexhaustible.

Stafford Cripps[i] lunched at my place today and told me the following story. Hitler desires very much to soften Labour's attitude towards him. Two years or so ago, before he came to power, he sent Cripps a draft party programme, requesting his comments. Cripps answered with a long letter that tore the draft to shreds. Nonetheless, having come to power, Hitler made several attempts to make contact with Cripps. About a month ago he sent special emissaries to Cripps, inviting him to visit Germany and to see whatever he wished, including prisons and concentration camps. Hitler even promised to give him the use of a special aeroplane. Cripps categorically rejected the Führer's proposal – but there's no denying the agility and resourcefulness of the German dictator!

Cripps told me some curious things about the Canadian premier Bennett,[ii] whom he saw during his recent visit to Canada. At a grand dinner in Ottawa, at which Bennett was present, Cripps made a speech inveighing against the capitalist system. The next day Bennett invited Cripps to see him. He told him that he had been mulling over Cripps speech all night and had to admit that he had not found a single serious argument in defence of capitalism. Cripps is right: capitalism is bankrupt. But what to do? Where to go?

Bennett discussed various issues of practical policy with Cripps at length. On parting, he shook the latter's hand firmly and exclaimed: 'You can't imagine what you've done for me. I haven't had such an important talk in all my life. You'll soon see.' And what do you think happened? A few months later, Bennett, to the considerable horror of his Conservative supporters, announced a New Deal programme modelled on that of Roosevelt.[iii] In a recent speech over the radio Bennett declared that three things played a decisive role in his change of policy: his talk with Litvinov in Geneva, Cripps's book on socialism and Strachey's[iv] book about the collapse of capitalism.

Just you think! Here it is, capitalism's 'hypocritical face'!

---

[i] Richard Stafford Cripps, left-wing British intellectual, Christian socialist and an eminent king's counsel; Labour MP, 1931–50; British ambassador to Russia, 1940–42; minister for aircraft production, 1942–45.
[ii] Richard Bedford Bennett (1st Viscount Bennett of Mickleham and of Calgary and Hopewell), Canadian prime minister, 1930–35.
[iii] Franklin Delano Roosevelt, governor of New York, 1928–32; 32nd president of the United States, 1933–45.
[iv] Evelyn John St Loe Strachey, a militant communist and Marxist theorist, he was editor of *The Socialist Review* and *The Miner* from 1924. Broke away from the Communist Party of Great Britain (CPGB) in 1940 and became a leading Labour politician in the post-war era.

4 March

Conversation with Lady Vansittart

As the senior lady guest, Lady Vansittart sat next to me at dinner in the embassy and described to me in the frankest terms the difficulties her husband is currently facing. The problems derive from Vansittart's and Simon's differing views on numerous matters. Moreover, Simon devotes little time to the Foreign Office and shifts the entire mass of routine business onto Vansittart. The latter is up to his neck in work from early morning till late at night, while Simon visits his country house every weekend and plays golf. Lady V. cited the events of the last fortnight as an example. The question of Simon's visit to various European capitals in connection with the Anglo-French agreement has turned Vansittart's life into absolute hell. Vansittart thinks that the question should have been resolved quickly and far-sightedly, i.e. it should have been decided right away that Simon would travel not only to Berlin, but also to Moscow. Vansittart had been working in this direction for the last fortnight, but Simon was constantly obstructing him: today it was yes, the next day no, and the day after that he would recommend postponing the decision. A decision was finally taken at the last Cabinet meeting on 27 February, but it only concerned Simon's visit to Berlin. Vansittart thought this a mistake: it would have been better to decide on Berlin and Moscow at once. But Vansittart was unable to push through his point of view, partly because the Soviet government's attitude to Simon's possible visit was still unknown on 27 February. After I told Vansittart about the Soviet government's positive attitude to Simon's visit, Vansittart felt it essential to push this issue through as a matter of urgency. But he could not get in touch with Simon for several days since, after returning from his lecture in Paris, Simon did not even look in at the Foreign Office, but went straight to his country house to play golf. Vansittart tried to get hold of him, but Simon was clearly doing his best to avoid meeting him. On Sunday, 3 March, his patience exhausted, Vansittart set off by himself to see Baldwin and then MacDonald. He had long talks with both and obtained their approval for Simon's visit to Moscow. The final decision will most likely be taken at the nearest Cabinet session, i.e. on 6 March. But all this has put extraordinary strain on her husband and frayed his nerves terribly. He returned from holidays only three months ago, and already he feels very tired again. I seized upon Lady V.'s remark and suggested that she and her husband might make a trip to Moscow for the Easter holidays – not on an official visit, but as tourists wishing to see the USSR. Vansittart, I believe, had had such intentions in the past. Lady V. replied enthusiastically that she wanted to go to Moscow very much, and that Easter would be a good time, but she was afraid Simon might put a spanner in the works. If, as she hopes, Simon goes to Moscow soon, he might start entertaining all sorts of suspicions:

why should Vansittart go there, too, so soon after him? Is Vansittart plotting something behind his back? In the course of further conversation, I asked Lady V. whether Simon would go to Berlin alone or with Eden. She answered with a sigh of relief: 'Fortunately, together with Eden. Simon is easily flattered, and Hitler is likely to be generous in this regard. This may prompt Simon to make some careless statements in Berlin. Eden will restrain him and put him right.'

5 March

Vansittart and his wife dined with us in the embassy. I had a talk with V. after dinner and gleaned the following from him.

Simon and Eden leave for Berlin on 7 March (according to my information, the Conservatives would not let Simon travel alone to Berlin; Eden goes with him as a commissar). Two or three Foreign Office men will accompany them. Both will return to London on the 10th, which Simon explains by the need to take part in the parliamentary debates on defence matters on 11 March. The Cabinet will take a decision on the visit to Moscow on 6 March. The chances are good, Baldwin and MacDonald are in favour. The visit may take place within the two weeks following the return of the British delegation from Berlin. Yet V. was once again evasive about who precisely will go to Moscow. I emphasized that we expect the same persons who will travel to Berlin, and added that if V., too, could come to Moscow, it would be even better. V. said that according to custom the foreign secretary and his permanent deputy cannot leave the country simultaneously. The British minister or ministers will spend two or three days in Moscow and visit Warsaw on the way home.

I drew V.'s attention to the obsequious servility to Hitler shown by the British press and some members of the Cabinet, Simon in particular. This is a poor tactic. It only inflames the Führer's appetite and makes him still more unyielding. Simon has not yet crossed the German border, but he has already proposed, in his talk with Laval in Paris on 28 February, to replace the Eastern Pact of mutual assistance with bilateral non-aggression pacts between Germany and her neighbours. What use will that serve? I added that we could make no concessions on the Eastern Pact issue.[10]

V. replied that the British government takes the following position on this matter: the goal of the British government is the appeasement of Europe. This is impossible without organizing eastern security. Let Germany agree with the states directly interested in this (the USSR, Little Entente, France, etc.) as to the forms of security suitable for both parties. The British government does not see the need to interfere in such negotiations. It makes no difference to the British government what agreement the East European countries reach – so long as they reach one. This is the line the British delegation will follow in Berlin.

* * *

I have information from Paris that Laval is also shifting. He was ready to discuss the following compromise with Simon on 28 February: a mutual assistance pact between the USSR and France and a non-aggression pact between all other participants. The Little Entente's protests made Laval abandon his plan.

What an unfortunate coincidence: Simon in England and Laval in France. One cannot think of worse foreign ministers from our point of view, and in such a serious period!

6 March

A totally unexpected surprise! Yesterday Hitler 'fell ill'. The day before he was seen in a perfectly healthy state at the automobile exhibition in Berlin, and the next day, don't you know, he managed to catch cold and become hoarse, so very hoarse in fact that he can't receive the British ministers. He requests that the visit scheduled for the 7th be postponed, and cannot name a new date as yet. He'll see. It all depends on the course of his illness.

What a poseur! The nub of the matter is the publication on the afternoon of the 4th of a White Book stating an increase in budgetary appropriations for military purposes of 10.5 million pounds. The British government justifies the increase by pointing to the unreliability of the collective security system and to Germany's militarization, which it sees as the main source of anxiety in Europe. Hitler took offence and decided to teach the English a lesson. The Foreign Office describes Hitler's prank as grotesque. Leeper (head of the press department) even made the spiteful witticism: Hitler caught cold between the damp pages of the English White Book.

In general, the British are shocked and vexed, but Simon, of course, will seek agreement with the angry dictator just the same. Presumably, Hitler will 'forgive' him… Hitler would never risk being so impudent, were the English not so wet and pathetic!

Hitler's illness has spoiled the game, and the Cabinet made no decision today on Eden's visit. Vansittart assures me that it will be made soon.

7 March

The decision has been taken!

Vansittart phoned me today and said that the Cabinet has decided to send Eden to Moscow. Simon will make an announcement after dinner in parliament.

V. wants to discuss the date of the visit and other details with me personally early next week (today is Thursday).

I made some complimentary remarks about Eden, but added that I had been authorized to hand the official invitation to Simon or to Simon and Eden. Now that the situation had changed, I would have to approach Moscow for instructions once again. Vansittart did not object. In conclusion he made a meaningful remark: he implores me to believe that the decision on sending Eden is the maximum that could have been achieved at the current stage. I understand.

So, Eden is going! Very good! There is no doubt that this is a historic step.[11]

8 March

Undoubtedly, the decision to send Eden and not Simon is a mild form of anti-Soviet discrimination on the part of the British government, although Simon's personal reluctance to go to the USSR also played its part. It also seems clear that the British government intends to scare Hitler and to make him more complaisant. Fine! The Bolsheviks have never made a fetish of prestige, have never sacrificed content for form. In actual fact, Eden is better for us than Simon, for Eden's star is rising, while Simon's is setting. Eden has been promoted by Baldwin, an influential Conservative, while Simon essentially represents no one. Compromised at home, he is liked neither by the Conservatives, nor the Liberals, nor Labour. Finally, Eden takes a tolerant attitude towards the USSR, while Simon is our inveterate adversary. Yes, Eden is much better! Walter Elliot, who entertained Agniya and me for lunch today, argued at length that a visit by Eden is preferable to a visit by Simon. Vansittart said the same. The press, especially the *Daily Telegraph*, commends Eden in every way and asserts that the lord privy seal ranks either fifth or sixth among the ministers. The press department has been soliciting for a sympathetic response in the Soviet press to the decision to send Eden. [Gordon-]Lennox[i] (diplomatic correspondent of the *Daily Telegraph*) even informed me today by phone that, according to 'the most reliable reports', Simon will leave the Foreign Office after the king's jubilee, to be replaced by Eden... The Foreign Office is really trying!

I sent a long telegram to Moscow today requesting that Eden be received courteously. We'll wait to see the reaction.

[The idea of a ministerial visit to Moscow was first mooted by Maisky in autumn 1934. The plan had been cooked up with Vansittart, behind the backs of Litvinov and Simon, long before the foreign secretary's visit to Berlin was contemplated. Maisky hoped the visit would drive a wedge between the different factions in the Foreign Office, which were divided over the attitude to be adopted towards Germany. He received little encouragement from Litvinov, who (it is seldom recognized by historians)[12] continued

---

[i] Victor Gordon-Lennox, diplomatic correspondent of the Conservative *Observer* and *Daily Telegraph*.

to view the British with suspicion, assuming them to be the main stumbling block in the attempt to extend security arrangements to Eastern Europe. He feared that any Russian initiative might be snubbed by the British or used as a card in their negotiations with the Germans.[13]

Maisky, who had great faith in his ability to carry out a coup together with Vansittart and Eden, pursued his plans systematically. He used the platform of the League of Nations Union to publicize and push through his own initiatives. A lunch at the embassy with Lord Cecil[i] and Professor Murray,[ii] the two architects of the Union, set the scene for the move.[14] On 11 February, Maisky pressed Litvinov to provide him with guidelines for a forthcoming meeting, which he claimed had been proposed by Vansittart, but in fact had been suggested by him. Litvinov reluctantly allowed Maisky to ascertain what the British attitude was, but remained highly sceptical of the outcome, complaining that even the Germans believed that the British 'were not in the least interested in the Eastern Locarno'.[15] Maisky did not shy away from seeking backing from some unexpected quarters: he approached Molotov, chairman of the Council of the People's Commissars and Stalin's right-hand man. An avowed rival of Litvinov, Molotov had acknowledged in his key report to the Seventh Congress of the Soviets, at the end of January, that 'relations with England have returned to the normal course'. In a private letter, Maisky cunningly flattered him for his speech:

> On the assumption that you may be interested in British political circles' reaction … Three speeches at the congress attracted the most attention and comment here: your fundamental report, your speech about the reform of the constitution, and Tukhachevsky's[iii] speech on the Red Army question … As for your reports … the tone of calm and confident strength that permeated them has been remarked on nearly always. It was impressive … the moods it has evoked in British political and public circles can be formulated roughly as: 'A new great power has finally arrived in the world. Whether one likes it or not, it cannot be overlooked.' Let me add from myself personally that I very much admired your report on the work of the government. It was impressive in its content, its architecture, and its tone. The only thing I regret is that I couldn't be in the congress hall at the time it was delivered.[16]

When Simon's intention of meeting Hitler in Berlin came to light, Litvinov finally gave way to the pressure exerted by Maisky, allowing him a free hand to decide when the time was propitious to tender an invitation. He continued to insist, however, that the visit to Moscow should be undertaken by the same British minister who went to Berlin. Moreover, in order to test the sincerity of the British commitment to the idea of an Eastern Pact, he pressed for the visit to take place promptly and not in conjunction

---

[i] Robert Gascoyne-Cecil (1st Viscount Cecil of Chelwood), president of the League of Nations Union, 1923–45; winner of the Nobel Prize for Peace in 1937.

[ii] Gilbert Murray, chairman of the League of Nations Union, 1923–38.

[iii] Mikhail Nikolaevich Tukhachevsky, marshal of the Soviet Union and a brilliant innovative military theoretician. Deputy and then chief of staff of the Red Army, 1924–28; deputy to the people's commissar for defence, 1934–36. A victim of the military purges, he was arrested, tortured and sentenced to death in June 1938; rehabilitated posthumously.

with the Berlin visit. Maisky, for his part, believed that Eden was a better prospect for the visit, particularly as he expected him to replace Simon in the near future. He therefore underplayed Litvinov's demands in his conversations with Vansittart on 28 February, to the point that Vansittart was able to comment, after consulting the Cabinet, that it was 'fairly sure that the visitor will be Mr Eden'. This was then presented by Maisky to Moscow as a final definite decision.[17]]

9 March

Hurrah! Moscow seems to look favourably on Eden. M.M. has asked me to deliver an official invitation and suggests that Eden come to Moscow as soon as possible, sometime between 13 and 15 March (unlikely!), or later – concurrently with Simon's departure for Berlin or after the Berlin talks.

* * *

I've just seen Vansittart and Eden. They were both in Vansittart's office. Vansittart remarked with a genial smile: 'When you asked for a meeting, we were intelligent enough to understand what it was all about. So we decided to see you together.'

As I had guessed, Eden will not be able to come between the 13th and 15th. Today is Saturday, then the weekend, then the great debates on the arms issue in the House on the 11th, so the government will discuss the date of Eden's visit no earlier than the 12th. Besides, I am a little worried about the influence of Simon, and also of Hailsham and Hoare – they are against a visit to Moscow in general. In short, the date of the visit remains unclear, but the main thing is that it has been finally agreed.

* * *

I've called Moscow to ask whether I should accompany Eden. It would be good if the answer were affirmative.

11 March

Zariņš[i] (the Latvian envoy) was looking for me today to inquire about Eden's route. He said that Riga had informed him that they would like to see Eden in Latvia on his way to Moscow or back. Of course they would!

Moscow, however, has instructed me to facilitate Eden's stopover in Prague. I'll do what I can. Moscow does not want Eden to stop in Riga, suspecting a German plot.

---

[i] Karlis Zariņš, Latvian envoy to Great Britain, 1933–40.

* * *

Ribbentrop met François-Poncet[i] in Berlin a few days ago and told him something to this effect: let us settle all controversial issues between ourselves. Forget Russia – it's an Asian power. Why should we, Europeans, allow it into Europe? François-Poncet replied that, according to physical and political geography, Russia is located in Europe.

Truly German gaucherie!

12 March

The Foreign Office is worried and perplexed at seeing no response to the decision on Eden's visit in the Soviet press. Indeed, it's not quite right. I'll have to push Moscow.

Nearly all the papers have decided to send their correspondents to accompany Eden: *The Times* (Reed),[ii] *Daily Telegraph* (Lennox), *Daily Herald* (Ewer),[iii] *News Chronicle* (Cummings),[iv] *Yorkshire Post* (Catlin),[v] and the Havas agency (Schuman).[vi] The *Daily Mail* needed my personal attention. The editor called on me twice and promised that his correspondent would behave decently in Moscow, so in the end I've given a visa to an enormous guy, 'weighing 24 tons' and with a very peculiar surname.

We shall see what will come of it. It's a risk, but it's worth it. M.M., however, categorically refused to grant a visa to the *Daily Express*, although I was against this sort of discrimination.

* * *

M.M. is still sceptical about Eden's visit. He even thinks it might not happen at all, or not for a good while. For this reason he has put off deciding whether or not I should accompany Eden. He has another reservation: Eden is not a Foreign Office minister. But I'll still go. I'll arrange it.

* * *

---

[i] André François-Poncet, French ambassador to Germany, 1931–38, and to Italy, 1938–40.
[ii] Douglas Reed, assistant Berlin correspondent of *The Times*, 1929–35 and the paper's Central European correspondent, 1935–38.
[iii] William Norman Ewer.
[iv] Arthur John Cummings, editor of the liberal *News Chronicle*, 1920–55; reported among other notable events the Metro-Vickers trial of British engineers (Moscow, 1933) and the Reichstag fire trial (Leipzig, 1933).
[v] George Edward Gordon Catlin.
[vi] Maurice Schuman, attached to l'Agence Havas in London and later Paris, 1935–39.

13 March

Presumably as a result of yesterday's telephone conversation with Eden,[18] Simon and Eden invited me to parliament today. I arrived at 3 p.m. We talked for some 40 minutes. The subject of the talk was the timing of Eden's visit to Moscow. Simon spoke nearly the whole time, admiring himself and skilfully juggling words. Eden spoke little.

The gist of the matter is as follows. The visit to Berlin has been fixed. Hitler's state of health improves. The British ministers (Simon and Eden) fly to Berlin on the 24th and spend two days there, the 25th and 26th. Simon returns to London on 27 March. As for Eden… Simon has worked out two alternatives: (1) Eden takes the train on the evening of the 26th and arrives in Moscow on the morning of the 28th; (2) Eden and Simon return to London on the 27th, and Eden departs for Moscow from London – not immediately, but in about a fortnight, since he will not be able to arrange things earlier. What do we prefer? What do we find more appropriate? (One should understand 'appropriate' as meaning appropriate from the point of view of our prestige.)

The British government, Simon said, would prefer the first alternative. The reasons: (1) to save time ('Time is very precious at the moment,' S. added); (2) if the interval between the Berlin and Moscow visits is too large, the British government will have to make statements in the House immediately after the Berlin visit about its outcome and the prospects for the future. The Germans will then assume the Berlin visit to be the major and decisive one, and the visit to Moscow of secondary significance. This should be avoided. It would be better, therefore, for Eden to proceed to Moscow directly from Berlin. In the meantime, he, Simon, would announce in the House that the British government does not wish to discuss the issue as a whole until Eden returns and will deliver its judgement after hearing the reports of both ministers on their visits to the two capitals. What was our opinion?

In essence, the directives I had received gave me the right to answer S. immediately, but I considered it profitable to draw things out a bit. So I said: we had been under the impression until now that the two visits were entirely independent of each other and that Eden would be in Moscow in a few days. Now it turns out that the Moscow visit depends on the visit to Berlin and that its date is being put back considerably. This is disagreeable. Since a new situation is arising, I ought to ask Moscow for new instructions.

S. was obviously disappointed. He asked: 'And when can you receive a reply?' I said: 'Probably tomorrow.'

Simon rubbed the bridge of his nose and entered into profuse argumentation. I was mistaken. The two visits were absolutely independent. If we were to fix and announce there and then the date of the Moscow visit, say 28 or 29 March, it would be final. No matter whether the visit to Berlin occurred or not, Eden would go to Moscow on the date that had been arranged. The British government, he argued, lent both visits equal value and importance. Furthermore, the visit to Moscow is of historic significance. Never since the time of revolution had a member of the British Cabinet visited Russia. Eden's visit bears the same significance as the USSR's entry to the League of Nations. It is visible evidence of the fact that Russia 'has returned to Europe and become an integral part of European politics'. Besides, it is a great step towards Anglo-Soviet rapprochement.

I replied that I understood Simon perfectly well, but that I still could not resolve the matter without consulting Moscow. S. made a helpless gesture and asked for a reply no later than tomorrow. He said the British government had already informed the Germans that the British ministers would arrive on the 24th. The German government was going to make the date public today or tomorrow. It would be undesirable if the public learned the date of the Berlin visit before the date of the Moscow visit had been set. I agreed with S. and promised to get the reply from Moscow straight away.

S. raised his eyes languidly to the ceiling and suddenly asked: 'Excuse my asking you this question, which may seem strange to you: but might the lord privy seal have a talk with Mr Stalin?'

I was waiting for this question and answered calmly: 'I don't know. Mr Stalin is not a member of the Council of People's Commissars and does not usually meet foreign ministers and diplomats.'

Once again S. set about trying to convince me. Oh, naturally he does not stipulate a meeting with Stalin as an indispensable condition of Eden's visit to Moscow. He knows Litvinov very well and respects and values him. Still, Stalin is the major Soviet figure for the British public. Attaching enormous importance to Eden's visit to Moscow, the British government would like to arrange his visit in such a way as to make the greatest possible impression on British public opinion. As I must know full well, not all in Britain approve of the government's decision to send a minister to the USSR; some influential circles frown on this move. It is important, therefore, to use this visit to effect a radical change in public opinion. For this it is highly desirable that Eden should meet Stalin.

I promised to make the necessary enquiries in Moscow.

At this point S.'s secretary rushed into the room to say that S. was expected in the House: he was supposed to give an answer to a question addressed to him. S. took his leave and hurried off. Eden and I were left alone. Eden said: 'I would most sincerely like to go to Moscow earlier, but it is quite impossible. We are going to Berlin and need to prepare ourselves on a number of issues, such as the aviation pact. Sir John [Simon] is up to his eyes in work and I can't burden him with all these preparations. I have to take an active role...' Then Eden added in a very particular tone: 'I ought always to be near Sir John, both during the preparatory work and during the negotiations with Germany.'

This can be understood as follows: the Conservative Party adamantly refuses to let Simon go to Berlin alone. The 'party commissar' – Eden – must assist him.

14 March

M.M. called me at 1 p.m. from Moscow, as I had asked in the telegram I had sent yesterday.[19] He spoke directly from Comrade Stalin's office. The reply was as follows: let Eden come to Moscow on 28 March; Comrade Stalin will receive him; I should accompany Eden, from Berlin onwards; it is desirable that Simon should make a public statement on the equal importance of the Berlin and Moscow visits; it would be good if Eden stopped in Prague on his way home.

I was back in parliament at 3 p.m., on this occasion in Eden's office. He asked me somewhat impatiently: 'So, what's the news?' I communicated to him the substance of Moscow's response. Eden was extremely glad. He remarked about the meeting with Stalin: 'You understand, of course, that I would hardly insist on this for my own sake. But for the British public, for the *man in the street*, such a meeting is very important.'[20] He was deeply moved on hearing that I would accompany him. Eden changed somehow, brightening up and exclaiming with unusual fervour: 'Please convey my deepest gratitude to Mr Litvinov.' Eden assured me that if Simon were to make a public statement on the visits, he would stress the equal importance of the Berlin and Moscow visits. At any rate, the press would be guided in this direction. *The Times* has already taken this line today on Eden's advice. Eden was evasive about Prague: he would have to stay away from England for a couple of days more. Besides, he might cause offence: why has he come to Prague and not Bucharest or Belgrade? People are already talking along these lines now. I pointed out the importance of the Little Entente in the cause of European appeasement and the opportunity to gather the three foreign ministers of the Little Entente in Prague. Eden promised to think it over, but it was clear that he did not like the combination...

Hurrah! M.M. has shown his charitable side: I have permission to go to Moscow together with Eden, or a day in advance – but on condition that Eden sets off soon. I don't understand this condition, but the main thing has been settled. Even if Eden sets off not so soon, I'll go with him all the same. It's a sure thing![21]

* * *

I have started organizing the tour. There are many details to think about: a special railway car for Eden should be sent to Nagoreloe on the border; the Nagoreloe–Moscow train must not fall two hours behind schedule en route; the restaurant car in the train should be clean and serve filling and inexpensive food; the meeting in Moscow should be properly organized, and suitable lodgings should be found for the English (Spiridonovka?).[22] After all our people can make completely unnecessary slips, simply through carelessness and inattention to detail. I'll call Moscow to ask about all this.

15 March

Judging by reports in English papers, von Hoesch (the German ambassador in London) will accompany Simon to Berlin and back, and the Polish ambassador Raczyński[i] will meet Eden in Stolbtsy on his return trip from Moscow. The ambassadors are on the move!

I saw Eden today at a Persian reception and learned that the British would be lodged in the British embassy. So, Spiridonovka is out. Only one room will be needed there – for me. When I asked what he would like to see in Moscow, Eden replied: first and foremost, the collection of French masters (Gauguin, Cézanne, Matisse, etc.), then architecture, theatre and the ballet in particular. He leaves the rest to our discretion. He should be shown something in the sphere of the military and aviation – this is spectacular, it makes an impression, and forces one to take the USSR more seriously…

* * *

There were two curious incidents at the Persian reception.

First, Matsudaira (the Japanese ambassador) looked absolutely delighted to see me and crossed the hall to shake my hand and congratulate me on the favourable conclusion of talks on the sale of the Chinese Eastern Railway. He said that the chances of concluding a Japanese–Soviet non-aggression pact were better now than ever before. Well, well! That's what it means to have a mighty air force in Vladivostok! Matsudaira had been extremely cool and even haughty towards me before. Being a relative of the Japanese emperor (his daughter is married to Prince Chichibu[ii]) and a 'friend' of the English king, Matsudaira considers himself a cut above other ambassadors, especially the Soviet one. Not once has he invited me to dinner or lunch during my stay in London. Now look how eager he is! He even walked over to me and shook my hand, his face

---

[i] Count Edward Bernard Raczyński, Polish delegate to the disarmament conference in Geneva, 1932–34; ambassador to Great Britain, 1934–45.
[ii] Prince Yasuhito Chichibu, Japanese prince and member of the imperial family, 1902–53.

shining like the sun. Yes, it's good to have a mighty air force! Stalin is right, ten thousand times right, that only the strong are reckoned with…

Second, the Lithuanian told me that on 13 March the envoys of Lithuania, Latvia and Estonia made a démarche concerning the Eastern Pact. There were nuances, however. The Lithuanian declared straightaway that his government supported the mutual assistance pact. The Estonian, not specifying which pact was meant, spoke of the indivisibility of western and eastern security. The Latvian first asked Simon about the British government's attitude to the mutual assistance pact, and having heard that the British government viewed it favourably, inquired how the British government would view an Eastern Pact of non-aggression. The Latvian's behaviour is quite typical: these are all German tricks!

16 March

Eden has been as good as his word. Yesterday, speaking at a large demonstration in Swansea in support of the government, Simon declared:

> The visit I shall be paying to Berlin, upon which the Lord Privy Seal will accompany me, is, of course, quite independent in origin from that which my colleague will pay subsequently to Russia and to Poland. Let me make it clear, however, that His Majesty's Government attach no less importance to the latter visit than to the former. They regard each visit as of exceptional importance and welcome most sincerely the opportunity which will thus be afforded in three great capitals of Europe to promote that international understanding which is the Government's chief concern.[23]

All right!

* * *

I've been asked again by Moscow to exert pressure on Eden in regard to Prague. There are no signs so far that he is planning to go there. I'll try to do something.

M.M. maintains that the communiqué of 3 February should serve as the basis of the Moscow talks. He recommends advising Eden in a delicate manner not to raise the issue of old claims. He asks me to indicate to Eden and Simon that any alteration of the design of the Eastern Pact of mutual assistance is inadmissible to us, that Hitler's opposition to the pact is a bluff that can be overcome with the assistance of Britain and France, and that in Berlin Simon should persuade Hitler to accept the pact rather than offer him any sort of compromise. I'll point it out to them, but I doubt any good will come of it. Simon is Simon.[24]

17 March

A great historic date: Hitler issued a new law yesterday: compulsory military service is being introduced in Germany, and the strength of the army has been set at 500,000.

A major step on the road to a new world war!

So, the cards are on the table. The Versailles treaty has been openly and ceremoniously torn to pieces. Nazi Germany is turning into a formidable military power. Her army will now surpass the French army in number. The Anglo-French platform of 3 February has been effectively liquidated. There is no point in Simon going to Berlin – what can he negotiate there in the new circumstances?

The consequences of the latest German move will be immeasurable. The attempt at a Franco-German rapprochement, dreamt of by Flandin and Laval, has been cut short. Next comes the conclusion of the Eastern Pact without Germany and possibly without Poland. The French have hesitated and tacked about on this matter throughout – but now there must be an end to all uncertainty. The evening news announces Laval's forthcoming visit to Moscow. Very good. The Eastern Pact might well be signed in Moscow. The English, of course, will spin the thing out and play both sides, but the logic of things will not let them do it for long. Tomorrow the British government will send a note to Berlin with the question: is there still a basis for talks between Simon and Hitler? Feeble! They'd be better off sending a stern note of protest. But MacDonald and Simon can't help trying to be clever. On the other hand, there was an official announcement over the radio that Eden's visit to Moscow will take place on the appointed date. Good news! This visit acquires special significance in the new circumstances, and I hope our people in Moscow will draw the appropriate conclusions.

The seal of death shows through ever more clearly on the face of the capitalist world. The cruel and idiotic Versailles treaty, the idiotic post-war policy of France and Britain towards Germany, Hitler's idiotically provocative behaviour… As a result, the world rushes ever faster and more uncontrollably towards a military catastrophe, in the womb of which is borne the proletarian revolution!

* * *

I spent the weekend in the country at the Webbs'. Wonderful old people! The cream of the world intelligentsia. In spite of their age (he is 75 and she is 77), they are working hard on their political testament, *Soviet Communism*. Two volumes of about 1,000 pages. Nine-tenths of it is ready. We spoke about the book at length, and I made a series of critical comments and corrections. The authors listened, sometimes objecting but mostly agreeing. Then Webb and I went for a stroll. He walked so quickly that I could hardly keep up with him. I got back drenched in sweat. How's that for 75 years! Agniya asked the old man about his heart. 'My heart?' he asked wonderingly. 'I never feel it.'

The Webbs have a wonderful country house: not very large, but extremely cosy, peaceful, and perfectly suited to mental work. A great deal of culture, thousands of books, hundreds of files with various materials, and silence – some kind of inspired silence...

18 March

The reaction of the English press to Hitler's actions has been weaker than might have been expected. The directing hand of the Foreign Office can be felt. The British government is obviously perplexed. It has to make a choice, and it doesn't like it. So it tries to buy time and defer the moment of decision-making. Maybe it will all come out in the wash!...

The Liberals and Labour, for their part, are also trying their hardest; conscience, not fear, directs them. They deal in abstract categories and an abstract notion of Germany, and are ready to applaud the liquidation of Versailles and the restoration of German 'equal rights', even in the sphere of arms, for the sake of 'eternal justice'. In addition, the Liberals and Labour are busy hunting for votes. They are against a further arms build-up because the British government is in favour. They oppose regional pacts because the government approves of them (though not sufficiently so, in our view), and so on and so forth. As a result, a strange situation has emerged: in the sphere of foreign policy we are presently much closer to the Conservatives (to such people, say, as Austen Chamberlain) than to Labour.

Among the newspapers, the *Manchester Guardian*, *News Chronicle*, *Daily Herald* and *Morning Post* support continued negotiations with Germany. The *Daily Telegraph* is more reserved and ends its editorial in meaningful fashion: 'In a certain sense, [Hitler's] melodramatic speech on Saturday cannot be considered a surprise. But the first real thunderbolt from a darkened sky always makes one shiver.' To my great surprise, *The Times* took a firm stand today – in favour of the negotiations, it must be said, but on certain conditions...

19 March

Having communicated with Moscow and Eden, I finally fixed the following timetable for Eden's stay in Moscow:

(1) 28 March: lunch at the British embassy (private), sightseeing tour of the city (3–4 p.m.), talk with Litvinov (approx. 4–6 p.m.), dinner at Litvinov's and grand reception at Spiridonovka in the evening.

(2) <u>29 March</u>: talk with Litvinov (approx. 10.30–12), visit to Molotov (12–1 p.m.), lunch at the British embassy (private), sightseeing tour of the Kremlin (3–4 p.m.), talk with Stalin (approx. 4–6 p.m.), ballet in the evening (*Swan Lake* with Semenova[i]).

(3) 30 March: Museum of western painting (the French) in the morning, lunch at Litvinov's dacha, visit to aircraft factory No. 22, dinner and reception at the British embassy.

(4) <u>31 March</u>: Tretyakov Art Gallery in the morning, the Red Army Central House, ballet or theatre in the evening, departure.

The schedule for the third and fourth days is, we have agreed, tentative. It might be changed depending on the circumstances (except for dinner at the British embassy). Eden likes the programme very much, particularly the visits to the aircraft factory and the Red Army Central House. He would not, I think, be against seeing more in the military sphere, but hesitates to ask. We'll decide what to do once in Moscow.

I spoke to Eden about Prague. He said that, taking into account Litvinov's request, he would be prepared to visit Czechoslovakia for a day, but could not give the final answer as yet. He will think it over.

Regarding the agenda for discussion, Eden proposed the communiqué of 3 February and the Berlin talks. But he is prepared to discuss other matters as well if we so wish. Moreover, Eden let slip a significant phrase: 'Who knows, following our Berlin talks Anglo-Soviet relations may just turn out to be a more important topic than the communiqué of 3 February.' Perfectly possible. Clearly, Eden is not very optimistic about the talks with Hitler.

I have been informed from Moscow that a limousine will be dispatched to Nagoreloe. Vainberg (deputy chief of the third western department) will meet the delegation.

* * *

M.M. is very angry – and rightly so – with the English note to Hitler concerning the decree of 16 March.[25] He considers it a complete capitulation to Germany.

I shall add a few humiliating details. The note was delivered by Phipps[ii] (the British ambassador in Berlin) at about 4 p.m. on the 18th. The reply was received at about 7 p.m. on the same day and sent to London by phone right away. At 9 p.m. the parliamentary session was interrupted (an unprecedented fact in history!) to let Simon communicate the joyous news: Hitler is prepared to grant the British ministers an audience after all!

---

[i] Marina Timofeevna Semenova, people's performing artist of the USSR, ballerina at the Bolshoi Theatre from 1930.
[ii] Eric Phipps, British minister in Paris, 1922–28, and in Vienna, 1928–33; ambassador in Berlin, 1933–37, and in Paris, 1937–39.

How shameful! What degradation! See what hatred of the Soviet Union can lead one to…

20 March

Yesterday's conversation appears to have had an effect: today Eden got the laissez-passer for Prague from the Czech chargé d'affaires! But Eden has not directly informed me or Čorny (the chargé d'affaires) about the trip.

* * *

Vansittart invited me to see him today. He was in a somewhat melancholy, even slightly despondent, mood as if he had had a bout of illness the day before and had not yet fully recovered. V. spoke of the extreme importance of the improvement of Anglo-Soviet relations, of his own struggle for this improvement, and of his delight at Eden's forthcoming visit to Moscow. Yes, he regards Eden's visit as a major historic event, and it is crucial that his visit should have major historic consequences. It would be good for the three of us to get together on the 22nd, on the eve of Eden's departure, and discuss the measures that could ensure the best outcome of the Moscow visit. I willingly agreed. In an almost trembling voice, V. added: 'For many months we have been working together in the cause of Anglo-Soviet rapprochement, and I have brought the matter to its present stage, at which you have initiated direct talks between ministers. Here, naturally, I had to efface myself and step back…'

I glanced at V. in some surprise, and my surprise only grew: it was obvious that he was jealous of my contacts with Eden or of the fact that the process of Anglo-Soviet rapprochement was progressing despite his playing a less active role than before!

* * *

Vansittart filled me in on a great many details regarding the events of recent days. The following transpired. In the British government, a struggle is being fought between two tendencies in regard to Germany – 'hard' and 'soft'. The same in the Foreign Office. Simon is for the 'soft' line, and V. for the 'hard'. The note of 18 March was sent by Simon against S.'s wishes and without his knowledge (this is a bit hard to believe). The French government knew nothing about the note and is most displeased with the British government. But the protests from Paris and Rome have done their job and Simon will take a fairly firm line in Berlin, all the more so as Eden will be with him. Simon, however, refused to pay a visit to Paris before going to Berlin, and so Eden has been sent to Paris now. V. expects nothing from the Berlin talks, but he considers the visit useful from the point of view of educating Labour-pacifist public opinion. We'll see.

21 March

I learned some curious things today from good sources. Simon, it seems, is obsessed with the quite fantastic idea of becoming prime minister after MacDonald, who, it has allegedly been decided, will step down immediately after the royal jubilee. Simon needs an impressive 'success' to achieve that. He has been planning to bring this 'success' back from Berlin. That's why, early in the year, he began 'secret' negotiations (unknown to the Foreign Office) with Hitler through Lothian, Ribbentrop and others. During these negotiations, Hitler pulled the wool over Simon's eyes, refusing to commit himself definitively, but sending the vague message that, under certain conditions (which?), he might be ready to 'consider' the question of arms limitation, a return to the League of Nations, and the preservation of the demilitarized zone on the French border. Simon believed, with peculiar naiveté, that all these concessions were more or less in the bag, hence the blatantly pro-German line he has been espousing for the last three months. Hence also his craving to travel to Berlin, and his servile attitude to Hitler with regard to the latter's 'hoarseness' and to the decree of 16 March. At a conference on Sunday, 17 March, which was attended by Baldwin, MacDonald, Eden, Simon and Vansittart and was held to discuss the reaction to the German decree, Simon and Vansittart argued so heatedly that Vansittart was on the point of declaring his resignation, before he was eventually persuaded to stay. Vansittart insisted that it was necessary to consult with the French government before deciding how to act. Simon, on the contrary, insisted on an immediate response. Simon was victorious, and the note was sent on 18 March. In order to ease the situation for Simon, Hitler promised that Ribbentrop would fly to London on 20 March and give an interview to the newspapers, where he would announce, in vague terms, the possibility of Germany returning to the League of Nations 'under certain conditions'. However, on the morning of the 20th, the French government resolved to appeal to the League of Nations against Germany's violation of the Versailles treaty. Hitler found out about this immediately and intercepted Ribbentrop, who had already departed for London, in Hanover, instructing him to return. As a result, Simon found himself in an awkward position. Serves him right.

22 March

We had talks between the three of us today: Eden, Vansittart and I. Both my interlocutors emphasized that they would like to make the visit a historic date in the sphere of Anglo-Soviet rapprochement. The circumstances are favourable. The Englishmen had nothing definite to propose, but they announced that in

Moscow Eden would bring up not only the communiqué of 3 February, but also the question of Anglo-Soviet relations. I, of course, had no objections.

But I did remark that we were a little anxious about the upcoming talks in Berlin.

'In this connection,' I added, 'I would like to express three wishes. First, that the British delegation should not make any binding promises in Berlin to Hitler (whether official or unofficial). Second, that it should not forget for a moment during its talks with Hitler that there can be no "European security" without the Eastern Pact of mutual assistance. Third, that in all its dealings with Hitler the British delegation should display firmness, firmness, and, once again, firmness.'

Eden and Vansittart assured me that we had nothing to worry about. The British ministers have not been authorized to decide or agree anything; their task is to elucidate and investigate. They understand the role of eastern security perfectly well. They will be firm with Hitler. I thought to myself: 'May your words come true. Let's see what comes of it...'

At 4 p.m. I saw Eden off at the Croydon Aerodrome. Kagan was with me. Strang[i] and Hankey[ii] were accompanying Eden. Eden's wife, a tall, nice-looking woman, was there. So was Hankey's wife. We were photographed in various poses and combinations, and Eden rapidly ran through his plans: today he is flying to Paris, tomorrow he will confer with Laval and Suvich[iii] (about the Berlin talks), on the morning of the 24th he will fly from Paris to Amsterdam, he'll meet Simon and his whole team there, and then they will all fly to Berlin. Talks with Hitler will begin in Berlin on the morning of the 25th (Monday) and end on the 26th in the evening. Simon will be back in London on the morning of the 27th, while Eden will meet me at the railway station in Berlin on the evening of the 26th, and from there we shall travel to Moscow through Poland...

As Eden's aeroplane rose heavily into the air – roaring, buzzing and generating a furious wind all around – I couldn't help thinking: 'This is the beginning of an important flight that may become truly historic... Will it?'

We shall see. For the moment I must think about concrete practical things. The day after tomorrow I shall set off, too, on a long journey to Moscow!

---

[i] William Strang, member of the British embassy in Moscow, 1930–33; head of the Foreign Office department for the League of Nations, 1933–37; assistant undersecretary of state for foreign affairs, 1939–43.
[ii] Maurice Hankey (1st Baron Hankey), secretary to the Committee of Imperial Defence, 1912–38, and to the Cabinet, 1916–38; minister without portfolio, 1939–40, and paymaster general, 1941–42.
[iii] Fulvio Suvich, Italian undersecretary for foreign affairs, 1932–36.

24. Maisky and Eden's wife seeing off the minister on his way to meet Hitler in Berlin and then Stalin in Moscow.

[Maisky accompanied Eden on his train journey from Berlin to Moscow. The ambassador's advice to pamper Eden was followed to the letter. Crossing into Russia, at the tiny hamlet of Nagoreloe, he was greeted by dignitaries and led to a 'palm-bedecked restaurant at the station, where a black-tied string orchestra played soft airs to beguile the tedium of the 90-minute wait' for the special coach which was to carry him to Moscow.[26] After a preliminary meeting with Litvinov, Eden was grudgingly shown the Pushkin Museum's prodigious collection of impressionists – 'bourgeois art' – which was closed to the general public. From there he was whisked off to Litvinov's dacha, which the latter had received from the Soviet government in recognition of the success of his Washington talks which had led to American recognition of the Soviet Union in 1934. A stiff walk on frozen ground in the surrounding woods was followed by a banquet-like lunch. Pats of butter were served in the form of rosettes; at the base of each appeared Litvinov's famous dictum: 'Peace is indivisible.' This evoked a wry warning from Strang when Maisky was about to help himself to a pat: 'Be careful how you cut that!'[27] After a long meeting in Litvinov's study, the guests enjoyed a game of billiards, 'as is done in England (to judge by the novels)'.[28] On his last day, Eden was taken for a ride on the first line of the spectacular Metro, which had just been completed. He was unaware, of course, that it had been constructed by inmates of forced labour camps. He was also entertained to lunch at Molotov's home, and dined at the home of Voroshilov, the minister of defence.

25. Eden, greeted by Litvinov and British Ambassador Chilston, at Moscow railway station.

But the highlight of his visit was clearly the meeting with Stalin on 29 March. Preliminary conversations with Litvinov had given the Russians an accurate and detailed picture of the forlorn talks in Berlin.[29] Indeed, on the way to Moscow, Eden had already cabled home his impression that Germany was unlikely to return to the League of Nations, but his recommendation to create a system of collective security under the umbrella of the League of Nations went unheeded.[30] Maisky's personal file, which is kept in the secret section of the Russian Foreign Ministry Archives, contains a record of Stalin's meeting with Eden in his office in the Kremlin. The document bears some amendments made in Maisky's hand.[31] The meeting lasted for an hour and a quarter. Eden resorted to flattering rhetoric, which was interrupted rather brusquely by Stalin, who demanded a clear and simple answer from Eden to the question of whether he believed the international situation was dangerous. In Eden's earlier conversations with Litvinov it had transpired that Hitler had tried to lure Britain by raising an alarm about the Soviet military threat, but that Eden did not appear to have been convinced by this aggressiveness. Moreover, it emerged, as Eden was forced by Litvinov to admit, that the main difference between the British and the Soviet points of view was 'that the former did not believe in the aggressiveness of German policy'.[32] 'Compared, say, to 1913,' Stalin challenged Eden, 'is the situation better or worse?' He was hardly convinced by Eden's assurance that it was better.[33] The aggressive postures of both Japan and Germany, Stalin argued, now posed an acute danger of war which could only be forestalled by a mutual assistance pact. Maisky was surely not amused at the metaphor Stalin chose to illustrate his point, after dismissing Eden's advocacy of bilateral agreements:

26. Eden given the honour of the first ride on the new Metro in Moscow.

Take the six of us present in this room. Suppose we concluded a mutual assistance pact and suppose Comrade Maisky wanted to attack one of us – what would happen? With our combined strength, we would give Comrade Maisky a hiding.

    Com. MOLOTOV (humorously): That's why Comrade Maisky is behaving so humbly.

    EDEN (laughing): Yes, I quite understand your metaphor.[34]

Despite the efforts invested by Maisky and Litvinov, the visit hardly advanced the idea of an Eastern Pact, and nor did it dramatically alter Eden's views.[35] He found Stalin to be 'a man of strong oriental traits of character with unshakeable assurance and control whose courtesy in no way hid from us an implacable ruthlessness'.[36]

In their memoirs, both Maisky and Eden hailed the visit to Moscow as the pinnacle of the diplomatic efforts to bring about a shift in Anglo-Soviet relations and to lay the foundations for an effective anti-Nazi coalition.[37] Maisky's expectations of Eden, however, were clearly too high. He was neither the first nor the last politician to be beguiled by Eden's lofty demeanour, his charm and the respect which he seemed to command, as well as by his ability to convey authority and power (which he completely lacked). The 'Welsh wizard', Lloyd George, who formerly had great faith in Eden and in his courage, now came to regard him as 'a funk'. His verdict was harsh: 'They all call him a darling, they say his heart is in the right place but I doubt if his spine is!'[38] 'Anthony,' Cadogan mused, 'was unlucky with his Chiefs: Baldwin could not be induced to take

27. Maisky's coup: Eden in Stalin's office at the Kremlin (left to right: Eden, Stalin, Molotov, Maisky, Chilston and Litvinov).

any interest in foreign affairs, Chamberlain took too much, Winston was a rather too oppressive thundercloud overhead!'[39]

While the negotiations were still in progress at the Kremlin, Litvinov received numerous reports that the British government demanded from the French that the Eastern Pact would conform with the statutes of the League of Nations, as well as with the Locarno Agreement. The French were discouraged from making any tangible commitments in their pact of mutual assistance, signed with the Russians on 2 May 1935, which left the nature of military assistance wide open.[40] Suspicion in Moscow was further aroused by the exclusion of Russia from the Stresa meeting in mid-April, when measures to check Germany were discussed by the Italians, the French and the British. An extraordinary session of the Council of the League of Nations on 17 April 1935 ended with a feeble denouncement of Germany's unilateral withdrawal from its international obligations. Even the sympathetic Vansittart told Maisky that it would be 'unwise not to pursue negotiations simultaneously with Germany on the basis of the German draft'.[41] Maisky did not write in his diary until early June, or possibly excised the entries when his position became precarious. He tried in vain to convince Litvinov that British public opinion, as well as government opinion, was slowly shifting against Germany. Litvinov in fact reprimanded him for failing to glean from Vansittart and Eden information vital for the progress of negotiations with the French.[42] The credibility of his reports that the British government did not object to the Treaty was shaken when

28. A visit to Litvinov, at his modest office in Narkomindel.

demands by the ever-suspicious Litvinov for such written assurances from Vansittart failed to materialize.[43]

Rather than turning against Germany (as Maisky predicted), the hardliners in the Foreign Office, led by Sargent,[i] were effectively prevailing on Cabinet to make further concessions to Germany. In his speech to the Reichstag on 21 May, Hitler rejected the Anglo-French proposals for disarmament and an eastern bloc, and countered with fresh proposals for the German fleet to be allowed to reach 35 per cent of Britain's naval strength. His offer to conclude mutual non-aggression pacts with each of Germany's neighbours was received positively. At the same time, he demanded 'a free hand' in Eastern Europe. Maisky, 'distinctly pessimistic', even found it difficult to convince Vansittart that Hitler had no intention whatsoever of signing any such agreement with Russia, and that the speech was merely an attempt to sow dissent among the 'peace-loving' powers. Worse still, from Maisky's point of view, Vansittart chose the moment to raise again the bogey of Soviet propaganda as the obstacle to improved relations between the two countries. Maisky would have been further upset had he been privy to Eden's approval of the way Vansittart spoke. During the meeting of the General Council of the League in Geneva, Eden deliberately avoided Litvinov, who came to realize the success of the strident and persistent Nazi campaign concerning the 'Bolshevik danger'. Maisky was instructed by Litvinov to acquaint the British government with the Russian belief that, pursuing *Mein Kampf* to the letter, Hitler's speech disclosed his determination

---

[i] Sir Orme Sargent, deputy undersecretary of state, 1939–46.

to expand eastwards and to frustrate the attempts by Russia and France to create a system of collective security. He was further to ascertain from Vansittart whether the British government went along with this by no longer pressing for the Eastern Pact to be part and parcel of any future agreement with the Germans.[44]]

23 March

Yesterday and today I've been thinking about the situation that has developed in England. A complicated picture! A contradictory picture!

There is a strong anti-Soviet movement in the country, which is consequently pro-German; a strong pro-French movement, which is consequently anti-German and tolerant towards the USSR; a strong pro-Japanese trend, which is thereby anti-Soviet; a strong pro-American trend, which is consequently anti-Japanese and tolerant towards the USSR; a very significant movement that tries to mobilize English public opinion against the 'yellow menace' (Japan and China) and therefore strives to establish 'order' in the family of the white nations, seeking routes of reconciliation with Germany. There is the National Government which, like any other coalition government, is torn by internal contradictions and suffers from internal weakness; and there is a strong pacifist opposition (Liberals and Labour), whose absurd tactics play straight into Hitler's hands. Elections are approaching; Labour's chances are steeply on the rise; the Conservatives are restive; and the government is afraid of giving its opponents more trump cards by making a major arms push or taking on 'new commitments' abroad. Diverse cliques and individuals are fighting for places and influence in the government camp... Such is the complicated, entangled, and contradictory background against which British foreign policy zigzags and vacillates!

3 June

I attended the dinner of the 'dying swans', as the diplomats called it. Any day now there will be a Cabinet reshuffle, and MacDonald will retire as prime minister. Many other ministers will also be replaced. Tonight, though, the old members of the government were still in their posts and they gave the annual dinner in the Foreign Office to mark the king's birthday. This time the celebration was on a larger scale than usual: the king has turned 70.

To the right of me sat Hilton Young,[i] the health minister, who is certain to be 'retired'. No wonder. This is what he told me at dinner: 'A military threat from Germany? Nonsense! All these rumours are terribly exaggerated. Even if there

---

[i] Edward Hilton Young (1st Baron Kennet), Liberal MP, minister of health, 1931–35.

is a threat, what do we, the English, have to do with it? We were stupid to send a million-strong army to the continent during the past war – we shall never do it again. We've had enough of war. If Germany and the USSR start fighting, that's their business. We would even gain from it – both sides would get weaker, and we would trade.'

No doubt, many Conservatives reason like this, but it's a bit much for 'His Majesty's minister'. There are obviously a few screws loose in Hilton Young's head.

To my left sat Halifax,[i] former viceroy of India and presently the minister of education. His stance was absolutely different. He himself began speaking about the German threat and inquired about our attitude to Hitler, the Franco-Soviet pact, etc. Summing up, Halifax said: 'It's extremely irksome that the German threat has re-emerged in Europe. I'd give anything for someone to persuade me that there is no such threat. But facts are facts. Since Germany's intentions are unclear, you need to base your practical calculations on the worst scenario, not the best.'

Cunliffe-Lister approached me after dinner and spoke to me about our air fleet, the prospects of limiting air forces, etc. One thing is clear: Cunliffe-Lister will be secretary of state for air in the new Cabinet.

5 June

A rather unusual neighbour moved in last year to house No. 12a (our embassy occupies No. 13), namely General Sir Bahadur Shamsher Jung Bahadur Rana, the Nepalese envoy extraordinary and minister plenipotentiary, together with his staff. I'd read in the papers that this Bahadur had arrived in London on a special mission, to bestow on the king the highest order of his country, and that he had fulfilled his mission successfully and with all due solemnity. Later, caught up in daily events, I forgot about Bahadur; I even thought that he had returned to his mountainous homeland.

Then it suddenly emerged that Bahadur was my neighbour! Taking into consideration the particular sensitivity of the English towards 'Indian affairs', I instructed the embassy staff to be reserved, even cold, with the neighbours, and not make friends with them. One fine summer's day, however, Bahadur himself paid me a visit. Even though our buildings stand side by side, he arrived in a car (oh, the Orient!). He wore national dress: a round lambskin hat, a long

---

[i] Edward Frederick Lindley Wood (1st earl of Halifax), a prize fellow at All Souls College, Oxford, he went on to become the viceroy of India, 1926–32; president of the Board of Education, 1932–35; chancellor of Oxford University, 1933–59; Conservative leader of the House of Lords, 1935–38; secretary of state for war, 1935; lord privy seal, 1935–37; lord president of the council, 1937–38; secretary of state for foreign affairs, 1938–40; and British ambassador to the United States, 1941–46.

black caftan (something between a frock-coat and a lapserdak) on a short fat body, close-fitting black trousers tight at the shins, and soft white shoes with no counters. Bahadur did not remove his black hat even indoors. It was the time of afternoon tea. The maid carried in a tray with two cups, a teapot, hot water, and the other necessary ingredients. With a cordial gesture, I invited Bahadur to partake... And then! And then sheer horror appeared on his face and his hands convulsed as if he wanted to shield himself from a blow with a cudgel. I looked at my guest in bewilderment. He said in an apologetic tone: 'The law of my country forbids my sharing a meal with foreigners.'

(Brailsford[i] later explained to me that this was a polite formula concealing a less than polite meaning. The point is that Bahadur, a Hindu, treats all Europeans as belonging to a lower caste than he; he would find it degrading to share a meal with them.)

I looked at Bahadur in surprise and asked: 'How do you expect to work in London? Here, people are forever meeting over lunch, dinner or high tea.'

'Yes, I am aware of that,' my guest replied, 'but there's nothing I can do.'

The maid left and I closed the door behind her. Bahadur looked around cautiously and said: 'You can't imagine how hard it is for me here in London. I understand perfectly well that I can achieve nothing here if I don't share meals with foreigners, but what can I do? It is the law of my country. I have already appealed to His Majesty my sovereign with a letter regarding these difficulties and I am waiting impatiently for Him to resolve this serious problem.'

See what problems may occur in the epoch of socialist revolution and in the eighteenth year of Soviet rule in the USSR! To eat or not to eat – this is the question!

I sympathized with Bahadur and he, a little moved perhaps or with my Soviet origin in mind, said to me in a half-whisper, casting wary glances at the door: 'Here, in private, I can make a small exception, but let it remain strictly between ourselves...'

Bahadur shyly took a cup of tea from my hands, but he refused outright the offer of a pastry. Having drunk half of the cup, he put it on the table and pleaded: 'This is strictly between ourselves.' I solemnly vowed to keep his secret.

Then the conversation turned to other subjects. We talked about our homes, the conditions of life in London, the weather, etc. For some reason my guest was terribly interested in the question of whether or not I had a cowshed. Flummoxed, I replied that I had a garage but not a cowshed.

---

[i] Henry Noel Brailsford, a publicist writing for the *Manchester Guardian, Morning Leader, The Star, Nation, Daily News* and editor of the *New Leader*, 1922–26; member of the Independent Labour Party, 1907–32. In 1935, Agniya referred to the Brailsfords as their 'most intimate friends in England', though this changed when he became a severe critic of Stalin's purges; Webb, diary, 18 Nov. 1935, p. 6092.

'But it's precisely a cowshed that interests me,' Bahadur repeated with obscure insistence.

I couldn't understand what he was on about. Why would a man in London suddenly need a cowshed? After some cautious interrogation, it emerged that Bahadur really did need a cowshed. In accordance with native customs and religious laws, he had brought with him from Nepal not only his national dress, interior decor and servants, but also his very own Nepalese cow. Upkeep of the cow has been causing my neighbour no end of difficulties. With no cowshed at home, he has had to rent separate premises for his four-footed friend, and this has proved highly inconvenient. That is why he was so keen to know whether or not I had a cowshed.

Other curious things transpired. Nepal is a semi-independent country in the Himalayas on India's borders. The country's mountainous character and the belligerence of the local population had prevented its complete subjugation by the British. So the British had acted in accordance with their proverb: if you can't strangle your enemy, embrace him. And they had embraced Nepal so skilfully and tightly that throughout the previous century the Nepalese contingent (the Gurkha) had been the most reliable of the Indian troops. An agreement on the exchange of diplomats was concluded between Nepal and England (represented by the East India Company) back in 1815. The British immediately took advantage of the opportunity, and a British resident minister has been present in the Nepalese capital for more than a hundred years now, exercising considerable influence over the political, economic and cultural life of the country (there are even English schools there). For a long time, however, Nepal had no official representatives in England, nor even in India. The reason? Because Hinduism forbids Nepal to have any dealings with foreign countries. It forbids foreigners from entering Nepal and Nepalese citizens from travelling to foreign countries. Theoretically, Nepal is a closed country (like Japan in the seventeenth and eighteenth centuries), but this did not prevent the British from having a resident minister there and Gurkha troops in India. However, it did prevent Nepal – through the efforts of her reactionary priesthood – from having its diplomats abroad. Only in recent times, with the growth of the national movement after the war, have attitudes in the country begun to change. The priests fought with the more progressive elements of the secular arm headed by the prime minister (Bahadur's father) about whether or not to send a representative to England. The struggle was fierce and stubborn. Bahadur's father finally won – but how? He reread all the books of the sutra (the sacred Hindu texts) and found a small note in one of them to the effect that although the Nepalese are not allowed to leave their country, they may do so in exceptional cases and for diplomatic purposes. That tiny note decided the outcome of the struggle. The priesthood was shamed, and Bahadur was sent to

England to represent Nepal's interests. But he has to be cautious: one false step and the priests could mount a campaign against him and his father...

That is why Bahadur refuses to eat with foreigners! I saw him at many receptions afterwards and even attended a reception given by him: never and nowhere did he touch any food (even in his own home, where all the guests drank and ate according to established European ritual). But I have seen him, on various ceremonial occasions, wearing the red uniform of an English general, while on his head he wears a Nepalese skullcap-like affair, with a tall and luxuriant light-brown plume. It is strewn with big diamonds, rubies and sapphires, and sparkles in the sun or under electric light with every colour of the rainbow. It is very heavy and costs fabulous money. Indeed, on such occasions my neighbour is wearing an entire fortune on his head. Oh, Orient, this is you!...

Something mysterious happened to Bahadur's wife. He arrived married in London. His wife fell ill and died, but from what I don't know. I only know that she fell ill during her husband's visit to Italy, where he bestowed the highest order of his country on Mussolini and the Italian king. Anticipating her death, Bahadur's retinue took his wife out into the country, to a clearing, and there she eventually died. Apparently this was done because, according to Hindu laws, it is bad for the deceased if his body is kept between stone walls. Out of concern for their mistress, the servants moved her away from stony London in good time. Once I happened to visit Bahadur when he was in mourning. He received me dressed in what seemed to be white pyjamas beneath a light summer coat, soft white shoes without counters, and a small white cap. It was quite an amusing sight (as if the man had just jumped out of bed at night), but it turned out to be Nepalese mourning dress.

A few months later, Bahadur left London and returned with a new wife, who never leaves the house. She does not even venture into the embassy garden.

What incredible things occur in our days! What remarkable contradictions exist side by side in the epoch of socialist revolution and in the eighteenth year of Soviet rule in the USSR!

6 June

I called on Vansittart. He met me cordially, but looked somewhat worn out and upset. Paler than usual. He took me aside and informed me on an entirely confidential basis (but with the request that I tell the Soviet government!) that Samuel Hoare had been appointed foreign secretary.[45] He had hoped for better, but this wasn't too bad. Yesterday he had an extensive conversation with his new boss and learned to his delight that their views were fundamentally similar. Vansittart fears, however, that the name Hoare might make an unfavourable impression in Moscow, and that the Soviet press might give him a hostile reception. One should not jump to conclusions. Just wait and see… Hoare will invite me for a talk immediately after Trinity Sunday. Vansittart hopes fervently that I shall try to reassure Moscow.

I replied that we view the restructuring of the British government with equanimity, and that we will judge the new Foreign Office, and indeed the new government as a whole, not by their words, but by their deeds.

I then asked what would happen to Eden. Vansittart replied that Eden would be promoted. He will enter the Cabinet, but it is not known yet in what capacity. In any event, he will represent the British government at the League of Nations and will be more independent than before.

Then I read out our appraisal of Hitler's speech of 21 May and handed it over. V. listened to the end and said, 'You will receive an official reply to this from the new foreign secretary.' In the meantime, he referred to Simon's recent speech in the House. (Its essence is as follows. The communiqué of 3 February is a single programme, but its separate parts may be discussed individually. In particular, negotiations on the air pact may be opened now. If agreement is achieved, the air pact will become part of the single London package.) It also transpired that the British government has not yet replied to the German note concerning Locarno. It wants to agree the reply with the French government – but there is no government in Paris at the moment. In any event, said V., the Germans will not rejoice at the British reply. We shall see.

So, the British government is concerned about Moscow's attitude to Hoare's appointment… Not a bad symptom! What will he be like, that Hoare?!…

* * *

We had a grand dinner in honour of Eden tonight. Twenty-seven guests were present… The atmosphere was not bad, even though Hoare had been appointed foreign secretary. Eden and Lord Cecil assured me that Hoare was a convinced advocate of collective security and that he would make a good foreign secretary. We'll see![46]

[One of the first issues to claim Hoare's attention when he assumed office was Litvinov's harsh analysis of Hitler's speech and demand from the British government to reassert its commitment to the principle of indivisible peace in Europe. While Vansittart and the northern department at the Foreign Office wanted to allay Russian fears, Sargent warned that any response to Litvinov's 'very cunning note' was likely to be distorted and exploited in the Soviet negotiations with the French. Vansittart disagreed. He reminded the new foreign secretary that it was in Britain's interests to maintain a friendly attitude towards Russia, and that this could only be realized if the Russians were treated as 'participants in the scheme of things'. Hoare, however, was more attentive to Vansittart's warning that the 'able and pertinacious' Maisky would return to the charge. He dreaded

29. Eighty-six-year-old Pavlov, the famous scientist, recruited to enhance Soviet prestige.

the idea of another meeting with Maisky, having himself gained the impression that Maisky was eager 'to indulge in a legalistic cross-examination'. Maisky was therefore put on hold while events unfolded.[47] To overcome the impasse, Vansittart assisted Maisky in setting up a powerful lobby within Conservative circles. The introduction of Maisky to the Fleet Street magnate Beaverbrook resulted in the first favourable mention of Moscow in the *Daily Express*, which, according to Maisky, hitherto had printed only 'obvious libels'. Maisky was further invited to a dinner *en famille* at Vansittart's home, where he met Churchill. 'I send you a very strong recommendation of that gentleman,' wrote Beaverbrook to Maisky. 'In character he is without a rival in British politics. I know all about his prejudices. But a man of character who tells the truth is worth much to the nation.' Churchill indeed told Maisky that, in view of the rise of Nazism, which threatened to reduce England to 'a toy in the hands of German imperialism', he was abandoning his protracted struggle against the Soviet Union, which he no longer believed posed any threat to England for at least the next ten years. He fully subscribed to the idea of collective security as the sole strategy able to thwart Nazi Germany.

Maisky further sustained his campaign with ambitious plans in the cultural sphere, which he had recognized earlier on – during his service in Japan – to be a vital means of influencing public opinion. Together with Keynes (whose young Russian wife was the famous ballerina Lidiya Lopukhova of the Ballets Russes), he propagated Russian culture in England, organizing performances at Covent Garden for the Soviet Ballet, Opera and the advanced Vakhtangov Theatre.[48] Likewise Ivan Petrovich Pavlov,[i] perhaps the greatest of the Russian scientists, was rushed to London at the age of 86 to attend a major international congress of neurologists and was paraded before the media.[49] The climax of such efforts was the Soviet participation in a well-attended and publicized international folk-dance festival in London at the end of July.[50]

---

[i] Ivan Petrovich Pavlov, a Russian physiologist known primarily for his work on conditioning. He was the first Russian Nobel Prize winner.

But strong opposition within the Conservative Party, as well as within the Foreign Office, was turning the tide against the rapprochement embarked upon by Maisky and Vansittart in 1934. The Franco-Soviet pact offered the Germans a convenient excuse for finally burying the idea of an Eastern Pact. Under the circumstances, in late autumn the Foreign Office examined the various options open to Britain. It rejected both the 'policy of drift' (waiting for events to occur) and the policy of 'encirclement' (the creation of an anti-German military alliance with France, Russia and the Little Entente), preferring the third option of 'coming to terms with Germany' – a policy that would signal the transition to 'appeasement'.[51]]

12 June

Just back from my first meeting with S. Hoare. He invited me according to the custom of receiving all diplomatic representatives accredited in London, but our conversation, which lasted some 40 minutes, far exceeded the bounds of mere etiquette.[52] What first impression did I gain of 'my' new foreign secretary?

First, the external details. The desk in the office has been moved – a new broom sweeps clean. What next, I wonder? Will H. limit himself to furniture rearrangement, or will he also start 'breaking the ceilings', in the spirit of Shchedrin?[i] Time will tell.

H. is dry, elegant and quite short. His face is sharp, intelligent and guardedly attentive. He is very courteous and considerate, but cautious. He still feels unsure of himself in his new position, is unfamiliar with the current problems, and is afraid most of all of committing himself in any way to anybody. He wants to keep his hands free and to have room to manoeuvre in all directions.

Our conversation fell into several parts. First, what you might call the preface. Hoare began with the current problems in the international situation: the world is in a state of military-nationalist fever that spills over from one country to another, creating problems, mutual suspicion, etc. – all said in very general terms, without alighting on anybody in particular. I listened to H. for a good while, and finally interrupted him, saying: 'This is all well and good, but it is important to localize the seat of the disease. Then it will be easier to fight the illness itself.' H. was a little shocked by my unceremonious approach, but he was quick to agree. I then said that in my view there were currently two major hotbeds of 'military-nationalist fever'. H. was once again quick to agree, noting that there were indeed two. However, neither Germany nor Japan was named.

Next came the chapter devoted to Anglo-Soviet relations. H. stated with satisfaction that although there had been difficulties in the past between Russia and England in Asia, they seemed to have vanished. I confirmed this, referring in particular to the Anglo-Soviet communiqué of 31 March (concerning

---

[i] Mikhail Evgrafovich Saltykov-Shchedrin, prominent Russian satirist of the nineteenth century.

Eden's visit to Moscow). Then we quickly ran through all the Asian regions (Constantinople, Persia, Afghanistan, India, the Far East), establishing that no conflict existed anywhere between the two countries. H. wanted to raise the question of 'propaganda' in connection with India, but I easily led him away from it. He acknowledged that this question had lost its urgency. H. was interested in trade relations between the USSR and England and, having listened to my account, asked how it might be possible to facilitate the expansion of trade. I made it clear that it would be possible only on the basis of (at least) a five-year loan, like with Czechoslovakia. H. promised to give thought to these considerations. I reminded H. that in Moscow Eden and M.M. reached agreement on the exchange of information – H. promised to continue this practice. He also remarked: 'We want peace. We believe that you want peace, too. Therefore, we have a great goal in common. If the powers that stand for peace do not stick together and cooperate, things may come to a very bad pass.'

We then moved on to the chapter devoted to European problems. I asked H. how he envisaged that peace could be secured in Europe. H. gestured his ignorance and refused to answer, emphasizing that he had only been foreign secretary for three days. I asked him what he thought about the communiqué of 3 February. Does the British government consider it indivisible as before? (I referred to my conversation with Vansittart on 6 June.) H. once again made a gesture and tried to evade a straight answer, pleading his insufficient familiarity with current issues. It sounded suspicious to me and I started besieging H. with various leading questions. Then H. started 'thinking aloud', and I soon had sufficient grounds to establish that my misgivings had not been unfounded. H.'s 'thoughts' boiled down to the following. The English are tired of endless, futile conversations. They want action, not talk. A small practical success is better than a truck-load of eloquent chatter. The disarmament conference failed because it set itself tasks that were too broad and all-embracing. If, 15 years ago, the powers had embarked on arms limitation via separate categories and not in general terms, we would currently be facing a very different situation. The British public now wants 'something, somehow, somewhere to be done'.

I replied that I found H.'s theory very dangerous. Disarmament cannot be fulfilled piecemeal, while the term 'somewhere' might easily be interpreted in the spirit of Hitlerite notions: 'security' in the west and a free hand in Eastern Europe. Does H. support such notions? Does he think that peace is divisible? H. replied that the British government would of course take our point of view into account in developing its foreign policy, but he again dodged my direct question. It became clear to me that this was a serious state of affairs. For H., the question of the 'indivisibility' of the communiqué of 3 February was still open at best. He obviously wants to leave himself the maximum room for manoeuvre.

As I was taking my leave, H. said, with a certain embarrassment: 'I hope that your government and your press will not hinder the development of the correct line of foreign policy through premature attacks on the new government.' I replied: 'I consider today's conversation to be a sort of preface to the book of deeds that will be written by the new government and the new foreign secretary in particular in the sphere of international politics. One judges a book not by its preface but by its full content. We shall do the same. If the book's content is good, the attitude of the Soviet government and the Soviet press will be good, too.' H. expressed the hope that all would be well. I added: 'Please remember, however, that it would be undesirable from all points of view to keep us waiting for good deeds for too long.'

What are my conclusions?

I'm somewhat alarmed. Although Vansittart reassured me that H.'s views basically coincided with his own, I think nevertheless that H. might prove more dangerous than Simon in the next few months. He is a novice, he underestimates the difficulties, and is prone to experimentation. He wants quick, concrete, demonstrative successes to justify his appointment in the eyes of the English public. He wants to oppose his 'sober', 'concrete', 'practical' policies to the 'foggy', 'baggy', 'spineless' policies of Simon. This is dangerous. Simon, for all his negative traits, had some experience. He had been bested more than once, and received many bloody noses in his attempts to regulate various international problems. He was skilled at knowing which sore spots should not be touched and which dangerous buttons should not be pushed. H. has still to master this tricky science. That is why I am a little anxious about the next five or six months. H. obviously wants to experiment in the sphere of Anglo-German relations – what will come of it? H. will learn, of course, but let's hope this process doesn't come at too great a price.

We must be doubly vigilant! France, the Little Entente and the USSR must demonstrate maximum activity![53]

15 June

Just back from a big Labour banquet. It was arranged by Hicks to mark the construction of the new building of the union. Up to 350 guests were present, including Lansbury, Morrison, Citrine and other Labour notables. Agniya and I were the only foreigners. As befits a faint-hearted reformist, Hicks invited me to the banquet, but handled it clumsily. To start with, my name was printed 'Ivan Maisky' in the seating plan, without reference to my ambassadorial rank. Then, naming all and sundry in his welcoming speech, Hicks 'forgot' a minor trifle – the presence in the hall of a Soviet representative. Agniya, in line with her temperament, unleashed her indignation on her neighbour Clynes. As I later learned, Walkden,[i] secretary of the clerks' union, immediately sent Hicks a note protesting about the chairman's incomprehensible behaviour. As a result, Hicks announced my presence in his second speech, and this elicited a round of applause. Clynes spoke and said a few heartfelt words about the USSR and my presence at the banquet. There was another burst of applause. Lansbury spoke, too. He took issue with the prince of Wales and suggested that those in power go not only to Berlin, but also to Moscow. This, too, was followed by a storm of applause in our direction. In general, the mood at the banquet was obviously pro-Soviet, and Hicks was taught a good lesson.

* * *

At the banquet, Lansbury related to me the following details about the 1907 Russian Social Democratic Labour Party (RSDLP) congress. One morning he received a telephone call from Fells, the owner of Sunlight Soap, asking him to come over. Lansbury and Fells were friends (J. Keir Hardie[ii] was also on friendly terms with Fells), and Fells often consulted with him on various matters. When Lansbury came into his office, Fells told him that Brailsford had asked him to lend 2,500 pounds to the Russian Social Democrats, who were holding their congress in London and didn't have the money to return home. Fells was unsure and asked Lansbury for his advice. Lansbury said that the Russians should be supported. Fells was still hesitant. Lansbury suggested that they should attend the congress and speak to the participants. Fells agreed. Lansbury does not remember whom they saw and spoke to at the congress, which was held in the Brotherhood Church, but afterwards Fells decided to give the money. The only thing he requested was an 'acknowledgement of debt' signed by all congress participants. This was done; moreover, it was declared in the letter that the RSDLP would return the money to Fells in the event of the revolution succeeding. When Krasin arrived in London in 1921, he asked his first secretary, Klyshko,[iii] to find Fells. Fells had since died, but his widow lived in England. Krasin, on behalf of the Soviet government, paid back the money lent in 1907 and asked in return for the paper acknowledging the debt of the 5th Congress. Lansbury was greatly moved by the old story and repeated several times that it was a *unique* episode in the history of the world labour movement. Incidentally, Lansbury told me that Fells was a Polish Jew by origin.

---

[i] A.G. Walkden, general secretary of the National Association of General Railway Clerks, 1906–36.
[ii] James Keir Hardie, founder of the Labour Party. Formed the Scottish Labour Party in 1888; Labour Representation Committee in 1900, changing its name to the Labour Party in 1906. Resigned as leader of the Labour Party in 1908.
[iii] Nikolai Klementevich Klyshko, Soviet ambassador in Estonia, 1920–21; head of the export department of the People's Commissariat for Foreign Trade, 1923–37. Arrested on charges of terrorism and shot in 1937; later rehabilitated.

16 June

During the naval parade in Spithead I found myself on the same ship (the *Maine*) as Leith-Ross,[i] chief financial adviser of the British government. He will soon leave for China to study the question of the strengthening of the Chinese currency. Our acquaintance until then had been entirely superficial, but today Leith-Ross suddenly started speaking to me on a very serious subject.

He had seen Ashton-Gwatkin[ii] the other day, who told him that I find it inadvisable to raise the question of the settlement of old debts. It's a great pity. This problem poisons Anglo-Soviet relations through and through. It should not be touched on, of course, if a favourable outcome is impossible, but is the debt problem really so hopeless? Would the USSR really refuse under all possible conditions to discuss, for instance, a plan of settlement such as that put forward by Cazalet?[iii]

I replied that Cazalet had himself described his plan to me, but I was still of the view that now was not the time to touch upon such a complicated and painful matter as British citizens' claims on old debts. This would be wiser precisely from the point of view of Anglo-Soviet relations. Moreover, I am sure that the London banks will not grant a 20- or 25-year loan to the USSR, as envisaged in Cazalet's plan.

Leith-Ross unexpectedly exclaimed: 'Who knows? The banks might be reluctant, but if the government were to agree to provide a guarantee, the whole situation would change radically.'

'The last person from whom I expect any indulgence toward the USSR is your chancellor of the exchequer (Chamberlain).'

Leith-Ross protested: 'Maybe you take an excessively pessimistic view of things. The government may not agree to a 25-year loan, but a 20-year one is a possibility. I talked with Colville[iv] on this subject recently, and he thinks that a loan of this type would of course be met by objections in the House, but it could be passed all the same.' I raised my hands and said: 'I still think it would be better not to awaken old ghosts.'

---

[i] Frederick William Leith-Ross, chief economic adviser to government, 1932–46; director-general, Ministry of Economic Warfare, 1939–42; chairman of Inter-Allied Committee on Post-War Requirements, 1941–43.
[ii] Frank Arthur Ashton-Gwatkin, acting counsellor at the British embassy, Moscow, 1929; first secretary, Foreign Office, 1930; policy adviser, Ministry of Economic Warfare, 1939.
[iii] Victor Alexander Cazalet, Conservative MP, 1924–43; suspicious of the expansionist intentions of the Soviet Union, he championed the Polish case after the outbreak of the Second World War.
[iv] Sir John Rupert 'Jock' Colville, assistant private secretary to Chamberlain, 1939–40, and to Churchill, 1940–41 and 1943–45.

17 June

I paid a visit to Guo Taiqi yesterday. He is in a foul mood. Small wonder. The Japanese have seized the Hebei province, including Beijing and Tianjin, are intending to grab Chahaer and Suiyuan, and plan to extend their influence as far as the Yellow River – and nobody moves a finger to stop it. Nanjing is powerless and is afraid even to appeal to the League of Nations or to the members of the Nine-Power Treaty, so as not to irritate the Japanese still more. The USA merely 'observes' the events in northern China. Guo paid a visit to Vansittart and informed him, on instructions from Nanjing, about what was going on in China. Moreover, on his own initiative, he drew Vansittart's attention to the violation of the Nine-Power Treaty by Japan. V. promised nothing, merely stressing that the British government was going to send its financial adviser, Leith-Ross, to China in late July or early August to examine the situation and work out measures for lending China financial and economic assistance. Guo doubts, however, that the British would render such assistance if Japan objected.

Guo also reported comments made recently by Raczyński (the Pole): that the position of Poland in Europe depends on the position of England. If England places itself firmly on the side of France and the USSR, Poland will betray Germany.

19 June

I've learned (admittedly, from a third party) some details of Stalin's meeting with Laval.

Having exchanged greetings, L. declared with the utmost French parliamentary courtesy that he was delighted about the very recent signing of the Franco-Soviet pact, which, he said, was not directed against any particular country. S. replied: 'What do you mean? It is absolutely directed against one particular country – Germany.'

L. was somewhat astonished, but he immediately tried to right himself and, with the same charming courtesy, expressed his pleasure at S.'s frankness. Only real friends could speak to one another like that.

Then S. asked him: 'You're just back from Poland. What is happening there?' In reply, L. fell into lengthy, polite and ornate explanations about how, despite pro-German attitudes remaining strong in Poland, there are signs of improvement that will eventually lead to a change in Polish policy, etc. S. interrupted L., declaring tersely, 'To my mind, there are no signs at all!' Then he added: 'You are a friend of the Poles, so try to persuade them that they are playing a game that will bring disaster on themselves. The Germans will trick them and sell them short. They will involve Poland in some adventure and when she weakens, they will either seize her or share her with another power.[54] Is that what the Poles need?' L. was again shocked by S.'s directness and frankness.

Referring in the course of their conversation to the power and influence of the Catholic Church, L. asked S. whether reconciliation could not be sought between the USSR and the pope,[i] perhaps by concluding a pact with the Vatican... S. smiled and said: 'A pact? A pact with the pope? No, that won't happen! We conclude pacts only with those who have armies, and the Roman pope, as far as I know, does not have an army.'

L. tried to touch on the question of debts and plunged into protracted discourse about the importance of liquidating old claims for the sake of political rapprochement. S. interrupted L., saying: 'I don't advise raising this issue.' In answer to L.'s query as to why he did not recommend it, S. said: 'For two reasons. One reason is minor: nobody pays his debts today – France does not pay either. The second is a major one: we have counterclaims against you.' L. brightened up and said that it would be an excellent thing to reckon up reciprocal claims, delegate experts from both sides, etc. But S. interrupted him again and said: 'I don't recommend doing it. Ours will be a heavy debt. It will include the cost of bloodshed, and the people's blood is an expensive item. I don't advise settling old claims.' L. had nothing to do but accept the fact.

At M.M.'s reception, Laval met Comrade Chernov,[ii] people's commissar for agriculture, and talked about farming with him. He asked, among other things, how we determine whether or not a cow is a milker, and whether or not its milk is fatty. Chernov began explaining to him in a lengthy and scientific manner what methods and instruments are used for this. L. listened to him for a while and exclaimed: 'That's all wrong! In France we have a simple and reliable method. Stick your finger in the cow's ear – a lot of earwax means a lot of milk, and a lot of good milk.' Chernov flung up his arms: 'You must be joking. In our collective farms, they wash cows' ears to remove earwax.' L. also flung up his arms and exclaimed: 'You poor farmers! You will never have milk!'

Joking and showing off, L. then asked: 'Will you hire me to work in a collective farm when the revolution occurs in France?' Chernov replied: 'That depends on the milkmaids – only if they approve of you!' Laval laughed and quipped with a sly wink: 'Well, if it all depends on milkmaids, I'm sure to get a job.' Alphand (the French ambassador in Moscow), who was standing alongside Laval, added in jest: 'Even if the milkmaids accept you, you'll fail the exam in political science.' Returning home, L. admonished Alphand for his joke, finding it inappropriate and tactless.

---

[i] Pope Pius XI, 1922–39.
[ii] Mikhail Aleksandrovich Chernov, a former Menshevik, was people's commissar for agriculture, 1934–37. He and his family were arrested in 1937 and shot.

27 June

More arias from the opera 'The Situation Changes'!

Two days ago Sir Harry McGowan[i] invited me to lunch. He is a big shot, head of the famous firm Imperial Chemical Industries, one of the most powerful British concerns and one which exercises great influence on foreign policy. I had heard that McGowan was a pillar of the Japanophile group in Great Britain – and all of a sudden he invited me to lunch tête-à-tête in his luxurious mansion on the Embankment. We had never met before and knew about each other only by hearsay. What had happened?

This emerged during our conversation. McGowan is most apprehensive about the future of the British Empire, especially in the Far East. Japanese aggression frightens him in the extreme. Japan is becoming a terrifying prospect for Great Britain economically and politically. McGowan visited Tokyo last year and negotiated the market carve-up in chemicals (in China, the Dutch and British Indies, the Middle East and Africa). The Japanese ministers made very good speeches and swore eternal friendship with England, but the Japanese industrialists refused to make any concessions. The negotiations failed, but McGowan still entertains the pious hope of coming to an agreement with his Japanese rivals in future. Nor did the English reach a compromise on textiles with the Japanese. Politically, Japan strives to subjugate China – what will happen to the British positions in Asia then? In short, the storm clouds have gathered. What hope is there? McGowan sees only one: close cooperation in the Far East between England, the USA and the USSR. Clearly, it was with the aim of communicating this brilliant thought to me that McGowan decided to invite me to lunch.

But there was also one further consideration: could Anglo-Soviet trade not be expanded? I explained that this was possible only on the basis of at least a five-year loan. McGowan had a think, nodded his head meaningfully, and then replied that my idea was very interesting and that he would discuss it with his friends in the City.

We shall see what we shall see.

* * *

Today – Act Two. I had a visit from the major owner of Imperial Chemical Industries, Lord Melchett[ii] (b. Alfred Mond), a young man of quite pleasant appearance. He said that he and a group of friends wanted to visit the USSR in

---

[i] Harry Duncan McGowan (1st Baron McGowan), vice-president of the Society of Chemical Industry, 1931–34; president of Imperial Chemical Industries (ICI), 1926–30 and its chairman, 1930–50.

[ii] Henry Mond (2nd Baron Melchett), Liberal minister of health, 1921–22.

September for a theatre festival. He was also interested in the Jewish colonies in the USSR. He asked me about travelling conditions and requested assistance.

Melchett told me an interesting fact. As a Zionist, he has many dealings with Palestine. Well, it turns out that the best colonists in this new Jewish homeland are the Russian Jews. Why exactly he could not satisfactorily explain, but he stated categorically that the fact itself was beyond any doubt. 'Unfortunately,' Melchett added, 'many of the Russian Jews wanted to go back to the USSR.'

* * *

One more interesting detail from my talk with McGowan. When I mentioned in the course of conversation that we have at our disposal a powerful air fleet in Primore, which, in the event of an emergency, is capable of destroying Japanese cities, McGowan's eyes lit up with delight and he exclaimed with joyous enthusiasm: 'That's really good! Really excellent!'

Oh, how the English desire it, how they wish to make a cat's-paw of us in the Far East! Nothing doing. Please join in within the frame of 'collective security' – then something might be arranged.

2 July

Abyssinia is the focus of attention today.[55] The English are in a bit of a fix. Yesterday's parliamentary session was interesting. The project of ceding to Abyssinia a tiny piece of British Somalia, including the port of Zeila, caused an absolute uproar in parliament! Yells from the members' benches when Hoare said that parliament should 'trust' the executive! Someone even shouted: 'Hitler!'

I don't know how the British government will extricate itself from this difficult situation, but if the genius of British diplomacy has not yet died, then Baldwin, taking his cue from long-distance imperialist policy, should have drawn up and implemented approximately the following plan: on the basis of the acknowledged indivisibility of the communiqué of 3 February, Great Britain agrees to form a united front with France and the USSR. Then the three governments immediately bring it to Mussolini's notice (while the war in Africa has not yet begun) that if the League of Nations declares Italy an aggressor, they will be forced to impose economic sanctions on her. In particular, Great Britain will close the Suez Canal to Italy. At the same time, Great Britain and France let Mussolini understand that if he renounces aggression against Abyssinia and agrees to allow the entire conflict to be resolved by the League of Nations, the latter will be prepared in a short while to give Italy, on the conditions of a League of Nations mandate, one of the former German colonies in Africa (say, Cameroon or Togo) that are presently the mandates of England and France. If Great Britain and France were to find the strength and resolution to implement a plan like this, not only would the Abyssinian problem be settled for many years to come, and not only would the prestige of the League of Nations be considerably raised, but the united front of Great Britain, France, Italy and the USSR against the German threat would be consolidated, and the paths to relative calm in Europe would be opened. Can Britain and France find the requisite strength and determination? I doubt it. But time will tell.

8 July

The more far-sighted representatives of the British bourgeoisie evidently share my views as to how Britain and France could settle the Italo-Abyssinian conflict while remaining true to their own system. Sir George Paish,[i] for example, unexpectedly called on me today. With a long preamble and a certain secretiveness, he shared with me 'the thoughts that came into his head'. Italy should be given a colony in Africa to calm her down. Which colony? Paish, for some reason, would like it to be Tunisia. I laughed and asked him why the 'bone' he intends to throw to Italy should necessarily wear a French costume?… Paish was a little embarrassed and hastened to add that England should certainly make its own 'sacrifice', too. Paish reckons that Italy might be presented with a former German colony in Africa, like Cameroon or Togo. Most remarkable of all, however, was Paish's final suggestion, 'of an absolutely confidential and amicable nature', that I should try to sway the British and French governments in the direction indicated. I laughed and said that it was none of my business. Since it is England and France who have to make 'sacrifices', let those Englishmen and Frenchmen who consider these 'sacrifices' essential raise the question. Paish had a long think and decided to discuss his plan with Sir Herbert Samuel.[ii]

9 July

Vansittart asked to see me in order 'to state his case'.

He began with the newspaper hoax started by [name indecipherable] (former diplomatic correspondent with the *Daily Telegraph*, a Germanophile) about V.'s putative appointment as ambassador in Paris. V. refuted the false rumours completely and assured me again (on the basis now of a month's work with Hoare) that the new foreign secretary was a 'realist' (meaning *pro-French* and *anti-German*) and that V. could get along well with him. He told me that the speech Hoare was going to make in parliament on 11 July would clear the air and please us: Hoare, it seems, is expected to make a firm statement about

---

[i] George Paish, English economist at London School of Economics, 1932–38.
[ii] Herbert Samuel (1st Viscount Samuel), Liberal MP, 1902–18 and 1929–35; secretary of state for home affairs, 1931–32; leader of the Liberal Party, 1931–35.

the indivisibility of western and eastern security and to say a few warm words about Anglo-Soviet relations. We'll see.

Naturally, V. defended the naval treaty.[56] He remarked in passing that he himself was also in favour of signing it. The reasons? There are two: (1) Better something than nothing – it was necessary to take Hitler at his word and oblige him to build no more than 35% of the British tonnage; (2) If agreement had not been achieved and the British government, spurred by the inevitable naval arms race, had to raise taxes in a year or two, there would be a great uproar in England and accusations that the British government had rejected Germany's promising proposal just to please France. Not only would the government have been harmed, but so too would the very idea of Franco-British cooperation, which V. considers fundamental.

These considerations do explain the British government's conduct in part, but only in part. In my view, there is more to it, namely: (1) electoral considerations: the Conservatives and Labour are desperately scrapping for the pacifist vote, and the naval treaty can be presented to the electorate as the first real step on the way to cutting or limiting arms in a sphere as important to England as that of the navy; (2) declining belief in the effectiveness of collective security and the ensuing desire 'to seize the moment' by concluding advantageous bilateral agreements, without worrying too much about possible implications; (3) the anti-Soviet factor: why not strengthen Germany in the Baltic just in case? Why not tie up the 'Soviets' in Europe? Who knows, perhaps one day they will want to bring the Communist Manifesto to the peoples of the West at the point of the bayonet? Who knows, perhaps one day the dream of many British Conservatives – a crusade by capitalist Europe against the workers' and peasants' state – will come true? To tell the truth, this dream has become less and less realistic over recent years, but who can know for sure?...

We also spoke about Lithuania, among other things. The British government is preparing a joint démarche with France and Italy. They want to demand 'free' elections to the Memel Seim on 29 September without any authoritarian violation of electoral law, and that the future government should be formed in accordance with the results of the ballot. V. believes that this is necessary in order to pave the way to an Eastern Pact. I objected sharply: why should pressure be exerted on Lithuania alone? Lithuania has her own well-founded grievances against Germany. Why is it not demanded that Hitler stop his Nazi propaganda in Memel? We do not believe that Hitler is delaying the conclusion of an Eastern Pact because of Lithuania alone. Were this pretext to be removed, he would find another. Moreover, we are not jumping for joy about an Eastern Pact stipulating non-aggression, consultation and isolation of the aggressor. Where is the guarantee that Hitler will observe it? But an Eastern Pact of mutual assistance is quite another matter… V. was a little confused, but he tried to defend himself according to the well-loved English argument: half a loaf is better than none. I can't say that V. made a particularly convincing case.

Another curious moment is worthy of note. While criticizing the methods by which the naval treaty was being concluded, I pointed out that a united front of 'collective security and peace', pooling Britain, France, the USSR, the Little Entente and other nations, had been forming gradually within the frame of the League of Nations in the past year, though not without difficulties and wavering. (The stages of the process: Barthou's visit to London last June, the communiqué of 3 February, Eden's visit to Moscow, Stresa, Geneva.) It could be expected that the front would be consolidated to such an extent in the next six to twelve months that the possibility might arise for more fruitful negotiations with Germany on the settlement of the European problem. V. suddenly interrupted me and exclaimed: 'Oh, no, that will need much more time.'

I smiled to myself. My manoeuvre had exposed an important element in V.'s general stand on the German question.

7 September

Here is an outline of Great Britain's position in the world as I see it:

(1) In general, GB belongs to the category of states which are satisfied with their possessions. This is 'satiated imperialism'. Its concern is not the conquering of new territories, but the retaining of old ones. Hence the support of the status quo and of peace and the fear of any serious war as a threat to the integrity of the Empire. A re-division of the world can only be carried out at the expense of GB – whether wholly or partially. From the point of view of world politics, GB is a <u>conservative</u> force striving to avoid, as far as possible, great changes in the current state of affairs.

(2) British imperialists experienced a sense of danger twice in the post-war period. First in 1917 through 1920 – the Russian Revolution (my conversation with Churchill on 14 June this year). The reaction was intervention and blockade, which failed in their purpose. This fear subsided gradually (in zigzag fashion) over the following 15 years. Today British imperialists, represented by such prominent figures as Churchill, Vansittart, Eden and others, subjectively believe that the USSR carries no immediate danger for GB because it is preoccupied with its internal affairs. Furthermore, they still cherish the hope (yet to be fully extinguished) of the internal regeneration of the Soviet Union, in the sphere of foreign policy at least. There is talk of the onset of NEP in Soviet foreign policy (entry to the League of Nations, mutual assistance pacts with France and Czechoslovakia, etc.), which might open up favourable opportunities for the bourgeois world. The above representatives of British imperialism are

opposed by others (like Montagu Norman,[i] Hailsham, Lord Lloyd,[ii] Hilton Young and others) who have not changed their attitude to the USSR; but their fear, too, has also dulled in recent times. So fear of the Russian Revolution as the major immediate threat to the British Empire has weakened considerably in conservative quarters. The possibility of a calmer attitude to the USSR has emerged. In the opinion of many Conservatives (such as B. [presumably Beaverbrook] for one), the 'capitalism vs. communism' problem may not become topical in England for another 40–50 years. In the meantime, why not try using the Soviet Union's rejuvenated might in their international political game? These cold utilitarian considerations, however, sometimes retreat when fear resurfaces, elicited by a revolutionary outburst in some country or a new event suggestive of the 'Red danger' (the Comintern congress).

(3) British imperialists felt themselves endangered for the second time when the Japanese seized Manchuria, and especially when Hitler came to power in Germany. They did not want to give credence to this danger. Even today they do not want to recognize it fully and draw the proper conclusions. Traditions of 'alliance' with Japan and the balance-of-power policy on the European continent stand in the way. So, too, even more prominently, do the deeply rooted and only temporarily subdued traditions of hostility towards 'Russia' and Sovietism. But irrefutable facts force the British imperialists, step by step and against their will, to arrive at the unpleasant conclusions that an ever-increasing danger is looming over the head of the Empire, primarily from Japan and Germany; and that they will once again have to think seriously about how to protect their gigantic possessions.

(4) How? At first, the British imperialists reasoned along habitual and traditional lines: the impending danger must be diverted in 'a safe direction'. Let the aggressive energy of Japan and Germany be directed against the USSR. Let the inevitable re-division of the world be carried out at our expense. In 1932–33, British imperialists dreamed persistently (and they did not only dream!) of a Soviet–Japanese war which, weakening both sides, would ease their own position in the Far East. Later they toyed with the idea of giving Hitler a free hand in Eastern Europe, in order to weaken both the USSR and Germany and divert the German threat from Western Europe. However, contrary to the expectations of the British imperialist leaders, these projects were hard to realize, for two reasons: (a) the rapidly growing might of the USSR; and (b) sharp disagreements between the imperialist powers, particularly Germany and France. The prospect of an imminent Japanese–Soviet war became quite

---

[i] Montagu Collet Norman, governor of the Bank of England, then president of the Bank of England, 1920–44.
[ii] George Ambrose Lloyd (1st Baron Lloyd), high commissioner for Egypt and Sudan, 1925–29; secretary of state for the colonies and leader of the House of Lords, 1940–41.

unrealistic in the spring of 1934 (or rather, the government arrived at the conclusion that a war between Japan and the USSR would likely result in victory for the latter, got scared, and set about opposing the outbreak of war in the Far East). The idea of using Germany against the USSR still excites the imagination of influential conservative circles, but more and more of them gradually perceive the enormous risk of such an adventure and the great likelihood of Britain's involvement in a new world war, with all the ensuing implications. Ultimately, although the British imperialist leaders have not parted with the idea of the 'safe channelling' of Japanese and German aggression at the expense of the USSR, the idea has lost its initial attraction in view of the difficulties and risks of its realization. The split in the British imperialist elite is evidence of that. While some of the Conservatives (Norman, Hailsham and others) are still dreaming of a crusade against the USSR and are looking for an agreement with Japan and Germany with the participation of France (and Italy if possible), another group (Churchill, Eden, Vansittart and others) finds it more practical at the given moment to establish a bloc of countries that do not want war, i.e. primarily those countries that are 'satisfied' with their possessions: GB, France, the Little Entente, the Balkan Entente, Scandinavia and, on certain conditions, the USSR. (Churchill: 'a defensive union of all countries fearing Germany'; a modernized Entente, according to Vansittart, etc.) Vacillation persists in regard to the USSR – to admit or not to admit? – and there are fears of the Comintern. The struggle between the two tendencies continues, which gives British foreign policy its zigzagging shape, its lack of clarity and uncertainty.

(5) The moment is gradually nearing, however, when the British government has to decide whether it is with or against the USSR. It tries to delay this moment any way it can, and is seeking the possibility of at least temporary and partial agreements with Japan (a modus vivendi in China) and Germany (the naval treaty). All the same, British imperialism will have to 'show its colours' in the not-too-distant future.

(6) GB's military weakness is another important factor leading to ambiguity and vacillation in British foreign policy. There is no doubt that British imperialism wasted no less than seven or eight years from the point of view of the 'normal' development of its armaments. The reasons: powerful pacifism among the masses; the influence of Labourites and pacifists such as Mander[i] and Cecil; the League of Nations; and the existence of Weimar Germany and (until 1931) a relatively peaceful Japan. As a result, when Nazi Germany and a highly aggressive Japan were born, GB turned out to be weak both at sea and in the air. GB will need two or three years to restore its minimum combat efficiency in the

---

[i] Geoffrey Le Mesurier Mander, a Midlands industrialist, art collector and impassioned Liberal parliamentarian, 1929–45; an anti-appeaser and a crusader for the League of Nations in the 1930s; parliamentary private secretary to Sir Archibald Sinclair (minister for air), 1942–45.

air and more time and far more money to achieve the same goal at sea (nearly half of the navy should be replaced). Hence the inevitable manoeuvring and the desire to avoid the worsening of relations with anyone – and primarily, at this moment in history, with Germany and Japan (and also the USSR).

(7) All this is vividly confirmed by GB's attitude to the Italo-Abyssinian conflict. The British government is definitely against the unleashing of war in Africa. The motives: (a) war there may easily trigger a world war and, consequently, a radical re-division of the world, which would hardly be beneficial for Britain; (b) more concretely: Italy, getting bogged down in Africa (which is inevitable), will cease to be an active factor in the European game; the present balance in Europe, poor as it is, will be shattered; Germany's room for manoeuvre will increase immensely, it will seize Austria in one form or another, and maybe Lithuania, thereby activating the abundant dynamic forces latent in this part of the world. The danger of a European war will increase tremendously, and GB will not be able to escape it – hence the very dangerous consequences for GB's position in the Far East and in other parts of the globe; (c) Italy's victory in Africa will give her the waters of Lake Tana (a threat to Sudan and Egypt), and inaugurate Italian expansion in Africa and Arabia, primarily to the detriment of British interests. Furthermore, a major European power would hover over the sea routes to India (Suez and Aden would lose their importance). On the other hand, Italy's failure would give a powerful impetus to the negro pan-African movement and create colossal troubles for GB in her numerous African colonies, where the rule of British imperialism rests mainly on the 'white man's prestige'. That is why GB will do her best to prevent an African war. If war does break out, GB will almost certainly do its utmost to localize and liquidate it as soon as possible (by offering to mediate, or by working out a compromise in which her own interests would not, of course, be forgotten). In the first period of war, especially if Italy were successful, GB would undoubtedly play dirty tricks on her, but in forms that would not lead to military conflict. If Italy were to fail, GB would also play dirty tricks on Abyssinia, but it would do so, once again, in a cautious manner, so as not to draw excessive indignation on the part of her numerous 'coloured' subjects.

(8) That group of British imperialists which supports the creation of a 'peace bloc' against Germany and Japan is currently groping for forms of closer contact with France (Baldwin's phrase: 'our frontier is on the Rhine', etc.) and with the USSR. As its next move in our direction, the group plans to grant the USSR a loan for a term of 20–25 years, with the simultaneous settlement of 'private claims' deriving from the Russian Revolution. A permanent trade treaty is also envisaged. Cazelet's and Marshall's propaganda and my talks with Ashton-Gwatkin and Leith-Ross this summer are highly indicative. The settlement scheme is approximately as follows. We agree to pay 10–15% of the 'private

claims' announced officially (about 250 million pounds during the 1929–31 talks). The 'homeless' gold of the tsarist government and former Russian banks that still sits immobile in the cellars of London banks (10–15 million pounds) will be used for this purpose. In addition, the USSR will obtain a loan to the tune of 30–50 million pounds for 20–25 years at 6% interest (the normal rate is 3.5%). The difference between the normal and actual interest will be spent on clearing 'private claims'. Such intentions prevail in the Finance Ministry and the Foreign Office (Ashton-Gwatkin). The Trade Ministry seems to prefer an alternative pattern: a loan for 5–6 years irrespective of debts and claims (Horace Wilson[i]), provided trade is secured. The Finance Ministry, on the contrary, would like to use the deal for strengthening its position in relation to other numerous debtors of GB who fail to pay. As for the Foreign Office, it wants to clear the decks and create the glue for the construction of a 'modernized Entente'. Now it is for us to decide whether or not to accept such a scheme for settling 'private claims'. It is a serious moment and much depends on our decision.

[Maisky spent his holiday in Copenhagen, Norway and Stockholm, on his way to a protracted stay at a sanatorium at Kislovodsk. Before his departure, he took his leave of Samuel Hoare. Their conversation left him with a grim impression that Hoare was 'fully prepared to reach a compromise with Germany on the basis of European Security'. His concerns were not allayed by his meeting with the more benign Baldwin, who constantly referred him to Hoare's speeches in parliament.[57] While in Moscow, Maisky found the Kremlin 'greatly perturbed' by rumours and snippets of information about French and British attempts to reconcile with Germany. The Anglo-German naval treaty made it 'doubt the friendliness of the Conservative government'. Maisky clearly feared that circumstances were propelling the Russians into an isolationist position. Although the danger of an immediate attack on the Soviet Union had receded, the Kremlin had become convinced that Germany was intent on breaking up Czechoslovakia and on bringing about *Anschluss* with Austria. The door to Germany, though, remained closed. While Schacht[ii] was anxious to promote trade, the embassy in Berlin was 'practically isolated from the German Government ... the diplomats might just as well not be there, they are made to feel "not wanted"'. At various meetings with Vansittart, some of which are described in the diary, Maisky appeared 'evidently very suspicious', posing endless questions, 'the one on which he was most pertinacious was whether there was any foundation at all for the rumours ... in regard to the possibility of an Anglo-Franco-German agreement, to which he added the corollary "at the expense of Russia"'. Maisky was little soothed by Vansittart's admission that it was 'an open secret that [Laval] liked, perhaps even preferred, the pastime of riding two horses at once ... it was quite possible ... that he would like to have some arrangement with Germany as well as with Russia'.[58]

---

[i] Sir Horace John Wilson, permanent secretary in Ministry of Labour, 1921–30; chief industrial adviser to the British government, 1930–39; seconded for special service with Chamberlain, 1937–40.

[ii] Horace Greeley Schacht, president of Reichsbank, 1923–30 and 1933–39; minister of economics, 1934–37; minister without portfolio, 1939–43.

Maisky now felt that the ground was quickly shifting under his feet. In a strictly personal letter to Litvinov, he expressed fears that he might be asked to replace Troyanovsky as ambassador in Washington, and raised fierce professional and personal arguments against his transfer:

> From the business point of view it would be completely irrational for me to leave England. I know well the country, the people, the mores and the customs. I have many varied connections here, accumulated over ten years ... As far as I can tell and judge, I have succeeded in winning a decent position here in governmental, public and political circles. In particular, I have very good relations with Vansittart. Each day many new doors open before me and endless opportunities emerge. It is only now, as plenipotentiary in England, that I am fully in my element ... and I am in a position to give the maximum diplomatic benefit to the USSR. It would be a shame if at this very moment I had to leave England, and a new plenipotentiary would have to start accumulating capital over again.
>
> From a personal viewpoint I prefer England to any other country except the USSR ... I would really not want to go to the USA: I have never felt any sympathy for that country, Washington's foreign policy is of little interest, it's deeply provincial, and it doesn't promise us anything positive in the near future. A.A. cannot think of crossing the ocean without horror.[59]]

4 November

The new Bulgarian envoy Radev[i] paid me a visit. A middle-aged man, of professorial appearance and build, speaks decent Russian. He is writing a treatise on the history of Russo-Bulgarian relations in a spirit antagonistic to tsarism. He has already published two volumes and is preparing the third. He asked for help in getting material from our archives. Radev has been somewhat infected by Pan-Slavism. He recalled the Slavophiles, who asserted that the Russian nation is destined to resolve the 'social question' and thereby fulfil its special global 'mission'. 'And now this has come true!' he exclaimed. He spoke at length about Bulgaria's desire to live in peace and tranquillity and to maintain good relations with the USSR, France and all her neighbours. He became agitated when I told him that we would welcome Bulgaria's accession to the Balkan Entente, insisting that it was not so essential: peace could be achieved without it. On parting, he expressed the wish to meet more often and to speak heart-to-heart.

6 November

Following my absence of nearly three months from England, I visited Hoare to renew contact. Hoare was so very polite that I began to feel somewhat ill at

---

[i] Simeon Radev, Bulgarian ambassador to London, 1935–38.

ease. There's too much sugariness and formality in this civility. You can't help being on your guard...

We spoke, of course, about the Italo-Abyssinian conflict.

Hoare started complaining about the French: they are far too optimistic in thinking that the conflict can be settled in a trice. The untangling of the African knot, alas, will be a lengthy process, to judge by the evidence. The Italian demands remain absolutely unacceptable to Abyssinia, as they do to the League of Nations and England. It would be best of all to end the war without winners and losers; peace in the future would be more stable. (H. listed the Vienna Congress, the 1866 Austro-Prussian war, and other historic examples.) But will it turn out like that? Nobody knows. Mussolini has taken the bit between his teeth, listens to no one, and decides everything by himself, while his advisers cringe before their dictator, telling him what he wants to hear.

I asked: does even Grandi behave like this?

H. spread his arms and said: 'All Mussolini's advisers strive only to please their Duce. As a result, he is misinformed. The harshness of the British response surprised him. He thought that Rothermere[i] and Beaverbrook had expressed the true opinion of the nation. That was a mistake. Now it is difficult for Mussolini to retreat.'

I briefed H. on our position. We have no quarrels with Italy. The political and economic relations between the USSR and Italy have been good for the last ten years. We have no interests in Africa. If we are currently taking a stand against Italy, it is only as a loyal member of the League of Nations and because we want to teach a lesson to serve as a warning for any future aggressors. Italy is not a very serious aggressor, but there are more dangerous candidates in the world, particularly in Europe. An appropriate precedent must be set for them.

H. assured me that the British position is exactly the same. England also has no interests of its own in the conflict. She is guided, he claims, purely by loyalty to the League of Nations and the desire to admonish a more dangerous potential aggressor who might appear in three, five or ten years (H., like me, does not regard Italy as a terrifying aggressor). H. formulated his thought in such a way that it was clear he had Germany in mind. The French, he said, do not understand the fundamental importance of sanctions in this case and hamper their application. True, the situation has improved, but insufficiently.

I inquired whether the rumours that someone was ready to offer Germany political and economic compensation for its participation in sanctions were true. H. categorically denied this. I expressed my satisfaction and added:

---

[i] Viscount Harold Harmsworth Rothermere, British newspaper proprietor and Conservative politician.

'Indeed, to reward Germany for participating in sanctions against Italy would be the same as treating influenza with an inoculation against typhus.'

H. laughed and said we shouldn't worry. He also said that Canada had proposed in Geneva to ban oil, coal, iron and other exports to Italy, without the knowledge of the British delegation, and that he was not optimistic about oil sanctions: the USA may sell them short. Roosevelt and Hull are ready to assist the League of Nations, but they do not control the powerful oil trusts. The announcement of oil sanctions without the USA's participation would have no practical significance.

In conclusion, I delicately expressed our dissatisfaction with a special agency organized in Geneva alongside the League of Nations, a certain 'Anglo-French conference' engaged in Abyssinian and other affairs. Our delegation in the League of Nations does not even know what this agency does or what decisions it makes.

H. blushed a little and shifted the blame onto the Belgian premier, Van Zeeland.[i] The latter, he said, overdid it at the last meeting when he spoke about a mandate allegedly obtained by Britain and France from the League of Nations to settle the Italo-Abyssinian conflict. That was absolutely false. There was no such mandate. H. had not known what Van Zeeland was going to say, otherwise he would have pulled him up. It had been awkward, but there was nothing to lose sleep over. Even if Britain and France undertake some preparatory measures to terminate the conflict, final termination will be carried out within the framework of the League of Nations and through its agency.

8 November

I saw Ashton-Gwatkin at the Foreign Office. He sits in the 'tower', as he calls his office on the fourth floor, admires the beautiful view of St James's Park, and guides the 'economic department' of the Foreign Office. In Moscow he said: 'I'm the same in London as Rozenblyum[ii] is in Moscow...'

A.G. is satisfied with his trip to the USSR, but now he is preoccupied with a very difficult problem: how to expand Anglo-Soviet trade. What do I think about it?

I replied that I evaluate the situation thus: (1) Anglo-Soviet trade based on the current trade treaty is nearing its natural limits; (2) further trade expansion is feasible if the USSR is afforded serious credit opportunities; (3) the system of Anglo-Soviet trade financing through the export department of the Trade Ministry has become outdated; we prefer buying for cash, which means that

[i] Paul Guillaume van Zeeland, prime minister of Belgium, 1935–37.
[ii] Boris Danilovich Rozenblyum, head of the economic department of the USSR People's Commissariat for Foreign Affairs, 1933–38. Victim of the repressions; rehabilitated posthumously.

we are limited in the scope of our purchases by current revenues from export and gold-mining; (4) if the British government really wishes to expand Anglo-Soviet trade, it should think about granting the USSR a long-term loan. We ourselves shall not take the initiative in this, for on the whole we are satisfied with the current state of affairs.

A.G. agreed with me and himself began to dwell on the necessity of granting a loan to the USSR. The trouble is, what to do with the old claims? If the old claims are not liquidated, it will be impossible to pass a loan in parliament.

I answered: 'Don't disturb old ghosts.' Debts and claims are highly unpopular in the USSR. Moreover, they bring back the spectre of intervention in the minds of the Soviet masses and stir up old, now half-forgotten feelings of hatred towards the interventionists, including England. What would be the point? Who needs it?...

A.G. rubbed the bridge of his nose and confessed I was right, while stating, on the other hand, that some elimination of 'old ghosts' was inevitable, otherwise they would always lie in our path. Summing up, he said: 'We need to give it some thought! We might think up some wheeze or other...'

I wished A.G. every success.

13 November

I called on Collier in the Foreign Office to 'renew contact' after my leave. I'd been expecting a general chat, but our conversation took a much more serious turn. C. informed me (on his own initiative, without my prompting him) that the draft of a 20-year loan to the USSR had been submitted for consideration to the Foreign Office and the trade and finance ministries. The Foreign Office supports the draft, but the final decision does not lie with the FO alone. In all probability, the draft will be brought to the Cabinet for consideration after the election. I asked whether the British government was going to tie the loan to a demand for compensation to old claimants, etc., and stressed that in that case a loan would be out of the question for us. We are not pursuing a loan, and certainly not one with 'addenda'. C. replied that the British government understood this perfectly well, and that the loan would be simply a loan, unrelated to the claims. We shall see. In any event, this information deserves serious attention.

Then C. expressed his opinion that Hitler is disinclined to embark on an adventure in Lithuania at the moment, mostly because of a lack of agreement with Poland on this question. But Austria and possibly Czechoslovakia are in greater danger. If the Italo-Abyssinian conflict lasts much longer, Hitler may yield to temptation. Which is why the British are so keen to terminate the conflict. This might be achieved in the next month or two.[60]

I inquired about the course of the British government's negotiations with Mussolini on the Mediterranean issue. The British government, it transpires, is playing cat-and-mouse with M. It is demanding that one more division should be withdrawn from Libya (two divisions all in all). In exchange, the British are prepared to remove two battleships from Gibraltar (but not from Alexandria). Whether the two actions should be synchronized is of secondary importance. The British are ready to make a fine gesture: if agreement is achieved, they may take the first step and withdraw the battleships from Gibraltar, keep them nearby in the ocean for a few days and see what M. does. It is not difficult to bring the battleships back to Gibraltar if necessary; much easier than to bring a division to Libya. Yet M. is evading the agreement offered to him and asks for a Mediterranean pact that would guarantee him freedom of communication with Africa in order to continue his Abyssinian adventure unhindered. C. added: Well, we shall wait! We can take our time. M. will see sense.

14 November

Reading the fresh issue of the *Daily Worker* on the morning of 7 November, Agniya showed me the following announcement:

DIMITROV'S MESSAGE TO ELECTORS

Dimitrov,[i] the helmsman of the Communist International, loved by the masses throughout the world for his heroic stand at the Reichstag fire trial, will write a special message to the electors of Britain in Saturday's 12-page 'Daily Worker'.

Readers are mobilising all over the country to get this important message and the pictorial supplement which exposes the National Government to wide masses of workers.

Extra orders for London so far are 23,716. Rhondda is out to sell 100 quires extra.

Those workers who recently left the ILP [Independent Labour Party] in London are right at the front in the preparations, and are out to show what they can do on Saturday.

North-West London have in most cases doubled the quantities they sold on the last sales day.

They aim to sell 3,024 extra copies.

---

[i] Georgi Mikhailovich Dimitrov, Bulgarian communist, served as the secretary-general of the Comintern, 1935–43.

This greatly alarmed me. The effect of such a message on Anglo-Soviet relations was beyond doubt. It could hardly help Pollitt[i] either: all types of Englishmen (including workers) dislike it very much when foreigners 'interfere in their domestic affairs'. I sent a telegram to Moscow. The reply came the next day: The message should not be published. So it was not published, either on the 9th or later. An unpleasant conflict had been averted.

That there would have been a conflict is certain. I visited Vansittart in the Foreign Office in the afternoon of 8 November, after the directive not to publish had been received from Moscow. We discussed different matters. At the end of the conversation, Vansittart raised the *Daily Worker* cutting from his table and said with the most charming smile:

I'll never understand you, Soviet people. Tell me, please, why should the Soviet citizen Dimitrov send such a message to Harry Pollitt by Soviet telegraph, which is controlled by the Soviet government? Please do not interpret my words as a formal political démarche – that's not what I want to do. But, being a supporter of Anglo-Soviet rapprochement, I must tell you that had Dimitrov's message been published on 9 November, it would have been treated as nothing other than explicit 'interference in the internal affairs' of Great Britain. Just think of the hullabaloo that would have followed in France if a British political figure had addressed French electors with an appeal for them to elect Herriot[ii] instead of Laval. Dimitrov wanted to do something similar with regard to England. He wanted to tell British electors: elect communists and Labourites, overthrow the National Government!

I interrupted V. and observed that the Soviet government and Comintern are different entities and that the Soviet government has no power over Dimitrov and is not responsible for him, etc. – things which I had had to repeat many times in similar circumstances and in various countries. V. listened to me quietly and uttered with the air of one augur addressing another: 'I would have understood if you'd had a chance of bringing, say, 150 deputies into the House. That might have been worth risking. But here the election of one or two communists is at stake. What practical significance can this have? Is it worth spoiling relations with England for this? I find the game not worth the candle.'

I laughed and repeated that V.'s admonitions were misaddressed.

---

[i] Harry Pollitt, one of the founders of the Communist Party of Great Britain (CPGB) in 1920 and its general secretary, 1929–39 and 1941–56.
[ii] Édouard Herriot, leader of the Radical Party, 1919–35; premier of France, 1924–25, 1926 and 1932; president of the Chamber of Deputies, 1936–40.

15 November

So, last night the five of us (Agniya, I, the Kagans and Mironov) sat in the Royal Automobile Club and listened to radio broadcasts about the election results until 2 a.m. We walked for a while along streets that were unusually calm for an election night. Today, we've learned the basic outcome of yesterday's voting. Well, the results are not bad, though they differ from my expectations. I thought that about 200 Labourites would win seats, but only 150 or 160 have been elected. As for the Liberals, my forecast was right: there are 20 in the new House! There is pleasant news: the Communist Gallacher[i] got in in Scotland. He is the first Communist since 1922, when the unfortunate Newbold[ii] was elected. There are grounds to believe that Gallacher will be more successful. The government majority is 250 (instead of the former 411) – a large majority, but significantly weaker than before. MacDonald failed pitifully, together with his son...

The election results are not bad from our point of view. The National Government has become considerably weaker, while the opposition has grown in quantity and quality. From having about a 30% mandate, the opposition has garnered nearly half the votes. Its political weight has increased. The National Government will have to pursue a more careful policy toward the USSR and it will have to emphasize its loyalty to the League of Nations. It will be more difficult for it to engage in any anti-Soviet intrigue. The chances of improving Anglo-Soviet relations are greater. If only Labour would not spoil everything with their absurd Germanophilia! We shall see.[61]

14 December

The situation becomes more and more mysterious.

On 11 September Hoare made his famous speech in Geneva, in which he resolutely stated that from now on British foreign policy would be the policy of the League of Nations. His speech was received here and abroad as a great, almost historic milestone in the sphere of international politics. For the next two months, Baldwin, Hoare, Eden and all the other members of the British government declared, emphasized and trumpeted their loyalty to the promise made on 11 September. When, in the run-up to the election, the Labourites (and especially Ewer in the *Daily Herald*) launched a campaign which accused the British government of using the League of Nations merely as an electoral

---

[i] William Gallacher, socialist agitator; chairman of Clyde Workers' Committee, 1914–18; leading member of the Communist Party and Communist International from 1920 onwards; president of the Communist Party, 1956–63; Communist MP for the Western Division of Fife, 1935–50.
[ii] John Turner Walton Newbold, first Communist MP, 1922–23; disillusioned with communism he joined the Labour Party and supported National Labour after 1931.

slogan that would be immediately forgotten, and which argued that Baldwin was preparing a reform of the League in order to render it innocuous from the point of view of the imperialists, the Conservatives were livid. Hoare delivered an indignant speech in Chelsea and castigated Ewer in the strongest terms during our conversation of 6 November. The government's declarations were taken seriously not only by the Conservatives, but also by the Liberals and many Labourites. Hundreds of Conservative deputies entered the House on the strength of their fidelity to the League of Nations. Mander, a Liberal MP and ardent supporter of the League of Nations, told me with satisfaction ten days ago, on 3 December: 'Whatever the shortcomings of the new government, we can say for sure that it will be a government of the League of Nations.'

I understood the situation in this way. Today it is advantageous for the British government to keep the League of Nations flag flying, because of the Abyssinian conflict. For this reason, it plays the part of incorruptible knight of collective security. In unfavourable circumstances, when such a position may prove disadvantageous for the British government, it will not hesitate to betray the League of Nations, but it will do so skilfully, smoothly, without a fuss and with a pious expression on its face.

I had assumed that loyalty to the League of Nations remained very much in the interests of the British government.

And, all of a sudden, the Hoare–Laval 'peace plan'[62] appears in Paris! A plan that marks the most brazen, most impudent betrayal of the principles of the League of Nations! And when? Three weeks after the election! And at what precise moment? The moment of the manifest failure of the Italian army in Abyssinia and of ever-increasing problems for Mussolini at home!

It's beyond understanding! What's it all about? Who is to blame?

There are two theories. The first, supported mostly by the *Manchester Guardian*, is that Hoare is guilty of everything. According to this version, he exceeded his authority and, pressed by Laval, who had skilfully put the wind up his British colleague, agreed to the 'peace plan', thereby committing the entire Cabinet. Baldwin, faced with the choice between Hoare's resignation and approval of the Paris agreement, took the course of rotten compromise and consented to the 'illegitimate child' of his foreign secretary, merely adding a few corrections and modifications.

The second theory, defended by the *Daily Herald*, asserts that the responsibility lies not with Hoare but with the Cabinet itself. The paper claims that the Cabinet began to prepare something like the Paris 'peace plan' some six weeks ago, and that Hoare signed his agreement with Laval with his government's blessing in his pocket.

Who is right? Hard to say at the present time.

But I am prepared to accept that both theories may be correct to an extent. Knowing the political and diplomatic customs here, I can easily imagine the following course of events. Six weeks ago the Foreign Office may have begun discussing various – minimal and maximal – versions of the future peace treaty (not for nothing did Vansittart express the hope to me on 8 November that the war in Africa would end by Christmas). Strict secrecy was maintained until the election. After the election, contact with Laval was established (Peterson[i] went to Paris). The potion was brewing in the imperialists' infernal kitchen. When Hoare went to Switzerland 'on holiday', he was given merely the most general instructions: do your best to end the conflict as soon as possible, even by 'correcting' Abyssinian frontiers and offering Italy some economic privileges in Negus's[ii] empire (after all, something must be given to Mussolini!). Hoare arrived in Paris. Laval pressed him, making it clear that England could not count on France in an armed conflict with Italy. He categorically refused to support oil sanctions... What was to be done? Hoare felt a surge of imperialist sentiments (which came so naturally to him) and decided to show that he was not some Simon or other, capable only of babbling on. He could be an Alexander the Great of British foreign policy. And he showed it. As for the details of the agreement, he reported them to the Cabinet only after Laval had informed Mussolini. The Cabinet, guided by the considerations mentioned above, dared not disown their foreign secretary.

Such are my conjectures. Am I right? I don't know. We shall see.

Meanwhile, a real political crisis has erupted in England. Today's newspapers report that Hoare is hurrying home and will speak in the House on 19 December. While skating in England, Hoare managed to break his nose. For this reason, he will not leave his home for a few days. How symbolic! Yes, Hoare has broken his nose politically as well as physically. Will he and will the government draw the proper conclusions? Will Hoare resign? We shall see. To tell the truth, I doubt it.

16 December

A visit out of the blue from Sir George Paish yesterday, even though it was Sunday. He'd obviously come on behalf of the League of Nations Union. He related the following details of the 'peace plan'. Baldwin, as well as Hoare, is responsible for it and was informed about it in due time. Laval 'frightened' Hoare (and Baldwin) by refusing to support the British fleet in the Mediterranean,

---

[i] Sir Maurice Drummond Peterson, acting high commissioner for Egypt, 1934; minister to Bulgaria, 1936–38; ambassador to Iraq, 1938–39; ambassador to Spain, 1939–40; undersecretary of state, Foreign Office, 1942; ambassador in Ankara, 1944–46, and in Moscow, 1946–49.
[ii] Haile Selassie, the Ethiopian emperor.

lest Mussolini decide to attack it as a result of oil sanctions. The British sounded out Yugoslavia, but she, too, refused (most likely at France's bidding) to help England in case of need with sea ports, aeroplanes, etc... That is why Hoare and Baldwin approved the Paris plan. How easily 'frightened' the British ministers are! It is as if they want to be 'frightened'. It's impossible to believe that Mussolini would take the risk of attacking the British navy, even under the worst circumstances. And suppose he did attack – would the British not be able to hit back? These are all children's tales. Nobody was 'frightened'. It seems to me that the British actions proceeded from the desire to have done with the Italo-Abyssinian conflict and free their hands to act in the Far East and Europe (Germany!). At the same time, they want an end to the conflict which would not harm the 'prestige' of the white man. Despite the widely spread rumours to the contrary, the English do not want to overthrow Mussolini: it is too dangerous in terms of foreign policy and in terms of facilitating class struggle.

But Paish did not come to see me just to share this information. He had a 'practical' project in store, as usual. Here it is. The British government, by all appearances, will defend itself by laying all the blame on the French. This may give rise to an outburst of anti-French sentiment in England, which would merely play into the hands of the Germans. There is only one way to prevent such a development: to overthrow Laval and put Herriot in his place. Couldn't I help in this matter? Needless to say, I politely declined this task.

1936

20 January

Wickham Steed[i] lunched with me. We discussed a variety of issues and happened to be in full agreement on matters of European politics. I presented my theory of German expansion to the south and south-east, and Steed concurred with me throughout. He said that Austen Chamberlain approved of his letter in *The Times* of 1 January.

Then we talked about the king's illness, and Steed related some interesting details concerning George V and his predecessors. On Victoria: in the 1880s, as a result of certain romantic involvements after the death of Albert,[ii] she began to lose her popularity, and the republican movement began to emerge in the country. But in the 1890s the affairs came to an end, the queen's reputation was re-established, and the republican movement subsided. On King Edward VII: Steed once found himself among the royal retinue in Karlsbad, where the king had gone for a cure. King Edward had to send a complimentary telegram to the Boy Scouts in England. The king's secretary asked Steed if he would write the draft. Steed did so. The next day the secretary ruefully informed Steed: 'Nothing doing, I'm afraid. The king read your draft and said: these are not the words of a father-king to his children, but an editorial from *The Times*. This won't do for me.' Edward composed the telegram himself; according to Steed, it really was much better than the one he had written.

King George also wrote most of his own speeches and addresses to the nation. A few years ago, when Steed was still working at *The Times*, the king's secretary asked him to send a man to draft the monarch's speeches. Steed sent a brilliant journalist. A month later the journalist returned to Steed in disappointment and said: 'I am not needed there at all. Whatever draft I tried to write, the king would rewrite it from scratch and barely a sentence of my

---

[i] Henry Wickham Steed, a BBC foreign correspondent and former editor of *The Times*, who endorsed 'The Protocols of the Elders of Zion', but despite his notorious anti-Semitism was early to warn of Hitler's intentions.

[ii] Prince Albert of Saxe-Coburg and Gotha, prince consort of Queen Victoria, 1840–61.

own would remain. I resigned my post in the palace.' Steed claims that in 1928, shortly before his illness, the king was in a very depressed frame of mind. He felt that he was coping poorly with his duties and steadily losing authority and respect among his subjects. He even toyed with the idea of abdication. Baldwin, who was prime minister at the time, tried to reassure the king and resolutely opposed abdication. In December 1928, George fell seriously ill. The general sympathy displayed by the public during his illness impressed the king deeply. He became calmer, having decided that the Empire needed him; his will to live came sharply into focus. This psychological state greatly facilitated the king's almost miraculous recovery seven years ago. 'Perhaps the same will to live will save the king even now,' Steed concluded. 'Who knows?...'

21 January

King George V died yesterday.

Rumours about his illness were already circulating at Christmas. They were officially denied. The king even broadcast his Christmas appeal to the Empire and many, including Bernard Shaw, complimented the king publicly on his skill at speaking over the radio. Then all the rumours faded. Not until the evening of 17 January did a medical bulletin appear dedicated to the state of the king's health. Listeners were informed that the weakening of the king's cardiac activity 'gives cause for concern'. That was a very serious symptom and a serious warning. Things went from bad to worse. A prominent cardiologist was summoned to Sandringham, bulletins began to come out more often and their contents were ever more disquieting. On Sunday, 19 January, I notified Moscow by telegram of the possibility of the king's death and requested that condolence telegrams be sent in that event to the queen and the royal family from Kalinin,[i] and to Baldwin from Molotov. On 20 January, Agniya and I went to the cinema. On leaving the cinema at about 11 p.m., we saw on newspaper posters: 'The King Is Dying.' When we got home, we tuned in to the radio and began listening. There was a bulletin every quarter of an hour. The Kagans came over to listen with us. At 12.15 a.m. the radio announcer said with emotion: 'It is with deepest regret...' All was clear. The king had died at 11.55 p.m. on 20 January.

We woke up Falin (our chauffeur),[i] and the four of us (the Kagans and we) drove into town to see what was happening. The traffic was unusually heavy. There was a long black queue near Buckingham Palace, which was slowly passing the gates, on which hung a notification of the king's death. The

---

[i] Mikhail Ivanovich Kalinin, member of the Politburo, 1926–46, and chairman of the USSR Supreme Soviet, the titular head of state of the Soviet Union, 1938–46. Although he survived the purges, his wife was arrested, tortured and sent to a labour camp, from which she was released in 1945, a year before his death.

square in front of the palace and the adjacent streets were crammed with cars. A large body of policemen had a hard time trying to keep order. There was a restrained, intent silence, but there were no tears or hysterics – or perhaps these were concealed by darkness. We drove on to Fleet Street, which was noisy and lively. Newspaper boys carrying huge piles of fresh print were running in all directions, shouting: 'The king is dead!' The passers-by stopped them and hastily bought newspapers still smelling of ink. We also bought some. They were the next day's issues of all the major papers (*Daily Herald*, *Daily Express*, *Daily Mail* and others) and were almost entirely given over to the king's death. They already carried editorials on the subject, lengthy surveys of the king's reign, character sketches of George V as monarch and man, and salutations to the new king, Edward VIII. I checked my watch: the time was not yet 1 a.m. The king's heart stopped beating only an hour or so ago. London journals work fast! There is no doubt that the editorials, recollections and salutations were written in advance, and that the printing presses were just waiting for the signal to unleash millions of copies on the world, but all the same...

Memories of Mongolia came to mind. It sometimes happens there that relatives who, having grown tired of waiting for an old man to die, may carry him, still breathing, into the fields and leave him to the mercy of fate. Corpse-devouring dogs gather in a circle around the dying man and wait, gnashing their teeth, for the end (the dogs do not touch the half-dead)... Another country, another culture, another age, but don't these journalists who pen obituaries at the bedside of a still living man somewhat resemble the Mongolian corpse-devouring dogs?

I sent a telegram to Moscow suggesting that Litvinov, who is nearby in Geneva, should attend King George's funeral. Will they consent? We'll see. They ought to, otherwise it will look like a demonstration of deliberate coldness on our part, which politically would be highly undesirable for us right now.

[When Maisky first met King George in November 1932, he was astounded by the king's resemblance to his cousin, Tsar Nicholas II.[i] 'I thought he would look upon me as a ... murderer,' he confessed to Lady Vansittart, 'but it was quite different from what I had expected.' Maisky resented such insinuations, which were frequently made: 'After all, if we are regicides, if we killed Tsar Nicholas, you killed King Charles and the French sent Louis XVI to the guillotine.' 'Yes,' retorted Lady Vansittart, 'but that was two centuries ago and more, and you killed the entire imperial family.' As Maisky recalled, she then added, in a characteristic English reflex: 'Why! You even killed their dog!' The observant Lady Vansittart noticed tears in the eyes of Maisky as he joined in the funeral procession for the cousin of the tsar.[2]]

---

[i] Nicholas Alexandrovich Romanov (Nicholas II) was the last Russian emperor, 1894–1917, forced to abdicate after the 1917 February revolution and shot with his family by the Bolsheviks in July 1918.

30. Maisky welcomes the Litvinovs to the Soviet embassy in London.

26 January

M.M. [Litvinov] has just arrived. I travelled to Dover to meet him.

Concurrent with my telegram of 21 January, supplemented by another the next day, M.M. sent his own telegram advising Moscow to send a special delegation to the funeral consisting of himself and someone from the top ranks of the Red Army. We had had the same thought. As a result, the Central Executive Committee will be represented at the funeral by a delegation of three: Litvinov, Tukhachevsky and myself. Tukhachevsky and Putna, who arrived in Moscow only recently, will be in London tomorrow.

Agniya is very busy with the wreath we shall lay on the king's coffin. The wreath is very fine: white lilies and lilies of the valley, with red orchids in the centre. The black-and-red ribbon bears the inscription: 'From the Central Executive Committee of the USSR'. The papers have noted both the beauty of the wreath and the very fact of its laying.

M.M. is bright and full of life. He has just won a brilliant victory in Geneva on the question of the severance of relations with Uruguay. Gershelman and Petrov are accompanying him. M.M. will spend about four days in London.

28 January

The king's funeral finally took place today. It was all most solemn and imposing, but I will not give a detailed description of the ceremony, which can be found in the newspapers. I would like to record something else here, which was not mentioned in the press and probably never will be.

We've seen a right old mess here over the last eight days!

The king died the night of 20 January. I expected the Foreign Office and the doyen to inform all diplomats the next morning what they were to do. Nothing of the sort! Nobody told us a thing. Having waited in vain until lunchtime, I set about making inquiries myself. Alas, Neither Monck (chief of protocol in the Foreign Office) nor the doyen were to be found. I phoned the Swede [Palmstierna], an old-timer in London. He was at work, but he had nothing sensible to say to me. I called Vansittart's secretariat: they had nothing definite to tell me either, although the secretary did observe that, in his personal opinion, it would be a good idea if I paid a visit to his boss to convey my condolences. I called in, and it was just as well: the Swede was already with V., and the Pole [Raczyński] was next in line after me. Next came the question of the embassy's flag: for how long should it be kept at half-mast? Again, neither the Foreign Office nor the doyen could give exact advice. I decided that I should keep it that way till the day of the funeral, and that also proved correct: the other diplomats did the same. On 23 January the king's body was brought from Sandringham to London and the coffin was placed in Westminster Hall in parliament. Hundreds of thousands were filing past the coffin. Should diplomats take part in the procession? Neither the Foreign Office nor the doyen knew. Finally, the marshal of the diplomatic corps gave us a dozen tickets to join the procession without queuing. Agniya and I, Kagan, Ozersky and a few others from our diplomatic staff, processed through Westminster Hall. Who would be present at the funeral from the diplomatic corps? Heads of missions alone or mission members as well? Three days of utter confusion before we were finally told: only heads of missions should attend. Two days passed and we received a new instruction: only members of delegations sent specifically for the funeral should be present. Mission heads who were not members of the delegations were to stay at home. And the ladies? Were wives of ambassadors and envoys to attend the funeral? All week the answer was the same: no. So Agniya ceased worrying about what she would have to wear. Then all of a sudden, at about 6 p.m. on Saturday, 25 January, the marshal of the diplomatic corps phoned and said that ambassadors' wives were to attend the funeral and that they were to be dressed in black and wear long black veils (18 inches at the front and 1.5 yards at the back). On Monday, 27 January, Agniya had to rush around town to equip herself for the funeral. What suits should men wear at the funeral?

31. Mourning the death of King George V, cousin of Tsar Nicholas II.

All week long we couldn't get a plain answer. Civil servants at the Foreign Office thought that long black frock-coats would be needed (though none of the diplomats owned them). It was only on Saturday, 25 January, late in the evening, that it was decided that the dress code was finally fixed: tails with black waistcoat and white tie. On the evening of 27 January, the king gave a reception for delegations and heads of mission at Buckingham Palace. The reception was to begin at a quarter past ten, following a dinner given to all the royalties who had come for the funeral. We arrived. The delegations were lined up along the wall in the picture gallery. Monck was running about and telling everyone: the king will come out now, walk around all the delegations, shake hands and make acquaintance. We got ready. And what happened next? The king came in and stopped, and all the delegations started walking up to him one by one – just the opposite of what Monck had said.

The funeral was to take place on 28 January. At the very last moment it became apparent that I would not be able to take part in the whole funeral ceremony. I had to choose: either to participate in the procession from the Westminster Hall to Paddington and not go to Windsor, or go to Windsor to attend the church service and not take part in the procession. Why? Because the procession was scheduled to arrive in Paddington at 11.45 a.m. and then the coffin with the king's body was to be carried on to Windsor by a special royal train that had seats for heads of the delegations only. In other words, it looked as if Tukhachevsky and myself would have to stay in London. However, the marshal of the diplomatic corps, surely pressed by mission heads and even more so by their wives, provided a special train for ambassadors and arranged special seats for them in the church. In my capacity as an ambassador, I was entitled to enjoy that privilege together with my wife. But our diplomatic train was leaving Paddington at 11.30 a.m., that is, a quarter of an hour before the procession was to arrive at the station. Therefore I had to choose. I could not understand why it was impossible to arrange the departure of the diplomatic train for Windsor at least ten minutes after the procession reached Paddington. On reflection, I chose to go directly to Windsor on board the diplomatic train. We arrived in Windsor at 12.05. The funeral service was to begin at 1.15. Thus, there was a one-hour gap. Why? What for? From the station we walked directly to St George's Chapel, sat down in pews before the altar, and waited. It was cold and uncomfortable. The ladies sat huddled up tight and shivering, wrapped in overcoats and capes. We spoke in half-whispers to our neighbours (I with a Spanish lady and Agniya with the French ambassador Corbin). The organ was playing, and from time to time dark female figures in long veils would appear, like shadows from another world, taking their seats in the pews. Like spectres from the other world. It was tedious. Time dragged on intolerably. I examined the faces opposite me, of members of government and their wives. There were Baldwin, Simon, Halifax, Duff Cooper, Elliot, Stanley[i] and others. Eden sat somewhere behind me where I couldn't see him. The clock struck one, then quarter past. No coffin. Half past one, a quarter to two... Still no coffin. What was the matter? We began feeling uneasy. After a long time, at around two o'clock, there came the loud tramp of thousands of feet, the noise of trumpets and commands, and the king's coffin upholstered with violet velvet was brought into the chapel. Why the delay? On the way to Paddington, it emerged, crowds had broken through the police cordons and filled up the streets and squares. It took about 40 minutes to clear the route. How odd! Couldn't all the necessary measures have been taken in order to keep to a strict schedule?...

The coffin was placed on a pedestal before the altar. The royalties all took their seats behind the coffin, and behind them the military, courtiers and numerous others. Final prayers, parting words, and all was over. The pedestal started its slow descent. The coffin sank further and further into the crypt. Now it was already at the bottom. The queen (I had a good view of her from my

---

[i] Oliver Frederick Stanley, Conservative MP, 1924–45; president of the Board of Education, 1935–37; president of the Board of Trade, 1937–40; secretary of state for war in 1940; secretary of state for the colonies, 1942–45.

seat) shuddered and shrank into herself, but she held her nerve. No tears. But the duchess of Athlone[i] wept openly. The new king threw pinches of earth into the open crypt three times. Then the royalties began a slow procession past the crypt. The diplomats and the government did not join and, turning away, left through another door. The Spaniard came up to me and asked: 'Can you tell me why they kept us in that cold for a whole two hours?' My thoughts precisely.

I looked to the right and there, to my surprise, was Tukhachevsky. How come? According to the initial plan, he was to accompany the coffin only as far as Paddington. But the authorities, it turned out, had changed their minds at the very last moment, and representatives of foreign armies were also taken to Windsor.

We returned to the railway station. One train left, then another, and a third... The diplomats were still waiting their turn. The marshal of the diplomatic corps was running along the platform and questioning railway officials, policemen and officers, but there was no progress. The marshal was displeased, but helpless. After a 40-minute wait, we boarded the diplomatic train, where lunch had been promised (we were all hungry by then). 'Lunch', though, consisted merely of tea and sandwiches. We reached London at four and got home half an hour later.

Such mess and confusion! I am sure the Germans would have organized everything infinitely better in a similar situation. Even we in Moscow would have probably avoided many of the *gaffes* committed by the English. I'm becoming more and more convinced that the English are good at managing events that come round every year (for instance, the air shows in Hendon). They accumulate experience and make good use of it. But when it comes to arranging something from scratch and – above all – in haste, you may confidently expect a flop. The English seem to have an inborn dislike of looking ahead and working out a detailed programme of action in advance. They are all too willing to rely on their ability to *somehow muddle through* in the event of an unforeseen development. It's an English modification of Russian *avos*.

29 January

A day of appointments and meetings.

Yesterday evening Eden invited Litvinov, Agniya and myself to have lunch with him today at 1.30. This morning the marshal of the diplomatic corps (Sir Sidney Clive[ii]) informed me that the king was granting a private audience to Litvinov at 2.30 in the afternoon. Then Baldwin's secretary phoned to say that

---

[i] Alice, duchess of Athlone, the last surviving grandchild of Queen Victoria.
[ii] Lieutenant General Sir Sidney Clive, marshal of the diplomatic corps, 1934–45.

the prime minister was expecting Litvinov today at 3.30. I had to phone Eden and ask him to shift our lunch to one o'clock.

We had lunch in Eden's private apartment. It was my first visit to Eden's home. Nothing special or splendid. An ordinary middle-class English house, rather cold, with second-hand furniture and a faintly Bohemian flavour. A pile of gramophone records lay on the floor of the drawing room: waltzes, foxtrots and polkas. There were a few fine pictures on the walls and a couple of Vigeland[i] prints in the dining room. We arrived a little bit early: Eden was still at a Cabinet meeting, and Mrs Eden was busy with housework. Eden arrived with Duff Cooper, the war minister. We sat down in a small dining room downstairs, at a table which could accommodate no more than ten. For some reason I found myself to the right of the mistress of the house, and Litvinov to her left. Duff Cooper's wife, an exceptionally beautiful and impressive lady, floated in half an hour late. There were no serious conversations. There was talk about the League of Nations' new building, the military programme of the British government, Eden's trip to Moscow, the Russian theatre and ballet. Duff Cooper hinted that he would like to make a trip to the USSR. His wife eagerly supported the project. M.M. invited them to come for 1 May. I chatted quietly with Mrs Eden on a variety of general topics and said that to my mind outstanding people always come from the provinces or the countryside. Capital cities wear people out quickly, consuming far too much of their nervous energy in vain. As a result, citizens in the capital (those who've lived there since childhood) become physically and mentally wasted. Even those with innate talents lack the juices to develop them properly. I illustrated my idea with a number of examples taken from British life. My words seemed to impress Mrs Eden greatly. She became concerned and agitated, and exclaimed at the end of our conversation: 'I shall now keep my sons in the provinces for longer.' On parting, we arranged with Duff Cooper to have lunch in our embassy, where he could meet Tukhachevsky. As he said goodbye from the staircase, Eden told Litvinov: 'If you would like to have a talk with me, I am at your service.'

Litvinov headed straight to the palace, while Agniya and I went home. The reception given by the king was very courteous and amicable. Litvinov had to wait about five minutes in Edward's anteroom, because the latter had an unexpected visit from the king of Norway,[ii] who was leaving that day. Edward sent his aide to Litvinov to apologize for the delay. When Litvinov was ushered in, the king made his personal apology. Their conversation lasted 50 minutes instead of the normal 15 or 20 – at the king's will. It was a very wide-ranging dialogue. Edward skipped from one topic to another, asking questions and

---

[i] Adolf Gustav Vigeland, Norwegian sculptor.
[ii] King Haakon VII of Norway (born Christian Frederik), 1905–57.

waiting for Litvinov to answer them. Some were of a very delicate nature. For example, Edward asked why and under what circumstances Nicholas II was killed. Was it not because revolutionaries feared his reinstatement? M.M. explained to Edward that Nicholas II was killed when the Czechoslovakians were approaching Ekaterinburg. The local authorities feared that the city would be captured by the Czechs. There was no time to contact central government, so they themselves made the decision to have the emperor executed. Edward asked: 'But *was* there a central government at the time?' M.M. gave him the necessary information. Then Edward mentioned Trotsky and asked why he was deported from the USSR. M.M. again gave the required explanation, stressing the debate about the possibility or otherwise of building socialism in one country. The king listened to him attentively and then said, as if the penny had dropped: 'So Trotsky is an international communist whereas you are all national communists.' Then Edward inquired about various aspects of the Soviet constitution, and M.M. gave the relevant explanations. In the sphere of foreign policy, the king was interested in our relations with Germany and Poland. M.M. said that we want good relations with both countries and work in that direction but, unfortunately, without much success so far. The USSR's policy is a policy of peace. 'Yes,' Edward responded, 'all nations want peace, nobody wants war.' In the course of conversation, he also remarked: 'Germany and Italy have nothing at all. They are dissatisfied. Something should be done to improve their condition as far as raw materials, trade, etc. are concerned.' M.M. added that there was Japan to think about, too. All three countries are either waging war or are preparing for one. They are aggressors. The King admitted that Japan also had to be included in the aggressive trio. As to the League of Nations, Edward had some doubts: he was afraid that the League might spread war all over Europe as a result of its efforts. There was the sense that Edward regretted the failure of the Hoare–Laval plan.

That is what I remember of M.M.'s account of his conversation with the king. On the whole, the king impressed M.M. as a lively and spirited man, with a keen interest in world affairs.

After his talk with the king, Litvinov went to see Baldwin. Their conversation was brief, lasting 15 or 20 minutes, and rather trivial. Litvinov later referred to it as an *innocent talk*. Baldwin told M.M. (as he also told me last summer) that he had studied Russian at the beginning of the war, that he was fond of Russian literature, that Sir Bernard Pares (director of the School of Slavonic Studies in London) was his schoolmate, and so on. No serious questions were touched upon.

We went to the cinema in the evening. A bad idea. We saw *Top Hat*[3] – a very silly comedy, which M.M. did not enjoy. After the movies we dined at Scotts, a restaurant opened in the 1850s.

30 January

M.M., Agniya and I had lunch at Vansittart's. Prior to Litvinov's arrival in London, I hinted to V. that it might be good for him to meet Litvinov in private. I proposed lunch at the embassy. V. declined my offer and insisted on lunch at his home. I did not object.

The lunch felt like a family affair. There were the three of us, V., his wife and his son. We discussed political issues: the Italo-Abyssinian war (V. did not conceal his disappointment at the failure of the Hoare–Laval plan), the situation in Central Europe, in the Balkans, and elsewhere. The entire conversation, however, was dominated by the spectre of Hitler. Speaking about the German danger and how to rebuff it, we came to the major issue of the day. I related my recent conversation with Austen Chamberlain (on 22 January) and emphasized the latter's idea that peace could be preserved only with the backing 'of a strong League of Nations', and that the League of Nations could be strong only if its great powers – Britain, France and the USSR – had a uniform policy and worked in close cooperation with one another. Chamberlain had never regarded Italy as a reliable supporter of the League, now less than ever. 'I subscribe entirely to Chamberlain's prescription,' echoed M.M. I was curious to see V.'s reaction. He hesitated for a moment and then set about arguing irritably that the great powers are great powers, but if we lay too much stress on their significance, we might, first, arouse suspicion and dissatisfaction among other members of the League and, second, give rise to 'demob tendencies'. Medium and small powers might want to shift all the concern for the preservation of peace onto the great powers and themselves sink into a state of prostration. In V.'s opinion, special attention should be given at the moment to the need for small and especially medium powers to be more active in the struggle for the preservation of peace and to accept the burdens imposed by that struggle, especially in the sphere of arms. Why should Great Britain or the USSR alone spend lots of money to maintain large armies and navies? Why shouldn't Sweden, for instance, or Holland or Denmark do the same, in accordance, of course, with their means and resources?

Every country with a place in the great front of peace must contribute its mite to the common stock.

I listened to V.'s arguments with mixed feelings. On the one hand, it was good that the Foreign Office, through his words, was taking a stand against the monopolization of international policy issues by great powers alone; on the other hand, I did not like the fact that he was using concern for the participation of small and medium powers to slur over the problem of cooperation between Great Britain, France and the USSR. M.M. told me afterwards that he was not altogether satisfied with V.'s position either. Still, the general mood at lunch was good, the atmosphere was most friendly, and on parting M.M. invited V. and his wife to visit the USSR.

At 5.30 p.m. M.M went to the Foreign Office to talk with Eden. I do not know the details of their meeting because, in his hurry before his departure, M.M. did not have time to tell me. His general impression after the talk was as follows: Eden was quite satisfied with the political line set forth by M.M., but did not want to draw any concrete inferences from the appraisal of the situation on which they were in agreement.[4]

Claire Sheridan[i] paid a visit to M.M. before he went to see Eden. Agniya and I were also present. Sheridan, who is still very beautiful, remembered the old days and her former acquaintances in the USSR, and invited us to visit her studio.

We saw *Ghost Goes West*[5] in the evening. M.M. loved it and roared with laughter in places.

31 January

M.M. left England today. Agniya and I accompanied him to Dover. The weather was damp, there was occasional rain, and the Dover cliffs were hidden in the fog. We shook hands firmly – till our next meeting. Where? When? Most probably in the summer, when I'll travel to the USSR on leave. But who knows?

We returned by car and stopped to see Canterbury Cathedral on the way. An enormous, ancient building full of historical, mostly bloody, memories. The church warden showed us around the chapels, corridors and vaulted spaces of the cathedral, telling us almost cheerfully, with little jokes and facetious remarks, about the executions, murders and crimes that the cathedral walls had witnessed in spades.

[If Maisky expected Eden to have been won over by his Moscow visit, he was to be disappointed. 'I have no sympathy to spare for Mr Maisky,' Eden minuted. 'I hope that next time M. Maisky comes with complaints he will be told that our goodwill depends on his Government's good behaviour; i.e. keep their noses and fingers out of our domestic politics. I have had some taste of the consequences of this lately ... I am through with the Muscovites of this hue.'[6]

Early in 1936, Maisky was in the middle of packing, about to depart for Moscow for consultations, when he received instructions to remain at his post owing to the 'present disturbed state of Europe'. This was clearly prompted by rumours that originated with Laval about a possible agreement between the Western countries and Germany. Eden's appointment as foreign secretary now put Maisky's expectations to the test, particularly against the backdrop of the swift British move towards appeasement. On 6

---

[i] Clare Consuelo Sheridan (Frewen), British sculptress and writer, Churchill's cousin.

January, Maisky met Eden briefly, as part of the foreign secretary's introductory round of meetings with foreign ambassadors. Reporting home, Maisky emphasized Eden's commitment to the stand he had taken in Moscow and his adherence to the Eastern Pact. The British records convey a different picture. Maisky appeared desperate to bring about a movement in relations. He did not conceal from Eden that 'it would be a great grief to him personally ... as well as a misfortune for Europe' if the opportunity was missed. He further bolstered his own position by reminding Eden that, like four other Soviet ambassadors, he was to be inaugurated in Moscow as a member of the Central Committee of the Party (which he rather oddly chose to depict as being a member of parliament 'untroubled either with constituents or election expenses').[7]

Maisky's request for a loan to Russia, which he proposed to use as a litmus test of British intentions, was foiled by Sargent, who warned that Hitler would represent the loan as British support for the French policy of encirclement, which would render 'still more difficult' the efforts of the government to 'come to terms with Germany'. Dithering, Eden did raise the issue in Cabinet, albeit reluctantly, though not before expressing his concern that some of the money would 'find its way into communist propaganda in the Empire'. 'The German propaganda against Russia and her allies,' the Czechoslovak ambassador, Jan Masaryk, alerted Maisky, 'is not altogether without success in this country.'[8] The overwhelming support for Sargent's views at the Foreign Office led Eden to finally concede that 'while I want good relations with the bear, I don't want to hug him too close. I don't trust him, and am sure there is hatred in his heart for all we stand for.'[9]

It was becoming increasingly apparent that Maisky's own personal safety was intertwined with the success of collective security. He could not afford to remain passive. On 11 February, he went on the offensive, confronting Eden with a long survey of the international scene. To his chagrin, he found Eden determined not to undertake any further commitment in Central and South-East Europe, expecting France to do 'the dirty work'. Maisky therefore resorted to a new plan. He encouraged Tukhachevsky, in London for the king's funeral, to fraternize with Duff Cooper, the secretary of state for war, over breakfast at the embassy. He hoped Duff Cooper's association with Churchill and his concern about Hitler's ambitions might make him an effective channel for exerting pressure on the government. The convivial atmosphere over breakfast led Maisky to float the idea of a visit by Duff Cooper to Moscow 'to inspect the state of the Soviet Armed Forces'.[10] In reporting home, Maisky suggested that it was Eden who turned the conversation to a possible visit by Duff Cooper. Eden's report, however, shows that the initiative clearly emerged from Maisky, who wondered whether the government 'would have any objection if the Soviet government were to extend to Mr Duff Cooper an invitation to go to Moscow'. It further emerged that the choice of 1 May, rather than August, when military manoeuvres were planned (a far more attractive prospect for Duff Cooper), was Maisky's. Eden's initial approval, however, encountered stiff opposition from the Foreign Office. In a memorandum that prefigures the machinations of the fictional Yes, Minister television series, Sargent reminded Eden that a Cabinet committee had been set up to investigate the possibility of 'a general understanding with Germany'. It was advisable, therefore, to avoid any negotiations with a third party which might be seen to conflict with the 'German Policy'. The timing for the visit was hardly propitious. Whatever hopes Maisky may have entertained of stopping the drift towards appeasement were dashed when Sargent specifically warned against any further conversations with Maisky on a common policy – conversations which Sargent expected to be put 'to very dangerous uses' by a man like Maisky. 'I agree,' minuted Eden. 'Let us beware of Mr Maisky – he is an indefatigable propagandist.'[11]

The extent of the drift towards Germany, however, had not yet fully sunk in. Maisky remained confident, 'full of beans about the change of opinion in high circles'. There was talk, he told the Webbs, 'of a parliamentary deputation to the USSR ... Winston [Churchill] wants to go to the Red Army manoeuvres; Samuel Hoare wants to revisit the Russia he knew under the Czar.'[12] However, the sobering moment came on 7 March, when Hitler abrogated the Locarno Treaty of 1925 and moved into the demilitarized Rhineland. Worse still, he justified the advance by the supposed incompatibility of the Locarno Treaty with the Franco-Soviet pact, ratified on 27 February. Baldwin admitted in Cabinet that, with Soviet help, France could possibly defeat Germany, but he feared it would lead to the Bolshevization of Germany. His heart, he asserted, would not break if Hitler went to the east. Eden followed suit, acknowledging that Hitler's fresh proposal for a revised agreement was 'deserving of careful study'. No wonder the 18 March resolution of the General Council of the League of Nations on the remilitarization of the Rhine zone recognized the German violation of the Covenant, but failed to reach an agreement on common action. Negotiation on a 'new Locarno' dragged on for nearly a year.[13]]

10 February

All that talking on the part of Collier, Ashton-Gwatkin, Leith-Ross and others, and all of Marshall's bustle have come to an unexpected and rather poor end.

Cabinet met the other day. The financing of English–Soviet trade was discussed. Two schemes were presented. One, from the Foreign Office, proposed a loan from the British to the Soviet government for a term of 20 or 25 years at a rate of 6–7% interest. The British government would raise the money on the London market at 1.5–3% interest, and the difference in the percentages would be paid as compensation to British citizens who had suffered losses as a result of our revolution. The loan was estimated at approximately 30 to 40 million pounds. The other scheme, from the Board of Trade, provided for ordinary financial credits for five years at 6% interest to the tune of 10 million pounds. The credits would not be linked to the old debts. The Board of Trade's idea prevailed, and Nixon (head of the export department at the Board of Trade) was advised to begin negotiations with Ozersky.

The reasons for the Cabinet taking this particular course are, in my view, the following: (1) In the current unstable situation, the British government does not want to bind itself to a lengthy term of 25 years, especially in relation to the USSR; (2) The British government wants to trade with the USSR, but does not want to make a political sensation out of it. Indeed, a 25-year loan really would have been a huge sensation; (3) The British are psychologically unaccustomed to sudden leaps. Switching from the current practice of giving

18-month credits to a 25-year loan would certainly have been a tremendous leap. The British government prefers something in between.

Should one be happy or sorry about such a turn of events? Collier was undoubtedly disappointed by the Cabinet's decision. He told me so himself during our recent lunch at the embassy. Marshall is even more disappointed. My feelings are ambivalent, but I see no reason to be distressed.

8 March

I don't like the British response to Hitler's 'coup' in the Rhineland. Today's Sunday press is appalling. In the *Observer*, Garvin chides Hitler mildly for his bad manners, then insists on the need to pay due to attention to 'the Fuhrer's brilliant and timely proposals' and to do so 'in a spirit of sympathy and good will'. The Labourite *People* regards Hitler's seven points as a basis for establishing peace in Europe. The *Sunday Times* alone takes a more decent stance, stating that 'the policy of the *fait accompli*' has destroyed all trust in Hitler's words and promises. I haven't met any influential people about this ('weekend!'), but I sense a new and very dangerous turn towards Germanophilia in British policy. Those '7 Points' will provide men like Londonderry and Rothermere with excellent ammunition and will sow terrible confusion in the minds of lily-livered pacifists and spineless Labourites who fancy that Hitler's declaration of his desire to return to the League of Nations solves the entire German problem at one fell swoop. If only France remains firm! A lot will depend on that.[14]

9 March

I was unable to meet Eden, who flew to France at four o'clock, so I spoke with his deputy Cranborne.[i] The mood of the English? They are in the mood to negotiate, of course. It is clearly a national English disease: negotiations, negotiations, negotiations... Therefore, the British government is prepared to begin *exploration* (what a lovely word!) on the topic of whether Hitler's '7 Points' provide a suitable basis for negotiations. Cranborne's words indicate that the British government hopes to restore Locarno minus the Rhine zone. Everything else is of far less interest to them.

I sharply criticized the intentions of the British government ('my personal view', as I have received no instructions from Moscow as yet), stating that the reinforcement of collective security would be the only adequate response to the

---

[i] Robert Arthur Gascoyne-Cecil (Viscount Cranborne, later 5th marquess of Salisbury), parliamentary undersecretary of state for foreign affairs, 1935–38; secretary of state for dominion affairs, 1940–42 and 1943–45; secretary of state for the colonies, 1942; lord privy seal, 1942–43 and 1951–52.

aggressor and should include whatever repressive measures against Germany the League of Nations could agree on.

Cranborne was unpleasantly surprised but defended himself feebly.

10 March

The directives arrived from M.M. They coincide entirely with what I told Cranborne yesterday.[15] M.M. maintains that the British standpoint signifies a reward for the aggressor, the break-up of the collective security system, and the end of the League of Nations. Talks with Hitler on the day after his speech will have more harmful consequences than the Hoare–Laval plan. Trust in Britain will be undermined for good. The League of Nations will lose its importance as an instrument of peace. The USSR is ready to support any action of the League of Nations adopted collectively. Quite right!

I saw Cranborne again today and stated our point of view on behalf of the Soviet government. Cranborne was a little *upset* and promised that he would immediately telephone Eden in Paris to inform him about my statement.

Late in the evening I learned that things had taken an unexpected turn: having met the French in Paris, Eden and Halifax had arrived at the conclusion that it would be useless to go to Geneva and decided to return to London and report to Cabinet. They invited representatives of the Locarno powers to come to London on 12 March, and, on the 14th, the entire Council of the League of Nations.

So, I'll see M.M. here in London soon. He left Moscow yesterday.

So these are the circumstances in which I will see M.M. again in London, just one and a half months after our January meeting. Yes, these days it is hard to predict the future, even just a couple of months ahead.

28 March

An unpleasant experience.

Martin,[i] the Abyssinian envoy in London, visited me and asked me on behalf of his emperor to convey an appeal for assistance to the Soviet government. The position of Abyssinia is critical, M. said. The rainy season will begin in early June, so the Italians have two more months to wage their campaign. The Abyssinians suffer most from the Italian planes, which drop explosive and gas bombs not only on the troops, but also on the Red Cross and peaceful civilians. The use of 'mustard gas' is particularly awful. M. set the Abyssinian casualties at about 15,000, but I think there are many more. The Abyssinians could resist the

---

[i] Dr Ajas Martin, Abyssinian minister in London.

Italians if they had aeroplanes, but they have none except for the three or four old machines by which the emperor travels. The Abyssinians can find pilots: M. has had about a thousand offers from all European countries. Couldn't we lend a hundred aeroplanes to Abyssinia on credit?

I asked M.: doesn't Abyssinia receive anything from England? I was under the impression that the British government gave her money and weapons on the quiet.

M. became terribly red in the face and angry. The English, it turns out, give nothing to the Abyssinians. Despite Eden's numerous promises, there is neither money nor aeroplanes. The little that the Abyssinians bought in Europe (in Britain, Germany, Czechoslovakia and Belgium) was bought for cash. Nobody (including the British) is giving credit. Eden also promised more than once that the League of Nations would help, but nothing has happened. The Abyssinians have become disillusioned with the League of Nations and with all the Western powers, who are merely engrossed in mutual intrigues and are ready to sell Ethiopia for a piece of gold. In this desperate situation, the emperor appeals to the Soviet government, which does not deal in intrigues, keeps to the side, and is guided in its policies by the interests of peace and justice.

M. was very agitated, his voice trembled, and his dark skin flushed.

What could I say? I told him that I would communicate with Moscow, although I knew from the very beginning that Moscow, threatened by Japan from the east and Germany from the west, would hardly wish to supply Abyssinia with aeroplanes.

M. left, and I paced my room for a good while, philosophizing about the complex and contradictory nature of the current situation. I had the feeling that a big lad was beating a child right in front of me and that I was unable to help.

2 April

I was right. Moscow is not going to sell aeroplanes to Abyssinia.

I also learned that David Hull, the Negus's special envoy, visited Moscow the other day. He brought the emperor's personal letter to Kalinin and a letter from the Foreign Ministry to Litvinov. Hull spoke mostly about restoring diplomatic relations. He also tried to test the ground on the question of arms supplies to Abyssinia, but our people refused.

3 April

A new memorandum from Hitler, brought by Ribbentrop from Berlin!

The British response to it is a bit better than to the former '7 Points'. There are two groups in the British government. The young Conservatives (Eden, Duff

Cooper, Elliot and Ormsby-Gore[i]) and, we are assured, N[eville] Chamberlain, do not believe Hitler, consider his proposals a camouflage by which to prepare better for war, and insist on rapprochement with France (in particular, on immediate talks between the military staffs) and with the USSR. The old Tories (Runciman,[ii] Simon, Hailsham, MacDonald, Cunliffe-Lister, Monsell[iii] and others) [sic] uphold a policy of wait and see and semi-isolation, trying to avoid both the fulfilment of their Locarno commitments and a quarrel with Germany. Runciman, my neighbour at the dinner given by the Shipping Chamber of Commerce, outlined this group's point of view with charming candour. He said to me: 'In such times as today, it is better *to go slow... Perhaps something turns up (sic).*' The very quintessence of British state wisdom! Baldwin, as always, wavers between the two groups.

Almost the entire press favours negotiations, but in a far calmer spirit than before. The *Daily Herald, News Chronicle, Manchester Guardian* and *Daily Express* emphasize the unfeasibility of settling European problems without Eastern Europe. That's progress! The broad mass of the population lives in mortal fear of war, but it is not much interested in foreign policy. Churchill told me today that over the last ten days he has received five times as many letters from his electors about the new soccer rules as about the Rhine crisis. With Bossom,[iv] the proportion is 500 to 5, and with Harold Nicolson[v] 120 to 4. Quite typical! Labour and the Liberals (except for Lloyd George) are gradually sobering up.

Eden is clearly playing for time. Just today he told Ribbentrop that Hitler's proposals needed a certain period of 'calm deliberation'. Then comes Easter, then the elections in France. An interval of a month or a month and a half is guaranteed. In the meantime, Eden hopes to re-educate 'public opinion' a little. He is also inclined to take negotiations out of the hands of the Locarno powers and redirect them to the League of Nations.

My personal opinion is that temporary isolation of Germany is a minimum requirement, as is the working out of a 'peace plan' (either within the League of Nations or outside it) by the other Europeans powers for the whole continent. This should then be offered to Hitler. Moscow is thinking along the same lines.

---

[i] William Ormsby-Gore, postmaster-general, 1931; first commissioner of works, 1931–36; secretary of state for the colonies, 1936–38; north-east regional commissioner for civil defence, 1939–40.
[ii] Walter Runciman (1st Viscount Runciman of Doxford), shipping magnate and National Liberal MP, 1931–37; president of the Board of Trade, 1931–37. Headed Chamberlain's inquiry mission to the Sudeten in 1938–39.
[iii] Bolton Meredith Eyres-Monsell (1st Viscount Monsell), first lord of the Admiralty, 1931–36.
[iv] Alfred Charles Bossom (Baron Bossom), British-born renowned architect of skyscrapers in the USA who was Conservative MP, 1932–59.
[v] Harold George Nicolson, Foreign Office official, 1909–29; National Labour MP, 1935–45; parliamentary private secretary to the minister of information, 1940–41.

8 April

Agniya and I lunched at the Vansittarts. I thought I would have an open talk with V. about the current situation, but he seemed to want to avoid this: for some reason, he had also invited MacDonald and Ishbel MacDonald, who chatted away pointlessly at table and immediately slipped away after lunch. Then I exchanged a few words with the host.

V. is in a sour mood. He gives the impression of a man who is not quite himself. Perhaps he has yet to get the Hoare–Laval plan and its consequences out of his system. He is greatly concerned by the Italo-Abyssinian conflict. As far as Germany is concerned, V.'s opinion is as follows. The Locarno powers must first agree among themselves, then ask Hitler a few specific questions, and after that pass the whole package over to Geneva for consideration. V. thinks it impossible to avoid negotiations: the British public would not comprehend a refusal to talk. The negotiations should be used for exposing Hitler. This is the easiest way of educating public opinion.

I asked Ishbel why she had suddenly decided to open a tavern. She replied: 'It just happened. I drive around the country a great deal and seldom see good taverns in the countryside. So the thought occurred to me: why not open a tavern that will be the envy of all England?'

* * *

We are leaving for France tomorrow for ten days: Easter. Time to blow away the cobwebs.

[An article in the official *Journal de Moscou* (which, Maisky impressed on Churchill – 'entirely entre nous' – was written by Litvinov and faithfully represented the Soviet point of view)[16] stirred Maisky to prod Litvinov into action. In the article, Litvinov had reluctantly yielded to the Kremlin that belligerence towards Germany was undesirable, and had called for a special meeting of the League of Nations to establish the necessary conditions for talks with Hitler. In a strictly personal letter to Litvinov on 24 April, Maisky, most likely inspired by what he had heard in Paris from Potemkin, whose ears were well attuned to the sounds emanating from the Politburo,[17] urged Litvinov to take the lead in a European conciliation, redressing what he recognized to be Germany's justified grievances:

Dear Maksim Maksimovich,
    I am writing to you in an entirely personal capacity and wish to share with you a few ideas which have popped up in my mind as a result of my daily encounters with the British public, especially in Labourite and Liberal circles. The issue at hand is how we should react, and what position we should take, faced with Hitler's 'peace plan'.
    Over the course of the last 2–3 years, our general attitude in questions of European politics has, for the most part, been to support the *status quo* ... If

we do not wish to severely weaken our authority and our influence among the democratic elements of Europe, then we should, alongside offering the severest possible criticism of Hitler's method of foreign policy, promote ... our own 'peace plan', under the auspices of which we can begin the mobilization of the democratic and pacifist elements of the east and the west.

The thoughts of Labourites, Liberals and Conservatives, who have an interest in maintaining the system of collective security ... move along the following lines: ... the current *status quo* is in many respects incomplete: it is coming apart at the seams and cannot hold together for much longer. Can we truly count on keeping Austria permanently from reunification (in one form or another) with Germany? Can we truly count on keeping Germany permanently from reunification with the German parts of Czechoslovakia, or Memel land, or Danzig? Isn't such a reunification of Germans with Germans in the very nature of things? Can we really be sure that a state of the size and structure of Germany will be able to survive for very long without raw materials from its colonies?

Don't you think the time has now come for us to put forward our own 'peace plan'?

... I do not want at present to go into the details about any possible USSR 'peace plan'. I will just make one or two brief remarks. First, it seems to me that this plan should be of a more practical nature than Hitler's plan ... Secondly, it should include not only regional pacts, but also some sort of pan-European mutual aid pact: it is only in this way that it will be possible to manoeuvre England into providing security for Eastern Europe... . The most difficult element in the creation of such a plan, of course, will be the avoidance of any harmful pressure on French or Czechoslovak interests. But I think that, within the conditions I have laid out, such a task will not be impossible.

These are the considerations which I thought it my duty to put down. Decide for yourself whether they can be realized. Only one thing is clear to me, that without some positive programme in place to resolve the European situation it will be very difficult for us to retain and strengthen our influence in England.[18]

Litvinov indeed adopted almost verbatim Maisky's proposals on how to meet the current indifference to Central and Eastern Europe in his outline plan for the Geneva session, which he sent Stalin in early September.[19]

Nevertheless, Maisky remained frustrated throughout 1936 about his failure to bring about any change in the British attitude. 'Europe,' he wrote to Beaverbrook, 'is at the cross roads just now ... and I am afraid that the eleventh hour chance of avoiding war will not be taken.'[20] He was particularly 'perturbed' to find Eden noncommittal and evasive, having practically dropped the demands for an Eastern Locarno in the fresh approaches to Hitler.[21] 'It seems to me,' he wrote to Bernard Shaw shortly afterwards, that 'the greatest sin of modern statesmen is vacillation and ambiguity of thought and action. This is the weakness which before long may land us into [sic] war. Happily Stalin is possessed, in the highest degree, of the opposite qualities!'[22]

In vain he sought new ways of breaking the stalemate. Attempts to enlist Labour's support registered only partial success. During Litvinov's visit to London, lunch at the embassy with Attlee, Greenwood[i] and Dalton proved to be a non-starter: Dalton seemed to be fascinated only by Rozenberg,[ii] Litvinov's representative in Geneva, 'a small slightly hunchbacked Jew, with a cruel mouth'.[23] Beatrice Webb found it awkward that Attlee proposed a toast to Maisky, who, despite being a foreign ambassador, was hailed 'as a colleague' at political meetings he organized with the leaders of the Parliamentary Labour Party and the Trades Union Congress at his residence.[24] Maisky even preached, to no avail, his own ideas on peace during an address to the Liberal Summer School at Oxford, widely reported in the press.[25] He further made great efforts to impress the military with Russia's increasing strength following the extensive reforms of the Red Army. In two well-publicized showings at the Soviet embassy, dignitaries were exposed to a full feature-length film of the Red Army's innovative manoeuvres the previous summer.[26]

Paradoxically, his only solace came from the champions of the British Empire, Beaverbrook and Churchill. Beaverbrook favoured a triple alliance with France and the Soviet Union to protect the status quo, motivated by the fear that Germany and Italy were out to absorb the British Empire.[27] Though recuperating at his country house from recurring bouts of psychosomatic illness, Beaverbrook was always eager to meet Maisky – 'for this I would jump at your invitation' – and the door of his own home was wide open to the Soviet ambassador: 'If you and her Excellency will come to Cherkley you have only to fix the day and time.' Their relations became most intimate: when Maisky fell ill in May 1937, Beaverbrook suggested he join him in the sanatorium 'where I am ill too. It is a most admirable place – the food is good, the sun shines brightly, and everything is comfortable.'[28]

Churchill had come to accept collective security as salvation for the Empire. The 'general outlook merits a chat between ourselves!' Maisky wrote to Churchill, proposing 'lunch à deux'. Churchill, as Maisky cabled to Moscow, appeared to be surprisingly frank and forthcoming. He shared the Soviet view both that peace was 'indivisible' and that the German danger was an immediate one and could only be confronted by a united Europe. But even Churchill was reserved, warning that the process of re-educating the pacifist public opinion was a long one and excluded military commitment or even the mention of an 'alliance'. He envisaged instead the fostering of a powerful Anglo-French defensive alliance, which the Russians might be invited to join sometime in 1937, when he expected the German danger to become imminent. 'We would be complete idiots,' he told Maisky, 'were we to deny help to the Soviet Union at present out of a hypothetical danger of socialism which might threaten our children and grandchildren.' Churchill, as was attested by Sir Maurice Hankey, had 'buried his violent anti-Russian complex ... and is apparently a bosom friend of M. Maisky'. Yet, as Maisky ominously reported to Litvinov, Churchill appeared to be most concerned about Russia's domestic affairs. Little did he know that Churchill's belief in the strength of Russia had been seriously shaken by an obscure book he had just read – *Uncle Give Us Bread*, written by a Danish farmer who had spent some time in Russia. From it Churchill gained the indelible impression that Russia might 'perhaps present only a façade with nothing behind'.[29]]

---

[i] Arthur Greenwood, deputy leader of the Labour Party, 1935–54; member of the War Cabinet, and minister without portfolio, 1940–42.

[ii] Marsel Izrailevich Rozenberg, deputy general secretary of the League of Nations, 1934–36; ambassador to the Spanish Republic, 1936; recalled in 1937, arrested and shot in 1938; rehabilitated posthumously.

3 May

Yesterday the Abyssinian Negus fled the capital to Djibouti, from where, if today's newspapers are to be believed, he plans to cross over into Palestine. Addis Ababa is in flames, there is plundering on the streets, rifle shots ring out… The war has ended (although peace is still far away), Abyssinia is conquered, Mussolini triumphs. This is also the final nail in the coffin of the League of Nations; and Europe is at a fateful junction. You can smell the gunpowder! A terrible storm is approaching at full speed!

I spent the whole morning in the garden thinking how and when to build a shelter under the embassy against gas attacks. We shall need it soon. I'll have to ask the commissariat for special credits and directions.

7 May

Muddle and confusion…

Nevertheless, in an attempt to find some patterns in the political chaos, I would depict the current situation in the following schematic manner.

In England the fight is on between three main tendencies:

(1) Complete isolationists (Beaverbrook, Rothermere and others, recently joined, quite unexpectedly, by the *Financial News*), i.e. withdrawal from the League of Nations, abandonment of Locarno, arms build-up in Britain, overt return to 'balance of power' politics, and the global development of the Empire.

(2) Semi-isolationists (most of the Conservatives and the British government, *The Times*, *Daily Telegraph*, *Morning Post* and others), i.e. annulment (*de jure* or *de facto*) of Art. 10 and Art. 16 of the Covenant, transformation of the League into a kind of 'conciliatory commission', the limitation of military obligations under the Locarno Treaty, search for an agreement with Germany, and reconciliation between France and Germany.

(3) Real collective security (Labour, the Liberals, Conservatives such as Cecil and Lytton,[i] *Daily Herald*, *News Chronicle*, *Manchester Guardian* and others), i.e. strengthening collective security and the League of Nations, a European mutual assistance pact admitting regional pacts, and firm commitments by the powers, including Britain, that, as a last resort, they will maintain collective security by force of arms in any part of Europe.

The second movement is the strongest today and, under certain circumstances, can easily obtain the support of the first. Objectively (and, to an extent, subjectively), these movements untie Germany's hands in the east and in the south-east. However, the third movement is also strong. So, to a

---

[i] Victor Alexander Bulwer-Lytton (2nd earl of Lytton), British statesman and diplomat, chairman of the League of Nations mission in Manchuria, 1932.

large extent, one side paralyses the other, which results in confusion and leads nowhere. As for the future, much will depend on the position of the USSR and the new French government, which looks like it will be headed by Blum.[i]

Corbin (the French ambassador) and Masaryk (the Czechoslovak envoy), with whom I had a chat the other day, corroborated my appraisal of the situation. Corbin maintains that the semi-isolationist attitudes derive from Britain's military weakness and the desire to somehow gain the two or three years needed to get its armaments in order.

Masaryk told me about Austen Chamberlain's tour of Central Europe and said that C. drew the following conclusions from what he saw and heard there: the independence of Austria is the central problem for Europe today; and cooperation with the USSR is essential in order to stabilize the situation, especially in Central and Eastern Europe. Upon his return C. had talks with Baldwin, Eden and the king. During the presentation of credentials on 5 April, the king asked Masaryk what he thought about C.'s visit to Central Europe. Does he think that it will have a positive influence on Central European affairs? Masaryk, of course, answered in the affirmative.

Incidentally, if we are to believe Masaryk, C.'s tour came about quite by chance. He is not rich (Masaryk estimates C.'s annual income at 1,000 pounds) and cannot afford the luxury of frequent travel abroad. Selby,[ii] the British envoy in Vienna whom C. promoted and whom he respects greatly, knowing about the straitened circumstances of his former boss, invited him to be his guest in Austria. C. agreed. When Eden learned about his trip, he asked C. to observe for himself what was going on in Vienna and then to inform him. So these were *holidays* intertwined with politics. When Masaryk learned about C.'s visit to Austria, he informed Beneš about it and Beneš invited C. to come to Prague. C. hesitated but finally agreed. While C. was in Prague, the British envoy in Budapest called him by phone and begged him to come to Budapest, too, so that the Hungarians would not think that C. was engaged in any anti-Hungarian intrigues. C. had to set off reluctantly for Budapest. The process resulted in a tour that the Germans are viewing as a premeditated, pre-prepared Machiavellian move on the part of 'perfidious Albion'. The reality was far simpler.

10 May

On 5 May, I presented new credentials to the new king. The ceremony was simplified and conducted in full accord with former precedents (as I was assured by the marshal of the diplomatic corps, Sidney Clive); and certainly

---

[i] André Léon Blum, member of the French Socialist Party from 1904 and of the Chamber of Deputies, 1919–28 and 1929–40; premier of France, 1936–37, 1938 and 1946, and vice-premier, 1937–38 and 1948.
[ii] Walford Selby, British minister in Vienna, 1933–37.

with the precedent created by the late George V. No court carriages were sent for me, and my 'retinue' did not accompany me: I just drove to the palace in my own car. All heads of mission gathered in the Bow Room and, in order of seniority, presented their credentials to the king, who was in the adjoining room. The doors to the hall were open, and those awaiting their turn could hear snatches of the king's conversation with the head of mission who was presenting his credentials. The king spent two or three minutes with each ambassador or envoy. It was, therefore, a presentation *en masse*.

As the Argentinian was absent, I was the fourth in line. That's how high I am now! A short step to becoming doyen. That would be amusing. Not that being doyen under the present king is such a frightening prospect. I entered the room and handed the envelope with my credentials to Eden, who was standing to one side and who placed it on top of similar packets already lying in a small basket. Meanwhile, Edward shook my hand and began asking questions befitting the occasion: How long have I been ambassador in London? Where did I serve earlier? I have been in London before, have I not? and so on. I gave similarly 'innocent' and superficial answers. At the end, the king said: 'In January I had a long and interesting conversation with Mr Litvinov.' I replied that I had heard about the conversation and that Mr Litvinov was *delighted* with his meeting with the king. That was all. It seemed to me that the king was chillier towards me than during our previous meetings when he was still the prince of Wales. Why? Was it the result of a general *muddle* in the sphere of British foreign policy? Or the reflection of Edward's allegedly growing Germanophilia? Or maybe I am mistaken and there was no particular coldness in the king's manner?

* * *

Leaving the palace, I met Monck, the Foreign Office chief of protocol, and told him that I was going to present new members of my diplomatic corps to the king at the nearest levee.

'Yes, of course!' replied Monck.

'But you know,' I continued, 'one of the new members is a woman: the deputy of trade, Mosina.'

The expression on Monck's face changed. Trying to conceal his embarrassment with a laugh, he exclaimed: 'Oh, that's a quite different matter!'

He hesitated for a moment before continuing: 'Maybe it would be better to present the lady not at the levee but at the summer *garden party*? What do you think?'

'Why?' I inquired.

'Oh, M. Ambassador, you are always so logical,' Monck joked, avoiding the question. 'We English are an illogical people. Well, I'll talk to the marshal of the diplomatic corps about it.'

Five days passed and this morning the marshal telephoned me himself. Here is our conversation.

Marshal: Today I am sending invitations to the coming levee to the heads of missions. Mr Monck told me that you wanted to introduce a lady, deputy for trade Mosina, to the king. May I ask you not to do it? It would be better if you introduced her at the summer garden party.

I: May I ask you why, Mr Marshal?

Marshal: I rummaged through the archives and found no precedent in our history of a lady attending a levee. Even when there were ladies in the Cabinet, they did not appear at levees. This matter was discussed for the last time in connection with Margaret[i] and the duchess of Atholl,[ii] when they were members of the government. There were heated debates, even quarrels, but it was decided finally that women should not be present at levees.

I: Tell me please, what would you do if a woman were appointed ambassador or envoy to London? Wouldn't you let her attend a levee?

Marshal (laughing): Oh, this is a highly unlikely situation!

I: Why do you think so? We have a lady envoy in Stockholm [Aleksandra Kollontay], and the USA has a lady envoy in Copenhagen. I'd not be surprised if tomorrow a woman came to replace me in London as ambassador. What would you do then?

Marshal (coughing in embarrassment): But... but... an ambassador or envoy should get an agrément before coming to London...

I: That's right. But are you trying to say that the British government might refuse the agreement on the grounds that the ambassador is a woman? Forgive me, Mr Marshal, but the British government would make a laughing-stock of itself.

Marshal (still more embarrassed, realizing that he had said a foolish thing): No, no! You misunderstood me! That's not what I wanted to say. I simply meant that the prospect of a lady ambassador is not at issue at the moment, so we do not have to rack our brains over how we would act if it were.

I: You are the hosts and we are guests. I find it my duty to follow the rules established by the hosts. Therefore, if you, Mr Marshal, find it improper to present Mosina at the levee, I'll postpone her presentation until the garden party. But I must let you know that at the garden party Madam Mosina will not be in the company of the ladies, the diplomats' wives, but in the company of the male diplomats, as she will be present there not in the capacity of a spouse, but as an appointed member of the diplomatic corps.

---

[i] Margaret Grace Bondfield, Labour MP 1923–31; parliamentary secretary to the minister of labour, 1924–29; minister of labour, 1929–31.
[ii] Katharine Marjory Stewart-Murray (duchess of Atholl), Conservative MP for Kinross and West Perthshire, 1923–38.

Marshal (musingly): You think she'll be with men? Hm... Hm... (reluctantly) Well, let her be with men.

I: Fine. So, I'll introduce Mosina to the king at the garden party together with the male diplomats. What should she wear?

Marshal: The usual *afternoon dress.*

I: Goodbye, Mr Marshal.

Marshal: Goodbye, Mr Ambassador.

* * *

My conversation with the marshal reminded me of Kollontay's story about the commotion caused by her appointment in the Swedish court and the protocol.

How was A.M. [Kollontay] to present her credentials?

Visiting the Foreign Ministry together with the perplexed and frightened chief of protocol – who, like Sir Sidney Clive, had consulted the archives in vain – she began to create an unheard-of 'precedent'.

The presentation of credentials takes place in the morning. Ambassadors who do not have uniform usually wear tails, that is, evening dress. What dress should she wear? An evening dress? It does not befit a lady to wear an evening dress in the morning. An afternoon dress? The chief of protocol was frightened. Then A.M. took matters into her own hands and announced: I'll wear a black long-sleeved dress with a white lace collar. The chief of protocol frowned but gave his consent.

Furthermore, according to Swedish etiquette, nobody may appear before the king with their head covered. Men present their credentials bareheaded. What was A.M. to do? She is a lady, and ladies wear hats on their daily business. A long and lively discussion followed. A.M. was for a hat and the chief of protocol against. Finally, the poor chief of protocol asked in exhaustion: 'What kind of hat do you have?' A.M. said: 'A small black brimless hat.' The chief of protocol raised his hands and cried: 'All right, all right! A small black brimless hat. But a very small one, please!' So, agreement was reached on this issue of global importance as well.

The next 'problem'. According to etiquette, envoys should enter the hall and go towards the king, who stays where he is. On the other hand, in Swedish society, on meeting a lady a gentleman must walk towards her and not vice versa. What should A.M. do? She is both a lady and an envoy. The chief of protocol insisted that A.M. should walk towards the king as men do.

One more 'problem'. After the presentation of credentials, the king converses with the envoy. Both should be standing. But, in Swedish society, when a man converses with a lady, he offers her a seat. What to do with A.M.? On the chief of protocol's insistence, it was decided that A.M. should talk while standing, like a male envoy.

In the event, nothing came out quite as planned. When A.M. appeared in the doorway with her credentials, the king, twitching in obvious embarrassment, made a couple of hesitant steps in her direction. They met halfway. When the credentials had been presented and the conversation began, the king became twitchy once again and said in some confusion, 'Now, it seems, I should ask you to be seated?' A.M. sat down and the king sat next to her, and it was from their armchairs that they conducted the rest of their conversation (in which, among other things, the king complained that there were now too many schools, and this made people unhappy). Thus, the gentleman won out over the man of the court.

In this way a new precedent was established in the Swedish court, and its every detail was entered into the book of Swedish protocol for the edification of descendants.

22 May

During all these difficult days I have seldom been as depressed as I was after today's conversation with Brailsford.

Brailsford published an article entitled 'The Nations of Europe Are Caught in a Cleft Stick' in the *Reynolds Newspaper* of 12 April.[30]

Brailsford also sent a letter to the editor of the *New Statesman* that was published on 9 May. He developed the same thoughts, came out strongly against the League of Nations and its reform, against collective security, Stresa, and the whole wide world. He drew the following conclusion: 'Those who believe in collective security – economic and military – must maintain a vigilantly disinterested attitude for as long as we live under the power of a capitalist government. When a socialist government comes to power, it will be necessary to make efforts to build, together with the Soviet Union as our main partner, a federation of states that are either socialist or close to socialism.'

B.'s literary-political statements astonished me so greatly that I decided to talk to him. Today we sat in the winter garden, drank tea and had a frank talk. I listened to B. and my heart sank...

Here was a clever, educated, brilliant representative of the English socialist intelligentsia, I thought. He has so much knowledge! He has a great store of observations and political experience! His remarks, appraisals and descriptions are subtle and shrewd! And the result? Confusion, lack of faith in the future, and pessimism. Even the best representatives of English socialism have a poor understanding of the mechanics of current events. When, criticizing B.'s position sharply, I set out the idea of a 'peace front' led by Britain, France and the USSR as the sole practical solution to the current situation, he objected: 'But it boils down to support for British and French imperialism, towards which I have no sympathy whatsoever!'

I argued that the cause of peace is the chief responsibility of every socialist in the present-day situation, and that the participation of the USSR in the 'peace front' leadership is the best guarantee that the front will not degenerate into some aggressive 'alliance' of the old type. B. listened to me attentively and, it seemed, sympathetically, but in the end uttered mournfully: 'If only the USSR were ten years older! If only the socialist member of this trio really were stronger than the capitalist members! Then it would be much easier to take a decision.'

He paused, as if trying to sum up our conversation, and suddenly said: 'If I were able to earn my living in some other way, I would quit "political journalism" now… I once had a good knowledge of Greek … One can live off it quite well in England – should I try?'

My heart just sank. It's complete capitulation! A flight of panic in the face of the imperialist Moloch!

26 May

[Arthur] J. Cummings told me about his conversation with Churchill. Churchill is ranting and raving at the government's spinelessness and indecision. Baldwin bears the brunt of the blame. Cummings asked when Baldwin would retire, and Churchill exclaimed irritably: 'He will never retire of his own accord! He wants to stay not only until the coronation but afterwards, too, if he can. Baldwin must be *kicked out* – this is the only way to get rid of him.' Then Churchill added: 'Baldwin reminds me of a man who has held on to the gondola of a rising balloon. If he lets go of it when the balloon is only 5 or 6 metres above ground, he will fall but he won't break his bones. The longer he hangs on, the surer he is to die when he does inevitably fall.'

Well put, in a true Churchillian manner. It reminded me how, some three months ago, Churchill answered a colleague's question as to why Baldwin had delayed the appointment of a defence minister with the following devastating witticism: 'Why, Baldwin is looking for a man smaller than himself as defence minister, and such a man is not easy to find.'

Churchill assured Cummings that the present government would soon collapse, but he was uncertain about when this would happen. Churchill flatly rejects all rumours and suggestions that he might join the Cabinet: 'I can't work in the same Cabinet as Baldwin. If I am to join the government, it will be a government where my influence will prevail.'

Churchill spoke little on this occasion about foreign-policy issues, but what he did say was in keeping with his general line: Germany is an enemy and a defence alliance against Germany must be set up.

28 May

Yesterday Sir Edward Grigg[i] and General Spears[ii] came to lunch, where they cursed and swore (insofar as this is possible in English and at the table of the ambassador of a great power) in the direction of Baldwin and the government. The Cabinet lacks spine, is unable to take decisions on serious matters, and has no policies, especially foreign policies. It has lost its way in broad daylight and is rapidly driving the country to disaster and Europe to war. But when I tried to discover my guests' political line, embarrassment followed: they, too, were confused and unable to make any definite statements. In Grigg's words, the masses at large are *all right*: they sense the growing danger from Germany and are ready to act, but they need the government's guidance. There is none. For this reason, if Hitler attacks Czechoslovakia, 'England will be unable to do anything – unless perhaps the USSR will help her?' (Grigg). Grigg would not mind Germany swallowing Czechoslovakia – he reckons that it would set off a salutary reaction in Great Britain which would seriously mobilize British public opinion against the threat from Berlin. Spears, who is the London director of the well-known Czechoslovak shoemaking company Bat'a, was not so casually inclined to sacrifice Czechoslovakia. Both guests asked me to arrange a showing of the film, *The Struggle for Kiev*, in the parliament building. Spears also wanted me to deliver a report on foreign policy (as I did last year) for his group of MPs…

At a lunch today for the journalists of *The Times* and the *Observer*, Glasgow,[iii] the *Observer*'s diplomatic correspondent, told me (as if echoing Brailsford): 'I have no policy whatsoever today. I did have a political line, but I have gradually lost all my views in recent months. It is difficult to reconcile the contradictions of the situation we are in. For the moment it is better not to try.'

12 July

At Garvin's request I received a correspondent of the *Observer* who wished to collect information about Chicherin.[iv] The article appeared today:

---

[i] Edward Grigg (1st Baron Altrincham), director of Reuters, 1923–25; Conservative MP, 1933–45; parliamentary secretary to the minister of information, 1939–40; joint parliamentary undersecretary of state for war, 1940–42.

[ii] Sir Edward Louis Spears (1st Baronet Spears), Conservative MP, 1922–24 and 1931–45; Churchill's personal representative to French prime minister, May–June 1940, and to General de Gaulle, June 1940; British minister to Syria and Lebanon, 1942–44.

[iii] George Glasgow, diplomatic correspondent for the *Observer*, 1920–42.

[iv] Georgii Vasilevich Chicherin, son of a retired diplomat, Chicherin was born into the nobility. An outstanding polymath and polyglot, he graduated from the historical-philological faculty of St Petersburg University and joined the archives department of the Ministry for Foreign Affairs. A highly accomplished pianist (he eventually produced an authoritative biography of Mozart), he was deeply interested in cultural modernism, and in 1904 took leave of absence and moved to

ARISTOCRAT AND COMMUNIST.

M. Chicherin's CAREER.

A REMARKABLE CHARACTER.

(BY A CORRESPONDENT)

M. George Chicherin, the Soviet Union's former Commissar for Foreign Affairs, whose death occurred last week, was inspired early in life by the ideals of the young revolutionaries of the land-owing class in Russia, who, twenty years before, had renounced their privileges and their fortunes to serve the people, then living under the most appalling conditions.

An aristocrat like them, he too renounced a fortune in order to spend it on the revolutionary movement. He carried his ideals even into his dress. He would wear the shabbiest of clothes, not because he could not afford to wear better, but because he believed it was serving the movement.

He was very fond of music and played the piano brilliantly. But when he joined the revolutionary movement he said, 'Music is a waste of time. I will indulge in it no longer.' So he gave up his music and stopped going to concerts and the theatre.[31]

LIFE OF MOZART.

When the Russian exiles in London gave a soiree in 1915 in celebration of May Day it was only with the greatest difficulty that they could persuade him to sit down at the piano that was in the room. But when he did play he played magnificently, in spite of the fact that he had not touched the keys of a piano for years before that night. He never played again, however, until after his retirement. Then he not only took up his music once more, but he also wrote a life of his favourite composer, Mozart.

He seldom used a typewriter and as rarely dictated his letters and reports. He preferred to write every word himself. When he was secretary of the Russian Social Democratic party, which had groups in every big city of Europe, he used to write to every group and often write several copies of his letters.

Later, when he became Commissar, he still kept up this practice. Sometimes notes and documents would get buried under the disorderly piles of papers that littered every corner of his rooms, but his memory

---

Berlin, where he joined the Menshevik section of the Russian Social Democratic Party. He spent the rest of the years until the revolution in political exile in Paris and (mostly) in London, where he befriended Maisky. Returning to Russia after the revolution, he joined the Bolsheviks and was appointed by Trotsky as his deputy people's commissar for foreign affairs and, from 1918–30, replaced him as commissar. In this capacity he was the architect of the Brest-Litovsk agreement and the Rapallo Agreement, and of the gradual accommodation with the capitalist world. His unconventional methods of work led to a fierce and open clash with his deputy, Litvinov, whom he regarded as boorish and amateurish, but who, in 1930, replaced him as people's commissar.

was such that he always knew exactly where he had placed them, and when others considered them lost beyond all hope of recovery he would find them in a moment.

A 'NIGHTBIRD'.

He had the extraordinary habit, too, of writing long into the night. This habit so grew upon him that at last he could not work in the day, and he would even make appointments for foreign ambassadors to meet him at one or two o'clock in the morning.

As there was only one 'nightbird' like himself, the German Ambassador at Moscow, Brockdorff-Ranzau,[i] these midnight interviews were not very popular. Nor were they good for Chicherin himself. Ill-health had always greatly troubled him, and his constant work late into every night certainly accentuated it.

He was extremely well educated, and spoke perfectly English, French, and German, besides his own language. He also read an immense number of books and newspapers in various languages, and he once remarked to a friend of his, 'If you read carefully the newspapers in various languages and of various shades of opinion you can always be *au courant* with every diplomatic "secret."'

[There follows a long gap in the diary at a rather crucial moment, marked by a swift deterioration in relations between the two countries and the unleashing of the political trials and terror in Moscow. The Anglo-French debacle in handling Mussolini, Maisky lamented, was leading the Soviet government to doubt 'whether it was worthwhile binding themselves up with such half-hearted partners as the British Government'. The Foreign Office was 'split from top to bottom … and the Cabinet did not know its mind'. With Japan, Germany and Italy 'greedy' for colonies, it was 'the British Empire which was in peril – and not the USSR', which deemed it 'wiser … to withdraw and mind [its] own business' even if that implied the establishment of a German 'Mittel Europa'.[32] Almost a year later, we still find Maisky disclosing the Kremlin's views that 'after the experience of Spain and the shilly-shallying of the British and French governments, the USSR might virtually withdraw from any further collaboration with Western powers and devote itself to the building up of socialism and the further development of defence'.[33] And yet, despite recurring setbacks, Maisky, unlike Litvinov, remained convinced – right up until the outbreak of war – that Anglo-Soviet interests were in harmony and that gradually the British were bound to seek Soviet assistance. As early as June 1936, he approached Brailsford (whom he held in great esteem as 'a better judge of the English character') to inquire whether he shared his view that the current 'drift and indecision'

---

[i] Ulrich Graf von Brockdorff-Ranzau, a Weimar German foreign minister and member of the German delegation to Versailles, he went on to become the German ambassador in Moscow, 1922–28.

was only 'a temporary phase and that before long the force of circumstance will compel Britain to take a definite attitude'.[34] For the moment, however, he obviously had to toe the Kremlin line, though he would make persistent subversive attempts to prepare the ground for an approach by Britain.

The swift turn of events, however, made it difficult for the Soviet Union to sit on the fence while Hitler appeared to be effectively wooing British politicians, largely by whipping up the 'red scare'. Lloyd George, who, in his conversations with Maisky, had praised the Soviet Union as the only country to be pursuing a 'lucid, precise, defined policy – a policy of peace', now dismissed the ideological tenets of Hitler's Russian policy contained in a chapter from *Mein Kampf* which Maisky had sent him.[35] Filled with admiration for the 'Führer', whom he had just met in Berchtesgaden, Lloyd George regretted the chill that had settled on relations with Germany following the outbreak of war in Spain, and confessed that he had 'never withdrawn one particle of the admiration which [he] personally felt for [Hitler] … I only wish we had a man of his supreme quality at the head of affairs in our country today.'[36]

On the other hand, the tentative feelers put out by the Russians in Berlin provoked a virulent response. Speaking to the party meeting in Nuremberg in mid-September, Hitler abused the Soviet Union as a country seeking 'the liberation of the scum of humanity'. He appeared to incite the Western powers openly, as Stalin marked in his thick black pencil on the text of the speech, to take concrete action against the USSR, when he warned that 'if the modern Girondins are succeeded by Jacobins, if Kerensky's[i] Popular Front gives place to the Bolshevists, then Europe will sink into a sea of blood and mourning'. From Berlin, Surits, the Soviet ambassador, warned Stalin that Hitler was provoking Russia to sever relations between the two countries. He, like Litvinov, wished to see a tougher attitude towards Germany. Instead, Stalin opted for further futile negotiations in Berlin, prompted by the British stand over the Spanish Civil War and the fear of becoming prematurely embroiled in hostilities.[37]

It took a while for the repercussions of the horrific Spanish Civil War, which erupted on 17 July when General Francisco Franco[ii] led a military revolt against the Spanish Popular Front government, to be fully registered in Moscow. The war undermined Litvinov's efforts to restore the First World War coalition against Germany. Back from the Montreux Conference (which reaffirmed the 1923 Turkish Straits' regime), he was coming under increasing criticism, while his personal life was in turmoil. His decision at the end of July 1936 to have Zina, a 17-year-old girl – described (by Ivy, Litvinov's wife) as 'nubile … decidedly vulgar, very sexy, very sexy indeed' – accompany him 'as his daughter' to the sanatorium at Kislovodsk led Ivy to pack and leave for remote Sverdlovsk. There, heedless of his distraught entreaties, she remained teaching schoolchildren English for three years, until his demotion.[38] Like most men, Ivy thought, he desired a wife and a mistress. 'I used to go about the town,' she recalled, 'walking about the streets, and suddenly our enormous Cadillac would dash by with Zina sitting beside the chauffeur, she'd gone out shopping … she turned up at the Foreign Office

---

[i] Aleksandr Kerensky, prime minister in the Russian Provisional Government, July–November 1917.
[ii] Francisco Franco, general, commander-in-chief, Moroccan army, 1935; chief of staff of Spanish Foreign Legion, 1935; commander-in-chief Canary Islands, 1936; commander-in-chief and head of state of Spanish Nationalist regime, 1936–39.

32. Ivy and Maksim Litvinov had seen happier days.

to fetch him in full riding kit.' Coming back into town from their dacha, Litvinov 'would have his arm round her, shrieking with laughter and giggling, tickling ... people in trams gazing down'. A large part of Litvinov's melancholy and resignation – often ascribed to the failure of collective security and the mortifying purges in his ministry – should clearly be attributed to personal aspects of his life.

Off to Kislovodsk, Litvinov encouraged Maisky to take his own summer leave, as the season had 'begun earlier than expected'. He continued, however, to fend off Maisky's efforts to rekindle the intimacy of their exile days and reiterated his position as *primus inter pares*. 'It would be difficult,' he responded to Maisky's pleadings to attend the September assembly of the League, 'to swap you for Potemkin or Shtein[i] for no good reason, as they have developed very good personal contacts over there.' Maisky was never to enjoy the warmth which infused Litvinov's relations with Kollontay. Not only was she encouraged to come to Geneva, but Litvinov would cut short tedious discussion within the delegation by turning to her: 'But now, Aleksandra Mikhailovna, where's that

---

[i] Boris Efimovich Shtein, general secretary of the Soviet delegation at the Geneva Disarmament Conference, 1927–32; chief of the second western department in the NKID, 1932 and 1934; member of the Soviet delegation to the League of Nations, 1934–38; ambassador to Finland, 1933–34, and to Italy, 1934–39; demoted to a lecturer position at the diplomatic academy of the NKID in 1939.

film about China showing, the one you praised? Is it worth watching? Come on then, let's go now.'[39]

Maisky left England for the Soviet Union on 11 August, first for Sochi and then – blissfully cut off from the world – for a delightful tour of the Caucasus.[40] Harsh reality awaited him on his return to Moscow. He was urgently summoned to the Foreign Ministry, briefed about the war in Spain and rushed to a nocturnal meeting at the Kremlin, where he was instructed to return to his post right away. The following day, he found himself on a train bound for London – a journey which would take two days and three nights via Berlin and Paris.[41]

In London, Maisky faced a grim situation which would trouble him for the next three years. During his absence, Britain and France had formed a 'non-intervention' committee, which the Soviet Union joined on 23 August. The scores of meetings of the committee over the next three years not only sapped his energy, but exposed even more the helplessness of Russia, which became increasingly alienated from the West.[42] Much of this was due to Hitler's success in wrapping the Civil War in an ideological mantle, harping on British fears that communism would spread from Spain to France, whose prime minister, the socialist Léon Blum, headed a Popular Front government. The lingering conflict only reinforced suspicion of Soviet intentions, and this suspicion was fuelled by the ongoing purges in Moscow. All this was to have disastrous consequences in the crucial years leading up to the war.

At a stroke, the war in Spain stripped Maisky of the limited success he had enjoyed in England. Eden's concealed hostility came to the fore in their first meeting, shortly after his return from Russia. Maisky found it difficult to convince Eden that the Soviet Union was not exploiting the war in Spain to advance communism. He emphatically dismissed the ideological dimensions of the war, insisting that Soviet assistance was solely motivated by the fear that Franco's victory might tilt the balance of power in Europe and encourage Hitler to expand further. 'Nobody governing Russia today,' he insisted, 'thought that [communism] could be achieved … in our lifetime.'[43]

Churchill, too, showed signs of wavering. While still committed to the idea of collective security, and recognizing the growing strength of the Soviet Union and its wish 'to be left alone in peace', he deplored in parliament her 'obscure, so double-faced, so transitional' state of affairs. 'Russia is in very great peril,' he concluded, 'and it is most surprising that a State thus threatened should act with such insensate folly.'[44] Maisky was greatly disappointed to find Lloyd George reprimanding the Soviet Union in public for sending volunteers to Spain.[45]

Litvinov, as Carley has rightly observed, saw the Spanish Civil War as a major threat to 'collective security', undermining relations with Britain while cementing the ties between Italy and Germany – ties which would indeed culminate in a short while in the anti-Comintern pact. Litvinov, far less optimistic than Maisky about the possible success of the Republicans,[46] was eager to contain the conflict and prevent it from shifting the balance of power on the continent by cooperating with the Non-Intervention Committee in London.

This committee, however, failed to prevent the Germans and Italians from directly assisting Franco. As is revealed by recently released archival material, Stalin's decision to assist the Republicans militarily was motivated first and foremost by political and Realpolitik considerations.[47] However, increasingly he was finding himself in a harsh predicament similar to the one he had to face during the 1926 British General Strike, when even half-hearted support of the miners led to the severance of relations in 1927. The pressure now from ideologists within his party and abroad for him to intervene on behalf of the left in Spain was nigh irresistible. The revolutionary situation had not been sparked by the Russians, and soon enough ran counter to Soviet national interests. Remaining passive, however, would have rendered Stalin vulnerable at home – particularly as the Trotskyites were trying to take the lead on the Republican side. Domestic and international politics were further bound up with the unleashing of the repressions marked by the trial of the veteran Bolshevik leaders, Zinoviev and Kamenev. Therefore, in September Stalin approved the despatch of war matériel to the Spanish Republicans and reluctantly supported the idea, put forward by the French communists, of 'international brigades'.

Alarmed at the harsh British reaction and the French threat to abrogate the mutual assistance pact, Litvinov finally succeeded in overcoming opposition from Stalin (whom he met six times in October and November) and from Maisky and arrest the Soviet attempts to maintain the military equilibrium. Not for the first time in Soviet history, when ideology and state interests collided, 'Realpolitik' gained the upper hand in the Kremlin.[48] With the fate of Madrid still very much in the balance, Litvinov informed Maisky in November that Soviet assistance would gradually cease. 'The Spanish question has undoubtedly significantly worsened our international position,' he explained. 'It has spoiled our relations with England and France and sown doubt in Bucharest and even in Prague.'[49]]

1 December

Lothian lunched with me today. Despite some wobbles along the way, we meet and talk from time to time. It's interesting. He is a bright representative and ideologist of the imperialist wing of the English bourgeoisie *par excellence*, and his pronouncements often reflect its latest moods…

Today the mood was vague and alarmed. Lord Lothian's Germanophilia has faded, owing especially to Hitler's colonial demands. 'I emphatically warned my German friends against raising this issue, for it can sow discord between Germany and England, but they just will not listen,' he said. L. criticized the German–Japanese pact, and the Franco-Soviet pact, too, saying that the latter had led to the former. L. is very afraid that Italy may join the German–Japanese pact. Then the world will split into two camps and, forced to choose, England will have no choice but to enter into alliance with France and the USSR (perhaps the USA will join in, too, if and when they recover from isolationism). Eventually, the history of 1914 may be repeated, and a new world war will become inevitable. L. clings to the hope that peace can be preserved for another three or four years; Hitler, Mussolini and the Japanese will be broken, and the global atmosphere will improve.

I laughed and added that it was precisely the process of 'broken dictators' that was most likely to trigger an armed conflict.

L. nodded in reply and said sadly: 'That is what I fear the most.'

Then L. returned to the question of the German–Japanese pact. He does not like it. In his opinion, it will result not in Nazi aggression against the USSR, since the USSR is far too strong, but in an increase of German pressure in Europe and of Japanese pressure in Asia. The British Empire, moreover, may easily suffer. Indeed, an attack against the USSR would be a very risky operation for Germany and Japan in any conditions. Far easier to make good at the expense of the 'huge, rich, fattened-up, slow-moving, and highly vulnerable body which goes by the name of the British Empire; all the more so as this is a democracy characterized by a diversity of opinions and slow operation' (L.'s own words). All this does not sound promising for the people represented by L.

As for the Spanish question, L. seems to be closer to us than I expected. Proceeding from the imperial interests of Great Britain, L. prefers the victory of the Spanish government. For this reason, he severely criticized the position of the British government. 'All intelligent people understand,' L. said, 'that we are currently seeing in Spain the first serious duel between the USSR on the one side and Germany and Italy on the other. Much depends on the outcome of this test of strength, including the future orientation of British policy. The English always gravitate towards the victor. If the fascist powers prevail in this conflict, England may ultimately, and very reluctantly, join them. If the USSR wins, an Anglo-Franco-Soviet alliance will become a *fait accompli* in the near future.'

The situation is not quite so simple, of course, but L.'s arguments are very interesting and symptomatic.

1937

The last two or three months have seen unmistakable shifts in British foreign policy. These have been suggested first by Eden's four speeches last November and December, and secondly by the change in the British government's attitude towards the Spanish question.

I'll begin with the speeches. But first I should say a few words about my conversation with Eden on 3 November. We had a long talk which was primarily devoted to the Spanish issue but which also dealt with a range of other international issues. On the Spanish question, I criticized the British position openly, before telling Eden: yes, serious disagreement exists between us. But we should not exaggerate its significance. We should do our best to localize it so that this specific disagreement should have the smallest possible effect on Anglo-Soviet relations in other parts of the world and in other important matters of world politics. We should not forget that besides Spain there exists an entire world – Europe, the Near East, the Far East, the League of Nations, etc. Let us make every effort to ensure that the course outlined by the Moscow communiqué which was issued at the end of Eden's visit to the USSR is pursued as closely as possible in all these spheres and problems, a course that proceeds from the fact that no serious clash of interests between the USSR and the British Empire can be found anywhere in the world. Meanwhile, life will resolve the Spanish question one way or another.

Eden agreed with my point of view and promised to assist in making it a reality.[1] Then we discussed Germany, Italy, the League of Nations, etc. It was then that Eden told me that the British government, thanks in large measure to his insistence, had decided to make one more attempt to revive the League of Nations and that he was busy developing various initiatives in this direction. I replied that this was all well and good, but that the most important factor in containing aggressive tendencies in Europe was the steadfast position of England and France, and particularly of England in regard to Berlin and Rome. Comically horrified, Eden exclaimed: 'You don't want me to be as impudent as Hitler, do you?'

'I don't mean impudence, I mean firmness,' I parried.

We continued discussing general political subjects for a while. I noticed that Eden's mind was in ferment, that he was looking if not for ways, then at least for forms through which he could carry out his policies.

And then there followed the four speeches made by the foreign secretary: in parliament on 5 November, in Leamington, his constituency, on 20 November, at the lunch arranged by the British Chamber of Commerce in honour of the Belgian prime minister, Van Zeeland, on 28 November, and in Bradford on 15 December. A summary of the content of the speeches would lead one to the following conclusions:

(1) The British government has decided to make one more attempt to revive the League of Nations and, in particular, to achieve the repeal of the unanimity rule, as set out in Article 11, and the de facto application of Article 19.

(2) The British government has recognized the indivisibility of peace in Europe in principle, but in practice it is prepared to render armed assistance against aggression only to France and Belgium (and, outside Europe, to Iran and Egypt).

(3) The British government has declared that it is ready to seek an agreement with Germany, but one which should not bear an exclusive character and which should not be directed against third countries. At the same time, the British government has made it clear that there can be no question of giving any serious assistance to Germany in the financial-economic sphere without a general European settlement, which must also include issues of disarmament.

(4) Finally, the British government has come out very firmly against the division of the world into two 'ideological blocs', the issue which the Nazis have been so hysterical about lately. It was with this in mind that the British government censured the anti-Comintern pact, while the British press has not held back in its sharp criticism of Hitler and Ribbentrop.

Appraising Eden's speeches, I would define the current position of the British government in the following way: England's prolonged retreat in the face of aggression has ended, at least for as long as the guidelines announced by Eden remain in force; but there has been as yet no counteroffensive against the aggressors. So far only the intention has been declared. In other words, the British government issued a political 'promissory note' of major importance through Eden's speeches. The future will show how this note is to be paid.

Now a few words on the Spanish question. Last October the British government clearly gambled on Franco winning. This was all too obvious in the notorious Non-Intervention Committee. Moreover, Eden himself ventured a rash statement against the USSR in parliament. Responding to the opposition's attacks concerning the failure by Germany and Italy to observe the principle of non-intervention, he lost his temper and said that those two countries were hardly the worst sinners in this respect. The arrow was manifestly aimed at the USSR. It is said that Eden's words slipped out at a moment of extreme vexation, under harassment from Labour MPs, and that afterwards he greatly regretted his lack of restraint... Perhaps. But facts are facts.

The British government's attitude has certainly changed for the better. Already in his Bradford speech (15 December), Eden declared that 'England is deeply interested in the integrity and inviolability of Spain and Spanish possessions', while during our conversation of 21 December he plainly admitted that the war in Spain was 'international', citing the German landing in Cadiz. Several days later, on 30 December, Burgin (deputy minister for trade) openly told me that England should in fact be deeply grateful to the USSR for what the latter was doing in Spain. One could hear similar views quite often here in recent weeks. Plymouth's[i] conduct in the Committee has also changed. I would characterize the British government's current position with regard to Spain roughly as follows: it is not supportive of the Republicans, but it has also stopped supporting Franco. Its position is close to genuine neutrality, with perhaps a slight bias towards Valencia. The British government does not itself want to render assistance to the Republic, but it is prepared to sympathize if somebody else does so. At least that's something!

What are the reasons for this shift in British foreign policy?

I would single out four major elements:

(1) England's increased fighting efficiency, particularly in the sphere of aviation.

(2) The reinforcement of Anglo-French rapprochement, which, with the rise to power of the Blum government in France, has effectively grown into an Anglo-French alliance.

(3) The activity of the USSR in Spain, which shows that we can be a serious factor in Western Europe and that the forces for peace in this part of the globe can count on the Soviet Union.

(4) The growing 'impertinence' of Germany, which takes the liberty not only of openly mocking Locarno, but also of furthering its colonial demands.

Of course, any illusions here would be dangerous. The English are infected to the core with the poison of 'compromise' and 'balance-of-power politics'. Besides, class hatred towards the USSR remains a fixed reality. Also, the current situation deters the City from effecting any drastic changes in the political and economic spheres. I do not know whether British policy will remain at its present level (if not above it), yet the aforesaid shifts are certainly interesting and cannot be ignored.[2]

---

[i] Ivor Miles Windsor-Clive (2nd earl of Plymouth), Conservative parliamentary undersecretary for dominion affairs, January–June 1929; parliamentary undersecretary at the Department of Transport, 1931–32, the Colonial Office, 1932–36, and the Foreign Office, 1936–39.

[The setback to collective security and the creation of the anti-communist German–Japanese Axis, which Italy soon joined, prompted the Kremlin throughout the second half of 1936 to project a sense of invincibility, based on rapid expansion of the military and the doctrinal avant-garde reforms of the Red Army.[3] The autumn manoeuvres of 1935 and 1936 certainly impressed observers such as General Wavell,[i] particularly when it came to the defensive and deterrent capabilities of the Red Army.[4] Maisky's unusual candour in assuring the Foreign Office that 'neither Germany nor Japan, acting separately, would venture to attack Russia' was dismissed as 'a good deal of whistling to keep his courage up'. Indeed, when the Latvian minister taunted Maisky with what he called 'cock-crowing' about Soviet military strength, Maisky replied with a smile: 'It is done deliberately, and it "has its effect".' But the confidence was genuine and on open display during a weekend he spent with the Webbs.[5] Maisky was scathing about the performance of the Wehrmacht, and sceptical about Germany's ability to launch an attack on the Soviet Union. The army, he argued, had 'neither the trained men, nor the mechanical equipment, for effective action … Half the tanks on the recent manoeuvres, attended by the military attachés of the Berlin embassies, failed to reach their destination either because the drivers were not skilled, or because the tanks were badly constructed.' The British 'far-flung empire' seemed to him to be more vulnerable, and without allies could not defend either its Far Eastern shores against Japan or the route to India out of the Mediterranean. Although the Soviet Union entertained no territorial ambitions, he feared that the British statesmen were 'bad imperialists, who were prepared to sacrifice the British Empire to their prejudice against the new social order of the USSR'.[6] The confidence, which might have encouraged the Russians to opt for isolation, was short-lived, however, and dissipated with Stalin's massacre within the armed forces.[7]]

16 January

The Japanese ambassador, Shigeru Yoshida,[ii] paid me an unexpected visit. The pretext of his visit was quite absurd: allegedly, he wanted to inform me personally why the lunch he had invited me to the day before yesterday had had to be cancelled (although I already knew the reason from a telephone conversation between our secretaries). But such *clumsiness* is quite in the spirit of Japanese diplomacy.

The essence of the matter was, of course, quite different. Yoshida had evidently come to provide some reassurance about the impact of the German–Japanese pact and, while he was about it, to demonstrate that he did not belong to the aggressive school of Japanese political thought. Certainly, Y. was very candid. He was sharply critical of the actions taken by the army and navy of his country and said that the Japanese people had to pay heavily for their

---

[i] Archibald Percival Wavell, field marshal, commander-in-chief, Middle East, 1939–41; commander-in-chief, India, 1941–43; supreme commander, south-west Pacific, 1942; viceroy and governor-general of India, 1943–47.
[ii] Shigeru Yoshida, Japanese ambassador to Great Britain, 1936–39; prime minister of Japan, 1946–54.

'stupidities'. By way of an example, Y. cited Japan's refusal to sign the agreement on the limitation of naval armament. He referred to the German–Japanese pact as another example. 'I can only hope,' the Japanese ambassador added, 'that this will be the last stupidity committed by my government.' In saying that, he hoped to gain my assurance that Japan would not have to pay too high a price for the German–Japanese pact. Naturally, I refrained from reassuring Y.; on the contrary, I gave him a bit of a fright.

Y. expressed his conviction that an excessively inflated budget and the drastically increased tax burden would quickly sober up Japan's leading circles, and that they would have to switch to a more reasonable foreign policy. I replied: 'Would that you were right! Let's wait and see. So far I see no signs of any sobering up.'

Y. also told me that trade complications between Japan and the British colonies were becoming increasingly aggravated, that the trade agreement with India was expected to be extended, and that economic talks between London and Tokyo were possible in the near future. Y. also intimated that the Japanese–Chinese talks could be resumed soon.

17 February

Today I gave Vansittart our declaration of adherence to the regulations of submarine warfare.

Then we talked about the present state of Anglo-German relations. According to V., it could be defined as 'running on the spot'. Neither Hitler's speech on 30 January,[8] nor Ribbentrop's recent talk with Halifax had changed a thing. Ninety per cent of that talk, which had lasted two hours, consisted of a monologue by Ribbentrop. Halifax merely made a few remarks and asked a few questions. Ribbentrop spoke on two issues: (1) regarding colonies, he demanded that all former German colonial possessions should be returned to Germany, and (2) regarding the French–Soviet pact, Ribbentrop argued, as ever, that this pact was the main obstacle to peace in Europe. Halifax, on his part, wanted to know when to expect Germany's response to the British note of 18 November 1936 concerning Locarno. Ribbentrop's answer was rather vague. Halifax then said that the satisfaction of Germany's colonial claims presented great difficulties. That was all. Since the talk was no more than a general exchange of views, the British government did not find it necessary to make any reply to Ribbentrop on the issues he raised.

As to Runciman's trip to the USA, V. noted that the current state of Anglo-American relations was very good, but he explicitly refuted the rumours circulating in Europe that Runciman was probing the possibility in America of granting a loan to Germany. According to V., the very assumption that such an issue could be raised at present is 'laughable'. Is it? I'm not so sure.

12 March

On 4 March, all heads of diplomatic missions submitted their credentials to the new king, George VI.[i] The procedure was simplified and carried out *en masse*. All the ambassadors and envoys were lined up in order of seniority in the Bow Room of Buckingham Palace. They were admitted one by one to the neighbouring room, where the king was expecting them, submitted their credentials to him, exchanged a few remarks as demanded by protocol, and left, giving way to those still waiting. The king devoted two or three minutes to each diplomat. Eden was present at the ceremony and gave some assistance, as the king is taciturn and easily embarrassed. He also stammers. The entire ceremony went smoothly. The only shock, which caused quite a stir in the press and in society, was Ribbentrop's 'Nazi salute'. When the German ambassador entered the room to meet the king, he raised his right hand in greeting, rather than making the usual bow. This 'novelty' offended the English deeply and triggered an adverse reaction in conservative circles. Ribbentrop was accused of tactlessness and was compared with me – a 'good boy' who greets the king properly, without raising a clenched fist above his head.[9]

To meet the diplomats' wives, the king and queen also gave a five o'clock tea party today, inviting the heads of missions and their spouses. Ribbentrop again saluted the king with a raised hand, but he bowed to the queen in the normal manner. The little princesses were also present: Elizabeth[ii] and Margaret Rose,[iii] both wearing light pink dresses and, it was clear, terribly excited to be present at such an 'important' ceremony. But they were also curious in a childish way about everything around them. They shifted from one foot to the other, then they began to giggle, and then to misbehave, to the considerable embarrassment of the queen. Lord Cromer[iv] led my wife and me to the royal couple and we had quite a long chat – I with the king and Agniya with the queen. The ladies were for the most part discussing children, whereas the king inquired about the state of our navy and the White Sea–Baltic Canal. The king expressed great satisfaction when I informed him that the battleship *Marat* would arrive for the coronation.

---

[i] King George VI, 1936–52. Strangely, Maisky does not relate much about the abdication crisis.
[ii] Since 1952, Queen Elizabeth II of the United Kingdom of Great Britain and Northern Ireland.
[iii] Princess Margaret Rose Windsor (countess of Swindon), daughter of George VI.
[iv] Rowland Thomas Baring (2nd earl of Cromer), lord chamberlain, 1922–38.

33. Setting off for an 'afternoon party' at Buckingham Palace.

10 April

Reviewing Anglo-Italian relations since the end of the Abyssinian war, one can distinguish two periods.

The first period, extending roughly over the second half of 1936, was marked by earnest attempts by both parties to bring relations back to normal. There were clear reasons for this. Italy was interested in the 'recognition' of its African conquests by Great Britain, in securing the City's financial aid (a hope it still retains), and in concluding an agreement with Great Britain on the restriction of the latter's armed forces in the Mediterranean. London, in its turn, was interested in gaining time for rearmament, relieving its position in the Mediterranean, driving a wedge into the emerging German–Italian axis and, finally, exerting some pressure on Italy with respect to the Spanish question.

As a result, the Italian press changed its tone considerably towards Great Britain after the Abyssinian war, while Mussolini found it possible to declare solemnly on 18 June 1936 that 'no contentious issues remain between Italy and Great Britain'. Italian policy stuck to that line throughout the second half of last year, including Grandi's conduct in the Non-Intervention Committee. He was always sharp and quick-tempered towards the USSR, but mild and considerate towards England.

Simultaneously, British government circles energetically promoted a policy of appeasement with respect to Italy (in so far as the circumstances, and especially the opposition's hostility to Mussolini, permitted them). The British government encountered many internal difficulties, but Vansittart was very active, while the traditional English habit of accepting *faits accomplis* facilitated the Cabinet's move toward the 'normalization' of relations.

The two sides' tendencies and efforts resulted in a gentlemen's agreement signed on 2 January 1937.

However, the next three months, which may be regarded as the second period, brought bitter disappointment to the supporters of Anglo-Italian rapprochement. There were several reasons for this. First, concurrently with the signing of the gentlemen's agreement, the Italians disembarked their 'volunteer corps' in Cadiz, whose strength reached 80–100 thousand by the end of March. Although the agreement did not mention the war in Spain directly, the Italian initiative was perceived in England as a swindle. That immediately undermined the precarious basis for 'normalization'. Second, an attempt on the life of General Graziani[i] was made in Addis Ababa on 19 February. Driven by fear and the desire for revenge, the Italians slaughtered as many as 6,000 civilians, regardless of sex or age. This prompted a furious anti-Italian campaign in England, joined even by the archbishop of Canterbury (his speech of 16 March). Third, in response to the British campaign the Italians resumed their anti-British campaign in the east, and Grandi refused to discuss the withdrawal of 'volunteers' from Spain – an issue to which the British government attached great importance – at a meeting of a subcommittee of the Non-Intervention Committee held on 23 March. At the same time, Mussolini made a theatrical trip to Libya, where he proclaimed himself 'defender of Islam' and shook his fist at the British Empire. Fourth, the British government reacted to the Italians' actions by inviting the Ethiopian emperor to the forthcoming coronation; Italy responded by refusing to send its own delegation.

Fifth, the British press reacted vociferously and rapturously to the Italians' defeat at Guadalajara.[10] Some newspapers even wrote that 'Basque fisherwomen' were throwing Italian soldiers (all armed to the teeth) out of the windows of their houses. This infuriated the Italian government and the Italian press. Sixth, Mussolini perceived the English rearmament programme, announced in March, as an arrow aimed at Italy, and quite lost his head.

In the final analysis, Anglo-Italian relations are so strained now that merely to speak of 'normalization' would be a joke in bad taste. In the past month, the

---

[i] Rodolfo Graziani (marquess di Neghelli), Italian viceroy of Ethiopia, 1936–37, chief of staff of the Italian armed forces, 1939; governor of Libya, 1940.

Italian government protested on four occasions to the British government in connection with the conduct of the British press.

On the whole, considering Britain's relations with Germany and Italy, current British foreign policy is closer to our line than ever before. But will this last long? It's difficult to say. Of course, Eden is prepared to go even further in this direction, but will he have the chance to do so? I'm not sure. I'm not even sure that Eden will be able to retain his present position for long, since Baldwin and Chamberlain are hardly allies in the resolute struggle against fascism and aggression.

16 April

My wife and I were invited by Eden to lunch at the Savoy. The guests were a mixed bunch: Minister for the Coordination of Defence Inskip,[i] Marshal of the Diplomatic Corps Clive, the Chinese ambassador [Guo Taiqi], the Austrian [Franckenstein],[ii] and others, all in all 25 people. I was the senior guest.

At lunch, Eden's wife couldn't stop complaining about how busy she was and, most of all, about the haste with which everything had to be done. Not a moment to reflect, or to catch one's breath. Everything moves at breakneck speed, and you find yourself caught in a maelstrom from which there is no escape. Truly, our fathers and grandfathers lived in better times! Everything in the world was quieter, calmer and steadier then. There was time enough for taking a walk, reading a book or having a think. 'Why wasn't I born in that time?' Mrs Eden sighed.

After lunch I talked with her husband. Our conversation revolved around Spain. Eden told me, among other things, that last September and October the British government was already nursing the idea of granting belligerent rights to both combatants. The Admiralty was particularly insistent on this point. Eden objected because he did not want to upset France, who could never agree to this for reasons of domestic politics. He sets great store by the close ties that have now been established with Paris. After Germany and Italy recognized Franco, granting belligerent rights became even more difficult, as it would look like semi-recognition of Franco and would have serious repercussions in England. So far Eden is succeeding in preserving the British government's current position, which does not recognize Franco's belligerent rights.

---

[i] Thomas Inskip (1st Viscount Caldecote), minister for coordination of defence, 1936–39; secretary of state for dominion affairs, January–September 1939 and May–October 1940; lord chief justice of England, 1940–46.

[ii] Georg Albert von und zu Franckenstein, Austrian ambassador to the United Kingdom, 1920–38. An opponent of Nazism, he sought asylum in London after being dismissed from his post.

Eden's position on the Spanish question is, in essence, rotten: on the face of it, England does not care which side wins, because Spain will be extremely weakened at the end of its civil war and it will have to start looking for money, which it can find only in London or Paris. The pound is more powerful than the cannon. Therefore, the British government does not worry too much about the outcome of the Spanish war. On the other hand, Eden is terribly afraid that England might get trapped in the Spanish events, since Spain, according to Eden, is a death-trap for anyone who tries to poke their nose into its affairs. Take Napoleon, Wellington and now Mussolini. Mussolini's prestige was much higher prior to his Spanish adventure than it is at the moment. And unless he hastens to leave Spain, he is headed for a bad end.

Here Eden added with a cunning smile: 'You are conducting your Spanish campaign brilliantly: you are doing whatever you consider necessary without getting bogged down. You even preserve the appearance of complete innocence.' I replied in the same tone: 'Now even Ribbentrop has stopped yelling about the fact that there is a large Soviet army in Spain.' 'An army, you say?' Eden exclaimed. 'You've given the Spaniards something far more important than an army, particularly an army like the Italian one.' I grinned and said: 'The Non-Intervention Committee deemed the USSR's participation in the war in Spain to be unproven.'

17 April

That was some lunch! Yoshida, evidently sticking to his course of trying to improve relations with the USSR, hosted a lunch at which I and the Chinese ambassador were senior guests. Also present were the Japanese ambassador in Moscow Shigemitsu,[i] Leith-Ross, Rendel[ii] (head of the Near East department of the Foreign Office), and some others. It turned out to be a sort of show of Japanese–Soviet–Chinese friendship. It was the first time during my stay in London that I received an invitation to lunch from the Japanese ambassador, and to a very exclusive lunch at that!

After lunch, Yoshida tried to bring it home to me that the newly appointed government headed by Hayashi[iii] would pursue a more conciliatory foreign policy, particularly with respect to the USSR and China, that the present government would be defeated at the forthcoming parliamentary election, that

[i] Mamoru Shigemitsu, Japan's vice-minister of foreign affairs, 1933–36; ambassador to Moscow, 1936–38; ambassador to London, 1938–41.
[ii] Sir George William Rendel, head of the eastern department, Foreign Office, 1930–38; envoy extraordinary and minister plenipotentiary to Bulgaria, 1938–41; British minister and (later) ambassador to the Yugoslav government in London, 1941–43.
[iii] Senjuro Hayashi, Japanese minister of war, 1934–35; prime minister of Japan, February–June 1937.

long-established parties would gain the majority of votes, and that Hayashi would have to form his new national party after the election by trying to split Minseitō and Seiyukai. It remains to be seen, however, whether he will bring this off. Then Yoshida began complaining about the 'aggressiveness' of the USSR, which keeps large military forces in the Far East. But were we to agree to transfer part of those forces to the country's interior, a peaceful atmosphere would immediately be restored in Japanese–Soviet relations. I turned his complaint into a joke, saying: 'Mr Ambassador, don't you know that all our military forces in the Far East have as their only task the protection of Soviet frontiers against "the bandits", who, according to your own Japanese sources, still teem in Manchuria?'[11]

Rendell spoke at length and with great enthusiasm about Comrade Litvinov, whom he met at last year's conference about the Straits in Montreux.

18 April

The Vansittarts came to us for lunch. The lunch was *à quatre* and our conversation was quite frank. Vansittart is certain that the Cabinet will be restructured after the coronation, with Baldwin resigning, Chamberlain taking his place, and Simon most probably becoming chancellor of the exchequer. Eden will remain in his post. When I inquired about Chamberlain's foreign policy, V. said that its general character would not change but that it would become somewhat better defined. As regards Germany, Chamberlain is considered *all right*. Well, we shall see. I'm somewhat sceptical about V.'s assurances. I recall how, in the spring of 1935, he also tried to set my mind at rest concerning Hoare, and we know how that turned out…

According to V., anti-German and anti-Italian sentiments are growing in England. A change in the position of *The Times* is particularly telling in this respect. Even Lothian treats Germany with increasing suspicion. The prospects for a new Locarno pact are very faint. The gentlemen's agreement with Italy, signed on 2 January, yielded nothing – Spain, Addis Ababa and other circumstances are to blame. The Berlin–Rome axis is getting manifestly stronger. Disagreements between Germany and Italy are not so great at present to prevent rapprochement. V. sees no point in concluding a new Locarno pact. Until Germany changes its current system of education, whereby the country's youth are brought up on the principle of expansion at the expense of others, V. will not believe in Hitler's readiness to observe the agreements he signs.[12]

V. said that the British government is concerned about Germany's attempts to strengthen its position in the Near East and, in particular, about its intention to have an air route across Iraq, Persia and Afghanistan. It was clear that V. disapproves of this project, but that his current position is to wait and see.

21 April

Eden and his wife came to dinner at the embassy. There were many diplomats, public figures and other guests. On the whole, it went off well.

After dinner I had a long talk with Eden about the commission for the settlement of the Syrian conflict (between France and Turkey), about England's conduct at the Disarmament Conference Bureau to be convened in May, and about the forthcoming coronation. Spain, naturally, occupied most of our discussion, and Eden, to my mind, displayed unjustified optimism. Here are his arguments.

Germany is increasingly inclined to leave Spain. The same tendency is growing in Italy, where the 'Spanish war' is becoming less and less popular. Furthermore, Abyssinia is eating up a great deal of money and effort. According to British information, the internal situation in Italy is becoming ever more difficult. Meanwhile, 'the Spanish adventure' (Eden's exact words) continues to require new and larger investments on the part of Mussolini, in terms of money, arms and manpower. These are unacceptable to him. Hence the conclusion: Mussolini is looking for 'a golden bridge' to leave Spain. Such a bridge needs to be built for him. That is the current task of the Non-Intervention Committee. If Germany and Italy leave Spain, one can count on the Spanish war ending by autumn. How? That's difficult to say. Eden favours a compromise between the two Spanish fronts and the formation of an interim government by Franco and Caballero.[i] Eden spoke with sympathy, although with certain reservations, about the *day dream* set out by Churchill at the Commons session on 13 April.

If Eden's expectations were to materialize (and he hopes they will), the ground would be cleared for the major European issues to be addressed by early winter. All the more so as British armaments will have increased considerably by that time, whereas the internal difficulties of Germany and Italy will have intensified.

I objected to this and criticized Eden's conception. In particular, I expressed my utter conviction that Mussolini was not going to leave Spain so easily. I sense this at every session of the Non-Intervention Committee. Eden stuck to his guns and finally said: 'You Soviets are eternal pessimists. You see dangers everywhere, even where there are none.'

'But don't you find that nine times out of ten we turn out to be right?' I retorted.

Eden laughed, but at that moment his wife came up to say good-bye.[13]

---

[i] Francisco Largo Caballero, prime minister of the Spanish Republic, 1936–37.

34. The sailors of the Soviet battleship *Marat* greeted by Maisky in the garden of the embassy.

24 May

The battleship *Marat*, which had arrived to take part in the coronation festivities, left yesterday. She was docked at Spithead for a week. The effect of her appearance was certainly positive. First, it was a sort of official recognition of the Soviet navy on the part of England. Soviet ships had never participated in naval parades in Great Britain before. Second, it was a good display of the efficiency of our navy. Two things particularly impressed the English: (a) during that week there was not a single case of drunken misbehaviour, a single fight or a single scandal involving sailors from the *Marat*. So the 'jail' prepared for Soviet sailors just in case remained empty, whereas similar 'jails' prepared for sailors from other countries had no lack of clientele; (b) on entering Spithead, the *Marat* moored in the space of 55 minutes, whereas warships of other nations spent several hours on this operation, while, at the previous coronation in 1911, it had taken a Russian battleship a whole 15 hours; (c) the arrival of the *Marat* was interpreted in court and political circles as a sign of the USSR's friendly disposition towards England. Churchill told me that the king and the government were particularly impressed by the 'Hurrah!' with which the Marat sailors greeted the passing royal yacht, as custom demands. It was an ordinary Russian 'Hurrah!' – broad, booming and repercussive. However, compared to the short and abrupt hurrahs of the English and most other nations, which sounded rather like the barking of dogs, it was perceived by court circles as especially warm and cordial. Even the press said the same.

We arranged trips to London on omnibuses for the *Marat* crew, and they visited the embassy in groups before touring the city and its sights. Our trade mission opened a shopping centre aboard the *Marat* selling essential goods. I gave a speech to the crew on the international situation. Then Agniya and myself inspected the battleship 'from head to toe'.

It all went rather well.

9 June

I went to see Vansittart. We discussed a variety of subjects, but there were two issues of particular importance.

The first was Germany. I said that I had observed a certain shift in Anglo-German relations lately. I listed a number of facts: the transfer of Phipps from Berlin to Paris; the appointment of Sir Nevile Henderson,[i] a fervent Germanophile, as ambassador to Berlin instead of Phipps, whom Hitler dislikes; a change in the tone of the British Conservative press with regard to Germany; the broad coverage in the English press of the dispatching of medical personnel by air to Gibraltar to render aid to the wounded sailors of the *Deutschland*;[14] and, finally, Henderson's speeches in Berlin, during the presentation of credentials and especially at the dinner arranged by the Anglo-German society.[15] All this induced certain thoughts. I stressed, in particular, that Henderson's last speech had caused 'amazement' in Moscow, not to mention other more definite emotions. What could V. say to explain all this?

V., of course, tried to persuade me that nothing had changed, that everything remained as before. Mere 'running on the spot'. The objective of the British government is to conclude an all-European agreement, though it would accept the restoration of the Locarno pact as a first step in that direction. But Locarno is static. Neither London nor Berlin is in a hurry to negotiate. The Foreign Office, for instance, has still not responded to the German note on Locarno received three months ago. As for Henderson, his Berlin speech at the English–German dinner was entirely his own creation; the FO was not responsible. The FO had not even seen the text of the speech before it was delivered. V. agreed that Henderson had said a lot of unnecessary things (there was even a question in parliament about his speech), but he pleaded 'mitigating circumstances': Henderson's inexperience and his poor knowledge of current European politics – he has been in South America until now. V. expressed the hope that Henderson would be more careful in future.

---

[i] Sir Nevile Henderson, British ambassador to Germany, 1937–39.

The second issue, which had been raised by the Australian premier Lyons,[i] was the Pacific pact. I asked V. what the British government thought of Lyons' idea. V. avoided giving a direct answer and started beating about the bush: Lyons himself has not thought out his proposal properly and is not yet sure whether the point in question is a pact of non-aggression or mutual assistance. Furthermore, Lyons' plan first has to be digested by the Imperial Conference before being submitted to the FO for consideration. Then things will be clearer. Meanwhile the issue remains in an embryonic state.

In conclusion V. informed me with great pleasure that Anglo-Japanese talks will begin in the near future on the entire package of issues that interest both countries (economic, political, etc.), and that the Japanese proposals were on their way from Tokyo to London.

[Vansittart denied a reorientation of British policy towards Germany but conceded – though Maisky neglected to report the fact to Moscow – that a change in atmosphere meant 'the prospects of reaching a result were perhaps slightly better' than a couple of months earlier. Vansittart further admitted (as Maisky did report to Moscow) that the propaganda campaign waged by 'Germanophile elements' in England had intensified considerably.[16] Chamberlain was indeed coming under increased pressure from various quarters to rein in the Foreign Office. Hoare strengthened his hand, complaining that 'the FO is so much biased against Germany (and Italy and Japan) that unconsciously and almost continuously they are making impossible any European conciliation'.[17] The drift towards 'appeasement' became the subject of conflicting appraisals in Narkomindel and the London embassy. It seemed to confirm Litvinov's growing belief that the British government was intent on washing its hands of Spain, enabling Germany and Italy to beat the Republicans. Maisky was less than comforted by Eden's assurances that 'as long as he was in the chair' there would be no change in policy. He attributed the drift to the British failure to detach Italy from the newly established German–Italian 'axis' following the war in Abyssinia. He was 'not inclined to attach much significance' to the overtures made to Berlin, as he expected Hitler to produce 'new tricks' in Spain or elsewhere in Europe, which would bring rapprochement to an end.[18]]

15 June

The Australian premier Lyons came to see me at the embassy and the two of us had a frank talk over tea.

I inquired about the Pacific pact. Lyons said that he preferred a mutual assistance pact to a non-aggression pact, but since he was sure that neither England nor in particular the USA would accept such a proposal, he was ready to concede to a non-aggression pact as an initial step in the desired direction.

---

[i] Joseph Aloysius Lyons, Labour prime minister of Australia, 1931–39.

But he conceives the non-aggression pact as one that stipulates the consultation of its participants in the event of aggression against a pact member by another power (irrespective of whether the latter is a pact member or not). Then Lyons told me about the outcome of his talks in London with representatives of various powers. To summarize: England's attitude to the idea of the pact is generally positive and the Foreign Office has been told to work on the details. New Zealand certainly supports the pact and so does Canada, but without such enthusiasm. The Chinese ambassador in London assured Lyons that the project had China's wholehearted sympathy. The Japanese ambassador, with whom Lyons also spoke, showered him with questions, but steered clear of expressing an opinion. In a conversation with Lyons two years ago, Roosevelt went along with the idea of a Pacific non-aggression pact, and now Bingham, the US ambassador in London, has confirmed this position. In conclusion, Lyons asked me where the USSR stood on this issue.

I replied that the Soviet government has a very positive view of the idea of a Pacific pact; that it prefers a mutual assistance pact but would be ready to join a non-aggression pact, too. In the opinion of the Soviet government, the only correct negotiation tactics are those that would make the Japanese understand from the very beginning that the pact will come about whether they join it or not. Only under this condition is there hope of forcing a degree of 'cooperation' from Japan.

Lyons was extremely glad to hear this and added that my words filled him with renewed energy. He agreed that our tactical line was correct and promised to continue his 'propaganda' in this vein among the interested powers, among which he includes the countries of the British Empire, France, Holland, the USSR, Japan, China, the USA and Portugal.

However, Lyons can hardly do much for the Pacific pact at the moment. On returning to Australia he will have to hold elections to the federal parliament. If he wins (and he is counting on the fact), the struggle for the Pacific pact will become his major foreign-policy objective. If the opposition wins, then, according to Lyons, the Pacific pact will be as good as dead, since the opposition is seriously infected with isolationism.

Then we talked at length about the USSR. Lyons asked me lots of questions and I gave him answers. His mental picture of our country is rather vague. He voiced his desire to visit the USSR personally one day, but not 'now', as 'now' he had no time.

The Australian premier is curious to look at: average height, sturdy, limping, strong-faced, and with a great big mop of lustrous grey hair that surrounds his head with a kind of radiance. Lyons' political significance for Australia is about the same as Ramsay MacDonald's for Great Britain.

16 June

Today I called on Titulescu,[i] who is staying, as always, in the Ritz Hotel and who is his usual noisy, dazzling, confident and even impudent self.

Titulescu has been in London for about a week. He has managed to see Chamberlain, Eden, Vansittart, Churchill and many others in high places, as well as to deliver two speeches: one at a Parliamentary Labour session and the other at the Royal Institute for International Affairs. While I was with him, he let me run my eyes over his speech to the Labour members.

Titulescu has been saying more or less the same things to everyone: peace in Europe and the integrity of the British Empire depend on whether a peace front led by England, France and the USSR can be set up in good time. If this happens, everything will be fine. If not, mankind in general and Great Britain in particular will have to endure a two-act tragedy: Act 1 is the forging of *Mitteleuropa* by Germany and Act 2 is the destruction of the British Empire by *Mitteleuropa*. The British should make their choice and do so urgently. To sweeten the pill, Titulescu has told the British that there is no need for them to undertake any firm commitments with regard to Eastern Europe. Undertaking such commitments with regard to France would do. 'The rest,' Titulescu added with a cunning smile, 'is sure to follow.' He assured me that his propaganda was successful, and this seems to be true: I have heard confirmation from various sources of the ex-minister's somewhat boastful statements. In particular, his speech in parliament made quite an impression on Labour MPs.

Titulescu also observed that Germanophile sentiments have grown considerably in England since his last visit to London in March 1936.

In reply to my question about his plans for the near future, Titulescu first told me the story, at very great length, of how the Germans have attempted to poison him three times in Switzerland and Bucharest. Then he said that he would return to Rumania in October. It was dangerous, of course, but he had to do it. He did not want to become a defector, as it would mean the end of his serious political activity and struggle. Titulescu, after all, is full of fire and determination. He dropped a typical remark on parting: 'If I am not assassinated within the first six months after my return home, Rumania will be mine!'[19]

28 June

I visited Beaverbrook at his country home. He was talking over the telephone with someone in Canada when I arrived. This immediately directed our conversation to the subject of the Imperial Conference that had just ended.

---

[i] Nicolae Titulescu, Rumanian foreign minister, 1927–28 and 1932–36; permanent representative at the League of Nations, 1920–36.

B. was far from enthusiastic about the conference. It had been dull and boring. It had added nothing to the cause of imperial unity. On the contrary, it seemed to have introduced a certain anxiety, for even as inveterate an imperialist as B., when summing up the results of the conference, stated frankly that the strength of imperial bonds could only be proven by the experience of war; he hoped they would stand the test. 'He hoped.' B.'s words did not express complete confidence, and this is highly symptomatic.

Then B. noted the lukewarm attitude of all dominions to the League of Nations in its current form. He said that Australia and New Zealand are in favour of collective security (but mainly in the form of a regional Pacific pact), while Canada and South Africa are strongly affected by isolationism. However, there is no danger of rapprochement between South Africa and Germany, given Germany's claims in South-West Africa.

B. views Chamberlain's foreign policy in the following way: the new premier will make every possible effort in the next few months to 'appease Europe', primarily by trying to strengthen ties with France and improve relations with Germany. Hence the unusual mildness of Chamberlain's speech in parliament on 25 May, which was sharply rebuffed by Lloyd George and the opposition. According to B., Chamberlain displays more interest in foreign affairs than Baldwin did, and therefore Eden will have less freedom of action than before.

1 July

Conversation with Lloyd George[20]

(1) My conversation with Lloyd George (in his country house) started with Spain. Lloyd George asked me for the latest news from the Non-Intervention Committee. I gave him a detailed description of the situation that developed after the subcommittee meeting on 29 June. The British and French governments had proposed to fill the gap in control created after the withdrawal of Germany and Italy with joint Anglo-French forces. Ribbentrop and Grandi agreed to pass the proposal to their governments for consideration. However, both delegates made it very clear through 'preliminary comments' that the British–French plan was unacceptable to Germany and Italy. The next meeting of the subcommittee is to take place on 2 July, and Ribbentrop and Grandi are expected to bring their governments' definitive responses to the British–French proposal. Judging by the behaviour of the German and Italian delegates at the meeting of 29 June, and considering the comments of the German and Italian press after the meeting, I am certain that neither Germany nor Italy will accept the proposals made by Britain and France. The situation may result in deadlock and the failure

of the entire system of non-intervention. To assess the situation correctly, one should not forget that Hitler and Mussolini have now come to the conclusion that the Spanish war, which has dragged on so long, must be ended as soon as possible. With this aim in mind, they want to make a new all-out effort in the nearest future to secure Franco's victory. After the elimination of the Basque front, Franco ought to concentrate his forces and aeroplanes against Madrid. Simultaneously, the Italian and German ships cruising along the Republican-controlled coastline may stage some new 'incident' and begin hostilities against the Spanish government by way of retaliation. Thus, squeezing the Republic by land and by sea, the Germans and Italians hope eventually to crush the Spanish government and rout its army. In the light of this plan, the behaviour of Ribbentrop and Grandi at the last meeting of the Subcommittee becomes absolutely clear. Germany and Italy are now striving to abolish naval control so as to have their hands free in their actions against the Republicans. That is where the major danger of the situation lies.

(2) Lloyd George listened to my information attentively. He readily agreed that the German–Italian plan I had outlined sounded perfectly realistic. 'A critical moment has been reached in the course of the Spanish war,' Lloyd George continued. 'The next few days will see the end of the entire Spanish campaign. What can be done to prevent the rout of the Republicans?' Lloyd George pondered and then, as if struck by inspiration, began to set out his plan. The entire opposition (both Labour and Liberal) should make it clear to the government that they will fight to the end against granting belligerent rights to Franco. He is sure that this is feasible. He had intended to stay a few more days in his country home, but in view of the extraordinary situation he will leave for London tomorrow and will meet the leaders of other opposition parties to work out concrete steps. 'I dislike it very much,' Lloyd George said,

> that Labour, campaigning in support of the Spanish government, proceeds from the interests of 'democracy' and appeals to the liberal instincts of the British population. They're missing the point. It is the Conservatives who hold power today, and no amount of yelling about the danger posed to 'democracy' by a victorious Franco will affect them. Let's be serious! The Conservatives do not care a fig about democracy. It would be more meaningful and effective to appeal to their imperial interests. Arguments to this effect could persuade even the diehards. For instance, yesterday I spoke at an election meeting in Walton, where the overwhelming majority of the audience were Conservatives. At first they were very hostile when I attacked the government on the Spanish issue. They shouted, whistled and tried to cut me short. Then I asked them: Are you patriots, or aren't you? That produced an immediate impression.

I continue: Do you want Franco to win? Do you want the Germans and
Italians to capture Spain? Do you want the Mediterranean to become a
sea controlled by the Italians? Do you want to leave our communication
lines to the east at the mercy of Italy and Germany? Tell me, has anything
remained in you of the spirit of Canning,[i] Palmerston,[ii] Disraeli[iii] and
Gladstone[iv] when they created our Empire? Or have you forgotten the
interests of the Empire? The longer I spoke the quieter the audience
became. When I finished, there was a burst of applause. I think that the
entire opposition, in its campaign in support of the Spanish government,
should now emphasize these concrete and highly important British
imperial interests.

(3) But the actions of the British opposition alone will hardly be sufficient
to prevent the government from taking dangerous steps. 'I sense,' Lloyd George
continued, 'that they (the government) are up to no good, and that to stop them
the assistance of the French government is required. I'll tell you frankly: the key
to the situation currently lies in Paris. Should the French government insist on
denying Franco belligerent rights, the British government will have to give in.
It values its good relations with France too much to jeopardize them by taking
a rash step. But will the French government take a firm stand?' Lloyd George
shrugged his shoulders and answered his own question: 'I don't know. Blum has
resigned and Chautemps[v] has replaced him. Blum was a real disappointment
to me. I had thought he was a strong man, but I was mistaken. I've never laid
eyes on Blum, but I've heard nothing about him to delight me. Blum is a very
refined, educated and likeable intellectual, but not a strong-willed and vigorous
statesman who can make the nation obey him. What to make of Chautemps?
I haven't the slightest idea. I've never met him. Foreign Minister Delbos[vi] is
weak and unintelligent. And what about the French ambassador here?' Lloyd
George asked me. I looked at him in surprise and asked, 'How come you do
not know Corbin?' 'Just imagine,' Lloyd George exclaimed, 'I've never met him,
not once!' I described Corbin's personality in a few words, without arousing
any enthusiasm in Lloyd George. But he exclaimed: 'No matter who Blum and

---

[i] George Canning, prominent British statesman of the late eighteenth and early nineteenth
century who served twice as foreign minister and became prime minister for the last four months
of his life in 1827.
[ii] Henry John Temple (3rd Viscount Palmerston), Tory foreign secretary, 1830–34, 1835–41 and
1846–51; prime minister, 1855–58 and 1859–65.
[iii] Benjamin Disraeli (1st earl of Beaconsfield), Tory MP, 1837–78; in House of Lords, 1878–80;
prime minister, February–December 1868 and 1874–80.
[iv] William Ewart Gladstone, Liberal prime minister, 1868–74, 1880–85, February–July 1886, and
1892–94.
[v] Camille Chautemps, French Socialist prime minister, February 1930, 1933–34 and 1937–38.
[vi] Yvon Delbos, French Radical politician; minister of foreign affairs, 1936–38.

Chautemps really are, we must do our best to strengthen the backbone of the French government. If only Attlee could go to Paris and see Blum. It would be very useful. But will he go?' Lloyd George thought for a moment and said: 'I'll talk about it with Attlee tomorrow.' I returned to the subject of the likely behaviour of the British government.

(4) The moment I mentioned the word 'government', Lloyd George all but leapt out of his seat. 'Government?' he asked sarcastically. 'Is it really a government? It's rather an assembly of mediocrities, a group of hopeless milksops. Do they have will? Or courage? Can they guard our interests? They inherited a rich legacy from their ancestors but they are managing it very badly, and I am afraid they will squander it. They are all wretched cowards. It is not cowardice, but daring that is needed to build and protect our Great Empire!' I observed that very few major figures could be seen on the European democratic horizon at the moment. 'You are absolutely right,' Lloyd George exclaimed.

'Where are they, the major figures? European democracy is in famine. There is only one big personality that democracy can boast of – Roosevelt. He knows what he wants and he knows how to get it. But Roosevelt is far away, and he doesn't want to meddle in European affairs. There's no point looking in England or France. Baldwin, Chamberlain, Blum or Chautemps – what are any of them good for? They have to deal with genuinely significant and powerful individuals – Hitler and Mussolini. Those fascist dictators are no fools. They are made of rough stuff and they use rough methods: force, impertinence, and intimidation. But they act, they are vigorous and energetic, and their countries follow after them. Are our ministers good enough to stand up for our interests in the face of dictators? Are they capable of that? Not a bit of it! If Winston Churchill were prime minister, he would know how to make the dictators reckon with him, but the Conservatives are terrified of admitting Churchill to the government. As a result, we have milksops dealing with men of action – Hitler and Mussolini. What a shame that both are fascists and opponents of democracy. But one has to admit that they are men of strength. Can you imagine what could happen if, say, Eden had talks with Mussolini? Mussolini would be sure to wipe the floor with him. That is exactly what happened at the time of the Abyssinian war. Your Stalin is a quite different matter. He is a big and very decisive man. He has a strong grip, he can impress dictators and he is capable of successfully repulsing Hitler and Mussolini. Ours are a sheer misfortune. Take Chamberlain – a narrow, limited and fruitless individual. A fish with a cold head – that's how I described him during the recent debates in parliament. Just look what he is up to at the moment. I know for sure that Chamberlain's 'master plan' amounts to the following: to make peace with Germany and Italy within the next year and to conclude a pact of four. As to Central and South-East Europe, Chamberlain is ready to rest satisfied with the dictators' vague pledges of non-aggression. Your country is to be shut out of the European mix and be left to its own devices.[21] After achieving all this, Eden wants to go to the polls. He will tell the voters: 'The insoluble problem of European appeasement has been resolved by me and my government. Now everything is all right. Vote Tory!' Having won the election, he'll secure his party's rule for another five years. The invitation to Neurath to visit London was his doing. Chamberlain's speech in parliament on 25 June was drafted in such a way that nothing, not a single word, could jeopardize the implementation of his intentions.

I argued that whatever Chamberlain's plans were, their realization did not depend on him alone. There are many factors that can prevent their implementation. Lloyd George livened up and exclaimed: 'Oh, of course, it is the height of naivety to believe that fascist dictators can be tamed merely with good words. They are a bloodthirsty pack and want their pound of flesh.'
(5) 'However,' Lloyd George went on,

I'll tell you frankly that our opposition, Labour in particular, is scarcely better than the government. It's worse and weaker in fact. The opposition has neither leaders, nor programme, nor energy, nor fighting spirit. They are still greater milksops than the government. Take Attlee. He is a nice man and he fought courageously in France during the war. But is he good as the leader of His Majesty's loyal opposition? He can make a fairly good speech now and then, but don't expect any actions – decisive actions – from him. I remember the time of Gladstone. We really had an opposition then, strong, full-blooded and capable of using every imprudent move of the government to launch a deadly attack. And what do we have now? The Liberal Party has quit the scene and is unlikely to rise again. As for Labour, they are yet to show they are capable of running the country. Our trouble is that we have no real opposition today. What we have are 160 MPs sitting on the opposition benches, but they are just an appendage to the Conservative Party. No wonder Labour have been losing heavily at recent by-elections. Instead of growing and developing, they stagnate and, of course, are quite incapable of rousing the enthusiasm of the masses. Strange as it may seem, there are only two Labour leaders who can muster and stir the masses at the moment: Cripps and Lansbury. The gatherings assembled by other leaders of the opposition are sparsely attended and deadly boring. Do you recall

Herodotus? Do you remember his story of the rebellion of the Parthian slaves? The Parthian king told his warriors then: 'Don't kill them; drive them back with whips.' Indeed, as soon as the warriors lashed at the slaves with their whips, the spirit of servitude immediately returned. The slaves screamed and dispersed, and the rebellion was suppressed. Our Labourites have a similarly powerful servile spirit. Age-old oppression and poverty nurtured in our workers the habit of obedience, submission, and a lack of faith in their own strength. That is why it is so easy for the Conservatives to frighten Labour with whips.

(6) I asked Lloyd George about his impressions from his visit to Germany last year. Lloyd George livened up and said:

I went to see Hitler and had a long talk with him. He struck me as a very unpretentious, modest, and quite well-educated man. One can discuss things with him and exchange opinions calmly. Yet, he has a sore point – communism. Every time Hitler mentioned communism or communists he immediately became deranged and his very face suddenly changed: his eyes flashed with sinister fire, and his lips began to twitch convulsively. Several times I tried to bring it home to him that unhealthy relations with your country could only put Germany at a disadvantage. But that made no impression on Hitler. He would begin shouting again, all but foaming at the mouth, about communism and the communist menace. He really believes that he was called to this world to accomplish a special mission: to save Western civilization and crush the hydra of communism. After all I saw at this meeting, I am entirely convinced that he will never agree to sign any sort of treaty with the Soviet Union, nor will he ever put his name to an international document alongside the signature of Stalin.

I inquired whether Lloyd George touched upon issues of European peace during his conversation with the Führer and what kind of response he received. 'Oh, yes,' Lloyd George exclaimed.

We spoke at length on this subject. Hitler kept trying to convince me of his love of peace. He advanced the following argument: it had taken Germany more than 40 years to build the powerful army it had had on the eve of the last war. He, Hitler, would need another 20 years to transform the Reichswehr into a major, battle-worthy force. How could it be in his interests to start a war before that time? I cannot deny that there is a grain of truth in Hitler's arguments. Hitler gave me permission to go anywhere and see whatever I wanted to see. By chance, when crossing Bavaria by car, I happened upon some large field exercises. I was permitted to drive through the training area, so I had the chance to take a closer look at the German army. I cannot say it impressed me much. True, there has been evident progress as far as weapons are concerned. I particularly liked the German anti-tank gun that later proved so helpful to Franco in Spain. But the men struck me as second-rate: the soldiers were small, puny, mere boys. Their training and discipline leaves much to be desired. An acute shortage of officers can be sensed. No, the German army today is not yet one that could risk a major war. It's a long way off the old German army which I saw and knew. So I am inclined to think that Hitler is right in saying that it will take him a great deal of time to make the German army genuinely battle-worthy – not 20 years perhaps, but 10 for sure. Until that time it's highly unlikely that Hitler will dare to attack France, us, or the USSR.

I replied that I could not entirely agree with Lloyd George's assessment. I am willing to concede that the German army is not yet ready for a major war, but what about a little war? A war against such countries as Austria, Czechoslovakia, Rumania and the like? It seems to me that the German army is ready enough to pave the way for Hitler to the south and south-east. What can prevent Hitler's expansion in that direction? Only the intervention of the great powers. Will they intervene? Will Great Britain and France take the risk? After the experience of recent years, I am rather sceptical. Lloyd George replied:

Well, if you put the question like that, you are right. I fully agree with you. This incurable weakness of our government and the French government, and these systematic retreats before the aggressors can only whet their appetite and make them more audacious. Hitler has got used to the cowardice of the Western democracies. One fine day he may indeed venture an attack on Austria or Czechoslovakia, in the expectation that he will get away with it as he has got away with much else in the past. The worst thing is that one cannot take Hitler at his word. The history of 'non-intervention' has taught me a great deal. The impression I had from my meeting last year did not prepare me in the slightest for such double-dealing on the part of the Führer, and I am coming more and more to the conclusion that all treaties and agreements with Germany are essentially meaningless. The signature of the German government is worth very little now. Hitler will observe a treaty for as long as he finds it profitable.

The moment he thinks the treaty restrains him, he will not hesitate to break it or tear it up. It is a graphic illustration of the degradation of international moral standards in Europe. And it is here that we find the greatest danger for peace.

That was the end of our conversation, and I returned to London.

P.S. I had the opportunity to observe the feebleness of the Labour opposition on the very next day after my meeting with Lloyd George. The 2nd of June was a Friday, the last day of the week in parliament. Unlike the sessions of the previous four days, which run from 2 p.m. to 11 p.m., the parliamentary session on Friday lasts from 11 a.m. to 4 p.m., after which MPs head off for their weekend. On 2 June I sat at the same table as Lloyd George in the parliamentary restaurant. It was two o'clock. The session was meant to last for two more hours, and the Labourites wanted to use the time to demand that the Spanish question be put on the agenda. Lloyd George was also going to speak. Suddenly a very embarrassed Attlee approached Lloyd George's table, waving his arms in confusion: 'They've closed the session!'

'How could they close the session if we have two more hours?' Lloyd George exclaimed in some amazement.

Attlee began to explain. It turned out that discussion of the item on the agenda had finished by two o'clock. Attlee was in his office at the time (the leader of the opposition has his own room in the parliament building) and there was not a single, remotely responsible individual on the opposition front bench to stand up and tell the Speaker that the opposition demanded adjournment, a technique regularly used by the opposition in parliament to put an urgent item on the agenda. So the Speaker announced that the agenda was concluded and immediately closed the session, without a single protest on the part of the opposition. Attlee stood before Lloyd George like a guilty schoolboy and asked what he should do next. He was quite lost and cut a pathetic figure. Lloyd George advised him to summon the leaders of the opposition in half an hour and discuss what steps could be taken. Attlee agreed and left. Lloyd George turned to me and said in a meaningful tone: 'See? That's our opposition for you! Could anything similar have ever happened in the past? In the past, when the Liberals were in opposition, we always left a few sharp-tongued men on the front bench to follow the debates and, if need be, demand adjournment. Then one of them would take the floor right away and, while he spoke, the party leader would be found and he would appear in parliament. And now? Now, Labour is incapable even of such simple tactics. Let me repeat: We do not have an opposition!'

27 July

Conversation with Eden

(1) Eden invited me to come to see him in the House of Commons. He told me that he was about to take a three-week vacation (but without leaving the country). Lord Halifax would act for him while he was absent. Eden wanted to discuss two issues with me: (1) the Far East and (2) Spain.

(2) Eden began with the Far East. Just this morning he received alarming news from Beijing.²² His initial optimism, it seems, has proved unjustified. The events in China are taking a very serious turn and the Japanese may enter Beijing any day now. This would be highly undesirable, as there are many British citizens and various British agencies in Beijing. Besides, the British have major interests linked to the regions of Beijing and Tianjin. (All this is highly regrettable.) The Guandong Army rather than Tokyo is the driving force of recent events. But this doesn't change the essence of the matter. In the morning, immediately after receiving the message from Beijing, Eden sent a telegram to Tokyo asking it to be brought to the attention of the Japanese government once again that Britain was following events in northern China with great concern and that it was firmly of the hope that war between Japan and China would be prevented. But it is hard to say how effective this démarche will prove.

(3) Then Eden asked for our evaluation of the events in China. I replied that their true nature was hardly in doubt any longer. Japan is trying to repeat the 'Manchurian incident' that happened six years ago. In other words, Japan is aiming to establish a second Manzhouguo in northern China. Her technique is identical to that employed in 1931. In her attempts to expand, Japan, like any aggressor, will be guided primarily by empirical, opportunistic considerations. She will probe how far she can go with impunity. Therefore the success or failure of the new Japanese venture will depend greatly on two factors: (1) the strength of Chinese resistance and (2) the behaviour of the great powers with interests in the Far East. Eden agreed that our analysis of the situation was more than credible, but added that China today was no longer the China of 1931 and that this time Japan will meet with much stiffer resistance. Jiang Jieshiⁱ cannot retreat beyond a certain limit, and in Eden's opinion the limit has been reached. So there is every reason to expect that major military actions may break out in the Far East soon.

(4) I asked Eden how other great powers planned to react to this prospect. Eden shrugged his shoulders and said: 'I don't know.' He told me that he had

---

ⁱ Jiang Jieshi (Chiang Kai-shek), former commander-in-chief of the army of the Chinese Revolutionary National Party (Guomindang); president of China, 1928–38 and 1943–49.

tried twice to draw the USA into a united front of three powers (Britain, the United States and France) against Japanese aggression, but without success. The Americans stubbornly reject this idea. They are willing to engage only in 'parallel action'. Unfortunately, 'parallel action' is far weaker than joint action. The USA has even undertaken a sort of 'parallel action' in Tokyo. The British and French governments have also made declarations to the Japanese government with the aim of preventing the worst scenario. But all this is not enough. Without the USA, Britain can do little more than make platonic démarches to the Japanese government.

(5) Then Eden asked me casually what sort of démarche was made by the Chinese ambassador[i] in Moscow. Has the Nanjing government made any proposals to us? He had heard something about this from the Chinese ambassador in London, but he would be very grateful if I could supply some details. I replied that the Chinese ambassador in Moscow had indeed had a talk with Comrade Litvinov and had asked him about the Soviet attitude towards a possible 'joint action' by the powers connected with the Far East. Comrade Litvinov replied to this: If a proposal was put to the Soviet government about a joint action, it would discuss it. Eden listened to this information with great attention and hastened to say that he found it very interesting. He would not go any further, however (the Chinese ambassador in London, Guo Taiqi, later told me that Eden had been careful not to draw the USSR into a joint démarche so as not to provoke irritation in Germany and Italy). Then Eden asked me to keep in touch with Cadogan, the undersecretary for Far Eastern affairs, during his absence from London.

(6) Then Eden moved on to Spain. Saying that he in no way wanted to thrust his advice on the USSR, Eden nevertheless announced that he would like to set out his views concerning the last session of the Subcommittee (26 July). During this session, I had stated categorically that the Soviet government found it impossible to recognize Franco's belligerent rights. Eden understands our motives perfectly well, as he does the fact that all non-intervention now hangs by a thread. Plymouth, for one, fell into deep pessimism after yesterday's session and scarcely seems to believe that any agreement is possible. The breakdown of non-intervention is highly probable. Eden finds, however, that it would be better from all points of view for the breakdown to happen as a result of Italy's and Germany's refusal to evacuate the 'volunteers', rather than as a result of a flat refusal by the USSR to grant belligerent rights to General Franco. Indeed, Ribbentrop and Grandi declared yesterday that they were ready in principle to discuss the evacuation of 'volunteers'. We declared that we could not, as a matter of principle, recognize Franco's belligerent rights. If non-intervention collapses,

---

[i] Jiang Tingfu (Ts'ang Ting-fu), Chinese ambassador to the Soviet Union, 1936–38.

it is we who will be blamed, not the Germans and the Italians, although Eden is not at all sure that the Germans and the Italians are really ready to withdraw their 'volunteers' from Spain. He does not quite understand why we should wish to make things easy for Italy and Germany. Would not it be better for us, the British and the French if the Soviet government agreed to second the British formula? And if we are not too pleased with the British formula, why could we not at least say: evacuate all volunteers first and then we shall see? If the Italians and the Germans, as we firmly believe, are not going to remove their troops from Spain anyway, then what are we risking? The matter won't progress as far as the issue of belligerent rights. On the other hand, if the issue of 'volunteers' falls through, responsibility for this will lie not with the USSR, but with Germany and Italy, who are in fact to blame for the present difficulties.

(7) Eden spoke with his usual air of great sincerity, but his zealous concern for our good name seemed somewhat suspicious to me. So I began to argue vigorously. I unfolded our principled stand on the matter of belligerent rights and explained our unwillingness to grant such rights to Franco. I stressed that for the past ten months we have constantly been trying to coordinate our actions on non-intervention with those of Britain and France. This was not always easy for us, but we were ready to make certain sacrifices both in view of the Spanish situation and out of general political considerations. But everything has its limit, and in this case the Soviet government has approached a boundary it cannot cross. Eden listened to me very attentively and said that he understood our position perfectly well, but asked me all the same to convey the content of our conversation to Comrade Litvinov. I promised to do that.

(8) While making my case to Eden, I mentioned that 100,000 foreigners at the minimum are fighting on Franco's side, including up to 80,000 Italians and 10–15,000 Germans, plus no fewer than 30–40,000 Moroccans. Eden affected surprise at these figures. To his knowledge, there were 50,000 Italians in early March, of which 10–15,000 have been sent home wounded or ill. Therefore, according to Eden's estimates, the number of Italians does not currently exceed 35–40,000. This is not a decisive sum for Franco, and Eden reasons that if the Italians were pressed a little, they might agree to withdraw the 'volunteers'. In reply, I made some ironic remarks about the sources of his information. Are not these the same sources that have failed to establish the calibre of the guns currently threatening Gibraltar? (The day before, Churchill, Lloyd George and others had criticized Eden sharply in connection with the fact that the Germans and Italians had brought 12-inch batteries up close to Gibraltar, dominating both the fortress and the Strait. In reply to their charges, Lord Cranborne asserted that the said batteries were not dangerous for Gibraltar, and that the exact calibre of the weapons was not known.) I repeated more than once that I had supplied the minimum figures and that I had heard other

estimates, according to which the number of 'volunteers' on Franco's side was much greater. Eden seemed rather confused and said he would ask for his figures to be checked once again for accuracy. He added at the end: 'If your figures are correct, much of what has been unclear will become clear to me. In that case I agree with you that the Italians and the Germans will certainly not withdraw their "volunteers" from Spain.'

(9) Having concluded our conversation about the last meeting of the subcommittee, I, in turn, asked Eden what Britain would do if non-intervention collapsed. Eden hesitated at first, but regained his composure and answered that in this case, as he saw it (he underlined that it was his personal opinion), the British government would have three choices. (1) To maintain the policy of non-intervention irrespective of what other countries might do. This would mean that Britain would not sell arms either to the Spanish government or to Franco. This choice would have its pros and cons. Its advantage would be that it would draw England closer to the United States in the matter of arms exports, and this would go down very well in the country. Its downside would be disagreement with France, and he, Eden, wishes least of all to jeopardize the present excellent relations between London and Paris. He values these relations very highly and considers them a priority. Furthermore, this choice would certainly entail internal difficulties for the government, too, since the prolongation of non-intervention would be better for Franco than for the Spanish government. Therefore, the opposition's attacks would continue and possibly intensify. (2) The British government restores free trade in arms and sells them solely to the Spanish government as the legitimate government in Spain. The opposition would be happy, but the Conservatives would not accept this, as in this case the British navy would have to use convoys to protect British ships heading for Republican ports. Such actions would look very much like intervention on the side of the Spanish government. (3) The British government resumes free trade in arms and sells them to both sides. Both sides are granted belligerent rights.

Eden did not say it in so many words, but it was evident from his intonation, gestures and so on, that he found the third option the most practical and desirable. I asked Eden why it was essential to tie the resumption of free trade in arms with the granting of belligerent rights to the Spanish government and the insurgents. Eden referred to various historical precedents, but it was clear that the main reason lay elsewhere. The main reason was that the British government did not want to make a move that would favour Valencia alone. Should circumstances force the government to permit arms exports to the Republicans, Franco must be compensated for this with belligerent rights. Eden tried to sweeten the pill by arguing that eventually the third choice would be good for the Spanish government: Franco has no money and is not in a position to buy arms from England, but the Spanish government has money and it can buy what it needs. True, having obtained belligerent rights, Franco could press Valencia at sea more than he can now, but this would not be of great significance because, with the collapse of non-intervention, the Franco-Spanish border would be open and the delivery of arms to the Republicans would come from or through France.

[After his appointment as prime minister in May 1937, Chamberlain hastened to seize the initiative from Eden and pursue his own foreign policy. He hoped to restore good relations with Italy (now a pariah after the conclusion of the war in Abyssinia) by recruiting her to a four-power pact together with Germany and France. Maisky first met Neville Chamberlain, then chancellor of the exchequer, on 16 November 1932. Though scornful of the 'revolting but clever little Jew', Chamberlain's early contacts with Maisky did not betray the animosity which would settle in later. In fact, his amiable approach was deplored in the Foreign Office.[23] Maisky might have been somewhat misled by his encounter with Neville Chamberlain's half-brother Austen, a former secretary of state, whom he found 'extremely sympathetic and responsive ... most satisfactory of all, we were in complete agreement on the international questions'.[24] Maisky does not seem to have been much influenced by Churchill's warning back in 1936 that it was 'better to have the Devil you know than the Neville you do not know'.[25] Nor does he appear immediately to have appreciated (as he later claimed he did) Lloyd George's scorching judgement: 'a provincial manufacturer of iron bedsteads'.[26] It took Maisky a while, as it did Eden, to realize that Chamberlain's appointment undermined the attempts to hitch Britain to collective security.

On 5 June, Maisky, who had been laid low by a severe bout of malaria, belatedly congratulated Chamberlain, concluding with the unheeded advice that 'the quality of Anglo-Soviet relations would profoundly affect the international situation as a whole and can influence decisively the issue of peace or war in Europe'.[27] It was, however, only on 29 July that Maisky first met Chamberlain in person. The contrast between Chamberlain's attitude to the Italian ambassador, Grandi, and Maisky – both of whom he met on the same day – set out in a letter to his sister, is most telling: 'My interview with Grandi seems to have made a very good impression in Italy and I see they have now "revealed" that I sent a personal letter to Mussolini ... My interview with Maisky was at his request and no doubt was intended by him to be a counter demonstration. But he hadn't really anything to say.'[28]]

29 July

Conversation with Chamberlain

(1) Following the English custom, I had long been planning to pay an official visit to the new PM. Other ambassadors in London had the same intentions. Chamberlain, however, postponed the visits week after week until the end of the parliamentary session. To tie up loose ends before leaving for holidays, the PM began to receive representatives of the great powers one after the other: the American, Bingham, the Italian, Grandi, and others. He received me in his

office in the House of Commons on 29 July. Knowing that he was very busy, I decided not to waste time and to take the bull by the horns. I already had information before visiting Chamberlain that the conclusion of a four-power pact and especially the improvement of relations between Britain and Germany represented the general line of his foreign policy. I wanted to check whether this was true and asked him straightaway: which in his view are the best methods to achieve the 'appeasement of Europe'?

(2) Chamberlain, who clearly hadn't been expecting a question of this sort, hesitated and looked at me either in surprise or embarrassment. Then he began his reply, articulating his words slowly and occasionally faltering. 'I cannot suggest a shortcut to achieving this result. The appeasement of Europe is a complicated and lengthy business. It demands great patience. Any means and any methods that might prove effective are good. Any available opportunity should be exploited.' The PM paused for a moment, pondered, and continued: 'I think that a successful settlement of the Spanish question could be the first direct step towards the appeasement of Europe. Spain is now the focus of attention. Events there generate many complications and conflicts in Europe. If the Spanish war does not end soon or is not at least fully localized, we can expect more serious perturbations in Europe in the near future. Spain needs to be dealt with – this is a prerequisite for the appeasement of Europe.' I asked Chamberlain what he meant by the expression, 'the settlement of the Spanish question'. Chamberlain paused again, pondered, and replied: 'In my view, to settle the Spanish question means to turn the Spanish struggle into one that is purely Spanish. We hope we shall eventually be able to achieve this – with your help, may I assume?' I accepted the challenge and said that the same idea prevails in the Soviet government's policy towards Spain. But how is this goal to be achieved? It is an open secret that a large Italian army and numerous detachments of German specialists – pilots, artillerymen, tank men and others – are fighting on Franco's side. Does Chamberlain think that the Italians and the Germans are really ready to withdraw their so-called 'volunteers' from Spain? I doubt it. The work carried out in the Non-Intervention Committee over 11 months makes me sceptical. Meanwhile, it is the evacuation of 'volunteers' that is currently at the heart of the entire problem of non-intervention today.

(3) Chamberlain did not answer at once. He first looked out the window, then at the ceiling, before beginning slowly: 'There is no doubt that Mussolini is very keen to see a fascist Spain. Just two days ago, Grandi communicated a personal message to me from Mussolini, assuring me that Italy had no territorial ambitions in respect of Spain, while also arguing that Franco has to win. In Mussolini's opinion, Franco's victory is needed to avoid Spain turning into a "Bolshevik state". If Franco fails, the triumph of communism in Spain is, he says, inevitable, and that is something Italy cannot accept. I don't agree

with Mussolini's appraisal. I don't think that communists can win in Spain now, whatever the conditions. But this is what Mussolini thinks. Nevertheless, I am not too despondent. I don't think that the head of the Italian state has said his last word. We must act with restraint and with patience. He will retreat from his present positions and then it will be possible to persuade him to withdraw the Italian legionaries from Spain.' I said: 'If only you were right. My government would be only too glad if your forecast came true. Unfortunately, I am yet to see any encouraging signs in this direction.' Chamberlain stuck to his guns, however, and repeated that we must be restrained and patient.

(4) Then the PM inquired what we think about the Spanish conflict and what position the USSR holds in the matter. I provided the requisite explanations and underlined our desire to eliminate intervention and turn the Spanish conflict into a purely Spanish affair. True to our common principles, we, too, are striving to secure 'the right to national self-determination' for the Spanish people. We do not aim to establish a communist or any other system in Spain. The Spanish people themselves should decide on their form of government. But we are trying, as best as we can, to prevent any kind of foreign intervention in Spain's domestic affairs. In our struggle to secure Spain's right to decide its fate independently, we have always tried to coordinate our actions with those of Britain and France. We happened to disagree on some practical matters relating to the Spanish problem over the past 11 months, and we may have disagreements in future. I hope, however, that the differences will not be exaggerated on both sides and that they will not hinder the joint efforts of the USSR and Great Britain in the cause of the strengthening of peace. Chamberlain listened to my account with great attention and evident sympathy, but afterwards it immediately became clear that he had understood it in his own way. The PM said: 'Mussolini wants to establish a fascist state in Spain, and you do not want this to happen. We are facing two extremes. Britain tries to hold an intermediate position between you and Mussolini.' I objected that he was giving a false picture of the actual state of affairs. In fact, Mussolini wants to establish a very definite regime in Spain – a fascist one – while the USSR is not striving to establish some particular regime there, whether socialist, communist or other. The USSR wishes only that all other powers should leave Spain alone and give it the opportunity to establish independently such a regime as is desired by the popular masses of Spain. There is a very great difference between the positions of Italy and the USSR. At this point Chamberlain had to acknowledge that there was indeed a difference, and that it was a serious difference. He expressed approval of our position and added that in principle it was very close to that of Great Britain. 'Unfortunately,' Chamberlain added, 'I fear that we shall not be able to resolve the Spanish problem very soon, and without that it is difficult to conceive of the possibility of any serious measures towards the real appeasement of Europe.'

(5) The PM paused again and turned to another subject:

I am constantly troubled by one particular thought: today's Europe is full of fear and suspicion. Countries and states do not trust each other. As soon as one power begins to arm, another instantly begins to suspect that these arms are set against it and also starts to arm to parry the real or imaginary threat. One thing leads to another, and as a result we are all spending a colossal amount of money unproductively on weapons of death and destruction – money that could be spent with far greater benefit on improving the lot of broad strata of the population. In saying this, I do not mean to reproach your country – we are arming, too, after all. I firmly believe that your country does not want war and is not a threat to its neighbours, and we would like to cooperate with you in the task of defending the world. Your country faces great problems to do with internal restructuring and the exploitation of its natural resources. I've heard and read a little about your magnificent country, and I know that its natural riches are truly immeasurable. Domestic work will occupy you for a good number of years and decades, and it would of course be disadvantageous and undesirable for you to interrupt its peaceful course because of external complications. But other countries in the world have a different attitude. Take Germany, for instance. The Germans keep going on about 'have' and 'have not' states. I don't know which category they place you in, but they refer Great Britain to the 'have' category and themselves to the 'have not'. There is a great deal of propaganda about this in Germany and very dangerous passions are being stoked. As a result, fears and tension are on the rise in Europe. This must be stopped. I understand that this cannot be achieved instantly. Years and years will be needed to appease Europe. But at least the first step could be taken towards creating a more benevolent atmosphere in our part of the globe, could it not?

I asked Chamberlain what exactly he had in mind. The PM answered:

Alongside the Spanish question, there is a second, very important and urgent question – the German one. I consider it very important to make the Germans move from general phrases about the 'haves' and 'have nots', the true meaning of which nobody understands, to a practical and business-like discussion of their wishes. If we could bring the Germans to the negotiating table and, with pencil in hand, run through all their complaints, claims and wishes, this would greatly help clear the air, or at least clarify the current situation. We would then know what the

Germans wanted and we would also know whether it would be possible to satisfy their demands. If it were possible, we would go as far as we could to meet them; if not, we would take other decisions. This, it seems to me, is what the current moment most urgently demands. Germany, of course, is not Europe's only problem, but she is the most important. I would like the European powers to take resolute and consistent strides towards resolving this problem, without being distracted by questions of secondary importance and without being held back by trivialities. It is clear that the appeasement of Europe does not depend solely on the solving of the German problem. There are other matters that need to be settled. We should aim for a general agreement in Europe – that is our goal, but we must in any case begin by resolving the German problem.

In reply, I briefly outlined my doubts concerning the effectiveness of this route to the 'appeasement of Europe' charted by Chamberlain. The PM was obviously not too happy about this, but as he did not want to enter into further argument, he hastened to say that we were discussing a very complicated issue and that naturally there could be entirely honest differences of opinion. Chamberlain said that in any event he was ready to listen to the views of those who thought differently.

(6) That was the end of the business part of our conversation. The rest was pure protocol and not worth recording. The conversation left me with the general impression that Chamberlain is seriously entertaining the idea of a four-power pact and of organizing western security, and is prepared to make considerable concessions to Germany and Italy in order to attain his goal. However, if it were to transpire in the course of events that an agreement with those two countries was impossible or that the price England had to pay for the agreement was unacceptable, he would take a far firmer stand towards the fascist powers than was taken by Baldwin.[29]

29 July

Vansittart told me today that King Carol of Rumania[i] has met Chamberlain, Eden and himself during his current trip to London. V. has the impression that Carol has 'developed politically' to a significant degree since his visit for the funeral of George V. Carol cannot be described as a Germanophile; on the contrary, he leans towards France and Britain (especially Britain), as is evident from his visits to Paris and London, but for obvious reasons he does not want to quarrel with Germany. The British ambassador in Bucharest corroborates this

---

[i] King Carol II of Rumania, 1930–40.

information. V. is sure that Carol will be very cautious towards the USSR and will not permit himself to do anything that might cause a quarrel between him and us. Time will tell.

1 August

The Far East is on fire. The consequences are hard to foresee, but they may be immense.

As soon as the Japanese launched an offensive near Beijing in mid-July, the Chinese ambassador in Moscow asked what we were planning to do. He was particularly interested to know whether we were ready to interpose separately or together with other powers. M.M. [Litvinov] answered that we would not interpose separately, but that if a joint démarche were proposed to us, we would discuss it.

The Chinese ambassadors in London, Paris[i] and Washington[ii] took similar steps. In addition, Nanjing sent a memorandum regarding the conflict to the members of the Nine-Power Pact.

The English became very concerned. Eden told me (on 17 and 27 July) that the British government was greatly alarmed and wanted to organize a joint London–Paris–Washington démarche in Tokyo, insisting on peaceful settlement of the conflict. But the Americans refused to take part in a joint démarche and were only prepared to take 'parallel' actions with Great Britain – a far weaker alternative. Consequently, Britain and France made identical statements in Tokyo and Nanjing calling for the cessation of arms and offering their mediation. The USA made an identical démarche separately. But Eden has little faith in the effectiveness of such actions. He has good grounds for his scepticism.

Chinese Minister of Finance Kong,[iii] who recently arrived in England from the USA, visited me on 23 July, accompanied by Guo Taiqi. Kong, a thickset vigorous man of about 50 with sharp gestures and rough manners, lost no time in demanding our aid to China, stressing rather clumsily that the seizure of Beijing by the Japanese would be merely a prelude to an attack on the USSR. In concrete terms, he suggested that we organize a military demonstration on the Manchurian border. Of course I refrained from giving Kong any reassurances along the lines he had in mind. Kong told me, among other things, that he had met Roosevelt not long ago and that the latter favoured a Pacific pact but considered a non-aggression pact insufficient (what are platonic promises worth

---

[i] Gu Weijun (Wellington Koo), former premier and president of China; Chinese ambassador to France, 1936–41; to Great Britain, 1941–46.
[ii] Shi Zhaoji (Dr Sao-ke Alfred Sze), first Chinese ambassador to the United States, 1933–37.
[iii] Kong Xiangxi (Hsiang-his K'ung), Chinese minister of finance, 1933–44; governor of the Bank of China, 1933–45.

today?) and wanted something more effective, although he did not refer to a pact of mutual assistance as such. But – and this is very important – Roosevelt does not consider it possible to engage seriously with the issue of the pact until the US naval programme is fulfilled! Kong also said that in Germany, before his visit to the USA, he spoke with the leaders of the regime and found Göring[i] to be utterly anti-Soviet and Schacht, on the contrary, to be a 'Sovietophile', while Hitler, allegedly as the result of a two-hour talk with Kong, began to yield to the thought that the normalization of relations between Germany and the USSR was *perhaps* possible.

Guo Taiqi invited my wife and me to lunch on 27 July, after which Kong, Guo and Gu Weijun, who had come from Paris, took me to an adjoining room and Kong again began to impress upon me rather clumsily that no matter how Britain and the USA conducted themselves, China and the USSR must come out in a united front against Japanese aggression, since they are the countries most threatened by the militarists of Tokyo. As I was very unforthcoming on the subject, Kong hastened to move onto practical matters. He no longer insisted on a military demonstration on the Manchurian border and only raised the question of the supply of arms to China from the USSR. I promised to communicate with Moscow on this matter.

Guo Taiqi visited me today. He told me that he had seen Eden twice and had insisted on the USSR being brought into a joint action in the Far East. Eden declined his request, however, arguing that this would only have complicated the situation. Guo is of the impression that Eden is simply afraid of Germany and Italy. In this connection he told me that the German and Italian ambassadors in Moscow have notified the Chinese ambassador in Moscow that as long as the USSR stands aside from the conflict between Japan and China, Rome and Berlin will occupy a neutral position. But if the USSR is drawn into the settlement of the Far Eastern conflict, Germany and Italy will support Japan.

Guo also informed me that Germany is continuing to send arms to China on the strength of the credit of 100 million marks given to Kong and in exchange for Chinese raw materials. Meanwhile, Italy has responded favourably to the recent Chinese request for certain types of weapons and ammunition. Such is the force of the contradictions rending the capitalist world today! But I am inclined to think that if the conflagration in the Far East intensifies, Rome and Berlin will finally show their ideological colours.

One more detail, but from a different sphere. According to Guo, the British ambassador in Berlin, Henderson, is trying to talk Dodd,[ii] the American

---

[i] Hermann Wilhelm Göring, Nazi president of the Reichstag in 1932; Prussian minister of the interior, 1933–34; founder and head of the Gestapo, 1933–36; Reichsminister for air and commander-in-chief of the Luftwaffe, 1933–45.
[ii] William Edward Dodd, American ambassador in Germany, 1933–37.

ambassador in Germany, into raising a joint Anglo-American loan for Hitler. Also, in his talks with the Nazi leaders, he expressed the opinion that Britain would easily be reconciled to the annexation of Austria and Czechoslovakia by Germany on 'federal terms'. Son of a bitch!

10 August

Masaryk called on me. I'll note the following from his accounts:

(1) He asked Vansittart bluntly the other day: What is the British attitude to Czechoslovakia's 'Russian policy', and particularly to the Czecho-Soviet pact? There is a widespread opinion in Europe that England disapproves of this policy and, in particular, of the pact. Is this true? Vansittart replied that it was absolutely untrue. Taking into consideration the current situation in Europe, Britain quite understands and even approves of the present relations between Czechoslovakia and the USSR. (2) Masaryk defines Britain's attitude to Czechoslovakia in this way: Britain is not indifferent to the fate of Czechoslovakia, it even sympathizes with Czechoslovakia as the outpost of democracy in Central Europe, but its sympathy is lukewarm and one can hardly count on an energetic response from London were Czechoslovakia to be endangered. It seems to me that Masaryk's description of the situation is correct. (3) Vansittart and the Foreign Office in general are unhappy about the PM's flirtation with Mussolini. They think that the ground is not yet ready for an agreement and, above all, they are annoyed by the fact that Chamberlain has completely ignored the FO in his attempts to reach an understanding with Italy.[30]

[Maisky wrote the following with no date mentioned but obviously during a visit to Paris in mid-August.]

It must be said plainly that the fair[31] is not very impressive. Everything looks unfinished, done in haste and without being thought through – and not only in its 'French aspect', but also in the 'foreign' one. Nearly all the pavilions are feeble, or at any rate feebler than the countries they represent. The only exception, perhaps, is Czechoslovakia, which has built a pavilion that fully reflects the true face of the country. All the other pavilions differ from each other merely in the extent to which they fail. The English pavilion is very poor: neither its appearance nor its exhibits give the faintest idea of the wealth and might of the British Empire. The Germans, who erected something halfway between a sarcophagus and a prison, failed to put up the good show that they are usually capable of. Our pavilion, which faces the German one and is surely the most original and dynamic in appearance (the sculptures at the top of the pavilion are truly beautiful), could also have been much richer and better inside. There are

35. A visit to the Communards' Wall, at the Père Lachaise Cemetery in Paris, where, in May 1871, 147 combatants of the Paris Commune were shot and thrown into an open trench at the foot of the wall.

too many diagrams, tables and photographs, and very few vivid and impressive exhibits. Our industry, for instance, is poorly represented. All the same – and this is an excellent sign – the Soviet pavilion attracts a huge number of visitors. In general, the fair suggests that the world has no time for demonstrations of peaceful, economic and cultural competition – it is too consumed by the spectres of war. In contrast to 1900 (when there was also a world exposition in Paris), 1937 has failed to bring the money, time, peace of mind, attention and energy that are needed to create a really vivid, full-blooded, rich and well thought-out fair. But such are the times we live in…

We went to the 'Artists' and saw *Anna Karenina*, *The Enemies*, and *Lyubov Yarovaya*. It was all well done, but the performances played to half-empty audiences. This was painful to see. Partly, August is to blame, since 'all Paris' is on vacation, particularly this year (the paid workers' holidays introduced by Blum); partly, the tour was not organized well enough. Another problem is language and the fact that the French do not understand our situation. Whatever the reasons, the theatre is half-empty…

23 August

I visited Vansittart and asked him what the British government had decided about arms supplies to China and about China's intention to raise the question of Japanese aggression at the forthcoming session of the League of Nations. V. was very reserved in his replies, stressing that the government had not yet discussed or taken decisions about the matters that interested me. He promised to inform me about the decisions once they were reached.

In general, V. was in a very pessimistic frame of mind, particularly with regard to the Far East and the Mediterranean. Things are getting worse and worse, the danger is ever nearer, yet no real measures are taken to fight it. Where is the world headed?

V. spoke bitterly about the fact that international complications have spoiled everybody's vacations this year. He himself has to remain in London permanently. Eden is having a holiday, but within England and for just three weeks – with trips to the capital every now and again.[32] Even the PM had to interrupt his holidays and convene an extraordinary meeting of the Cabinet. This is the first time since the war that the PM has not been able to spend his holidays in peace. This is what we have come to!

I listened to V. and smiled to myself: if only the spoilt vacations were the only trouble!

25 August

Guo told me today that the export of arms from England to China goes on unhampered so far. The Chinese recently bought – partly for cash and partly on credit – a few planes in France. Kong placed big military orders with Škoda in Czechoslovakia.

The most interesting thing is that China gets arms from Germany, too, in exchange for raw materials and under the credit of 100 million marks obtained by Kong. Italy promised China to sell her arms, too. These are the contradictions of capitalist reality! Indeed, they raise a sardonic laughter.

12 September

The Mediterranean is to be patrolled mainly by Britain and France... The insecurity of shipping in the Mediterranean is caused by one main circumstance, the denial of belligerent rights... The elementary nonsense of still talking of Valencia as 'the Government of Spain' has become a menace to the peace of Europe. (*Observer*, 12 September 1937)

So, today's *Observer* carries an account of the 'anti-pirate conference' in Nyon.[33] The account is by no means accurate. One thing is certain, however: we've played the round well. We took the rook at the chessboard of Europe. The *Observer*'s concern shows that our arrow hit the target.

14 September

Hore-Belisha,[i] the new war minister, came up to me unexpectedly at the Foreign Office dinner on 9 June and began to speak to me in very animated tones about his great interest in the USSR and his desire to visit us, to see the country, the people and, of course, the army. I expressed polite approval of his idea, but promised nothing, since it was not yet clear to me what Moscow would think of the war minister's intention. He continued, even more vigorously than before: 'When do you do manoeuvres?' I replied that we usually conduct manoeuvres in the autumn, in August and September. Looking at me cunningly through squinted eyes, Hore-Belisha suddenly said: 'Well, if I were to get an invitation to see your manoeuvres, I would probably come.'

I contacted Moscow. They had no objections to the war minister arriving for the manoeuvres that were scheduled for September. They promised to send him a special invitation, if it could be guaranteed that he would accept it. They advised me not to be importunate and to leave everything to Hore-Belisha. I have not, therefore, raised the issue again on my own initiative. Nor has the war minister. Consequently, Hore-Belisha's visit has not yet taken place.

He is presently in France, at manoeuvres near Strasbourg. General Deverell,[ii] chief of the imperial general staff, is at manoeuvres in Germany. The English demand 'reciprocity'!

Hore-Belisha uttered an interesting phrase during our conversation on 9 June: 'If I come to you, then only by bypassing Germany.' The war minister is no admirer of Hitler. What's more, he is a Jew.

19 September

This evaluation of all that happened in Nyon and Geneva last week[34] is even more revealing than the quotation I gave on 12 September. Even the *Observer* has to admit, gritting the teeth, that Russian diplomacy drove Italy away from the conference, bringing non-intervention to an end.

In actual fact, the importance of the Nyon conference is much greater: the gulf between the aggressors and the 'peace front' was demonstrated to the world for the first time, while the logic of events and the skill of Soviet diplomats forced Britain and France to take their places in the peace front against the aggressors. No doubt the French, and especially the British, will try more than once to bridge the gulf and confuse the issue. Nevertheless, the Nyon conference will always remain an important stage in the consolidation of

---

[i] Leslie Hore-Belisha (1st Baron Hore-Belisha), secretary of state for war, 1937–40; member of the War Cabinet, 1939–40.
[ii] Sir Cyril Deverell, general, chief of the imperial general staff, 1936–37.

the 'peace front' and 'collective security'. But will the peace front have time to form before the aggressors unleash war? This is the question of the day.

27 October[35]

The first five-year plan of my ambassadorship in England has come to an end!

I vividly remember 27 October 1932...

Five years have passed since then. What years they were! A thought runs through my mind, like lightning: 'How much time have I to spend here? What will I see? What will I live through? And what will the future bring me?...'

6 November

Martin, the Abyssinian minister, told me at a party given by the lord mayor's wife that a month ago Mussolini suggested to the Negus that he return to Abyssinia as a vassal monarch. The Negus flatly refused. Then Mussolini began to cajole the crown prince, who was in Jerusalem. As a precautionary measure, the Negus hastened to summon his son to London, where he currently resides. According to Martin, the total number of refugees from Abyssinia has now reached seven to eight thousand, scattered over various countries (Kenya, Palestine, Egypt and elsewhere). Their material status is very grave. Money is being collected for them everywhere. The Negus's coffers have been greatly depleted (he gave abundantly to support the Abyssinians' struggle against Italy), but newspaper reports about his 'destitution' are unfounded.

* * *

I saw Collier. He told me a piece of quite pleasing news. In the opinion of the Foreign Office, the project of a German airline to fly via Afghanistan to China and Japan has been set aside for a long time, if not forever. The reasons are the war between Japan and China, the failure of two maiden flights to Xinjiang, flown by German pilots, and British pressure. The British were particularly unhappy about German planes flying frequently near the Indian border this summer, allegedly in connection with the quests for the lost German pilots. If there really is no way of avoiding it, the British might let the German line to the Far East pass through India along the route currently used by British and Dutch planes, but the border between Afghanistan and India must be free of German intrigues.

16 November

Today Agniya and I attended the 'state banquet' given by George VI in honour of King Leopold of Belgium, who has arrived on a four-day visit. It was a banquet like any other: 180 guests, the entire royal family, members of government, ambassadors (but not envoys) and various British notables. We ate from gold plates with gold forks and knives. The dinner, unlike most English dinners, was tasty (the king is said to have a French cook). Two dozen Scottish 'pipers' entered the hall during the dinner and slowly walked around the tables several times, filling the palace vaults with their semi-barbarian music. I like this music. There is something of Scotland's mountains and woods in it, of the distance of bygone centuries, of man's primordial past. Pipe music has always had a strange, exciting effect on me, drawing me off somewhere far away, to broad fields and boundless steppes where there are neither people nor animals, and where one feels oneself young and brave. But I saw that the music was not to the taste of many guests. They found it rough, sharp and indecently loud in the atmosphere of palatial solemnity and refinement. Leopold was one of the disgruntled diners…

After two speeches made by George VI and Leopold, who proclaimed unbreakable friendship between their states, the guests moved to the adjacent halls and we, the ambassadors, were gathered in the so-called Bow Room, where the two kings, ministers, and some high-ranking courtiers were located. The ladies were in a neighbouring hall with the young queen and the old queen mother. Here, once again, everything was as it always is at 'state banquets': first the kings talked between themselves while the ambassadors propped up the walls like expensive 'diplomatic furniture'. Then Lord Cromer and other courtiers began buzzing among the guests and leading the 'lucky few', who were to be favoured with the 'very highest attention', to one or other of the kings. Leopold conversed with Chamberlain, Hoare, Montagu Norman (governor of the Bank of England) and, from among the ambassadors, with Grandi, Ribbentrop and Corbin. There was an obvious orientation towards the 'aggressor' and the aggressor's collaborator.

Naturally enough, I was not so honoured: the USSR is out of fashion today, especially in the upper echelons of the Conservative Party. The Japanese ambassador Yoshida, who skulked in a corner, was not invited to pay his respects either. No wonder: Japanese guns are currently firing on British capital and British prestige in China!…

I eventually tired of this dull spectacle and I was already planning to slip out to the other rooms, where I could see many interesting people I knew. But at that moment there was a sudden commotion in the Bow Room. I looked up and realized what was happening. Lord Cromer, emerging from a neighbouring room, led Churchill to Leopold and introduced him. George soon joined them. The three of them carried on a lively and lengthy conversation, in which Churchill gesticulated forcefully and the kings laughed out loud. Then the audience ended. Churchill moved away from the kings and bumped into

36. A friendship is born in defiance of Chamberlain.

Ribbentrop. Ribbentrop struck up conversation with the famous 'German-eater'. A group immediately formed around them. I did not hear what they were talking about, but I could see from a distance that Ribbentrop was, as usual, gloomily pontificating about something and that Churchill was joking in reply, eliciting bursts of laughter from the people standing around. Finally Churchill seemed to get bored, turned around and saw me. Then the following happened: in full view of the gathering and in the presence of the two kings, Churchill crossed the hall, came up to me and shook me firmly by the hand. Then we entered into an animated and extended conversation, in the middle of which King George walked up to us and made a comment to Churchill. The impression was created that George, troubled by Churchill's inexplicable proximity to the 'Bolshevik ambassador', had decided to rescue him from the 'Moscow devil'. I stepped aside and waited to see what would happen next. Churchill finished his conversation with George and returned to me to continue our interrupted conversation. The gilded aristocrats around us were well-nigh shocked.

What did Churchill have to say?

Churchill told me straight away that he considers the 'anti-communist pact' to be directed against the British Empire in the first place and against the USSR only in the second. He attaches a great deal of importance to this agreement between the aggressors, not so much for the present as for the future. Germany is the chief enemy. 'The main task for all of us who defend the cause of peace,' Churchill continued, 'is to stick together. Otherwise we are ruined. A weak Russia presents the greatest danger for the cause of peace and for the inviolability of our Empire. We need a strong, very strong Russia.' At this point, speaking in a low voice and as if in secret, Churchill began asking me: what was happening in the USSR? Hadn't the most recent events weakened our army? Hadn't they shaken our ability to withstand pressure from Japan and Germany?

'May I reply with a question?' I began, and continued: 'If a disloyal general commanding a corps or an army is replaced by an honest and reliable general, is this the weakening or the strengthening of an army? If a director of a big gun factory, engaged in sabotage, is replaced by an honest and reliable director, is this the weakening or the strengthening of our military industry?' I continued in this vein, dismantling the old wives' tales which are currently so popular here about the effect of the 'purge' on the general condition of the USSR.

Churchill listened to me with the greatest attention, although he shook his head distrustfully every now and again. When I had finished, he said: 'It is very comforting to hear all this. If Russia is growing stronger, not weaker, then all is well. I repeat: we all need a strong Russia; we need it very much!' Then, after a moment's pause, Churchill added: 'That Trotsky, he is a perfect devil. He is a destructive, and not a creative force. I'm wholly for Stalin.'[36]

I asked Churchill what he thought about Halifax's forthcoming visit to Berlin.[37] Churchill pulled a wry face and said that he regarded the trip as a mistake. Nothing will come of it; the Germans will only turn up their noses even more and treat the visit as a sign of England's weakness. This is no use either to England or to the cause of peace. But at least Halifax is an honest man and will not succumb to any 'disgraceful' schemes, such as betraying Czechoslovakia or giving Germany a free hand in the east. All the same, they should never have bothered with this visit!

Churchill shook my hand and proposed that we should meet more often.

[The three waves of purges at Narkomindel commenced at the end of 1937, gathered momentum after the Munich Conference, and peaked with the dismissal of Litvinov in early May 1939 and the subsequent cleansing of the Commissariat for Foreign Affairs. The deployment of terror by the state was aimed at instilling fear in the population and enforcing obedience through violence. Historians are still deeply divided over the motives for the terror. It may have been inspired by the ideological predisposition of a 'utopia in power', marking a continuity of the Leninist and Stalinist perceptions of terror as a useful tool of control; it could have been a spontaneous reaction to changing historical circumstances, which naturally brought Stalin's personality to the fore as instigator and pursuer; or, widening the scope further, it might be ascribed to fear among the leadership about their continuing survival and domination.

The constant factor in the emergence of the terror, as the Russian historian Oleg Khlevniuk has convincingly shown, was the Stalinist fear of the formation of a 'Fifth

Column' in the likely event of war sparked by the rise of Nazism. The intensification of the terror coincided with growing international tension and threat of war, and was amplified by the experiences of the Spanish Civil War. The lessons drawn from that war were that the social upheaval caused by war could breed treachery at home, which had to be nipped in the bud.

Within the sphere of foreign policy, the terror highlighted the long-standing conflict between Stalin's Politburo and the elite of the Commissariat for Foreign Affairs, which was by no means a cohesive monolith blindly following Stalin's diktat. Naturally it aroused his 'suspicion of his comrades-in-arms who could recall the heyday of party democracy'.[38] Stalin was determined to break up the old cliques and, above all, to stamp out the prevailing dual allegiances – to him and to patrons in the various party and state institutions. The Commissariat for Foreign Affairs was especially vulnerable, as the recruitment of key personnel was conducted personally by Chicherin and Litvinov from a cosmopolitan, polyglot and independent-minded retinue, in many cases members of the revolutionary intelligentsia from the tsarist days. Cosmopolitanism in particular implied contamination through direct contact with the seductive bourgeois environment. The old cadres were to be replaced by a new generation of leaders, devoid of an 'inflated sense of their own worth, due to revolutionary service', who owed their promotion to Stalin personally.

The terror affected Soviet foreign policy at two levels. First of all, the old guard at the Commissariat was almost completely wiped out: at least 62 per cent of top-level diplomats and officials were eliminated by the *ezhovshchina*, while only 16 per cent remained in post; Narkomindel was infiltrated by NKVD officials. The all-consuming purge and basic survival instincts set diplomats against each other both secretly and publicly. Second, and just as significant, was the ravaging image of the terror abroad. This had direct repercussions on Western foreign policy. Surprisingly few diplomats defected, and not necessarily the most prominent ones.[39]

Certain precursors to the terror exposed Stalin's personal intervention. In July 1936, he reproached Karakhan,[i] the ambassador in Turkey, whose recall, arrest and execution in December 1937 heralded the cleansing in Narkomindel: 'Your treatment of, and demands from, the Turks create a bad impression. Never allow nerves to interfere with politics. Hold yourself calm and maintain dignity.'[40] Far more alarming was the execution of Litvinov's deputy, Krestinsky,[ii] who was replaced by Potemkin, a cunning and ambitious diplomat. In her diary, Kollontay describes how, while 'wriggly, adulatory' in Litvinov's presence, out of his superior's sight Potemkin left no one in any doubt that he could be at least as good a commissar for foreign affairs. He associated Litvinov, of whom he was contemptuous, with the 'old underground workers'. In Litvinov, he told Kollontay:

> are firmly embedded the habits of illegal work, tea and sausage, and cigarette-ends on the table. It is time we forgot the asceticism of war communism times and went over to underlining our external prosperity and riches, our ability to display the values of a great country like Russia and our Russian style ... It's

---

[i] Lev Mikhailovich Karakhan, deputy people's commissar for foreign affairs in 1918–20 and 1927–34, he was later ambassador to Poland, China and Turkey.
[ii] Nikolai Nikolaevich Krestinsky, deputy commissar for foreign affairs, 1930–37. Shot in 1938; rehabilitated posthumously.

the task of the people's commissar to surround himself with wealth and artistic values.

Potemkin's appointment as deputy commissar for foreign affairs undermined the position of both Litvinov and Maisky. He now spread the word that Litvinov was getting ready to retire.[41] Potemkin, as Kollontay found out while on a stroll with him and Litvinov on the shores of Lake Geneva, was not only a proponent of keeping the German door wide open, but was also subservient to the Kremlin:

'I am puzzled, Maksim Maksimovich, by your wealth of ideas and by the new assertions in your speeches,' Potemkin reproached Litvinov. 'I cannot but wonder: when did you manage to receive the consent of the Politburo to all of that?' ...

Litvinov: 'Well, I did not. If I oversee our foreign policy, then it's natural that at the Assembly I can set out its fundamental line ... It's not all something I've come up with myself; my thoughts and propositions are a conclusion based on our whole foreign policy and our perspectives.'

Potemkin: 'But don't you yourself think, Maksim Maksimovich, that your hostile attitude to Germany crossed the line?'

Litvinov suddenly stopped and looked carefully at Potemkin: 'Have you been sent something from Moscow? Come out with it, there's no point messing around.'[42]

'The past winter and the current summer,' Maisky lamented to his brother, 'have been very agitated in the sphere of international affairs, and this has significantly affected my health. What is more, I have been on average 50% busier this year than before ... With time this has had a significant effect on my nerves, my attention, and – taken together – my day-to-day work.'[43] One can only imagine how Maisky felt when Aleksandr Barmin,[i] one of the few defectors from the Soviet diplomatic service, wrote a long article in the New York Times, describing not only the pitiful situation of Litvinov, but also that of the three survivors Surits, Troyanovsky and Maisky, the last mentioned had fought the Bolsheviks in the Civil War together with the White Russian Admiral Kolchak.[44]

Maisky's oblique reference above to the trying situation is typical of the mood of subdued depression which had enveloped the Soviet diplomatic corps throughout Europe as the wave of repressions started to lap at Narkomindel's door.[45] Earlier on, Beatrice Webb, though still an admirer of the great social changes in the Soviet Union, was nonetheless concerned about 'the big blot on the picture, the terror, suspicions, suppression of free opinion, the arrests, prosecutions, death penalties ... Those amazing confessions which would not be considered as evidence in an English Court, how are they obtained?' She was particularly worried (as undoubtedly was Maisky) by the fact that his predecessor Sokolnikov was 'still in prison, apparently [he has] not yet confessed'.[46]

Circumspection had clearly become the order of the day, as is well illustrated by the paucity of entries in Maisky's diary for the second half of 1937. An indiscreet comment or an emotional outburst could be fatal for a diplomat in the event that he or she was indicted; yet the need for self-expression and empathy was nigh irresistible. The solution

---

[i] Aleksandr Barmin, a former military intelligence officer, he served as chargé d'affaires at the Soviet embassy in Athens, 1935–37.

often came in the form of seemingly innocuous hints and innuendos, even allegories, that were tacitly understood by the correspondents but were hardly incriminating. Kollontay, for instance, concluded a brief note to Maisky with her fondest greetings and a cryptic, but well-understood, comment on how precious were 'genuine sympathy and feelings of friendship in life which made them so much dearer'.[47] A love letter written by Maisky to Agniya on their wedding anniversary is drenched in allusions to the fragility of the future and the need to celebrate the fleeting moment – and above all the past. It is prefaced by two lines from Nikolai Nekrasov's portentous poem 'A New Year':

> ... And what has once been taken from life
> Fate is powerless to take back.

> Dear, beloved and ever-so-slightly-crazy Agneshechka! The poet's right. The future will bring what it brings, but the 15 years we have spent together are ours, and nobody can do a thing to change that. In memory of these 15 years, which, despite the occasional shadow, were years of love, life, fight and movement ... please accept this modest gift from me. As for the future ... let us stride on, in friendship and good cheer, towards our 'silver wedding'.
>   Mikhailych[48]

Freda Utley, an ardent communist and intimate friend of the Maiskys, whose Russian husband had been arrested and was eventually shot, remembered coming to plead with Maisky. Noticing a Mongolian ring on her finger, he 'quoted the Chinese saying: "Everything passes"'.[49]

No wonder, therefore, that when the time arrived for his summer vacation, Maisky was determined to avoid Moscow on his way to the sanatorium. He intended to explore the remote corners of the country, on the rather flimsy pretext that this would better acquaint him with 'the achievements of socialist construction' and would be 'extremely useful' in countering anti-Soviet propaganda in England.[50] Litvinov, too, was cracking under the pressure: he relished the cure he took in Czechoslovakia, and even more so the five days he could spare before the Assembly met, when he toured Austria and Switzerland and tried to avoid thinking about the gathering clouds on the international scene 'and other unpleasant things'.

Litvinov now protected his ambassadors by conferring with them in Geneva rather than in Moscow. Maisky, who a year earlier had been discouraged from attending the Assembly,[51] was now welcomed, and at the same time was instructed to defer his holiday in Russia and remain at his post.[52] Two prominent members of the Soviet delegation in London, the military attaché Putna and Ozersky, the head of the trade delegation, were recalled and executed, while the able first secretary Kagan, who had worked with the discredited Sokolnikov, was recalled to Moscow, like so many other experienced diplomats – ostensibly to prevent them from 'being too acclimatized to particular countries'.[53] Rumours were rife in the London press about Maisky's own imminent withdrawal.[54]

Kollontay's diary captures the depressing and terrorizing impact of the purges, only alluded to in Maisky's diary and letters. She describes how, like Litvinov, she was relieved by the 'holiday mood' over breakfast at the restaurant in the Palais de Nations 'from which there is a long view out to the Alps'. She tried desperately 'not to think about the troubling news from Moscow which Surits had shared with me that morning'. On her way back to Stockholm the following day, she could be found dejectedly sipping her coffee at the railway station in Basel and avoiding the newspapers, which contained rumours of her recall and even of her defection. She was consumed with thoughts about the vicissitudes of life that had overwhelmed her friend David Kandelaki.[i] Only recently he had been engaged in clandestine negotiations in Berlin on Stalin's behalf; now he had been withdrawn from the German capital, sacked from Narkomindel and arrested.[55]

It was hard enough to pursue level-headed policy at the time of the purges; but just as testing for Maisky were the constant demands from friends and foes alike to come up with explanations for them. He would, Beatrice Webb noted, be 'reserved about the arrests and rumours of arrests; justifies some, denies the fact of others'. Meanwhile Agniya, whose brother-in-law had just been arrested and sent to a gulag,[56] was 'tired and I think, depressed'. Beatrice Webb was seriously concerned 'whether he will last long as ambassador in England'. 'The sickening vilification of all who differ from the policy of the governing clique,' she moaned in her diary, 'the perpetual fear of innocent citizens of being wrongly accused and convicted is a terrible social disease. It must need strong nerves to be a Soviet diplomat even in a democratic country ... Any intercourse with the rulers of the country, or even with any citizen might be interpreted as incipient treachery to their own government. The poor Maiskys, what a life they must be leading!'[57] No wonder Agniya suffered a nervous breakdown, from which she emerged only at the beginning of 1938.

When Dalton met Maisky at his office in the embassy to inquire about the purges, he had a strong feeling that 'there was an unseen listener to our conversation'. Maisky defended the execution of the generals, particularly of Tukhachevsky, and of Putna, arguing that they were

> definitely pro-German, anti-French and anti-British. When Tukhachevsky had been over here for the funeral of King George V he had spoken openly and contemptuously of Britain and France, both as regards their Parliamentary institutions and their armed forces. He was a great admirer of the efficiency of Germany. Putna was the same ... I told him that I still did not find this part of the story convincing.[58]

In a conversation with Dalton, Vansittart, clearly echoing Maisky, appeared to be 'very sceptical about the earlier blood baths, but he was satisfied that the Generals were guilty; that they had been in close relations with Germany and were planning a military dictatorship and the elimination of Stalin and Voroshilov'. Tukhachevsky, Maisky told Beatrice Webb, wanted 'to be the *Napoleon of the Russian Revolution*' (emphasis in original). Putna, Maisky's former military attaché, was 'a fellow conspirator'. They could not be trusted if Germany were to attack Russia and 'had to be liquidated'.[59]

Like Kollontay, Maisky never repudiated the terror either privately or publicly. He shared with her, as did many of their revolutionary generation, the pain brought about by the 'widely prevalent ... brutality, intolerance, injustice and the suffering of human

---

[i] David Vladimirovich Kandelaki, trade representative at the Soviet embassy in Berlin, 1934–37. Recipient of the Order of Lenin in 1937, shortly after which he was arrested; condemned to death in July 1938; rehabilitated posthumously.

beings', but, like her, he regarded the terror in a determinist fashion, as a transitional stage that was indispensable for the radical political and economic transformation which the Soviet Union was undergoing.[60]]

17 November

Lothian visited me after nearly a year's absence. We drank tea and talked about world problems.

Lothian is obviously frightened by the bloc of three aggressors. The anti-communist pact signed in Rome on 6 November is directed against England and France in the first place and against the USSR only in the second. 'It's fine for you,' Lothian exclaimed. 'You enjoy an excellent geographical position; you are almost invulnerable. Moreover, everyone knows that Russia can't be conquered. But what about us? We can be attacked from a dozen directions.' Lothian questioned me thoroughly about the terms under which the USSR would be prepared to help England in the Far East. I replied that my personal opinion boiled down to the following. An agreement between the USSR and Britain on the Far East alone is of no value to us; only a general agreement of mutual assistance in both Europe and the Far East is conceivable. The simplest means of achieving this would be to revive the League of Nations: the USSR was and remains an ardent advocate of collective security. Lothian seemed somewhat disappointed.

What should be done to repel the menace looming over the British Empire? In Lothian's opinion, help should be given to the Spanish government and China should be supported with money and weapons. If China could fight on, say, for another year, Japan would not be able to cope and would crack.

However, Lothian makes less sense on the subject of Central Europe. He considers the Anschluss and the annexation of Sudeten Germans to Germany to be preordained and finds nothing wrong in them: 'The self-determination of nations!', don't you know. He is less happy about the prospect of German influence spreading to the Balkans, but here he would like the Soviet Union to assume the task of wrestling with Berlin. Just think how British statesmen of a previous generation would have reacted to attitudes of this kind!

Lothian expects little from Halifax's visit to Berlin. In general, the whole trip has been poorly conceived and carried through. Chamberlain is to blame. He is very naive in matters of foreign policy and thinks that disputes between states can be settled in the same manner as disputes between two trading houses. Halifax complained to Lothian yesterday that the press had raised such a racket that he was ready to abandon the whole idea, but things had already gone too far and there was no way back.

On the whole, Lothian struck me as an extremely troubled and even frightened man. The British bourgeoisie must be having a very bad time of it, if even Lothian was speaking in such terms.

18 November

Oh, perfidious Albion! Corbin told me today that the French government had not been informed about Halifax's forthcoming visit. He himself learned about it from the *Evening Standard* and then asked the Foreign Office what it all meant. The FO confirmed the fact of the visit and showed him the text of the announcement made by Simon in the Commons on 12 November. Paris is terribly irritated by the 'two-faced' position taken by the English. Corbin consoles himself that an identical episode had occurred 25 years ago (he checked it in the embassy's archives), in connection with Haldane's[i] visit to Berlin. Corbin hopes that Halifax's mission will end no better than that of his predecessor. We shall see.

I met Vansittart at the dinner in honour of King Leopold of Belgium in the palace. He takes a sour view of Halifax's visit and is evidently displeased. He said that there had been no diplomatic preparation for Halifax's visit and that no programme of talks had been established. V. does not expect any good to come of the trip and fears that Germany may regard it as a sign of weakness that Cabinet came to a decision about the visit four days after the signing of the Rome pact.[61]

[Maisky included in his diary a draft undated letter to Litvinov, excerpts of which are reproduced here.]

(1) Just over two weeks have passed since the tripartite anti-communist pact (Germany, Japan and Italy) was signed in Rome, and it is now possible to make a preliminary appraisal of the reaction elicited by the pact in Great Britain. This reaction is most certainly negative. With the exception of a small group of English fascists and associated elements, the anti-communist pact has found no supporters at all – either among Labour and the Liberals, or among the Conservatives. One only has to look through the editorials devoted to the pact in the most important British papers to convince oneself of this beyond any doubt. I hardly need quote the left-wing papers (*Daily Herald*, *News Chronicle* and *Manchester Guardian*), for their position was clear in advance. The response of the Conservative press is far more revealing. *The Times*, wishing to soften the impression produced by the pact in England, tries to belittle its importance in every way in its editorial of 9 November. However, even this paper, known for its tendency to conspire with the fascist powers, is forced to acknowledge that the pact 'cannot guarantee peace' and that 'its future depends on the course of events'. The evaluation of the pact in the *Daily Telegraph* is far more striking.[62]

---

[i] Richard Burdon Haldane (1st Viscount Haldane), paid a visit to Berlin, in his capacity as minister of war (1905–12), in a futile attempt to stop the naval arms race.

(2) Meetings and conversations with political and public figures corroborate the impression gained from reading the papers. I have already sent a telegram to you about my talks with Churchill and Lothian. Both are greatly alarmed and think that the pact is aimed not so much at the USSR as at England and France. I heard similar judgements from Elliot (secretary for the affairs of Scotland) and Lord De La Warr[i] (the lord privy seal). Inskip, minister for the coordination of defence, thinks the same. I sat next to him at the lord mayor's banquet on 9 November, and in the course of our conversation, when we touched upon the anti-communist pact, he said with obvious envy: 'Well, your geographical and strategic position is such that nobody can really hurt you. Our situation is quite different: our Empire is vulnerable from every direction.' You will hear similar opinions and statements wherever you go here. One can confidently state, then, that the anti-communist façade of the pact has deluded fewer people in the British Isles than it did a year ago. All authoritative politicians, public figures and journalists have clearly understood that the anti-communist pact pursues purely practical, and not 'ideological', objectives: it is intended to formalize and organize the brotherhood of aggressors who aim to refashion the world, primarily at the expense of Britain and France, along with their appendages Holland and Belgium. Given all this, can one really be surprised that the anti-communist pact has been met with firm disapproval and even hostility in the British Isles? And can one be surprised that one of the by-products of this pact should be a growing hostility toward Ribbentrop, Hitler's chief commissioner in the anti-communist crusade? This hostility has become so acute that it may be hard for Ribbentrop to remain in London for long. If he leaves, I'll be sincerely sorry. I have written to you before that Ribbentrop, owing to his phenomenal tactlessness and his rare ability to rub the English up the wrong way, has been my best ally in the struggle against the growth of German influence in Great Britain over the past year.

(3) Although the reaction to the anti-communist pact in England has been sharply negative, this does not mean that the immediate practical conclusions drawn by the ruling elite of the Conservative Party follow a course close to that of our policy. I have informed you more than once about Chamberlain's foreign-policy plans: he wants to reach an agreement at all costs with Germany and Italy over some form of 'western security' and then go to the polls in the role of 'appeaser of Europe' so as to consolidate the power of his party for the next five years. Eden is against this policy, finding it short-sighted and an affront to all the principles of the League of Nations. That discord exists between the PM and the foreign secretary about the general line of British policy is beyond doubt.

---

[i] Herbrand Edward Dundonald Brassey Sackville (9th Earl De La Warr), parliamentary undersecretary of state for the colonies, 1936–37; lord privy seal, 1937–38; president of the Board of Education, 1938–40; chairman of the National Labour Party, 1931–43.

However, Eden is not a sufficiently major, independent and resolute figure to be in a position to defeat Chamberlain's line. He is supported by 'young' Conservatives such as Duff Cooper, Elliot and Stanley, who are promising but not yet very influential, and by a few National Liberals (like Hore-Belisha) and National Labourites (such as Lord De La Warr). Chamberlain, in turn, finds support among the more influential 'old men', like Halifax, Simon and Hoare. As regards the latter two, their political considerations are mixed with considerations of personal animosity towards Eden. As a result, Chamberlain's line prevails, but its practical implementation is held back to a certain extent by the opposition provided by Eden's group. I take the rumour that Chamberlain is going to replace Eden, possibly with Halifax, with a grain of salt.[63] It is hard to believe that Chamberlain would part with Eden in the capacity of foreign secretary, since Eden is very popular in England and is held in respect by the opposition. Besides, the London diplomatic corps treats him very well, and he has an excellent reputation among the French. To throw Eden out would be to deliver a blow to the Cabinet's prestige and to make it appear utterly reactionary, which would increase the chances of the opposition. And what would be the point? In spite of his disagreements with the foreign secretary, the PM knows full well that Eden wants a career for himself and that, in the final analysis, it is possible to 'get on' with him. Eden is not made of iron, but rather of soft clay which yields easily to the fingers of a skilful artisan.

(4) Now, to turn back to Chamberlain's plans, I am more and more convinced that he is ready to go a long way to implement them. He is ready, for instance, to sacrifice Spain. He is ready to accept German hegemony in Central and South-East Europe, provided the forms it takes are not too odious. It goes without saying that he would not move a finger to help the USSR in the event of an attack on it by the fascist bloc. In general, Chamberlain would be glad to pay a very high price in Europe for the organization of 'western security'. Only two issues, it seems to me, might check Chamberlain's retreat before the aggressors and provoke his retaliation: the colonies and England's rule of the seas; but even in the matter of the colonies he would be prepared, it seems, to seek a compromise with Hitler. (I have not mentioned a direct attack on Great Britain (including the problem of Belgium and Holland) since the attitude of any British statesman to a menace like this is obvious enough.) Chamberlain's position also affected the response of the British government to the anti-communist pact. Instead of taking a cool, expectant stance, if not a stance of active opposition, the Cabinet in London decided to send Halifax to Berlin merely four days after the signing of the Rome protocol. True, Vansittart assured me that the date of Halifax's visit had been set long before, when nobody knew that the pact would be signed on 6 November, and that afterwards it would have been awkward to make changes to the plans. But of course this is a mere

excuse. As far as I know, there was talk quite a while ago among Chamberlain's entourage about Halifax going to Berlin for a hunting fair, but nothing was fixed and nothing was published before 6 November. It was after the signing of the Rome protocol that Chamberlain, contrary to Eden's opinion and taking advantage of the latter's absence from London (Eden was in Brussels), pushed the decision on Halifax's visit through Cabinet. As you know from my telegram, this was done without notifying the French government and struck the general public like a bolt from the blue. Chamberlain was obviously in a hurry: the first news about Halifax's visit appeared on 10 November. Simon made an official announcement about the government's decision in parliament on the 12th, and the visit was scheduled for 17 November, but the date of departure was changed at the last moment, and Halifax actually left London on the afternoon of the 16th.

(5) I don't think that Halifax had any far-reaching plans when he left for Berlin. Vansittart was probably telling the truth when he assured me there had been no serious diplomatic preparation for Halifax's meeting with Hitler and no definite programme of talks had been envisaged. Judging by abundant evidence, Chamberlain's aim was to size Hitler up, to clarify his present mood, and, should these signs prove at all encouraging (from the point of view of the prime minister), to pave the way for more official negotiations. As I write these lines, Halifax is still in Germany and it is too early to judge the outcome of his visit. It should be noted, however, that Chamberlain's undertaking was somewhat damaged at the very beginning by a clever move on the part of Augur (Polyakov), a person well known to you. Now a diplomatic correspondent of Beaverbrook's *Evening Standard*, he published a sensational report on the evening of 13 November claiming that Hitler would propose the following compromise during his talks with Halifax: Germany's freedom of action in Central Europe by 'peaceful means' in exchange for Germany steering clear of the colonial question for the next ten years. Freedom of action 'by peaceful means' is to be understood as England's agreement to a plebiscite in Austria and to Germany's demand for autonomy for the Sudeten Germans. The *Yorkshire Post* corroborated Augur's information on 15 November, and the *Manchester Guardian* on 17 November. The German press angrily rebuffed Augur's article, stating categorically that Germany would not bargain about such issues as its fundamental right to possess colonies. As a result, 'the atmosphere of the visit' was somewhat poisoned and although the press of both countries hastened to affirm by the time Halifax arrived in Berlin that the incident was closed, there is no doubt that Augur's sensational report nevertheless had an effect. What guided Augur in his conduct? His anti-German sentiments undoubtedly played a part, but I think that Mussolini's gold played the most important role. Augur is currently in the pocket of the Italians, and they, for quite understandable

reasons, would not mind spoiling the atmosphere of the Anglo-German attempt at rapprochement.

(6) How to explain the 'general line' of Chamberlain's foreign policy, and in particular the sending of Halifax to Berlin in reply to the Rome protocol? There are two major points: (1) his fear of communism (Chamberlain is a prominent spokesperson for this tendency among the English bourgeoisie); and (2) his desire to buy time to conclude the British rearmament programme and for various political schemes and manoeuvres in the international arena. The second point has even more immediate significance than the first. Inskip, for one, told me in the conversation I mentioned that the preparation work on the programme took much more time than the government had envisaged. Actually, British industry has only just started full-scale implementation of the programme. According to Inskip's estimate, the programme will be fully completed in the middle of 1940, but by the middle of 1939 will have already reached the stage at which England will be able to 'breathe easily'. I'm inclined to think, therefore, that Chamberlain's reasoning, in sending Halifax to Berlin, was as follows: 'In the best scenario, we set in train negotiations that will give rise to the organization of western security; in the worst, having once again kindled the hope in Hitler's heart that an agreement with England is possible, we will have gained a few extra months to make further progress in rearming – why not try it?' It is difficult to say for sure at the moment which of the two alternatives will come true, but I would not set great store by the chances of a serious agreement between England and Germany in the near future. There are so many obstacles on the path to an agreement that, even in the best case, it would take a very considerable amount of time to clear them ...

24 November

The London Trades Union Council, together with the Anglo-Russian Parliamentary Committee, arranged a grand dinner on the occasion of the twentieth anniversary of the October Revolution. More than 400 people were present. Attlee proposed a toast in honour of the twentieth anniversary. Elvin, the current chairman of the General Council, responded with another. The dinner was opened by Wall,[i] secretary of the London Trades Union Council. I spoke in reply.

Everything turned out well, especially considering the current situation. Attlee's and Elvin's speeches were quite *all right*. Wall, following Blum's recent example, even raised the question of cooperation between England, France and the USSR for the cause of peace. I drew up my speech with the intention of

---

[i] Alfred M. Wall, a former communist he became an active trade unionist.

emphasizing Anglo-Soviet relations and our attainments over 20 years, with only a few glances at issues of international politics. I bore it in mind that it is hardly desirable for us at this time to come out with general declarations about the course of Soviet foreign policy or to set ourselves up as initiators of an attack on fascist countries. Our position is clear to all. Let 'Western democracies' reveal their hand in the matter of the aggressors. What is the point of us pulling the chestnuts out of the fire for them? To fight <u>together</u> – by all means; to serve as cannon fodder for them – never![64]

1 December

The French ministers have finally left London, and it is now possible to sum up the results of the *exciting month* that has just passed. The following picture transpires.

In October, the 'Cliveden Set' proved especially lively and active. It is grouped around Lady Astor's salon and it has *The Times* and the *Observer* as its mouthpieces. The key figures in this clique are Lady Astor, Garvin, Geoffrey Dawson[i] (editor of *The Times*) and Lothian. The latter appears to have been wavering recently, but he has not yet broken with the Cliveden Set. Dawson is particularly energetic.

Lady Astor's group has a powerful representation in Cabinet: the majority of the 'old men', including Hoare, Simon, Halifax, Kingsley Wood[ii] and Hailsham. Hoare plays the most active role among the 'Cliveden' ministers. He hates Eden and wants to take his place. Chamberlain, as PM, tries to be neutral, but he basically shares the attitudes and views of the 'old men'.

The 'old men's' programme roughly boils down to the following.

A deal with Germany and Italy (at least in the form of a four-power pact), even at the cost of great sacrifices: Germany will be given a free hand in Central, South-East and Eastern Europe; Spain will lose out; certain colonial compensations will be granted to Hitler.

Political 'realism', acknowledgement of the collapse of the League of Nations, abandonment of any 'League of Nations prejudices' and of 'sentimental' lamentations in regard to collective security and universal peace.

Turning France into an appendage of Whitehall, the liquidation or at any rate 'freezing' of France's eastern pacts and above all of the French–Soviet pact.

---

[i] Geoffrey George Dawson, elected fellow of All Souls College, 1898; editor of *The Times*, 1912–19 and 1923–41; a proponent of appeasement.
[ii] Sir Howard Kingsley Wood, minister of health, 1935–38; secretary of state for air, 1938–40; lord privy seal, April–May 1940; chancellor of the exchequer in Winston Churchill's Cabinet, 1940–43.

In essence, this is pure Germanophilia and a complete capitulation to the aggressor.

This group of 'defeatists' is opposed by another group led by Eden and comprising mostly 'young' members of the government and the Conservative Party, among them Elliot, Ormsby-Gore, Stanley, Hore-Belisha, De La Warr, MacDonald Jr.[i] and others. Duff Cooper ought also to be numbered in this group, but he recently 'kicked the bucket' and became an Italophile. Eden is supported in parliament by Churchill, the duchess of Atholl, Adams[ii] and other Conservatives of the same ilk.

The programme of the 'young' can be summed up as follows.

Alliance with France as the cornerstone of British foreign policy.

Cooperation with the USSR. (This group presently prefers 'for tactical reasons' not to talk about cooperation with the USSR, but thinks intensely about it while foregrounding the Anglo-French alliance, which is more acceptable to public opinion.)

Maintenance of the League of Nations as a useful instrument in the struggle for peace and a convenient form of closer cooperation with the USSR (an Anglo-Soviet pact of mutual assistance, etc. is ruled out).

Activation of British policy in Spain and Central Europe, but without any definite commitments undertaken in advance in respect of Austria and Czechoslovakia.

In summary: Francophilia, the League of Nations, and a not entirely confident attempt to take on the aggressor.

The first group, the group of 'old men', relies on mass Conservative support. The second group, the group of the 'young', counts on the support of the Labour–Liberal opposition and of that part of the Conservatives which is led by Churchill. These groups do not represent clearly defined, closed corporations: each has many individual shades and nuances, and defections from one group to the other are not infrequent. But the existence of these two fundamental trends in British foreign policy is not in doubt.

Such was the balance of forces at the beginning of October.

Next comes that which many call, with a smile, the Cliveden Conspiracy.

Here are the stages of the 'conspiracy'.

The 'conspirators' gather in Lady Astor's country estate in Cliveden throughout October. They work out a 'plan' of major action in order to change the general line of British policy in a decisive manner, shifting it towards a four-

---

[i] Malcolm John MacDonald, son of the former prime minister; secretary of state for the colonies, 1938–40.
[ii] Vyvyan Trerice Adams, Conservative MP, 1931–45, opposed to appeasement.

power pact and rapprochement with Germany. Hoare plays the leading role. Halifax and Kingsley Wood are active participants.

The Field journal sends Halifax an invitation to attend the world hunting fair in Berlin that will be held in November. The 'conspirators' decide to seize the opportunity and organize a 'private meeting' between Halifax and Hitler. Simon and Hailsham are all for it. Chamberlain gives his blessing without himself getting involved. Nevile Henderson (the ambassador in Berlin) tests the ground in Hitler's company. Hitler agrees to meet Halifax. Eden and Vansittart are bluntly against the venture from the very beginning, but cannot prevent it.

In early November, prior to the signing of the tripartite anti-communist pact in Rome (6 November) a preliminary platform for the discussions, evidently drawn up by Göring, arrives from Berlin via Henderson. The main points of the 'platform' are as follows.

[Attached is an article from the *Manchester Guardian* of 24 November 1937 conveying the essence of the 'orientation platform' proposed by Göring. Britain would consent to the reshaping of the Czechoslovak state along the lines of the federal model of Switzerland; the Sudetenland would acquire a status similar to that of a Swiss canton and would undertake to refrain from rendering any diplomatic, political or military assistance to Austria.]

Eden and Vansittart once again categorically object to Halifax's trip, especially in the light of the 'platform'. Chamberlain finds that German demands 'go too far', but thinks that Halifax should still go: why not talk to Hitler all the same? No harm can come of it. A lengthy struggle ensues in Cabinet. Eden, who left for the Brussels conference[65] on 1 November, returns on the 5th for the weekend and tries once again to hinder Halifax's visit. He goes back out to Brussels on the 8th. The question of Halifax's visit remains undecided.

On 10 November, in the absence of Eden, the 'big four' (Chamberlain, Halifax, Hoare and Simon) rush the decision on Halifax's visit through Cabinet and Halifax goes to Germany on 16 November. Eden protests and threatens his resignation (but he does not resign). The *Manchester Guardian* uses its channels in the Foreign Office to bring Göring's preliminary 'platform' to the notice of the opposition and the diplomatic corps.

Hitler and Halifax meet in Berchtesgaden. Hitler lectures Halifax and Halifax listens, only occasionally asking questions or making a remark. Hitler speaks in general and relatively modest terms. He asks for the recognition in principle of Germany's right to have colonies without any compensation and the right to adjust relations with Central European countries bilaterally, and intimates that he would be ready to return to a 'reformed' League of Nations under certain conditions. Halifax states that the British government is not antagonistically disposed to Germany and that it admits the possibility of certain changes in Central Europe, but only by peaceful means and with the consent of France. Practically no mention is made in the conversation of the USSR and communism.

Hitler's entourage – Göring, Hess,[i] Neurath and others – dots the i's and crosses the t's. In concrete terms (1) Germany gives up its former colonies in the Pacific, but demands an 'African Empire' comprising Togo, Cameroon, Angola and the greater part of the Belgian Congo. Germany is prepared to receive Angola and Congo in the form of mandates (while joining the 'reformed' League of Nations) or in the form of a right to exploitation through 'trade campaigns'. The entourage does not mention Tanganyika, Kenya and South-West Africa – neither giving them up nor even raising the issue. Evidently, they are putting the problem aside for the time being. (2) As to Central Europe, Germany demands that Britain and France should stop interfering in her affairs and give Hitler freedom of action. (3) At the same time, they intimate that Germany might agree to postpone the matter of colonies for a few years in exchange for a free hand in Central Europe.

Halifax returns to London on 22 November, rather disheartened. Chamberlain is also disappointed. But Eden rejoices and puts on a feast for a few of his friends in a restaurant on the evening of the 22nd (as Masaryk told me). Mrs Eden is delighted and joyfully announces that the dark clouds looming over her husband have dispersed. In our conversation of 26 November, Harold Nicolson confirms that the outcome of Halifax's visit strengthened Eden's position. However, the danger has not passed, since Chamberlain will certainly try again to come to an understanding with Germany. All the more so as Chamberlain's attitudes are quite widespread among the Conservatives (Nicolson was able to verify this at the meeting of the Foreign Policy Committee of the Cabinet on 25 November). Vansittart, in his turn, states in his conversation with me on the same day, 26 November, that Halifax had promised nothing to Hitler and that there is no reason for Czechoslovakia and Austria to panic, since the British government 'does not sell countries either in the direct or metaphorical sense of the word'.

The peripeteia of the Cliveden Conspiracy ends at this point, and the counteraction of Eden's group begins.

On 24 November Voyt, diplomatic correspondent of the *Manchester Guardian*, publishes a sensational article disclosing the preliminary 'platform' cited above. Similar information appears, in slightly modified form, in the

---

[i] Rudolf Hess, deputy Nazi Party leader, 1933–41. Flew to Scotland on 10 May, on his own initiative, with a peace offer.

Yorkshire Post (Mrs Eden's paper). The press kicks up a storm. In parliament, Chamberlain hurls invective at the 'irresponsible reports' of the press in connection with Halifax's visit. The Germans are ranting and raving and declare that it is impossible 'to do any business' with the British: everything always has to be made public in the end. Voyt's article has a tremendous effect.

By way of compensation and to prevent false rumours, Eden demands that Chautemps and Delbos should be invited to London right away in order to demonstrate the inviolability of Anglo-French closeness. The Cabinet accepts his request, all the more so as a visit by the French ministers had already been planned. The visit has now been brought forward: the Anglo-French meeting will be held on 29 and 30 November.

On 28 November, on the eve of the arrival of the French, Eden himself receives the English press and states that the aim of the Anglo-French meeting is not to conclude some agreement with Germany and Italy at the expense of third countries, and that the British government is not going to exert pressure on France in connection with its eastern pacts (especially the Franco-Soviet pact), but it will try to find ways of easing tension in Central Europe. A serious discussion of Germany's colonial demands is also possible.

The Anglo-French meeting was held on the 29th and 30th. Unlike Baldwin, who would usually keep silent at meetings of this sort, granting an active role to the foreign secretary, Chamberlain kept a tight rein on the talks from the very beginning. Eden was pushed to the background a little, but Chamberlain repeatedly emphasized that there were no differences between himself and his foreign secretary. Corbin, who was present at the meeting, asserted that the prime minister was generally objective and showed much less Germanophilia than Halifax. Chamberlain demonstrated a strikingly practical, business-like approach to all the problems discussed.

A pleasant disappointment was in store for the French. Leaving for London, they had feared that the British government would insist on 'freezing' the pacts and ask France to exchange agents with Franco, as England had done. Their expectations did not materialize. The PM said in his opening speech that the British government was far removed from the idea of influencing the foreign policy of France, while Eden, in his conversation with Delbos, pronounced that any weakening of the Franco-Soviet pact would be undesirable. The talks on Spain were short: both governments reaffirmed the policy of non-intervention. The matter of agents was not even mentioned by the British. The PM had clearly learned some lessons over the previous weeks.

No wonder that under these circumstances the atmosphere at the meeting was most cordial (much better than at the meeting at the end of January 1935, when France was represented by Flandin and Laval), and that all decisions were taken quickly and easily. The French left London elated.

The decisions themselves boiled down to the following. (1) The British and the French are ready to discuss Germany's colonial claims, but only as part of a 'general European settlement'. The English were firmer in this matter than the French. (2) As far as Central Europe is concerned, the British declared that they adhered to the positions formulated during Barthou's visit to London in 1934, i.e. they would not make any definite commitments in advance, but would continue to be interested in the state of affairs in this part of the globe and would formulate their position when necessary, depending on the circumstances. (3) Delbos announced his forthcoming tour of Central and Eastern Europe and gained approval for it. (4) The two governments agreed to follow a common line in Far Eastern matters. Here, too, the British were more energetic than the French. One minor episode is worthy of attention. The French drew the attention of the British to an editorial in *The Times* of 29 November that defended the idea of giving Germany a free hand in the east and asked anxiously what this meant. The British explained to them that *The Times* does not express the government's line, and the French sighed with relief.

On the afternoon of 30 November, Chamberlain summoned the Labour leaders, Attlee and Greenwood, and communicated the results of the Anglo-French meeting to them. He especially emphasized that the British government had not exerted any pressure whatsoever on the French government (particularly in regard to the Franco-Soviet pact), that it had adhered to a platform of 'general European settlement', and that the attempt to achieve this settlement was still at a very early stage and would take a great deal of time. On the whole, the PM showed little optimism and the Labour leaders even had the impression that Chamberlain was concerned more about buying time – through further negotiations – to complete Britain's rearming. Attlee stated on behalf of the Labour Party that the British Labour movement would not tolerate the division of Europe into 'western' and 'eastern' and allowing Germany freedom of action in the east. Chamberlain promised to take this into consideration.

I saw Corbin and Vansittart after the meeting. Corbin said somewhat cynically that a 'general European settlement' was rather like a square peg in a round hole and that the Anglo-French decision on the colonial question was essentially an irrelevance. First the British and French will collect material on this matter, then they will study it, then they will formulate points of view, then they will negotiate with other colonial powers, etc. Months will pass before things get moving, if they ever do. When I asked him what he understands by the phrase 'general European settlement', Vansittart answered that there is no sense racking one's brains over its interpretation now, for this is all the music of the rather distant future and nobody knows whether a discussion of the 'settlement' will ever take place at all. When I mentioned *The Times*, Vansittart became highly agitated and exclaimed with manifest fury: 'Fortunately, it's not

Geoffrey Dawson (the editor of *The Times*) who directs British foreign policy, but Anthony Eden!'

This is how this *exciting month* ended.

What are my conclusions? Here they are.

The 'Cliveden Conspiracy' has evidently suffered defeat. The attempt to change the course of British foreign policy failed. The policy remains as it was before: that is, weak, vacillating, zigzagging, retreating before the aggressor; but not, at least, a policy of alliance with the aggressor at the expense of third countries.

Chamberlain was taught a good lesson. Eden's position has been greatly strengthened. The PM will clearly have to 'straighten' his line in the near future.

What are the causes of the failure? They are very complicated and diverse. The resultant force, in my view, was formed from the following basic elements: Hitler's uncompromising formulation of the colonial question; growing fears in British ruling circles in connection with the conclusion of the tripartite 'anti-communist pact'; the opposition of France and the Little Entente to a deal with Germany; the unfavourable response of the USA to Halifax's visit; fear of spoiling relations with the USSR; the hostile attitude of the Labour and Liberal opposition to the idea of giving Berlin a free hand in the east; the resistance of the Francophile group in Conservative circles, especially of the Foreign Office with Eden and Vansittart at its head; and, finally, Eden's personal popularity among both the 'young' Conservatives and the opposition parties, which understand that Eden is the best possible British foreign secretary in the present government. Consequently, the Germanophile attack was rebuffed.

So can we put our minds at rest about the future? We can't, by any means. The Cliveden Set will undoubtedly continue its conspiracies and will resume its attack at the first opportunity. The line of attack is predictable: the Germanophiles will insist on rejecting a 'general European settlement' and on resolving its constituent problems one by one. Chamberlain could easily be tempted by the idea, as he has the psychology of a typical *businessman*. In addition, the Germanophiles have circulated an absurd theory: the appeasement of Europe is necessary to obtain freedom of action in the Far East. Any serious change in the correlation of forces in Spain and any new fascist adventure in some other part of Europe could exert a very strong influence on the conduct of the British government.

The final conclusion: we must be on the alert!

[The ferocious purges meant that Maisky's personal survival had become bound up with the success of collective security, for which the extraordinary connections he had forged in London were vital. This was an extremely delicate balancing act: he had to manoeuvre between the need to provide Moscow with objective evaluation and the need to keep alive the prospects of an alliance with the West. Early in the summer, he had already expressed in private his concern that the failure of non-intervention in Spain might lead to 'an interval of isolation policy on the part of the UK and the USSR – each distrusting the other'. From Lloyd George he had gleaned the fact that Eden was indeed toying with the idea of adopting a neutral position in Spain, were non-intervention to collapse. Chamberlain, on the other hand, was seeking to change the committee of non-intervention into 'a four-power pact ... detaching itself from the Soviet Union'.[66]

Maisky by no means shared the view that isolation was being imposed on the Soviet Union. He pleaded with Litvinov to seek compromise.[67] Whether intimidated by Stalin[68] or, more likely, following his own convictions,[69] the defiant Litvinov waved away Maisky's appeals, arguing that: 'We sometimes prefer to be isolated rather than go along with the bad actions of others, and that is why isolation does not scare us.' However, when Maisky resorted to the 'isolation' card to raise concern in London over the plans for a four-power pact, he was severely reprimanded for causing 'unnecessary nervousness and distress'.[70] In fact, Maisky persevered in his efforts to seek collaboration with Eden, and even obtained Stalin's personal approval. In December, he went out of his way to expose the futility of Halifax's trip to Germany, referring to Eden's opposition to Chamberlain's policy and the frailty of the 'Cliveden Set' in exerting influence on the prime minister. His report to Narkomindel concluded that 'all attempts by the Germanophiles to bring about a change in the course of English foreign policy have proved unsuccessful'. British policy, he insisted, could not be 'characterized as a direct association with the aggressors'. He believed that Chamberlain, confronted by Eden, had finally understood that the road to a 'four-power pact' was far from smooth.[71]

Following the withdrawal of Germany and Italy from the League of Nations, Maisky contemplated countermeasures to reinstate the League as the genuine framework for collective security. 'The USSR,' he explained to Noel-Baker[i] in an attempt to mobilize Labour's support, 'would co-operate to the full in any such joint action based on the Covenant and worked through the League. But it cannot take isolated action.'[72] He further contested Potemkin's judgement that the British were bent on discrediting the Soviet Union's pacts with both France and Czechoslovakia. He referred to Chamberlain's disclosure to Attlee that he harboured little hope of reaching an agreement with Germany, but regarded the move as a necessary breathing space in which to rearm Britain. However, it could hardly escape the Kremlin's attention that the soothing words were only a response to Attlee's warnings that the Labour movement objected to 'a free hand' being given to Hitler in Central and Eastern Europe.[73]]

4 December[74]

Good riddance!

Ahlefeldt[ii] is a typical diplomat of the pre-war generation, obsessed with etiquette and clueless in politics. Over five years I have failed to observe any real intelligence in him. Only *bonhomie*.

---

[i] Philip John Noel-Baker, Labour MP, 1929–31 and 1936–70.
[ii] Count Preben Ferdinand Ahlefeldt-Laurvig, Danish envoy to Great Britain, 1921–37.

But his wife! Good grief! Tall as a pole, flat as a plank, with a neck so long and dismal that she always had to keep it propped up with a high collar made of spangles, stones and celluloid. The countess was truly hideous. A nose a yard long, eyes like a frog's, and skin that had darkened from decay and spite. Every time I had to look at her I started feeling sick.

In addition to all these charms, Countess Ahlefeldt was from the Russian White Guard. She had once been a maid of honour in the court of Mariya Fedorovna[i] and lived in the Anichkov Palace.[75] Then she fled the revolution and married her splendid 'consort'. Of course she hated us with a visceral loathing, and this was the seed of conflict between the Soviet embassy and the Danish mission; it lasted throughout the five years of my time in London. The gist of the conflict was as follows.

Although, according to the old-fashioned etiquette of the Vienna Congress, newly appointed ambassadors pay first visits only to other ambassadors upon arrival and not to envoys (who should themselves pay first visits to new arrivals), I have never followed this absurd custom. I thought that the newcomer ought to pay the first visit to all his colleagues, as old-timers, irrespective of their rank. Therefore, having handed my credentials to the English king I began to do the rounds of both ambassadors <u>and</u> envoys. I called on Ahlefeldt, too. Ahlefeldt returned my visit. Then Agniya began making her calls in the same order as I did. When it was time to visit the Danish lady, my secretary called the Danish mission to set the date and hour for Agniya to see the countess. A brief reply followed from the Danish mission: the countess was unwell. A few days later we read in the papers that Ahlefeldt and his spouse had attended a diplomatic dinner. Agniya concluded that the countess must have recovered, and my secretary called the Danish mission once again. This time they answered that the countess was leaving for Denmark and could not receive Agniya. The matter was taking a strange turn. I suspected that something was amiss (I did not know then that the countess was from the Russian White Guard). So, when we were refused a second time, I asked my secretary to ask the Danish countess to inform my wife when she returned from Denmark, so that my wife could pay her a visit. That was the end of it. The countess never got round to calling all these five years. As a result, my wife remained 'unacquainted' with Countess Ahlefeldt and, on meeting in the palace, at receptions, etc., they never greeted one another. Nor did we ever invite the Ahlefeldt couple to our receptions; and they paid us in the same coin. Relations between the two missions were essentially broken, although relations between the USSR and Denmark remained friendly throughout.

---

[i] Mariya Fedorovna, wife of Tsar Alexander III.

In the end, the countess got angry. Being untouched by genius, she began to pour her hatred on us by spreading the most absurd rumours about Agniya among the diplomatic community. Thus on one occasion an English journalist we knew told us that Countess Ahlefeldt was going round telling everybody (including that journalist) that when Agniya met her at a reception at Buckingham Palace and saw the last tsarist medal on her breast, she came right up to her and spat on it.

'And what did you do?' the journalist asked the Danish lady mischievously.

She did not understand that he was provoking her and answered: 'What did I do? Of course I spat back in that Bolshevik bag's face.'

The journalist roared with laughter.

'Why are you laughing?' the countess asked in alarm.

'I know Mrs Maisky too well to believe a story like that,' exclaimed the journalist.

The countess turned bright red and abruptly walked off.

That's what lady diplomats can be like!

12 December

Today, spending the weekend with the Webbs, I put to this old couple the possibility of a united front in England (not to the left with the communists, but to the right with Liberals of all stripes, National Labourites, etc.).

My arguments were as follows. As far as I can judge, Labour's hopes of gaining a parliamentary majority for themselves are ill-founded. The Conservatives may well stay in power for some ten years more. This means that British foreign policy will hold to its zigzagging course, systematically retreating before the aggressors. Such a policy will inevitably serve to unleash war. Aren't there ways and means to establish an alternative, stronger and more resolute government in the near future? Couldn't there be a united front in power oriented to the right, if Labour is so very scared of a united front oriented to the left?

Sidney Webb entirely shares my fears about Conservative dominance for another ten years. In his opinion, the term might be reduced to seven years at best. The outlook is grim. Yet a united front oriented to the right offers no salvation. The Liberals would not accept Labour's programme of the nationalization of banks, railways, mines, etc., and if Labour made major concessions to the Liberals, then the Labour Party would be split. Moreover, Webb suspects that even if a Lib–Lab government did come to power, it would not be any more daring or resolute in foreign policy than the Conservative government. The heart of the matter is that a close relationship, perhaps even an alliance, needs to be established with the USSR. A Liberal–Labour government would never do this for fear of the Conservatives. Webb comes to the conclusion that however deplorable the outlook, it is hardly possible to change it (on the assumption, of course, that no catastrophic events of an extraordinary nature happen within the next few years). Beatrice Webb is more optimistic. True, she also thinks that Labour has no chance of gaining a majority for itself in the near future. But this is by no means essential in order to straighten the course of British foreign policy. The best combination would be this: a weak Conservative government with a strong Labour opposition (say, 313 Conservatives, 280 Labourites and 12 Liberals). Beatrice thinks that such a government could make an alliance with the USSR. The political history of Great Britain shows that most of its radical reforms and actions have been carried out by Conservative governments with a narrow parliamentary majority. The Conservatives can permit themselves the luxury of greater boldness with regard to the USSR than the Liberals or Labour. Being very familiar with Labour's cowardly heart, I am inclined to think that there is considerable truth in Beatrice Webb's judgement. Eden is surely more capable of concluding an alliance with the USSR than Dalton or Archibald Sinclair.[i]

* * *

Beatrice told us the amusing story of Bernard Shaw's marriage.

The year was 1908. Shaw was earning no more than six pounds a week and living in the countryside with the Webbs. He had a rakish temperament, his affairs never ceased, and the writer's 'girlfriends' made scenes that gave the Webbs no end of trouble. For instance, some of Shaw's jilted girlfriends blamed Beatrice for their frivolous lover's betrayals. They were jealous of her and pestered her with scenes of indignation and despair. Finally Beatrice got bored of all that and decided to have Bernard married.

At that critical juncture, Beatrice's old school friend, Charlotte Townsend, came to visit her. Charlotte was not married and she had a yearly income of some 5,000 pounds following her father's death. Charlotte decided to move in with the Webbs. Beatrice warned her that two men were living there, Shaw and Graham Wallas[ii] (the well-known Fabian writer). Charlotte had nothing against it. Beatrice, discussing her matrimonial projects with Sidney, told her husband regretfully about her apprehension that Charlotte, with her character and tastes, would get along better with Wallas (he was a bachelor, too) than with Shaw. To her great surprise and joy, Charlotte and Bernard became the closest of friends

---

[i] Archibald Sinclair, secretary of state for Scotland, 1931–32; secretary of state for air, 1940–45; leader of Liberal parliamentary party, 1935–45.

[ii] Graham Wallas, political psychologist and educationalist, dominant during the Fabian Society's early years along with Sidney Webb, Sydney Olivier and Bernard Shaw. Resigned in 1904 in disagreement over the Society's sympathy for imperialism and the Conservative Education Act 1902.

37. Bernard Shaw entertained at the embassy.

in three days. They had a stormy and fast-paced affair, but Shaw did not want to marry, for how could he, a pauper, marry a wealthy woman?

At this time, the Webbs were about to go to America. Beatrice summoned Shaw and told him bluntly: either get married immediately or leave my house. If you stay here without us your relationship will become too obvious to everyone and it will bring a great deal of trouble.

Shaw refused to marry, moved out on the next day and settled in a garret in London. Charlotte also left. She went to see Rome. The Webbs departed for America.

Some time later, when they were already in America, the Webbs received a telegram from Wallas saying that Shaw was dying (Shaw had tuberculosis and life in the garret was taking its toll). The news shocked the Webbs and they were about to return to England. However, on the next day they received a second telegram from Wallas that greatly surprised them: Bernard had married Charlotte.

The Webbs were perplexed. Clarification came later. Wallas had first sent a telegram to Charlotte, notifying her that Shaw was ill. Charlotte rushed to England and lodged Shaw in a splendid villa. She summoned doctors and a serious course of treatment began. Then Bernard told Charlotte: 'If this is how it is, then we have to marry. It must be fate.' They married the same day. Bernard and Charlotte still live together now. Shaw is 80 and Charlotte 82.

14 December

The British are increasingly troubled by events in the Far East.[76] Serves them right. It's high time for them to be taught a good lesson in one part of the world or another. It will be very beneficial in cleansing their brains, which have gone to fat.

I've seen many people over the last few days: the duchess of Atholl, Layton (*News Chronicle*), the Webbs, the chemical tycoon McGowan, the machine-tool builder Alfred Herbert,[i] Horace Wilson (Chamberlain's chief secretary), Roderick Jones (head of Reuters) and others. They all scold Japan, ooh and aah over British losses in China, raise their hands hopelessly and exclaim: 'Ah, what can we do now?' They speak about cooperation with the USA as a cure-all. The trouble is that the Americans do not want to cooperate, since they fear, not without reason, that the English want to use them and make the Americans pull chestnuts out of the fire for them.[77]

Some of my interlocutors (the duchess of Atholl and McGowan in particular) cautiously tried to sound me out about whether we would agree to support England in the Far East and what our terms might be if we did agree.

I replied in the following way. The USSR is well protected against any attack from the outside and can just wait for events to unfold. We see the struggle against Japanese aggression only as part of the struggle against any aggression within the framework of collective security. Why should the Far East be seen as an exception? Just because the English are being squeezed there? At any rate, I cannot conceive the possibility of any special agreements with England in a joint campaign against Japanese aggression alone. If, at long last, Great Britain wants to begin a serious campaign against aggression, all well and good. We shall support it and make our contribution, provided the struggle is carried out on a general scale, in the Far East and in Europe within the framework of the League of Nations. All the more so that now, with Italy having left the League and all major aggressors having fled from Geneva, peace-loving nations have an opportunity to turn the League of Nations into a united bloc of all peace-loving states. My interlocutors were somewhat disappointed.

---

[i] Sir Alfred Edward Herbert, managing director of Alfred Herbert Ltd, the largest machine tool company in the world.

1938

4 January

I found Vansittart's name in the New Year's Honours List. But what kind of an 'honour' is this? As yet, it's hard to tell.

V. has been accorded a lofty award and a new position to boot: he ceases to be permanent undersecretary (a most important post as effective head of the Foreign Office staff and thus to a significant extent head of the FO itself) and becomes 'chief diplomatic adviser' to the foreign secretary. What does this mean?

No one is quite sure, because the post has only just been created. There is no precedent in the history of the FO. But all the information I have been able to muster, together with the observations of experienced people, adds up to the following.

If V. succeeds in working his way into the PM's entourage (like Horace Wilson, chief industrial adviser to the British government) and in gaining the latter's trust, then the new appointment will represent a major promotion for him and his influence will grow. If, however, V. fails in this and remains in the capacity of 'adviser' only to the FO, the new appointment will have to be regarded as a demotion or, more precisely, as a retirement ticket, only with uniform, decorations and a pension. We shall see what we shall see.

It is beyond doubt that V.'s new appointment is a typical British compromise in the struggle occupying government circles between the Francophiles and Germanophiles. The latter wished to get V. away from London and pack him off as ambassador to the United States, whereas the Francophiles insisted on V.'s retention in his former post. Eventually, V. stayed in London, but lost direct control of the FO.

The *Observer* was hostile about Vansittart's appointment, and so was *The Times*. These are good signs, but who knows what tomorrow will hold.

[Chamberlain's appointment as prime minister proved to be a severe blow to Maisky and Litvinov, and added to the fear that Britain was seeking new allegiances, leaving the Soviet Union out in the cold. Frustrated at the League of Nations' failure to sustain peace, Litvinov wavered, sharing the Kremlin's increasing sense of marginalization and passivity in the face of an imminent war. But, like Maisky, he did not yet abandon his expectations of a long-term shift towards collective security.[1] As the New Year dawned, Maisky could only hope that the brazen display of German aggressive intentions might lead to 'something completely unexpected' in Britain. His hopes that the Republican victory in the battle of Teruel on the Aragon front, in December 1937, might tip the scales were, however, shattered when the town was recaptured by Franco on 21 February 1938.[2] To make things worse, the British drift towards appeasement intensified following the resignation of Eden and the 'promotion' of Vansittart to the lofty but powerless position of chief diplomatic adviser. The Soviet retreat from collective security into isolation was, therefore, enforced rather than self-inflicted.

The diary, as well as related documentary material produced in this volume, clearly indicates the extent to which Soviet foreign policy remained reactive, and did not dogmatically pursue Lenin's 1916 ideological premise, which dictated the need for 'isolation' in a war that was perceived to be inevitable.[3] Speaking in Geneva on 27 January, Litvinov reaffirmed that, although some members had withdrawn from the League, the Soviet Union was 'prepared as before for full cooperation with the remaining loyal members of the League'. Maisky, however, disclosed to the Webbs that 'the Soviet government was tending towards isolation and though she will not leave the League she will cease to be interested in it. Collective security must be applied everywhere or nowhere – to Germany in the west as well as to Japan in the east'.[4] He was certainly attentive to Zhdanov's[i] frontal attack on Litvinov a couple of days earlier, during which he castigated Narkomindel's policies. Zhdanov now chaired the Foreign Affairs Commission of the Supreme Soviet, which gradually took over the formulation of foreign policy from the deflated Politburo and Narkomindel. As will be seen below, Maisky most likely learned that, in his despair, Litvinov had composed, but not sent, a letter of resignation addressed to Stalin.[5]]

15 January

[Attached to the diary is an article from the *Evening Standard* of 15 January 1938 offering two versions of an incident which occurred in the British embassy in Tokyo on 15 January. According to the police report, a certain Japanese citizen, Makato Watanabe, met the British ambassador, Robert Craigie,[ii] and told him that Great Britain must revise its policy toward Japan. He then pulled out a long sword and handed it to the ambassador. The man was arrested and interrogated. According to the official version of the Japanese news agency Domei, the sword was given to the ambassador in recognition of his efforts to improve Anglo-Japanese relations.]

---

[i] Andrei Aleksandrovich Zhdanov, replaced Kirov, after his murder in 1934, as general secretary of the Communist Party in Leningrad; chairman of the RSFSR Supreme Soviet, 1938–47; member of the Politburo, 1939–48. Actively involved in the purges of the 1930s, he introduced the Zhdanov Doctrine – the rigorous communization of Eastern Europe – as well as the cultural purges of the post-war era.

[ii] Robert Leslie Craigie, assistant undersecretary of state in the Foreign Office, 1934–37; British ambassador in Japan, 1937–41.

Typical Japanese goings-on! The Domei agency's explanation is sheer nonsense.

I can't help recalling my own experiences in Japan: 1928, a dark night, I am working alone at the embassy. All my embassy colleagues, including Ambassador Troyanovsky, have gone to a Kabuki show. Two deafening explosions under the embassy windows, alarm, a thorough torch-lit search of the garden by our staff, and... a white silk handkerchief pinned with a dagger to a tree opposite the embassy entrance and inscribed in Japanese: 'Bolsheviks, go home!'

All this had been carried out by a secret Japanese fascist organization. Fortunately, they used petards, not bombs...

Another memory. When a Kabuki company returned from their trip to Moscow, Japanese 'patriots' staged a hostile demonstration at their first performance back home: they scattered live snakes under chairs all around the hall, just before it began. During the show, the snakes began hissing and crawling amidst the audience. A fearful panic broke out. Men snarled, women shrieked, children cried, the curtain had to be lowered and the performance was interrupted. Only after all the snakes had finally been caught and carried out of the theatre did the performance resume...

That was in 1928. The same is happening now.

The Orient never changes.

20 January

China remains high on the agenda.

Guo Taiqi came over the other day. He complains that the British refuse to give the Chinese enough weapons and aeroplanes, claiming a shortage of their own. In addition, they demand cash for everything. Guo has raised the issue of arms sales on credit, but there has been no answer as yet from the British government.

When I visited Cadogan on 12 January, he assured me that Jiang Jieshi was firmly set against capitulation. Jiang Jieshi rejected Japan's peace terms, which were passed to him by the German ambassador in China, and is now turning to guerrilla warfare. Jiang Jieshi still has considerable military resources, including his best divisions and significant stockpiles of weapons. Weapons are shipped to him from the United States, Britain, France and, most intriguingly, from Germany, via either Indochina or Hong Kong. Cadogan also spoke with great satisfaction about Soviet supplies to China, and turned out to be better informed on this matter than me...

25 January

Today Chamberlain received a delegation of the National Council of Labour (the trade unions, the Labour Party Executive Committee, and Parliamentary Labour), which made a formal submission to the PM about the urgent need to intensify the struggle against Japan and assistance to China. Citrine, Noel-Baker and Dallas[i] spoke on behalf of the delegation. Chamberlain replied that any serious action against Japan could only be taken in the form of naval military operations, for which the cooperation of the US was essential; but the latter had shown little desire to do anything. Chamberlain mentioned in passing that the Soviet Union was powerful on land and in the air, but weak at sea; so cooperation with Moscow was of no relevance in this context.

So, the British government is still unwilling to combat aggression in the Far East. Well, sometime or other, probably not too far in the future, it will bitterly regret this.

27 January

I visited Vansittart and inquired about his new position and duties.

Judging by what V. told me, matters stand as follows. He remains in the Foreign Office, keeps his old office and reads all the correspondence, but is no longer involved in administrative affairs (appointments, staff, finance, and so on) and takes no part in the daily management of FO staff in London or elsewhere. The two latter tasks are to be assumed by Cadogan, the new permanent undersecretary. V. will focus wholly on drawing up and giving advice on the main issues of foreign policy.

What will the relations between V. and Cadogan in the sphere of 'advice' be like, given the fact that, according to the FO constitution, the permanent undersecretary must also counsel the foreign secretary?

V. could not clarify this issue at all. The problem evidently persists both for him and for Cadogan. Friction and conflicts are possible. But V. does not intend to surrender. He told me with a laugh: 'I have always given advice, both when I was asked and when I wasn't but thought it necessary. I intend to do the same in the future, too.'

Since V. is a much sturdier and bigger man than Cadogan, he will probably remain in charge, provided, of course, that there are no unexpected changes at the top and, in particular, at the head of the FO.[6]

I asked V. about the rumours that he would be spending most of his time on trips abroad. He gave a sarcastic response: 'I knew that the "Cliveden FO", after

---

[i] George Dallas, trade unionist.

suffering a defeat in their plans to pack me off to Washington, were now hoping that I would at least be in London as little as possible. Lady Astor is in for a great disappointment: I'll be spending at least three-quarters of my time here (V. pointed to his desk), because all major foreign-policy decisions are taken in London and not in foreign capitals.'

We talked about Spain, Germany and Italy. V. believes that now, after Teruel, the widespread belief in the inevitability of Franco's immediate victory has to be reviewed. The Republicans have displayed great vitality and fortitude. Even taking into account foreign intervention on its current scale, Franco will hardly be able to overthrow the Republic on his own. I voiced my fear that Italy and Germany could expand the scope of intervention. But V. expressed his doubts about this.

As regards talks with Germany and Italy, V. thinks that rapid developments are most unlikely. Britain and France are still 'studying' Hitler's colonial claims. Any loan to Germany in the terms of Van Zeeland's report is out of the question.[7] Furthermore, any agreement with Germany must be part of an 'all-European settlement'. Practical decisions will be long in coming (if they ever do!). The British government is now pursuing a wise policy of wait-and-see towards Italy: following the events in Abyssinia, Spain and Austria, Mussolini's position is growing weaker with every passing month. So what cause can there be to hurry with the talks in Rome? The longer Britain keeps its composure, the easier it will eventually be to come to an agreement with Italy.

Finally, V. began probing me on the Far East issue, inquiring about our intentions in this part of the world and the possibilities for cooperation there between London and Moscow. I answered in the same spirit as I answered all other Englishmen who asked me this question. In particular, I emphasized the inviolability of our position in the Far East. V. was somewhat disappointed and argued at length that even on the strength of its purely selfish national interests, the Soviet Union could in no way reconcile itself to Japan's victory in China; after all, peace is indivisible. I remained adamant. V. was very evasive when I asked him what he thought about engaging the League of Nations against Japan.

[On 24 January, Maisky begged Litvinov confidentially to allow him to proceed to Geneva within days, ostensibly for consultations over pressing issues concerning Anglo-Soviet relations. But 'above all', Maisky impetuously got to the point, 'I have a highly important personal question which I would like to discuss with you'. If it could not be justified as a business trip, he was even prepared to make the journey as 'a private one'.[8] Though there is an absence of any reports on what transpired in Geneva, corroborative evidence seems to confirm Maisky's growing concern about the future of Litvinov, his guardian and mentor, no less than about his own continued stay in London. Life had become unbearable, with rumours of his imminent withdrawal circulating widely in the press and with the intrusion of the NKVD into the embassy and an attempt to recall Kagan, his loyal first secretary, from an embassy that was already seriously understaffed.[9] The circumstances surrounding the hastily arranged encounter between Maisky and Litvinov are reminiscent of Maisky's similar approaches at the outset of his career, prompted by Agniya, who was determined to return to the homeland.[10]]

28 January

Eden had a talk with M.M. [Litvinov] in Geneva. First, Eden showed M.M. the statement he was going to make at the Council session and then asked M.M. what statement he would make. M.M. replied half in jest that he had reckoned on finding everything ready, since it followed from my report from London that Eden was planning a joint statement. Eden got very embarrassed and tried to assure him that there was some kind of misunderstanding. Apparently, he hadn't spoken to me about a joint statement. I must have meant the possibility of Council adopting a resolution. Such a resolution would turn out to be rather bland and thin, however, so it would be better to forgo it. Eden then began fervently trying to convince M.M. that he must say something because it was important, through individual statements, to demonstrate the solidarity of the permanent members of the Council. M.M. gathered from Eden's behaviour that he had really spoken to me about a joint statement, but, for whatever reason, was now beating a retreat...

The explanation seems simple to me. During our conversation on 31 December, Eden did tell me about the possibility of a joint statement, but Chamberlain evidently did not consent to the idea and the foreign secretary had to dig himself out of the hole in Geneva.

7 February

So, Hitler has struck a blow at his army![11] The legal 'opposition' to the dominance of the 'party', which grouped around the Reichswehr and included big industrialists, landlords, old-school diplomats and so on, has been broken for good. The removal of Schacht was a sign of the approaching climax. Blomberg's[i] marriage to a plebeian was the last straw. Is the 'purge' over? Hard to tell. I am inclined to think that the disgraced military will come in for more exiles, arrests and so on. To give Hitler his due, he carried out the operation very skilfully and with lightning speed. Even if this is only a 75% victory, it is a victory none the less.

---

[i] Werner Fritz von Blomberg, German minister of defence and later of war, 1933–38; commander-in-chief of the German armed forces, 1935–38.

What were the differences between the 'opposition' and the 'party'? As far as we know, the army was displeased with attempts at its 'Nazification'; it took a critical view of the persecution of the Church, the four-year plan, the destruction of agriculture, the disregard for tradition, Italy and the notorious Axis, the alliance with Japan which threatens to sow conflict between Germany and the USSR and China, and the party's failure or unwillingness to reach an actual agreement with Britain. In general, the army was a restraining factor in German policy: it opposed the occupation of the Rhineland, and it was very unenthusiastic about the Spanish adventure. The army believed that Germany was not ready for a big war and, for this reason, should not take excessive risks.

What can we expect now, after this crackdown on the military? Increasing aggressiveness in German policy (not for nothing has Ribbentrop been appointed foreign minister), the strengthening of the Axis and the anti-communist bloc and, as a result, the accelerated formation of two fronts, although the latter process may not be a linear one. More purposeful attempts to seize Austria and, perhaps, Czechoslovakia are also very probable, as are a more contentious approach to the issue of colonies and more active support for Japan in the Far East and Italy in Spain.

The events of 4 February have made a profound impression in England. Even the *Daily Mail* is somewhat taken aback and predicts further complications. It has affected not just the political world; the City, too, is ruffled. Yesterday the Reichsmark fell on the London Stock Exchange. But the English, as is their custom in difficult moments, try to conceal their concern. They invent all manner of consolations. In particular, they pin too much hope on the dispute between Rome and Berlin because of Austria. I have no doubt that the British government's first response will be to expedite Anglo-German negotiations. Chamberlain and Co. will argue that the last chance must be taken to avoid a war. Oh, these eternal appeasers! Is there any end to their short-sightedness and cowardice?

It was not without reason that at a private meeting of City representatives a few days ago (before 4 February), Simon recommended that credits be granted to Germany, arguing that England had come to the point where it had to make a definite choice: either to go to war against Germany or to pay her off. Simon, of course, was in favour of a pay-off.

If Hitler manages not to behave like a bull in a china shop, and particularly if he says a few encouraging words in his speech on 20 February,[12] Chamberlain will be just dying to meet him halfway. The slow pace of the Anglo-German talks, which Vansittart recently spoke to me about, will then speed up and the outline of a four-power pact at the cost of Central, South-East and Eastern Europe will loom clearly on the horizon. It is also very likely that the British will try to give the Axis a tug at its Italian end – who knows what might come of it?

11 February[13]

Went to see Eden. The immediate reason for my visit was the 'consular conflict'.[14] On 11 January, Potemkin notified Chilston of the Soviet government's decision to ask Britain to close down its consulate in Leningrad for reasons of parity, retaining only the consular department at the embassy in Moscow. The proud Brits took offence. Chilston had a few sour conservations with M.M. and then submitted two notes. The British decided to resort to punitive measures. They closed down the consular department in Moscow and announced that parity was thereby observed, as they had only one consulate in the USSR, in Leningrad. They suggested that we should now receive all ordinary visas in Leningrad (they agreed to issue only diplomatic and business visas in Moscow). I was instructed to meet Eden in order to resolve the conflict in some way. He knew nothing about it and promised to ask me over next week after he had familiarized himself with the essence of the dispute...

But this is all by the by. For, quite to my surprise, today's meeting with the foreign secretary ended up dealing with much more serious matters.

I had hardly crossed the threshold when Eden began firing questions at me: what do I think about the German developments? What will be the effect of Goga's[i] resignation? Is Mussolini really going to withdraw from Spain? etc. Eden was in such an animated, even excited state that I had to ask him what he was so pleased about.

Eden confessed that he had not been so happy for quite a while and that there were three main reasons for this. First, Goga's cabinet had resigned. This was excellent, and Eden was very pleased that he would no longer have to deal with Micescu[ii] (the Rumanian foreign minister), whom he had disliked since meeting him in Geneva. 'He seems to have made an unfavourable impression on Mr Litvinov, too,' Eden added with a grin. He also said that in recent weeks he had been putting pressure on Carol [the Rumanian king], particularly in connection with the Jewish problem – this circumstance had evidently contributed to the fall of the Cabinet.

Second, Germany is bound to become weaker for a while due to the latest events. True, the party had won out over the 'moderate' elements, but the newly created 'balance' is by no means fixed and various unexpected things may happen. Eden then listed the various branches of government activity in Germany and, after indicating the changes in personnel since 4 February in the army, economy, Foreign Ministry and so on, concluded that smaller, less experienced men had replaced figures of greater weight. This cannot but affect the efficiency of the machinery of state. When Eden mentioned the Foreign

---

[i] Octavian Goga, Rumanian prime minister, 1937–38.
[ii] Istrate Micescu, Rumanian foreign minister, 1937–38.

Ministry, he made a startled comic gesture, as if he were fending off a ghost that had suddenly appeared before him, and exclaimed with a laugh: 'For reasons of diplomatic etiquette I must be silent, but you know what I think!' I laughed out loud. Ribbentrop's shade was hovering over us at that moment. I sharply refuted Eden's optimism and said that, on the contrary, I was now expecting an intensification of German aggression in various directions. Specifically, what would happen to Austria and Czechoslovakia? Eden tried to defend his case, but he was not particularly successful. Eventually, he said that Germany would probably behave more scandalously than ever, but that it would actually become less dangerous. I shook my head distrustfully. Eden expressed the hope that Czechoslovakia would not be endangered immediately, but he could not conceal his concern for Austria. It is in that direction, in his view, that Germany would be most likely to strike.

Third, the time has almost come when Italy will have to 'put the brakes on'. Mussolini, in Eden's opinion, has a highly stretched front – Abyssinia, Spain and Austria – as well as major financial and economic difficulties in Italy itself. He will have to narrow the front one day soon, but where exactly? Everywhere! Eden thinks this will happen in Spain. In any case, we must do our best for this to happen in Spain.

Eden does what he can. Last week, after announcing Italy's consent to step up the struggle against piracy in the Mediterranean, Grandi added that Italy would be prepared to engage in the settling of all issues disputed by the two countries.[15] Grandi insisted, however, that the Spanish question should be excluded from the forthcoming talks. Eden replied by saying that Spain was the main obstacle and that a constructive discussion of all other issues was precluded without a satisfactory solution to this problem. He also added, quite deliberately, that the Cabinet shared his view. A few days later, Grandi informed Eden that the Italians were ready to discuss the Spanish question as well. Moreover, the Italian government was inclined ('as it had always been inclined') to seek ways of speeding up the evacuation of 'volunteers'. Yesterday, Eden handed over Plymouth's latest formula to Grandi to define 'substantial evacuation' and is now waiting for an answer from Rome. Grandi's response was rather curious: 'Just a few days ago I would have turned down this formula without further deliberation, but today I am ready to send it to my government for consideration.' Eden believes that Mussolini's answer regarding the formula will also represent a reply to the question: is Mussolini just blackmailing or does he really intend to withdraw from Spain? Eden thinks he is going to withdraw.

I criticized Eden once again for his complacency. I would like him to be right, but I do not see sufficient grounds for that to be the case. Mussolini's front is indeed overstretched, but I rather think that he will shorten it at the cost of Austria, not Spain. If one takes a sober view, the game is up for Mussolini in Austria: if not now, then in six months, a year or two years, Hitler will seize it and Mussolini will be in no position to avert it. Mussolini has probably reconciled himself mentally to the loss of Austria and just wants to 'sell' it to his partner at a high price. For what price? Most likely, Spain. That is why I fear that in the near future we shall witness another desperate attempt by Italy to win the war for Franco, with Germany rendering aid more energetically than before. And that is why I think that Mussolini is just double-dealing with Britain about the pull-out of volunteers and that he has no intention of honouring his promises. It would be no surprise if the British government were made a fool of once more, as has happened on more than one occasion in the past. Eden listened to me very attentively, and my words evidently made some impression on him because he replied in precisely the following manner: 'Italy's words and promises are not enough for me. I am ready to enter into general negotiations with Rome only once the issue of the withdrawal of volunteers has been favourably settled. And Italy will receive not one single concession until all the volunteers actually leave Spanish territory. But if this will be accomplished, won't it be worth paying something for Spain?'

Eden added, with a particular tone: 'I hope there will be no objections to this line on the part of Mr Litvinov.'

Eden is definitely competing with M.M.! Or, more precisely, at every political turn he wants to remain in contact with the USSR. This is very reassuring. It is this new quality which I have been observing in him recently and which was expressed so vividly during our meeting just before the New Year.

But relations between Eden and Chamberlain are not improving at all. I've learned from various sources that Eden regards settling the Spanish question as a basic prerequisite for an agreement with Italy, while Chamberlain is prepared to give up Spain as a last resort. So far, Eden has evidently succeeded in convincing the Cabinet to back his point of view, but there is no guarantee that tomorrow Chamberlain might not get his revenge.

[Two threads intertwine when it comes to 'appeasement': retrospective attempts by the main actors to portray themselves as having been conscious of the German danger, and the common dismissal of the alarmists by contemporaries as oddities or warmongers. It should be noted, though (as the diary entry above attests), that just a week before his resignation Eden appeared to be rather complacent, convinced that the German danger to England had receded.[16] It was Chamberlain's decision to pursue negotiations with Mussolini behind Eden's back which led to the latter's resignation on 20 February.[17] Chamberlain confided to his sister that he had gradually reached the conclusion that 'at bottom Anthony did not want to talk either with Hitler or Mussolini, and as I did he was right to go'.[18] Seen from Chamberlain's perspective, both Halifax and Cadogan were pliant, whereas Vansittart had been openly hostile and Eden difficult to manage, particularly when it came to Mussolini. Halifax was an ideal choice for the post of foreign secretary. He found Eden's 'preconceived prejudices' against the dictators 'too strong … in as much as you have got to live with the devils whether you like them or not'. Presumably that should have rendered him more amenable to Stalin than Chamberlain was, but class bias, historical legacy (reinforced by his experience as viceroy in India) and his High Church leanings coloured his views of the Soviet Union. Moreover, he doubted his own competence for the position of foreign secretary, and finally accepted it reluctantly and only after receiving assurances that he could continue to spend the weekends hunting on his estate and would be exposed to a reduced load of material, which could be consulted 'on train or at home'. His laidback demeanour enabled Chamberlain to bypass the Foreign Office and to call on his own advisers, particularly Horace Wilson.

Maisky, who penned a portrait of Halifax following his appointment, described him as 'a typical representative of the old generation of Conservatives'. While praising his intellectual and administrative abilities (he had been a prize fellow at All Souls College, Oxford), Maisky dismissed his outlook on foreign policy, which was geared towards achieving a 'balance of power and Western security … an indifference to Anglo-French cooperation and a proclivity towards a rapprochement with Germany and Italy. His attitude to the Soviet Union is hostile but so far he has made no anti-Soviet appearance.'[19] Maisky was, however, particularly concerned lest the appointment of Lord Halifax meant that foreign policy in the Commons would be personally handled by Chamberlain (who was dismissed by Churchill as 'that provincial undertaker taking an interest in foreign affairs').[20] Once in office, Halifax, who was 'particularly averse to conversations with Russians and Japanese', tended to delegate such meetings to Butler,[i] his parliamentary undersecretary of state.[21]]

25 February

After the disturbances and worries of the past few days, life is returning to its normal course. Chamberlain got his way after all, and Halifax was appointed foreign secretary, but it is the PM who will be speaking in the Commons on all the more important foreign-policy issues. A certain Butler, former parliamentary assistant minister of labour, has replaced Cranborne. He is a newcomer to foreign policy, but an obedient type. It transpires that up to a hundred coalition government members sympathize with Eden, but only Vyvyan Adams voted against the government, and 22, including the duchess of Atholl, abstained. The rest did not dare to cross Chamberlain: such is the power of the 'party machine'.

The latest reshuffle has greatly displeased the Foreign Office. The following incident is being reported: the PM ordered the FO to gather material for a White Paper, with the intention that the White Paper would refute Eden's assertion

---

[i] Richard Austen Butler (Baron Butler of Saffron Walden), Conservative MP, 1929–65; undersecretary of state, India Office, 1932–37; undersecretary of state for foreign affairs, 1938–41; minister of education, 1941–45.

that the talks with Italy had opened under Mussolini's threat of 'now or never'. FO civil servants refused to make such a biased and fallacious selection of material. Chamberlain eventually had to announce to the Commons that there would be no White Paper.

A large-scale campaign has been launched in the country against the government and in defence of the League of Nations. The campaign proceeds along two channels: (1) The Labour Party, which is arranging 3,000 meetings to demand new elections in view of the government's breach of its 1935 election promises about the League of Nations etc.; (2) The League of Nations Society, the International Peace Campaign, and Lloyd George's Council for Action. Eden's attitude will be critical now. Both the government and the opposition, including Churchill, are trying to talk Eden round. It seems to me, from what I know of Eden, that he is hardly likely to rebel against his party, at least for the moment.

1 March

Today Halifax received all the ambassadors, one after the other. Monck met them in the lobby and supervised the visits, notifying each ambassador that he would have 10 to 15 minutes with Halifax.

'Well, that'll be enough,' I remarked jokingly, 'to put some questions to the foreign secretary that will spoil his mood.'

'Alas! Alas!' Monck answered with a touch of melancholy. 'In the old days, it was not the done thing to touch upon serious matters during one's first visit to a newly appointed foreign secretary. The aim of the first visit was merely to establish contact between the minister and the ambassador. Nowadays, it's all mixed up. No one pays any attention to time-honoured traditions, and ambassadors will talk about whatever they fancy during their first visit, even complicated financial matters.'

I could only offer my sympathy to Monck, without expecting it to be taken at face value.

Conscious of having so little time at my disposal, I asked Halifax just two questions.

(1) What is Britain's stance toward Central Europe? The answer was barely intelligible: Britain considers itself an interested party in this region, but cannot take on any commitments in advance. Everything will depend on the circumstances. This attitude seems almost deliberately designed to excite Hitler's appetite and provoke him into aggression.[22]

(2) What is Britain's stance toward Spain? More specifically, is an agreement between London and Rome, which would ignore the 'resolution' of the Spanish question in terms of the evacuation of foreign troops from Spain, conceivable?

The answer was again vague and evasive. Halifax first declared that the British government regarded the 'resolution' of the Spanish problem as part of a general agreement with Italy. But when I pressed him with more insistent questions, he gave in and admitted that much would depend on whether or not it was Mussolini who was to blame for the fact that the 'volunteers' could not be withdrawn speedily from Spain.

My questions certainly spoiled Halifax's mood, but at least I now know *where we are*. The new leaders of British foreign policy will not move a finger in regard to either Central Europe or Spain. I even have the feeling that Chamberlain has already decided in his soul to 'sell' Spain to Mussolini for whatever price he deems fair.

Halifax's manners are those of a well-bred English lord. He is polite, almost friendly. Talks little and uses platitudes. Likes to appeal to exalted feelings and noble principles, in which he half believes and, playing the hypocrite, half pretends to believe. He is always mindful of his own interests. Let's see how we get on.

On leaving Halifax, I ran into the doyen, the Brazilian ambassador, Oliveira.

'Tell me,' I asked the doyen, 'how many foreign secretaries have you dealt with during your stay in Britain?'

Oliveira thought for an instant before replying: 'This is my ninth foreign secretary: Lord Curzon,[i] MacDonald, Austen Chamberlain, Henderson, Lord Reading,[ii] Simon, Hoare, Eden, Halifax. And you?'

'It's my fourth: Simon, Hoare, Eden, Halifax. Don't you think it's a bit too many for my five and a half years in London?'

'Indeed,' Oliveira agreed. 'They change their foreign secretaries rather too often here.'

When I returned to the lobby, Monck was saying to the Belgian ambassador: 'Just imagine, the new American ambassador, Kennedy,[iii] is arriving in London tomorrow morning at four o'clock! His steamer reached Southampton behind schedule. Of course, I won't be meeting him. Not at such an ungodly hour!'

And Monck added with a little laugh: 'While discharging my official duties, I wear either tails – until midnight, that is – or a morning coat from 8 a.m. From midnight till eight in the morning I'm in pyjamas, which means I'm off duty.'

---

[i] George Nathaniel Curzon (1st Marquess Curzon of Kedleston), prize fellow, All Souls College, Oxford, 1883; viceroy and governor-general of India, 1899–1905; lord privy seal, 1915–16; foreign secretary, 1919–24.
[ii] Rufus Daniel Isaacs (1st marquess of Reading), secretary of state for foreign affairs in first National Government, 1931.
[iii] Joseph Patrick Kennedy, American financier and major contributor to Roosevelt's presidential campaign; US ambassador to London, 1937–40.

8 March[23]

(1) <u>Neville Chamberlain</u>. In order to better understand the origin and significance of the ministerial crisis that ended in Eden's resignation, we must have a clearer understanding of the personality of the current prime minister – Neville Chamberlain. As you probably know, he is certainly not a man of great stature. He is narrow-minded, dry, limited, lacking not only external brilliance but also any kind of political range. Here, he is often called the 'accountant of politics': he views the whole world primarily through the prism of dividends and exchange quotations. It is for this reason that Chamberlain is a darling of the City, which places implicit trust in him. At the same time, Chamberlain is very obstinate and insistent, and once an idea has lodged in his mind he will defend it until he is blue in the face – a rather dangerous quality for the prime minister of a great power nowadays, but such is his nature. A particularly important trait of Chamberlain's character is his highly developed 'class consciousness', which, of course, is the 'class consciousness' of a great-power British bourgeois. Lloyd George recently told me (and this is corroborated by information from other sources) that Baldwin, the current PM's predecessor, was a quite different man in this regard.

Naturally, Baldwin also embodied the ideas and aspirations of his country's ruling classes, but he was a lazy and rather inert 'philosopher', plagued by scepticism and doubts. There was something of the ancient Petronius in Baldwin. According to Lloyd George, he was not at all convinced that capitalism was the best of all possible systems in the world. Baldwin tended more towards the opinion that the capitalist system had entered its period of decline and that another system, most probably socialist, would take its place. It is not accidental that Baldwin's favourite son, Oliver, is in the Labour Party. Accepting that capitalism's disintegration and the creation of a new social system on its ruins might be inevitable, Baldwin prayed to God for just one thing: 'Let it happen after me! I want to die under capitalism. I'm accustomed to it and I haven't fared so badly under its conditions. The new generation can do what it wants.' Chamberlain is different. He believes in capitalism devoutly. He is firmly convinced that capitalism is not just the best, but also the only possible socio-economic system, which was, is, and will be. Capitalism for Chamberlain is as eternal and unchanging as the principle of universal gravitation. This makes him a vivid and self-confident representative of bourgeois class consciousness, which in our days, as we know, can come decked only in deeply reactionary colours.

Indeed, Chamberlain is a consummate reactionary, with a sharply defined anti-Soviet position. I remember my first conversation with him about five years ago when I had just been appointed ambassador to Britain. The signing of a new trade agreement was on the agenda of Anglo-Soviet relations. Chamberlain complained to me about the insufficient number of our purchases in Great Britain, contrasting their relatively modest quantity with the major German exports to the USSR. I replied by referring to the better credit terms granted by Germany at that time. Chamberlain gave a sudden start and, with an icy expression, remarked: 'Credit? Why on earth should we lend out our money to our blatant enemies?' This may not have been very diplomatic, but it was entirely sincere, and I sensed that it came from the bottom of his heart. I retorted in the proper manner, but that is not the point. The point is that Chamberlain's remark vividly illuminates the very essence of his mental profile. He both acknowledges theoretically and feels with his every fibre that the USSR is the principal enemy and that communism is the main danger to the capitalist system that is so dear to his heart. (Such was Chamberlain five years ago and such he is today; for, in the opinion of all who know him well, Chamberlain never changes.) Such is the prime minister we have to deal with now in England.

(2) Two paths. When Chamberlain became head of government in the spring of 1937 and came face to face with the complex problems of British foreign policy, which now essentially boil down to the question of how to defend the Empire and maintain British positions in the world, two possible paths were open to him. The first was the path of effective resistance to the aggressors (Germany, Italy and Japan) via the League of Nations and collective security, which in practice required the creation of a London–Paris–Moscow axis. That was the only reliable and efficacious path, but it demanded close cooperation with the 'Bolsheviks'. Eden accepted that path and, judging by my last talks with him, he seemed to believe that the Western democracies, in their retreat before the fascist aggressors, had reached a certain critical line where they had to stop and say firmly: 'Thus far and no further!' Eden wanted to entrench himself on that line and gather strength, i.e. revive the League of Nations and cement cooperation between Britain, France and the Soviet Union, before going on the offensive against the aggressors. For Chamberlain, with his acute 'class consciousness' of a British bourgeois, this path was inconceivable. He just could not stomach the prospect of close cooperation with Moscow. But if he was to reject this first path, the PM had no choice in the current situation, which is so very difficult for Great Britain, but to take the second path – the path of a direct deal with the aggressor, which in fact meant something very close to capitulation before the aggressor. This is the path Chamberlain has taken. Of course, he now tries to sweeten the pill for himself and his party with various reassuring arguments. He thinks (as I have heard from reliable sources) that Italy and Germany are in considerable difficulty and so he will manage to get off quite lightly. Furthermore, he tends to exaggerate the significance of Austria's role, as a bone of contention between Hitler and Mussolini which

can easily be exploited in order to all but destroy the Rome–Berlin axis. All these political notions are highly dubious – not so much, perhaps, because Chamberlain obviously exaggerates the present difficulties of Germany and Italy, as because the British PM, through his cowardly tactics, is massively strengthening his opponents' positions and inflaming their appetite out of all proportion. There is good reason to assume that by virtue of his diplomatic inexperience Chamberlain grossly underestimates the difficulties he will meet on the way to an agreement with the aggressors. There is also good reason to assume that major disappointments await the PM on the road he has taken. It is quite possible that, one sad day, Chamberlain will find himself left with nothing; and if this happens, very different forces may rise to power, which will be obliged, by the logic of things, to engage the aggressor in open conflict. But for the moment all this is just idle speculation. Today it is Chamberlain who stands at the helm of the ship of state, and the next few months promise a phase of 'new experimentation' in British foreign policy. Besides, we must realize that the PM will stop at nothing to achieve a 'success', or at any rate to reach an agreement with Italy and Germany such as could be presented to the voting public as a success. For, as I have informed you more than once by telegram, Chamberlain has staked both his reputation and the fate of his Cabinet on one card: cutting a deal with the aggressor. If this card fails him, he will be done for and the Conservative Party will find itself convulsing in the most severe internal turmoil.

(3) The gathering crisis. I'll try to outline a few specific patterns against this general political background. From the very first days of his premiership, Chamberlain took the following course in regard to Eden: either to 'tame' the foreign secretary and make him an obedient tool of his policy or (if this failed) to get rid of him as quietly as possible. Naturally, Chamberlain preferred the first option, since Eden was undoubtedly the most popular member of the government and there were even many in the opposition who were well disposed to him. The loss of Eden would significantly diminish the Cabinet's prestige under any conditions. The foreign secretary, however, turned out to be a much tougher nut than the PM had expected. Attempts to control Eden ended in failure. Relations between the PM and the foreign secretary worsened to a sometimes critical extent, as in the case of Halifax's visit to Germany. As is known, the issue of Eden's dismissal was already in the air at that point, but conflict was averted for a while. The Cliveden Set (the Astors, Halifax, Samuel Hoare, The Times editors, Garvin, etc.), who had arranged Halifax's visit, continued their stubborn attack on Eden, despite their own temporary setback. In the PM's own office, something like a parallel FO was formed, headed by Chamberlain's first secretary Sir Horace Wilson, who acted independently from, and even against the wishes of, the real Foreign Office. Chamberlain acquired his own 'unofficial' and unaccountable agents in various countries,

who supplied him with information contradicting that of the ambassadors and envoys; but the PM trusted this intelligence more than he did Foreign Office reports. This state of affairs, naturally enough, could only widen the gulf between the PM and the foreign secretary. Time and again Chamberlain and Eden were at variance on issues pertaining to the League of Nations, the Far East, Spain and other matters. Let me note here that, as I recently learned from absolutely reliable sources, Eden sympathized on a personal level with the Spanish government, but was forced to pursue a somewhat different policy under Cabinet pressure. The relationship between PM and foreign secretary thus grew more strained with every passing month, and their disagreement over the Italian negotiations was merely the straw that broke the camel's back.

(4) The crisis. The specific details of the crisis take approximately the following form. Since last summer, Chamberlain has had a great desire to normalize relations with Italy in one way or another in order to create a more peaceful situation in the Mediterranean. He constantly strove to further his ploy, which began with an exchange of letters with Mussolini in July, but Eden held him back, using information supplied by the Italians themselves: piratical submarine adventures in the Mediterranean, Mussolini's insolent bragging about the role of Italian troops in the capture of Santander, Italy's ostentatious walk-out from the League of Nations. Eden's reckoning was very simple: as he clearly intimated to me during our recent talks, he was playing a wait-and-see game, being fully aware that Mussolini's position in Abyssinia, Spain, Austria and inside his own country was becoming ever more difficult with each passing month. Eden expected that in, say, six months Mussolini would be much more pliable, and so he was in no hurry to begin official negotiations. When, in early February, Grandi himself began to force the issue of serious talks, Eden simply sabotaged their progress.

In particular, Eden made a favourable resolution of the Spanish question a prerequisite for opening formal negotiations. In our talk on 11 February, he clarified this point as follows: negotiations with the Italians would not open until the evacuation of 'volunteers' began, and the concessions that Britain would be prepared to grant to Italy after the talks would not be effected until the last 'volunteer' left Spain. Such was the foreign secretary's policy. Chamberlain did not like any of it. He, on the contrary, was eager to open negotiations with Mussolini as soon as possible.

One further consideration, in addition to those mentioned above, played a very significant role in causing Chamberlain's impatience, namely: if Mussolini was not helped out in time, he might be done for, and what then? Who would take his place? The 'Reds'?... The mere thought of a left Republican government, let alone a communist one, appearing in Italy on the ruins of the fascist dictatorship sent shivers down the spine of the 'class-conscious' PM. He was therefore indignant with the foreign secretary for his Fabian tactics and grew ever more convinced that a break with Eden was inevitable. A circumstantial factor played its part here.

The widow of the late Austen Chamberlain[i] went on holiday to Rome a while ago. Mussolini decided to 'conquer' her, and did so. He showered kindnesses and attention on the honourable Lady Chamberlain and managed to convince her that he was ready to sell Great Britain his 'friendship' for a very modest price. At the same time, however, Mussolini told Lady Chamberlain outright that he could not conceive of an agreement with Britain while Eden remained foreign secretary. Lady Chamberlain assailed her brother-in-law with letters demanding quick and resolute action. Her message to Chamberlain from Mussolini was that the question of reconciliation between Britain and Italy was at the point of 'now or never'. There is every reason to believe that Lady Chamberlain's influence played no small part in preparing the crisis.

It is also worth noting here another curious fact indicative of the role played by 'unofficial' persons and influences in the methods of Chamberlain's foreign policy. As I have already mentioned, Grandi had been holding rather fruitless talks with Eden on Anglo-Italian issues since the beginning of February. On 17 February, in the afternoon, Sir Horace Wilson received a phone call from... Augur (alias Polyakov), an agent on Mussolini's payroll for the past two or three years. Augur told Wilson in a raised voice that the Italians were highly dissatisfied with the slow pace of the talks and that Mussolini had sent a telegram to Grandi asking him to put the dilemma, 'now or never', before the British government in the starkest of terms. Wilson panicked and immediately reported this to Chamberlain, who also panicked and on the following morning, 18 February, asked Grandi to see him without consulting Eden. Although Eden was also summoned to attend the meeting, it was Chamberlain who conducted the entire conversation: Eden merely observed, intervening with the odd remark. Chamberlain first asked Grandi whether Italy was prepared, in compliance with the Stresa agreement, to take part in consultation on the fate of Austria (the agreement, as it is known, envisaged the possibility of consultation on this issue between Britain, France and Italy). Grandi replied that he had to confer with his government. Then Chamberlain began an exchange of opinions with Grandi on other points disputed by Britain and Italy. No binding statements were made, but the two sides sounded one another out extensively. With that, the morning meeting concluded.

After lunch, Grandi visited Chamberlain again and told him, on Mussolini's behalf, that Italy would not take part in consultation on the Austrian issue. Despite this affront and Italy's violation of yet another international agreement,

---

[i] Lady Ivy Chamberlain, wife of Austen Chamberlain.

Chamberlain did not even frown, but made a renewed and more resolute statement to Grandi that serious talks in Rome were highly desirable. After Grandi's departure, Eden pointed out to the PM the danger of such an approach vis-à-vis the Italians and added that if Chamberlain was intent on sticking to his guns, he, Eden, would have to resign. This was beginning to look like a crisis.

So Chamberlain, sidestepping hallowed British tradition, convened a special Cabinet meeting after lunch the following day (19 February), a Saturday, where he raised the question of the immediate commencement of negotiations between Britain and Italy. A great battle followed, in which, as was to be expected, most of the ministers, headed by Chamberlain, Hoare and Simon, spoke against Eden. A minority, consisting mainly of the so-called young Conservatives (Elliot, Morrison,[i] Ormsby-Gore, Stanley and others), as well as a few National Labourites and National Liberals, supported the foreign secretary. At the end of the meeting, Eden left for the Foreign Office, across the road from the PM's residence, and returned a quarter of an hour later with his letter of resignation. Eden then went home, but there was great agitation among the members of the government. Fearing the repercussions of Eden's resignation, Chamberlain implored several of Eden's closest friends in the Cabinet to persuade him to revoke his resignation. I know that, throughout the evening of 19 February and the morning of 20 February, Elliot, Morrison and young MacDonald went to great lengths to try to keep Eden in the Cabinet, but Eden would not budge.

On Sunday, 20 February, another special Cabinet meeting was set for 3 p.m., at which Chamberlain himself, supported by a large number of his colleagues, tried to get Eden to reverse his decision. This attempt also ended in failure. Eden was adamant. That evening, the press was informed about the foreign secretary's resignation. Cranborne resigned together with Eden. In the heat of the moment, several 'young' ministers (Morrison, Elliot, Ormsby-Gore, Bernays[ii] and others) were also about to follow Eden, but Chamberlain held another hastily convened Cabinet meeting late on Sunday night and persuaded the 'rebels' to abandon their plan. In truth, this was not all that difficult for him. The so-called 'young' ministers were all too keen to hold on to their portfolios, and none wished to jeopardize their positions.

On the following two days, 21 and 22 February, debates were held in parliament in connection with Eden's resignation. In accordance with British customs, Eden and Cranborne were to explain their moves. They both spoke in a fairly tough manner and emphasized the serious fundamental disagreements

---

[i] William Morrison (1st Viscount Dunrossil), minister of agriculture, fisheries and food, 1936–39; minister of food, 1939–40; postmaster-general, 1940–42.
[ii] Robert Hamilton Bernays, parliamentary secretary to the Ministry of Health, 1937–39, and to the Ministry of Transport, 1939–40.

between the Foreign Office and the premier. Cranborne even described Chamberlain's policy as 'capitulation to blackmail'. Both received resounding ovations, not just from the opposition, but also from a significant section of the Conservative Party. Chamberlain gave his own account, while striving all the time to show that there had been no fundamental discord between him and the Foreign Office, and that Eden had resigned on a 'secondary matter' of a procedural nature, namely, the question of when to open talks with Italy: now or a little later? Chamberlain also received an ovation from his supporters, but it was weaker than that accorded to the disgraced foreign secretary.

On the second day of the debates, a vote of no confidence in the government was discussed, having been proposed by Labour. The opposition accused the Cabinet of betraying the League of Nations platform, on the basis of which the National Coalition won the last election of 1935. This predetermined the outcome of the ballot, since a vote of this sort was a clear case of party politics and forced government supporters, even those who disagreed with Chamberlain's policy, to vote against for reasons of party discipline. That is what ultimately happened. The no-confidence vote was rejected by a majority of 330 to 168, with 22 official abstentions. Only one Conservative, Vyvyan Adams, voted with the opposition, although 60 to 70 government supporters abstained 'informally', that is, they either did not attend the meeting or left it before the voting began. The total number of abstentions thus amounts to 80–90 (out of the 431 members on the government benches). This figure shows the approximate number of Eden's supporters in the National Coalition. The opposition stars spoke on the second day of the debates: Churchill on behalf of the Conservatives, and Lloyd George and Herbert Morrison on behalf of the Liberals and Labour. Their speeches were very unpleasant for the government, especially Churchill's.

In defending himself, Chamberlain committed two major tactical errors. First, he openly announced that he no longer believed either in the League of Nations or in collective security, and thought it imperative to neutralize the League by removing Article 16. This elicited vigorous protests from the opposition and furnished the pro-League elements – whose number, in spite of everything, is still large in the country – with a powerful weapon for propaganda against the government. Second, Chamberlain revealed all too clearly that he associated his reputation and the fate of his Cabinet with the outcome of the Anglo-Italian talks. This will greatly weaken his position in negotiations with Mussolini and will again play into the hands of his adversaries in Britain itself. Be that as it may, however, the Cabinet withstood the storm and has now emerged from it, albeit with torn sails and serious leaking below the waterline. I am fully justified in using these colourful nautical phrases, because, in the informed opinion of the most experienced parliamentarians (Attlee, Lloyd

George, Nicolson, Margesson,[i] the chief whip of the Conservative Party, and others), this recent crisis has seriously damaged the government's prestige. If an election were to be held now, say these same political experts, Chamberlain would lose at least 100 to 150 seats and, at best, would return to parliament with a negligible Conservative majority. But since the government has no plans to call an election now, Chamberlain has the opportunity to retain his post on the captain's bridge and to chart a course for the ship of state with greater freedom than before.

(5) What prospects are now in store? The events described above certainly represent an achievement for the *Cliveden Set*. Eden's replacement as foreign secretary by Halifax has made this particularly clear. The opposition and some members of government launched a major campaign against Halifax's candidature, but Chamberlain eventually got his way, albeit by assuming personal responsibility in the Commons for all major foreign-policy issues. Undersecretary Butler, who has been appointed to replace Cranborne, is a newcomer to foreign affairs, but is a man who will diligently obey his superiors. The Chamberlain–Halifax–Butler combination leaves not the slightest doubt that from now on Chamberlain will be the real foreign secretary. What is Chamberlain's programme? Everything that is known to me of the PM's foreign-policy ambitions and everything that surfaced so clearly in the course of this recent crisis allows one to formulate Chamberlain's programme according to the following four points:

(1) Renunciation of the League of Nations and the principle of collective security (couched in an indirect form, of course), and a more or less patent return to traditionally English 'balance-of-power politics'.

(2) The opening of Anglo-Italian negotiations is the first step towards a four-power pact. It is quite possible that talks with Germany will be carried on in parallel, but it is more likely that serious negotiations between London and Berlin will open when (if ever) talks between London and Rome are successfully completed.

(3) Isolation of the USSR as the first stage on the path towards various more ambitious plans (an attack by the fascist aggressors against the USSR, etc.) which Chamberlain may not yet be thinking about as practical political objectives.

(4) Vigorous build-up of Great Britain's armaments.

Such is the general outline of Chamberlain's foreign-policy programme. Were he to succeed in implementing the second point, i.e. in securing a four-power

---

[i] David Reginald Margesson (1st Viscount Margesson), chief whip of the Conservative Party, 1931–40; secretary of state for war, 1940–42.

pact, he would undoubtedly go to the polls to consolidate the Conservative majority for another five years. One should not discount the possibility of the PM risking election even if the Anglo-Italian agreement alone were to be signed, providing that the latter proved remotely advantageous to Great Britain. The present parliament has entered the third year of its term; a general election is traditionally held in the fourth year, but no one can know what 1939 will bring. New foreign-policy problems and an economic depression, or even a crisis, are highly probable. In such a situation, how could one fail to take electoral advantage of so favourable a development as the 'appeasement' of Europe, resting on an agreement with Germany and Italy?

But will Chamberlain succeed? There are arguments on both sides. Undoubtedly, the intensification of the class struggle at a global level paves the way for the realization of a four-power pact. The personal ambitions of Hitler, Mussolini and Chamberlain also point in this direction, abetted by France's feeble and wavering political line. On the other hand, there are many obstacles on the path to a four-power pact. There are serious economic and political conflicts between Britain and France on the one side, and Germany and Italy on the other, which are not easy to bridge. Naturally, the typical tactlessness of German diplomacy only makes these difficulties harder to overcome. What will the final outcome be? Nobody could give a definite answer at the moment.

One thing is certain, however: France's position will play a critical role, however the issue is resolved. Labour and Liberal opposition inside Britain, which is now launching a major movement in defence of the League of Nations and against the government, can also play its part. The events of the next six to eight months will prove critical, and future historians may one day mark 1938 as a decisive year in the development of foreign politics in our era. Meanwhile, we should prepare ourselves for a spell of deterioration in Anglo-Soviet relations, the duration of which will depend directly on the fate of the four-power pact.

[The resignation of Eden, whom Maisky had been meticulously cultivating, was yet another blow to collective security. This was further undermined by the muzzled reaction in Britain to Hitler's annexation of Austria on 12 March – a precursor to the Czechoslovak debacle six months later.[24] 'Extremely pessimistic', Maisky expected Chamberlain to 'throw overboard' the League of Nations and try to resuscitate the four-power pact, 'excluding the Soviet Union'. He had no high hopes of Chamberlain, who, he assumed, was guided exclusively by his ideological bent, vividly remembering his comment during the 1932 negotiations for a British loan: 'Why on earth should we lend out our money to our blatant enemies?' Consequently, Maisky feared that the crisis might reinforce the drift towards isolation which had 'already been discerned in Moscow for quite some time'. Had it been possible to bring about a closer and more effective alliance between the USSR, France and Britain, he told the French ambassador in London, 'his government would certainly have engaged in a more active policy of European collaboration. The successive disappointments inflicted on her led to the gradual turnabout.'[25] Chamberlain, Maisky told Lloyd George, 'was playing with one card, on which he had put all his money'.[26] His observations were spot on, as Chamberlain indeed confided to his sister on 18 March that he had 'abandoned any idea of giving guarantees to Czecho-Slovakia or to France in connection with her obligations to that country'.[27]

Although Litvinov had succeeded in convincing Stalin that Russia could not remain 'completely passive', he did not really anticipate a favourable response to his 'final appeal to Europe for a collective action'. This move was aimed as much at exonerating Russia of possible accusations of isolationism as it was at scotching the widespread rumours that the purges had rendered her militarily weak. However, with Cadogan now secure at the helm of the Foreign Office, Vansittart's faint support for Maisky could do little to persuade the Foreign Office to respond to Litvinov's appeal. It had become apparent to Maisky that Vansittart (who now consistently referred to the government and the Foreign Office as 'they') had been pushed aside. His successor Cadogan, who was well attuned to the prime minister, warned about the possible repercussions the Soviet overtures might have in parliament: 'The opposition will say "Here is collective security: march under the brave Litvinoff's banner". The Russian object is to precipitate confusion and war in Europe: they will not participate usefully themselves: they will hope for the world revolution as a result (and a very likely one, too).'[28] But Maisky had also to protect himself against the storm brewing in Moscow, where the third public trial of former Trotskyists, accused of plotting with the Germans and Japanese to topple the Soviet regime, had just commenced. Among the accused were the 70-year-old Christian Rakovsky, the first Soviet ambassador to Britain, and Arkadii Rosengolts, who was Maisky's superior in London in 1926. Both were eventually shot.]

11 March

Last night, Agniya and I attended a grand dinner at the Spanish embassy. The guest-list was surprisingly exalted. Among those present were Cadogan and Plymouth with their wives, Sir Sidney Clive (marshal of the diplomatic corps) and his wife, Lord Robert Cecil and his wife, who usually stayed away from such functions, and a host of other diplomats and politicians. Taking into account the current situation in Spain, this was not at all bad. I even congratulated Mrs Azcárate,[i] who sat next to me at the table, on the success of her dinner.

After dinner, a Labour MP whom I knew came up to me and asked anxiously: 'How long do you think all this will last?'

He nodded at the smart crowd in the embassy's smart drawing room, with Azcárate's bald head visible at the centre.

I evinced as much optimism as I could. Referring to the history of our Civil War, I began arguing that nothing was lost yet. Yet, I do not feel quite calm at heart. I do not like one bit the offensive launched by Franco two or three days

---

[i] The wife of Pablo de Azcárate y Florez, Spanish ambassador in London, 1936–39.

ago on the Aragon front. The rebels have been victorious so far, but that is not the point. I am disconcerted by the virtual absence of resistance on the part of the Republicans. What does it mean?

22 March

Today I returned a visit to Kennedy, the new US ambassador to Great Britain. He is quite a character: tall, strong, with red hair, energetic gestures, a loud voice and booming, infectious laughter – a real embodiment of the type of healthy and vigorous *business man* that is so abundant in the USA, a man without psychological complications and lofty dreams.[29]

When Kennedy came to visit me, he stayed for a full hour and exclaimed on leaving: 'Just give me a chance to cope with all these visits and formalities and I'll come and see you. We can spend a couple of hours together discussing all the questions I'm interested in. I like you. You know your business. None of the diplomats here in London have talked to me in such plain, human language. I value that. I'm not really a diplomat. I like to have real conversations.'

Today I visited Kennedy in his new office on Grosvenor Square. It's a four-storey office-type building which houses not just the US embassy, but also all its affiliates: the air and naval attachés, commercial and agricultural counsellors, and others. The entire staff of the embassy, including service personnel, totals 170 employees. Not bad!

Kennedy was roaring with laughter again and, by the by, told me a very interesting thing.

'Tell me something,' he exclaimed. 'All the Brits keep assuring me that, according to the most reliable sources, a profound domestic crisis has taken over your country (which is why trips to the USSR have lately become so complicated for foreigners) and that your army is falling to pieces and is unfit for serious military operations. So, the Brits claim, you would not be able to help Czechoslovakia if it were attacked by Germany, even if you wished to. They are saying the same to the French and asking them: in these circumstances, is it worth you running risks by following to the letter your agreement with Czechoslovakia?'

I ridiculed the English insinuations and clarified the true state of affairs to Kennedy.[30] He thanked me and confessed that he knew virtually nothing about the USSR. He hoped that one day he would visit our country.

So that's what the English are like! Chamberlain wants to tear France away from its eastern allies and to that end he is exploiting our recent trials. That won't work.

23 March

Conversation with Churchill

(1) Randolph Churchill[i] rang me up and said that his father wanted very much to see me. We agreed to meet at Randolph Churchill's apartment for lunch. I found Winston Churchill greatly agitated. He took the bull by the horns and addressed me with the following speech:

Could you, please, tell me frankly what is going on in your country? Tomorrow, during the debates after Chamberlain's speech, I intend to speak and to touch upon various sensitive issues of foreign policy. You know my general standpoint. I deeply detest Nazi Germany. I believe it to be an enemy not only of peace and democracy but of the British Empire, too. I think that the only reliable means to restrain this beast could be a 'grand alliance' of all peace-loving states within the framework of the League of Nations. Russia should occupy one of the most prominent positions in this alliance. We badly need a strong Russia as a counterweight to Germany and Japan. I have been working, and continue to work, on bringing about an alliance, despite the fact that I often find myself in a minority in my party. But lately I hear from all quarters, particularly from Conservative friends, and from ministers and officials close to them, that Russia is currently experiencing a grave crisis. They say, referring to supposedly reliable sources, that a bitter domestic struggle is under way in Russia, that your army is on the verge of degeneration as a result of recent events and has lost its fighting capacity, and that Russia, broadly speaking, has ceased to exist as a serious factor in foreign politics. I am not going to repeat some of the more fantastic stories I have heard and I am not disposed to take all that I was told on trust. Yet still I say to myself: there is no smoke without fire. There must be something to it. But what exactly? Over the years that we have known each other I have become accustomed to trusting your words, so could you please make it clear to me what is actually going on in your country. It is important for me to know this for my general bearings, and it is important in view of tomorrow's debates in parliament.

Churchill's look, tone and gestures left no doubt of his sincerity. I had to take the floor and lecture my interlocutor at some length on elementary politics, providing him with the clarifications of recent events that he had

---

[i] Randolph Churchill, Conservative MP, 1940–45.

requested. Churchill listened to me most attentively, occasionally interrupting me with brief remarks and questions. When I had finished, Churchill seemed to brighten up a bit, gave a sigh of relief, and exclaimed: 'Well, thank God. You've reassured me a little.' Then he continued with a crafty grin: 'Of course, you are ambassador and your words have to be taken *cum grano salis*; yet much is becoming a great deal clearer to me and I'm beginning to grasp what is going on in your country.' Then, after a minute's pause, Churchill went on: 'I hate Trotsky! I've kept an eye on his activities for some time. He is Russia's evil genius, and it is a very good thing that Stalin has got even with him.' Another minute's pause and Churchill, as if answering his own thoughts, exclaimed: 'I am definitely in favour of Stalin's policy. Stalin is creating a strong Russia. We need a strong Russia and I wish Stalin every success.'[31]

Then Churchill, returning for a moment to the slanderous propaganda about the USSR, added: 'In order to put an immediate end to all these fairy tales about the USSR's weakness, which I assure you many people here and in Paris take in good faith and which damage the prestige of your country, it would be most helpful if Russia could show the rest of the world the falsehood of the rumours being spread about it through some major action. This would have enormous significance not only for you, but also for us, France, Czechoslovakia, and for the consolidation of peace.'

I asked Churchill what sort of action he had in mind, before adding in good humour: 'Surely you don't want the USSR to suddenly annex a foreign state, do you? We, the Soviet people, are a peaceful nation and we don't go around plundering foreign territories.' Churchill retorted in a fitting tone: 'Oh, no! I wouldn't sit down with a gangster. I mean something quite different. Why, for example, don't you make a declaration, couched in a particularly impressive form, that you will render substantial military assistance to Czechoslovakia in the event of an attack by Germany? That would really make an impression. All the more so as you are quite entitled to do this in accordance with the Czechoslovak–Soviet pact.' I told Churchill that I did not quite understand his idea. It is well known that the Soviet Union respects its commitments. In twenty years of foreign trading, there has been not a single instance of our failing to meet our obligations on time. Churchill nodded in agreement and said: 'Yes, it is well known that you pay punctually.' 'We pay our political debts just as punctually,' I went on, 'and this is also well known to all.' So what would be the point in making the declaration proposed by Churchill? But Churchill would not accept my reasoning. 'I know,' he said, 'that Stalin is a solid and reliable man; he will do what he says, and he is able to keep his promises. Yet it would still be useful if the USSR declared once again now for the whole world to hear: we will help Czechoslovakia in earnest! I assure you it would be of great importance for both the USSR's prestige and the cause of peace.'

(2) When we had finished discussing the USSR's domestic situation, I decided to pay Churchill back in his own coin, and asked him: what was happening now in England? In the course of my professional duties, I have been keeping close track of foreign and domestic policy in my country of residence throughout the last five years, and I have to say that with every year I have been growing increasingly pessimistic about everything connected with British foreign policy. These five years have been marked by England's continuous retreat in the face of aggressors – Germany, Italy and Japan – in all parts of the world. Manchuria, Abyssinia, the Rhineland, Spain, Eden's resignation, Austria – these are the major landmarks on the backward journey taken by Great Britain right before my eyes. And the retreat seems to be far from over, for Chamberlain is clearly pursuing a course towards a deal with Italy and Germany. Instead of collective security and fighting aggressors, he is trying to construct a four-power pact which would require major concessions to the aggressors on the part of England and France. And it is not known yet whether the four-power pact is the last concession Chamberlain is prepared to make. I cannot conceal it from Churchill that sometimes I find myself asking: is there anything in the world that people like Chamberlain might fight for? Will they take up the sword if only to protect the British Empire? I may be wrong, or perhaps I do not understand the English spirit well enough, but when I am following parliamentary debates from the top of the diplomats' gallery, it often seems to me that the leading Conservative circles have completely lost their courage, the courage displayed by their predecessors, without which the Empire cannot be held together. I am hardly about to make any utopian demands on these Tories. I am fully aware that they cannot be the crusaders of socialism; but I am quite astonished to find that they are such exceptionally poor imperialists, even though they swear allegiance to the Empire every step of the way. Strange as it may seem, the only opinions one hears in parliament about the paths that should be taken to secure the Empire come not from the government, but from the benches of the Labour–Liberal opposition. How is all this to be explained? Would it be fair to assume that the ruling classes of Great Britain are too far gone in their decadence to be able to protect the British Empire?

Whatever the explanation, there is no doubt that this phenomenon echoes loudly across the globe. The feebleness and indecision of the British government and its continuous yielding to the aggressor greatly diminish Great Britain's prestige and raise the stock of Germano-Italian fascism. What is more, all this is very damaging to the cause of peace and gives rise to isolationist sentiments in other countries, including the USSR. I do not mean that the Soviet government is embracing a policy of isolationism. It certainly is not. The Soviet government adheres, as before, to the principles of collective security and to the Covenant of the League of Nations. The best evidence of this are the statements made by Litvinov a few days ago in Moscow. (Churchill broke in at this point: 'I fully agree with Mr Litvinov's proposals.') Yet I have to say that more and more people in the USSR have begun asking themselves the question: are the 'Western' democracies capable of any kind of energetic response against the aggressors? Soviet public opinion has been particularly affected by the example of Spain.

Many people in our country say: 'If Britain and France did not find it possible to do their duty as members of the League of Nations with respect to Republican Spain, a country which is virtually on their doorstep and which is linked to them by great military strategic interests, what can the USSR expect of them at a time of danger? Wouldn't it be better in this case to give up all illusions about the likelihood of assistance on their part and rely solely on our own resources? The USSR is a big, rich and mighty country, and it can survive on its own if the worst comes to the worst.' Let me repeat: this is not the policy of the Soviet government, but the mood of a considerable and growing number of Soviet citizens.

(3) My critique of Great Britain's ruling classes was deliberately emphatic, being designed to arouse Churchill's patriotism and to galvanize him in the struggle against the tendencies represented by Chamberlain in British politics. I had anticipated protests and objections from my interlocutor, but I was mistaken. He responded quite differently. Churchill admitted that there was much truth in my critique of the Tories, and his face reflected his bitterness. Over the last five or six years, the leading group of the party had indeed displayed cowardice and short-sightedness on a scale with few, if any, precedents in history. Churchill was particularly spiteful and outspoken when he turned his anger on the *Cliveden Gang*: Nancy Astor and her American husband, Garvin (editor of the *Observer*), Dawson (editor of *The Times*), Hoare, Simon and others. Churchill snatched a fresh issue of the *Evening Standard* (23 March) from the table and triumphantly showed me a very malicious caricature by David Low, devoted precisely to this 'gang of quivering sisters'.[32] Churchill had to admit that in matters of foreign policy and of the Empire's rational protection, the voice of reason and courage was much more audible from the opposition's benches than from those of his own party. On these matters, Churchill is much closer to Attlee and Sinclair than he is to Chamberlain.

But all is not yet lost. There are healthy elements in the Conservative Party. They are often suppressed by the party machinery, but they are tenacious and will show their worth when the occasion arises. Last week, even Chamberlain told Churchill that he agreed in principle with his idea of a 'grand alliance' and admitted that the course of events might bring him to the point where the formation of such an 'alliance' became inevitable. But the PM thinks that the time has not yet come for this, and that political manoeuvring and other approaches need to be tried out first – who knows if they might not help. Should the situation become truly unbearable, they will have to turn toward the grand alliance. What's more, Chamberlain is one of the 'oldies'! Younger Tories are more sensitive. If the party were to suffer several defeats at by-elections, the effect would be considerable and the government line could be radically altered.

Replying to my question, Churchill noted that a week ago the Cabinet's situation had been rather difficult and a reshuffle had appeared possible, but Chamberlain's position was now somewhat stronger, as he had finally agreed to make an official statement in parliament concerning the course of his foreign policy (something he had previously avoided) and this statement might represent some kind of progress. (He, Churchill, will certainly criticize the government tomorrow, because he will certainly not be satisfied with what Chamberlain proposes. But some progress is nevertheless visible and further advances are possible.)

Via a series of cautious leading questions, I learned that Churchill had received some assurances from Chamberlain and that this seemed to be the main reason why Churchill had given up his trip to Paris, planned for last weekend. Then I asked Churchill whether he thought a restructuring of the government was possible in the immediate future. Churchill replied that it was not only possible, but highly probable. For, in the light of the rapid deterioration in international relations, it is becoming imperative to hasten the fulfilment of rearmament programmes and to introduce various forms of 'civil conscription' to strengthen the country's defence capacity. These measures cannot be carried out without the consent of the opposition, and of the trade unions in particular. When the government comes face to face with the necessity of carrying out these measures (negotiations with the trade unions concerning labour mobilization have already begun), it will be forced into a reorganization. At that point, one cannot even rule out the possibility of a coalition government being formed, with the participation of the opposition. Should the opposition not be included in the Cabinet for whatever reason, the present composition of the Cabinet would still have to be radically restructured.

I asked who could become prime minister in a reorganized Cabinet. Chamberlain? Churchill shrugged his shoulders and replied: 'Things become very complicated at this point. The Conservative Party won't let anyone tell it who should be its leader. On the other hand, the opposition simply cannot accept Chamberlain. The idea has been floated of bringing Baldwin back in so that he, as a member of the House of Lords, could serve, in essence, as a merely nominal head, while the government would actually be led by somebody else. However, it is too early to judge.'

I should note in passing that I had already heard about this suggestion a few days ago, and that the supporters of this alternative named Churchill as the real head of the government, representing the Cabinet in the House of Commons. As if reading my thoughts, Churchill began to ponder aloud about how much he enjoyed his position as a 'freelance Tory' who could afford to criticize the government, and said he would not exchange it for a Cabinet post.

'It is far more pleasant,' Churchill remarked venomously, 'to read books or write articles than to try to convince ministerial nonentities that twice two is four.' But it was clear that he was merely showing off and being coy. I inquired about Eden's intentions. Churchill replied that it was too early to tell. He has the impression that Eden won't want to clash with the Conservative Party. Quarrels like that are always unpleasant. It causes the 'rebel' no end of difficulties. Besides, Eden has already grown used to power and his high standing. This can spoil a man. Therefore, in Churchill's opinion, Eden will sit this out. When the time comes for the anticipated restructuring, Eden will undoubtedly return to the Cabinet and take up a major post. Then I asked about Vansittart's standing. Churchill answered that Vansittart was going through a difficult period, but he hoped that his position would be strengthened in the near future. Vansittart currently has influence but lacks power.

(4) Our conversation moved on to international questions. Churchill sees the general situation in a menacing light. Where is Hitler headed? Churchill is in no doubt that Hitler's dream is a 'Central Europe' extending from the North Sea [sic – Maisky possibly means the Baltic Sea] to the Black and Mediterranean Seas, possibly as far as Baghdad. He has an excellent chance, unless he meets proper resistance from the other great powers. Hitler will require only a modest period of time to carry out his plans, some four or five years at most. In this he will be aided by Italy's rapid transformation into Germany's appendage, particularly following the appearance of German troops at the Brenner Pass.

However, Churchill is not inclined to think that Hitler will attack Czechoslovakia in the nearest future. What good would it do him? Open aggression against Czechoslovakia might bring France and the USSR onto the scene, which would be undesirable, since Hitler is not yet ready for a full-scale war. Far simpler for Hitler to act in a different way. The next stage of his expansion, according to Churchill, will be Hungary, which Hitler will be able to assimilate with no great difficulty. Via Hungary he can push his way into Rumania, exploiting the latter's sizeable Hungarian minority.

Meanwhile, Hitler will use Henlein's[i] party to cause internal difficulties for Czechoslovakia and undertake various economic initiatives (exploiting, in particular, the importance of Vienna as the crucial transit junction of Central and South-East Europe) to strangle her economically. When Czechoslovakia

---

[i] Konrad Henlein, leader of the fascist Sudeten-German Home Front Party in Czechoslovakia, 1933–38; Gauleiter of Bohemia and Moravia, 1939–45.

becomes isolated from the outside and shattered from the inside, it will lose its nerve and fall without a fight into Hitler's hands, like a ripe fruit. Such are the calculations of the German fascists. And Churchill believes many of these calculations to be correct.

I observed that unexpected developments can easily arise in ploys of this sort (separatist actions by Henlein, for example), which may wreck Hitler's cunning plans, if he has any. Churchill agreed with me, but insisted that the pattern of events he had outlined was the most probable. Should it materialize, a 'Mitteleuropa' would present a most serious danger to the world at large, and specifically to Britain, France and the USSR. In particular, Churchill would like to draw our attention to the fact that we would find ourselves in a very difficult situation, should Hitler succeed in realizing his dream. Certainly, it is beyond doubt that eastward expansion exerts a strong pull on Hitler: in the direction of grain-rich Ukraine, the oil-rich Caucasus, and Asia Minor, Arabia, and so on. Making Rumania his own, Hitler would not only get his hands on the Rumanian oil which he needs so badly, but he would also build up a fairly powerful fleet in the Black Sea (submarines, in particular) that would endanger Soviet shores and Soviet navigation. Using his advantages, Hitler could start putting pressure on the USSR, demanding a supply of raw materials, provisions, etc. In view of these considerations, Churchill finds the isolationist sentiments which, by my account, can be observed in certain quarters of Soviet public opinion to be rather dangerous. For Churchill thinks it nearly inevitable that Hitler's next step after setting up a 'Mitteleuropa' would be an eastward attack against the USSR, with its vast territories and immeasurable resources.

(5) I objected by saying that I had a rather different picture of the prospects for the more distant future. Even if we assume that Hitler will succeed in creating a 'Mitteleuropa', I do not believe that he would then focus his aggression on the east. Taking into account my interlocutor's psychology and habits of thought, I put forward three major arguments to substantiate my way of thinking. First, it is a well-known historical fact that Russia, a great power, can be neither conquered nor crushed (Churchill nodded his assent). At best, Hitler could count on grabbing some Soviet provinces, which would bring him more headaches than benefits. In return, he would reap the deadly hatred of his eastern neighbour which, even after a military operation of this sort, would remain a great power possessing immense human and natural resources. Second, a huge proportion of the population in 'Mitteleuropa' would be Slavs. Under these conditions, it would be highly risky for Hitler to wage war against the USSR, the majority of whose population is Slavic. The experience of employing Czechoslovakians against Russia during the last war is very indicative in that respect. The third argument is particularly important: if Churchill is correct in his calculation that Hitler would need four or five years to set up 'Mitteleuropa' (provided he

meets with no resistance from other great powers), it means that peace for the USSR would be guaranteed during this period. In turn, this means we would manage to fulfil our third five-year plan.

This fact is of the utmost importance. We already feel that we are quite capable of successfully resisting any simultaneous attack on our western and eastern fronts. (Churchill grinned at this point and remarked with obvious satisfaction: 'Oh, yes. You scared the living daylights out of the Japanese. They treat you with greater respect now because they understand perfectly well that in the space of a few hours your air force can turn Tokyo and Osaka into piles of ash.') The fulfilment of the third five-year plan, I went on, should result in a boom in the military and economic power of the USSR as compared to the present day. An assault on us by Hitler thus becomes all the more questionable. In view of all these considerations, it seems more probable to me that German aggression would take a westward, rather than an eastward, course following the creation of a 'Mitteleuropa'. It is in the west that Germany can gain the wealthy colonial kingdom that its fascist leaders currently yearn for.

(6) My reasoning seemed to impress Churchill because he replied: 'Let's assume that a "Mitteleuropa" is equally dangerous to both of us. Doesn't this suggest that we should join forces in the struggle against Hitler's Germany?' I answered that we had always been and remained active supporters of the collective struggle against aggression, wherever it might be committed, and that we had joined the League of Nations for this very purpose. It's up to his country now, not ours. As far as I can judge, Chamberlain intends not to fight aggression, but to make a deal with the aggressors in the form of a 'four-power pact' at the expense of Central and South-East Europe, and also of the USSR, which would be isolated. Churchill would do better to address his arguments first and foremost to his own prime minister.

Churchill gestured in annoyance and replied contemptuously: 'A four-power pact? What nonsense! What sort of four-power pact could there be? Poland already has an agreement with Germany and Italy that in the event of the four-power pact becoming reality, it would become the fifth member. And if Poland becomes a member of the "four-power pact", then how could the Little Entente be excluded? Indeed, how could the USSR be excluded? Chamberlain is a complete ignoramus in matters of foreign policy and that is why he can talk in all seriousness about a four-power pact.' Churchill began to elaborate his idea. At present he advocates the idea of a 'grand alliance' within the frame of the League of Nations. It would be intended, first and foremost, to unite Great Britain, France, the Little Entente and the USSR.

Churchill stresses the particular importance of establishing a Danube federation as a counterweight to German expansion in Central and South-East Europe. It would be excellent if the USSR could actively support the idea of such a federation. But in the event of these designs failing to materialize, of the 'grand alliance' falling through and 'Mitteleuropa' becoming a reality, Churchill conceives a close, heavily armed alliance of Great Britain and France as a last resort. With its backs to the ocean and commanding world sea routes, the alliance would be capable, temporarily at least, of securing crucial positions of both 'Western democracies'. It could rely, at any rate, on the tacit indirect support of the USA and the USSR, which, without being bound to the alliance by any formal obligations, would, by the very fact of their existence, serve to some extent as a counterbalance to the might of the aggressors – the fascist states. 'It would be not the policy of *isolation* advocated by Beaverbrook, but the policy of *bisolation*, as I like to call it.'

(7) 'But this,' Churchill continued, 'is of course only the very worst, the very last solution. Less a solution, in fact, than a dire necessity. I still haven't given up the hope of something better. I believe that the time of the grand alliance will come. I believe that, through their joint efforts, England, France and the USSR will be able to put global affairs in order on the basis of collective security. Twenty years ago I put my every last ounce of energy into the struggle against communism, since at that time I believed communism, with its idea of world revolution, to be the greatest menace to the British Empire. Today, communism does not represent such a danger to the Empire. Today, the greatest menace to the British Empire is German Nazism, with its idea of Berlin's global hegemony. That is why, at the present time, I spare no effort in the struggle against Hitler. If, one fine day, the German fascist threat to the Empire disappears and the communist menace rears its head again, then – I tell you frankly – I would raise the banner of struggle against you once more. However, I don't anticipate the possibility of this happening in the near future, or at least within my lifetime (Churchill is 63). In the meantime, we are walking the same path. That is why I am advocating the idea of a "grand alliance" and perhaps of closer cooperation between London, Paris and Moscow.'

Finishing his speech, Churchill asked me with a subtle grin: 'Tell me, what do you, the USSR, demand from us?' I answered: 'We do not demand anything; but we would just like you, Great Britain, to be a good member of the League of Nations.' Churchill exclaimed: 'That's my wish too. And it's the wish of many of my friends.' I replied: 'It will be a great deal easier for our countries to agree on matters pertaining to the struggle for peace if the ideas inspiring you and your friends become the dominant principles of British foreign policy.'

29 March

I attended a session of the House of Lords for the first time ever during my life in England – whether in exile or after the revolution.

Foreign-policy issues were on the agenda. There were at most 100 or 120 people sitting on the red leather benches. They looked like flies in milk, since the chamber can house three times as many. But today was a 'big day'! Normally, no more than 30 to 40 peers are present, while the quorum in the House amounts to… 3!

In the side galleries, I noticed some two dozen ladies, all dressed-up. The diplomats' box was occupied by the Japanese envoy, the Belgian, the Swiss, and Agniya and me. Guo (the Chinese ambassador) arrived with Sun Fo,[i] who is in London for a while, but on seeing the Japanese envoy they made themselves scarce and several minutes later I saw them in a vacant box on the opposite side of the chamber.

The session lasted from 4.15 p.m. to 7.40 p.m. Only three and a half hours! Not like the House of Commons, where a normal session starts at 2.45 p.m. and ends at 11 p.m. The speeches, too, were much shorter here than in the Commons – 15 or 20 minutes. Even Halifax, answering on behalf of the government, did not exceed 25 minutes. Well, lords do not like putting themselves to any trouble!

But what a session it was! It was opened by the leader of the Labour opposition, Lord Snell,[ii] with an attack on the government's foreign policy. I had heard more or less the same things a few days ago from Attlee and Noel-Baker in the House of Commons. But what a difference, what a terrific difference in presentation! The speaker's voice was subdued, his appearance expressly respectable, his gestures almost those of a preacher, and his words as though rolled in cotton. Snell was followed by a Liberal lord who spoke so quietly that I couldn't understand a thing. He looked around 80. Then the archbishop of Canterbury took the floor and… gave his full and unconditional backing to Chamberlain! What had become of his old loyalty to the League of Nations? What had become of his anti-German tendencies? In his white mantle, which looked crumpled and unkempt from afar, the archbishop resembled a large bird with a hooked beak. After him spoke other lords, whose names I do not know, claiming that Hitler was a wonderful man who did the right thing by occupying Austria: after all, by doing so he saved the world from another 'civil war' in Europe – incredible! One speaker called for the publication in English of an unabridged translation of Hitler's *Mein Kampf* at the price of no more than a shilling per copy – so impressed was he by the profundity and foresight of the Führer's writings. To unstinting cheers from the government benches, Ponsonby[iii] explained why England should not worry itself about the

---

[i] Sun Fo (also known as Sun Ke), chairman of the Executive Yuan government of the Republic of China, 1938–39.
[ii] Henry Snell (1st Baron Snell), Labour chairman of London County Council, 1934–38.
[iii] Arthur Ponsonby (1st Baron Ponsonby of Shulbrede), Labour MP, 1922–30; leader of the opposition in the House of Lords, 1931–35.

League of Nations and why it was against her interests to assist Czechoslovakia, a country whose whereabouts are unknown to 99% of her people. In the second part of his speech, losing all the enthusiasm of the Tories, Ponsonby demanded immediate disarmament, for the best policy was the policy of non-resistance. What a nutter! But that's the way of all absolute pacifists, starting with Leo Tolstoy.[33] Lord Samuel (a Liberal) declared in his turn that the policy of collective security was bankrupt, the policy of isolation impossible, and the policy of balance of power and alliance-making dangerous. Therefore, the best and only policy for the present time was merely one of peaceable opportunism, i.e. the absence of any policy and unprincipled day-to-day manoeuvring in an attempt to avoid war. Strabolgi's[i] closing speech, on behalf of Labour, was not bad – lively, forceful and sensible. Replying to him and to all the other speakers of the opposition (including Lord Cecil, who today attacked the government from the League of Nations' point of view), Lord Halifax made the kind of speech that might have been expected of him. Straight out of Chamberlain's book. Viewed strictly as a piece of oratory, however, it was a good speech and was even leavened by flashes of wit. Frankly, I hadn't expected such agility from Halifax.

How can I sum up my impressions?

Never in my life have I seen so reactionary a gathering as this House of Lords. The mould of the ages lies visibly upon it. Even the air in the chamber is stale and yellow. Even the light through the windows is gloomy. The men sitting on these red benches are historically blind, like moles, and are ready to lick the Nazi dictator's boots like a beaten dog. They'll pay for this, and I'll see it happen!

But we need to be as sharp-eyed as the devil. For today's session of the House of Lords definitively convinced me that the British bourgeoisie, fleeing its historical nemesis, will make a new and resolute attempt to divert the lightning towards us. It's harder than it looks!

31 March

I have rarely experienced such a sense of disgust and loathing as I did at today's meeting of the Subcommittee,[34] presided over by the chairman.

Non-intervention has always been a farce. Along with rampant hypocrisy, there has always been an *air of unreality* about the meetings of the Committee and the Subcommittee. Indeed, what kind of reality could there have been when, from its very inception, the Committee was led by two great powers who

---

[i] Joseph Montague Kenworthy (10th Baron Strabolgi), opposition chief whip, House of Lords, 1938–42.

had set themselves the very definite task of maximum interference in Spanish affairs on the side of Franco?

But today the hypocrisy and unreality reached their apogee. And no wonder! The Italo-German intervention has expanded as never before. Hundreds of German and Italian planes, dispatched in recent weeks to help Franco, are dropping bombs on Republican lines and Republican cities. Hitler and Göring keep saying that they will not permit the triumph of 'Bolshevism' on the Iberian Peninsula. In his speech yesterday, Mussolini boasted openly of the exploits of the Italian air and ground forces in Spain. The Italian press glorifies the 'heroism' of the fascist 'legionaries' in the war against the Republic. Franco's ambassador in Rome sends his gratitude to the Duce for aid rendered to the insurgents in recent battles...

And at such a moment, Lord Plymouth suddenly convenes the Subcommittee to discuss the final version of the 'Plan for the Evacuation of Volunteers and for Granting Belligerent Rights under Certain Conditions', the very same plan that the Subcommittee had been drafting and redrafting for the past six months and that had never seemed particularly realistic. Now that the Spanish Republic might cease to exist within three or four weeks, it is merely a mockery of common sense and the most elementary decorum.

Yes, it was a foul and repulsive show! Especially the sight of the dandified and perfumed Dino Grandi, who turned up at the meeting with the look of a victor. There was nothing to be done. I had to listen to all the nonsense spoken at the meeting while maintaining a serious, business-like air and making occasional remarks. But I did manage to spoil the script somewhat for Grandi. He had prepared a long and doubtless boastful speech (I saw him pulling a thick roll of typewritten pages out of his pocket at the beginning of the meeting) and was waiting for any kind of statement from me in order to assail the Subcommittee with it. So I decided not to speak at all, even though I also had something ready. That upset the Italian ambassador's apple cart. The speech he'd prepared could not be used. He fidgeted nervously with the text throughout the meeting, turning over the pages and rereading certain passages, but he didn't manage to employ his poisoned weapon. At the very end, when the communiqué was already being drawn up, Grandi made an attempt to use at least part of his speech against Corbin, but he was unlucky here, too: it was late, everyone was hurrying to have lunch, and Plymouth, with uncharacteristic firmness (he must have been very hungry), rejected the Italian's attempt to keep us longer under the pretext of his objections to the French ambassador's remarks.

I had one more reason to refrain from any serious declarations. Chamberlain had clearly made his mind up to sell Spain to Mussolini and to sign an agreement with Rome whatever the cost. Labour–Liberal public opinion, along with that of many Conservatives, will protest against the Spanish price to be paid for the agreement. The PM needs a scapegoat onto whom he can shift the blame for his failure to have the volunteers withdrawn as he had promised, and he would like it best if the USSR took that role. Chamberlain's calculations must be upset.

At the end of the meeting, Corbin approached me and asked: 'Can you explain to me why Plymouth convened this completely pointless meeting?'

'That is not difficult to explain,' I replied. 'When he answers questions in the House, Chamberlain can now say: "The Non-Intervention Committee is at work. The British government submitted new proposals to the Committee that are currently being studied by interested governments."

'You may be right,' concluded Corbin with little enthusiasm.

The French ambassador has grown noticeably older in the past year. He now walks with a stoop, his hair has turned white, and his face is covered in wrinkles. He is the very picture of the crisis which France is undergoing!

12 April[35]

A very interesting conversation with Sun Fo. (Incidentally, he is not the son of Sun Zhongshan,[i] as many believe. The only connection is that his second wife is the daughter of the great Chinese revolutionary's sister.)

Sun Fo has spent six weeks in Moscow, seeking an agreement with the Soviet government on aid to China. He left content and he expressed his gratitude for our thorough implementation of the agreements reached in Moscow. Initially, however, Sun Fo was not quite so pleased with the Moscow negotiations. As far as I could understand from his rather foggy explanations (he usually speaks clearly, precisely and frankly), he had hoped to convince the Soviet government of the necessity of a joint military action with China against Japan. The Soviet government declined the proposal, but it did promise active assistance to China by sending arms, aircraft, etc. The results have been obvious in military operations in China. There is no doubt that the Chinese successes of the past three weeks have been due in no small measure to the arrival of our planes, tanks, artillery, etc. No wonder Sun Fo feels almost triumphant.

The details of his crucial meeting with Stalin are interesting. 'I was told the date of my meeting with your leader,' Sun Fo said, 'but not the time of day. I got ready. I sat at the embassy and waited. Evening came: eight o'clock, nine o'clock, ten o'clock, eleven o'clock… Nothing! Somewhat disappointed, I decided to call it a day. I got undressed and went to bed. Then all of a sudden, at a quarter to

---

[i] Sun Zhongshan (Sun Yat-sen), Chinese revolutionary; founder of Guomindang (National People's Party) in 1912; leader of the Republic of China, 1921–22 and 1923–25.

midnight, people came for me: "Please, you are expected." I jumped up, got dressed, and set off. Molotov and Voroshilov were with Stalin. Towards the end of the meeting Mikoyan[i] and Ezhov[ii] also arrived. The conversation lasted from midnight until 5.30 in the morning. That's when it was all decided.'

According to Sun Fo, it was during that conversation that the Soviet government dismissed the idea of direct military involvement in the war against Japan. The reasons given by Stalin to justify this line of behaviour boiled down, in Sun Fo's account, to the following: (1) Military action by the USSR would immediately rally the entire Japanese nation, which at present is far from unified in its support of Japan's aggression in China. (2) Military action by the USSR, on the other hand, might well frighten right-wing elements in China and thereby split the United National Front which has recently emerged there. (3) Military action by the USSR, with its prospect of victory, would alarm Great Britain and the USA and might transform their current sympathy towards China into its direct opposite. (4) Military action by the USSR, and this is particularly important, would be exploited by Germany for an attack on our country in Europe, and that would unleash a world war. For all these reasons, Stalin considers open military action against Japan by the USSR to be inexpedient. But he is quite prepared to render assistance to China by providing it with arms and so on.[36]

This assistance, according to Sun Fo, is being rendered in smooth and regular fashion. The motor road to Lanzhou via Xinjiang is satisfactory. Transportation from the Soviet borders to Lanzhou takes two to three weeks on average. During winter, those living along the road have been voluntarily removing snowdrifts, and as a result traffic along the route has not been interrupted even for one day. Planes reach China in summer time. The Soviet aircraft are first-class. They were so fast that at first the Chinese pilots could not fly them properly. Now they are gradually mastering them. Soviet experts are rendering the Chinese great assistance in the training of pilots. The majority of German instructors in the Chinese armies were recalled by Hitler. Only 30 or 40 men were left who refused to leave for Germany and took an oath of allegiance to the Chinese government. Germany also terminated arms deliveries to China. The Italian instructors left China long ago. The Chinese government has as many as 600 foreigners (mainly Americans, Englishmen, Dutchmen and others) serving in the air force. It now numbers 500 to 600 aircraft. Some arms come from

---

[i] Anastas Ivanovich Mikoyan, Politburo member, 1935–52; people's commissar for external trade, 1938–49; member of the State Defence Committee, 1939–45.

[ii] Nikolai Ivanovich Ezhov, people's commissar for interior affairs (NKVD) and general commissar of state security, 1936–38, who oversaw the 'Great Terror'. He was demoted to the position of people's commissar for water transport, 1938–39. Arrested in April 1939, he was charged with conspiracy and espionage, convicted and shot in February 1940.

the USA, some are delivered from Great Britain (about 60 planes as of today), Belgium, France and Czechoslovakia (the Bren machine-gun), but not much on the whole. But then the British government keeps Hong Kong open for arms transit, which is very important, and keeps the motor road in good nick between Burma and Yunnan on the Burmese side. The Chinese government, for its part, is hurriedly completing the same road on the Yunnan side, where as many as 170,000 workers are employed. The road will be opened in June, and then, besides Hong Kong, there will be a new and absolutely safe route to deliver all essential imports to China from the Indian Ocean.

Speaking about communication routes, Sun Fo suddenly remembered the following: 'During my conversation with your leaders I advanced the idea that it would be helpful if a railway connecting Alma-Ata, Xinjiang and Lanzhou was laid to facilitate Soviet deliveries to China. Stalin took an interest in my idea. He took out a map and we studied it to see where exactly the railway could be laid. We calculated that the length of the line would be about 3,000 kilometres and that, under the most favourable conditions, three years would be needed for its construction. When this had become clear, Stalin noted: "A railway there is not of primary significance today, at least as far as the current war is concerned. This is a peace-time task." To which I replied: "Why do you think the line we are talking about is not of immediate military importance? China is prepared to wage war for five years." Stalin laughed, but he was obviously pleased and said that in that case my idea should be taken more seriously.'

I asked Sun Fo about his negotiations in England. His objective was to raise 20 million pounds in the form of a loan or credits for Chinese tungsten and antimony. He had made scant progress. Halifax was full of amicable sentiment towards China in his conversation with Sun Fo but vague in matters of supply and finance. Simon sympathized, too, but thought that the City would not grant a loan without the government's guarantee, which would be difficult to push through the House (sheer nonsense!).

As a result, Leith-Ross was assigned to draft a project for a group of British companies that need tungsten and antimony and might provide the Chinese government with an advance in exchange for future supplies. This is patently a lousy scheme! The higher echelons of the Tory Party have decayed to such an extent that they have lost their ability to defend their own interests, even with the help of the gold they are still rolling in.

Sun Fo seemed flattered by the big lunch I arranged in his honour on 8 April. On 6 April I had attended lunch in his honour at the Chinese embassy, and on the 7th I attended the reception there which was held on the occasion of his arrival.

14 April

The Abyssinian envoy Martin came to see me. A tragic figure. He still shows up everywhere – at official receptions, in society, among diplomats – wearing his tunic covered in gold and a green-red-yellow sash over his shoulder. Outwardly, everyone still shows him respect and sympathy (some do so emphatically), but behind his back they ask: 'How long will this last?'... Martin walks about as a living ghost, and at the same time as a bleeding wound on the conscience of 'Western democracies'. His dark-skinned, full figure is a daily reminder of the triumphant insolence of the fascist aggressors, the myopic weakness of Western democracies, and the flagrant injustice committed right before our eyes with the connivance of England and France...

'Do you see how they are toying with us?' Martin exclaimed as he entered my office.

I understood at once that 'they' were the British government. Then Martin unburdened his heart to me. He told me about various trivial instances of 'chicanery' to which the Negus had been subjected by the British authorities and courts, the growing coldness on the part of so-called society, the icy propriety of the Foreign Office that freezes his heart, and much else in the same vein. Incidentally, when Martin paid his first official visit to Halifax in early March (he is still, formally speaking, an accredited envoy at St James's!), he addressed the foreign secretary with the words: 'I hope that in your work you will not forget the principle called justice.' Somewhat disconcerted, Halifax replied: 'Unfortunately, justice does not always triumph in our world.'

Today Martin came to request that I inform Moscow that the Negus and the Abyssinian people, who, despite everything, are waging a heroic partisan war against the Italians, are pinning their hopes on the USSR. Let Chamberlain's plans for some members of the League of Nations to be relieved of their obligation not to acknowledge the conquest of Abyssinia fail! Let the Soviet government express its weighty opinion about the deeply treacherous plan plotted by the British government! As a last resort, let the Soviet government ensure that the question be postponed until the Assembly of the League of Nations, that is, until autumn. That would give four or five months, and then we shall see.

As I did not know Moscow's decision on this question, I had to be very cautious. I tried to console Martin, telling him not to despair, but I must confess that my heart was heavy and troubled.

[An Anglo-French summit meeting in London on 28–29 April revealed the hegemony of the hosts. Daladier's[i] passionate advocacy of stiff resistance to Hitler in Czechoslovakia,

---

[i] Edouard Daladier, French minister of defence, 1932–34, 1936–38 and September 1939–March 1940; prime minister, January–October 1933, January 1934 and April 1938–March 1940.

with Soviet help if necessary, did not carry the day. It was, Cadogan commented, 'Very beautiful, but awful rubbish'.[37] Masaryk disclosed to Maisky that the British had been 'highly defeatist', arguing that 'neither France, nor the USSR was in a position to render any effective help to Czechoslovakia'. He further revealed that on the eve of the talks, Hore-Belisha, the secretary of state for war, who was just back from Rome, had intimated that 'the expansion of Germany in the direction of Czechoslovakia, Hungary and the Balkans was inevitable, that England was not prepared for war, that as long as Hitler's actions were confined to Europe there would be no war'.[38] Briefed by Halifax, Maisky was left in no doubt that Britain, determined not to get involved directly in the conflict, was at best prepared to act as a go-between, though only once Beneš had made further substantial concessions.[39]]

10 May

Sir Horace Wilson came over for lunch. His fate has followed a rather bizarre course. I was acquainted with him in late 1932 upon my arrival in Britain as ambassador, in connection with the newly opened negotiations on a trade agreement. The previous agreement of 1930 had been denounced and a new agreement had to be signed. I headed the Soviet delegation at the negotiations, while Wilson, who at that time was on the Board of Trade and had the high-sounding title of 'chief industrial adviser to the government', was the *de facto* head of the British delegation. I say '*de facto*' because the British delegation was nominally headed by Walter Runciman, president of the Board of Trade. The negotiations were tough and abounded in dramatic turns. They were broken off for four months during the Metro-Vickers trial and the trade embargo, and resumed only after the conflict had been settled. We tussled and argued over the new trade agreement for a whole 15 months and signed it only on 16 February 1934. During this time, I had the opportunity to get to know Wilson well and establish an acquaintance. He always struck me as a clever, cunning and somewhat cynical fellow, well versed in the politics of trade, a dab hand at formulating compromises, and an ardent defender of the interests of British industrialists and traders. I never saw him display an understanding of international politics, still less a desire to be engaged in those complex and sensitive matters.

Sometime later – in 1935, I believe – Wilson moved from the Board of Trade to 10, Downing Street, where he became Baldwin's economic adviser. However, right up until Baldwin's resignation at the end of May 1937, Wilson remained in the shadows, playing no particular role and attracting no particular attention. The situation changed dramatically when Chamberlain came to power. I do not know how and why it happened, but the new prime minister discerned a kindred soul in Wilson, and his rapid, dizzying ascent began: first he was promoted from economic adviser to Chamberlain's chief secretary and, soon after, to chief adviser – and mainly on international affairs! The Foreign Office was incensed but could do nothing. Wilson played a major part in Eden's resignation, and someone told me that the last conversation between Eden and Wilson, which took place a few days before 20 February, was a very stormy affair.

Today Wilson and I had lunch tête-à-tête. We spoke, of course, about international affairs. I advanced and substantiated the thought that Hitler's immediate objective was to set up a 'Mitteleuropa' and that Chamberlain's policy only facilitated his attainment of this aim. Meanwhile, 'Mitteleuropa' would, it seems, threaten the interests not only of the USSR, but also, and perhaps to an even greater extent, of Britain.

In a subtle but perfectly clear manner, Wilson suggested that Hitler's next blow after 'Mitteleuropa' would be directed eastward, against the USSR, and this would accord with British interests. I ridiculed these suppositions, drawing on approximately the same arguments I had used in my recent conversation with Churchill. They seemed to hit the mark. Wilson immediately became hesitant and pensive. After a brief silence, he said: 'I confess that your considerations have a sound basis. There is a possibility that Hitler may not move eastward. Still I am not inclined to think that even in this case "Mitteleuropa" would pose such a terrible threat to Britain. You see, today Germany is a monolith: one nation, one state, one leader. That is her strength. "Mitteleuropa" will be different: a conglomerate of nationalities, state organizations, and economic regions. Internal contradictions, friction, struggles and conflicts are inevitable. All these mitigating factors shall certainly come into play. As a result, "Mitteleuropa" may prove weaker than present-day Germany. And I have no doubt that it will be less aggressive. Germany's empty stomach will be filled. She will grow heavy and calm down...'

So this is what Wilson's, or for that matter Chamberlain's, 'philosophy' amounts to![40]

[The time had arrived for Maisky's obligatory summer vacation and, far more terrifyingly, the newly instituted procedure of annual hearings for ambassadors at the ministry. His gloomy reports to Narkomindel on appeasement were now tempered by an illusionary conviction, largely sustained by conversations with members of the opposition, such as Churchill, Lloyd George and Beaverbrook, that 'the ground was systematically shifting under the English Government's feet, though that process does not make headway fast enough'.[41] As insurance, before he left for Moscow, Maisky extracted from Lloyd George 'a warm message of admiration to Stalin, as the greatest statesman alive!' At the same time, he did not fail to keep the elderly Liberal informed of his whereabouts in Russia and, though well aware that it was monitored, kept up a constant flow of correspondence while he was away. This served to boost his standing in England: 'I look forward to your return,' wrote Beaverbrook, 'and that view is held by most Englishmen, but not by all foreigners' – a clear reference to the Germans and Italians.[42]

By the same token, in a report to Narkomindel, Maisky highlighted 'the Soviet demonstration' by Chamberlain, who, at the royal reception on 11 May, made a point of approaching him and of displaying interest in his vacation plans, allegedly eager to find out when he could be expected back in London. The unusual approach, Maisky hastened to add, was well covered by journalists, who had been ringing the embassy since the early hours of the morning.[43] At the same time, Maisky had to project a sense of complacency, in order to dispel rumours of his permanent recall, insisting that he was 'on the best of terms with his own government'.[44] A ray of hope for Maisky was Stalin's unusual personal approach to him on 12 May. Obviously not trusting the embassy in Tokyo or Narkomindel, Stalin instructed Maisky 'not to avoid' meeting the Japanese ambassador in London and to try and glean from him what the Japanese intentions were, as well as to convey the Soviet wish to improve relations with Tokyo. Maisky not only obliged, but also transmitted the ambassador's suggestion that further negotiations be pursued in London, emphasizing his own invaluable position in the British capital.[45] However, the probability of a recall was very much on Maisky's mind. Taking her leave of the Webbs, Agniya, for instance, revealed her determination 'to have six months in the USSR, to regain her contact with her beloved country; she dislikes her life in the hostile atmosphere of the London society'.[46]

It was Agniya who, despite being 'a poor sailor', was eager for them to travel by steamboat via Leningrad, and she also hoped to entice Litvinov to join them. The pretext was the recent birth of Maisky's first grandson to his daughter in Leningrad. But perhaps as significant was the opportunity for Maisky and Litvinov to continue the talks Maisky had initiated in Geneva on their future during the five-day uninterrupted sea voyage. Uncertain about what lay ahead, the Maiskys had hastily bought new furniture for their Moscow flat, and they hoped to ship it at the same time. The cruise would also have provided some sense of security, as they would arrive at Narkomindel accompanied by the commissar in person.[47] Litvinov was 'most tempted', but, unable to get there in time, he proposed that they travel together by the Nord-Express from Paris.[48] Litvinov further explained to the wife and daughter of the ambassador in Italy, Shtein, who were pleading with him to allow the ambassador to return to Moscow for a vacation, that it was 'better for him to sit in Rome than to be here'. Shtein, whose nerves were cracking, was advised by a private doctor he saw in Geneva to let off steam by 'destroying a dinner service once a month, powerfully and angrily crashing it on the floor'.[49] Kollontay, who was recalled at the same time, wrote a morbid farewell letter – practically a will – to an intimate friend, entrusting her with her diary and personal correspondence 'in the event of my death (something can always happen while travelling)'. She instructed her friend to deposit the papers in the archives of the International Labour Organization in Geneva, 'in case you do not hear anything from me in the coming years, or you are certain that I am no longer alive'.[50] She then confided in her diary: 'The world is now so terrible, tense. It is frightful for many friends. I worry, my heart is torn for them … If I don't fall "underneath the wheel [of history]" it will be almost a miracle.'[51]

Unlike his previous vacations, which had been spent in the Caucasus and travelling all over the country, this time Maisky was confined to a sanatorium outside Moscow, surrounded, as he tried to impress his friends in England, by 'beautiful and most invigorating pinewoods' – but from where he could obviously be summoned at any moment to the capital. His unenviable position was rendered particularly dire when the *Sunday Express* chose now of all times to harp on his 'unpopularity with the Soviet rulers', alleging that he had 'refused for many months to obey orders to return to Russia'.[52] This was not too far from the truth. Maisky was indeed summoned to Narkomindel and forced to compose a confessional autobiographical sketch, in which he admitted to political short-sightedness and failure to recognize the 'enemies of the people' within his embassy. He was confronted with testimonies extracted from his former subordinates, Putna, the military attaché at the embassy, and Ozersky, the head of the trade delegation in London. Both had given compromising evidence against him before being shot. Together with Litvinov, he was then rushed to the Kremlin on 1 June, where, in the presence of Molotov and Voroshilov, Stalin urged them to keep a low profile in the future and act prudently. Consequently, he was let out 'on parole', well aware of the vulnerability of his situation.[53]

Maisky and Agniya returned to London at the end of July, having spent a few days in Stockholm, recuperating in the company of Kollontay. Obviously relieved, they projected a feeling of being 'jolly and well ... at once exceptionally self-confident and self-assured about their beloved country and cool and cautious about the rest of the world'. Maisky did not conceal from the Webbs the Kremlin's 'coldness towards Great Britain, hatred of Chamberlain as their enemy, concern about Czech-Slovakia and coolness towards the present French Government'. While admitting that, given the international situation, the Soviet Union preferred to 'keep out of a European war', Maisky reaffirmed that it would remain 'loyal to its pact'. In further candid talks with Harold Nicolson and Vansittart, Maisky again warned of 'the incipient movement towards isolation in Russia', which he attributed to the West's intention of keeping Russia 'at arm's length', but which 'he hoped would not go too far'. He vowed, though, as he had done at his meeting with Halifax a few days earlier, that 'If France and Great Britain, in the event of an invasion of Sudetenland, came to the armed support of Czechoslovakia Russia would come in on our side.'[54]

Maisky had obviously become convinced that his personal salvation lay in the success of collective security. With Litvinov increasingly hamstrung by the vacillating and sceptical attitude of the Kremlin, and further crippled by the purges in his ministry, Maisky would henceforth become the main driving force in trying to bring about a change in British policy. This he hoped to achieve by resorting to unconventional methods. Throughout the following year, sharp discrepancies between his reports to Moscow and the British records, as well as his misleading and tendentious memoirs, reveal painstaking efforts on his part to attribute his own ideas to his interlocutors. In so doing, he hoped to elicit from Moscow a positive response, which might spark a chain reaction that would advance the ideas of collective security and extricate the Soviet Union from its increasingly forced isolation.

Perhaps as striking was his unabashed interference in British domestic politics, as he incited the anti-Chamberlain opposition in wishful anticipation that the worsening international situation would encourage it to overthrow the prime minister and install either Eden or Churchill in his stead.[55] Maisky lost no time in seeking a meeting with Eden and his 'English friends'. In order to dispel the rumours of his poor standing in

Moscow, he depicted in rosy colours the 'very pleasant and refreshing holiday' he had had there. His hopes were dashed, though, when Eden, instead of seizing the reins in the run-up to the Munich Conference, opted for a long break from politics to go on 'a motoring tour in Ireland'. He did not expect to return to London, so he informed Maisky, before the end of September.[56] Maisky nonetheless went out of his way to deliberately convey to Moscow the fallacious impression that the anti-Chamberlain forces were on the rise. He suggested, for instance, that Vansittart had recovered his voice within the Foreign Office; that a highly agitated Churchill advocated patience in anticipation of the forging of an Anglo-Franco-Soviet alliance; and that Horace Wilson appeared to be disillusioned with Hitler.[57]]

4 August

Guo Taiqi came to see me, together with the newly appointed Chinese ambassador to the USA (I forget his name). He was interested in the impressions I had gained during my trip to the USSR and told me about his affairs.

Alas, his news was not very reassuring. While I was on leave, the British government refused the 20 million pound loan to China that had been negotiated in spring. The reason: Japan might 'take offence'. The talks begun by Sun Fo to obtain an advance for the Chinese secured by mineral resources in southern China have also yielded no results as yet. Negotiations are under way to supply China with export credits for ten years, at an amount of up to 15 million pounds. Even if this last scheme comes off, the Chinese government will be able to use the credits obtained for buying motor vehicles, railway equipment and the like, but not for the purchase of arms. Guo also told me about the growing 'Japanophilia' of Craigie, the British ambassador in Tokyo, who wants to restore 'friendship' between Tokyo and London whatever the cost. But his efforts are to no avail: whatever agreements Craigie comes to with the Japanese government in Tokyo are insolently overturned by the Japanese military in China.

∗ ∗ ∗

I have received interesting information about the Anglo-French talks held during the king's visit to Paris. Halifax promised Bonnet[i] that the British–Italian agreement would not be implemented until the Spanish question was resolved, but he did not agree to link this to the conclusion of a similar French–Italian agreement. On the issue of Czechoslovakia, Halifax maintained the following: Czechoslovakia is an artificial state incapable both of defending itself and of getting assistance from the outside.[58] Great Britain will not detach itself from Central European developments, but France should exert greater pressure on

---

[i] Georges-Etienne Bonnet, French ambassador to the United States, 1936–37; finance minister, 1937–38; minister of foreign affairs, 1938–39; justice minister, 1939–40; member of the National Council, 1941–42.

Prague, demanding more serious concessions to Henlein. The Czechs must be made to come to terms with the Germans. In particular, France must obstruct the immediate introduction of the nationality code into the Czech parliament. (The English are afraid that the code may tie the hands of the Czech government on the one hand, and fail to satisfy Henlein on the other.) If the Czechs persist, Henlein might raise the question of a plebiscite, to which the British government would not be able to object. Chamberlain has constantly to keep in mind that public opinion and the dominions are against Great Britain's meddling in Central European affairs. Phipps, the British ambassador in Paris, has put forward a plan of how to neutralize Czechoslovakia (it envisages the annulment of the pacts signed by Czechoslovakia with France and the USSR, in exchange for a joint guarantee of Czechoslovakia's independence by France, Germany and the USSR). He did so on his own initiative – the British government allegedly had nothing to do with it. Wiedemann[i] came to London to pave the way for Göring's visit and to assure the British government of Hitler's wish to bolster friendly relations with Britain. He also broached the question of arms limitation. But Halifax replied to Wiedemann that no foundations existed for successful Anglo-German negotiations without a peaceful resolution of the Czechoslovak issue. Wiedemann claimed that Germany posed no threat to Czechoslovakia. Bonnet just echoed Halifax.[59]

* * *

It transpires that the signing of an open Anglo-Italian agreement on 16 April coincided with a secret agreement by the parties of a financial nature. The Italians agreed, for a term of 66 years that could be extended to 99 years, to cede the right to the utilization of the water of Lake Tana in Abyssinia to an Anglo-Egyptian consortium. In return, the English agreed to make an advance payment to the Italians under this concession, covering a period of 530 years.[60] In other words, Chamberlain promised Mussolini a fairly large loan, albeit in covert form.

That's why, when the agreement of 16 April was made public, neither party uttered a word about its financial and economic aspects.

6 August

Masaryk had much of interest to tell me.

(1) The British démarche in Berlin on 21 May[61] was accompanied by moments of high drama. First, under strict instructions from London, Henderson (the British ambassador to Germany) pointed out to Ribbentrop

---

[i] Fritz Wiedemann, Hitler's adjutant, 1935–39.

that the concentration of German troops on the borders of Czechoslovakia might have grave consequences for the world; that Czechoslovakia would respond to any German aggression with armed resistance, which would entail military interference by France and the USSR; that in this case the war would assume European dimensions; and that Britain would not be able to stay out of the conflict. Let Hitler consider whether it would be in his interests to see the British Empire among Germany's enemies and, in the light of this prospect, assess his subsequent moves.

Henderson's words enraged Ribbentrop, who, with characteristic tactlessness, screamed: 'Your British Empire is an *empty shell*. It is rotten and decaying. It would have collapsed long ago were it not for Germany's support. What right have you to come here with your advice and to interfere in affairs which do not concern you?'

It was Henderson's turn to fly into a rage and, banging his fist on the table, he exclaimed that he would not tolerate language of this kind against his country. He then grabbed his hat and made for the door. Ribbentrop shouted after him: 'Britain is governed by Jews, ha-ha-ha! Isn't it so?'

Stunned, Henderson paused on the threshold, turned round and cried: 'We, at least, are governed by gentlemen!'

Slamming the door, the British ambassador left Ribbentrop's office.

(2) Upon receiving Henderson's report about his talk with the German minister for foreign affairs, Halifax felt somewhat embarrassed and approached Lothian with a request to inform Hitler privately that the British démarche on 21 May was not meant to insult him, that the British government believed in his peaceful intentions, and that Britain was not going to defend Czechoslovakia with arms in hand. Halifax was extremely shaken when Lothian not only categorically refused to carry out this mission, but also expressed his disapproval of the British government's capitulatory policy. Lothian, it transpires, has drastically altered his stance over the last few months and now thinks that the main menace to the British Empire resides in Berlin. His views, of course, have found an instant echo in the Astors' salon and, as Masaryk heard with his own ears, Lady Astor now declares her disappointment with 'those dictators' and has even become an opponent of Franco. Lady Cunard,[i] who until recently kept her salon open to Ribbentrop, is also unhappy with the Germans, telling all and sundry that they want to occupy the whole of Europe. Even Londonderry told Masaryk the other day that he no longer trusts Hitler, that he feels indignant at the treatment of Jews in Vienna, and that he will no longer visit Germany. Astonishing! Are the Germanophile sentiments in the higher echelons of the British bourgeoisie fading away? I find it difficult to believe.

---

[i] Maud Cunard, a society hostess and supporter of Wallis Simpson during the abdication crisis.

(3) During his unexpected visit to London, Wiedemann stayed at the house of Princess Stephanie Hohenlohe,[i] born Richter, a Viennese Jew by birth. Stephanie is intimately involved with Rothermere and is constantly wringing money from him. Wiedemann's residence in Stephanie's home has become common knowledge in Germany and has created a great scandal. This explains why Wiedemann's second visit to London failed to take place. The fact that Hitler chose his aide for such an important mission, rather than Ribbentrop or Dirksen[ii] (the German ambassador in London), is interpreted by Masaryk as a sign of Ribbentrop's decline.

By the way, yesterday Ewer revealed to me curious details of how he managed to find out about Wiedemann's visit to London and to be first to announce it in the press. The visit was kept under wraps, but rumours still spread about Wiedemann being in London. To find out if it was true, Ewer sent a reporter from the *Daily Herald* to the house of Princess Hohenlohe, expecting Wiedemann to be staying there. Ewer's envoy was lucky. Coming to the house, he saw a taxi approaching the entrance and Wiedemann jumping out of it. So, the fact of Wiedemann's presence in London was established and became immediately known to Ewer. But he still had to find out whom Wiedemann was seeing here. How was this to be done? Ewer's lad was a quick thinker. When Wiedemann entered Stephanie's house, he ran up to the taxi and asked the driver where he had picked up his passenger. The driver responded ingenuously: from *Eaton Place*. Ewer grabbed the *Directory* to see who was living in Eaton Place. It turned out that this was a 'ministerial quarter': Colville, Walter Elliot and others had their houses there. Ewer ran through the list of distinguished residents, trying to guess whom Wiedemann could have visited. It all seemed improbable. And then – eureka! Halifax's apartment was also located in Eaton Place. Wiedemann must have been on his way back from the foreign secretary! But how was this fact to be firmly established? Ewer had nearly despaired when it finally dawned on him. He called Halifax's apartment and asked for the butler. When the butler took the phone, Ewer said in a heavy German accent: 'Hello, butler. This is Wiedemann's secretary speaking. My boss was at your place and left behind his umbrella. Please send it back immediately.'

The unsuspecting butler responded: 'Oh, no, you must be mistaken. Mr Wiedemann hasn't left anything with us. He must have left his umbrella somewhere else.'

Hurrah! Now everything was clear, and the next day the *Daily Herald* carried front-page headlines breaking the sensational news about Wiedemann's

---

[i] Stephanie Julianne (von) Hohenlohe, German princess, who during the inter-war years took up residence in London and socialized with Britain's elites.
[ii] Herbert von Dirksen, German ambassador in Moscow, 1928–33, in Tokyo, 1933–38 and in London, 1938–39.

visit and his meeting with Halifax. It caused a tremendous scandal and Halifax had to acknowledge publicly that he had had a talk with Hitler's envoy.

(4) Heavens above! The zigzags and shifts of British policy! Masaryk also told me the following: ever since the Austrian Anschluss, Halifax has ceaselessly demanded that Czechoslovakia should grant maximum concessions to the Sudeten Germans, and that she should do so as soon as possible.

'You see,' Masaryk said in his sweeping, sarcastic manner, 'for three months I felt like a boy running along the rails before a locomotive, unable to get away since there are high walls on both sides of the track. Halifax kept summoning me to persuade me, advise, instruct, warn and even threaten... And what could I do? How could I resist a locomotive? Almost every week I flew to Prague and harassed Beneš, Hodža,[i] Krofta[ii] and whoever I could. By the end, they simply came to loathe me in Prague. As soon as I appeared in Krofta's office, I would hear: "What, another British demand?"'

Just imagine how shocked Masaryk must have been when Halifax invited him over in mid-July and began singing a quite different tune. Speaking on behalf of the British government, he expressed his concern that the talks between the Czechoslovak government and Henlein were moving too fast, given the very serious issues at hand; that there was no need to rush; and that it would indeed be a very good thing if the Czechs could drag out the talks till late autumn. At first Masaryk failed to understand a thing, but shortly afterwards the mystery cleared up. The British government had learned that Hitler was preparing an open assault on Czechoslovakia and that he intended to exploit the breakdown of talks between the Czechoslovak government and Henlein as a pretext. The British government was frightened. The gap between the demands made by the two sides was too great to hope for a compromise. Did that mean the talks would soon fall through? That Hitler would soon act? This danger had to be averted at all costs. Especially if was to fall in August and September, holiday season for the British ministers (their rest is not to be spoiled) and also the time of the German Nuremberg.[62] But how to do it? Then Chamberlain hit upon 'the brilliant idea' of dragging out the talks and buying time.

Hence Runciman's mission.[63] The mission was thought up by Chamberlain himself (or, as seems to me more probable, Horace Wilson). Neither Halifax, the Foreign Office, Corbin, Masaryk nor the Czechoslovak and French governments had the vaguest inkling about the PM's 'genius plan'. All rumours and claims to the contrary are false. Half an hour before Halifax's departure, together with the king, for Paris, Chamberlain told his foreign secretary, 'By the way, could you sound out the French government's attitude to this project...',

---

[i] Milan Hodža, prime minister of Czechoslovakia, 1935–38.
[ii] Kamil Krofta, foreign minister of Czechoslovakia, 1936–38.

and proceeded to outline his plan for Runciman's trip to Czechoslovakia. That is how foreign policy is carried out now in England!

As a matter of fact, Runciman's mission, which was readily supported by the French, met with a degree of resistance in Czechoslovakia. At first, Beneš's reaction was extremely negative, as he perceived Chamberlain's intentions as direct interference in the internal affairs of his country, but then the French started to work on the Czechoslovak government. Eventually, a compromise was reached: Runciman went there, but as a private person who has nothing to do with the government. Runciman is phenomenally lazy and thus ideally suited to 'playing for time'. But that will hardly be his only occupation. Runciman is just another link in the chain of British policy towards Czechoslovakia: to restrain not the aggressor but the victim of aggression.

(Hillman from *The International News Service* communicated to me the putatively reliable news that Runciman brought a plan approved by Chamberlain for the resolution of the Czechoslovak question. The first stage: to reach any compromise immediately and at any cost in order to avert the danger of a conflict between Czechoslovakia and Germany. The second stage: at some later juncture, when the situation had calmed down, the German and Czechoslovak governments should unite in guaranteeing the neutralization of the Sudetenland, and this agreement should be entered as a protocol in the future pact of the four.)

7 August

Beaverbrook phoned me to welcome me back to England and invited both of us to have dinner at his country house. There were about a dozen guests, mostly staff from his newspapers, and a beautiful young lady presented by the host as a Jewish refugee from Vienna.

During and after the dinner, Beaverbrook spoke to me on various topics. The most interesting points:

(1) Ribbentrop's star is waning. Hitler is mad at him. Why? Ribbentrop is said to have misinformed Hitler about the state of affairs in Britain and in Europe in general, and now this has come to light. The foreign minister is expected to resign soon. The Führer himself is going through one of his periods of 'trance': for almost a month he has not seen anyone, spoken to anyone or consulted anyone. He lives in solitude and 'converses with his soul'. Those around Hitler quiver and worry. They don't know what to expect.

(2) The bombing of British ships by Franco's planes has finally affected the soul of the English philistine. There has been a marked shift in public opinion in favour of the Spanish government. The latest successes of the Republicans on

the Ebro were met with great satisfaction in England. Beaverbrook expressed the hope that the Spanish government would hold out, at least till next spring.[64]

(3) As I left for the USSR, Beaverbrook was very well disposed towards Chamberlain's policy. Now I sensed something different. Beaverbrook accused Chamberlain of selling out Spain for his friendship with Mussolini. Moreover, he berated him viciously for his attitude towards agriculture (in one of his speeches Chamberlain expressed the opinion that it was more profitable to buy grain overseas than artificially stimulate the development of agriculture in England).

Someone told me that Beaverbrook has become very fond of the songs of the International Brigade in Spain. He has the music and lyrics of these songs and asks people to play them for him. So the *Daily Express* wants to support the Spanish government after all!

10 August

Resuming contact after my vacation, I visited Oliphant.[i] He's just the same. Hasn't changed a bit.

I asked him about the meaning of Runciman's mission. Oliphant gave me a caustic glance, pulled at his long red moustache and said with a tone of barely perceptible irony: 'What is Runciman doing in Prague? He is taking in the atmosphere.'

I couldn't help laughing. According to Oliphant, Runciman will spend four to six weeks in Czechoslovakia. He has no fixed plan, just a few ideas. Of course, regardless of all the denials, Runciman is in essence a representative of the British government. But, in the end, what's wrong with that? If Runciman succeeds in reconciling the Czechs with the Germans, then wonderful. If he fails, that's also no reason to cry: at least we'll have gained some time.

'Are you displeased? I can see by your face that you resent our policy in Czechoslovakia. Why?'

'Yes, we are dissatisfied with your policy,' I agreed, 'for you are constantly striving to restrain not the aggressor, but the victim of aggression. Runciman's mission serves the same end.'

Oliphant tried to argue but eventually realized that such an impression could indeed have been formed on the continent.[65]

In his turn, Oliphant asked me about the events in Manchuria. He was eager to know whether we provoked the conflict deliberately to render support to China. I had to disappoint him and later he himself admitted that, according

---

[i] Lancelot Oliphant, deputy undersecretary of state for foreign affairs, 1936–39.

to British sources as well, the aggressors in this case were the Japanese. To my question about the British response to the events in Manchuria, Oliphant replied: 'The Japanese have sown the wind, now they are reaping the whirlwind. They deserve it. This is the average British attitude to the conflict over Zhanggufeng.'[66]

Then Oliphant asked me if the conflict in Manchuria could grow into a big war.

'It entirely depends on the Japanese,' I answered. 'The USSR doesn't want a war, but we are determined to protect our rights and our territory.'

'So there is no question of mediation?' Oliphant went on.

'That's correct.'

True world brokers! Mad about mediation!

In the end, Oliphant complained about Craigie's difficult position in Tokyo. Over the last year he has effectively turned into a solicitor defending British interests in China (customs, trade, navigation, etc.). He's had few successes.

'The time will come,' Oliphant concluded, 'when we shall be able to get even with Japan, but the moment has not yet arrived.'

11 August

So, the hostilities in Manchuria have ceased. The armistice has been signed. Both sides remain where they are, i.e. we hold Zhanggufeng. Very good. The outcome is definitely in our favour.

The conflict was provoked by Japan, not us. The Japanese wanted to occupy Zhanggufeng, or at least to prevent us from fortifying it. They failed on both counts. We hold Zhanggufeng and we are bound by no promise to clear the mountain-top. The conflict was provoked by local militarists. The Japanese government was afraid it would spread and searched for an immediate cessation of hostilities. It came up against the will of the military and Shigemitsu.

Be that as it may, Japan has been taught a good lesson, as have the 'Western democracies'.

15 August

In London, nerves are on edge; there is even alarm. People are frightened by the large-scale German manoeuvres. What are they for?

There are two theories:

(1) Hitler is preparing to 'jump' on Czechoslovakia and, anticipating war to be inevitable, is mobilizing his country in order to have an initial advantage over France, whose army is still in a peace-time condition.

(2) Hitler is not planning to fight, but merely wants to scare Czechoslovakia, Britain and France so that he can swallow up Czechoslovakia all the more easily, without unleashing a major war.

I see no contradiction between the two alternatives: Hitler will first try scare tactics and, if that fails, he will start shooting.

The situation is aggravated by the fact that, according to information available in London, the Germans are sending a great number of camouflaged assault groups, rifles and machine-guns to the Sudetenland. Moreover, the eight regiments of the recently formed Sudeten Legion, based in Germany, are being readied for war.

Chamberlain has interrupted his vacation and hastily returned to London. The official cause of his return is nasal catarrh; the genuine one is the German manoeuvres.

16 August

Masaryk came over straight after a weekend spent at Eden's country house in Yorkshire. He told me many interesting things about Eden.

Eden is cheerful and bubbling with life. He thinks and reads a lot, studies economics, particularly the problem of unemployment, and prepares himself for the forthcoming battles. Chamberlain's foreign policy has failed. All Eden's forecasts have been borne out to the letter. The PM's Italian affair ended in a hangover. A Cabinet reshuffle can be expected in late autumn. Eden does not intend to attack the government's foreign policy as yet, but he won't vow to remain silent either. If crisis breaks out, he will have to speak. In the meantime he prefers to speak on various matters of domestic policy. He regards unemployment as the most important challenge.

Eden talked at length with Masaryk about Czechoslovakia. He tried to convince him to fight, not surrender. That is the only way to save Czechoslovakia. Prague's firm stance will force France to defend it. Britain will have no choice but to support France in the long run. Eden is most unhappy about the German manoeuvres. He does not rule out the possibility of war breaking out before the end of the year. The only way to avert war is to form a London–Paris–Moscow axis with the friendly backing of the United States. But is Chamberlain up to it? His position is to ignore the USSR, as if this gigantic power did not exist. This is an ostrich policy. A four-power pact? Such a pact is nonsensical without the USSR. But the prime minister fails to understand all this and does not wish to understand. Halifax, on the other hand, displays some capacity for evolution. Eden meets with him from time to time and eagerly chats to him. Halifax is gradually giving in. He is learning from life, from facts. He has already stopped believing that it is easy to reach an agreement with Germany. Now he thinks it very difficult, if it is even possible. Halifax looks to the future of Europe with great pessimism. He has even begun doubting the Spanish policy of the British government. There are visible signs of a rift between Halifax and Chamberlain...

Eden's views of the Spanish question are very interesting. He told Masaryk that when he was in the Cabinet he fought desperately against the pro-Franco tendencies in the government. His chief opponents were Lord Swinton, air minister (retired recently), and Kingsley Wood (former minister of health, who replaced Swinton as air minister). The latter was particularly poisonous: he is a close friend of Chamberlain and a diehard reactionary. Alas, Eden's struggle against Franco within the Cabinet was not always effective. Eden believes that even now Franco cannot regard his victory as decisive. The Republic can still win. Just give it arms. Returning to the PM's Italian policy, Eden said with a chuckle: 'Chamberlain devised his plans without taking Russia into account, and now he is being mercilessly punished.'

17 August

Bidding farewell to me before my vacation, Halifax asked me to visit him as soon as I got back from Moscow. I planned to do so immediately upon my return. However, the developments on the Manchurian border forced me to postpone my visit to the foreign secretary: the press might kick up a racket and interpret it as a request for mediation. Such rumours did begin to circulate on Fleet Street after my visit to Oliphant on 10 August – imagine what would have happened if I had gone to see Halifax! While I lingered and put the meeting off, the mountain itself came to Mahomet: today, Halifax invited me round.

The conversation began with vigorous questioning by Halifax about the events in Manchuria. Where and why were the battles waged? What was the essence of the Hunchun treaty?[67] Is it true that our OKDVA [Red Army's Special Far Eastern Troops] is an autarkical, self-sufficient organization which does not rely on supplies of food, ammunition, etc. from the central regions of the country? What are Japan's objectives in Manchuria? What can I tell him about the Japanese army? Then Halifax asked: can it be said that the conflict on the Manchurian border has been nullified? Or is there still a danger of its growing into a real war?

I replied that it all depends on Japan's conduct. We don't want war and seek to settle all conflicts with Japan peacefully, but Moscow is quite determined to protect our rights and territory against any aggression, regardless of the consequences. If the Japanese try to violate our state borders once again, they will meet with an even stronger rebuff than in this case. But we think that the

Japanese have been taught a good lesson. Our readiness to strike back is the best way to avert genuinely major conflicts.

I had expected my ideas to elicit corrections and qualifications on Halifax's part. How astonished I was when he pondered them for a minute before saying calmly: 'Perhaps you are right and it is the best way to avoid war.'

Then Halifax asked what I thought about the problem of Czechoslovakia. I took the opportunity to discuss the matter at length. I told Halifax that on my arrival in the USSR I noticed great disappointment in the policies of Britain and France. In the opinion of my Moscow friends, these policies demonstrate the weakness of 'Western democracies' and thereby encourage the aggressors. The governments pursuing such policies are making themselves responsible for unleashing a new world war.[68] Czechoslovakia is a fine illustration of the view I have just expressed. It seems to us that the course pursued by Britain and France on this issue represents an unhealthy distortion. Britain and France strive to restrain the victim of aggression rather than the aggressor. In Prague they raise their voices to such an extent that the Czechs feel offended, whereas in Berlin their voices are so soft that Hitler pays no heed to them. What's happened to impartiality and justice? It is quite understandable that the Soviet government cannot sympathize with policies of this kind. The Soviet government maintains that the fate of Czechoslovakia is in the hands of 'Western democracies'. If Britain and France are willing and able to take a firm stand with regard to Germany, Czechoslovakia will be saved and a lasting peace in Europe will be secured.

My words were hard, almost harsh, and I had expected Halifax to respond with a vigorous defence of British government policy. But I was mistaken once more. Halifax had no thought of remonstrating. His whole bearing and behaviour, his gestures and rare remarks showed quite clearly that a significant part, if not all, of what I had said met with his approval.

In turn, I asked Halifax what he thought about the state of affairs in Central Europe. Halifax replied that, in his opinion, the situation is very serious, that the German manoeuvres are causing alarm in England, that Runciman (Halifax has received 'two private letters' from him) is far from optimistic, and that in the final analysis everything depends on Hitler. The latter's behaviour is highly enigmatic and nobody knows for sure what course of action he might hit upon next. All this was hardly encouraging.

Then Halifax broached the Spanish question and wanted to know our opinion. I gave a resolute description of Moscow's attitude towards the notorious policy of 'non-intervention'. I pointed out that we had never been enthusiastic about it, but in its present-day form it arouses nothing but indignation. We stay in the Committee solely out of solidarity with Britain and France. However, the Soviet government will make no further concessions. Our decision to accept the British plan is our final word. All the more so as Mussolini is not evacuating the Italians.

'So, you think,' Halifax asked, 'that the policy of non-intervention is definitively bankrupt?'

'It certainly is.'

At this point, for the first time during our talk, Halifax started to defend British government policy. His arguments were not new, but he presented them with feeling. In particular, he referred to the worsening internal situation in Italy and concluded that the 'volunteers' could be evacuated in the foreseeable future. I gently ridiculed these naive hopes, but I felt sick at heart: it meant that nothing had changed in the British government's Spanish policy. No light at the end of the tunnel.

Lastly, I asked Halifax what he thought about the recent decision of the Oslo Group in Copenhagen. These countries essentially wish to abrogate Article 16 of the Covenant.[69] This question will surely be raised at the next session of the Assembly of the League of Nations – what position is the British government going to take?

Halifax was a bit embarrassed by my question, but he pulled himself together and replied that, although the question had not been definitively resolved, he thought that the only way out of the current situation would be to recognize the sanctions as optional.

I objected strongly to Halifax's capitulatory stance, but I was unable to convince him that I was right. So, yet another retreat before the aggressors!

20 August

Yesterday Agniya and I visited Lloyd George in his country house in Churt. The old man told us many interesting things.

In his opinion, the government is unpopular, but it may still hold on for a long time because the country has no alternative. The opposition is too weak in terms of quantity and, most importantly, quality. The voting masses will not entrust the helm of state to them at such a difficult time. L-G, meanwhile, concedes the possibility of new elections this very year if Chamberlain scores a major 'success' in foreign policy (e.g. the 'withdrawal of volunteers' from Spain or at least a temporary resolution of the Czechoslovak question). His electoral slogan would be: 'I saved the country from war!' It would appeal to many.

Speaking of political prospects, L-G expressed the opinion that Eden is obviously set on the premiership. Baldwin is guiding him. For the time being, Eden remains in the background. He makes few appearances and what speeches he gives are devoted exclusively to domestic politics (unemployment in particular). He tries to play the 'gentleman' towards the PM: I don't agree with your line, but I won't get in the way – show us what you're capable of. The old man thinks that it's clever of Eden to behave like that.

L-G told me a very amusing story about Beaverbrook. The other day Beaverbrook paid him an unexpected visit. During their talk, L-G uttered ironically: 'your friend Chamberlain'. Beaverbrook leapt out of his chair and exclaimed heatedly: 'My friend! My friend! Right!'

He said it in such a tone and with such an expression that L-G realized: something had come between Beaverbrook and the PM. But what? L-G could not tell me, but I heard the following story from another source. Beaverbrook had decided that it was time for him to occupy some lofty official post and had his eye on the position of minister for production (for the army, navy, air defence, etc.). Beaverbrook came to Chamberlain with his idea, but the latter snubbed him, without sparing his feelings. As a result, Beaverbrook joined the opposition.

I asked L-G what Britain and France were going to do if matters in Czechoslovakia took a turn for the worse. L-G's reply was categorical: 'Neither the British government nor the French government will take any genuinely effective action to defend Czechoslovakia against German aggression.'

My hunch is the same. L-G is afraid that developments in Central Europe may take the following course. At a certain moment, Henlein will claim that the negotiations have reached a deadlock, he will declare the Sudetenland independent and summon Hitler's assistance. However, the Germans won't attack Prague. In such a situation, the English and the French are sure not to do a thing for Czechoslovakia. The whole matter will be limited to protests on paper.

L-G was almost in raptures when he spoke about the firmness shown by the USSR in Manchuria.

'You have taught a good lesson not only to the Japanese, but also to the Western democracies,' he exclaimed.

Agniya took a few pictures of me and L-G outdoors.

24 August

Nicolson confirms that Eden is aiming for the post of prime minister, yet he may need some time to realize his ambition. He also confirms that Chamberlain is still strong ('he saved us from war!'), although so-called 'solid Conservative opinion' is turning against his foreign policy more and more. But it is considered unpatriotic to challenge the PM openly.

According to Nicolson, Eden is very uneasy about the following prospect: it is highly probable that in the next few months, especially if some kind of even temporary solution is found for the problem of Czechoslovakia, Hitler will propose 'reconciliation' between Britain and Germany on the basis of 'western security', an air pact, a willingness not to force the colonial issue, etc., but on condition that 'Germany's special political and economic interests in the Danube basin and in the BALKANS' are recognized. Eden believes that acceptance of such an offer would mean the end of the British Empire. And he is afraid that the proposal would be a great temptation not just to Chamberlain, but to broad swathes of the Tory Party. At present Eden prefers not to speak on foreign-policy matters, but if the moment that he fears arrives, he will strain every sinew to ensure that such offers are rejected.

Eden is still very popular. The following curiosity is evidence of the fact. Not long ago, Eden and his wife went to Glasgow to see the Empire Exhibition. He was there as an ordinary tourist, but as soon as word of his presence spread around the pavilions, a huge crowd gathered to greet him with a thunderous ovation. Women in particular were in raptures. All cried: 'When will you be back in office?'

Eden, according to Nicolson, said that before the signing of the Anglo-Italian pact, on 16 April, Mussolini assured Chamberlain that Franco would be in Barcelona no later than 1 May. Relying on this promise, the PM not only agreed to sign the pact but also ventured to make a promise to the opposition in parliament that the pact would not come into effect before the Italians were evacuated from Spain.

The prime minister's calendar was approximately as follows: April – Franco's victory, May – the withdrawal of at least part of the Italian troops from Spain, and June – ratification of the pact. He made a slight miscalculation: the Republicans proved much stronger than Mussolini and Chamberlain had thought, the USSR rendered timely assistance with arms and ammunition, and Franco is now farther from Barcelona than ever before. Eden concluded with a laugh: all his forecasts had come true to the letter, whereas Chamberlain suffers failures, mainly because he dislikes the USSR and tries to ignore it.

26 August

What an awful life!

Masaryk came to impart the latest news to me. It is distressing. The anti-Czechoslovak campaign in Germany is growing daily. Henlein rejects all concessions. For his own part, he would certainly agree to a compromise, but Hitler does not allow it. Runciman's mission is on the brink of collapse. The German 'manoeuvres' are taking their course and tension is mounting both in Germany and outside. What is the purpose of the manoeuvres, which have put more than a million people under arms? Is it a demonstration of force to scare Britain and France, or the preparation for real war? Two days ago, the German envoys to Bucharest and Belgrade made similar démarches on instructions from Berlin. Both declared to their respective foreign ministers that although Germany was striving for a peaceful resolution of the Sudeten problem, the German people's patience was wearing thin and, if Henlein's demands were not met quickly, the Germans would have to interfere and render assistance to their brothers on the other side of the border. Fabricius,[i] the envoy in Rumania, added that if France dared to interfere, the responsibility for the consequences would fall on France, not Germany. Clear enough, isn't it?!…

The only bright spot in this gloomy picture is today's communication from Moscow, relayed to Masaryk from Prague. The German ambassador, Schulenburg,[ii] made a statement to Comrade Litvinov, similar to those made in Bucharest and Belgrade, and then, stressing Germany's neutral conduct in the recent Japanese–Soviet conflict in Manchuria, expressed the hope that the USSR would reciprocate if Germany had to take the settlement of the Sudeten problem into its own hands. M.M., however, replied that the USSR would not be able to stand aside in this case, that the USSR would meet all its commitments under the Czechoslovak–Soviet pact, that France would also have to interfere, and that in the long run Britain would be drawn into the war, too. I confess that I have not been informed by Moscow of Schulenburg's talk with Litvinov as yet, but perhaps the Czechs, being the most interested party, learned about it earlier?

Masaryk asked if Litvinov could make a similar statement in public, before the press. It would be of great significance and would greatly reinforce France's resolve to come to the aid of Czechoslovakia. I promised to convey his request to Moscow.

I asked Masaryk: what was the stance of the British at present?

Masaryk waved his hand in despair and said: 'Well, you know the English! Just yesterday Halifax said to Cambon[iii] that although the British government deemed the situation in Central Europe to be very serious, it would hardly go beyond its declarations made on 24 March (Chamberlain's speech)[70] and on 21 May (Henderson's démarche in Berlin).' Simon is going to speak in the same vein tomorrow. Curses! What's the use of ambiguous gestures and slippery half-promises? Today, when one must bang one's fist on the table to avert the disaster?

Masaryk was livid, and at the same time you could sense the mortal agony in his mood. I felt ill at ease.

---

[i] Wilhelm Fabricius, German ambassador to Rumania, 1936–41.
[ii] Friedrich-Werner Graf von der Schulenburg, German ambassador to the USSR, 1934–41.
[iii] Roger Cambon, counsellor at the French embassy in London, Cambon stayed on as chargé d'affaires after the resignation of Ambassador Corbin on 26 June 1940, before himself resigning on 5 July 1940.

I recalled a motion picture I had recently seen (*Her Jungle Love*). It includes a ghastly scene. A semi-barbarian people on an island somewhere in the Pacific make a human sacrifice once a year to their god, the Crocodile. A huge crowd of negroes gathers on the shore of a lake half hidden by crags. A man tied hand and foot lies on the ground by the water's very edge. Dull beats of the tambourine summon the Crocodile. Finally a huge monster emerges from under the dark crags, its small eyes glittering carnivorously. It slowly approaches the shore, its gaze fixed on its victim, filling the air with roars from an open mouth that has long, sharp teeth… Closer and closer… The wretched victim, facing the inevitable onset of death, writhes in convulsions… His face is a picture of inhuman horror… Wild screams burst from his mouth… In vain! The terrible Crocodile is already at the edge of the lake. It breathes heavily and produces a joyous growl… Another instant and the doomed victim and cruel Crocodile vanish under the water…

What an awful life!

27 August

On his return from Germany several days ago, Schulenburg, the German ambassador in Moscow, started 'frightening' diplomatic circles in the USSR. The Sudeten problem is very acute. The military and right-wing nationalists in Czechoslovakia are unwilling to make any concessions to their German population. They are blocking Beneš's efforts to reach a compromise. If this dispute is not resolved satisfactorily in the nearest future, an armed confrontation will be inevitable. Runciman is the last hope for peace. Will he succeed? The purpose of Schulenburg's talks is clear: to exert moral pressure on Czechoslovakia, France and the USSR.

Schulenburg was out of luck with us at least. Two days ago, before his departure for a new trip abroad, he began a discussion about the European situation with M.M. He sighed and moaned over a probable war and tried to sound out our mood. M.M. replied with characteristic clarity: 'In the event of German aggression, Czechoslovakia will put up armed resistance, France will certainly come to its aid, and the USSR will carry out its obligations under the Czechoslovak–Soviet pact.'

Schulenburg was deeply *impressed* and upset.

28 August

Vansittart invited me over lunch. We were alone in his apartment. We spoke almost exclusively about international affairs.

V. attaches the utmost importance to Czechoslovakia, as it holds a key position. If it is lost, 'Mitteleuropa' will become an established fact, which would be dangerous to both Britain and the USSR. At this point I added and explained that 'Mitteleuropa' would be more dangerous to the west than the east. V. raised few objections.

'This is a critical moment,' he went on. 'We have to act and act quickly. France has already declared that, if need be, it will come to the aid of Czechoslovakia. In his speech of 27 August, Simon has expressed England's opinion also, albeit with insufficient clarity and certainty. But what about the USSR? The Soviet government continues to maintain silence. Neither London nor Paris knows anything about your intentions. This weakens the standing of the peace front.'

I replied that I was very surprised by V.'s rebukes. It is common knowledge that the USSR has always met its economic and political commitments. The same applies to the Soviet–Czechoslovak pact. But we don't see the need to get ahead of ourselves in this matter. After all, the observance of peace treaties is the business of Britain and France in the first place – they bear responsibility for them. Since the USSR does not bear such responsibility, it cannot act as champion of the Versailles order. Of course, our general notion of the fight against aggression disposes us to support Western powers in their efforts to preserve peace, but we cannot take the lead and the initiative. The complaint that London and Paris know nothing about our intentions is more than strange. Do London and Paris deem it necessary to inform us about their plans and actions in Central Europe? Why should we act differently?

V. started to object, pointing out that now is not the time to harbour past grudges. It is an exceptionally critical period. Next week in Nuremberg, Hitler may say something that could unleash a war. It is imperative to put strong pressure on him prior to Nuremberg.

I asked: what does the British government propose doing if the situation is so critical?

V. gave an evasive answer, adding only that important decisions are expected to be taken at a Cabinet meeting tomorrow morning...

I had not seen V. for almost four months and today I found him in a far more active, combative and decisive mood than in May. He looked like an invigorated man who had once again found his footing. The rumour that V. is regaining his strength seems to be true. All the better. His temporary *eclipse*, particularly after Eden's resignation, had an extremely harmful effect on British policy.

29 August

Vansittart invited me to a lunch *tête-à-tête*. We talked with complete frankness.

At first the host inquired about my impressions of the general mood in Moscow. I replied in the same vein as in my talk with Halifax on 17 August. Vansittart was apparently alarmed at the growing disappointment in Moscow over Anglo-French policy and our shift toward isolation. He began arguing passionately that we should not despair and that major processes were unfolding in the thick of British life and would soon produce concrete results. He concluded: 'For Britain and the USSR to pass to an isolationist policy means to serve Europe to Germany on a platter.'

I answered that I had to agree with his formula. Yet if, contrary to our will, we had to face this eventuality, Great Britain would bear the brunt of the responsibility. It was Great Britain that for the last three years had been delivering blow after blow to the League of Nations and collective security.

Vansittart was in raptures about the Spanish Republicans. What fighters! What resistance! He asked me anxiously how long Barcelona could hold out. When I assured him that it would hold out for a long time, he cheered up at once and exclaimed: 'That's very good! Very good!' Vansittart also expressed the opinion that the French government wouldn't be able to keep the border closed for long following Franco's response to the Committee's evacuation plan.[71]

'Perhaps the British government could ask Paris to open the border?' I asked ironically.

Vansittart got slightly embarrassed and once again referred to the internal processes unfolding in the thick of British life.

Vansittart's view of China is as follows: if Jiang Jieshi could hold out for another 12 months (even with the loss of Hankou), Japan would find itself in a critical position. I gained the firm impression from today's meeting that Vansittart has found his feet again. Good luck to you, old chap! But for how long?

30 August

The Cabinet held its meeting today, and the government took one really 'important decision': to do nothing. Nevile Henderson attended the meeting to shed light on some issues. Tomorrow he is returning to Berlin, but contrary to yesterday's rumours he is not carrying a 'personal letter' from Chamberlain to Hitler. He is not even meant to seek a meeting with Hitler or Ribbentrop.

So, 'wait and see'. England's favourite policy!

* * *

An acquaintance of mine passed Halifax's words to me: even though no decisions were taken at today's Cabinet meeting, it was ascertained after three hours of debate that all ministers except one (who could it be? Kingsley

Wood?) consider it impossible for Britain to stand aside if war breaks out over Czechoslovakia.

Very good. But what practical conclusions can be drawn from the above? There may be two possible conclusions. The first is to provide effective support to Czechoslovakia now, scare Hitler, and thus avert a war. The second is to exert 'friendly' pressure on Czechoslovakia to the extent that it would surrender entirely to Hitler without fighting, and thus avoid war. I have a strong suspicion that the Cabinet might draw the second conclusion.

[Unbeknownst to Maisky, Chamberlain had just come up with the most 'unconventional and daring' plan 'Z', which 'took Halifax's breath away': if the crisis in Czechoslovakia continued, he proposed to fly to Germany and meet Hitler to avert war.[72]

At just the same time, on the eve of his departure for Geneva on 2 September, Litvinov asked Payart,[i] the French chargé d'affaires in Moscow, to convey to Bonnet, the French foreign minister, that the Soviet Union stood steadfastly by its contractual commitments to Czechoslovakia in the event of an attack on her by Germany. He called for an immediate conference between Great Britain, France and the USSR to coincide with consultations between the representatives of the Soviet, French and Czech armed forces. He further urged that the crisis be placed on the agenda of the Assembly of the League of Nations. The same message was reiterated by Potemkin a couple of days later, but Payart concealed the essence of the message and conveyed the impression that the approach was not sincere, as Litvinov assumed Russia would not be called upon to fulfil its obligations.[73] Confronted by Litvinov in Geneva on 11 September, Bonnet was likewise devious: in an attempt to relieve the pressure on the French government, he suggested that the Soviet Union was seeking 'an escape clause to justify its abstention at a moment when France itself is already committed'. Briefed by Litvinov, Maisky followed his own counsel, disclosing to wide circles the content of the proposals made to Payart. Spilling the beans, though ostensibly aimed at countering the 'whispering campaign of the Cliveden Set',[74] would become Maisky's trademark in his desperate efforts to resuscitate 'collective security' and prevent the Soviet government from becoming reclusive.[75]]

31 August

Sir Horace Wilson visited me today and we had lunch together. The last time I saw him was in May, just before I left for my vacation. I was curious to see him now and feel his current political pulse.

This time Wilson's mood was completely different from how it had been four months ago. Then he had been full of energy, self-confidence and optimism. He believed that together with Chamberlain he was about to inscribe a new and glorious page into the book of European 'appeasement'. Now W. looked

---

[i] Jean Payart, French chargé d'affaires to Moscow, 1931–41.

somewhat gloomy, anxious and faded. And conversations with him assumed a despondent, almost panicky tone.

Indeed, the flowers have shed their petals and the fires died out...

W. avoided talking about Italy. Hitler clearly inspires panic in him. He expects little but trouble from him. The four-power pact has retreated to a hazy distance. Czechoslovakia is the key problem today. If it is lost, the creation of 'Mitteleuropa' will be inevitable. Wilson has thought through what I was telling him about 'Mitteleuropa' in May. He now fully agrees with me that such a formidable imperialist combination is more dangerous to Britain and France than to the USSR. But what is to be done? How to act? You could feel from W.'s mood that he was prepared to pay off Germany at any price.

'But if you are so well aware of the paramount importance of the Czechoslovak problem,' I remarked, 'why is Britain unwilling to take a clear and resolute stand? It could indeed restrain Hitler and prevent war.'

In reply, W. began to harp on the usual English tune. Public opinion 'won't understand' a war over Czechoslovakia, the dominions are against the interference of their mother country in European affairs, the British rearmament programme is far from being completed (the production of aeroplanes only began to accelerate last July). France, Britain's closest ally, is internally weak in financial, political and military terms (French aviation is not up to the mark, etc.). If only the conflict could be postponed for twelve or at least six months, Britain would feel stronger and everything would be different.

This familiar tune drove me out of my wits and I took the bull by the horns: 'Let us assume,' I began, 'that public opinion won't agree "to fight for Czechoslovakia", as you say, though in fact the matter concerns not so much Czechoslovakia as the future of the British Empire. Let us assume this is really so, but isn't it possible to put forward a slogan that is more comprehensible and closer to the ordinary Englishman, such as, "We will back France under any conditions"? You know perfectly well that such a slogan can be presented to the public in a very impressive and convincing way (W. nodded his head in consent). Why can't you do this? Why can't the British government, instead of just flowing with the stream of public opinion, take the lead and direct it? Isn't this within the British government's capabilities? (W. nodded once again.) Were England to tell the world that it would back France under any circumstances, i.e. also in the event of a war with Germany caused by the Czechoslovakia issue, then everything would be done and dusted! Hitler wouldn't risk "jumping" into Czechoslovakia.'

'But we have never gone so far in our promises to France,' Wilson exclaimed in virtual despair.

'Tell me,' I rejoined, 'if France were for any reason dragged into a dangerous war that posed a threat to her very existence, would Britain leave her to the mercy of fate?'

'Of course not!' W. replied firmly.

'Then why not say so openly? All the more so as such a declaration would assure not only the safety of Czechoslovakia, but also the preservation of peace in Europe.'

W. shrugged his shoulders and began thinking aloud. Of course, a resolute statement like that could, quite probably, forestall a war. But that means challenging Germany! What for? To avert a hypothetical danger that will not become pressing for a few more years? How can one take responsibility for this? Fine if Hitler becomes scared. But what if he doesn't? What if he charges on? It's terrifying! No, better to wait and see. Maybe things will sort themselves out one way or another.

This is how the chief adviser to the prime minister feels today.

W. told me many amusing things about Runciman's 'work' in Prague.

'You know Runciman,' he said with a smile, 'he is a nice man but phenomenally lazy, physically and intellectually. He never listens to the people he is talking to. His secretary takes notes of the conversation and gives him a report. It has been the same in Prague up to now. Deputies from various parties and groups came to Runciman and delivered long speeches (the continentals are fond of talking). Runciman would sit there like a sage – the pose that he manages so brilliantly – turning a deaf ear to his visitor's words. At the end of the speech, he would ask the man to give him a memo so that he could make a better evaluation of his wishes. Of course, no one refused. As a result, Runciman was inundated with reports, dissertations, etc., which he wouldn't read, but would pass on to Ashton-Gwatkin or someone else on the staff.'

Such is life in its prosaic, unvarnished state.

However, the initial stage of Runciman's 'work' is coming to an end. 'Absorbing the mood' cannot last forever. Now he has to sum things up and draw conclusions. So far Runciman has merely been putting pressure on the Czechs, urging them to make 'reasonable concessions' and trying to arrange negotiations between the two parties. The 'third base' recently offered by the Czechoslovak government is a major step forward, but it is still not enough. If Henlein rejects the 'third base', Runciman will probably try to work out his own plan and offer it to the parties concerned for consideration. His plan will certainly be more amenable to Henlein than the 'third base' (the country's division into 20–30 cantons, based on the Swiss pattern).

'Do you expect Runciman's plan to resolve the Sudeten problem?'

'If Hitler allows it. It wouldn't be too difficult to reach a compromise between the Czechoslovak government and Henlein if the latter could act on his own. But Hitler is shadowing him – that's the problem.'

'And what are you going to do if Runciman's mission eventually fails and Hitler decides on direct action?'

W. shrugged his shoulders and made a helpless gesture.

As he departed, W. asked me about the functioning of the Anglo-Soviet trade agreement, in the drawing up of which he had played a leading role on the British side. I replied that we were satisfied with the agreement and were not planning to raise the question of any revisions. W. greeted this piece of information as an author would accept a compliment on his work, and expressed the opinion that, despite the opposition of some British industrialist groups, it was not worth changing the agreement. Should the industrialists' complaints become too vociferous, specific ways could be found to satisfy their claims. I fully agreed with W.

'There is nothing more solid than the temporary!' I laughed, alluding to the fact that our agreement bears the name, 'Temporary Trade Agreement'.

'You are absolutely right,' rejoined W.

1 September

Yesterday Winston Churchill invited me for dinner. We met in the apartment of his son, Randolph.[76]

Churchill-*père* took the bull by the horns right away. The situation in Europe is exceptionally serious. War can break out any day now. Should Czechoslovakia resist German invasion with arms, France shall undoubtedly come to her aid. Even Britain will have to interfere, though not, perhaps, from the very beginning. The mood in the country has taken a sharply anti-German turn over the past ten days. A 180-degree shift may happen quite suddenly. Merely a couple of days before war was declared in 1914 – Churchill remembers it well – only four members of the entire Cabinet advocated the immediate support of France. On 3 August these four, including Churchill himself, were ready to resign. Then suddenly everything changed. When the earliest news arrived of German guns firing in Belgian territory, a genuine explosion occurred in the country. Yesterday's pacifists and isolationists were now the loudest in crying, 'War!' The same may happen now...

But the most important thing is to prevent war. How? Churchill has such a plan. At the critical moment, when the Prague talks eventually reach a dead end and Hitler starts rattling his sabre, Britain, France and the USSR should deliver a collective diplomatic note to Germany – it must be collective, Churchill emphasized – in protest against the threat of an attack on Czechoslovakia. The exact wording of the note is not so crucial, and could even be toned down if necessary. It is the very fact of a joint move by the three powers that is crucial. A démarche of this kind, which would undoubtedly receive the moral support of Roosevelt, would scare Hitler and lay the foundations for a London–Paris–Moscow axis. Only the existence of such an axis can save humanity from fresh carnage. Churchill discussed his plan today with Halifax, who asked him to set it down on paper. Churchill did so. He is awfully glad that Halifax did not reject his proposal outright and asked him to write it out. This offers hope. It opens up possibilities. All the more so as Vansittart is regaining power and will undoubtedly support Churchill.

What do I think of his plan? What would the Soviet government make of it?

I answered that it's not for me to speak for the Soviet government. As for me personally, I think the plan is a good one, but it has no chance of being implemented. I simply can't believe that Chamberlain would agree to join with the USSR in standing up to Germany. Our view of what needs to be done to oppose the aggressors was set out quite fully by Comrade Litvinov in an interview of 17 March, directly following the Anschluss of Austria (immediate consultations between peace-loving powers to determine the measures to be taken against aggression). What he said is still valid today. But would Britain and France agree to such consultations? I doubt it.

Then we spoke about many other subjects. I even conveyed to him some of what I had seen and heard during the Revolution and the Civil War. Churchill showed great interest. As for him, he hurled thunderbolts at Germany and finally announced that he had found a new slogan: 'Proletarians and freethinkers of all countries, unite against the fascist aggressors!'

2 September

Azcárate, who recently returned from Spain, told me that Barcelona, after Franco's response, regards the opening of the French border as its priority. About two days ago, Azcárate visited Vansittart, who treated him with the utmost attentiveness and asked him many questions about the situation at the front lines, at the rear, etc., and did not conceal that his sympathies lay with the Republicans. In conclusion, V. asked Azcárate to set out in a private letter his personal considerations concerning the Spanish question as it stands today. Azcárate has already done so. Later, he also visited Halifax, where he received a quite different reception. Outwardly, Halifax observed all the proprieties, but when he heard Azcárate declare that England and France, having actively insisted in July on the immediate adoption of the Committee's plan for Barcelona, were now morally obliged (following the plan's rejection by the insurgents) to free the Republic from the shackles of non-intervention, he could do nothing better than lecture the Spanish ambassador on the benefits of non-intervention. Further proof that Chamberlain will never give up this damned Committee!

* * *

A visit from Corbin, who has just returned from holidays in Évian-les-Bains. In Paris he met Daladier and Bonnet. The situation in Europe is critical, according to them, and Corbin wants to be in as close contact with me as possible. Simon's speech in Paris is considered insufficiently clear and firm. France itself will fulfil its obligations to Czechoslovakia.

Very good. Yet there was something I didn't quite like. I asked Corbin what the French government would consider to be an act of aggression sufficient to oblige it to stand up against Germany? Imagine the following scenario: Henlein declares the independence of the Sudetenland, he forms a provisional government, the latter invites Hitler to send his troops to Bohemia, and then German divisions enter the territory of Czechoslovakia. What would this be – an act of aggression in the terms of the Franco-Czech agreement or not?

Corbin was confused and began 'treading water'. He eventually announced that it was hard to discuss hypothetical situations in detail.

Corbin and I nearly had an argument over the Spanish question. He's all for doing nothing. No need to call the Committee together; instead, Hemming[i] should be sent to Burgos[77] for a *clarification* of Franco's reply.

* * *

Yesterday, Kennedy, the American ambassador, had a lengthy talk with Chamberlain. The prime minister asked him to approach Roosevelt and find out what would be the US interpretation of their neutrality law in the event of a European war. Can the democratic countries rely on getting weapons and money from America? Kennedy promised to contact the president.

It seems that even Chamberlain is losing hope of an easy agreement with the aggressors.

* * *

Plymouth invited me over and passed on to me the British government's memorandum, which boils down to sending Hemming to Burgos (probably to Barcelona as well) for talks with Franco (possibly with Negrín,[ii] too) about the Committee's future plans. Franco, you see, doesn't grasp all the subtleties of the plan, and Hemming will clarify them. Plymouth asked me what I thought about the memorandum, but I merely declared that I would convey its content to Moscow.

An outrageous idea! If the British do not want to do anything to implement the plan and stop the intervention, that's their business. But then let everyone

---

[i] Arthur Francis Hemming, secretary, Economic Advisory Council, 1930–39.
[ii] Juan Negrín, Spanish minister of finance, 1936–37; premier of the Republican government, 1937–39; following Franco's victory in 1939, he fled to Paris, where he tried to organize a government in exile; found refuge in England when the Germans invaded France in 1940. Maisky spent most weekends at his country house in Bovingdon.

see that they do not wish to do anything. Why assist them in their pretence through the appearance of activity and of efforts to implement the plan on the part of the Committee?

Azcárate was beside himself with rage when I showed him Plymouth's memorandum.

3 September

An exceptionally important conversation took place yesterday in Moscow between M.M. [Litvinov] and Payart, the French chargé d'affaires.

Payart came at Bonnet's behest with an official inquiry: how could the USSR come to the aid of Czechoslovakia in the event of German aggression, given the reluctance of Poland and Rumania to allow Soviet troops and aircraft to pass through their territory?

M.M. noted with typical acidity that in fact the USSR should pose a similar question to France, since France's obligations to Czechoslovakia are unconditional, while those of the USSR would come into force only once France implements hers.

Payart either could not or would not give a clear answer to M.M.'s question, but M.M. continued unperturbed.

Provided France fulfils its obligations, the USSR is also determined to carry out its obligations under the Soviet–Czech pact. Rumania's unwillingness to let Soviet troops pass through its territory could, most probably, be overcome, should the League of Nations recognize Germany as the aggressor and Czechoslovakia as the victim of aggression. To Payart's comment that the League of Nations could hardly be expected to reach a unanimous decision on this issue, M.M. noted that even if only a majority of League members voted for this formula (especially if they included the great powers), the moral effect of the decision would be immense and would exert the necessary influence on Rumania, which, he hoped, would itself vote together with the majority. In view of the sluggishness of the machinery of the League of Nations, M.M. would consider it desirable to start preparing for such a move as soon as possible, using provisions of Article 11 of the Covenant.[78]

M.M. further suggested that it was senseless to speak of the military defence of Czechoslovakia by three countries (France, the USSR and Czechoslovakia) without preliminary preparation of the respective military plans. This requires negotiations between the general staffs of the three armies. The USSR was prepared to take part in such negotiations.

The crucial thing at the moment, however, was to prevent the outbreak of war. In this regard, M.M. thinks that the proposals made by him in his interview of 17 March, right after the Anschluss of Austria, are now assuming particular significance. All peace-loving powers of the world are to get together to consult and seek measures against aggression. A joint declaration made by Great Britain, France and the USSR, with the guaranteed moral support of Roosevelt, could do more than anything else to prevent violent acts on the part of Hitler.

Unfortunately, we have very little time, and we must act quickly.

M.M. suggested that Aleksandrovsky[i] should make the contents of this talk known to Krofta.

So, our position in the Czechoslovak crisis has been set out with absolute clarity.[79] We are ready to offer armed assistance to Czechoslovakia, if the others are ready to fulfil their duty. Will they rise to the demands of this terribly serious historical moment? We'll see. But in any case, even if Czechoslovakia should still suffer ruin and Germany becomes the hegemonic power in Western Europe, responsibility for this cannot be laid at the door of the USSR.

4 September

I visited Churchill on his country estate.

A wonderful place! Eighty-four acres of land. A huge green hollow. On one hillock stands the host's two-storey stone house – large and tastefully presented. The terrace affords a breathtaking view of Kent's hilly landscape, all clothed in a truly English dark-blue haze. On the other hillock is a beautiful wood. There are ponds in three tiers down the slope of the hill, all with goldfish of varying size: in the upper pond they weigh up to 3–4 pounds, in the next they are somewhat smaller, while the really tiny ones are in the lowest pond at the bottom of the hollow. Churchill is fascinated by his big and small fish; he happily holds forth on their every detail and obviously considers them to be one of England's most characteristic attractions.

The estate also contains an artificial pool for swimming and bathing, a fine garden, an abundance of fruit (plums, peaches, etc.), a tennis-court, cages with blue birds that can speak in human voices, and a great deal else besides. Churchill took me to a pavilion-cum-studio with dozens of paintings – his own creations – hanging on the walls. I liked some of them very much. Finally he showed me his pride and joy: a small brick cottage, still under construction, which he was building with his own hands in his free time.

'I'm a bricklayer, you know,' Churchill said with a grin. 'I lay up to 500 bricks a day. Today I worked half the day and, look, I've put up a wall.'

He slapped the damp and unfinished brickwork with affection and pleasure.

---

[i] Sergei Sergeevich Aleksandrovsky, Soviet ambassador to Czechoslovakia, 1933–39; dismissed from the Foreign Ministry in 1939; associated with the partisan movement during the war, he was arrested in 1943, accused of espionage for Germany and shot. Later rehabilitated.

It's not a bad life for the leaders of the British bourgeoisie! There's plenty for them to protect in their capitalist system!

Churchill must have guessed my thoughts because, taking in his flourishing estate with one sweeping gesture, he said with a laugh: 'You can observe all this with an untroubled soul! My estate is not a product of man's exploitation by man: it was bought entirely on my literary royalties.'

Churchill's literary royalties must be pretty decent!

Then the three of us had tea – Churchill, his wife and I. On the table, apart from the tea, lay a whole battery of diverse alcoholic drinks. Why, could Churchill ever do without them? He drank a whisky-soda and offered me a Russian vodka from before the war. He has somehow managed to preserve this rarity. I expressed my sincere astonishment, but Churchill interrupted me: 'That's far from being all! In my cellar I have a bottle of wine from 1793! Not bad, eh? I'm keeping it for a very special, truly exceptional occasion.'

'Which exactly, may I ask you?'

Churchill grinned cunningly, paused, then suddenly declared: 'We'll drink this bottle together when Great Britain and Russia beat Hitler's Germany!'

I was almost dumbstruck. Churchill's hatred of Berlin really has gone beyond all limits!

His wife made a good impression on me. I'd barely known her before now. A lively, intelligent woman who was interested in politics and understood it. With a glance at his wife, Churchill genially remarked: 'I tell her everything. But she knows how to keep mum. She won't spill a secret.'

Randolph Churchill wasn't present. He's doing three months' training in the army.

[The diary conceals the main purpose of this second meeting with Churchill in two days: to disclose to him 'in detail' Payart's statement to Litvinov and to prod him to relay the information to Halifax. Maisky was acting on his own initiative. Churchill recalled how Maisky asked to come down to Chartwell to see him 'at once upon a matter of urgency'. He attached such significance to the meeting that a whole chapter – 'The Maisky Incident' – appeared in an early draft version of his memoirs and was later dropped, while the final account of the meeting was criticized by his literary agent for lacking colour.[80]]

5 September

Today I saw Corbin and was surprised to find out that he still knew nothing about Litvinov's conversation with Payart on 2 September. I had to relate it to him in its every detail. Strange! Such an important talk at such a crucial moment should, it seems, have been conveyed to the French ambassador in London right away and yet… Something is wrong here! Equally strange is the fact that, despite the talkative nature of the French, not a word has been written about the Moscow conversation in the French press. Bonnet, it seems, is trying to hush up the news...

Citrine is playing a disgraceful role at the Trades Union Congress conference currently taking place in Blackpool. The Czechoslovakia problem is being discussed there. A number of delegations have put forward a motion demanding that the British government take genuinely effective measures to protect Czechoslovakia from German aggression. The response? Citrine created a veritable scandal. He stated, *inter alia*, that he would be ready for a split in the workers' movement should such a resolution be adopted. Our trade-unionist heroes chickened out as usual, and a compromise resolution was adopted and published in newspapers. Chamberlain and Citrine – these are the two most sinister figures in England today.

[*The Times* leader of 7 September, which was appended to the diary, floated a *ballon d'essai* on behalf of the inner Cabinet. The fateful lines were written by the editor Geoffrey Dawson, whose close All Souls College connections with Halifax made him an '*ex officio* member of the Cabinet', with exclusive access to the proceedings of the crucial 30 August meeting. The article urged the Czechoslovak government to cede the Sudetenland, as 'the advantages to Czechoslovakia of becoming a homogeneous state might conceivably outweigh the obvious disadvantages of losing the Sudeten German districts of the borderland'.[81]]

7 September

I have seldom felt such indignation as I did reading the above citation.[82] So, the English already want more than 'the fourth plan' which was adopted by the Czechoslovak government the day before yesterday under the very greatest pressure from London and Paris. Hitler wrinkled his nose – so let's throw him yet another bone. Now *The Times* suggests a revision of the Czechoslovak borders! Of course, it's not just *The Times*; it's Chamberlain launching his *ballon d'essai*. And tomorrow Runciman will present it as his own 'plan'.

Vile betrayal not only of Czechoslovakia but of the whole European world! A stab in Czechoslovakia's back at the most critical moment in her history! That's English politics.

Why should Hitler put himself out? Why risk a war? The English and the French will do the dirty work for him.

* * *

Halifax sent over the main points of his upcoming speech in Geneva concerning the reform of the League of Nations. Very nice of him. But the things he's planning to come out with! I can hardly believe my eyes.

Halifax intends to make Article 16 optional and turn Article 19[83] into a 'reality'.

To come forward with such a proposal right now, when Czechoslovakia is in mortal danger – isn't this just another flagrant betrayal of Czechoslovakia and the European world as a whole?

The day will come when Britain will have to pay dearly for its present policies. But what good will that do Czechoslovakia and Europe?

Capitalism is obviously moving ever further towards its dead end. On days like this one feels especially acutely that only communism can lead mankind out of the bloody bog of the present.

8 September

An unexpected invitation to see Halifax.[84] It turned out that he wanted to ask me to convey his apologies to Litvinov for not being able to meet him in Geneva, on account of the European crisis. He is really very sorry, he was greatly looking forward to meeting and speaking to M.M., but sadly there is nothing to be done. The British delegation to the League will be headed by Lord De La Warr.

Then Halifax turned to current affairs, expressing his concern that Henlein might reject the fourth plan. I noted with some irritation that the editorial in yesterday's *Times* would surely contribute to Henlein's decision. Halifax suddenly became animated, even turned a little pink in the face, and said that the editorial was a regrettable fact, that it did not express the opinion of the British government and that both Prague and Berlin had already been informed about this. 'Unfortunately,' Halifax added somewhat naively, 'nobody believes our denials.'

I made no comment, but I didn't believe them either. And I was right. Because when I asked Halifax whether the British government considered the fourth plan to be Czechoslovakia's absolute limit, the foreign secretary seemed confused and merely said that it represented a 'big step forward'. To clarify this position definitively, I put to him the following question: does the British government consider further concessions on the part of Czechoslovakia to be possible? Halifax replied that the British government was first and foremost interested in the peaceful resolution of the dispute. The rest was of secondary importance. 'But aren't you interested in the price?' I asked again. Halifax shrugged his shoulders and said that the price was determined by the circumstances. 'And what will you do if Henlein rejects the "fourth plan" and refuses to enter any negotiations with the Czechs?' I inquired. Halifax replied: 'In this case all the resources available to humanity should be used to persuade the two sides to resume negotiations.' The position became clear to me. Lloyd George was right when he impressed on me on 19 August that the British government would take no effective steps to protect Czechoslovakia. Yesterday's editorial in *The Times* was nothing but a *ballon d'essai*. Perhaps Halifax himself had a hand in it.

In conclusion, Halifax enquired about our position on the question of Central Europe. He had heard something about Litvinov's talk with Payart on 2 September (evidently from Chilston) and wanted to get additional information from me. I conveyed the contents of the talk to him in detail. Halifax heard me out, thought a little and declared that he now understood the Soviet point of view very well. But he disclosed nothing of his own attitude towards it.

                                        *   *   *

Tomorrow morning, Agniya and I are going to drive to Geneva to attend the session of the League of Nations.

[Appeasement, as Paul Kennedy has convincingly argued, was entrenched in the 'pragmatic, conciliatory and reasonable' British approach to conflict resolution. This assumed that, unless national interests were 'deleteriously affected', the peaceful settlement of disputes was preferable to war.[85] British historiography of the Munich Agreement has undergone radical metamorphosis: from the 'Guilty Men' verdict of contemporaries (pinning all the blame on Chamberlain for his naivety, ignorance and arrogance in the pursuit of foreign policy), through the revisionism of the 1970s (which convincingly introduced the constraints on Chamberlain – economics, pacifist public opinion, the poor state of British armaments, etc.).[86] Conspicuous by its almost total absence is an analysis of the Soviet Union's role in Munich – a role which, by and large, sustains the 'counter-revisionist' view that, although Britain's position was fraught with exceptional difficulty, 'the way in which issues were perceived and tackled reflected *a priori* principles and choices'.[87] Pessimistic assessments were selected to justify a preconceived policy. Taking into account the constraints, recent research has nonetheless reverted to and reinforced earlier appraisal that Chamberlain's judgement was clouded by personal prejudices, obstinacy, self-righteousness and dictatorial proclivity. The resurgence of a viable Soviet alternative in the Munich crisis is clearly validated by the diary and the recent stream of thoroughly documented works by Carley and others. The extensive archival sources and subtle arguments expose the impact of embedded cultural anti-communism on the failure to erect an effective all-embracing anti-Hitler alliance in 1938–39.[88]]

11 September

Here we are, in Geneva at last.

We left London on 9 September at about nine in the morning. At noon, we boarded the ferry in Dover. The sea was *rough*, but Agniya bore it bravely. In Calais, against our expectations, we had a rather unpalatable lunch in the restaurant at the railway station. We were in Paris by 11 p.m., with little to report

38. The warrior's respite on the way to Geneva.

about the journey. What surprised me was the emptiness of the French roads: very few cars, and we rarely had to overtake. Quite different from England.

The embassy was empty too. Surits and his family have already left for Geneva. Girshfeld[i] is on leave in the USSR and will stay to work in Moscow. A number of the embassy staff are away, either on holiday or on business. The only person to be found wandering around the enormous building is Biryukov,[ii] the first secretary, temporarily acting as chargé d'affaires, or, as he himself puts it, Mr Unfairly Charged. He really does have far too much on his plate. We spent the night in the Blue Room, while our driver stayed in a neighbouring hotel. On the morning of the 10th we walked around the city and did some shopping. At about three o'clock, having lunched in a restaurant we found on our way, we set off. We wanted to get to Dijon before nightfall, but the evening was dark and wet, so we decided to make a stop in Avalon. We put up in a small and primitive hotel on the way to this little town, where they served us a magnificent supper. I am fairly indifferent to the qualities of food, but on this occasion even my taste buds were astonished by the exceptional quality of the *poulard* which we were served. At eleven in the morning we were back on the road. Lunch in Dijon, the capital of Burgundy. Excellent yet again. The French are simply geniuses in matters culinary. We had a fantastic Burgundy with our meal. Whether

---

[i] E.V. Girshfeld, first secretary at the Soviet Union's Paris embassy, then Litvinov's general secretary at Narkomindel.
[ii] I. Biryukov, first secretary to the Soviet embassy in France, 1940–41.

because of the wine or for some other reason, I left my Baedeker to France in the restaurant. Before lunch, Agniya and I had taken a lengthy stroll around Dijon. A nice old town, French to its core. We were greatly surprised to find, in a dark corner behind a church, 'Rue Babeuf'.[89] Agniya photographed the corner bearing the sign. In a good mood (improved further by the fine weather) and with a pleasant weight in our stomachs, we left Dijon at about three and, after crossing the Jura, reached Geneva at about seven that evening.

We found the *Richmond* empty. It was Sunday and M.M., accompanied by the whole delegation and the 'undersecretary' Sokolin,[i] had set off in the morning, as always, for an outing to France. They were expected to return late in the evening. After settling in the hotel, Agniya and I quickly toured the town. We dined at the Bavaria.

PS 1 October

How funny! On the way back from Geneva, Agniya had lunch in the same restaurant in Dijon where we'd eaten on the way down, and they returned the Baedeker I'd lost there.

12 September

The three-day trip from London to Geneva was a true rest for me. Today working life resumed.

I attended the opening of the League's Assembly, but that is hardly important. The thoughts of Assembly members are now turned in a quite different direction. A dark and terrifying cloud hovers in the political atmosphere. In the corridors of the League everyone was asking one another: 'What will Hitler say, do you think?'

That's all that matters.

At tea-time I went to a reception organized by the Women's International League for Peace. I made the acquaintance of delegates from all over the world. Every lady asked me one and the same question: 'What do you think Hitler will say?'

The delegate from Czechoslovakia, after a firm handshake, looked at me like a wounded doe and almost pleaded: 'You're our only hope... Please, don't betray us...'

We had dinner at Café Landolt, so well known to me from my distant years in emigration.[90] Hitler was yelling from the loudspeaker, making his speech in Nuremberg. But Agniya and I were sitting quite far away and I could not make

---

[i] Vladimir Aleksandrovich Sokolin, counsellor at the Soviet embassy in Paris, 1936–39.

everything out. One thing was clear though: Hitler has made up his mind to stake his all.

Back in the hotel I learned the latest news from London. Yesterday Attlee saw Chamberlain and insisted that Britain, France and the USSR issue a joint declaration concerning assistance to Czechoslovakia in the event of German aggression, but Chamberlain found such a move 'inexpedient'. Eden visited Halifax, and Churchill met Chamberlain: they both demanded that the British government make a clear declaration of its position, but without success. Masaryk handed a note to the Foreign Office, informing the British government that Czechoslovakia could not agree to a plebiscite in the Sudetenland, a subject of talks in recent days both inside and outside Germany. The Cabinet met, discussed and decided: they would do nothing until they had heard the speech of the 'Führer'.

13 September

Taking advantage of the fact that the commissions had not yet started working in earnest, Agniya and I drove out to Montreux. The weather smiled on us: the Lake of Geneva shone in its dazzling way, but a light haze, unfortunately, covered the French shore. We visited the Castle of Chillon. I'd been there during the emigration years and it had struck me as gloomy, menacing and majestic – perhaps I was under the fresh influence of the famous poem by Byron,[91] whom I'd been so fond of in my childhood and youth. The castle now seemed much less impressive, something between a museum and a hotel made out to look old. The romanticism had gone, leaving only the prose of life. I even felt bored. Or maybe it's the years that have taken their toll? After all, 30 years have passed since I first set foot in the castle of Chillon – and what 30 years they've been!

On our way back from Montreux we stopped to have lunch in Ouchy (Lausanne). I found the Hotel d'Angleterre where Byron, so impressed by his visit to the Castle of Chillon, wrote his famous poem in 1816. A metal plate on the wall of the hotel recalls this fact...

* * *

The debate on the League of Nations began today in the Assembly. Article 16 was the main issue. Sandler[i] (the Swede) and Patijn[ii] (the Dutchman) made speeches. They advocate complete capitulation: Article 16 must be made optional. The Dutchman, an ancient and sickly creature who can hardly move on his legs, was particularly insistent. Is the struggle against aggression really a

---

[i] Rikard Sandler, Social Democrat prime minister of Sweden, 1925–26; foreign minister, 1932–39.
[ii] Jacob Adriaan Nicolaas Patijn, Dutch foreign minister, 1937–39.

fit concern for such a man?! On hearing these speakers, Petrescu-Comnen,[i] the Rumanian foreign minister, exclaimed in my presence: 'But this means the end of the League of Nations!'

Comnen seemed outraged. Maybe because I was standing two feet away from him? It would be interesting to hear what he tells the French and the British.

* * *

The situation is becoming increasingly acute. After Hitler's speech yesterday, Henlein announced today that the Karlsbad Programme was already obsolete and that a plebiscite was now the order of the day. Disturbances and provocations have begun in the Sudetenland. The tension grows with every passing hour. Attlee has again been to see Chamberlain and said that a plebiscite in the present situation would mean a partition of Czechoslovakia, which is why the British workers' movement was against it. The PM replied that he, too, was against a plebiscite, but he did so in such a manner that Attlee departed full of suspicion…

I have the impression that the world is sliding uncontrollably towards a new world war… The only uncertainty is when it will begin.

14 September

The day was spent in boring committees. I sat, kept silent and listened. M.M. thinks there is no sense for us to be active at the moment in these committees, except perhaps one or two. There was no Assembly today. We spent the evening in the Lignon Castle. M.M., Surits, Shtein and E.N. played bridge, while I interviewed the *sous-secretaire* on various issues surrounding the League of Nations.

Late in the evening K[agan] telephoned from London with the latest sensation: it has been decided at today's Cabinet meeting that Chamberlain will fly out tomorrow for a meeting with Hitler in Berchtesgaden.[92]

Incredible! The leader of the British Empire goes to Canossa cap in hand to the German 'Führer'. This is how low the British bourgeoisie have fallen!

[Butler, whose support for appeasement and the Munich Agreement exceeded even that of Chamberlain, was the first to insist in his memoirs that he 'was left in no doubt that the Russians did not mean business' and that 'Litvinov had been deliberately evasive and vague'.[93] However, the diary and corroborative material sustain the argument that Stalin's caution and Litvinov's vague public statements reflected a Soviet dilemma. Any public statement might be provocative towards Germany and have unimagined repercussions if the Anglo-German negotiations did indeed reach a positive conclusion,

---

[i] Nicolae Petrescu-Comnen, Rumanian foreign minister, 1938–39.

as was anticipated. While unilateral assistance was therefore not on the cards, the Soviet Union's commitment to its contractual obligations, provided the French first fulfilled their obligation, remained unshaken. Such an outlook, a precursor to the following year's negotiations on a triple alliance, drew on the lasting and clear lesson of the failure to turn the 1934 agreement with France into a full-blown military alliance and the dismal experience of acting alone in Spain while appeasement of Germany was in full swing. It was one thing fighting the Germans and Italians on the edges of Europe, but quite another having to face Germany alone on the Soviet border, with an insouciant Western Europe looking on. What Litvinov vainly sought in Geneva, therefore, was the inception of military talks in London and Paris (which might have deterred Hitler), rather than negotiations with Beneš at the Castle in Prague.[94]

The session of the morally bankrupt League, which practically ignored the Czech crisis, coincided with Chamberlain's negotiations with Hitler leading to the Munich Conference. It turned out to be Litvinov's swan song. The British delegation was reduced to De Le Warr, the lord privy seal, and Richard Butler, then holding a junior position at the Foreign Office. Halifax preferred to remain in London, where the real drama was unfolding. The French delegation was likewise low key. Bonnet made a brief appearance on 11 September, but his meeting with Litvinov lasted only 'for a moment and did not go beyond generalities'.[95] Kollontay, who happened to be on the same train to Geneva as Bonnet, was startled by the melancholic mood surrounding him. The following morning she bumped into Litvinov as he emerged from his meeting with Bonnet, 'waving his hand impatiently and with obvious irritation: "Results? None ... The French don't intend to fulfil their obligations to Czechoslovakia. When it comes to our Soviet proposal, Bonnet dodges and prevaricates, claiming he needs to consult London first. A delaying tactic, in other words. And right now every hour counts."'[96]

The French were visibly surprised and embarrassed by the unexpectedly 'firm position' of the Soviet Union. They played down the significance of the shift, mounting a rather successful disinformation campaign (which has subsequently misled many historians). The British dominions, for instance, were convinced that the Soviet commitment was a mere feint and was aimed at impressing the League, ensnaring the West and, above all, at benefiting from a capitalist war.[97] Litvinov could only give vent to his frustration in a fierce speech to the Assembly that criticized Anglo-French attempts to water down the Covenant of the League and make collective action voluntary. While reiterating the Soviet proposals made to Payart, Bonnet and Beneš and reasserting Soviet loyalty to the League, Litvinov ended with an ominous warning that Anglo-French 'capitulation' was bound to have 'incalculable and disastrous consequences'.[98]

Maisky complained to Lloyd George that throughout the crisis the British steered clear of the Russians in both London and Moscow, whereas the meetings in Geneva were confined to an 'exchange of the latest bits of news' and the British delegation 'particularly stressed ... the informal character of the conversations'. Litvinov himself, as Boothby observed in Geneva, had 'burst into bitter complaint' about the lack of consultations when the two met.[99] At the meeting with the British delegation on 23 September, Litvinov 'reiterated the firm resolve of the Soviet government to fulfil all her obligations under the Soviet–Czech Pact ... and in turn suggested certain measures which in his opinion it would be necessary to take forthwith'. However, his demand for an emergency meeting of the powers involved, either in Paris or London, to coordinate

39. A day off with Agniya.

military plans against the backdrop of the collapse of the Godesberg talks, was dismissed out of hand by the Foreign Office as being 'of little use', since it was bound to 'certainly provoke Germany'. The meeting, indeed, ended with an ominous British reservation that the questions raised related only 'to the unhappy eventualities that might occur' if the deadlock in the negotiations with Hitler at Godesberg was not resolved.[100]]

15 September

In the morning Agniya and I drove to Lac de Lucerne and on the way back stopped in Lausanne. Lunched again at Hotel d'Angleterre. Then we had a good long stroll around town. I found the street and the house where I lived in the summer of 1908, right after my emigration from Tobolsk province. The house is 17, Avenue Eduard Dapples. Agniya photographed it. I stood opposite the familiar building and thousands of reminiscences crowded in my mind. How much water has flowed under the bridge since then! How the times have changed! How I, too, have changed! 1908 and 1938 – they are like two quite separate worlds, divided by centuries.

* * *

Chamberlain's visit to Hitler is the focus of attention.[101]

Attlee and Greenwood met Chamberlain and he explained to them the purpose of the trip. It's necessary, don't you see, to find out what Hitler wants on the Sudeten issue, and at the same time to inform him of 'England's intentions'. The PM has no concrete proposals. He will take no binding decisions in Berchtesgaden. Typical English tricks. Smells fishy.

Kagan informs me that London is greatly alarmed, and that the British government is gradually mobilizing its army and navy. Live ammunition has even been loaded onto the vessels on the open sea.

16 September

M.M. [Litvinov] told me about his meetings with Bonnet in Geneva (11 September) and Herriot (somewhat later).

Bonnet was, as always, mischievous and evasive. He wanted to know our position concerning Czechoslovakia. M.M. repeated what he had said to Payart in Moscow on 2 September, but much more decisively. I am not sure what impression it made on Bonnet. Probably not a very good one. Bonnet is doing whatever he can to avoid fulfilling the obligations under the 1935 French–Czech agreement. Our resolute stance spoils his plans. He may well try to muddy the issue…

M.M.'s conversation with Herriot bore a quite tragic character. Its most interesting and important aspect was Herriot's candid admission that France is no longer capable of playing the role of a truly great power: its population is falling, its finances are in complete disarray, internal strife has reached a state of extreme tension, aviation is neglected, the ties in Central and Eastern Europe have been severely damaged and are nominal at best. All this is very sad, but sadly it's a fact. The time will soon come when France will be forced to draw the appropriate conclusions from its situation.

This is what the Third Republic has come to!

40. Maisky and Kollontay in the countryside near Geneva, mourning the fate of their colleagues.

* * *

So, Chamberlain is in Berchtesgaden today. According to the press, he will be Hitler's guest for one or two days at least.

The Times, of course, is quick to put a fly in the ointment. Its Riga correspondent insinuates that the intentions of the USSR are unclear and that Czechoslovakia can hardly expect any real help from it. An ulterior motive must exist. Yesterday, Mander said at the meeting of the executive committee of the League of Nations Society that, according to his information, Britain and France would exert strong pressure on Czechoslovakia: she should abrogate her pact with the USSR, which in fact is more a *liability than* [an] *asset*. It seems that this process has already begun: today, the Czechoslovak government addressed the Soviet government with an official request – can it count on the local fulfilment of the Soviet–Czechoslovak pact by us?

The National Labour Council in London has elected a delegation of Morrison, Citrine and Dalton for talks with the government.

18 September

Sunday. The whole delegation headed by M.M. [Litvinov] went to the French Savoy. We ate well, had a walk, talked and were home in the evening.

Events keep developing at breakneck speed. Contrary to all expectations, Chamberlain had only one meeting with Hitler, on 16 September, and then decided on an immediate return to London. Yesterday, on the 17th, he landed in Croydon. What happened? Two possibilities: either Hitler demanded a price that even Chamberlain could not pay (i.e. the meeting in Berchtesgaden ended in failure), or Hitler made Chamberlain some proposals which the latter considers acceptable but does not wish to agree to at his own risk, so he has returned to consult the Cabinet (i.e. the meeting was a success from the PM's point of view). Knowing Chamberlain, I favour the second hypothesis. This is confirmed by the fact that upon his return the PM immediately invited Daladier and Bonnet to come to London for an urgent conference. This conference began today.

Late in the evening, the first news arrived from London. Chamberlain has put forward a proposal at the meeting to cede to Germany the Sudetenland areas where the German population exceeded 50%, to provide guarantees for the rest of the Czechoslovak territory on the part of the four Western powers, and to establish a canton system in the spirit of Beneš's 'fourth plan' for the Germans residing in Czechoslovakia. This is all quite probable. But will the French really swallow the pill? The meetings between the English and French ministers are still ongoing.

Kagan informs us that he has been visited, at Layton's request, by a very worried Cummings. A member of the Cabinet told Layton that even if France came out to protect Czechoslovakia with arms in hand, the USSR would do nothing more than raise the question of German aggression in the League of Nations. Is this true? Kagan, of course, ridiculed and refuted this canard. But where has it flown in from?

Chamberlain received a Labour deputation, which kept insisting on a tripartite declaration by Britain, France and the USSR. The premier again rejected the proposal. Chamberlain complained about the difficulty of the situation, insufficient British armaments, the weakness of the French air force, and the unclear position of the USSR. Once again, suspicion of our intentions – where does this come from? At the same time, the PM revealed what Hitler said to him in Berchtesgaden: 'I can crush Czechoslovakia in the space of one week.' One thing is clear: Chamberlain is feverishly seeking justifications for his defeatist line and, of course, he finds them. But what do we have to do with it?

News has arrived from Rome that the British chargé d'affaires saw Ciano[i] and, acting on behalf of the prime minister, conveyed the latter's wish to bring the Anglo-Italian agreement into effect as soon as possible in view of the sharp deterioration in the general situation in Europe.

Yes, Chamberlain is demonstrating great activity.

19 September

What a dead place Geneva is today! The Assembly, the commissions, the meetings, the protocols, lunches and dinners, the political gossiping in the corridors… Who needs all this right now? And does it really matter? Events of the greatest importance are unfolding in the world, events on which the future of Europe and perhaps all humanity depends in the most literal and immediate sense; yet here, in bourgeois, obtuse, dull Geneva we wander like sleepy flies along the corridors of the League of Nations and our hotels, waiting for news from that big and real (even if vile and repulsive) life, which tears along like a violent stream somewhere beyond these beautiful, hidebound mountains.[102] What a pity that I'm here, in Geneva, and not in London! Surits is dying to go to Paris and I quite understand him. But M.M. keeps him here and, from the point of view of political tactics, he may be right. I'm calmer than Surits and I stay silent, but I'm fed up to the back teeth with Geneva and I'm simply desperate to be in London. Well, we'll just have to stick it out…

---

[i] Gian Galeazzo Ciano, Italian fascist chief of the press bureau, 1933; undersecretary of state for press and propaganda, 1934–35; Italian foreign minister and member of the fascist Supreme Council, 1936–43; Italian ambassador to the Vatican, 1943.

News from London that the meetings of the English and French ministers have produced a so-called three-point 'Anglo-French plan' to settle the Sudeten problem: (1) areas with a German population of more than 50% go over to Germany; (2) areas with a smaller German population remain within Czechoslovakia but are granted cantonal self-government; (3) the borders of the new Czechoslovakia are guaranteed by the 'big four'. There are some other, more obscure details about a plebiscite and other matters, but this is less important now. The Anglo-French plan was passed on to Czechoslovakia with a request for a very urgent reply (Hitler said to Chamberlain in Berchtesgaden that the Sudeten problem must be resolved before 1 October). Having done this excellent deed, Daladier and Bonnet returned to Paris, where the French Cabinet approved the plan worked out in London after a single session lasting one and a half hours! Where are the opponents of capitulation gone, such as Mandel[i] or Reynaud?[ii]

It is rumoured that Osouský,[iii] the Czechoslovak envoy in Paris, was in tears after his meeting with Bonnet. In London, Masaryk was cursing obscenely (he knows Russian all too well!) after receiving the text of the plan from Halifax.

The Labour delegation had a stormy talk with Chamberlain. It demanded that Hitler be met with a decisive rebuff, declaring: 'Now or never!' The PM agreed that, sooner or later, a fight with Germany was inevitable, but he deemed the present moment unsuitable. Then he set about frightening the Labourites. Hitler had allegedly told him quite bluntly: 'I'm 49 and I've set myself the goal of uniting all Germans under the banner of the Reich in my lifetime. Plebiscite or no plebiscite, it's all the same to me, but the Sudeten Germans must become part of Germany. For this I'm even ready to risk a new world war.' This wasn't enough for the PM, who decided to play the pauper: Britain is poorly armed, France has a weak air force (only 21 top-class flying machines to rival the best German ones, and about 500 planes of acceptable quality), while Russia's intentions remain unknown. There is nothing left to do but give ground.

Dalton (one of the three members of the delegation) interrupted Chamberlain, saying that, according to information in his possession, the Soviet position was quite clear, while the readiness of the Soviet government to fulfil its obligations under the Soviet–Czechoslovak pact was beyond any doubt.

Chamberlain was slightly embarrassed and said that he had received his information on the Soviet position from Bonnet, who recently met Litvinov

---

[i] Georges Mandel, French journalist and politician; minister of colonies, 1938–40; minister of the interior, May–June 1940.
[ii] Paul Reynaud, French minister of justice, 1938; minister of finance, 1938–40 and 1948; prime minister, 1940.
[iii] Štefan Osouský, Czechoslovak ambassador to France, 1920–39; minister in the émigré government in Great Britain, 1940–42.

in Geneva. It was also from him that he learned about the condition of French aviation.

Bonnet! So he's the source of all the fabrications about the USSR's position! A despicable individual.

After their talk with Chamberlain, the Labour delegation convened the National Council of Labour, which was in session the whole day. They decided to invite representatives of the French socialists to London for a joint meeting. They will defend the platform agreed at Blackpool.

Churchill, Eden and Sinclair arranged a meeting. They are all livid. They decided to make contact with Labour.

An intriguing detail. During discussion of the Anglo-French plan in Cabinet, Hoare, Simon and Kingsley Wood spoke in favour of transferring the Sudetenland to Germany, without a guarantee from England of the new Czechoslovak borders. Chamberlain supported transferring the Sudetenland, but with a guarantee, and Halifax was against the transfer altogether. In the end, Chamberlain's point of view prevailed.

20 September

On 18 September, the Czechoslovak government officially asked Moscow for the first time whether it could count on a unilateral fulfilment of the pact by the USSR. An entirely positive reply followed from Moscow on the 19th. The Czechs took heart. On the very same day they were given the 'Anglo-French plan'. The Czechs were indignant. Only today, towards evening, did they send their reply to the 'Western democracies': without rejecting the plan directly, the Czechoslovak government suggested using the 1926 German–Czech treaty, confirmed at one time by Hitler himself, to settle the present controversy by arbitration.

Reports come from Prague that in recent days the Soviet embassy has become the focus of overwhelming popular demonstrations. Crowds walk up to the building in their thousands, hailing the USSR, sending deputations to the ambassador, and imploring with tears in their eyes that Czechoslovakia not be abandoned in its hour of need... In Prague, people have ceased hoping for help from Britain or France. They are no longer expecting anything from the 'Western democracies'. I am reminded of the Czechoslovak delegate at the reception of the *J.W.P.C.*, who said to me just a few days ago: 'You are our only hope... Don't betray us!'

21 September

M.M. [Litvinov] delivered a major speech at the Assembly today. A forceful, venomous, terrific speech! The audience listened with bated breath. The house was packed for the first time during the entire Assembly. I watched their faces: many expressed sympathy and many could not conceal their smiles at those points where M.M. gave free rein to his malicious wit. What's more, it wasn't just the Spanish, Chinese, Mexican and our other friends, but also those whom you'd hardly suspect of being particularly fond of the USSR. He received loud, universal applause.

A Frenchman spoke before M.M. In view of his disagreement with his government's policy, Paul-Boncour refused to speak. The speech was made instead by [name erased]. Goodness, what a speech it was! Long, flowery, empty and… devoted almost entirely to the <u>economic</u> tasks of the League of Nations. Economic tasks – at such a moment! In such a situation! The entire decline of present-day France could not have found a more vivid expression than that speech delivered today from the rostrum of the League of Nations.

Surits has finally got what he wanted: with M.M.'s permission he left for Paris today.

*　*　*

The baseness of the English and the French knows no bounds! Yesterday evening, after receiving the Czechoslovak reply with its proposal to settle the German–Czech dispute through arbitration, Chamberlain contacted Daladier and late at night (at 3 a.m., I'm told) the two premiers, without even informing their Cabinets, sent an ultimatum to the Czechoslovak government: <u>either Czechoslovakia accepts the 'Anglo-French' plan, or London and Paris leave Czechoslovakia to the mercy of fate in the event of a German attack</u>. The French even announced that in such a case they would no longer consider themselves bound by the terms of the Czech–French treaty. <u>The Czechs were given six hours to respond.</u> The Czechoslovak Cabinet convened in the night and was in session until the morning. Some members of the government insisted on rejecting the ultimatum and fighting Germany with the help of the USSR alone. Others objected resolutely, arguing that in this case a hue and cry would be raised everywhere (including Britain and France) about a war for the 'Bolshevization of Europe', from which Czechoslovakia would only stand to lose. It was a hopeless situation, and early on the morning of 21 September the Czechoslovak government accepted the 'Anglo-French' ultimatum with death in their hearts.

When Prague learned about last night's events, the masses' indignation against Britain and France knew no bounds. Huge crowds swamped the streets of the capital. It seemed that the tension would culminate in some terrible explosion. There was the smell of the Commune in the air. But the Czechs demonstrated once again their calm courage and iron self-control. No explosion followed.

This day, 21 September, will forever remain a momentous historical landmark. It brought to an end the entire post-war development of Europe and opened the gates to the events which, in the nearest future, may change entirely the face of the earth.

* * *

Reports from London that Attlee and Greenwood had another talk with Chamberlain and Halifax today. The Labour leaders demanded a fundamental change in British policy towards Czechoslovakia. They stated, among other things, that after reading Litvinov's speech at the League of Nations (the most important parts were sent from Geneva to London early in the morning, before Litvinov made the speech), they must declare openly that the information about the Soviet position which they had received from Chamberlain beforehand was in total contradiction to the Soviet foreign minister's speech (and to all the information that they had held previously on the subject). The PM was greatly embarrassed and referred once more to Bonnet. Attlee and Greenwood then addressed Halifax, asking him point-blank whether the Soviet ambassador had informed him about the Soviet position before his departure to Geneva. Halifax was also embarrassed and replied that indeed he had discussed Czechoslovakia with Maisky, but that Maisky had palmed him off with general phrases, stating merely: 'We will do our best.' (In fact, I answered Halifax's question by conveying to him in great detail M.M.'s talk with Payart in Moscow on 2 September.) In conclusion, Chamberlain told the Labourites that there could be no more talk about any change in British policy toward Czechoslovakia: the Cabinet had adopted it.

22 September

The Czechoslovak government has resigned. Stormy demonstrations in Prague and all over the country. Indignation against 'Western democracies' is growing. It is now dangerous to speak French or English on the streets of Czech towns. Towards evening a new government was formed, headed by General Syrový[i] – its character is more business-like than political.

Jubilation and festivities in Germany. Entirely merited. It's not just that Hitler is getting the Sudetenland without a fight, but that it's being handed to him on a plate by the British and the French. Chamberlain and Daladier have done all the dirty work for him. England and France have become the maidservants of German fascism. Why shouldn't the Germans be happy? But how low, how very low the once proud 'Western democracies' have fallen!

---

[i] Jan Syrový, commanded the Czechoslovak Army Corps in Russia during the Civil War, 1918 and 1919–20; minister of defence, 1926 and 1938–39; president of Czechoslovakia, September–November 1938.

Today, Agniya left for a tour of Switzerland by car. Why shouldn't she see a bit of the country? Who knows whether we'll have occasion to be here again? After all, tomorrow Hitler might extend his paws to Switzerland with equal right and with equal success. In the evening, I went on my own to the Finns for a reception. I met De La Warr there. He had just returned from London – he'd flown there from Geneva for a Cabinet meeting.

According to De La Warr, tension in England is growing by the day. The 'Anglo-French plan' is extremely unpopular. Unfortunately, the French are taking a stance of complete capitulation. The conduct of Daladier and Bonnet during the recent meetings in London was a savage blow to the hopes of English supporters for a more active policy. The crucial thing now is to boost Czechoslovak morale for at least the next couple of days and to lean on France to rectify its position. Then there will be a great swell in Britain and everything will sort itself out. Frankly speaking, De La Warr's reasoning seemed too optimistic to me, but... after all, he'd just returned from London, where he is a member of the Cabinet!

* * *

The General Council of the Trades Union Congress and the Labour Party Executive Committee held a meeting yesterday evening in London, following Attlee's and Greenwood's visit to Chamberlain. The PM's statement was considered unsatisfactory and the decision was taken to send another delegation to him. Chamberlain declared that it was physically impossible for him to receive it (he is flying to Hitler in Godesberg). So it fell to Halifax to meet the new deputation, consisting of Dalton, Morrison and Citrine.

The deputation demanded an immediate démarche in Berlin by Britain, France and the USSR. In this connection, Dalton, referring to Litvinov's speech, called Bonnet a 'disgraceful liar'. The foreign minister dodged Dalton's question as to the content of his meeting with Maisky on 8 September. As for the essence of the Labourites' demand, Halifax replied: 'At present, no European political manoeuvre can prevent the crushing of Czechoslovakia. The British government does not intend to threaten Germany with war because it is not ready for it. The demand of the Labour deputation cannot be met.'

The deputation reported the outcome of their meeting with Halifax to the Plenum of the General Council and the Executive Committee. Having judged the outcome as unsatisfactory, the Plenum took the decision to appeal to the nation and to organize about two thousand protest meetings against Cabinet policy next weekend (24 and 25 September).

In addition, the Plenum elected a delegation to be sent to Paris. The meeting of British and French trade unionists and socialists in London yesterday was a clear failure: the French (Vincent Auriol[i] and others) took a very feeble position.

---

[i] Jules-Vincent Auriol, French minister of finance, 1936–37; minister of justice, 1937–38.

They returned to Paris the same day. That is why the Labourites have decided to go to France themselves to try to prod the French into action. I wonder whether anything will come of their efforts.

23 September

Vague rumours have been spreading since the morning that the second meeting between Chamberlain and Hitler is not running as smoothly as the first. A Foreign Office functionary assigned to the British delegation told me in a corridor of the League of Nations that the first meeting between the British PM and the Führer took place last night, but that the talks did not continue today because Chamberlain found it more expedient to address Hitler with a letter – he is currently waiting for a reply.

What's the matter? It is obvious that some unforeseen difficulties stand in the way of an agreement. What are they? Some time later I met Butler in the League corridors, but apart from confirming the very fact of a break in the talks, he also had little more to add. Tension and alarm grew by the hour. The League building and the lobbies of the Geneva hotels swarmed with new information and new rumours. Nobody was making much sense, but the general impression was unanimous: matters in Godesberg were not running smoothly and had probably already reached a deadlock... So is a break inevitable? This gave rise to the most heated speculations and to the most reckless wagers.

I went for a lunch given by Avenol.[i] I was accompanied by A.M [Kollontay]. There were about 15 guests at the table, including the Spaniards (del Vayo[ii] and Azcárate with wives) and Kayser,[iii] one of the leaders of the French Radicals. The latter asserted categorically that the Anglo-French plan represented an absolute limit, beyond which the French would not go. I had a rather unpleasant talk with Avenol: at M.M.'s request I voiced a protest against the appointment of Munters[iv] as spokesman for Article 16, since the man had a very clearly defined position on this issue. Avenol argued that Munters was the best of the possible spokesmen. We failed to reach an agreement but at least Avenol has been notified of our attitude on this matter.

From three o'clock onwards, I attended the 6th Commission, where the discussion of Article 16 continued. M.M. was not there (he was at home, preparing his speech). I spoke with Munters and told him frankly that we object to his appointment as spokesman but that this was not a personal matter.

---

[i] Joseph Louis Avenol, deputy secretary-general of the League of Nations, 1923–33; secretary-general, 1933–40; French foreign minister, 1933–34, 1936 and 1938.
[ii] Julio Álvarez del Vayo, foreign minister of the Spanish Republic, 1936–39.
[iii] Jacques Kayser, journalist and general secretary of the Radical Socialist Party.
[iv] Vilhelms Munters, foreign minister of Latvia, 1936–40; chairman of the September 1938 session of the Council of the League of Nations in Geneva.

We would simply prefer a spokesman who was not following a party line on Article 16.

Many people spoke at the Commission, including Paul-Boncour. His speech was unclear and vague, and he either could not or would not divorce himself from the capitulatory stance of the French government. M.M. arrived towards the end of the session and asked for the floor. His speech was very sharp and cut many to the quick, but the audience still applauded him vigorously. Paul-Boncour was openly quivering when M.M. mentioned the 'German–Anglo-French' ultimatum to Czechoslovakia. Butler started tittering in embarrassment when M.M. declared that only the USSR had a 'clear conscience' and 'clean hands' in the matter of meeting self-imposed obligations. Our arrow found its target.

Just before the meeting came to a close, a secretary of the British delegation approached M.M. and said that De La Warr and Butler would like to have a talk with him and me right away. A quarter of an hour later, we all gathered in the office of the British *sous-secretaire*. It was about eight in the evening, and a somewhat romantic semi-darkness filled the room.

De La Warr spoke first. He had just received instructions from London to see Litvinov and me as soon as possible. Things are bad in Godesberg.[103] The collapse of negotiations can be expected any hour. The British and the French governments have already informed Czechoslovakia that they no longer believe they have the right to prevent her from mobilizing. Prague will probably declare mobilization tonight. Germany will certainly not tolerate such a situation. So we can expect an armed move by Hitler against Czechoslovakia. What then? What would be the position of the USSR in these circumstances?

M.M. answered that he would like to know the facts first. What is happening in Godesberg? What are they talking about there? What difficulties have they met?

De La Warr and Butler, however, didn't know much (or pretended not to know). They explained this by saying that the Godesberg–London telephone line was tapped by the Germans, so the British delegation in Godesberg had to be very careful. Sheer nonsense! But I certainly do not rule out the possibility that London is deliberately keeping De La Warr and Butler in the dark about what is really happening. Such are the methods of foreign-policy work introduced by Chamberlain. But the two Englishmen did say that Hitler had put forward a series of new and unacceptable claims and that the PM was returning to Britain tomorrow. Most likely, a new meeting of British and French ministers will be immediately convened in London. But what do we think of the situation?

M.M. answered that our position was stated with sufficient clarity in his speeches at the League of Nations on 21 September and today. We are sincerely prepared to meet our obligations under the Soviet–Czechoslovak pact. It's up to France. England's position is also important.

De La Warr tried to find out whether the Soviet government has already taken some military measures. Has the army been mobilized, at least partially? Have the troops been moved to the border?

M.M. avoided answering these questions directly, saying that he had been abroad for almost three weeks.

De La Warr made another attempt to discuss military affairs, asking how many air divisions we could send to help Czechoslovakia and whether Rumania would let them through.

M.M. replied that he was not a military man and could not satisfy De La Warr's curiosity. That was why, in his talk with the French chargé d'affaires on 2 September, he had recommended urgent talks between the general staffs of the three armies. As for Rumania, M.M. thought that if Britain and France supported Czechoslovakia, Rumania would follow suit.[104]

De La Warr interjected that, according to his information, the Rumanians would not impede the passage of Soviet troops sent to assist Czechoslovakia.

Butler, for his part, said he would like to clarify the question of when and under what conditions the USSR would be ready to *move*. Only after France moves? Or earlier?

M.M. replied with absolute clarity that this was the case: only after France. Those were the obligations undertaken by the USSR under the Czechoslovak–Soviet pact.

'What then should be the next practical step?' asked De La Warr.

'If the British government has seriously decided to intervene in the developing conflict,' M.M. answered, 'then the next step, to my mind, should be an immediate conference of Britain, France and the USSR with the aim of working out a general plan of action.'

De La Warr agreed with this and asked M.M. where this conference might be held.

M.M. observed that the choice of place was of secondary importance, with one reservation. The conference should not be held in Geneva. Hitler is so accustomed to identifying Geneva with irresponsible talk that any conference convened there would fail to make an adequate impression on him. And this impression is now more important than anything.

De La Warr and Butler conceded the truth of this observation, and De La Warr asked M.M. whether he had any objections to holding the conference in London. M.M. replied that he did not.

'Who could represent the USSR at the conference?' continued De La Warr. 'Would you be able to attend yourself?'

M.M. replied: 'If the ministers of other countries are present at the conference, then I am ready to come to London.'

De La Warr expressed his full satisfaction with today's talk and promised to inform the Foreign Office about it immediately. Further details could be discussed the following day once he had received a reply from London. Then we took our leave. On parting, De La Warr and Butler said a few times, with emphasis: 'Let us consider today's meeting as the first "*informal step*" on the way to establishing contact between the two governments. "*Informal*", of course! Only "*informal*"!'

On the way home, M.M. and I exchanged views about our meeting with the British. M.M., as usual, was most sceptical. I am also not in a very optimistic mood, but one thing is clear to me: if London is so eager to seek at least *informal contacts* with the Soviet government, then Chamberlain must be having a very hard time of it.[105]

Late in the evening, De Valera,[i] president of the Assembly, gave a big reception in the hotel Les Bergues.

Up to a thousand people gathered, of every appearance and rank. It was hot, stuffy and crowded, but nobody seemed to notice. Everyone's thoughts were elsewhere. News of mobilization in Czechoslovakia had arrived late in the afternoon. Godesberg was being spoken of as a complete failure. The rumour was passed around that tomorrow the French government was also going to announce mobilization. A leaden cloud hangs over the world. The spectre of war rose in all its horror before those gathered at the reception... A war very close at hand – tomorrow, the day after...

All evening I myself could not get rid of the thought that there was no longer a way out, and that war was inevitable. Here is the logical line of my reasoning. The 'Anglo-French plan' is the absolute limit. If Hitler has demanded any more from Chamberlain, then neither London nor Paris can accept it. At any rate, they cannot exert pressure on Prague to accept Germany's new demands. So Czechoslovakia will reject the demands. Hitler, of course, will use force. Czechoslovakia will respond by resorting to force as well. War will break out and France will have to come to Prague's aid. We shall follow France. And then events will run their inevitable course. As if all this were right and logical... As if there were no other way out of the current situation...

But who can tell? Life is often far more complicated than logic. Besides, the English, who are destined to play a major part in this whole story, love to call themselves an 'illogical people'. Well, we'll see.

---

[i] Eamon (Edward) De Valera, president of the Sinn Fein Party in 1917; prime minister of Ireland, 1932–48, 1951–54 and 1957–59; president, 1959–73.

24 September

A lovely, bright, sunny day. From the windows of our hotel we can see the cumbersome dark mass of Le Salève; the green fields and trees; the blue lake that seems to be laughing; the yellow anthill of the town drenched in the cheerful, spring-like sun...

In this magical setting you can hardly believe that the world is on the brink of a great catastrophe. Or maybe it isn't?

It's Saturday. Very few League commissions hold their sessions today. M.M. [Litvinov] and I devote the morning to strolling and shopping. Everybody recognizes M.M. They gaze and even point their fingers at him – not with animosity but, on the contrary, almost always with sympathy and respect. As we crossed a small square near Rue de Rhone, a touching episode occurred. A cyclist, who looked like a skilled worker or a junior clerk, was riding towards us. He stopped abruptly under our very noses, quickly jumped off his iron horse, raised his hat and exclaimed: 'Bravo, Litvinov!'

We wandered about for quite a while, buying barometers, thermometers, envelopes, paper and other small things. Crossing the bridge and looking down at the clear blue water foaming along noisily beneath us, I couldn't help remarking: 'What a glorious day. Such fine weather.'

'Stop it,' M.M. grumbled back. 'You're inviting bad weather for tomorrow.'

Tomorrow, Sunday, he plans his usual jaunt into the countryside by car.

'When Surits plays cards, he always begins by yelling, "Wonderful cards! Beautiful!", and then, as a rule ends up with nothing.'

M.M. was half-grumbling, half-laughing. But still!... Even he is not immune from something like superstition.

Towards evening Agniya returned from her trip around Switzerland. She's got a tan, looks refreshed and is simply delighted with everything she's seen and heard. Excellent.

* * *

Chamberlain was back from Godesberg in time for lunch in London. The details are gradually emerging.

In Godesberg, it transpires, Hitler presented the British prime minister with a series of new and unexpected demands. Chamberlain had assumed that only the details of the implementation of the 'Anglo-French plan' remained to be discussed with the 'Führer', following its acceptance by Czechoslovakia; but now he found himself caught in a trap. Yesterday he had to break off the talks and resort to correspondence. Chamberlain sent two letters to Hitler in the course of one day. In the first, he asked Hitler for guarantees that force would not be used while the talks were ongoing, and offered his 'compromise' solutions. As I was informed today, there are two major difficulties: (1) Hitler's claims now extend not only over the territories with 50% German population but also over a number of areas with a predominantly Czechoslovak population; and (2) he absolutely insists that the territories to be transferred to Germany under the Anglo-French plan should be occupied by German troops on 1 October. Hitler is not interested in compromises. He answered the prime minister's first letter with a lengthy statement about the persecution of Sudeten Germans in Czechoslovakia and held fast to his positions. Then Chamberlain sent Hitler a second letter, in which he said that he was ready to communicate Germany's new claims to Czechoslovakia and that, seeing no use in his remaining in Godesberg, he was returning home immediately. Late in the evening of 23 September, Chamberlain had one further meeting with Hitler, at which the latter handed some sort of a memorandum to the British prime minister. What kind of memorandum? What is its essence? Nobody has anything definite to say about it.

* * *

News arrived from London in the evening. The mystery of the memorandum has been cleared up. Its essence is as follows:

(1) By 1 October the Czechs are to evacuate and transfer to the Germans all the territories that are specified as subject for transfer in the 'Anglo-French plan', i.e. the areas where the German population exceeds 50% (shaded in red on the map appended by Hitler to the memorandum).

(2) A plebiscite shall be held no later than 25 November in a number of other areas where the German population is less than 50% (shaded in green on the map). Most of these areas are of great economic or strategic importance.

(3) The territories to be evacuated shall be transferred to the Germans 'complete and intact', i.e. with all the military, economic, transport and other facilities, including radio stations, aerodromes, etc. Also subject to transfer are: raw materials, rolling stock, commodities, foodstuffs, livestock, etc., including those owned by private persons. Germany agrees to attach Czechoslovak representatives to the German army headquarters for the settling of all details concerning the evacuation.

(4) The Czechoslovak government shall immediately set free all the Germans doing service in the Czechoslovak army and police, as well as all the Germans kept in prisons on political grounds.

(5) The final border between Czechoslovakia and Germany is to be fixed by a Czech–German or an international commission. The plebiscite is to be organized under the supervision of an international commission on the basis of the census taken on 28 October 1918, with both sides withdrawing their troops from the respective territories during the plebiscite.

(6) Germany proposes the creation of a Czech–German commission to agree all subsequent details.

Such are the contents of this intriguing document. Appetite comes with eating. After Berchtesgaden, it would seem, Hitler's appetite grew considerably. That's no surprise, given Chamberlain's conduct there. But will even Chamberlain be able to swallow Hitler's impertinent demands? And will the French swallow them? This is the crux of the matter now. It would seem that London and Paris ought to choke on the Godesberg ultimatum. But who knows?

Chamberlain sent Hitler's memorandum to Prague directly from Godesberg. But the plane that was meant to bring this document to the Czechoslovak government landed somewhere on the way. So Halifax handed the memorandum to Masaryk today. The following conversation took place:

Halifax. Neither I nor the prime minister thinks it possible to advise you on Mr Hitler's memorandum. But I would like to tell you man to man: think well before giving a negative answer. The prime minister is convinced that Mr Hitler desires only the Sudetenland and that, if he receives it, he won't make any further demands.

Masaryk. And you believe this?

Halifax (sharply). I told you, the PM is convinced of it.

Masaryk. If neither you nor the prime minister wants to give us advice on the memorandum, what then is the role of the PM?

Halifax. The role of a postman, and nothing else.

Masaryk. Should I understand that the British prime minister has become an errand boy for that killer and brigand, Hitler?

Halifax (embarrassed). Yes, if you so wish.

* * *

News from Moscow that Potemkin summoned the Polish chargé d'affaires yesterday and made an official statement to him that if Poland crossed Czechoslovakia's border, the Soviet government would view it as an act of aggression committed by Poland and would instantly renounce the Soviet–Polish non-aggression pact of 1932. Late in the evening, the Polish chargé d'affaires handed the Polish government's reply to Potemkin. The Polish government stated that Poland was not obliged to inform anyone about the measures it was taking for its defence and that she was familiar with the texts of agreements she had signed. Ha-ha! One can spot Polish haughtiness at a glance.

Our démarche made a huge impression on Geneva and raised spirits in Prague considerably.

Yesterday Beneš, concurrently with the declaration of Czech mobilization, notified the Soviet government about the measures he had taken and asked the USSR to do its utmost to defend Czechoslovakia in compliance with the Soviet–Czech pact.

* * *

Comedy is running hand in hand with tragedy.

Yesterday it was announced on the London radio that the Soviet chargé d'affaires had been summoned for a talk at the Foreign Office. This sounded highly significant. So significant that yesterday, during a meeting with M.M. and myself, De La Warr referred to it as a symptom and a démarche parallel to the one he was presented with in Geneva. As soon as I returned to the hotel, I phoned Kagan to ask him what all the fuss was about.

I burst out laughing once I had heard Kagan out. He did indeed visit the Foreign Office today. What for? Plymouth had invited him. Why? Plymouth wanted to talk to him about Hemming's forthcoming trip to Burgos, where he was going to hold talks with Franco about the notorious plan for the evacuation of 'volunteers'. So far we had been categorically opposed to such a trip, but perhaps we had changed our minds?

Truly, comedy is running hand in hand with tragedy. Today De La Warr confessed to me that when he mentioned the fact of Kagan's visit to the Foreign Office yesterday he had no idea about the matter at hand. He had simply relied on the radio and had drawn his own conclusions.

25 September

Sunday. The League of Nations is not working. Indeed, outside Geneva, in the great world where ominous events are unfolding, the thermometer still shows 40°. In Prague, people are getting ready to die for the freedom and independence of their country. In London, the British Cabinet was in session yesterday for many hours, while today a fresh meeting of British and French ministers is to be held on the subject of the Godesberg ultimatum.[106] But here in Geneva it is Sunday: silence, calm and rest from toil, as once we sang as children.

We all, excepting A.M., make another trip to France. M.M. wants to find some new, as yet untried restaurant somewhere in Doucier (Jura). On the way we get out of the car, stroll, talk, and make bets. M.M. asks me: 'Well, what do you think: will there be a war or won't there? Yesterday at Lac Léman our views diverged. I believe that the English and the French will yield again and that there won't be a war.[107] Yakov Zakharovich [Surits] agrees with me; Boris Efimovich [Shtein] and Vladimir Aleksandrovich [Sokolin] hold the opposite view. And what do you say?'

Shtein barges into the conversation and starts arguing that the Czechs will reject the ultimatum, the English and the French will not be able to exert

41. With the League of Nations on hold, the diplomat-survivors of the purges find refuge in the French Alps (right to left: Maisky, Litvinov, Surits and Stein).

pressure on them in such a situation, the Germans will attack, the Czechs will resist, the French will have to support the Czechs, and then the course of events will resemble a spontaneous avalanche. I listen to Shtein and his logic seems irrefutable. Yet a voice deep in my soul tells me: 'Will Chamberlain and Daladier stand their ground when the time comes to say plainly: war! I doubt it.' So, answering M.M.'s question, I say: 'Knowing my English friends, I'm inclined to agree with you. Yet there are other factors in the current situation which have not been taken into account and which are capable of playing a great role: for instance, the Czechs' behaviour at the moment of danger. Therefore, I can't make a bet.'

The restaurant in Doucier was superb. The food was heavenly. After lunch, Agniya and I asked for tea. The owner, who was attending our table himself (and why not? M.M. was immediately recognized and an atmosphere of amicable sensationalism constantly surrounded us), grimaced in horror and disbelief: 'Tea?' he asked again, almost dumbstruck. 'You would like tea?'

We realized we had committed a sacrilege. The owner went on: 'I have first-class coffee!… Wonderful coffee… You won't find such delightful coffee anywhere else!'

We were defeated. They brought us fragrant black coffee…

Late at night, when we returned to Geneva, the news came that Czechoslovakia had rejected the Godesberg 'memorandum'.

26 September

Moscow instructed us today that Surits, Merekalov,[i] and I should be back in our places. Surits has already been in Paris for five days. After consulting M.M., Merekalov and I decided to leave tomorrow. I shall go by train in order to arrive by 28 September, when a session has been planned in parliament, at which Chamberlain will make a statement about his talks with Hitler and at which, who knows, a decision might be taken about war. Agniya will return by car one or two days later.

Before the French ministers' departure from Paris, the French government held a special meeting which resolved that the Godesberg ultimatum was unacceptable. That's good. The hands of Daladier and Bonnet are now tied and they won't get too far in London. The British and French ministers spent the whole of yesterday afternoon in meetings. Gamelin[ii] also arrived in London this morning.

A propos, I heard the following story. Bonnet, whose role throughout the crisis has been of the most sinister kind, insisted in his talks in London on the need to avert a war whatever the cost. In the main, Daladier supported him. It goes without saying that the French ministers met with Chamberlain's full 'understanding' and 'sympathy'. As an argument in favour of capitulation, Bonnet cited the unpreparedness of the French army, particularly its air force for a large-scale war. Gamelin found out about this and immediately decided to go to London personally in order to renounce Bonnet's slander and restore the honour of the French army. When Daladier learned about the forthcoming arrival of the chief of the general staff, he deemed it best to legalize his appearance in London and sent Gamelin an official invitation to the conferences. In London, Gamelin admitted to certain flaws in the French armed forces (especially in aviation), but he declared categorically that, although he was against preventive war, France would emerge victorious if war were to break out now. According to Gamelin, the Siegfried line does not yet pose an insurmountable obstacle. The Germans have not had sufficient time to reinforce it properly. Gamelin is said to have used the following expression: 'The Siegfried line is just a wall of marmalade.'[108]

* * *

When Chamberlain returned from Godesberg, Attlee and Greenwood went to see him. Halifax was also present at the meeting.

---

[i] Aleksei Fedorovich Merekalov, deputy people's commissar for foreign trade, 1937–38. Stalin's personal appointee as ambassador to Berlin in April 1938, he initiated rapprochement with Germany a year later, but was recalled to Moscow in May 1939 and sidelined to direct the country's meat industry.
[ii] Maurice Gustave Gamelin, chief of the French general staff, 1931–40.

42. Maisky with the other survivor, Surits, in Geneva.

Chamberlain began with lengthy deliberations on the theme that Hitler is 'an honest man', and that, having received the Sudetenland, he would be appeased. The speech bored Greenwood, who interrupted the prime minister and asked him: 'Have you read Hitler's *Mein Kampf*?'

Chamberlain got angry and answered irritably: 'Yes, I have, but I have conversed with Hitler and you have not!'

The Labour leaders wanted to know whether the Godesberg memorandum was forwarded to Czechoslovakia with or without a recommendation that it be accepted. The prime minister replied that no recommendations had been made from his side.

'What will happen,' the Labourites went on, 'if Czechoslovakia rejects Hitler's demands?'

'That will depend on the behaviour of France,' responded the prime minister.

'And what if France supports Czechoslovakia? What stand will the British government take in that case?'

Chamberlain avoided answering this question directly, but said that 'a new situation would be created' which the Cabinet had not yet discussed. Neither could the prime minister give a clear and definite answer to the question about the guarantees of Czechoslovakia's new borders. Concluding the conversation, the Labour leaders returned once more to their initial point: What foundations were there for assuming the Sudetenland to be the Führer's last demand?

Chamberlain exclaimed once again with renewed annoyance: 'I saw Hitler and I believe him!'

27 September

I started preparing for the journey in the morning. Agniya and I did our last bits of shopping and paid our last visits. A grey and foggy day. Some occasional drizzle. In the evening a *black-out* was enforced in Geneva. The city was plunged into complete darkness. The cars moved about with their lights a deep shade of blue. Despite the fact that it was a trial alarm or, perhaps, precisely because of that, the streets quickly filled with people. You could hear footsteps everywhere, along with the sound of restrained laughter and people talking. Young people came out in particularly large numbers. For them this was such *fun*!

It was pitch-black at the railway station. I had some trouble finding a porter and then my carriage. I said goodbye to Agniya and the train moved off. Louis Fischer[i] turned out to be my travelling companion. We had a long talk about Spain and European affairs. He told me, among other things, that Chamberlain had spoken on the radio that evening. The prime minister was almost weeping, his voice trembled, and he couldn't reconcile himself to the thought that the war could begin any moment now.[109] That's bad. A speech like that augurs ill. True, the partial mobilization of the French army began today, and the mobilization of the British navy was also announced. This must make some impression on Hitler, but the trouble is that Hitler shows utter contempt for bourgeois politicians, being sure that their nerves are weaker than his own. In this he is certainly right. And the kind of speech that Chamberlain made today can only further encourage the 'Führer' to stake his all.

As it happened, M.M. was in Lignon when I was leaving. It would have been risky to drive over there in full darkness. I might have missed my train. So we parted over the telephone.

28 September

The train arrived in Paris on time. It was around seven o'clock in the morning. I was met at the station and went to the embassy for half an hour. In view of the early hour, I decided against waking up Surits. I saw only one or two employees at the chancellery. My train for London was leaving at 8.20. I had deliberately chosen an early train, arriving in London at 3.21 p.m., as I planned

---

[i] Louis Fischer, American journalist who gained access to the Soviet leadership in the post-revolutionary years.

to go straight from the station to the parliament session where Chamberlain was expected to speak at 3.30.

On that early, rainy morning Paris looked somewhat grey, disgruntled and unwelcoming. The general picture, though, barely differed from normal. At the embassy I was told that, on the previous day, the railway stations with trains bound for the east were crowded with reservists and relatives seeing them off. The mood of the mobilized soldiers was sullen and unenthusiastic, but quiet and determined. There were no disturbances or incidents. They all felt that they had to drain their cup of woe; it was unpleasant, but nothing could be done about it. Today, however, the stations were back to normal.

The journey from Paris to London passed without incident. The sea was calm. Even though I have crossed the English Channel many times before, today was the first time I noticed that, on a clear day, you can see the British coast from Calais and the French coast from Dover.

A great disappointment lay in store for me on the British shore. The 'war alarm' of the last few days had already affected the regularity of the trains. Our train from Dover to London was one hour late. This had very unpleasant consequences for me. I had hoped that, with nine minutes at my disposal, I would have got from Victoria station to parliament in time for the beginning of Chamberlain's speech. But I arrived in London at 4.25 p.m., instead of 3.21 p.m. At the station, I couldn't help wondering: wasn't it too late to go to parliament? But I dismissed the thought, jumped out of the carriage and rushed to Westminster.

When, panting for breath after a brisk walk along the corridors of parliament, I ran up to the entrance to the diplomatic gallery, the fat good-natured policeman at the door, who knew me well by sight, broke into a happy smile and said hastily: 'Have you heard the good news? The prime minister has just informed the House: Mr Hitler has invited him to a new conference in Munich. Tomorrow.'

I ran upstairs. Not only all the galleries, but even all the approaches to them were crammed with people. With great difficulty I pushed my way to the front row, but there was no way of getting through to the diplomatic gallery. To make it worse, there were no vacant seats there. I stood where I was and focused my attention on my surroundings. Down below, the chamber was black with MPs. Not only were all the benches taken, with no room left to swing a cat, but thick crowds of MPs thronged the gangways. You could sense a tremendous tension. It seemed unbearable, as if on the brink of a spontaneous explosion.

Chamberlain was speaking. When I entered, he was coming to the end of his speech. He had just announced Hitler's invitation and his consent to fly to Munich the following day.

Chamberlain took his seat. Attlee got to his feet and said a few words. The leader of the opposition wished the prime minister success in his mission and only at the end added in haste that principles should not be sacrificed in Munich. He didn't even say what principles he had in mind. It was a very weak speech. Sinclair, speaking on behalf of the Liberals, was much better. But Gallacher gave the best speech of all. He protested against Czechoslovakia's division and called for peace based on freedom and democracy. Lansbury and Maxton[i] were in raptures as they expressed their gratitude to the prime minister. It was simply disgusting.

The session was then closed. The MPs and the guests dispersed, excited and alarmed, conversing loudly and gesturing with great animation. One and the same question was on everyone's lips: 'What's it to be? War or peace?'

The majority was inclined to think: peace.[110]

29 September

Halifax invited me over. He began with justifications. The British government fears that the conference of the four which convened today in Munich could arouse certain suspicions in the Soviet government, for it is very familiar with our attitude towards anything resembling a 'four-power pact'. Halifax wants to dispel our suspicions. Although only four powers are meeting in Munich, the British government has always desired and still desires to maintain good relations with the USSR and fails to understand why this should not be possible.[111]

Then Halifax moved on to an account of the circumstances under which the Munich Conference originated. In his desperate attempts to avert war, the prime minister made a final appeal to Hitler and Mussolini on the morning of 28 September. At 4 p.m., while speaking in parliament, Chamberlain received Hitler's invitation to come to Munich on the 29th for a conference that would be attended by Mussolini and Daladier as well. Chamberlain gave his consent without consulting the French, as the matter seemed absolutely clear to him. Daladier also gave his consent to come to Munich without consulting the British. The British government did not raise the question of sending an invitation to the USSR because, first, time was terribly short, with not a minute to spare and, secondly and most importantly, it knew beforehand the reply that it would get to such a proposal from Hitler. The last chance to preserve peace could not be wasted because of an argument about the composition of the conference. But the prime minister did wire Beneš, asking him to send his representative to Munich either for participation in the conference or, if this proved impossible, for consultation in the course of the conference.

---

[i] James Richard Maxton, chairman of Independent Labour Party, 1926–31 and 1934–39.

43. A caricature by David Low.

44. Gloomy Litvinov, Maisky and Surits, stranded in Geneva.

After hearing all this, I asked about the programme of the conference. Halifax threw out his hands and said they had had no time to work out a programme and that the agenda would depend to a great extent on the intentions and mood of the 'Führer'. In any case, Halifax does not rule out the possibility that questions may be raised in Munich regarding not only Czechoslovakia, but also other problems, such as Spain, general European 'appeasement', and so on. Halifax made the following remark in this connection: 'I still have in my mind the idea of an Anglo-Franco-Soviet consultation which was put forward during Mr Litvinov's talk with Lord De La Warr in Geneva.'

Since Halifax had mentioned the guarantees which should be given to Czechoslovakia, I asked him to clarify the British government's understanding of the guarantees. Halifax replied that so far they had conceived them as follows: Germany and Czechoslovakia sign a non-aggression pact, while Britain, France and the USSR ('if it so wished, of course') shall guarantee the borders. The question of Italy and the limitrophes being drawn into the guarantees is very problematic and remains open for now.[112]

* * *

Attlee and Greenwood came to talk to me. They can't have been feeling especially brilliant in the wake of yesterday's parliament session, for they began by making excuses.

In the circumstances it would have been wrong to speak out against Chamberlain's visit to Munich. It was necessary to wish him success, if only for the sake of appearances. After all, this was a matter of war or peace, of the life or death of millions of people. If the Labourites had acted differently, their party would have been accused of being a party of war. Moreover, Attlee ended his speech by saying that principles should not be sacrificed in Munich!

'And which "principles" do you think will triumph?' I asked.

Both Attlee and Greenwood shook their heads dejectedly. They are certain that Chamberlain will capitulate once again in Munich.

But the mood of the masses is wonderful! The two thousand meetings arranged across the country last weekend went terrifically well. The trades unions are holding firm. Even Citrine is *all right*.

Marvellous! But the capitulation and the sale of Czechoslovakia are still inevitable! So what is there to be happy about?

30 September

The gloomy forebodings of the Labour leaders have materialized. Yesterday I didn't go to bed until almost 4 a.m., and sat listening to the radio. At 2.45 it

45. Maisky cheering up Masaryk.

was finally announced that an agreement had been reached in Munich and the peace of Europe had been secured. But what an agreement! And what peace!

Chamberlain and Daladier capitulated completely. The conference of the four essentially accepted the Godesberg ultimatum with minor and negligible adjustments. The one 'victory' won by the British and the French is that the transfer of the Sudetenland to Germany will take place not on the 1st but on the 10th of October. What a tremendous achievement!

I paced the dining room for a long time, lost in thought. My thoughts were distressing. It is difficult to grasp at once the true meaning of all that had just happened, but I feel and understand that a landmark of enormous historical significance was passed last night. In one bound quantity became quality, and the world suddenly changed...

I woke up in the morning with a headache and the first thing that occurred to me was that I should immediately visit Masaryk.

When I entered his reception room there was no one there. A minute later I heard someone's hurried steps on the stairs and the host sidled in. There was something strange and unnatural about his tall, strong figure. As if it had suddenly iced over and lost its habitual agility. Masaryk threw a passing glance at me and tried to make polite conversation in the usual manner: 'What fine weather we are having today, aren't we?'

'Forget the weather,' I said with an involuntary wave of my hand. 'I have not come here for that. I have come to express my deep compassion for your people at this exceptionally hard moment and also my strong indignation at the shameful behaviour of Britain and France!'

A kind of current seemed to pass through Masaryk's tall figure. The ice melted at once. Immobility gave way to quivering. He rocked rather comically on his feet and fell all of a sudden on my breast, sobbing bitterly. I was taken aback and somewhat bewildered. Kissing me, Masaryk mumbled through his tears: 'They've sold me into slavery to the Germans, like they used to sell negroes into slavery in America.'

Little by little, Masaryk calmed down and began to apologize for his weakness.

I shook his hand firmly.

* * *

In the afternoon, Cadogan invited me to his office and gave me a brief account of the decisions taken in Munich. Obviously, he was fulfilling the promise made to me yesterday by Halifax. Then Cadogan set about interrogating me for my opinion on these decisions.

I decided to cut to the chase. I bluntly stated my belief that England and France had suffered a crushing defeat in Munich; that an important historical landmark had been passed last night, ushering in a new era in European history – the era of German hegemony; and that the result would be a succession of further retreats by 'Western democracies' and, perhaps, the collapse of their current empires.

Cadogan tried to refute my statements, stressing the importance of the fact that peace had been preserved and war had been averted; but eventually he had to confess that he could not be sure about the future and that only subsequent developments would show whether Munich was worth the price.

* * *

I had a long talk with Churchill yesterday. This was before the news came from Munich, and Churchill expressed his almost total confidence that this time Chamberlain would not be able to make any serious concessions to Hitler. In any event, Chamberlain would not be able to retreat from the Anglo-French plan of 18 September! How terribly mistaken Churchill was!

Churchill is satisfied with the position taken by the USSR during the crisis. In particular, he liked the speech delivered by M.M. [Litvinov] in the League of Nations on 21 September and our Polish démarche of 23 September. He thinks that the USSR has carried out its international duty in this critical period, while Britain and France have capitulated. In connection with this he pointed out how the prestige of the USSR and sympathy towards it was growing, not only in Liberal and Labour circles, but also among Conservatives, even among the diehards. Four days ago, Churchill spoke at a special joint meeting of the Conservatives of both Houses arranged by Amery[i] and Lord Lloyd. The resolution adopted unanimously at this meeting was quite something!

Churchill gave me a sheet of paper on which I read the following: the gathering welcomes the establishment of direct contacts between the governments of Britain and the USSR; it believes that from now on close political and military cooperation will be maintained between the British, French and Soviet governments; and it hopes that Hitler will be made to understand, before he takes an irreversible step, that the said three powers will act as a united front against a German assault on Czechoslovakia.

This resolution was handed to Halifax. Churchill also told me that it was at his urgent request that the communiqué issued in London on 26 September said that, in the event of German aggression against Czechoslovakia, Germany would come up against a united front of Britain, France and the USSR. Churchill believes that the statement had a sobering effect on Hitler and that it may be regarded as a truly historical event. Chamberlain was forced to swallow this mention of the USSR. But how absurd and criminal is his attitude to the Soviet Union!

I asked Churchill about the state of affairs in the Cabinet and in the country at large. According to him, major shifts occurred in public opinion during my two weeks' absence from England. If Germany unleashes war, the entire country will rise to fight. This mood has been reflected in the government, where there are now considerable disagreements. Duff Cooper, Hore-Belisha, Stanley, Elliot and others are opposed to the prime minister. Halifax guardedly backs the opposition, but he does not want to break with Chamberlain as yet. The presence of an opposition has forced the prime minister to agree to the guarantees of Czechoslovakia's borders, which in the past he could not even bear to hear mentioned, and also to the mobilization of the navy carried out by Duff Cooper.

In conclusion, Churchill told me about the campaign against the USSR being conducted in London. It transpires that the *Cliveden Set* and other related elements have been busy spreading rumours that Soviet aviation is weak; that the recent 'purges' have deprived it of nearly all of its qualified personnel; that owing to this fact the USSR presently has no more than a thousand first-line aircraft at its disposal; and that all this played a major part in determining

---

[i] Leopold Amery, Conservative MP, secretary of state for India and for Burma, 1940–45.

the Anglo-French position in the Czechoslovak crisis. Churchill learned from Cabinet circles that the British government has received a document confirming that between 60% and 70% of the officers in our air force have been 'liquidated' in some form or another. When relating all this, Churchill tried to smile sceptically, but I could see that the 'information' he had received worried him. I scoffed at the *Cliveden Set*'s idle talk and tried to reassure Churchill. I don't know to what extent I succeeded.

1 October

I visited Lloyd George in Churt. We had a long talk about the crisis. Among other things, Lloyd George told me an extraordinary story. A week ago, Baldwin came to Chamberlain and said: 'You must do everything in your power to avoid a war, however humiliating the cost. Just think what will happen if it comes to war! Our complete unpreparedness will immediately become apparent and then the indignant public will have us both hanging from the street lamps.' Lloyd George is convinced that this consideration played a major role in the capitulation in Munich.

Lloyd George sees the near future in a very bleak light. A crushing defeat has been inflicted on Western democracies in Munich. France has turned into a second-rate power (Daladier is weak, and Bonnet is a traitor). The League of Nations and collective security are dead. The world has entered the era of the mailed fist and of wild outbursts of coarse violence. England is in a deeply reactionary state. Power is in the hands of the most conservative circles of the bourgeoisie, who fear communism most of all and calculate their every step accordingly. Chamberlain's next objective, in the sphere of foreign policy, is the 'Pact of the Four', and, in domestic politics, elections, at which he will try to capitalize on his 'success' in Munich.

'The sole bright spot against this dark background,' concluded Lloyd George, 'is the USSR. It has conducted itself with dignity during the crisis. It is the sun of world democracy today. There were times when all the democratic elements in various countries looked up to us, England and France. It is not so any longer. Now all democratic elements all over the world turn their gaze on you, the USSR.'

Lloyd George was interested in the Soviet response to the Munich Conference. I replied that I had not been fully informed as yet, but I had no doubt that the response would be sharply negative. Disappointment and irritation with Britain and France would undoubtedly grow and isolationist tendencies would intensify among the general population. Of course, the Soviet government, with its inherent realism (far removed from that of Chamberlain), will hardly take any serious decisions in a hurry. Most likely, it will wait, think things over, weigh up the current situation and examine subsequent developments before undertaking any changes in our foreign policy. But I am speaking now not about the Soviet government, but about the mood of the general public.

'Just don't leave Spain, whatever you do!' exclaimed Lloyd George.

And then he began to argue at great length that isolationism would be a bad policy for the USSR. I reassured my interlocutor once again that the Soviet government is not pursuing any consciously isolationist policies, but that isolationist sentiments do exist in some circles of our population, and that events such as Munich could only serve to intensify them.

Lloyd George has been reading a lot of Turgenev lately. He showed me a big pile of books – English translations of Turgenev – and asked me which one in particular I would advise him to commit to memory. I recommended *Fathers and Sons*.

[For the Soviet Union (and for Litvinov and Maisky personally), the Munich Agreement was a horrific setback. Litvinov's 'year-long and untiring efforts to realize his policy of collective security against Germany,' reported the British ambassador from Moscow, 'would appear ... to have fallen into the water'; he 'has scarcely been visible since his arrival' from Geneva.[113] Increasingly identified with isolationist tendencies, Litvinov's deputy, Potemkin, was little impressed by Maisky's attempts to assure Narkomindel that the situation 'was slowly beginning to change'.[114] Maisky was severely reproached for the failure to respond critically to the 'deceitful inventions' of Halifax and others regarding presumed 'cooperation' and 'consultation' with the Soviet Union prior to the Munich Agreement. Their objective, it was implied, had been to exonerate themselves and pin the blame on Moscow. 'In your reports of these conversations,' Maisky was reprimanded, 'we fail to see a critical reaction ... One gets the impression that you seriously accept this eyewash, which, however, should have been all too obvious to you.'[115] No wonder Maisky spared no effort in alerting both Churchill and Lloyd George, at great length, to the 'absolutely false' claims that the Russians had been privy to the Anglo-French settlement of the Czechoslovakia case.

As indicative of Maisky's mood were his desperate attempts to meet an elusive Eden and the strikingly disproportionate space devoted in his diary to his public repudiation of Lord Winterton's[i] claims that, because of its military weakness, the Soviet Union 'confined itself to merely making vague promises'.[116] To satisfy Moscow, Maisky even arranged for a parliamentary question to be put to the prime minister. This led to a major (and disproportionate) debate on Winterton's statement a week later.[117] It is hardly surprising that Maisky appeared henceforth to be 'vague, mordant, and ominous', barely concealing his 'unutterable disgust with the Chamberlain policy', which he feared would spawn a four-power pact leading to the institutionalized isolation of Russia.[118] He now regarded Chamberlain as 'The Enemy', while he nicknamed Halifax 'The Bishop' who 'retires to pray and comes out a worse hypocrite than before'.[119]

---

[i] Edward Turnour (6th Earl Winterton), chancellor of the duchy of Lancaster, 1937–39; deputy to secretary of state for air, March–May 1938; member of the Cabinet, March 1938–January 1939.

The Soviet Union's raging denunciation of the Munich Agreement should have alerted Chamberlain to the likelihood of Soviet reclusion and possibly its corollary, an accommodation with Hitler. Spending a leisurely weekend with the Webbs, Maisky revealed his cards: 'he thought that the USSR would be cautious and discreet in her policy: she would tend to withdraw from world affairs *in effect*; meanwhile staying at Geneva awaiting a "change of heart" in the democratic powers'.[120] But in the absence of an alternative policy, Stalin was, for a while, dissuaded by Litvinov from withdrawing into isolation, particularly after Hitler's seizure of Prague in March 1939. Yet Maisky's existentialist need to preserve collective security led to an ambivalence, whereby ominous threats of isolation were combined with assurances to the contrary. 'Whatever happens,' Maisky assured Lord Strabolgi, 'the USSR will continue its constant policy of peace and the resolute struggle against aggression.'[121]]

6 October

Barely left parliament for four days running because of the debates on the Munich Conference. On the first day, 3 October, the diplomatic gallery was full, but then it began to empty until only I and the Belgian were left. The latter, the old hereditary Baron Cartier de Marchienne,[i] a typical diplomat of the pre-war school, is for reasons incomprehensible to me a regular visitor to parliament. You can always find him in the diplomatic gallery during any remotely interesting session. Corbin, Guo Taiqi and some others reappeared towards the end of the debates. Masaryk did not show up at all, and this was quite understandable.

My impressions of the debates? I would sum them up as follows.

The debates were accompanied throughout by considerable tension, with feelings spilling over at times. No fewer than sixty speakers took the floor. The dividing line was markedly apparent. On one side were members of the Cabinet and the overwhelming majority of the government coalition; on the other, the Labour–Liberal opposition plus the 'rebels' from the Conservative camp. There is no disputing, however, that the debates took an unfavourable turn for the government, not in terms of the voting results (which were predetermined), but in terms of the political effect in parliament and in the country at large.

The speeches on the government side were mostly ineffective. Chamberlain was nervous, over-excited, and kept losing his thread. He couldn't cope with the numerous shouts and rejoinders flung at him from the opposition benches, and was generally feeble. His speech showed more vividly than ever that he is a poor orator and one incapable of captivating an audience. Inskip, Burgin and Hoare in the House of Commons and Halifax and Stanhope[ii] in the House of Lords

---

[i] Baron Emile de Cartier de Marchienne, Belgian ambassador to London, 1927–46.
[ii] James Richard Stanhope (7th Earl Stanhope), parliamentary undersecretary of state for foreign affairs, 1934–36; president of Board of Education, 1937–38; first lord of the Admiralty, 1938–39;

also won no laurels. Hoare was simply impossible: he got confused, played with his spectacles, and mumbled incoherent phrases. Burgin, on the contrary, spoke very smoothly, with artfully feigned enthusiasm and almost military gusto, but he failed to observe any restraint and thereby spoiled the whole show. If one were to believe Burgin, nothing had really happened, all was marvellous in this best of all possible worlds, and the division of Czechoslovakia sanctioned in Munich was to be put down to *minor adjustments* in Central Europe, ensuing from the principles of justice and self-determination. Listening to Burgin was quite disgusting. The only skilful and well-delivered speech on the government side was that of Simon. It was a cut above the rest.

But these were all ministers. The *backbenchers* preferred to keep silent, and to do their bit for the government by voting. This created the impression, most unfavourable for the Cabinet, that its policy was defended almost exclusively by its members, i.e. the persons who shaped and carried it out. Moreover, not all of the ministers spoke. Elliot, Stanley, Hore-Belisha and some others kept their lips sealed. Elliot would not even sit on the government bench. Equally unconvincing was the ovation given to Chamberlain, which the Conservatives had prepared with such care. The plan was that as soon as Chamberlain appeared in the House, all the government's supporters would stand up and greet him with loud *cheers* for several minutes. It was expected that at least the Liberals would also stand up, while the Labourites, even if they remained in their seats, wouldn't interfere with the Tory ovation. But things turned out quite differently. The government's supporters did all that was expected of them when the PM appeared, but the Liberals would not join them, while Labour not only remained seated, but started hissing. The result was a *flop*.[122]

In the debates themselves, Chamberlain's opponents stacked up points against the government. First, in terms of quantity: most of the speakers were against Chamberlain. Second, in terms of quality: it turned out that not only the entire opposition, but also all the more eminent and intelligent members of the government coalition who were well versed in international affairs (Churchill, Eden, Cranborne, Nicolson, Duff Cooper, Amery, Richard Law,[i] son of Bonar Law,[ii] and others) disagreed with the prime minister and the Munich Agreement. Duff Cooper's speech was of particular importance. He resigned on 1 October and following parliamentary tradition he was the first to take the floor on 3 October, prior to Chamberlain, to explain the reasons for his retirement. Duff Cooper's speech was forceful and stinging. Someone later said that his speech was too 'literary'. There is a grain of truth in that,

---

lord president of the council, 1939–40; leader of House of Lords, 1938–40.
[i] Richard Kidston Law, British Conservative politician; financial secretary to the War Office, 1940–41; parliamentary undersecretary of state for foreign affairs, 1941–43.
[ii] Andrew Bonar Law, Conservative prime minister, 1922–23.

but nevertheless his speech made a very strong impression on the House and instantly 'poisoned' the atmosphere of the debates. Chamberlain, who took the floor after Duff Cooper, was unable to rectify the situation. As for the other anti-Chamberlain speeches, I best liked those delivered by Churchill, Cranborne, Nicolson and Herbert Morrison. Archibald Sinclair was not bad either. The rest of the opposition speeches were of poor quality.

Be that as it may, the 'old hands' in parliament, summing up the debates, reached the conclusion that they had gone against the government.

* * *

There is much truth in this. The best evidence is that the government decided not to call an election in the immediate future. Boothby told me that the party apparatus headed by Kingsley Wood insisted on making a prompt gain out of the Munich Agreement. Chamberlain hesitated at first. By the end of the debates, he had decided not to call an election now. Why? According to Boothby (I heard the same from other sources), there are three reasons: (1) the euphoria of the first days following the Munich Conference is quickly evaporating, thanks in large measure to the debates; (2) the Churchill–Eden group has threatened to act against the government at the election if Chamberlain takes the 'capitalization' route; and (3) the rearmament programme is to be implemented as quickly as possible in the nearest future, which is feasible only with the cooperation of the trades unions. A general election would only widen the gap between the government and the workers' organizations. I can't vouch for the 100% accuracy of Boothby's statements, but it is unquestionable that there is a great deal of truth in what he is saying, and that the recent parliamentary debates have played their part in starting to bring the general public to its senses.

One of the most heated moments in the debate concerned the USSR. The opposition of all shades and hues accused the government of ignoring the USSR throughout the crisis and doing everything in its power (even slandering the USSR) to prevent close cooperation between London, Paris and Moscow in the struggle against Hitler. This issue was raised by Attlee, Dalton, Morrison, Sinclair, Churchill and others. The pressure they exerted was so great that the government had to justify itself and afford at least a certain verbal satisfaction to the opposition. In the House of Lords on 3 October, Halifax more or less repeated what he told me on 29 September: namely, that the Munich Agreement did not signify a weakening in the desire of the British government, as of the French government, to maintain relations of mutual understanding with the USSR. In the House of Commons on 4 October, Simon confirmed that although the British government intended to develop 'friendly consultations' between the four powers, it did not intend to 'exclude Russia from the resolution of European questions in future', and he added that he hoped to see the USSR among the guarantors of Czechoslovakia's new borders. Hoare and Inskip spoke in the same vein. Of course, these are mere words, and Chamberlain would rather lose half the Empire than agree to genuine cooperation with the USSR; even so, these words are somewhat symptomatic.

Most disgusting of all were the people in the Independent Labour Party. These 'r-r-revolutionaries', if you will, praised Chamberlain to the skies. They say they are against a 'capitalist war' and for the transformation of capitalism into socialism (by what means?), and they are grateful to the PM for saving them from such a war and for preserving peace, which is so essential to them for the fulfilment of their ideals. Maxton got a genuine ovation... from the Conservatives! That's how low they've sunk!

11 October

In the morning papers today I came across an account of the speech delivered by Lord Winterton (member of the Cabinet and chancellor of the Duchy of Lancaster) in Shoreham on 10 October. 'Russia,' he stated there, 'had offered no aid during the crisis over Czechoslovakia and, as a result of its military weakness, had confined itself merely to promises of a vague and general nature.'

I decided to act immediately, without even making preliminary contact with Moscow. First of all, I sent off my reply to Winterton's slander to the press, and then I asked Halifax for a meeting. He received me at 5 p.m.

Having familiarized the foreign minister with the content of Winterton's speech, I made the following statement: 'Recently, certain high-ranking individuals in Britain and France, including some who hold high public office, and even ministerial positions, have been spreading lies and slander about the USSR's stance on the issue of Czechoslovakia. These fabrications basically boiled down to two points: (1) the USSR has no intention of fulfilling its obligations under the Soviet–Czechoslovak pact and (2) the USSR cannot fulfil its obligations owing to the weakness of the Red Army and deficiencies in the Soviet air force.'

Halifax had been listening to me silently and motionlessly, but at this point he stirred a little, made a gesture with his hand and nodded as if to say: 'Yes, I too have heard rumours of this sort.'

I went on: 'The purport of the slander being disseminated by the persons I have mentioned is absolutely clear. They simply wanted to shift the blame from the sick to the healthy party and make it seem as if the responsibility for the systematic retreat of Britain and France before the aggressors, culminating in Munich, lies with the USSR. I had thought that Litvinov's speech in the League of Nations on 21 September and the recent debates in the British parliament had delivered a fatal blow to all these rumours. I had assumed that now every

British citizen, let alone every Cabinet minister, could be in no doubt that the USSR had never had anything to do either with the policies that led to Munich or with the Munich Agreement itself, which, I am deeply convinced, will bear catastrophic consequences for peace in our days and will be severely condemned by history. So it is all the more astonishing to hear those slanderous fabrications repeated publicly by Lord Winterton, a responsible Cabinet minister! In view of the aforesaid, I consider it my duty to lodge a protest against the speech made by the chancellor of the Duchy of Lancaster.'

Halifax heard my statement calmly and then, turning slightly to towards me, said that he acknowledged the validity of my protest and understood my reasons. Unfortunately, British politicians sometimes take the liberty of saying too much. Halifax regrets Winterton's speech, all the more so as mutual reproaches and accusations concerning things that have already happened and cannot be changed needlessly aggravate relations. Meanwhile, as he assured me on 29 September and later confirmed in the House of Lords on 3 October, the British government wishes to maintain good relations with the USSR. Even if the British government has to conduct further separate talks with Germany and Italy, it certainly does not intend to exclude the USSR from attempts to resolve common European problems. Halifax concluded by adding that he would immediately contact Winterton and take measures to prevent such incidents in future.

I replied that the USSR also aims to maintain good relations with Britain, but it has to reckon not with kind words and assurances but with concrete facts.

Halifax pondered for a minute, as if he were turning over my words in his mind. Then he uttered slowly: 'That is a very wise and reasonable approach.'

I smiled to myself, and said that, recalling recent developments, especially Munich, I cannot be sure that it will be so easy to maintain those good relations between the USSR and Britain which, according to Halifax, his government desires. Not because we shall try to erect any obstacles, but because the facts, including the Munich Agreement, have a logic of their own.

I was already preparing to leave, thinking that my mission had been accomplished, when Halifax, apparently provoked by my last remark, stopped me and began to speak: 'It seems to me that you, like many others in Europe, do not understand England's position clearly enough. We think that nowadays the world is witnessing the struggle of two ideological fronts – fascism and communism. We, the English, support neither one nor the other. Moreover, we dislike both. We have our own notions and institutions, developed over centuries. We do not want to change them for anything else. In the struggle between the two fronts, we occupy a neutral or, if you please, a middle position. It is precisely for this reason that we are misunderstood so often on the continent and attacked so frequently from both sides.'

I have heard this 'philosophy' of the cowardly Brits a thousand times already, and I had little difficulty finding the necessary arguments in reply. I remarked with a hint of mockery that the notorious 'anti-Comintern pact', which was supposedly geared primarily against the USSR, was so far operating against China, Spain, Czechoslovakia, Abyssinia, and against the interests of the British and French empires.[123] On the other hand, we had good relations with Italy over a period of 11 years (1924–1935) despite our polarized 'ideologies'. These were ruined only when Italy embarked upon the path of external aggression – against Abyssinia and Spain. That is no accident. Current developments in the world signify <u>not the struggle of two ideological fronts, but the struggle of two trends in foreign policy: aggression and peace</u>. One cannot remain betwixt and between in this situation. One cannot be lukewarm. Anyone trying to hold a neutral position in the struggle between aggression and peace objectively encourages aggression and, in the long run, will suffer most of all. I gave Munich as an illustration: it has presented Hitler with the opportunity to set up 'Mitteleuropa' in the shortest possible time, and this is fraught with the gravest consequences not only for the cause of peace, but for Great Britain itself.

'Well, should I understand,' Halifax interrupted me, 'that you would like to ward off German expansion in South-East Europe by war?'

'Not by war,' I replied, 'but by pursuing a sound policy. Why do you always frighten people with war? War can and must be avoided, if timely measures are taken. Unfortunately, neither England nor France has been willing to take such measures. All illnesses are easier to cure at an early stage. If the illness is neglected, then the moment may come when, in spite of the most desperate efforts, and in spite of the doctor's sincere sympathy, the patient will die.'

My words clearly made an impression on Halifax for he suddenly interrupted me and, nodding in consent, observed: 'Even surgery may not help.'

After a moment's pause, Halifax went on: 'Let us assume that Germany will form its "Mitteleuropa", which is quite probable in my mind. What will it do next?'

I smiled to myself again and, fully aware of the true meaning of Halifax's question, replied: 'Naturally, Hitler will turn to the west!'

'Why do you think so?' Halifax asked.

I put forward a few arguments to support my notion, which I had advanced more than once in my talks with the English (for instance, in my conversation with Churchill last March), and concluded by saying: 'Hitler is afraid of a big war. He prefers bloodless victories. Judging by the experience of recent years, he knows how to win them without firing a shot. Why? It is certainly not because he is especially strong. Britain and France are basically much stronger than Germany. Hitler scores his bloodless victories because he is an expert at fraying one's nerves. His nerves are stronger than yours. That's why you lose one game after another. But Hitler is well aware that this method would not work in the east, that is, against the USSR. The Soviet government's nerves are yet stronger than Hitler's. If he tried his luck at the expense of the USSR, he wouldn't get away with bluffing. He would have to fight, to fight in earnest. And without any hope of ultimate success. What for? Wouldn't it be simpler and easier to head west where, to all appearances, Munich is far from being his last bloodless victory?'

Halifax made not so much as a sound or a movement in dissent. Then, after a long silence, he asked: 'What do you think Hitler will play for next?'

'The colonies,' I answered without a moment's hesitation.

Halifax nodded and said: 'I think so, too.'

On parting, I asked whether the British government considers Mussolini's promise to evacuate 10,000 volunteers an adequate price for the ratification of the Anglo-Italian agreement.

Halifax seemed almost to choke and began saying something obscure and vague.

It's quite clear: the British government is preparing another betrayal of Spain.[124]

13 October

Recently I met the Labour leaders – Cripps, Morrison and Dalton. All maintain that there is great excitement among the working masses, but also great confusion. Where to go? What to do? How to fight against Chamberlain's policy?

There is a growing tendency towards a 'united front' without communists (Labourites, Liberals, the Conservative opposition, and Independent Progressives). *Transport House* is against it, of course, but the probing and groping for opportunities to form such a front are nonetheless ongoing. Cripps and Dalton, in particular, are engaged on this. I am sceptical: there is strong resistance to a united front in the Labour Party, while the Conservative opposition lacks determination. Moreover, the Tories are a motley crew. Also, one cannot rule out the possibility that Chamberlain, with a view to sowing confusion in the ranks of his Tory opponents, may offer ministerial posts to one or two of them. They may just fall for the bait. We'll see. But it seems to me that, for the moment at least, prospects for a united front are slim.[125]

All the Labourites keep asking me anxiously whether we intend to 'leave' Europe? Do we propose to move to a policy of isolationism? The Labourites admit that after Munich the USSR has every moral right to turn its back on Europe and say: 'You can stew and perish in your own juice.' Yet they all beseech me: 'Don't leave!' For our withdrawal would mean the final breakdown of democratic forces and the absolute triumph of the reactionary policies of Chamberlain. Meanwhile, the Labourites are hoping that the masses will recover from their recent shock in due course and progressive forces will begin to build up once more. Our 'presence' in Europe might facilitate this process enormously.[126]

Interestingly, Vansittart, showing great concern, asked me the same question when we had lunch together today. In his opinion, the situation will become clearer by the beginning of 1939 and take a turn for the better; moreover, the Germans are likely to do some foolish things in the intervening period. As for Vansittart himself, he does not intend to leave the Foreign Office, contrary to the rumours that have been circulating. He will stay on and fight for his line. He would very much like the USSR to 'remain' in Europe.

(I responded to them all in the same way: the USSR is *disgusted* by the behaviour of Western powers, but does not intend to take any hasty steps. We are studying the current situation and keeping a close eye on it. We'll draw conclusions in due time. This seems to more or less satisfy them.)

Incidentally, Dalton explained to me the essence of Chamberlain's foreign-policy 'philosophy', citing highly competent sources. Here it is. All international affairs must be regulated by truly great powers, of which there are six: the USA, the British Empire, Germany (with its vassals), Japan (with its empire) and the USSR. Chamberlain has no doubts concerning the participation of the first four powers in the world directorate, but what should be done with the USSR? Nothing has occurred to him as yet. France is to become Britain's 'satellite'. There may be a struggle for Italy between London and Berlin. All the other countries will serve as small change in transactions between members of the 'directorate'. Not bad! Real 'super-imperialism'!

Dalton also mentioned that Henderson, the British ambassador in Berlin, told him right after his appointment last year: the object of my mission is to form an Anglo-German alliance. He let it be understood that this was the prime minister's point of view. The very same Henderson developed the following theory: to satisfy Germany's colonial claims, it is necessary to draw up a subscription list for each colonial power to make its donation. Would Hitler be satisfied with such a solution? I doubt it.

The German embassy lodged a protest against Morrison's speech in parliament on 4 October.

15 October

In spite of Halifax's promise to 'take measures', which was given to me on 11 October, I was surprised to find among the newspapers of 13 October an account of a new speech made by Winterton, in which he repeated his initial false statement in an even sharper form. This enraged me. I immediately sent a second statement to the press, very scathing and biting, where I publicly denounced the 'noble Lord' as a liar. I also wrote a letter to Halifax, asking him what all this meant. Two hours later I received Halifax's reply by special delivery. He expressed a belief that his letter to Winterton, which he had forwarded promptly after our talk on 11 October, did not reach the addressee in time; but now he would speak to his colleague personally and he was sure that from now on everything would be *all right*.

Halifax was right. Winterton stopped making such statements. Moreover, today I received a letter from Winterton inviting me, with true English politeness, to have lunch with him in order to clarify and end our dispute.

Well, let's have lunch and talk about it. The entire incident is taking a curious turn.

17 October

The Protest of the USSR Ambassador in London Comrade Maisky

LONDON, 13 October (TASS). On 11 October the USSR ambassador in London Comrade Maisky visited the British foreign secretary, Halifax, and entered a protest against the mendacious insinuations made by Lord Winterton in his speech in Shoreham.[127]

… The *Manchester Guardian*, *News Chronicle* and *Daily Herald* carry excerpts from the article devoted to the foreign policy of the French government published in *Journal de Moscou*. Besides, the British press features the full text of the Soviet embassy's refutation of 11 October concerning Lord Winterton's false statement that the Soviet Union allegedly did not intend to render assistance to Czechoslovakia.

The *Manchester Guardian* writes in its editorial about the Soviet Union's stand in the Czechoslovak crisis. Isn't it time for the British government, the newspaper asks, to define its attitude to the USSR? Does the government wish to cooperate with the Soviet Union or does it intend to keep away from it in future? Chamberlain tried, the newspaper continues, to establish cooperation with Germany and Italy. As a result, these countries brought Britain to an imminent threat of war. At the same time, although Chamberlain's attitude toward the USSR was exceptionally cool, it was eventually hailed as our ally in the event of war.

Simon and Hoare did everything possible during the debates in the House of Commons to somewhat repair the damage inflicted. They announced that there was no design to confine the Soviet Union to the east and expressed a hope that the USSR would join the new international guarantees for the changed borders of Czechoslovakia. The newspaper writes further that the international situation Britain found itself in after signing the Munich Agreement requires that the policy of close and friendly cooperation with the Soviet Union should be chosen not only for reasons of common sense, but also as a necessity. However, Lord Winterton evidently holds a different point of view.

It is only natural that the Soviet ambassador in London made a strong protest to the British Foreign Office against Winterton's speech and recalled Litvinov's speech in Geneva, where the latter confirmed that the Soviet Union intended to fulfil all its obligations. Apart from everything else, there is yet more evidence of the actual intentions of the USSR. At the peak of the crisis, on 27 September, the world press published a statement originating from 'authoritative British circles in London'. Everyone understands what is implied by 'authoritative circles'. The statement read that if Czechoslovakia was eventually attacked by Germany, France would be compelled to lend aid to it immediately, and Britain and the Soviet Union would certainly side with France.

So, the newspaper proceeds, the statement pointed out directly that the three powers would act in concert, and, in the opinion of other persons (whether they are right or not is another question), this particular statement made Hitler agree to the Munich Conference at the last moment. Anyway, it was an exact, formal and 'authoritative' declaration from London about the Soviet Union's solidarity with Britain and France. A time may come when we shall be glad to hear about solidarity from the USSR once again.

It is strange that the British ministers speak in the same spirit as Winterton. Members of the House of Commons will undoubtedly not be slow in asking Chamberlain what the Cabinet's real stand is. Is it really possible to suggest that the British government assumes no responsibility for Lord Winterton's statement?[128]

19 October

Beaverbrook came for lunch. As always, he had many interesting things to say.

According to him, Chamberlain firmly believes in the possibility of European 'appeasement' by way of negotiations with Hitler and Mussolini. This is hardly surprising, considering that the PM is prepared to retreat even further at the cost of third countries and, as a last resort, even at the cost of the British Empire. The prospect of creating a 'Mitteleuropa' does not frighten Chamberlain at all. On the contrary, it even pleases him: won't it lead to a confrontation between Germany and the USSR?

When I asked what the PM thought about the colonial issue, Beaverbrook replied that Chamberlain was ready to return to Germany all its former colonies in Africa, with the exception of Tanganyika and South-West Africa, and to compensate her with Angola and the Congo. This, of course, would result in a serious split in the country and within the Conservative Party, but Beaverbrook thinks that the PM might manage to carry it through nonetheless.

Generally speaking, Beaverbrook is in a vague and irritated state of mind. He supports Chamberlain's Munich policy, but he is flatly against the PM's rearmament policy. For what is happening now? Convinced that he will be able to come to terms with Hitler and Mussolini, Chamberlain tarries with rearmament. The proof: his unwillingness to mobilize industry and to set up a ministry of supply. He is altogether against any kind of 'heroic measures'. His slogan is 'business as usual'. And this happens despite the fact that Inskip's total failure as 'minister for coordination'[129] is acknowledged by all, even by the PM himself!

Beaverbrook does not anticipate any major changes in the government in the near future. The PM will on no account let Churchill into the Cabinet. He would willingly take in Eden, but Eden himself will hardly agree, since for him this would be tantamount to political suicide. The result is bad! Very bad!

'What we need most of all,' Beaverbrook exclaimed a couple of times, 'is a strong government! Where it comes from and what it will be like is a secondary issue. Just so long as it's strong!'

This sounded almost fascistic.

* * *

Attlee and Greenwood came for dinner. We discussed at length current events and Labour's plans. A sad picture. Both fail to understand or sense that the present situation is absolutely extraordinary and requires extraordinary measures to be taken – in particular, some 'heroic' steps to change Britain's foreign policy. In their opinion, everything should continue as normal. They must campaign, make speeches in parliament, assail the government in the press, etc., and wait for the nearest election, which will probably be held in a year at the earliest. That's the sum of their philosophy, strategy and tactics.

* * *

Layton, who had tea with me today, told me a strange story. During the crisis, none other than Samuel Hoare told him one day: 'The more I reflect on the situation, the closer I come to the conclusion that if we really want to preserve our empire, we have no choice but to go along with Russia. Indeed, Russia is not an expansionist country today and poses no danger to the British Empire. Germany, on the contrary, is breaking forth from its borders in all directions and undoubtedly constitutes a threat to the Empire. Why, in such a situation, shouldn't we come to an agreement with Russia about cooperation?'

Hoare also voiced his pleasure apropos De La Warr's and Butler's meeting with M.M. [Litvinov] and me in Geneva. Sir Samuel is evidently not as hopeless as I thought.

Layton is pessimistic about the political situation. He thinks Chamberlain is *safe*, as at least 70% of the voters are definitely behind him.

20 October

The position of the small powers today is an unenviable one! I had the chance to feel this when the Greek ambassador Simopoulos,[i] sitting in the armchair opposite me, lamented their unhappy lot.

He was in a panicky mood.

'We used to fear our enemies, but now we have to fear our "friends" more,' he said.

These are terrible times. Force triumphs everywhere. Who knows what tomorrow will bring. One must be cautious. Keep a low profile. Sit quietly in one's corner and wait. Maybe things will 'blow over'.

I asked whether England, which is so interested in maintaining good relations with Greece, offers any support?

Simopoulos gestured vaguely. Yes, England certainly plays the role of Greece's 'protector', but… isn't it kind of a strange 'protector'? You can never be sure of her. Especially now, after Munich.

Take Italy, for example. Greece is mortally afraid of Italy. Should the Italian navy appear in Piraeus, everything will be over in 24 hours. What's to be done? Can one say with confidence that England will not betray Greece? Who knows? Everything is so vague. If only the Anglo-Italian agreement could come into effect soon. Perhaps the situation in the Mediterranean would become a little more stable. But in the meantime Greece has to bow down low before Italy.

The economy is another example. The total debt of Greece to Britain and France amounts to 60 million pounds, with the annual interest totalling 4–5 million. Greece is unable to pay this much and offers about half the sum. That's not so bad, is it? But the English won't have it. Meanwhile, Greece has a trading deficit with Britain of 1.5 million pounds. How can Greece pay its interest in such circumstances?

I inquired about the particulars of Greek foreign trade. Simopoulos was very keen to answer: 'Tobacco and currants are our main export items. Britain purchased huge amounts of both before the war, and what now? Currants are no longer exported to Britain at all because of Australian competition. Tobacco exports to Britain amount to virtually nothing. It's three years now that I've been doing my utmost to persuade the Imperial Tobacco Co. to add some Greek tobacco in its cigarettes. If they agreed to mix in even just 5%, Greece would be happy and her entire economy would recover. But the ITC has its

---

[i] Charalambos Simopoulos, Greek ambassador to London, 1935–42.

own plantations and does not want to use our tobacco. What should we do? We've tried to obtain export credits in Britain, but to no avail. We've asked for armaments on credit, but failed again. Greece is building two destroyers in Britain, which will be completed in about four months, and now what? The company flatly demands that we pay on the nail. We lack the funds to make an immediate payment for the guns that are to be mounted on the destroyers, and now what? The company refuses to grant us credit. We'll have to send the destroyers to Greece unequipped and mount German guns on them at home.'

'Why German?' I asked.

'Very simple,' Simopoulos answered. 'The Germans, unlike the British, take nearly half Greece's exports and supply us with arms and ammunition on a clearing basis.'

The Greek ambassador concluded: 'You know, I am an Anglophile. My wife is English. But what are we to do? You rack your brains and sigh, and finally go cap in hand to Funk.[i] There is nowhere else to go.'

22 October

Canton fell yesterday. Guo Taiqi called on me urgently today. He was worried and upset. He immediately turned to the difficulties being faced by China. Britain does nothing to help her. The Chinese received merely 36 planes from Britain during the war, and had to pay in cash. The British give neither money nor credits. The United States is assisting China indirectly (by buying Chinese silver, informally prohibiting its industrialists to supply aircraft to Japan, etc.), but this is not enough. France gives neither money nor arms and seriously slows down transit through Indochina. In general, all the 'Great Democracies' have turned their backs on China. Thank you USSR – it alone provides real help. In particular, it supplies China with excellent planes.

Now, however, with the fall of Canton and the imminent cleansing of Hankou, the situation is becoming critically serious. The supply of arms and aircraft will not suffice. More effective means are needed.

I asked Guo what he meant.

Guo said: we need another Zhanggufeng! Otherwise, the movement for peace with Japan among the Chinese population will become irrepressible.

I couldn't say anything to encourage Guo, of course. However I assured him that the USSR was not going to 'leave' the sphere of active foreign policy, and that our attitude to China, which is fighting for its independence, would remain most friendly.

---

[i] Walther Funk, press chief and undersecretary in the Nazi Ministry of Propaganda from 1933; minister of economics and ambassador general for war economy from 1938.

After Guo's departure, I wondered for a long time: was this a 'spontaneous' move by Guo himself, prompted by the fall of Canton? Or was he sounding me out on instructions from his government? Or was this a plot on the part of Wang Jingwei,[i] with whom Guo has long been on friendly terms?

Time will tell.

25 October

War Minister Hore-Belisha came over for lunch. Also present were Butler, the undersecretary for foreign affairs, Sir William Brown,[ii] the permanent undersecretary for trade, Leith-Ross and others.

Hore-Belisha was jovial, drank Russian vodka at a gulp, and said some quite interesting things. The German to British aircraft ratio is 3:1. The production capacity of German aircraft factories is 800 units a month, while the British plan to increase their output to 700 aircraft a month no earlier than the end of 1939. I asked how the British government was going to deal with its air *inferiority* and when. Hore-Belisha raised his hands and said: 'I don't know. We face great challenges.' I then asked whether the Cabinet was at least planning to set up a ministry of supply in the near future and to mobilize industry?

'Not yet,' answered Hore-Belisha.

'Why?' I insisted.

'Why?' Belisha shrugged his shoulders and said in a sarcastic tone, 'Have you been to 10, Downing Street lately?'

'No, I haven't.'

'There you are. Had you been there, you'd have seen that the PM's apartment is strewn with flowers sent to him by female admirers from all over the country. The PM seriously considers Munich a victory, and is convinced that if he takes a delicate approach towards Hitler and Mussolini he will succeed in appeasing Europe.'

Translated into the language of politics, this means that Chamberlain intends to retreat even further. Hore-Belisha confirmed this: although no official Cabinet decision has been taken, the general opinion of the majority of ministers is that a 'colonial deal' should be struck with Hitler.[130]

26 October

So, my squabble with Lord Winterton is over. Today I had lunch with him at his place (various specific reasons had prevented us from meeting earlier). We were alone and the conversation was very open.

---

[i] Wang Jingwei (Wang Chiang-wei), leader of the pro-Japanese faction in the Guomindang, headed the government set up by Japan in Nanjing from 1940 to 1944.

[ii] Sir William Brown, permanent secretary, Board of Trade, 1937–40.

Winterton began by making apologies. He begged pardon for his speech, which he thought a mistake, and assured me that not only he, but all members of the Cabinet desire the best possible relations with the USSR. Hmm! Let's suppose. I said a few conciliatory phrases in reply, as the occasion demanded.

We then began to talk seriously about the current situation. We spoke frankly. Winterton put forward the notion, shared by many Englishmen at present, that Hitler's next move will be the Ukraine. I disappointed him by advancing approximately the same arguments that I had used in my talk with Halifax on 11 October. My words evidently made an impression on him, because he hastened to admit the justice of my thesis about the small probability of a German advance to the east. At the same time he tried to contest my assertion that Britain was in imminent danger, claiming that Hitler would not dare to encroach upon the integrity and inviolability of such a great power as the British Empire. In this respect, the chances of the USSR and the British Empire are even. 'Isn't it so?' Winterton asked me.

'Not exactly,' was my reply.

Then I told him what I thought about this question not as an ambassador, but as an impartial and unofficial political observer:

There are two types of great powers: natural and artificial. A natural great power, as I term it, is one that possesses a great, compact and rich territory and has a large, vigorous and stable population. There are three natural great powers in the world today: the USA, the USSR and China, in spite of the latter's misfortunes in the past century. Presently, Germany is making a desperate attempt to become a natural great power: having a large and vigorous population, she is trying to obtain a great and compact territory by extending her sphere of influence to the countries of Central and South-East Europe. It is too early to tell how successful she will be. I call an artificial great power one that, lacking the two basic prerequisites mentioned above, has built its might on the possession of overseas territories (colonies, mandates, etc.) and a number of other economic, financial and political factors. Great Britain belongs to the great powers of the second type. Given the conditions and dimensions of the twentieth century, the island of Britain is not a natural great power by itself. Great Britain is a great power only thanks to its Empire. But the Empire is scattered all over the seas and continents and is strategically vulnerable from a dozen directions. Prior to the appearance of aeroplanes, Great Britain together with its Empire probably could be called a natural great power by virtue of its absolute supremacy at sea. All this changed, however, with progress in aviation. Great Britain lost the features of a natural great power and turned into an artificial great power. Hitler, no doubt, has taken all this into account. Furthermore, he regards the English as a nation running to seed. My conclusion: Lord Winterton is unduly optimistic when he assumes that Hitler will never raise arms against such a mighty power as the British Empire. The Soviet Union and Great Britain are incomparable in this respect.

Evidently, the honourable lord had hardly ever been subjected to such an appraisal from anyone, let alone a foreign ambassador. And clearly he did not feel at ease. While I was speaking, his tall, stick-like figure fidgeted nervously on the chair. But the England of today is no longer the proud great-power England that I observed during the years of my emigration and that took any doubting of its strength or future as utter sacrilege. Winterton, therefore, had to resign himself to my words. When I finished, he tried to defend himself, but he did so rather feebly and unconvincingly. To sweeten the pill, I made a few compliments about British self-possession and administrative talents. Winterton cheered up. We then talked for a while about various aspects of the current situation and parted as 'friends'. Winterton expressed a desire to meet again, together with our wives, and added in conclusion: 'My friend Lord Halifax told me that you would lunch with him next week. It would be very good if you could repeat to him what you expounded so convincingly to me today.'

Well I never!

Leaving Winterton's place, I recalled the English rule: if you can't strangle the enemy, embrace him.

27 October

Today is the sixth anniversary of my arrival in Britain as ambassador. Some six years!…

28 October

Two high commissioners, Jordan[i] (New Zealand) and Te Water[ii] (South Africa), as well as Arthur Salter,[iii] Vyvyan Adams and Harold Macmillan came over for lunch.

The high commissioners are both interesting men. Jordan is a large, broad-shouldered, awkward bear who resembles a London policeman. Not without reason. He did indeed work as a policeman in London in his youth, before

---

[i] William J. Jordan, high commissioner for New Zealand in London, 1936–51.
[ii] Charles Theodore Te Water, high commissioner for the Union of South Africa in London, 1929–39; president of the League of Nations, 1933–34.
[iii] Arthur Salter, Gladstone Professor of Political Theory and Institutions, Oxford University.

emigrating to New Zealand, joining the Labour Party and making his career. He has a harsh, loud voice, and uses popular sayings; a bit naive, but honest. At the League of Nations, he often ruffles feathers among the British delegation. Te Water is a different type. A tall, elegant and intellectual Dutchman with 'soul' and 'sentiments'. A handsome face, or a pleasing one at any rate. A glaring contrast to Jordan.

We talked, of course, about the current situation. I emphasized the colonial issue. Emotions ran high. Te Water made a really passionate speech… in favour of granting colonies to Germany – only not South-West Africa. The latter must not be touched. South Africa is the sole seat of European culture on the African continent. It must be guarded and protected against dangers. Therefore, South-West Africa cannot be yielded to Hitler, because this would threaten Kaapstad [Cape Town]. Why not give Hitler something in some other place, in equatorial Africa, for instance? Colonies are not a commercial enterprise for Hitler, but a matter of honour. The Boers, who have been through the mill of military defeat and national oppression, understand the German mentality perfectly well. If the British had not displayed great political tact in 1926 by recognizing the equality of South Africa with the mother country and all other dominions, South Africa would be outside the Empire today. Similar tact must be shown towards Germany. The feeling of bitter resentment will then vanish from its mentality, and it will become less aggressive.

A dispute broke out. Adams and Macmillan objected vigorously. Salter also objected, but rather cautiously. I remarked that one should not bracket a rapacious imperialist power with a non-imperialist small country that presents no danger.

Te Water was highly agitated. I asked him whether the British government had conducted any exploratory talks with South Africa about returning South-West Africa to Germany. He answered in the negative. Salter inquired what South Africa would do if Britain agreed, at another Munich-like conference, to give South-West Africa to Germany. Te Water argued that this could not happen. Salter made his question more specific: 'Let's assume that at a Munich Conference No. 2 the British government gives its consent to the transfer of South-West Africa to Germany and promises not to give any support to South Africa during the implementation of such an agreement. What stand will South Africa take in this case? Will South Africa fight on its own?'

Te Water was confused and probably somewhat frightened by such a prospect. He just said: 'In that case, an absolutely new situation would emerge, and no one can say in advance what my government would do under such circumstances.'

After lunch I went to see Masaryk and congratulate him on the twentieth anniversary of independence of Czechoslovakia – which finds itself, alas, in a grievous plight. Masaryk told me that he had sent in his resignation, but that he would remain in office until 1 January at the request of the Czechoslovak government ('And not a day longer!' Masaryk added). He would live in London and occasionally travel to America, where he had spent many years as an émigré. He has already rented a small flat in Westminster and is going to write, lecture and broadcast on the radio.

'I'll survive one way or another,' he added. 'I'll exploit the good name of my father. And it is a good name! It means something today. There are fewer and fewer good names left in the world.'

* * *

Sir Bernard Pares dropped in. He is 71, but very active. He delivers lectures and speeches. Chamberlain makes him indignant. Pares follows a very sound course in politics. He contends that the country will not tolerate the present foreign policy of its government for long. That would be fine – but is it really so?

30 October

Just back from visiting the Webbs in the country, where we spent a few hours in lively conversation with our hosts. Sidney has recovered after the stroke he had in the spring. He walks, speaks and reacts more or less normally. Beatrice carries herself wonderfully for her 80 years – fresh and hale and hearty. Incidentally, they both complain about 'getting old' and tiring. Pull the other one! What I'd do to be like them at 80!

The old couple are in a very pessimistic mood, politically speaking. The latest events have consolidated their belief that England and France are in steep decline. France has already become a minor power, and England has embarked upon the road that will reduce it to the same status. In a historical perspective, the great dispute about the advantages of capitalism and socialism will be resolved through the rivalry between the Soviet Union and the United States. England will quit the scene as a possible rival much earlier. As for the fascist states, such as Germany and Italy, the Webbs dismiss the possibility of their return to bourgeois democracy, but they do not exclude the possibility that they will develop into communist powers. Organizationally, and in part also mentally, they are better equipped to turn to Soviet planned economy than to capitalist anarchy.

The Webbs take a gloomy view of Britain's immediate prospects. Chamberlain will hold out until the next election, which will return the Conservatives to power. However, when I told them about Chamberlain's plans for a *colonial deal* with Hitler, of which they knew very little, the old couple came to the surprising conclusion that the Conservative Party as a whole would not accept

it, that a split in its ranks would be inevitable, and that it could all end in an
Eden–Churchill cabinet coming to power.

31 October

The Elliots came for lunch. We talked *a quatre*. Most openly. Elliot said the
following: 'This is not a talk between an ambassador and a member of the Cabinet,
but between two students sitting in a café somewhere in Kiev or Glasgow.'

The Elliots are in low spirits. Her position is better than his. Yet, Elliot
himself also admits – contrary to the official version – that the 'democracies'
suffered a defeat in Munich and that the main task now is to avert the recurrence
of similar or even worse defeats in future. But how is this to be done? Here
Elliot falls silent and throws up his arms. For he is not a student after all, but a
member of the Cabinet, and he does not want to spoil his career.

A curious detail. Speaking about the lack of contact between the USSR and
Britain during the [Czechoslovak] crisis (a lack which he fully acknowledges),
Elliot offered the following explanation both of this fact and of the general chill
in Anglo-Soviet relations of late: 'Let's be frank. One thought weighed upon the
minds of the members of the Cabinet and their supporters throughout the crisis:
the Bolsheviks want to set Britain and Germany at loggerheads while keeping
themselves out of the way, and then, at a certain moment, when both sides grow
weaker, to interfere and engineer a world revolution. I can believe that Moscow
might have entertained such a thought. Probably you also feared that we wished
to set you and Germany at loggerheads and to gain by it ourselves. Distrust on
one side bred distrust on the other. As a result, it was Hitler who won.'

Reasoning in this way, Elliot comes to the conclusion that the recovery of
trust between London and Moscow is a prerequisite both for the strengthening
of Anglo-Soviet cooperation and for an effective response to German
aggression. But how is this to be achieved? Here, Elliot once again becomes
obscure and vague.

Elliot is essentially right: the heart of the matter lies in the class prejudice that
the English bourgeoisie cannot get rid of, even for the sake of saving the Empire.

1 November

Liddell-Hart[i] conveyed the following interesting information to me today.

The German air fleet totals <u>only</u> 7,000–8,000 aircraft. The monthly output
amounts to about 800 planes.

---

[i] Basil Liddell-Hart, a leading scholar of military history and war correspondent of the *Daily
Telegraph*, 1925–33 and then of *The Times*, 1935–39.

The British air fleet totals <u>only</u> some 3,000 aircraft, and the monthly output is 250 to 300 planes.

The rearmament of the British armed forces will be completed in approximately 12 months, but the size of the army is not expected to increase.

The anti-aircraft defence could be put in order in the course of six months, but Chamberlain will probably stretch it out for much longer.

In Liddell-Hart's opinion, Chamberlain does not intend to set about arming properly as (a) he is afraid to annoy Hitler and (b) he has no expectation of enlisting real support from the workers and their trade unions (on account of his present policy), without which serious arming is unthinkable.

Liddell-Hart had been Hore-Belisha's closest adviser for a whole year, but he parted with him not so long ago. Why? For the same reason. The British government does not want to arm properly, and Liddell-Hart does not want to serve as a tool by which the government can sell to the public those military pseudo-reforms to which it agrees.

3 November

Halifax invited Agniya and me to lunch. We first received a luncheon invitation from him on the eve of our departure for the USSR in mid-May and, if I am not mistaken, it was scheduled to take place on 24 May. That time we declined. Now the lunch has taken place. Apart from the hosts, there were Inskip, De La Warr and Butler with their wives. The food was good and homely. Nothing serious was discussed. After lunch, Inskip had me in hysterics with his sudden complaints about his inability to grasp military terminology: 'What is a division? There is a peace-time division and a wartime division, a continental division, an imperial division, a stationed division and a territorial division, and in every division there is a different number of men. Sometimes, the difference is as much as 50 or 60%! Or take air squadrons. How many planes are there in a squadron? Nine? Twelve? Fifteen? You can never tell. Or the navy. How many vessels are there in a flotilla? I'm completely lost in all these terms. Why can't the military make its terms more simple and specific?'

That is how the minister for [the coordination of] defence of Great Britain speaks! Is it any wonder that the defence of his country is in such a poor state?

I gleaned two things from Halifax. First, the ratification of the Anglo-Italian agreement 'bears no relation' to the recognition of belligerent rights. The latter issue is still wholly under the supervision of the Non-Intervention Committee. Second, the Franco-German talks are of a very general nature so far. Hitler did not make any special proposals to François-Poncet during their recent meeting. It looks as if France itself must put forward certain proposals. Halifax does not anticipate any rapid developments in this area.

46. Sir Frank Bowater, lord mayor of London, welcomes the Soviet ambassador.

Speaking to Agniya at lunch, Halifax said that the return of Germany and Italy to the League of Nations would be a great boon but, unfortunately, it was very difficult to arrange. The 'purge' of personnel initiated by Avenol was quite insufficient for the purpose. But it seems that Halifax (like Bonnet) nevertheless gave his blessing to Avenol to carry out such an operation.

9 November

Once again I attended the traditional banquet of the lord mayor of the City of London. For the sixth time. It's becoming boring, as the same ceremony is repeated every year. Just one episode is worthy of note. According to the ritual, every guest is to walk all the way along the famous Guildhall library to shake hands with the new and former lord mayors and their wives. Crowded on both sides of the strip, in their very finest attire, are the British notables of every hue – economic, political, military and cultural. They welcome every guest with applause. Its duration reflects the audience's attitudes. This time they clapped me for a fair length of time, longer than last year. So I can assume that the barometer of Anglo-Soviet relations shows 'fair' for the time being. The new Japanese ambassador Shigemitsu elicited just a few sparse claps.

47. Maisky entertaining the writer Alexei Tolstoy.

Grandi and Dirksen went before me and I have no idea how they were greeted. Chamberlain received a lengthy ovation, but it seemed to me that much of it was quite deliberately artificial. Simon was not given a big hand.

At the table I was seated between the Hoares, husband and wife, and I had a very interesting conversation with Sir Samuel. At first, I avoided politics on purpose and spoke mainly about literature. Hoare said he reads a lot, in Russian, too. He enjoys Stendhal and Mérimée. He lavished praise on Alexei Tolstoy's *Peter the First*, which he read in translation. Hoare is also a passionate admirer of Pushkin – he has read all his works in the original. He bought an old edition of the great Russian poet's works in Moscow many years ago. Hoare spoke exceptionally highly of Leo Tolstoy's *War and Peace*. 'It is not an ordinary novel,' he remarked, 'It is an epic.' I suggested that *War and Peace* was the greatest novel in world literature and Leo Tolstoy the greatest novelist of all times and peoples. Hoare very nearly agreed, but with the reservation that Walter Scott's novel *Waverley* should be bracketed with *War and Peace*.

Little by little, however, our conversation shifted to political themes, and what I heard from Hoare was highly characteristic and instructive.

According to Hoare, home secretary and member of Chamberlain's 'inner Cabinet', it transpires that the prospects for peace in Europe are better today than they were six or twelve months ago. Why? Simply because the Czechoslovak question, the only one that could have been the cause of a European disaster, has been settled. The German expansion to the south-east is a 'natural process' and cannot lead to a European war. Spain is no longer a threat to peace in Europe. So there are no more political entanglements which might erupt in a European war.

'And the colonies?' I inquired.

'Ah, the colonies,' Hoare echoed. 'That problem will be resolved sooner or later. But I don't think that Hitler will raise the colonial issue very soon. Even if he does, it won't be in a brutal form, but in the form of negotiations, and we'll be able to find a compromise that will suit both parties. In short, I believe that we can confidently rely on at least two years of peace.'

With that, Hoare pounced with relish on the piece of roast beef on his plate.

'Why are you so sure that Hitler won't raise the colonial question in a brutal form?' I asked.

'Why?' Hoare answered with a note of superiority in his voice. 'If only for the simple reason that, in contrast to Czechoslovakia, Hitler cannot flood the colonies with his troops.'

I laughed: 'He can't flood the colonies with his troops? He doesn't need to. There is a much simpler way: to intimidate the mother country!'

Hoare choked on a bit of roast beef and looked up at me in alarm: 'What do you mean?'

'It's very simple,' I answered. 'Is Hitler incapable of intimidating Belgium and making it cede the Congo?'

Hoare said nothing, but my words obviously spoilt his mood.

'And another thing: can't Hitler confront France with the alternative – the colonies or war?'

'But that's impossible!' Hoare exclaimed. 'We shall never agree to this!'

'Fine,' I summed up, 'but then why are you so sure that the colonial issue cannot lead to a European war?'

Hoare's mood deteriorated still further.

I then started questioning him about what the British government was thinking of doing to increase the country's defence capacity, particularly in the air. Was it intending to set up a ministry of supply? Or to mobilize the defence industry?

Hoare reverted to his 'optimistic philosophy'. He argued that since the British government had at least two years at its disposal, there was no need for extraordinary measures and that everything required for rearmament could be done in the normal manner without upsetting the ordinary course of economic life.

I voiced my doubts about this and asked him what goals the British government was setting itself in the sphere of air force rearmament. Parity with Germany?

Hoare affirmed that the British government was for parity and that it would never sign a pact perpetuating German air supremacy. But then he set about arguing, at suspicious length, that parity as such is an abstract notion, for it depends not only on mathematical equality in the number of aircraft, but also on many other factors, including the strategic needs of the country. Passing on to figures, Hoare said that Germany had approximately 10,000 aircraft, including as many as 3,000 up-to-date first-line planes, while its monthly output amounted to 800. He would not give any exact figures for Britain, but admitted that the British air force was between two and three times weaker. Referring to those very figures, I repeatedly asked Hoare how in that case the British government was expecting to achieve parity with Germany in two years, all the more so as Germany could increase – and undoubtedly was increasing – its present level of aircraft production. Hoare was unable to give me an articulate reply.

I concluded from my talk with Hoare that the British government is not planning to arm in earnest and has evidently reconciled itself to the prospect of German air supremacy. What lies behind this?

The main reason, it seems to me, is that Chamberlain has not yet lost hope of 'coming to terms' with the aggressors at the expense of third countries and of setting them, especially Germany and Japan, against the USSR.

15 November

The South African minister of defence, Pirow,[i] currently finds himself *in the limelight*. A man of our times.

A South African of German origin, Pirow has a great liking for present-day Germany. At home, he is jokingly called 'our Führer'. A man of great ambitions and strong will. His *idée fixe* is that a universal revolt of 'blacks against whites' is nigh, bringing the destruction of the only citadel of 'European civilization' in Africa, i.e. the Union of South Africa. This basic idea defines Pirow's worldview and politics. A few years ago, at a parade of military school graduates in Johannesburg, Pirow made a speech in which he stated that the arch enemies, with whom the officers must be ready to fight, were the African aborigines. In the Union of South Africa he was and remains an advocate of a policy of ruthless suppression of blacks. It is beyond doubt that even today Pirow is a key

---

[i] Oswald Pirow, South African minister for defence, 1933–39.

figure among the Boers, and there are grounds to expect that after Hertzog's[i] death he will become leader of his party and prime minister.

Pirow flew out of South Africa three weeks ago and embarked on a 'political tour' of European capitals. His itinerary covers Lisbon, Burgos, London, Berlin, Brussels, Rome and Paris, i.e. all the countries with colonies or dominions in Africa. The purpose of his tour was to pave the way for a colonial deal with Germany.

In what form? Pirow's project can be reduced to the following. Togo and Cameroon should be returned to Germany, but not Tanganyika and South-West Africa (the latter should not be given away on any account). Angola (or at least part of it) and a certain part of the Belgian Congo should be given to Germany as compensation for keeping Tanganyika and South-West Africa within the British Empire. Germany will thus obtain a compact 'African empire' on the Atlantic coast in equatorial Africa. This solution of the colonial problem strikes Pirow as almost ideal. The point is not so much that Versailles will thus be liquidated forever and 'Germany's honour' fully retrieved. <u>Far more important is the fact that German fascism will gain a firm foothold on the African continent and will surely manage to establish order in Africa, safeguarding the whites against any kind of revolution contemplated by the aborigines.</u> In Pirow's view, German rule must be established precisely in equatorial Africa, because it is there that 'negro nationalism' has flourished more than anywhere else under flabby British, French and Belgian governance, and it is there that it must be struck a heavy blow to the head. Incidentally, there is one further very serious argument in favour of this solution of the 'colonial problem': friends are friends, but all the same it would still be better to keep Germany at arm's length from the boundaries of the Union of South Africa!

Chamberlain is ready to sacrifice and is indeed sacrificing the vital interests of the British Empire for the sake of the narrow class interests of the bourgeois elite that he represents. Pirow is ready to sacrifice the interests not only of the British Empire, but also the very independence of the Union of South Africa for the sake of the chauvinistic class interests of the bourgeois elite which he represents. What vivid examples of the profound decay of capitalism in our time!

Leaving for this tour, Pirow set himself two tasks: (1) to persuade Britain, France, Portugal and Belgium to make the sacrifices demanded by his plan, and (2) to persuade Hitler to find the plan satisfactory. Pirow was out of luck in Lisbon: the Portuguese made it clear that they would never agree to any colonial sacrifices whatsoever. Things went better for him in London: after all,

---

[i] James Barry Munnik Hertzog, South African political leader; assistant chief commandant of the Orange Free State forces in the Boer War, 1899–1902; National Party (from 1914) MP for the Smithfield constituency, 1907–40; prime minister of the Union of South Africa, 1924–39.

Pirow's thoughts accord with those of Chamberlain. But then Jewish pogroms broke out in Germany, the atmosphere changed radically, and even the PM himself had to admit that it was a quite inappropriate moment to discuss plans for the 'colonial gratification' of Germany. At the same time, Daladier made a statement to the effect that France would not give up its colonial territories, while Smuts made a speech in South Africa in which he threatened war against anyone who attempted to assault South-West Africa.

Yesterday Te Water said to me: 'Pirow's mission is in limbo. True, he has decided not to change his itinerary and is therefore leaving for Berlin tomorrow. Then he will go to Brussels, Rome and Paris, but it is clear to everyone that after the recent events in Germany it is out of the question for her to be given any territory inhabited by another race.'

...Out of the question... Completely or for the time being? Te Water meant 'completely', but I don't believe it. This critical moment will pass, the present wave of indignation will ebb, and Pirow, together with Chamberlain and his ilk, will once again set about weaving their treacherous plots.

16 November

King Carol of Rumania has arrived on an official visit to the king of Britain. Carol's long-cherished dream has come true. Some three years ago, during one of his frequent 'raids' on London, I asked Titulescu what he was up to, and he answered with his typically ironic, impish smile: 'I'm paving the way to London for my sovereign. He's dying to pay a social visit to his august relative on the royal throne. We've had no luck so far: Lupescu[i] gets in the way. But I'll surely arrange it!'

The highly respectable George V was still reigning then, and the times were quieter. One could afford the luxury of worrying about Madame Lupescu.

Now Carol is in London as a guest of George VI. Accompanying him is the heir Mihai, a lively boy of 17 in a military uniform and epaulettes. There's also the foreign minister Petrescu-Comnen and several notables. Everyone is amazed that Carol has brought neither the minister of finance nor the minister of trade with him, because it was known in advance that, apart from improving Carol's prestige, the primary purpose of the visit was 'metallic': if not a loan, then at least some British investments in Rumania (particularly in port construction in Constanta), export credits, and the expansion of Anglo-Rumanian trade. But Grigorcea (the Rumanian ambassador in London) gave me the following explanation yesterday: the king just wants to explore whether any basis exists for the realization of these plans and, if it does, to agree in

---

[i] Madame Magda Lupescu, wife of King Carol II of Rumania.

principle. The experts will come later to negotiate the details. We shall see what will come of it all. Frankly speaking, I'm rather sceptical.

Carol was received very much in the same style as the Belgian king last year. A red-carpet welcome in Dover and at Victoria Station, a ceremonial procession from Victoria to Buckingham Palace, a state banquet for 180 guests in the palace yesterday, a 'levee' for the diplomatic corps in the palace this morning, where Carol and the heir greeted all the ambassadors and envoys, a ceremonial lunch with the lord mayor, dinner with the royal couple in the Rumanian mission, and a reception for 700 guests in the palace. For tomorrow, dinner in the Foreign Office and an air show.

Not everything was the same as last year, however. The speeches given by the kings at the state banquet were more vacuous and politically insubstantial. Neither Churchill nor Lloyd George nor Eden was present at the banquet. Chamberlain is obviously getting his own back! And another thing: the attitude of the royal family, and particularly of the king and queen, towards me and Agniya as representatives of the USSR was much more hostile, detached and strained. It's natural: the crisis of capitalism has advanced one step further.

17 November

Lothian paid me a visit today after a very long interval. During that time he managed to travel the world and to attend a unique imperial conference in Australia – a conference not of statesmen but of political party representatives, public figures, writers and so on, devoted to the prospects of the British Empire. Lothian published his first article about the conference in the *Observer* of 12 November.

I was more interested, however, in Lothian's views on European policy. He visited Berlin about three years ago, talked with Hitler, and returned home a staunch Germanophile. Later on he began to retreat. He criticized the 'Führer' mildly, displayed interest in the fate of Czechoslovakia and concern about possible German aggression. Today, I found Lothian's thoughts and sentiments to be overtly anti-German.

Munich, of course, was a crushing defeat for Britain and France. Hitler secured free access to the resources and raw materials of Central and South-East Europe. 'Mitteleuropa' is being created before our very eyes, though it is not yet complete. Where will Hitler go next? East or west? Both directions are possible. The odds are even. The urgent task is to unite democratic forces (England, France, the United States) against the aggressors, first and foremost Germany, and to arm them urgently. For tactical reasons, it is better not to raise the question of Soviet participation. The USA cannot be relied on very much for the time being: isolationism is too powerful there. However, even in

America all thinking people, including the president and the army and navy chiefs, have come to realize that the fall of the British Empire would constitute a deadly danger for the USA, because supremacy at sea would then pass to the fascist aggressors – Germany, Japan and Italy. Fascism would triumph in Latin America, too. In such circumstances, US security would be jeopardized. That is why intelligent America understands that it cannot keep out of the democracies' struggle for their existence. Nevertheless, for the moment one cannot rely on the USA as an active force in international affairs. The responsibility of Britain and France is thus all the greater. If they fail to arm quickly and mightily, the world could be in for a dismal fate. Will they succeed? This will become clear in a few months. Much time has been lost. To overtake Germany in the sphere of air arms is very difficult, if not impossible. Let the USSR also arm. Even without any formal pacts or commitments, the simultaneous arming of the 'Western democracies' and the USSR can play a tremendous role in preventing the further expansion of the aggressors.

Such is Lothian's present mood. True, he is an inconsistent sort, but it is still rather interesting to take his temperature at this particular moment.

Lothian says that he no longer has anything to do with *The Times*. Clearly, the Astors do not delight him much either.

25 November

Eden and his wife came for lunch. They examined the walls of the yellow drawing room and the upper dining-room with a connoisseur's eye. They were very complimentary about Kustodiev's[i] and Grabar's[ii] paintings, as well as the furniture. They praised some other pictures and engravings as well. I recalled that when Eden was planning his trip to Moscow, he asked me to include in his schedule a visit to the museum of Western painting. His artistic background shows!

There were four of us at table. The conversation was very frank. Far more so than when Eden was foreign secretary.

I asked Eden what he thought about England's immediate prospects? Will Chamberlain and his policy of 'appeasement' hold out for long?

Eden shrugged his shoulders and answered that the current situation is very unclear. Chamberlain certainly enjoys his party's support and can hold out until the next election. When will the elections be held? It is hard to say. The

---

[i] Boris Mikhailovich Kustodiev, Russian painter and stage designer, best known for portraits and scenes from traditional country life.
[ii] Igor Emmanuilovich Grabar, Soviet painter of landscapes of ancient Russian or old country estate architecture. Head of the Tretyakov Gallery, 1913–25; director of the Scientific Research Institute of Art History, 1944–60.

party machine wanted to have the election right after Munich, but Chamberlain refused for various reasons. The issue was postponed. In early November the party machine raised the question again, proposing to hold a general election in February 1939, and this time Chamberlain agreed. But the Jewish pogroms in Germany changed the situation, and this date was cast aside. It is unclear what will happen next. The election could be postponed until the autumn of 1939. Other dates are also possible. In any case, Eden does not think that the election will be on the agenda in the immediate future.

'It follows,' I reasoned, 'that there is no hope of a change in British foreign policy as yet?'

'What can I say?' Eden responded. 'A change in policy is conceivable even without elections. Events might force the hand even of the present government.'

Eden stopped for a moment before continuing: 'If I were in Chamberlain's shoes, I would do the following. I would address the party and the nation and say: I have done everything in my power to reach an agreement with Germany and secure the "appeasement" of Europe. I have made every kind of concession for the sake of this. I have made many sacrifices. I have been ready to forgo my own and my country's pride, to endure assaults, criticism and accusations for the sake of achieving the goal... But now I see that all my efforts have been in vain: Germany does not want an honourable peace for both sides, it wants a *pax germanica*. I cannot agree to this. That's the limit. We can do no more. We must defend ourselves. If the prime minister put the question like that, he would have a united country behind him and could carry out a firm and dignified policy of genuine peace.'

'And you think that Chamberlain is capable of performing an about-turn of this kind?'

Eden grinned: 'No, of course he won't do that.'

'So how do you expect a change in foreign policy under the present PM?' I went on.

'I'm speaking about the government, not about the PM,' Eden replied. 'Of course, a change in policy is possible only if the present Cabinet is substantially refreshed.'

I asked him whether the rumours were true that Eden was thinking about setting up a new 'middle' party. Eden shook his head.

'Our political traditions make it very difficult to form a third party, especially a "middle" one,' he said. 'The creation of any new party in Britain is an extremely troublesome and unpromising business. I think it more effective to work within the Conservative Party and gain influence in it step by step. By the way, the supporters of the views I advocate have greatly increased in number and standing over the past few weeks.'

Eden further informed me that while the Conservative opposition as such numbers approximately 50 party members, at least 50 more are tacit sympathizers. About 100 members support the PM staunchly, and the other 200 make up the 'swamp'. The trouble is that the power of the party machine has increased immensely and terrorizes many MPs. Some twenty-five years ago there were many Conservative MPs with their own private means, who felt independent and paid little attention to the instructions given by the *chief whip*. They spoke and voted as they wished. Nowadays the overwhelming majority of Tory MPs are subsidized from party funds at election time, so they seek to ingratiate themselves with the *chief whip*.

'Isn't that so, Beatrice?' Eden concluded, turning to his wife.

Beatrice agreed with her husband and cited her late father as a characteristic example. For the remainder of our talk Eden would repeat, after stating his opinion: 'Isn't that so, Beatrice?'

Evidently, Beatrice is not only Eden's wife, but also his adviser.

Despite all its difficulties, the Tory 'opposition' is growing and should continue to grow in influence. At least half of Conservative voters are dissatisfied with and alarmed by the current state of affairs and the government's foreign policy. They sense that the integrity of the Empire is at stake. The result is that not only 'left-wing Tories like me' (Eden went on), but also right-wing imperialists like Amery and Lloyd are against Chamberlain.

I asked Eden whether he thought it possible to organize a broad national opposition comprising Tory opposition, Labourites and Liberals.

'That would be very difficult, at least at present.'

He then began scolding the Labourites for their very negative attitude towards the idea of a united front.

I complimented Eden on his latest speech in parliament on 10 November – this obviously pleased him – and asked him to comment on the throw-away remark he made in his speech to the effect that the present system of democratic governance requires 'reorganization and, first and foremost, the speeding-up of its work'. Eden said that he had not thought this issue fully through yet, but it seemed to him that if the British parliament adopted, for example, the method of commissions practised in the French Chamber, they would gain considerable time. Some other reforms are also conceivable.

I remarked that Eden's speeches differ greatly from the speeches of other Conservative oppositionists in one very important respect: he always ties together the problems of foreign and home policy. He demands not only struggle against the aggressors, but also social reforms. My words hit the mark. I had touched a very sensitive spot in Eden's heart. He livened up at once, gained some colour, and straightened his figure.

'In leftist circles,' said Eden, 'there's an absurd theory that I speak this way on Baldwin's instructions. Nonsense! Baldwin has nothing to do with my fight with the government. It's just that as a person who understands the current situation and the emerging trends I believe that a progressive foreign policy must harmonize with a progressive home policy – otherwise the British Empire will perish.'

Eden then developed the following syllogism: the strength of a nation depends not only on its armaments, but also, and to a much greater degree, on the happiness and prosperity of the population. In the case of Britain, this means the happiness and prosperity of the working masses. This goal can be attained exclusively by means of large-scale social reforms (affecting unemployment, specific districts and so on). In turn, large-scale social reforms are feasible only if the Empire remains intact, while the Empire's integrity is impossible without a progressive foreign policy, i.e. collective security, the League of Nations, a united front of peace-loving powers, and, as a minimum, the London–Paris–Moscow axis.

I added that a lengthy engagement with the policy of 'appeasement' would render the British Empire non-existent within a decade.

'You think we have that much time?' Eden responded. 'I'm more pessimistic. If Chamberlain stays in power for long, the disintegration of the Empire will proceed much faster.'

We then discussed my episode with Winterton, and I told Eden about my talk with him concerning two types of great powers. Eden accepted my thesis with certain reservations. He, too, thinks that Hitler's next step will be toward the west rather than toward the Ukraine.

'But what is Hitler going to demand from us?' Eden reflected. 'Colonies? Most likely. But in the present conditions, in the atmosphere created by the Jewish pogroms, not a single British statesman will dare even to raise the question of transferring any territories with national minorities to Germany. And what will Hitler do? He can't cross the sea to grab the colonies!'

'But can't Hitler intimidate the mother country?' I asked.

'No, that's out of the question,' Eden exclaimed. 'Britain will stand united to resist Germany on the colonial question!'

Eden condemned Chamberlain's foreign policy most harshly. It is leading directly to the downfall of the British Empire. The PM's policy on rearmament is virtually criminal. The immediate prospects in France worry Eden greatly. He is very interested in our stand on international affairs and was clearly glad to hear that we are not hurrying to make definitive conclusions, but are merely following the course of events in Europe. He repeated that in his opinion salvation lies only in the London–Paris–Moscow axis, and added in this connection that he was including the speech he gave at the dinner in Moscow during his 1935 visit in a collection of speeches to be published imminently.

During our conversation, I remarked in passing that capitalism was a spent force. I was surprised to hear Eden reply: 'Yes, you are right. The capitalist system in its present form has had its day. What will replace it? I can't say exactly, but it will certainly be a different system. State capitalism? Semi-socialism? Three-quarter socialism? Complete socialism? I don't know. Maybe it will be a particularly pure British form of "Conservative socialism". We'll see.'

27 November

Agniya and I made a trip to the country. Grey and rainy. A real English autumn. We went to the Plough Inn near High Wycombe – an old, authentically English inn with low ceilings and crude wooden chairs and tables. The hostess is Ishbel MacDonald, daughter of the former prime minister. The food was tasty and inexpensive.

7 December

A week ago, the parliamentary committee for Spanish affairs sent two Labour MPs, George Strauss[i] and Aneurin Bevan, to see me. The food situation in Spain is desperate. Private benefactors and public charitable organizations cannot cope with the problem. Wouldn't the Soviet government agree to the following plan: the USSR publicly announces that it is sending a certain number of ships with provisions for Spanish women and children, and proposes to the governments of Britain, France and the USA that their countries should join in the effort by sending a certain number of ships and providing convoys for the vessels bearing provisions. According to the committee, the advantages of this plan are the following: (1) If the four powers named above do arrange food supplies to Spain, then that's marvellous. (2) If they don't, which is more likely, Chamberlain will find himself in a very difficult position, his standing inside the country will weaken, and his intention of reaching an agreement with Mussolini about granting belligerent rights to Franco during the forthcoming visit to Rome on 11 January will be in jeopardy. (3) The prestige of the USSR and sympathy towards it will increase, especially in the USA. (4) Thanks to the Soviet action, the gathering in England of donations and food products for Spain will be facilitated. Moreover, the British government will have to assist with this collection in whatever form it finds most convenient.

I contacted Moscow on the subject. Moscow turned down the proposal.

---

[i] George Russell Strauss, militant Labour MP, 1929–31 and 1934–50.

11 December

What will Hitler's next move be? Where will he strike next?

The question is in the air. It is written about in the press, debated in political circles, and discussed in private homes. Vansittart, who is just back from a six-week vacation in Monte Carlo, tried to convince me at lunch the other day that the arrow of German aggression was turning ever eastward. Lloyd George also told me this recently. Wilson openly admitted that the British government is proceeding on the premise of an inevitable German strike to the east, and that many things follow from this assumption, including the government's attitude to rearmament. Why should there be a ministry of supply and other extraordinary measures if Britain is not threatened with war in the immediate future?

Mutatis mutandis, this is a repeat of what I observed here in the winter of 1932–1933. The British ruling circles then put their stake on a Soviet–Japanese conflict and did their best to provoke it. Today they seem to be inclined to stake on a German–Soviet conflict, and someone will probably take a hand in trying to unleash it as soon as possible. It's doubtful, however, that the hopes of the English reactionaries will be fulfilled.

I accept that Hitler may turn for a while to the east. Since now is an unfavourable moment to raise the colonial question seriously, it would not at all be surprising if he decided for the time being to focus his attention on eastward expansion, which is in fact one of the cornerstones of his programme. The Franco-German declaration of friendship signed by Bonnet and Ribbentrop last week, the apparent preparations for the annexation of Memel, the stirring up of Ukrainian nationalism in Transcarpathian Ukraine and Poland (yesterday the Ukrainian group in the Polish Sejm tabled a bill concerning the national autonomy of the Ukraine within the bounds of the Republic of Poland), and attacks by the German press on the Rumanian king – all this and much else seems to testify to an imminent German strike to the east.

What does 'a strike to the east' mean exactly? It is still difficult to say with any certainty. It seems clear to me, however, that it may involve, at the most, some German operations against Lithuania, Poland and the Balkan states, but not against the USSR.

The seizure of Memel and Danzig is probable,[131] fomentation of Ukrainian irredentism is probable, and encouragement of the separatist movement among Germans and Hungarians in Rumania is also probable. Let us imagine that Germany strikes Poland, recovers the corridor and Silesia, and establishes a Ukrainian vassal state made up of Transcarpathian and Polish Ukrainians. Hitler might possibly regard such a state, which would share a border with the USSR, as a milestone on the way to tearing Soviet Ukraine away from the USSR. All this is conceivable (but not inevitable) in 1939.

But I refuse to accept the possibility of a German attack on us in the immediate future. We are too strong and threatening for this, and Hitler is afraid of big wars. His sense of smell is as keen as a raven's for carrion. Wherever there is a smell of decay and bloodless conquest, there he is. But wherever serious fighting is required, there he is not.

13 December

Today's *Evening Standard* features Duff Cooper's article 'Another French Revolution?', where the author arrives at the conclusion, which he finds comforting, that there will be no revolution. The following passage caught my attention:

[Attached in the diary is a long excerpt from the article arguing that the propertied classes of France were apprehensive of the growing military might across the Rhine as well as of the spread of communism in France.]

Duff Cooper is undoubtedly correct. The fear of a pending proletarian revolution and communism is forcing the French (as it does the English) bourgeoisie to sacrifice the most important national interests.

A few months ago Corbin complained to me that France's foreign policy had become a problem in domestic policy and this explained a large number of its shortcomings and errors. Duff Cooper has the same idea. Only he expresses it much more poorly, in the bureaucratic and idealistic vernacular of a professional bourgeois diplomat.

18 December

[A report in the *Observer*, attached by Maisky to the diary, emphasized the signs of detachment from 'the spirit of Munich' which had appeared on the eve of the new parliamentary session in Britain. The correspondent attributed it to the German attacks on British ministers and politicians, and to the 'krystal nacht', on 9 November 1938, the pogroms of Jews which shocked the world. Such events elicited a 'bitter sense of disappointment' and questioned the motives of Berlin and Rome, which were postponing for an unknown period the process of peaceful settlement.]

Meanwhile, in the course of his article, Garvin discusses the chances of an 'alliance' between Britain, France and the Soviet Union! True, he comes to the conclusion that the USSR is a dubious entity, and that it is better to rely on the USA; but what progress compared with what he has been writing over the past two years!

Clearly, the 'umbrella policy' is having a very bad time of it.

Masaryk, whom I saw two days ago, told me that during his farewell audience the king complained to him at length about the difficulties which Chamberlain faced in trying to carry through his policy of 'appeasement' while dealing with people such as Hitler and Mussolini. Then the king said *verbatim*: 'These people (i.e. Hitler and Mussolini) were once useful to their nations. They united them and inspired them with courage and confidence. But the useful mission of Hitler and Mussolini is over. Everything they do now is directed against us and against civilization.'

And Halifax asked Masaryk, during his farewell visit, to convey to Roosevelt, whom Masaryk hopes to meet on his trip to the USA, that 'neither the prime minister nor I cherish any illusions about Germany'.

Symptomatic.

19 December

Today we had a farewell dinner for Masaryk. He resigns on 30 December: he cannot serve the new Czechoslovak government. He will then go to the USA, where for the next 2–3 months he will give lectures, speeches, etc. He also hopes to see Roosevelt. He wants to educate the Americans a little about European affairs and to earn some money. Masaryk evidently has no means of his own, or very few, and one has to make a living. He expects to get two or three thousand pounds which, by his reckoning, would be enough to keep him going for some three years. Later, he'll see. Masaryk has rented a small flat in Westminster (his permanent residence will be in London) and invited me to a house-warming party after his return from the USA. His plans are still vague. He only said to me: 'I want to do something useful for democracy and progress.'

The number of defecting ex-diplomats is rapidly growing: Franckenstein, the Austrian, now naturalized and bearing the title Sir George Franckenstein; Martin, the Abyssinian, who has not been invited to a single official reception since 15 November (the date when the Anglo-Italian agreement came into force); and now Masaryk. All this in the course of just one year! What speed! The question arises: who next?

Today's dinner was attended by Cecil, Lytton, Snell, Layton, D. Low, Grenfell,[i] Nicolson, Murray and others, about 20 guests all in all. I said a few words appropriate for the occasion. Lytton, Cecil and Layton also addressed the guests. Masaryk spoke in reply. There were two memorable moments. Speaking on behalf of the Englishmen present, Lytton said that he was 'ashamed' of his country's behaviour during the Czechoslovak crisis, but he hoped to live to see

---

[i] David Rhys Grenfell, Labour MP, member of the Forestry Commission, 1929–42, the Royal Commission on Safety in Mines, 1936, and the Welsh Land Settlement Commission, 1936–56; secretary for mines, 1940–42.

the time when he would not be ashamed to welcome Masaryk again. In his endearing but very muddled speech, Masaryk uttered: 'I'll fight for the *Lorelei* to be sung in Germany again!'[132]

[Munich had confirmed for Litvinov how futile it was to seek to recruit Britain and France to collective security. His outlook now conformed very much to the isolationist views held in the Kremlin, but his paralysis reflected his association with the discredited idea of collective security and his apparent refusal to consider the obvious alternative of reconciling with Germany. Maisky, whose room for manoeuvre had been significantly narrowed, retained some vestige of hope that the damage could be repaired. He tried relentlessly to galvanize into action oppositional elements inside government circles. Within the span of a single month, he entertained to lunch *à deux* at the embassy a wide array of politicians, including the high commissioners of New Zealand and South Africa, Cranborne, Harold Macmillan, Walter Elliot, Liddell Hart, Thomas Inskip, De La Warr, Eden, Vansittart, Butler, Samuel Hoare, Philip Kerr (Lord Lothian), William Seeds[i] (the newly appointed ambassador to Moscow), Randolph Churchill, Lord Cecil and Horace Wilson.[133]

Beyond fraternizing, Maisky went on wooing his collaborators with gifts of caviar and vodka as the year drew to a close.[134] However, attuning to his master's voice, Maisky conveyed to Litvinov his conviction that Chamberlain's policy would be aimed 'not at resistance but at a further retreat in the face of the aggressor'. He had heard from Chamberlain's entourage the following remark: 'What sense is there in feeding a cow which Hitler will slaughter anyway?' Likewise, following his long-sought meeting with Eden, who he had hoped might challenge Chamberlain's leadership, Maisky hastened to confirm to Litvinov that 'Chamberlain has his hands firmly on the wheel.' 'I was glad to observe in your last report,' responded Litvinov, 'that you do not overrate the successes of the English opposition.' He was suspicious of the self-flagellation indulged in by Cabinet ministers at Maisky's lavish luncheons, viewing this as a misleading 'manifestation of correctness' aimed at concealing the conspicuous deterioration in relations.[135]

A series of post-Munich by-elections, which Litvinov followed closely, saw the opposition fail to capitalize on growing public doubts about the agreement. And not until May 1940 did the opposition within Conservative and Liberal ranks succeed in creating a cohesive bloc that could seriously challenge the parliamentary majority, although the oratory of Churchill and Lloyd George would 'enliven many a debate'.[136]

The year 1938 thus ended miserably for Maisky. He had become estranged from Litvinov, his sole remaining succour in Moscow – himself teetering on the edge of the abyss. Earlier in the year, Maisky had – tongue in cheek – welcomed Narkomindel's infusion of 'new blood' to the embassy and promised to 'help these new people stand on their own two feet'. However, in what seems likely to have been a move aimed at self-preservation, he warned that the new cadre 'had no experience of diplomatic work,

---

[i] Fulfilling a lifetime ambition, William Seeds, who had studied Russian and spent time in the Russian capital at the turn of the century, was appointed ambassador to the Soviet Union in 1938, conducted the negotiations on the triple alliance in Moscow, and was recalled to London after the Soviet invasion of Finland in December 1939.

48 & 49. The hall of the residence of the ambassador before and after the 'cult of personality'.

particularly considering the difficult and sensitive work which takes place in centres such as London'.[137]

Having been reprimanded in Moscow during his early summer vacation, his private sphere was now invaded. This culminated in a harsh report by an investigation committee concerning the décor and workings of the embassy. The precarious and degrading position of a Soviet ambassador at the time is well reflected in Maisky's rebuttal:

> … Over the last few years I have tried to augment and renew the embassy's collection of paintings in order to represent suitable works by old and new artists. Thus I have added … a few paintings by contemporary Soviet artists, some portraits of Comrade Stalin … a bust of Lenin and other works … I can confirm that modernity is more in evidence in the London embassy at the current moment than in the majority of other embassies.

> … The way in which clause 7 [of the report] is formulated might lead one to think that there are no portraits of the leader in the embassy. The truth is entirely the opposite. In the very reception room under discussion there is a large, life-size, well-executed portrait of Comrade Stalin by Sokolov,[138] so displayed as to dominate the room. Given the architectural features of the room, I consider it unnecessary for there to be any other portraits here either for political or artistic reasons. There are many further portraits of the leader in other rooms and areas of the embassy.[139]

50. A portrait of Comrade Stalin towering over Maisky.

Notes to Volume 1

Introduction

1. The other exception was Aleksandra Kollontay, the Soviet ambassador in Stockholm, who, prompted by Maisky, kept a scrappy diary.

2. J. Hellbek, *Revolution on My Mind: Writing a diary under Stalin* (Cambridge, MA, 2009); for an innovative and penetrating observation of diary writings during Stalin's time, see M. David-Fox, 'Stalinist Westernizer? Aleksandr Arosev's literary and political depictions of Europe', *Slavic Review*, 62/4 (2003), and B. Farnsworth, 'Conversing with Stalin, surviving the terror: The diaries of Aleksandra Kollontay and the internal life of politics', *Slavic Review*, 69/4 (2010).

3. See the chapter 'The Price of Fame'.

4. Archives of the Russian Academy of Sciences (hereafter RAN) f.1702 op.2 d.77 l.15 & d.49 l.639.

5. See final commentary in 1941.

6. Perfect examples are the first volume of S. Kotkin's biography, *Stalin: Paradoxes of Power, 1878–1928* (London, 2014), the more popular biography by S. Montefiore, *Stalin: The Court of the Red Tsar* (London, 2003) and R. Service, *Trotsky: A biography* (London, 2009). A ground-breaking work on Soviet personalities and the role of diplomats in the formulation of Soviet foreign policy is S. Dullin, *Men of Influence: Stalin's diplomats in Europe, 1930–1939* (Edinburgh, 2008). See also M.J. Carley, 'A Soviet eye on France from the Rue de Grenelle in Paris, 1924–1940, *Diplomacy and Statecraft*, 17 (2006) and G. Roberts, *Molotov: Stalin's cold warrior* (Washington, DC, 2011).

7. Lenin.

8. See D. Reynolds' eye opener, 'Churchill's writing of history: Appeasement, autobiography and *The Gathering Storm*', *Transactions of the Royal Historical Society*, 11 (2001), pp. 221–2, 227; RAN f.1702 op.4 d.282 ll.5–6, 10 Sep. 1928.

9. See diary entry for 19 January 1943.

10. The intimacy established between the Churchills and the Maiskys is apparent as well from a personal letter that Maisky sent Clementine; Churchill papers, CHAR 20/94A/122–3, 13 Sep. 1943; RAN f.1702 op.4 d.1172 l.3., 25 Sep. 1943. The accounts of Maisky's extensive conversations with Churchill belie the suggestions made by historians such as John Charmley and D.C. Watt that Churchill 'fell into the clutches' of Maisky, who 'deceived a wishful-thinking, old fool' about Soviet intentions. See the balanced views of M.J. Carley, in

'Generals, statesmen, and international politics in Europe, 1898–1945', *Canadian Journal of History*, XXX (1995). Churchill asked Maisky in a jocular way whether he 'wanted to turn him into a Communist', to which Maisky replied: 'No, only into an enlightened Imperialist'; Stamford papers, diary, 18 July 1941.

11. See S. Dullin, *Des Hommes d'Influences: Les ambassadeurs de Staline en Europe, 1930–1939* (Paris, 2001), pp. 334–8. The number of diplomats deployed in Europe was halved. Only 8 out of the 83 diplomats serving in Europe were kept in their posts after 1939.

12. See commentary following diary entry for 16 June 1943; see also Richard Beeston, *The Times*, 9 March 2002.

13. I. Maisky, *Before the Storm* (London, 1943), pp. 120–1; Webb, diary, 12 June 1939, p. 6667. The last thirty years of his life were indeed spent at the Institute of History at the Soviet Academy of Sciences.

14. I. Maisky, *Spanish Notebooks* (London, 1966), p. 17.

15. RAN f.1702 op.4 d.1495 l.10, 4 July 1944.

16. See diary entry, 29 January 1940.

17. See diary entry, 25 November 1938.

18. *Before the Storm*; *Journey into the Past* (London, 1962); *Who Helped Hitler?* (London, 1964); *Spanish Notebooks*; *Memoirs of a Soviet Ambassador: The war, 1939–43* (London, 1967).

19. *New York Times*, 20 March 1961.

20. Russian State Archive of Socio-Political History (hereafter RGASPI) f.17. op.171. d.466. l.201–10, report of the interrogation of Beria, 19 Aug. 1953.

21. RAN f.1702 op.2 d.79 l.34, letter to Bulganin, 25 Oct. 1956.

22. RAN f.1702 op.2 d.79 ll.9–13 & ll.17–18, Draft and final letter to Khrushchev, 7 & 30 Dec. 1955.

23. RAN f.1702 op.2 d.79 ll.9–13, Maisky to Voroshilov, 5 Aug. 1955 (emphasis in original); the politicized nature of the projected memoirs became even more pronounced two years later. In a long personal letter to the president of the Soviet Academy of Sciences, Maisky unfolded a concrete plan (which was later adopted) to launch such a programme; RAN f.1702 op.3 d.478 ll.40–1, Maisky to Nesmeyanov, 14 Feb. 1957. Maisky skilfully exploited the campaign against the falsifiers of history, which had been initiated by Stalin. See G. Roberts, 'Stalin, the pact with Nazi Germany, and the origins of postwar Soviet diplomatic historiography', in *Journal of Cold War Studies*, 4/4 (2002).

24. RAN f.1702 op.2 d.79 ll.49–51, 20 March 1957.

25. RAN f.1702 op.4 d.275 ll.8–10; see also his letter to Zarubin, deputy foreign minister, in RAN f.1702 op.3 d.527 ll.1–2, 10 Oct. 1958 and a month later a further letter to Khrushchev, again proposing to introduce any required amendments to the text, which would make it hard for 'our enemies' to use them against the Soviet Union; RAN f.1702 op.4 d.275 ll.22–4, 18 Nov. 1958.

26. A.M. Samsonov (ed.), *K 100-letiyu so dnya rozhdeniya akademika I.M. Maiskogo* (Moscow, 1984), p. 14. The uncritical reception in Russia, overlooking his arrest and the consequences, is well discerned in an article by V.F. Neganov in the same collection (pp. 18–56). Indeed, the earlier reviews, by those who had known Maisky closely, pointed out

the apologetic nature of his work. See the review of Maisky's *Who Helped Hitler?* and *Spanish Notebooks*, by I. McDonald, in *The Times*, 17 Feb. 1962 and 28 Feb. 1966, respectively. See also the obituary of Maisky in the *New York Times*, 4 Sep. 1975, and a letter to the paper by the 'baffled' Brzezinski, 12 July 1971, criticizing Maisky's 'restatement of the official Soviet line', his 'false' statements and frequent 'omissions'.

27. This provoked a strong reaction from the Harvard historian of Soviet foreign policy, A. Ulam, in the *New York Times*, 23 Sep. 1971, as well as from *The Times*, 7 July 1971.

28. G. Bilainkin, *Diary of a Diplomatic Correspondent* (London, 1942), pp. 37–9. The first to suggest it was S. Aster in his excellent contribution 'Ivan Maisky and parliamentary anti-appeasement 1938–1939', in A.J.P. Taylor (ed.), *Lloyd George: Twelve essays* (London, 1971), pp. 317–57.

29. J. Rothenstein, *Brave Day Hideous Night, The Tate Gallery Years, 1939–1965* (London, 1966), p. 32. It has been argued that whereas French dignitaries frequented the Paris embassy and spoke frankly, Maisky's contacts were confined mostly to Labour circles. Despite the claim made by Dullin, *Men of Influence*, pp. 59–62, the list of politicians, journalists and intellectuals frequenting the London embassy clearly exceeded that of Paris and comprised mostly Conservatives.

30. I. McDonald, *A Man of the Times* (London, 1976), p. 62.

31. V. Sheean, *Between the Thunder and the Sun* (London, 1943), p. 203.

32. I. McDonald, *The Times*, 6 September 1975; Webb, diary, 12 June 1939, p. 6667.

33. Beaverbrook papers, BBK\C\238, 12 Nov. 1936. See also A. Foster, 'The Beaverbrook press and appeasement: The second phase', *European History Quarterly*, 21/5 (1991).

34. Beaverbrook papers, BBK\C\238, 29 June 1939.

35. Beaverbrook papers, BBK\C\238, 17 May 1939.

36. RAN f.1702 op.4 d.1373 l.1, 22 Dec. 1936.

37. RAN f.1702 op.4 d.1225 l.3, 2 Jan. 1938.

38. The National Archives, London (hereafter TNA) FO 371 36996 N753/753/38, mins. 3 Dec. 1942.

39. TNA FO 800/300, Cadogan to Kerr, 1 May 1942.

40. See Maisky's views on the new diplomacy in the chapter 'Making of a Soviet Diplomat' and his letter to Narkomindel, following the diary entry of 8 April 1940.

41. RAN f.1702 op.4 d.1141 l.37, 7 April 1934; D.C. Smith, *The Correspondence of H.G. Wells* (London, 1996), III, p. 474, 24 April 1934.

42. F. Williams, *Nothing So Strange: An autobiography* (London, 1970), pp. 120–1.

43. Webb, diary, 23 Jan. 1938, pp. 6434-35.

44. N. Nicolson (ed.), *Harold Nicolson: Diaries and letters, 1939–1945* (London, 1967), p. 155.

45. E. Spears, *Fulfilment of a Mission: The Spears mission to Syria and Lebanon, 1941–1944* (London, 1977), p. 286.

46. Webb, diary, 18 April 1937, pp. 6316-7.

47. Nicolson, *Diaries*, pp. 255–6. Reading the memoirs years later, Maisky thought the 'references to me and Soviet Embassy are not very profound but at times very amusing. I didn't realise being in London that he is such a "gourmand" – always writing about

food which he is offered'; RAN f.1702 op.4 d.1031 l.26, Maisky to Montagu, 2 March 1967. Others were more complimentary about his hosting: Maisky would 'pour out tea at attractive side table; put milk in his cup. I had lemon and sugar tea. On lower shelf of trolley many tiny sandwiches with caviar, caviar on white and brown toast, meringues (one for the Ambassador), smoked salmon sandwiches; chocolates, cream cakes, and other sandwiches whose contents were difficult to see'; Bilainkin, *Diary of a Diplomatic Correspondent*, pp. 37–9.

48. Rothenstein, *Brave Day*, pp. 31–2.

49. H. Morrison, *An Autobiography by Lord Morrison of Lambeth* (London, 1960), pp. 226–7.

50. B. Pares, *Russia and the Peace* (London, 1944), p. 158.

51. R. Bruce Lockhart, *Comes the Reckoning* (London, 1947), p. 256.

52. R. Bruce Lockhart, *Comes the Reckoning*, p. 257.

53. L. Fischer, *Men and Politics* (London, 1941), pp. 467–8.

54. RAN f.1702 op.4 d.155 l.28, 10 Jan. 1939.

55. V. Gollancz, *Reminiscences of Affection* (London, 1968), p. 132. At times her brazenness could have devastating repercussions for Maisky; see commentary following the diary entry for 6 April 1942.

56. The song from the 1937 musical *Me and My Girl* lent its name to a fashionable Cockney dance describing working-class life in London.

57. Morrison, *An Autobiography*, p. 226.

58. Webb, diary, 16 March & 18 April 1935, pp. 6317 & 6360; *Hansard*, HC Deb 28 April 1948, vol. 450, cols 521–62.

59. Webb, diary, 22 Aug. 1934 & 12 June 1939, pp. 5827 & p. 6664.

60. See also diary entry for 1 July 1937, and conversations with Churchill in the same vein on 23 March 1938.

61. Conversations with American ambassador, Joseph Kennedy and Churchill, diary entries for 22 March and 30 September 1938.

62. Diary entries for 7, 8 and 12 March 1935.

63. Diary entry for 24 November 1937.

The Making of a Soviet Diplomat

1. V.S. Myasnikov (ed.), *Ivan Mikhailovich Maiskii: Izbrannaya perepiska s rossiiskimi korrespondentami* (Moscow, 2005), I, p. 7; Webb, diary, 15 Oct. 1939, p. 6734.

2. Gollancz, *Reminiscences of Affection*, p. 132.

3. Maisky, *Before the Storm*, pp. 101–2, 114, 131.

4. Maisky, *Before the Storm*, p. 37.

5. Maisky, *Before the Storm*, pp. 33, 52–3.

6. Maisky, *Before the Storm*, pp. 12–14, 16, 19–23, 63–4.

7. Nekrich papers, conversations with Maisky, 7 Aug. 1973.

8. Passfield papers, II.4.l, 117a, Maisky to the Webbs, 28 Aug. 1940; Maisky, *Journey into the Past*, pp. 173–4.

9. RAN f.1702 op.4. d.149 ll.33–4, 25 March 1910; Maisky, *Before the Storm*, pp. 27, 33–4, 52, 131–2. On the rather ambivalent attitude to Europe on the part of Maisky's revolutionary generation, see the ground-breaking work by David-Fox, 'Stalinist Westernizer?', and *Showcasing the Great Experiment: Cultural diplomacy and Western visitors to the Soviet Union, 1921–1941* (Oxford, 2011).

10. RAN f.1702 op.4 d.1184 ll.2–3, 20 Jan. 1936.

11. RAN f.1702 op.4 d.279 ll.75–6, letter to his uncle E.M. Chemodanov, 20 Oct. 1912.

12. Maisky, *Journey into the Past*, p. 54.

13. RAN f.1702 op.4 d.149 ll.73–4, 28 Dec. 1912; Maisky, *Journey into the Past*, pp. 53–5.

14. Regarding himself as a writer, Maisky was particularly drawn to the British literary circle, regardless of their political 'deviations'. He would be amused by Shaw's observation that the world was 'not populated only by the bourgeoisie and the proletariat. Among the British proletariat there are probably as many bourgeois than among the capitalists. In any case, for me it is easier to understand an intelligent bourgeois, than the descendants of the proletarians'. Maisky's close friendship with Shaw survived the entire period of his ambassadorship, despite Shaw's growing criticism of Stalin. See I. Maisky, 'Bernard Shou – Vstrechi i razgovory', *Novy Mir*, 1 (1961).

15. Ivy Litvinov papers, unpublished biography. See also J. Carswell, *The Exile: Life of Ivy Litvinov* (London, 1983), pp. 62–8.

16. Maisky disclosed this to Beatrice and Sidney Webb while spending a weekend at their country cottage. Webb, diary, 8 Aug. 1933, p. 5502.

17. Quoted in Myasnikov, *Maiskii: Izbrannaya perepiska*, pp. 152–4. See also Myasnikov's insightful observation, pp. 8–9; Maisky, *Journey into the Past*, pp. 58–9.

18. A typical example is a severe lashing of Maisky for failing to follow Litvinov's directives during the Spanish war. See Maisky's apologies in RAN, f.1702 op.4 d.143 ll.57–8, 10 Jan. 1937. In July 1937, Litvinov returned to Maisky a draft article intended for publication in *Izvestiya* on the international situation, heavily corrected in red ink, informing him that it needed 'substantial changes' before it could see the light of day; RAN f.1702 op.4 d.546 ll.39–40.

19. G. Hilger and A. Meyer, *The Incompatible Allies: A memoir-history of German–Soviet relations, 1918–1941* (New York, 1950), p. 111. In a more subtle way, Kollontay formed a similar impression: 'He does not reveal much in his words, but it is necessary to be attentive to his mood.' A. Kollontay, *Diplomaticheskie dnevniki, 1922–1940* (Moscow, 2001), I, p. 249. See also A. Roshchin, 'People's Commissariat for Foreign Affairs before World War II', *International Affairs*, May (1988).

20. Z. Sheinis, *Maxim Litvinov* (Moscow, 1990), pp. 261, 284.

21. See commentary following diary entry for 10 May 1938.

22. RAN f.1702 op.4 d.143 l.41, 9 Dec. 1933.

23. Maisky, *Journey into the Past*, pp. 89–94; Kollontay, *Diplomaticheskie dnevniki*, II, pp. 125–6.

24. S.B. Smith, *Captives of Revolution: The socialist revolutionaries and the Bolshevik dictatorship, 1918–1923* (Pittsburgh, 2011), pp. 95, 102. Maisky remained associated with the

opposition even when in Mongolia, see J.D. Smele, *Civil War in Siberia: The Anti-Bolshevik Government* (Cambridge, UK, 1997), p. 556.

25. Y. Martov, 'Vospominaniya renegata', *Sotsialisticheskii vestnik*, 9 Dec. 1922. See also V.N. Brovkin, *The Mensheviks after October* (Ithaca, NY, 1987), pp. 275–6; E. Mawdsley, *The Russian Civil War* (London, 2001), pp. 63–6.

26. Maisky wrote an authoritative book on Mongolia, *Sovremennaya Mongoliya*, which was published in Irkutsk in 1921.

27. A. Liebich, 'Diverging paths: Menshevik itineraries in the aftermath of revolution', *Revolutionary Russia*, 4/1 (1991), pp. 28–30.

28. RGASPI f.2 op.1 d.12945 ll.1–4, 20 Feb. 1921.

29. Maisky, *Journey into the Past*, p. 77.

30. Webb, diary, 16 March 1935.

31. Nekrich papers, conversations with Maisky, 7 Aug. 1973, and A. Nekrich, 'The arrest and trial of I.M. Maisky', *Survey*, 22/3–4 (1976), p. 315; RGASPI, Secret Archives of the TsK VKP(b), Protocol No. 66, meeting of the Politburo of 24 November 1920.

32. Maisky, *Journey into the Past*, p. 59.

33. Trotsky, for instance, continued to reprimand Stalin for appointing Maisky, Potemkin and Surits, 'who had stood on the other side of the barricades during the October revolution', to prominent diplomatic posts; Leon Trotsky, *The Revolution Betrayed* (London, 2004), p. 71.

34. Deputy people's commissar for foreign affairs in 1918–20 and 1927–34, he was later ambassador to Poland, China and Turkey. His recall, arrest and execution in 1937 triggered the purges at Narkomindel.

35. RGASPI f.82 op.2 d.1452 l.2, 10 March 1924.

36. RAN f.1702 op.4 d.149 l.141 & d.546, l.1, 30 Aug. & 17 Oct. 1925.

37. RAN f.1702 op.4 d.153 ll.2–3.

38. Manchester Guardian Archives, A/m29/12, Maisky to Scott, 30 May 1927.

39. RAN f.1702 op.4 d.1141 ll.8–12 & d.862 ll.3–4, 12 Nov. 1927 & 27 May 1928.

40. I. Maisky, *B. Shou i drugie: Vospominaniya* (Moscow, 1967), pp. 3–12.

41. Diary entry for 15 January 1938; RAN f.1702 op.4 d.862 ll.1–2; RAN f.1702 op.4 d.940 ll.3–5 (a long description of the episode), letter to Eden, 19 Jan. 1938; Maisky to Brailsford, 5 Nov. 1927 and Maisky to H.G. Wells, 2 Jan. 1928, d.1141 ll.13–18.

42. RAN f.1702 op.3 d.50 l.41, Maisky to Trenovskaya, 6 Dec. 1928.

43. F. Utley, *Odyssey of a Liberal: Memoirs* (Washington, 1970), p. 99.

44. RAN f.1702 op.4 d.282 ll.5–6, 10 Sep. 1928.

45. RAN f.1702 op.4 d.143 l.6, 23 Jan. 1939.

46. RAN f.1702. op.4 d.143 ll.3–4 & d.546 l.2, exchange of letters between Maisky and Litvinov, 8 Nov. & 6 Dec. 1928; RGASPI f.17 op.3 d.721 l.1, 10 Jan. 1929; Myasnikov, *Maiskii: Izbrannaya perepiska*, I, p. 506.

47. RAN f.1702 op.4 d.1141 ll.26–9, 26 Aug. 1930.

48. RAN f.1702 op.4 d.1248 ll.8–9 & d.862 ll.8–10, exchange of letters between Brailsford and Maisky, 27 June 1928, 25 Aug. 1929 & 6 March 1930; see also ll.1–7, Brailsford's letters

to Maisky, 16 March, 5 & 30 April & 19 Dec. 1927; RAN f.1702 op.4 d.1628 ll.1–5 & ll.10–11, letters from H.G. Wells, 30 March, 16 April, 25 May, 8 Dec. 1927 & 6 March 1930.

    49. RAN f.1702 op.4 d.1141 ll.26–9 & d.143 ll.14–15, 19 & 26 Aug., 2 Nov. 1930 & 9 June 1931.

    50. RAN f.1702. op.4. d.143. l.17 & d.546 l.8, 10 & 14 Feb. 1931.

    51. RAN f.1702 op.4 d.143 l.43, 1 March 1931; Kollontay, *Diplomaticheskie dnevniki*, p. 111.

    52. RAN f.1702 op.4 d.143 l.19, 9 June 1931.

    53. Kollontay, *Diplomaticheskie dnevniki*, II, pp. 136–7.

    54. A.A. Gromyko, *Pamyatnoe* (Moscow, 1990), II, pp. 416–7. His somewhat critical portrait of Maisky is omitted from the English edition of his memoirs.

    55. On the 1927 crisis, see G. Gorodetsky, *The Precarious Truce: Anglo-Soviet relations, 1924–7* (Cambridge, UK, 2008), ch. 6, and M.J. Carley, *Silent Conflict: A hidden history of early Soviet–Western relations* (London, 2014), ch. 9.

    56. TNA FO 371 16339 N5131/5131/38.

    57. RAN f.1702 op.4 d.153 l.8, 9 Feb. 1934.

    58. TNA FO 371 16339 N6160/5131/38, 20 Oct. 1932.

    59. Kollontay, *Diplomaticheskie dnevniki*, II, pp. 136–9.

    60. Webb, diary, 20 Feb. 1930, 24 Nov. 1932, 11 April 1933 & 12 June 1939, pp. 4882, 5375, 5474–7, 6667; TNA FO 371 16290 N5909/3509/56 (emphasis in original).

    61. Webb, diary, 25 July 1937, pp. 6630–1.

    62. RAN f.1702 op.4 d.1184 l.7 & d.1687 ll.64–6, correspondence with Bernard Shaw, 16 and 18 Nov. 1936; Webb, diary, 15 Nov. 1936, p. 6262.

    63. RAN f.1702 op.4 d.546 ll.10–11.

    64. On this point, see Dullin, *Men of Influence*, pp. 92–5.

    65. Indeed Maisky had few expectations of Ramsay MacDonald, the Labour prime minister, whom he found 'cold and officious' during their first meeting. He surely was not amused by the prime minister's sniping reminder that the last time they had met 'he was a very active Menshevik'. TNA FO 371 16321 N6617/22/38, 15 Nov. 1932; I. Maisky, *Vospominaniya sovetskogo diplomata, 1925–1945 gg.* (Moscow, 1971) (hereafter *VSD*), p. 169.

    66. See diary entry for 27 October 1932; Maisky, *Who Helped Hitler?*, p. 17; *VSD*, pp. 146–7, 154–9. See also Aster, 'Ivan Maisky and parliamentary anti-appeasement', p. 317.

    67. RAN f.1702 op.4 d.862 ll.11–14, 1 April 1930; Webb, diary, 11 April 1933, p. 5474.

    68. Myasnikov, *Maiskii: Izbrannaya perepiska*, II, pp. 229–301; RAN f.1702 op.4 d.282 l.1–2, 2 June 1928. A. Gromyko in *Memoirs* (London, 1989), p. 310 conveyed the same feeling, recalling how Litvinov presented himself as 'accredited to the British working class rather than to the Court of St James, but Lenin had been sharply critical and had ticked him off about it'.

    69. RAN f.1702 op.4 d.282 ll.1–2, 2 June 1928.

    70. RAN f.1702 op.4 d.143 l.13.

    71. See for example A. Kocho-Williams, 'The Soviet diplomatic corps and Stalin's purges', *Slavonic and East European Review*, 86/1 (2008), p. 207.

    72. RAN f.1702 op.4 d.143 ll.7 & 10, 14 Oct. 1929 & 4 May 1930.

Prelude

1. Reflections on the fifth anniversary of his arrival in England, entered in the diary on 27 October 1937.

2. *Narkomindel*, People's Commissariat for Foreign Affairs. By the early 1930s, it was being referred to (though not officially) as the Soviet Foreign Ministry, and the *polpreds* were more often than not referred to as ambassadors.

3. Maisky reissued an updated version of his book *Sovremennaya Mongoliya* under the title *Mongoliya nakanune revolyutsii* (Moscow, 1959).

4. Maisky was always bemused when he recalled how, exactly 20 years earlier, he had almost been denied entry at Folkestone, arriving on the ferry from France with a third-class ticket and failing to possess 'an immigrant's minimum' – the sum of £5. Only after producing from his pocket a crumpled letter from Chicherin, attesting to his status as a 'political refugee from Tsarism', was he grudgingly allowed to proceed to London; G. Bilainkin, *Maisky: Ten years ambassador* (London, 1944), p. 13; RAN f.1702 op.4 d.282 l.17, Maisky to Chicherin, 25 May 1934.

5. Maisky, *Journey into the Past*, pp. 266–7.

1934

1. An excellent and balanced account of the relations and negotiations is in R. Manne, 'The Foreign Office and the failure of Anglo-Soviet rapprochement', *Journal of Contemporary History*, 16/4 (1981).

2. *The Times*, 6 September 1975.

3. RAN f.1702 op.3 d.98 ll.1–2, draft communiqué.

4. Webb, diary, 11 April 1933, pp. 5474–7 (emphasis in original).

5. Maisky was told by the Foreign Office that the government 'could not allow British subjects to be the victims of a stage trial'. J. Bullard and M. Bullard (eds), *Inside Stalin's Russia: The diaries of Reader Bullard, 1930–1934* (Charlbury, 2000), p. 168. He had been privy to a decision to release the engineers in return for the lifting of the embargo on trade imposed by the British; Samuel papers, A/93/2, 24 May 1933; N. Smart (ed.), *The Diaries and Letters of Robert Bernays, 1932–1939: An insider's account of the House of Commons* (London, 1996), p. 73.

6. G.W. Morrell, *Britain Confronts the Stalin Revolution: Anglo-Soviet relations and the Metro-Vickers crisis* (Ontario, 1995). On the economic aspects see G.L. Owen, 'The Metro-Vickers crisis: Anglo-Soviet relations between trade agreements, 1932–1934', *Slavonic and East European Review*, 49/114 (1971). For a well-documented, excellent survey of the Soviet wavering, see Dullin, *Men of Influence*, pp. 111–17.

7. Garvin papers, 8 March 1934.

8. RAN f.1702 op.4 d.114 ll.42–3. On Maisky's contribution to the reconciliation, see the report by Herbert Samuel in Samuel papers, A/93/2, 24 May 1933. For Maisky's own lively and insightful recollections see I. Maisky, 'Mirovaya ekonomicheskaya konferentsiya, 1933g. v Londone', *Voprosy istorii*, 5 (1961). Litvinov further exploited his presence in London to pave the way for an American recognition of the USSR, as well as to secure credit from the French and to prepare the ground for a pact of non-aggression with the Soviet neighbours;

Webb's conversations with Litvinov in Webb, diary, 10 July 1933, p. 5528. Maisky was a master of initiating policies by pulling strings behind the scenes. His major role in securing the Soviet Union's entrance into the League, using the Chinese ambassador in London, Guo Taiqi, as a go-between, has not yet been appropriately acknowledged in the literature, but is revealed in a folder of correspondence in the Noel-Baker papers, NBKR 4/637. On prodding Moscow to join the League, see his reported conversations with Lord Cecil, *Dokumenty vneshnei politiki SSSR* (hereafter *DVP*), 1934, XVII, doc. 44.

9. Quoted in M.J. Carley's highly useful and informative 'Down a blind-alley: Anglo-Franco-Soviet relations, 1920–39', *Canadian Journal of History*, 29/1 (1994), p. 157.

10. Kollontay, *Diplomaticheskie dnevniki*, II, pp. 169–70. The 'Little Entente' comprising Czechoslovakia, Yugoslavia and Rumania under the aegis of France aimed at preserving the status quo in Central and South-East Europe. Soviet attempts to incorporate the entente in a comprehensive collective security system faltered after the Munich Conference.

11. *DVP*, 1933, XVI, pp. 876–77, Litvinov to Paul-Boncour, 28 December 1933.

12. Argued most persuasively in Manne, 'The Foreign Office and the failure of Anglo-Soviet rapprochement', pp. 728–30.

13. *DVP*, 1934, XVII, docs. 250 and 258, Litvinov to Maisky, 16 and 19 July, and doc. 254, to the Soviet ambassadors in the UK, Germany, Italy, Czechoslovakia and the Baltic States, 17 July; TNA FO 371 18305 N4029/16/38, 3 July 1934.

14. Persuasive arguments in this vein are presented in B.J.C. McKercher, 'The last old diplomat: Sir Robert Vansittart and the verities of British foreign policy, 1903–30', *Diplomacy and Statecraft*, 6/1 (1995), pp. 1–38; S. Bourette-Knowles, 'The global Micawber: Sir Robert Vansittart, the Treasury and the global balance of power 1933–35', *Diplomacy and Statecraft*, 6/1 (1995), pp. 91–2; and P. Neville, 'Lord Vansittart, Sir Walford Selby and the debate about Treasury interference in the conduct of British foreign policy in the 1930s', *Journal of Contemporary History*, 36/4 (2001), pp. 628–9.

15. M.L. Roi, 'From the Stresa Front to the Triple Entente: Sir Robert Vansittart, the Abyssinian crisis and the containment of Germany', *Diplomacy and Statecraft*, 6/1 (1995), pp. 63–4; M.L. Roi, *Alternative to Appeasement: Sir Robert Vansittart and alliance diplomacy, 1934–1937* (Westport, CT, 1997), pp. 1–4 and 169–75. See also J.R. Ferris, '"Indulged in all too little?"': Vansittart, intelligence and appeasement', *Diplomacy and Statecraft*, 6/1 (1995), pp. 132–3.

16. Cadogan papers, ACAD 7/1, draft chapter for an autobiography. Maisky shared the same view, *VSD*, pp. 128–30, 234.

17. G. Bilainkin, 'The Ivan Maisky legend', *Contemporary Review*, 211 (1967), p. 195; Bilainkin, *Maisky*, pp. 123–4; I. Colvin, *Vansittart in Office* (London, 1965), p. 33; and N. Rose, *Vansittart: Study of a diplomat* (London, 1978), p. 292.

18. D.C. Watt, 'Sir Nevile Henderson reappraised', *Contemporary Review*, March (1962).

19. B. Pimlott (ed.), *The Political Diary of Hugh Dalton* (London, 1986), p. 209.

20. *VSD*, p. 315; Maisky, *Who Helped Hitler?*, pp. 43–5. On the special relations between the two, see also K. Neilson, *Britain, Soviet Russia and the Collapse of the Versailles Order, 1919–1939* (Cambridge, UK, 2006), pp. 108–9.

21. A full report is in *DVP*, 1934, XVII, doc. 246.

22. Welcoming Russia's inclusion in the League of Nations, Simon emphasized that the mutual assistance pact would 'connect Russia with the existing Locarno Treaty'. The statement should have addressed Russia's fear of isolation, brought about by the conclusion of the Locarno Agreement leading to the 'war scare' of 1927. Unlike Maisky and Vansittart, Simon believed deterrence would pave the way to disarmament (*Hansard*, HC Deb 13 July 1934, vol. 292, cols 691–2). Litvinov indeed attached great significance to the change; but, like Maisky, he remained suspicious of British intentions due to the apparent disagreements within the Foreign Office; *DVP*, 1934, XVII, doc. 258.

23. The initiative came from Barthou, who did the main preparatory work in Geneva and London. Maisky reassured Lord Cecil on 28 March 1934 that the USSR was prepared to cooperate with the League of Nations in the interests of peace. The 15th Assembly of the League of Nations resolved to admit the USSR in September and offered her permanent membership of the Council; *DVP*, 1934, XVII, fn. 128, p. 792 & doc. 133; TNA FO 371 18298 N1741/2/38. See also Maisky, *VSD*, p. 313.

24. Under the New Economic Policy (NEP), the British company Lena Goldfields resumed its concession for gold mining in Siberia, but unresolved issues came before an arbitration court, which was boycotted by the British firm. The improvement in relations led to a positive solution of the conflict in November 1934; *DVP*, 1934, XVII, doc. 380.

25. Vansittart was apparently more blunt: 'What would be the position in any club card-room if members were continually accusing each other of having the fifth ace and a Thompson sub-machine gun under the table?' Persistent mutual suspicion continued indeed to mar relations. 'I shall tell M. Maisky again the next time I see him,' minuted Vansittart, 'that it is of no use whatever to speak of improved relations in one breath and to blackguard us systematically with the other.' TNA FO 371 18305 N4027/16/38 & 18299 N4718/2/38, 13 July and 9 Aug.1934.

26. The year 1933 saw hunger all over Europe; however, collectivization and the forced acquisition of grain to finance the Five Year Plan led to a horrific famine in the Soviet Union, resulting in around 5–7 million deaths. It further brought about stagnation in industrial productivity in 1932. Some historians argue that the famine, affecting mostly the Ukrainian population, had the ingredients of deliberate ethnic cleansing. See T. Snyder, *Bloodlands: Europe between Hitler and Stalin* (New York, 2010), ch. 1. The havoc, leading to the repressions of the 1930s, was more likely a consequence of Stalin's domestic consolidation of power, much influenced by the hitherto little-known waves of rebellion in the countryside and even within the Communist Party. Stalin was blamed for conducting a reckless policy, inciting an unjustified confrontation with the peasantry; see O. Khlevniuk, *Master of the House* (New Haven, 2009), pp. 7–9 and ch. 2.

27. Maisky shared a passion for travel with his fellow Russians in exile – a passion which was to set them apart from Stalin and Molotov and the Bolsheviks who stayed behind in Russia. In her unpublished biography, Ivy Litvinov noted that 'Like all Russians, Maxim was an indefatigable tourist, I had been taken for rambles in the home-counties before, but no Englishman had ever shown such an intimate knowledge of their byways as the Russian emigrants.' Ivy Litvinov papers, draft memoirs.

28. RAN f.1702 op.4 d.1141 l.44, Maisky to H.G. Wells, 12 Dec. 1934.

29. RAN f.1702 op.4 d.143 l.44 & d.546 l.22.

30. RAN f.1702 op.4 d.143 l.45 & d.546 l.26 & l.28, exchange of letters between Maisky and Litvinov, 11 June, 24 July & 4 Aug.1934.

31. For the tremendous significance attached to the Far East, and particularly to a possible Anglo-Japanese collusion targeting the Soviet Union, see *DVP*, 1934, XVII, doc. 164, Maisky to Krestinsky, deputy commissar for foreign affairs, 11 May 1934.

32. K. Young (ed.), *The Diaries of Sir Robert Bruce Lockhart* (London, 1980), II, p. 285.

33. *DVP*, 1934, XVII, doc. 71, Maisky to Narkomindel, 2 March 1934.

34. TNA FO 371 18305 N6328/16/38, Boothby to Eden, 6 Nov. 1934, and minutes.

35. TNA FO 371 18305 N6462/16/38, minutes, 23 Nov. 1934.

36. Following the economic crash of 1929, MacDonald's second Labour government broke up in 1931 on the issue of unemployment benefit cuts. MacDonald then formed the National Government, a coalition with a majority of Conservative ministers, including Baldwin and Chamberlain. It also comprised Liberals, headed by Samuel, and Labourites. MacDonald and the Labourite ministers, who were consequently expelled from the Labour Party, formed a marginal National Labour Party, which carried little weight.

37. Garvin papers, 10 March, 12 Dec. 1933, 1 Jan., 20 and 26 Feb., 1935. Maisky paid equal attention to journalists, such as J. Cummings, the political editor of *News Chronicle*, who were highly critical of the Soviet Union; see *VSD*, p. 304, and I.M. Maisky, *Vospominaniya sovetskogo posla v Anglii* (Moscow, 1960), pp. 99–100.

38. Although nowadays little distinction is drawn between 'Near East' and 'Middle East', Maisky does use two different expressions to denote the regions. For the sake of accuracy, the same distinction is made in this translation of the diaries.

39. In his report home, Maisky, anxious to advance the negotiations, glosses over the obstacles raised by Simon and his explicit statement that improving relations with Russia also meant 'that we hoped to preserve and promote good relations with other countries, such as Japan'; *DVP*, 1934, XVII, doc. 384, and TNA FO 371 18305 N6462/16/38. Well-censored and selective reporting to advance his case would become the trademark of Maisky's ambassadorship.

40. The German diplomat Count Harry Kessler observed in *The Diaries of a Cosmopolitan, 1917–37* (London, 1971), p. 454, that Maisky 'sits at home and is completely ignored by society'. The event is also covered by George Bilainkin, 'Mr Maisky sees it through', *Contemporary Review*, 162 (1942), p. 264.

41. A few days earlier, Maisky attended the opening of the new session of parliament. In his memoirs, he recalls how he sat 'with the other Ambassadors to the right of the throne, and my wife with the wives of other Ambassadors to the left. Etiquette also requires that the most honourable place be given to the wives of the Ambassadors, and only after them come the Court ladies of the highest rank. My wife at that time was the most junior of the Ambassadors' wives, and therefore it turned out that by her side sat a senior female representative of the British aristocracy. She was a Duchess, as old as Methuselah and as ugly as a deadly sin, but all glittering in silks and diamonds. Before the ceremony opened, the Duchess began a conversation with my wife and, realizing that she was a foreigner, asked: 'And what country

do you represent?' My wife calmly answered: 'I represent the Soviet Union.' The effect of these words was shattering. The Duchess suddenly changed countenance as though she had stepped on a poisonous snake. She coloured frightfully, veins swelled on her scraggy neck, angry little lights glittered in her eyes. She brusquely drew away from my wife and cried out angrily: 'Do you know, I hate the Soviets!' (Maisky, *Who Helped Hitler?*, pp. 24–5). According to Beatrice Webb, it was the duchess of Somerset: 'It shows,' she entered in her diary, 'what the Soviet Embassy has to put up with in Capitalist circles'; Webb, diary, 24 Nov. 1934.

42. After the split in the Labour Party, the Socialist League was organized by Sir Stafford Cripps (Beatrice Webb's nephew) on its left fringes. It tended towards Marxism and used *Tribune* as its vehicle. Early in 1937, the Socialist League launched a campaign for a united front with the Communist Party, which led to the expulsion of Cripps from the Labour Party in 1939. See P. Clarke, *The Cripps Version: The life of Sir Stafford Cripps 1889–1952* (London, 2002), pp. 55–6.

43. Maisky told Beatrice Webb (but did not report home) that the prince of Wales had actually intimated his wish to visit the Soviet Union. See N. MacKenzie and J. MacKenzie (eds), *The Diary of Beatrice Webb* (London, 1985), IV, p. 345.

44. Simon told Maisky that he could not respond to Litvinov's overtures without consulting the Cabinet, but he was increasingly sceptical about a positive response. MacKenzie and MacKenzie, *Diary of Beatrice Webb*, IV, p. 345.

45. The description of the meeting with Eden is typical of the subversive methods Maisky would adopt throughout his ambassadorship to convey to Moscow his own ideas, while attributing them to his interlocutors. It was the only effective way of doing so, particularly in the stifling atmosphere in Moscow following the purges in the late 1930s. In this particular case, it was Maisky's plea for Litvinov to attend the League of Nations session, supposedly proposed by Eden, so that the two could meet and reinforce the rapprochement by further driving a wedge between Eden and Simon. This part is missing from the diary, but is in his official report in *DVP*, 1934, XVII, doc. 394 and in *VSD*, pp. 314–16.

46. Successive loans made by the Japanese government to Chinese warlords in 1917–18, which served to increase Japanese control over raw material sources and railway construction in China.

47. The duke of Kent married Princess Marina of Greece and Denmark, his second cousin, on 29 November 1934, at Westminster Abbey.

48. V. Bartlett, *I Know What I Liked* (London, 1974), p. 97.

49. *VSD*, pp. 198–201, 238–40; Maisky, *Who Helped Hitler?*, pp. 54–66, 69.

50. Astor papers, 1416/1/2/144, 21 May 1934; see also Astor papers, 1416/1/2/145, 161 & 223, 14 June 1935, 6 July 1936 & 4 Sep. 1942.

51. Astor papers, 1416/1/2/188, 28 Nov. 1938.

52. *Time* magazine, 3 April 1939.

53. *Hansard*, HC Deb 7 March 1950, vol. 472, col. 257.

54. N. Rose (ed.), *Baffy: The diaries of Blanche Dugdale, 1936–1947* (London, 1973), p. 9.

55. K. Martin, *Editor* (London, 1968), II, p. 141.

56. J.P. Wearing (ed.), *Bernard Shaw and Nancy Astor* (Toronto, 2005), p. 96, and a letter in this vein to Charlotte F. Shaw, 13 Sep. 1941, p. 97. This is attested by other observers, such

as Stephen Duggan, *A Professor at Large* (London, 1943), pp. 205–6. On the visit by Shaw and the Astors to Moscow, see Maisky's diary entry of 5 April 1940.

57. At the 17th Congress of the CPSU, the so-called 'Victory Congress', Kirov delivered a fiery speech which received a tumultuous ovation – in contrast to the reception of Stalin's rather uninspiring oratory. It has since often been suggested that the assassination was related to the political threat Kirov posed to Stalin in 1934. Earlier on, J. Haslam in *The Soviet Union and the Struggle for Collective Security in Europe, 1933–39* (New York, 1984), pp. 408–9, had discharged any evidence as being 'thin and based largely on conjecture'. More recently, Khlevniuk in *Master of the House*, pp. 65–8, 108–16, 128–9, has convincingly dismissed the persisting entrenched views on the basis of a thorough survey of the Russian archives. Both have further demonstrated how Stalin exploited the event to unleash the Great Terror, issuing a directive on the day of the assassination advocating harsh treatment (including the death penalty) for suspected terrorists. See also R.J. Overy, *The Dictators: Hitler's Germany and Stalin's Russia* (New York, 2004), pp. 51–3. Stalin's complicity was vehemently denied by Molotov, who was present when Stalin received news of the assassination and personally took charge of the investigation the following day in Leningrad, interrogating the assassin, Nikolaev; see A. Resis (ed.), *Molotov Remembers: Inside Kremlin politics, conversations with Felix Chuev* (Chicago, 1993), pp. 218–22. Amy Knight adds no fresh evidence, though in *Who Killed Kirov? The Kremlin's greatest mystery* (New York, 1999) she attributes its absence to the efforts undertaken by the Russians to block access to relevant archival sources. Recently declassified archival documents pertaining to Kirov's death, however, confirm that Nikolaev acted on his own initiative and that his was a crime of passion, not a plot by counter-revolutionary terrorist groups, as Stalin's baseless version would have it. It was typical of Maisky to initially take Stalin's account at face value and endorse it, but then later, perceiving the consequences, to maintain a low profile.

58. The reference is to Baldwin's hope of helping India attain 'dominion status'. Support came from Halifax and from Geoffrey Dawson, editor of *The Times*, but he faced fierce opposition from a militant section of Conservatives, led by Churchill and Croft and supported by the press magnates Rothermere and Beaverbrook. The joint select committee finally adopted a resolution stipulating the establishment of an All-India Federation with a central government, whose authority, however, did not extend to the vital spheres of defence and foreign policy. See L.S. Amery, *My Political Life* (London, 1955).

59. The quotation is taken from *The Times*, 5 December 1934.

60. The sailors of the British Atlantic Fleet took industrial action, protesting against a 10 per cent pay cut.

61. Following the refusal of Germany and Poland to participate in an Eastern Pact, the Russians reverted to a joint protocol with the French, signed in Geneva on 5 December 1934. France and the USSR undertook not to enter into negotiations with potential members of the pact that might lead to multilateral or bilateral agreements, which would thus undermine an Eastern Regional Pact. They further undertook never to denounce the protocol and to inform each other of any overture made to them by the parties concerned. Czechoslovakia acceded to the protocol two days later. From Geneva, Litvinov instructed Maisky to inform Vansittart that the protocol was evoked by Hitler's attempt 'to sow mistrust' between the

Soviet Union and France through rumours of separate negotiations, 'now with the USSR, now with France'. But his main concern, shared by Maisky, was of a possible British overture to Germany which might tie French hands; RAN f.1702 op.4 d.472 l.1, Litvinov to Maisky, 7 Dec. 1934, and *DVP*, 1934, XVII, docs. 415 & 416.

62. A declaration of members of the Labour Executive and Trades Union Congress (TUC) against the execution without trial of the so called 'enemies of the people' in the Soviet Union following Kirov's murder.

63. On 15 December, Maisky added a note to his diary that late the previous evening a messenger had arrived at the embassy and delivered by hand a letter from the Coles (whom Maisky referred to as 'Sentimental idiots!') and the 'Declaration of the 43'.

64. Maisky was advocating a blueprint for the improvement of Anglo-Soviet relations. It sought the eradication of suspicion over British intentions in the Far East, and a ministerial visit to Russia. Vansittart was favourably disposed, the more so when he learned shortly afterwards that Maisky's complaints were justified. But the idea of a ministerial visit, similar to the French radical Édouard Herriot's, was discouraged in the Foreign Office, which feared that a visitor would be shown 'Potemkin's villages'. Vansittart condoned a visit by a minor official and further adopted Maisky's idea of a statement by the foreign secretary in parliament denying any Anglo-Japanese collusion. Simon, however, was less responsive to Soviet suspicions, and far less enthusiastic about rapprochement. He, as the British record of Maisky's meeting with the dismayed Vansittart on 27 December reveals, was more interested in raising Comintern subversion as a counter-argument; TNA FO 371 18306 N7104 & N7155/16/38.

65. The International Dimitrov Committee was set up by leftist intellectuals, among them André Malraux and André Gide, to secure the release of Dimitrov, head of the Bulgarian Communist Party, who was interned in Leipzig and charged with setting the 1933 fire which destroyed the Reichstag.

66. Relates directly to Maisky's own situation, were he to find himself in Germany. On his Jewish roots, see the 'Prelude'.

67. The article under the headline 'Terror in Russia' concluded with the words: 'The Russian executions are barbarous and unworthy of a regime which professes to be the most advanced in the world.'

68. Maisky had been instructed by Litvinov that any future agreement with Germany, France or England should be conditional on adherence to the 'Eastern Pact' and should exclude any revival of the 'Pact of Four', which had been signed by Britain, France, Italy and Germany on 15 July 1933 but which never came into force due to major disagreement between the signatories; *DVP*, 1934, XVII, doc. 437, 21 Dec. 1934.

69. Maisky's report home was extremely succinct and, as would become his practice, attributed to Vansittart initiatives of his own that clearly exceeded his authority. It was Vansittart, he insisted, who 'established' that no points of necessary friction existed between the Soviet Union and Britain, while in fact the undersecretary of state was only cajoled into confirming Maisky's long exposé. Maisky further concealed from Litvinov the fact that he had been wrong to assume that the foreign secretary intended to raise the whole scope of

Anglo-Soviet relations in Cabinet and then send for him again. In fact, the FO records show that, when he did raise the issue with Vansittart, he was told that 'in the case of normal and satisfactory relations the usual course was to let them take care of themselves, seeing only that they were maintained by normal diplomatic contacts'. Moreover, the northern department examined the record of the interview with Simon and established (tongue in cheek) that Maisky was 'doubtless under a misapprehension'; *DVP*, 1934, XVII, doc. 431, and TNA FO 371 18306 N6953/16/38.

70. This dictum could hardly apply to Maisky. For his views on the role of personalities, see the 'Introduction'.

71. Undated memo attached to the diary, written around 3 January 1935.

72. The repercussions of Kirov's assassination and the introduction of the reign of terror increasingly undermined Maisky's attempts to bring about genuine rapprochement. Citrine stated matters far more bluntly than Maisky suggests: 'If Hitler had known as much about the art of repression as Stalin the world might never have heard of Dimitrov. He would have been shot in a cellar'. This argument was then adopted by Maisky in his communications with the Soviet government when he advocated open trials. Citrine, he argued, had finally accepted the Soviet arguments, but would not abandon his '"fetish" of a public trial'. Ironically, Maisky's campaign might have contributed to the decision to conduct the Moscow mock 'show trials'. The executions further led to an estrangement with H.G. Wells, after Maisky failed to provide him with a convincing answer to a blunt question: 'What is going on over there?' Maisky never openly condemned the purges. In fact, he went so far as to pin the blame for them on the Western intelligentsia and the way it had turned its back on the Soviet Union; W. Citrine, *Men and Work: An autobiography* (London, 1964), p. 126, and Maisky, *B. Shou i drugie*, pp. 80–2.

73. Not reproduced in this edition.

1935

1. It is doubtful whether Maisky was privy to the recruitment in Cambridge at that time of Philby, Burgess, Blunt and Maclean as Soviet spies, though he was well aware of – and exploited – the great sympathy felt towards the Soviet Union in certain student circles.

2. French Prime Minister Pierre Étienne Flandin and his foreign minister, Pierre Laval, visited London on 1–3 February and met MacDonald and Simon.

3. On the 'Little Entente' see note 10 in 1934. Maisky reported home that the British government was divided on the issue. While MacDonald wholeheartedly supported Hitler, Simon was ambivalent; Baldwin and Eden were 'cautiously' supportive of France; while Vansittart strongly advocated rapprochement with Italy; *DVP*, 1935, XVIII, doc. 42, fn. 23.

4. A typical allusion to the perception Maisky had of the centrality of his own ambassadorial position *vis-à-vis* Stalin.

5. The Franco-British communiqué agreed to abolish the limitations set by the Versailles Agreement on the German armed forces and called for a new arms agreement to coincide with Germany's return to the League of Nations, the conclusion of an Eastern Pact, and the preservation of Austrian independence; see Z. Steiner, *The Triumph of the Dark: European*

international history, 1933–1939 (Oxford, 2011), p. 83. The Soviet position is in *DVP*, 1935, XVIII, doc. 68.

6. Vansittart's report, in TNA FO 371 18826 C1321/55/18, does not mention at all the conversation concerning Eden's proposed mission to Moscow, but he raised it during the Cabinet meeting of 25 February; TNA FO 371 19450 N1111/17/38.

7. The importance attached by Maisky to his presentation is attested by his rebuke aimed at Garvin's editorial in the *Observer* for failing to realize that 'Peace and security in Europe [were] indivisible.' The matter was rectified by a second editorial the following week; Garvin papers, 20 Feb. 1935.

8. The Russian version is in *DVP*, 1935, XVIII, doc. 72. Simon, as is obvious from his own account, left Maisky in no doubt that the main objective of the Eastern Pact was to 'give confidence necessary to make an arms agreement possible'. 'The sooner the Russians get used to this idea,' it was minuted in the Foreign Office, 'the better.' This view was not shared by Vansittart and Eden; TNA FO 371 18827 C1429/55/18. The reason for the persistent gulf in the two countries' attitudes (and the essence of the emerging appeasement) was the British government's belief that a general European arms limitation agreement could still be achieved if Germany's legitimate grievances were addressed. The Russians meanwhile had become convinced that Hitler could only be checked by resort to force. Maisky told Dalton: 'By all means talk with Hitler, and come to agreements and compromises. But talk to him with a rifle in your hand, or he will pay no regard to your wishes.' Pimlott, *Political Diary of Hugh Dalton*, p. 188.

9. The meeting took place on 28 February.

10. Maisky was faithfully following Litvinov's instructions of the previous evening; *DVP*, 1935, XVIII, doc. 93.

11. In conveying the decision, Maisky pressed Litvinov to receive Eden, producing a misleading argument that 'at present the whole Berlin visit hangs in the air and it is not clear whether it will take place at all'; *DVP*, 1935, XVIII, doc. 102 & fn. 60.

12. One notable exception is Carley, 'Down a blind-alley', pp. 157–8.

13. TNA FO 371 19450 N1072/17/38, Chilston to Vansittart and FO minutes, 2 and 5 March 1935.

14. See his letter to Gilbert Murray in the Murray papers, Box 129, 2 Feb. 1935.

15. *DVP*, 1935, XVIII, docs. 51, 63 & fn. 29.

16. Quoted in Myasnikov, *Maiskii: Izbrannaya perepiska*, II, p. 13.

17. TNA FO 371 19450 N1110/17/38, 28 Feb. & 6 March 1935; this is the extended version of Vansittart's instructions to Chilston, but Simon then used it for his own purpose of pushing through his reconciliation plans in Berlin, while keeping Russia in the picture by dispatching to Moscow a minor minister, devoid of any authority. See also TNA FO 371 18827 C1429/55/18, 20 Feb. 1935.

18. Maisky pleaded with Eden to ensure that the visit took place 'with the least possible delay', so as not to create the impression that the British government was postponing the visit 'until such time as Berlin was prepared to receive a similar visit'. According to Eden, Maisky sounded 'both insistent and worried', and he feared he was 'unable wholly to reassure him'; TNA FO 371 19468 N1270/1167/38.

19. Maisky had impressed on Litvinov the significance that Eden and Simon attached to a meeting with Stalin, who, in the past, had met Bernard Shaw, Lady Astor and Lord Lothian. Eden would be the first Western minister ever to be received by Stalin; *DVP*, 1935, XVIII, doc. 108.

20. Maisky explained to Eden that Stalin was no longer only the secretary of the Communist Party, but now held a 'special position on the Executive of their elected Assembly. M. Maisky incidentally informed me with a grin that he himself was now an MP'. Maisky was elected to the Central Committee of the Communist Party; TNA FO 371 19468 N1329/1167/38.

21. Maisky spent the weekend at the Webbs' 'very triumphant – glad that it is Eden and not Simon, whom he is chaperoning to Moscow on the 27th – he dislikes Simon intensely – mainly because he feels that, in this slippery lawyer, the USSR had an enemy. Also Eden represents the conservative party and is an "English gentleman" – qualifications which Simon lacks according to the ambassador'; Webb, diary, 16 March 1935, pp. 5944–5.

22. The palatial lodgings of a former Russian merchant turned into the guest house of the Soviet Foreign Ministry in the Moscow countryside.

23. Quoted from *The Times*, 16 March 1935.

24. Litvinov's instructions in *DVP*, 1935, XVIII, doc. 115.

25. Without consulting the French, on 18 March the British government sent a note of protest to the Germans over their unilateral action, ending by asking whether the Germans were still interested in a meeting between Simon and Hitler; Steiner, *Triumph of the Dark*, p. 86.

26. *The Times*, 27 March 1935. Maisky's full itinerary of the visit is in RAN f.1702 op.3 d.105 ll.1–2.

27. J. Gleasor, *War at the Top: Based on the experiences of General Sir Leslie Hollis* (London, 1959), p. 125; and Sheinis, *Litvinov*, pp. 272–3.

28. Kollontay, who happened to be on leave in Moscow, left her vivid impressions in *Diplomaticheskie dnevniki*, II, p. 280. See also A. Eden, *The Eden Memoirs: Facing the Dictators* (London, 1962), pp. 158–9, and Maisky, *Who Helped Hitler?*, p. 51. A candid description of the visit by Chilston is in TNA FO 371 19468 N1871/1167/38.

29. See Maisky's detailed report of the meeting in *DVP*, 1935, XVIII, doc. 146, 28 March 1935. The British records (TNA FO 371 18833 C2726/55/18) and the circumstances which led to the Berlin and Moscow visits hardly sustain the idea that Stalin was subjected to a distorted account underlining a British desire to pacify Hitler. See C. Andrew and V. Mitrokhin, *The Mitrokhin Archive: The KGB in Europe and the West* (London, 1999), pp. 71–2. Eden attests in his memoirs that his report of the talks was 'rather fuller than that which Simon had given to the French'; Eden, *Facing the Dictators*, p. 145.

30. Eden, *Facing the Dictators*, pp. 142–3. An excellent but forgotten source is D. Bardens, *Portrait of a Statesman* (London, 1955), pp. 125–9.

31. It was published in *DVP*, 1935, XVIII, doc. 148. Part of it is reproduced here, since Maisky made no further entries until June.

32. TNA FO 371 18833 C2726/55/18.

33. Once Eden became foreign secretary in early 1936, Maisky cabled Litvinov: 'In March 1935 Eden still expressed doubts concerning the correctness of the Soviet judgement

of Hitler as a potential aggressor. Today his sentiments are absolutely different ... He is convinced that Hitler is a potential aggressor. Eden is uncertain and hesitant only about when Hitler will come out'; *DVP*, 1935, XIX, doc. 42.

34. In *Facing the Dictators* (p. 154), Eden recalls that Stalin 'chuckled at the idea, Maisky grinned somewhat nervously'.

35. See the commentary following the diary entry for 31 January 1936.

36. Quoted in Neilson, *Britain, Soviet Russia and the Collapse of the Versailles Order*, p. 135. In retrospect, Eden would form a more positive impression of Stalin. 'His personality,' he recalled, 'made itself felt without effort or exaggeration. He had natural good manners ... I respected the quality of his mind ... perhaps this was because of Stalin's pragmatic approach. It was easy to forget that I was talking to a Party man, certainly no one could have been less doctrinaire ... I have never known a man handle himself better in conference. Well-informed at all points that were of concern to him, Stalin was prudent but not slow. Seldom raising his voice, a good listener, prone to doodling, he was the quietest dictator I have ever known'; Eden, *Facing the Dictators*, p. 155.

37. Maisky, *Who Helped Hitler?*, pp. 50–2. It was already discernible in his briefings from Moscow to the correspondent of *The Times*, 29 and 30 March. A well-informed evaluation of the talks is in Manne, 'The failure of Anglo-Soviet rapprochement', pp. 735–7.

38. Sylvester papers, diary, A32 & A40, 6 July 1936 & 15 Oct. 1937.

39. Cadogan papers, ACAD 4/4, letter to Lord Birkenhead, 12 Oct. 1964. The gap between Eden's expectations and his ability to deliver would be accentuated during his famous second summit with Stalin in December 1941. See commentary at the end of the year 1941.

40. *DVP*, 1935, XVIII, doc. 201, Litvinov to Maisky, 29 March 1935. A well-documented discussion of the rather neglected history of the agreement is in M.J. Carley '"A fearful concatenation of circumstances": The Anglo-Soviet rapprochement, 1934–6', *Contemporary European History*, 5 (1996). See also his 'Prelude to defeat: Franco-Soviet relations, 1919–39', *Historical Reflections*, 22/1 (1996).

41. TNA FO 371 18838 C3523/55/18, 30 April 1935.

42. *DVP*, 1935, XVIII, doc. 195. See also Manne, 'Failure of Anglo-Soviet rapprochement', pp. 738–41.

43. TNA FO 371 18838 C3554/55/18.

44. TNA FO 371 19467 N2761/998/38, 28 May 1935; *DVP*, 1935, XVIII, docs. 247 & 250, 2 & 3 June 1935.

45. In the reorganization of the Cabinet, Baldwin became prime minister, while Hoare replaced Simon as foreign secretary. Sixteen out of the 22 Cabinet members were Conservatives.

46. Having placed his bet on Eden, Maisky, in reporting home, went out of his way to explain that, although Eden had failed to receive any significant portfolio, Maisky had been assured by Vansittart that Eden would become a full member of the Cabinet and as such would have 'more influence in the conduct of foreign policy than before'; *DVP*, 1935, XVIII, doc. 261.

47. TNA FO 371 18845 C4564/55/18, 15 June 1935.

48. See the voluminous correspondence between Beaverbrook and Maisky; Beaverbrook papers, BBK\C\238. Maisky was even invited to spend a weekend at Beaverbrook's country house. See also correspondence with Lady Astor in Astor papers, 1416/1/2/144 and the memoirs of the duchess of Atholl – K.S. Atholl, *Working Partnership* (London, 1958), p. 200; *DVP*, 1935, XVIII, doc. 272, Maisky to Narkomindel, 15 June 1935; Keynes papers PP\45\207\4, exchange of letters with Maisky, end of July 1935; Webb, diary, 12 July 1935, pp. 6003–5.

49. Maisky, who came in person to greet him at the station, was particularly excited. He proudly shared with Pavlov his childhood memories of their earlier meetings, when he had accompanied his father to the Institute of Experimental Medicine in Moscow, where Pavlov had pursued his research; *Before the Storm*, pp. 52–3. The visit was covered *inter alia* by the *New York Times*, 29 July 1935.

50. *DVP*, 1935, XVIII, doc. 302 & fn. 168.

51. By far the best account is still Manne, 'Failure of Anglo-Soviet rapprochement', pp. 740–2.

52. The lengthy meeting was more likely forced on Hoare, who complained that 'although it was [Maisky's] first and on that account a ceremonial visit, he soon plunged into European politics'. He emerged from the meeting, though, with the wrong impression that Maisky 'seemed pleasantly surprised with an interview between himself and one like myself who is known to have continuously disapproved of the Bolshevik regime'; TNA FO 371 19451 N3187/17/38. See also Neilson, *Britain, Soviet Russia and the Collapse of the Versailles Order*, p. 146.

53. Maisky reported home that he had gained a 'strong impression' that Hoare would strive to achieve a quick agreement with Germany. Indeed, five days later the naval agreement was signed; *DVP*, 1935, XVIII, doc. 268. Hoare 'is trying to experiment in the foreign policy field,' Maisky wrote to Kollontay. 'He is gradually learning, but it would be good if the learning process didn't cost England itself and many others too dear'; RAN f.1702 op.4 d.111 l.11.

54. Maisky's diary is a vital source for the meeting. Perhaps this clairvoyant comment, suggesting a possible deal between Germany and the Soviet Union at Poland's expense, has prevented the Russians from declassifying the official report of the meeting.

55. Obsessed with the idea of restoring the fallen Roman Empire, Mussolini sought his empire in North Africa and Ethiopia, after securing a veiled agreement from Laval. In September 1935, Italian troops invaded Ethiopia. The League of Nations condemned the invasion and imposed economic sanctions on Italy, but these were frustrated by Germany and the United States, which continued trading with Italy. The results exposed the bankruptcy of the League of Nations and hastened the rapprochement between Hitler and Mussolini, which finally led to the formation of the 'Axis'; see R. Overy, *The Road to War* (London, 1999), pp. 183–8.

56. The Anglo-German naval treaty of 18 June 1935 sanctioned the building of a German fleet up to 35 per cent of the tonnage of the British navy and of a submarine force that did not exceed 45 per cent of the tonnage of the British submarine fleet. It was abrogated by Hitler on

28 April 1939. Entertaining Ashton-Gwatkin to tea at the Soviet embassy, Maisky remarked that 'In signing the Naval Agreement with Germany, Great Britain had snatched at an apparent advantage, as a greedy boy will snatch at a cake on the table; the result is likely to be an attack of indigestion. This action by Great Britain was a shock to the confidence of France, Italy and the USSR.' He dismissed the suggestions made by his interlocutor that Germany was simply tired of being a second-rate country but did not wish to fight. 'Tell this story to *babouschka* (little Grandmother!),' Maisky responded. 'Hitler's ambitions were recorded in *Mein Kampf*, which he had never repudiated'; TNA FO 371 19460 N3423/135/38, 4 July 1935.

57. *DVP*, 1935, XVIII, docs. 327 & 330.

58. TNA FO 371 18851 C7596/55/18 & C7730/55/18, 9 & 18 Nov. 1935; Webb, diary, 18 Nov. 1935, p. 6092.

59. RAN f.1702 op.4 d.143 l.50, 2 Dec. 1935. To bolster his position and show off his extraordinary standing in London, Maisky presented Litvinov the following day with a report of two meetings – with Churchill and with Beaverbrook – the latter had just been a guest of Hitler's. He reported Beaverbrook's impression of Hitler's irreconcilable hostility towards the Soviet Union. By contrast, the press baron took an optimistic view of the future of Anglo-Soviet relations and promised to use his press to improve them further. Maisky emerged from the meeting with Churchill encouraged by the 'great sympathy' the latter had shown towards any form of rapprochement between the two countries; *DVP*, 1935, XVIII, docs. 430 & 440, 3 Dec. 1935. Maisky further intensified his contacts with Garvin, editor of the *Observer*; see Maisky's letter to Garvin, Garvin papers, 14 December. From 1937 onwards, Garvin became increasingly associated with the 'Cliveden Set' and there was a degree of estrangement from the Maiskys; see, for example, Agnes Maisky to Garvin, Garvin papers, 2 April 1937. To dispel rumours in the ministry concerning his dire situation, Maisky tried hard to convince Kollontay that there was 'little particularly new right now' and relations with Britain were 'as satisfactory' as possible; RAN f.1702 op.4 d.111 l.12–14, 2 Dec. 1935.

60. Russian historiography still hails the Soviet moral and political support for Ethiopia (see V.S. Myasnikov et al., *Ivan Mikhailovich Maiskii: Dnevnik diplomata, London, 1934–43* (Moscow, 2006), I, p. 462, fn. 39). Maisky was, in fact, instructed by Litvinov to inform the British government 'explicitly' that the Soviet government 'was not opposed to any attempt at reasonable settlement' of the conflict and was 'interested in shortening the war'; TNA FO 371 19161 J7786/1/1, 13 June 1935.

61. The Conservative Party won 432 seats in parliament, Labour 154 and the Liberals 21.

62. The Hoare–Laval plan of 8 December 1935 proposed a settlement of the Italo-Ethiopian conflict, whereby the Ethiopian government would cede large parts of its territory to Italy, in return for the sea port of Aseb in southern Eritrea and a narrow corridor connecting it with the mainland. The League's defiance prompted Mussolini to pursue his campaign, which led to the occupation of Addis Ababa on 5 May 1936. Indignation in Britain led Baldwin to abandon Hoare as foreign secretary and replace him with Eden, an advocate of the League of Nations.

1936

1. Maisky could hardly trust his own driver, who had clearly been set up in the embassy to watch over his movements. Beatrice Webb recalls a party, attended by the Maiskys, Lord William Percy and a certain Captain Bennett, who had been caught by the Bolsheviks while fighting with the White Armies in southern Russia – but had escaped. When Maisky's chauffeur appeared on the scene to take them back 'there was an instantaneous recognition between former gaoler and escaped prisoner – the Soviet chauffeur turning out to be a GPU [Soviet Secret Service] official. They chummed up and were joined by Dick and Lord William Percy – both of whom were connected with the British Secret Service – whereupon the four "mystery men" strolled off together for a friendly glass and a smoke – much to the astonishment of Their Excellencies and the other guests!'; Webb, diary, 27 August 1934, p. 5763.

2. *VSD*, pp. 138–40; see also Colvin, *Vansittart in Office*, pp. 33–4, 56; RAN f.1702 op.4 d.940 l.1, Maisky's condolences to Eden.

3. The quintessential Fred Astaire and Ginger Rogers film.

4. On Litvinov's irritation with Eden's evasive attitude, see *DVP*, 1936, XIX, doc. 32.

5. Most profitable movie in the UK in 1936, directed by René Clair.

6. TNA FO 371 19452 N5966/17/38, C7730/55/18, 20 Nov. & N6030/17/38, 21 Nov. 1935. Maisky told Beatrice Webb that he was extremely careful not to be associated with the British Communist Party, whose members were not even invited to functions at the embassy. She herself noticed that militant Labour leaders, such as Stafford Cripps and herself, were always met 'alone and not "in company"'; Webb, diary, 18 Nov. 1935, p. 6092. M.J. Carley is one of the few historians to recognize Eden's shortcomings and the fact that he turned out to be 'a false friend'; see Carley, '"Fearful concatenation"'.

7. *DVP*, 1936, XIX, doc. 3; TNA FO 371 20338 N125/20/38 & N120/20/38, conversations with Collier and Eden, 6 Jan. 1936 and minutes. See also Neilson, *Britain, Soviet Russia and the Collapse of the Versailles Order*, p. 157.

8. RAN f.1702 op.4 d.1460 ll.1–4, 30 July 1936.

9. Quoted in Manne, 'Anglo-Soviet rapprochement', pp. 747, 748–50.

10. In reporting home, however, he attributed the idea to the secretary of state; RAN f.1702 op.4 d.1407 l.1 and *DVP*, 1936, XIX, doc. 36.

11. *DVP*, 1936, XIX, doc. 42; TNA FO 371 20339 N833/20/38, 19 Feb. 1936.

12. Webb, diary, 25 Feb. 1936, p. 6128.

13. Steiner, *The Triumph of the Dark*, pp. 136–55; R. Lamb, *The Drift to War 1922–1939* (New York, 1991), p. 192; and P.M.H. Bell, *The Origins of the Second World War in Europe* (London, 1987), p. 210.

14. See I. Kershaw's impressive work, *Making Friends with Hitler: Lord Londonderry and the British road to war* (London, 2004).

15. The directive is in *DVP*, 1936, XIX, doc. 71. Expressing his personal views, Maisky warned against Hitler's proposal for a non-aggression pact with Czechoslovakia and Austria. He expected the Germans to concoct some internal agitation which would 'lead to an Anschluss'. Negotiation on Germany's return to the League could only take place after a show of force by the 'three great nations of the League' – England, France and Russia. At a

follow-up meeting, he conveyed the Soviet government's grave concern and opposition to any negotiations or exploratory conversations with the German government. It was 'the last in a long chain of actions which ... could only end, if not stopped, in the complete destruction of the League and collective security'. Germany had become, 'to use an American phrase, "Aggressor No. 1"' and the Soviet Union was prepared to 'take part in any action, whatever it might be, which was decided by the League'; TNA FO 371 19889 C1602/4/18 & 19890 C1716/4/18. The Soviet opposition to any negotiations was conveyed by Maisky through Corbin, the French ambassador in London, and provoked strong German reactions, *Documents on German Foreign Policy* (London, 1956) (hereafter *DGFP*), V, 141. See also H. Ragsdale, *The Soviets, the Munich Crisis, and the Coming of World War II* (Cambridge, UK, 2004), p. 28.

16. Churchill papers, CHAR 20/253/134, 24 April 1936.

17. Kollontay, *Diplomaticheskie dnevniki*, II, pp. 356–7.

18. RAN f.1702 op.4 d.143 ll.51–4.

19. Quoted in Dullin, *Men of Influence*, p. 129.

20. RAN f.1702 op.4 d.854 l.1, 4 May 1936.

21. TNA FO 371 19904 C3231/4/18; *DVP*, 1936, XIX, doc. 142, 28 April. See also Corbin to Flandin, in P. Renouvin and J.B. Duroselle (eds), *Documents diplomatiques francais* (hereafter *DDF*), 2 Serie, II, Doc. 125.

22. RAN f.1702 op.4 d.1184 l.5, 4 May 1936.

23. Pimlott, *Political Diary of Hugh Dalton*, p. 200.

24. Webb, diary, 27 May 1936, p. 6174.

25. *The Times*, 3 August 1936; Richard S. Grayson, *Liberals, International Relations, and Appeasement: The Liberal Party, 1919–1939* (Abingdon, UK, 2001), p. 161.

26. For Maisky's efforts, see correspondence with *inter alia* Churchill in Churchill papers, CHAR 2/251/53 & 76, 15 & 18 Feb. 1936; also with Cranborne, Elliot and H.G. Wells, RAN f.1702 op.4 d.1399 l.1, d.1192 l.1 & d.1141 l.45, 17 & 18 Feb. 1936.

27. Webb, diary, 6 Aug. 1936, p. 6208.

28. Invitations, Beaverbrook papers, BBK\C\238, 21 July. See also 8 and 29 April, 10 June and 18 July 1936, and 25 May 1937. Maisky left a candid portrait of Beaverbrook in *Who Helped Hitler?*, pp. 57–8: 'a short, extremely lively restless man, with a round mobile face and acute, piercing eyes. There poured from his lips a firework torrent of wisecracks, opinions, assessments, characterizations of people and events. He did not restrain himself in his expressions.'

29. Churchill papers, CHAR 20/252/92, CHAR 20/253/7 & 9 (1936); *DVP*, 1936, XIX, doc. 115. See also J. Barnes and D. Nicholson (eds), *The Empire at Bay: The Leo Amery diaries* (London, 1988), p. 348. Maisky's evaluation was used by Litvinov to exert pressure on the French: see Alphand to Flandin, 4 April 1936, in *DDF*, 2 Serie, II, Doc. 22. M. Gilbert, *Winston S. Churchill*, Companion Vol. V, Part 3, *The Coming of War, 1936–1939* (London, 1982), p. 108. Reynolds, 'Churchill's writing of history', p. 238, suggests that in 1936 Churchill definitely leaned towards Franco and 'the Anti-Red' forces, but the following year he was already admitting in parliament that 'if I had to choose between Communism and Nazi-ism, I would choose Communism'.

30. The article appears as an attachment in the diary.

31. Nonetheless, his motto for his work on Mozart's operas was: 'There are great ideas floating in the world but above them floats the figure of Mozart.' This led to the suppression of the work until the 1970s.

32. Webb, diary, 11 May 1936, pp. 6158–60.

33. MacKenzie and MacKenzie, *Diary of Beatrice Webb*, IV, 27 Feb. 1937.

34. RAN f.1702 op.4 d.862 l.15, 3 June 1936.

35. *DVP*, 1936, XIX, doc. 208; A.J.P. Taylor (ed.), *Lloyd George: A diary by Frances Stevenson* (London, 1971), pp. 324–5.

36. Sylvester papers, Lloyd George to Conwell Evans, A40, 18 Dec. 1937, and diary entry of 3 Sep. 1936.

37. RGASPI, Stalin papers, f.558 op.11 d.214 ll.31–6; see also Dullin, *Men of Influence*, pp. 137–9.

38. Ivy Litvinov's papers, draft memoirs. Litvinov was crushed by her decision to leave. This European bohemian way of life, as Montefiore suggests in *Stalin: The court of the Red Tsar*, pp. 246–7, could hardly endear Litvinov to the puritanical Stalin. There is nothing to suggest, as Dullin does in *Men of Influence*, pp. 216–17, that Litvinov deliberately encouraged her to depart to protect her from the Stalinist carnage.

39. RAN f.1702 op.4 d.546 ll.34–6, 31 July 1936; Kollontay, *Diplomaticheskie dnevniki*, II, pp. 356–7.

40. RAN f.1702 op.4 d.878 l.3, Maisky to Webb, 20 Oct. 1936; Beaverbrook papers, BBK\C\238, letter from Maisky, 9 Nov. 1936.

41. Maisky, *Spanish Notebooks*, pp. 20–2. Maisky expected to spend a couple of months in Russia; see RAN f.1702 op.4 d.854 l.2, Maisky to Beaverbrook, 10 Aug. 1936.

42. For a candid description of the *dramatis personae* on the committee, see Maisky, *Spanish Notebooks*, ch. 7. See also G. Martel (ed.), *The Times and Appeasement: The Journals of A.L. Kennedy, 1932-1939* (CUP, 2000), p. 273; and Girard de Charbonnières, *La plus evitable de toutes les guerres* (Paris, 1985), pp. 109–22. On the confusion surrounding Soviet policy at the outset of the conflict and its impact on Maisky, see exchanges between Kaganovich, Litvinov and Stalin, in O. Khlevniuk et al. (eds), *Stalin i Kaganovich: Perepiska, 1931–1936 gg.* (Moscow, 2001), especially doc. 861.

43. TNA FO 371 20584 W15074/9549/41, 3 Nov. 1936. A convincing dismissal of the ideological premises of the war are in Ragsdale, *The Soviets*, pp. 188–9.

44. *Hansard*, HC Deb 5 November 1936, vol. 317, cols 318–19. Maisky had warned Narkomindel that while Churchill still perceived an Anglo-Soviet–French combination to be the only effective means of stopping Hitler, he was 'unhappy about the Soviet "intervention" in Spanish affairs', which, he warned, could harm Anglo-Soviet relations; *DVP*, 1936, XIX, doc. 341, 1 Nov.; and Churchill papers, CHAR 2/259/81, Maisky to Churchill, 19 Oct. 1936.

45. RAN f.1702 op.4 d.994 l.2, Maisky to Lloyd George, 8 Dec. 1936.

46. A most convincing argument is presented in Dullin, *Men of Influence*, pp. 133–5. Maisky told the Webbs that he had 'little fear of getting involved in a war through helping the Spanish government … implying that the Kremlin was willing to run the risk in order

to prevent the rise of a fascist Spain'; Webb, diary, 15 Nov. 1936, pp. 6260–1; M.J. Carley, 'Caught in a cleft stick: Soviet diplomacy and the Spanish Civil War', in G. Johnson (ed.), *The International Context of the Spanish Civil War* (Newcastle upon Tyne, UK, 2009).

47. Most decisively, R. Radosh, M.R. Habeck and G. Sevostianov, *Spain Betrayed: The Soviet Union in the Spanish Civil War* (New Haven, CT, 2001). While exposing the absence of any pure ideological drive in Spain and the rather superficial 'anti-fascist' cloak, the recent works fail to perceive the vital international perspective of the intervention which emerges from Maisky's diary and the commentary.

48. Blum warned Litvinov that on no account would France intervene in Spain, and that Soviet intervention was jeopardizing the collaboration between the two countries. Dullin, *Men of Influence*, pp. 126–7.

49. Quoted in Carley, 'Caught in a cleft stick', p. 163. This thorough and documented work should be considered the most reliable and up-to-date account of Soviet foreign policy during the Spanish Civil War. His narrative questions the conclusions of Z. Steiner, *The Triumph of the Dark*, pp. 230–1, who, following in the footsteps of Haslam, *The Soviet Union and the Struggle for Collective Security*, suggests that the diversion to the east in the wake of the outbreak of the Japanese–Chinese war in July 1937 and the logistical constraints, mostly naval weakness, were prime reasons for the detachment from Spain and the withdrawal into isolation, as advocated by Zhdanov and Potemkin.

1937

1. The conversation took place on 3 November 1936; TNA FO 371 20584 W15074/9549/41. Eager to present a rosy picture, in his report home Maisky concealed Eden's continued irritation with communist subversion in Spain; *DVP*, 1936, XIX, doc. 344. Eden had, in fact, commended Vansittart for 'his excellent plain speaking' when Maisky came to see him on 6 January, complaining that Maisky tended to 'presume too far'. Maisky, however, cabled to Moscow that Vansittart saw eye to eye with him; TNA FO 371 21318 W647/7/41 and *DVP*, 1937, XX, doc. 2.

2. 'Self-preservation' would increasingly lead Maisky (as so many other Soviet diplomats during the terror) to amplify his successes in ameliorating relations with Britain and to cautiously temper his observations. A typical example is a telegram to Litvinov in mid-March, suggesting that 'The past three to four months have witnessed a step-by-step increased coldness in relations between London and Berlin.' This he attributed to the Nazi threat to the West. However, Maisky qualified his judgement with a warning that a change in the international situation could easily lead again to a thaw in Anglo-German relations; *DVP*, 1937, XX, fn. 129.

3. S. Naveh, *In Pursuit of Military Excellence: The evolution of operational theory* (London, 1997).

4. By far the most lucid presentation of the Western perceptions is in K. Neilson '"Pursued by a Bear": British estimates of Soviet military strength and Anglo-Soviet relations, 1922–1939', *Canadian Journal of History*, 28 (1993).

5. An example of such bravura is Maisky's address to the National Congress of Peace and Friendship with the USSR, reported in *The Times*, 15 March 1937.

6. TNA FO 371 20348 N5866/287/38, 19–25 Nov. 1936, and TNA FO 371 21103 N1479/270/18, 23 March 1937, respectively; Webb, diary, 15 Nov. 1936, pp. 6260–1.

7. See note 58 below.

8. Hitler once again demanded equal rights for Germany and refuted Eden's earlier statement in parliament that Germany was intent on isolating itself from the rest of the world, citing as an example the recently concluded anti-communist pact with Japan.

9. In *Spanish Notebooks*, p. 86, Maisky summed up his impression of Ribbentrop: 'Since I sat for a whole year diagonally opposite the German Ambassador at the table of the Committee for "Non-intervention", I had the opportunity of studying him at close quarters. And I must without mincing words say that this was a coarse, dull-witted maniac, with the outlook and manners of a Prussian NCO. It has always remained a mystery to me how Hitler could have made such a dolt his chief adviser on foreign affairs.'

10. The Republican army defeated the Italian and Nationalist forces which were seeking to encircle Madrid on 23 March.

11. See also *DVP*, 1937, XX, fn. 7.

12. A far more distanced report of the conversation, passed on to Stalin, appears in RGASPI, Stalin papers, f.558 op.11 d.214 ll.60–3.

13. A detailed account of the meeting, but deprived of his own thoughts, is in *DVP*, 1937, XX, doc. 115.

14. The German cruiser *Deutschland* was shelled by the Republican forces on 29 May 1937, leading Germany and Italy to withdraw temporarily from the Non-Intervention Committee and the patrolling of the Spanish coast. Maisky warned Moscow on 3 June that the British were seeking to bypass the Committee by making separate arrangements with Germany, Italy and France, a 'four-power pact in practice'; *DVP*, 1937, XX, doc. 192. The patrolling of the Spanish coast was discontinued on 16 September.

15. A society set up by various bankers in the City in conjunction with the Imperial Policy Group aimed at drawing Great Britain closer to Nazi Germany and Japan.

16. TNA FO 371 20735 C4229/270/18; *DVP*, 1937, XX, fn. 121.

17. A competent survey of the discussion is in Neilson, *Britain, Soviet Russia and the Collapse of the Versailles Order*, pp. 216–17. It did not prevent Hoare from sending Maisky a most friendly letter on his move from the Admiralty to the Home Office; RAN f.1702 op.4 d.1657 l.6, 10 June 1937.

18. *DVP*, 1937, XX, doc. 195, Maisky's report on meeting Eden, 11 June 1937; No. 211 & No. 212 for the meetings on 23 & 24 June 1937.

19. Titulescu had been removed from office by King Carol at the end of 1936, having floated the idea (which came to naught) of a mutual assistance pact with the Russians. He met Lloyd George on 11 June and expressed the view that the 'spirit in France was so bad' that France would 'certainly hesitate to fulfil her obligations' to the Franco-Soviet pact. Both agreed that it was Beneš who had wrecked Lloyd George's scheme at the 1922 Genoa Conference for integrating Russia into Europe. Where they disagreed was over Titulescu's conviction that 'Moscow was turning its thoughts' towards a Russo-German reconciliation and entente. His own friendship with Russia 'was not based on any liking for Moscow, but on a desire to keep Russia sweet, and prevent her from claiming

Bessarabia'; Lloyd George papers, LG/G/130, 11 June 1937. See also Steiner, *The Triumph of the Dark*, pp. 288–90.

20. Maisky's official report can be found in *DVP*, 1937, XX, doc. 226.

21. Lloyd George's assessment was spot on and led Maisky to argue hitherto that Chamberlain was bent on concluding a four-power pact without the Soviet Union and ultimately supported direct German expansion eastwards. See Aster, 'Ivan Maisky and parliamentary anti-appeasement', pp. 320–2.

22. An incident between Japanese and Chinese troops, provoked by Japan on 7 July 1937, served as a pretext for the Japanese to mount a major offensive against China.

23. R. Self (ed.), *The Neville Chamberlain Diary Letters: The Heir Apparent, 1928–33* (London, 2002), III, pp. 357–8, 19 Nov. 1932; TNA FO 371 16321 N6619/22/38; RAN f.1702 op.2 d.3 d.101 ll.7–11, FO and Maisky's reports of the meeting, 16 Nov. 1932.

24. Gilbert Murray papers, Box 75, Maisky to Murray, 24 Jan. 1936.

25. Sylvester papers, diary, A32, 6 July 1936.

26. Maisky, *Who Helped Hitler?*, p. 68.

27. RAN f.1702 op.4 d.1168 l.2.

28. R. Self, *The Neville Chamberlain Diary Letters: The Downing Street Years, 1934–40* (London, 2005), IV, p. 264. Thirty years of revisionism introduced the notion of economic and military constraints as a justification for Chamberlain's appeasement, but overlooked his ideological bias concerning Russia. Recently, however, many of the early charges against Chamberlain in what turned out to be the iconic *Guilty Men*, published in 1940 under the pseudonym of 'Cato', have been resurrected. Sidney Aster, who has examined the year 1939 in depth using Chamberlain's papers, has launched a devastating criticism of Chamberlain's 'misplaced trust, unwarranted optimism and erroneous judgements'. Chamberlain showed, he argues, 'a blind conviction that there was no alternative to the policy he had decided upon'; quoted in D. Dutton, *Neville Chamberlain* (London, 2001), p. 184. His analysis dovetails with Margesson's observation in 1939 that 'Chamberlain had never met anybody in Birmingham who in the least resembled Adolf Hitler. He had always found that people he had met ... were reasonable and honest and it had always proved possible, with a certain amount of give and take, to make a deal with them that should prove satisfactory to both sides ... He has as little chance in a Europe dominated by Stalin and Hitler as Little Lord Fauntleroy would have of concluding a satisfactory deal with Al Capone'; Margesson papers, MRGN, 1/5.

29. Repeated in *DVP*, 1937, XX, doc. 269. In a typical retrospective attempt to prove that the Munich Agreement had been foreordained, Maisky presented a crude picture (as he did throughout his memoirs). Writing to *The Times*, 8 June 1971, he did quote Chamberlain as saying 'Oh, if we could sit down with Hitler at the same table with pencils in our hands and go over all the differences between us, I am sure that the atmosphere would clear up immensely!' This was a deliberate retrospective distortion, which is also evident in Maisky, *The Munich Drama* (Moscow, 1972), p. 13, and in *Who Helped Hitler?*, pp. 68–9. As is obvious from the conclusion of the talk, Maisky saw fit to stress the qualifying and, as it turned out, misleading comments made by Chamberlain that failure to reach an agreement would lead him to seek an alternative solution. A few months later, however, Maisky grasped, as he told

the Webbs, that 'that hard grained but frank reactionary' was set on a renewal of the four-power pact for peace in the west, while the Soviet Union 'was to be left outside to mind her own business'; Webb, diary, 27 Oct. 1937, p. 6393.

30. Vansittart further advised Masaryk to make the necessary concessions to the Sudeten Germans, though he declined to specify which measures he had in mind; *DVP*, 1937, XX, fn. 141, Maisky to Narkomindel, 10 Aug. 1937.

31. Maisky refers to his visit to the Paris Art and Technology Exhibition of 1937. In the midst of the Civil War, the Spanish pavilion attracted particular attention, displaying Pablo Picasso's depiction of the horrors of war in his famous *Guernica* painting, Alexander Calder's sculpture *Mercury Fountain* and Joan Miró's *Catalan Peasant in Revolt*. Strangely enough, that pavilion is not referred to by Maisky. The two pavilions of Nazi Germany and the Soviet Union (the latter hailed by Frank Lloyd Wright as the most fascinating pavilion at the exhibition) were placed directly across from each other. Hitler wanted to withdraw from the exhibition, but was persuaded by Albert Speer to present it as a bulwark against communism; the best description is in M. Kitchen's riveting biography, *Speer: Hitler's architect* (London, 2015), pp. 60–1, 74 and 281.

32. Chamberlain exploited Eden's absence to embark on negotiations with the Italians behind his back, aimed at liquidating the Abyssinia conflict; *DVP*, 1937, XX, fn. 161, Maisky to Narkomindel.

33. Upon receiving information about attacks on Soviet ships from NKID, Maisky placed a proposal before the committee of non-intervention on 5 May to appoint a special expert commission to work out practical measures against piracy; *DVP*, 1937, XX, doc. 136). In September 1937, Britain and France convened a conference in Nyon, Switzerland, which was attended by Great Britain, France, the USSR, Turkey, Bulgaria, Greece, Yugoslavia, Rumania and Egypt. The conference resulted in an agreement signed on 14 September entrusting Britain and France with patrolling the Mediterranean; *DVP*, 1937, XX, docs. 322, 326 & 328–34; see also the notes on pp. 750–1.

34. The Nyon Conference was convened to address the unrestricted submarine warfare carried out by Italy. Seen from Maisky's point of view it forced France and Britain to adopt a more belligerent attitude towards Italy and Germany. Maisky is referring to an attached press cutting from the *Observer*, which stated that 'In a subtle way Britain is being forced to take sides against Germany and Italy.'

35. This entry describing his appointment has been moved to the 'Prelude'.

36. In a less glaring report to Narkomindel, clearly aimed at bolstering his continued indispensable presence in Britain against the backdrop of the purges at the ministry, Maisky emphasized the demonstration of Churchill's 'friendly feelings towards me', as well as the latter's acknowledgement that 'above all we now need a strong Russia'; *DVP*, 1937, XX, doc. 411.

37. Halifax accepted an invitation to Germany in his capacity as the 'Master of the Middleton Hunt' to attend an international hunting exhibition in Berlin, in the course of which he had a lengthy talk with Hitler. Maisky gleaned from Lloyd George, on 21 November, that the reconciliation with Germany had become Chamberlain's main goal, even if it meant sacrificing Spain, Austria and Czechoslovakia and was pursued against Eden's specific will.

Eden's popularity, however, prevented Chamberlain from removing him from office, as he was bound to become the nucleus of a powerful opposition; *DVP*, 1937, XX, docs. 415 & 420. See also Ragsdale, *The Soviets*, pp. 3–4.

38. Forcefully argued by O. Khlevniuk, 'The reasons for the "Great Terror": The foreign-political aspect', in S. Pons and A. Romano (eds), *Russia in the Age of Wars, 1914–1945* (Milan, 2000), and by G. Roberts, 'The fascist war threat and Soviet politics in the 1930s', in the same edited volume.

39. T. Uldricks, 'The impact of the Great Purges on the People's Commissariat of Foreign Affairs', *Slavic Review*, 6/2 (1977); S. Dullin, 'L'Union soviétique et la France à un tournant: conjoncture extérieure et évolution interne en 1936–1937', *Matériaux pour l'Histoire de Notre Temps*, 65-6 (2002).

40. RGASPI, Stalin papers, f.558 op.11 d.214 l.24.

41. See Haslam, *The Soviet Union and the Struggle for Collective Security*, p. 132.

42. Kollontay, *Diplomaticheskie dnevniki*, II, pp. 356–7. Back in Moscow, Potemkin was scathing of the British and (particularly) the French, who were 'slavishly following London's orders' and whose country was being led 'to the complete loss of its independence'. Quoted in Carley, 'Caught in a cleft stick', p. 171. On the rivalry between Potemkin and Litvinov, see Dullin, *Men of Influence*, pp. 218–19. On Litvinov's independence, see Uldricks, 'Impact of the Great Purges', p. 197.

43. RAN f.1702 op.4 d.152 l.50, 27 Aug. 1937.

44. *New York Times*, 25 December 1937.

45. On the wide scope and extent of the purges in the ministry, see Haslam, *The Soviet Union and the Struggle for Collective Security*, pp. 148–50.

46. Webb, diary, 25 Nov. 1936, p. 6265.

47. RAN f.1702 op.4 d.509 ll.31–2.

48. RAN f.1702 op.4 d.155 l.20, 24 July 1927. I am grateful to Oliver Ready for his translation, as well as his wise comments. 'Mikhailych' is the colloquial form of his patronymic; similarly, the endearment Agneshechka of his wife.

49. Utley, *Odyssey of a Liberal*, p. 125. Lord Inman recalled in the Lords that Maisky used to have on his desk a large card bearing the words 'This also will pass'; *Hansard*, HL Deb 16 April 1946, vol. 140, col. 830.

50. Quoted from Myasnikov, *Maiskii: Izbrannaya perepiska*, II, pp. 56–7.

51. See commentary following the diary entry for 12 July 1936.

52. RAN f.1702 op.4 d.546 l.41–2, Litvinov to Maisky, 8 Sep. 1937.

53. Webb, diary, 27 Oct. 1937, p. 6393.

54. Bilainkin, *Maisky*, pp. 160–1.

55. With hindsight, it is mind-boggling that despite the misery and pain, Maisky and Kollontay, having thrown their lot in with the Bolsheviks, accepted the purges as an inevitable and necessary purification, justified by the revolutionary process and the subversion by Russia's enemies. And yet, by 1937 they had obviously modified their views. 'All the plots and intrigues of the papal court in old Rome,' Kollontay entered in her diary, 'all the perfidy and hypocrisy of the Medici courts, with their poisoned gloves and daggers in the back,

pale before their maleficence and perfidy. The work of the Jesuits at the courts of absolute monarchs in Renaissance Europe seems child's play. Hypocrisy and perfidy are flourishing, schemes and conspiracies are afoot'; Kollontay, *Diplomaticheskie dnevniki*, II, pp. 389 & 391, 29 & 30 Sep. 1937.

56. Interview with Alexei Voskressenski, Maisky's great-nephew.

57. Webb, diary, 5 July 1937, pp. 6358–92 & 6431, 23 Jan. & 8 March 1938; MacKenzie and MacKenzie, *Diary of Beatrice Webb*, IV, pp. 398–9, 12 December 1937.

58. Pimlott, *Political Diary of Hugh Dalton*, p. 212, 26 June 1937. As Haslam has correctly established, the purges of the military weakened the Soviet Union's credibility as a partner in collective security, but they served mostly as 'a convenient alibi' for those who harboured ideological hostility and 'tended to confirm existing doubts rather than lead to a completely new evaluation'; Haslam, *The Soviet Union and the Struggle for Collective Security*, p. 140.

59. Webb, diary, 25 July 1937, pp. 6358–9. In his old age, Maisky would cover his tracks, hailing both men, see 'V Londone' in Ya.I. Koritskii, S.M. Melnik-Tukhachevskaya and B.N. Chistov (eds), *Marshal Tukhachevskii: vospominaniya druzei i soratnikov* (Moscow, 1965). The left remained divided. Maisky's friend, the renowned publisher Gollancz, for instance, did not hesitate to propose Stalin – who, he believed, was 'safely guiding Russia on the road to a society in which there will be no exploitation' – as the man of the year for a British news magazine; Gollancz papers, MSS 151/3/U/1/30, 3 Nov. 1937.

60. Ada Nilsson papers, Letter to Ada Nilsson, 21 July 1938.

61. The protocol on Italy's joining the anti-Comintern pact of 6 November 1937.

62. The *Daily Telegraph* suggested that the overt hostility to Soviet Russia may assume the form of challenging not only the Bolsheviks, but also France, Britain and the United States, encroaching on their vital interests in the Baltic, the North and the Mediterranean seas and in the Pacific Ocean.

63. However, that is precisely what happened a couple of months later.

64. This speech is an early harbinger of 'isolation' in Soviet policy and was clearly rephrased by Stalin in his famous 'chestnuts' speech of March 1939.

65. The Brussels conference was held on 3–24 November, following a decision by the League of Nations to examine the conflict between Japan and China. The USSR proposed to apply Article 16 of the Covenant and impose collective sanctions against the Japanese, but the Western powers objected. Litvinov ascribed the adverse outcome of the conference to the British desire to act as an intermediary between Japan and China; *DVP*, 1937, XX, doc. 421.

66. Webb, diary, 25 July, p. 6359; *DVP*, 1937, XX, doc. 261, 26 July 1937.

67. *DVP*, 1937, XX, docs. 380, 381 & 385, 26 & 27 Oct. 1937.

68. Dullin, *Men of Influence*, pp. 150–1.

69. One might think, Litvinov lamented on reading the French newspapers, that 'France has a mutual assistance pact, not with the Soviet Union, but with Germany or Italy'; quoted in Carley, 'Caught in a cleft stick', p. 169.

70. *DVP*, 1937, XX, doc. 390, 29 Oct. 1937. Maisky leaked information in the same vein to the press; see *Time* Magazine, 8 November 1937.

71. *DVP*, 1937, XX, doc. 427, 3 Dec. 1937.

72. Noel-Baker papers, NBKR 4/639, 23 Dec. 1937. At the Foreign Office, the head of the northern department, Laurence Collier, indeed gained the impression that Soviet policy might become 'increasingly passive', but hardly believed it would lead to 'an open declaration of "isolationism" or a departure from the League of Nations'; Neilson, *Britain, Soviet Russia and the Collapse of the Versailles Order*, p. 232.

73. *DVP*, 1937, XX, doc. 230, Potemkin to Maisky, 7 July 1937; RGASPI, Stalin papers, f.558 op.11 d.214 ll.115–16, Maisky to Narkomindel, 1 Dec. 1937. A similar comment was made by Eden to the French ambassador in London; *DDF*, 2 Serie, VII, Doc. 299.

74. This entry was written in response to an announcement in *The Times*, 4 December, that the Danish minister was being withdrawn from London and sent to Madeira.

75. The former imperial palace in St Petersburg.

76. Refers to the Japanese capture of Shanghai in November 1937, and of Nanjing a month later.

77. Unknown to Maisky, Roosevelt consented to have periodical secret meetings of the British and US staffs. He insisted, though, that he wished to restrain Japan without resorting to belligerent action; D. Reynolds, *The Creation of the Anglo-American Alliance 1937–1941: A study in competitive cooperation* (Chapel Hill, 1982), p. 30.

1938

1. S. Pons, *Stalin and the Inevitable War: 1936–1941* (London, 2002), pp. 95–6, 103–8. Litvinov resorted to the German card in press interviews, probably as a means of exerting pressure on England and France. Maisky's main concern was that the nature and timing of the Cabinet changes might enhance the Soviet tendency to retreat into isolation; Lloyd George papers, LG/G/14/1/4, 10 Feb. 1938. See also RAN f.1702 op.4 d.111 ll.15–16, Maisky to Kollontay, 6 Feb. 1938.

2. RAN f.1702 op.4 d.111 ll.15–16, Maisky to Kollontay, 6 Feb. 1938.

3. In her magnum opus, *The Triumph of the Dark*, pp. 439–40, Steiner attributes the terror to Stalin's desire for absolute power and 'his ideologically based belief in the coming war', a point which historiography has yet to establish firmly. She relies heavily on J. Harris, 'Encircled by enemies: Stalin's perceptions of the capitalist world, 1918–1941', *Journal of Strategic Studies*, 30/3 (2007), who claims that the way Stalin handled the intelligence reports submitted to him evinced his ideological predisposition. However, it reflects, at best, a cultural revolutionary bias, hardly different from the ideological bias discernible in the official British and French reports on Russia, the content of which were well known in the Kremlin but which Harris tends to overlook. The Western bias is convincingly presented in the prolific works of J. Carley (cited within this volume), as is the revolutionary culture, which by no means signifies a dogmatic *modus operandi*. T.J. Uldricks, 'Soviet security policy in the 1930s', in G. Gorodetsky, *Soviet Foreign Policy, 1917–1991* (London, 1994), continues to serve as a sound and objective compass. Similar subtle, complex and convincing arguments were produced by Pons in *The Inevitable War*. Naturally the synoptic nature of Steiner's masterpiece leads to inconsistent presentations of Stalin, who occasionally is also viewed as 'the pragmatic Soviet leader' (*The Triumph of the Dark*, p. 443). The inconsistency reflects the

absence of consensus among experts in the field, even after the partial opening of the Soviet archives. The failure to reach a single common explanation for the purges leads Steiner to reach a final verdict that the terror was 'rooted in Stalin's fierce determination to establish his absolute control over all men and institutions that might threaten his monopoly of power' (ibid., p. 461). She does, however, overlook a significant corroborative element – the struggle for power and ideas within the Soviet elite, which goes beyond the simple selfish interests characterizing the totalitarian model. See J.A. Getty and O.V. Naumov, *The Road to Terror: Stalin and the self-destruction of the Bolsheviks, 1932–1939* (New Haven, 1999).

4. *DVP*, 1938, XXI, doc. 27; Webb, diary, 23 Jan. 1938, p. 6433. An isolation, contingent on military might and economic autarky, was ordained from the outset by the failure of collective security and was first enunciated by Molotov in January 1936. See Haslam, *The Soviet Union and the Struggle for Collective Security*, p. 93. The entire work of Pons, *The Inevitable War*, presents a fusion of the ideological and pragmatic approach, but Pons's narrative, based on impressive archival findings, overwhelmingly underlines the reactive nature of the policy.

5. Suggested by Pons, *The Inevitable War*, pp. 106–10.

6. The dismissal of Vansittart and the unrelated resignation of Eden a month later, against the backdrop of Chamberlain's personal handling of foreign policy, were a tremendous blow to Maisky's networking in the Foreign Office. His wishful thinking that Vansittart might emerge as the more influential was short-lived. Cadogan accepted the appointment on the condition that Vansittart would 'not come between' him and Eden in the conduct of foreign affairs. The long and degrading process of Vansittart's demotion is unfolded in detail in Cadogan papers, ACAD 4/5, Cadogan to Eden, 25 Jan. 1962.

7. Van Zeeland was entrusted by the French and British governments with a mission to investigate possible measures to alleviate obstacles to international trade. The report is in *World Affairs*, 101/1 (1938).

8. RAN f.1702 op.4 d.143 l.63 & d.111 ll.15–16, letter to Kollontay, 6 Feb. 1938.

9. In a personal letter to Litvinov, Maisky wrote that Kagan 'himself told me a few days ago that if he goes away on holiday then he will never return to London. All the more reason to complete his recall in the normal way. It is important for London, for all those many connections and colleagues that he formed or made over the years of his work in England.' RAN f.1702 op.4 d.143 ll.64–5, 26 April 1938.

10. On Agniya's influence, see the 'Introduction' and on the impact of the purges on her see the commentary following the diary entry for 16 November 1937 and the commentary following 10 May 1938.

11. On 4 February, Hitler concentrated power in his own hands, replacing Werner Fritsch, the army's commander-in-chief, with General Keitel and assuming command of the Wehrmacht and abolishing the Defence Ministry. Whether or not inspired by Stalin, Hitler went on to purge the Foreign Ministry of its hard core of professional diplomats, replacing Neurath with Ribbentrop at the head of the office.

12. In his speech on 20 February, Hitler announced his intention of redressing the grievances of the German population in Austria and Czechoslovakia.

13. The entry evolved into Maisky's report to Narkomindel, *DVP*, 1938, XXI, doc. 41.

14. In an attempt to further curtail the power of Narkomindel, as well as the flow of Westerners to the Soviet Union, the Kremlin reduced the number of Soviet consulates abroad and forced European consulates to withdraw from Russia; *DVP*, 1938, XXI, fn. 59.

15. Eden made the conclusion of a treaty conditional on Mussolini's withdrawal from Spain. However, the evacuation of foreign 'volunteers' remained a thorny issue. On 4 November 1937, the Non-Intervention Committee adopted a resolution which stipulated that both parties in the Spanish conflict could be granted belligerent rights, provided substantial progress was achieved in the evacuation of volunteers. However, the members of the Committee failed to agree on what 'substantial evacuation' constituted. Negotiations dragged on until 16 April 1938 (by then Eden had been replaced by Halifax).

16. This emerges as well in Cadogan's comments on Eden's draft autobiography; see Cadogan papers, ACAD 4/5, 25 Jan. 1962. On Eden's subsequent exaggeration of his rift with Chamberlain on matters of principle, see A.R. Peters, *Anthony Eden at the Foreign Office, 1931–1938* (Aldershot, 1986), pp. 338–9.

17. R. Mallett, 'Fascist foreign policy and official Italian views of Anthony Eden in the 1930s', *The Historical Journal*, 43/1 (2000). An admission of that is in Cadogan papers, ACAD 4/5, letter to Eden, 22 Nov. 1961.

18. Self, *Chamberlain Diary Letters*, IV, p. 303.

19. P. Neville, 'Sir Alexander Cadogan and Lord Halifax's "Damascus Road" conversion over the Godesberg Terms 1938', *Diplomacy and Statecraft*, 11/3 (2000), pp. 81–2; M.J. Carley, *1939: The alliance that never was and the coming of World War II* (Chicago, 1999), p. 88. Maisky's portrait of Halifax is in RAN f.1702 op.9 d.110 l.1, 25 Jan. 1938.

20. *DVP*, 1938, XXI, doc. 48, Maisky to Litvinov, 20 Feb. 1938; Sylvester papers, diary, A45, 21 Feb. 1938.

21. Lord Butler, *The Art of the Possible* (London, 1970), p. 75.

22. In retrospect, Maisky regarded this response as the blueprint for the surrender in Munich, where Hitler is given a free hand in the east; Maisky, *Munich*, p. 21. See an even more blunt version in *VSD*, pp. 336–7.

23. The entry appears to be a draft of a letter sent by Maisky to Litvinov.

24. In his Commons speech on 14 March, Chamberlain condemned the *Anschluss*, but in the same breath acknowledged German interests in Austria. Both Britain and France refrained from raising the issue at the League of Nations. See Maisky's observations in *DVP*, 1938, XXI, doc. 82.

25. *DDF*, 2 Serie, VIII, Doc. 254. Identical words were used by Maisky over lunch *à deux* with Harold Nicolson; see Nicolson, *Diaries*, p. 238. On his pessimism, see telegram to NKID, 17 March, *DVP*, 1938, XXI, doc. 88.

26. A.J. Sylvester, *Life with Lloyd George: The diary of A.J. Sylvester, 1931–1945* (London, 1975), p. 197. See also a similar prognosis in Maisky's long telegram to Litvinov, 26 Feb., *DVP*, 1938, XXI, doc. 52.

27. Self, *Chamberlain Diary Letters*, IV, p. 307, 20 March 1938. Self dismisses out of hand the story spread by 'the less than reliable Maisky' as a 'slip of the tongue' by Chamberlain, p. 18.

28. Pons, *The Inevitable War*, pp. 114–15 and *DVP*, 1938, XXI, docs. 59, 88, 102 & fn. 59. Cadogan's minutes from 17 March, following a meeting with Maisky in which he had

submitted Litvinov's appeal for an international conference, are in TNA FO 371 21626 C1935/95/62.

29. 'The Americans,' Maisky told Beatrice Webb, 'had no civilisation of their own: they were first rate as mechanics, good organisers, open and alert minded; but fundamentally without a national culture or traditional background, in the sense that these are present in Great Britain, France, Germany and Scandinavia'; Webb, diary, 8 Aug. 1933, p. 5503.

30. Kennedy informed Roosevelt that Maisky, who gave him a long explanation of the trials, 'look[ed] scared to death himself'. He gained the impression that 'if the telephone had rung and said "Come back to Russia", he would have died right on my hands', to which the president responded: 'Poor old Russian Ambassador! I hope he will not die of fright if he is sent for'; reproduced in A. Smith (ed.), *Hostage to Fortune: The letters of Joseph P. Kennedy* (New York, 2001), pp. 242–3; and E. Roosevelt (ed.), *F.D.R. His personal letters, 1928–1945*, II (New York, 1950), p. 769.

31. The full entry contains a far more detailed and colourful account of the meeting than the report sent to Narkomindel, in which Maisky, rather cunningly and with great circumspection, exploited Churchill in order to convey to the Kremlin the damage inflicted by the trials on Soviet interests, while at the same time praising Stalin's leadership; *DVP*, 1938, XXI, doc. 103, 23 March 1938. Maisky succeeded in swaying other politicians towards a benign view of Stalin. He widely distributed Alexei Tolstoy's *Peter the Great*, which had just been published, drawing from Lloyd George the comment: 'it gives me the historical background of Russia which explains better than any book I know on the subject the why, the wherefore and the whither of the great Revolution. Peter was a great fellow, but he would not have won through without adopting ruthless methods'; Sylvester papers, copy of letter to Maisky, A45, 4 Feb. 1938; and response in the same vein by Maisky in Lloyd George papers, LG/G/14/1/4, 10 Feb. 1938. Likewise, Trevelyan praised the book 'giving a vivid picture of the society which Peter tried, with his titanic energy, to bring into some sort of order'; RAN f.1702 op.4 d.1616 l.5 & d.1132 l.1, exchange of letters with Trevelyan, 1 & 13 Jan. 1938.

32. Reference to David Low's caricature 'Shiver Sisters Celebrate', in which he implied that Astor, Garvin and Dawson were in fact susceptible to Nazi propaganda.

33. In his speech, Lord Redesdale argued that 'Austria had to relinquish her independence in favour of joining up with Germany', as it reflected 'the sincere desire of the large majority of the Austrian people'. The enthusiastic reception accorded to Hitler in Vienna, he claimed, 'came straight from the hearts of a people for the man they looked upon as their saviour'. Lord Ponsonby dwelt on the artificial nature of Czechoslovakia, warning that 'if the Government had committed us to fight for Czechoslovakia, who in this country would have had any sort of enthusiasm for a war of that description, when there is not one person in a hundred who knows where Czechoslovakia is?' It was Lord Stonehaven, the former governor-general of Australia, who, fascinated by Hitler's prophecies in *Mein Kampf* which 'turned out to be correct, every one of them', found it distressing 'that Mein Kampf cannot be read in this country ... it would be a very good deed and a very patriotic action if some prosperous man would have Mein Kampf translated word for word from the original edition ... and made available at a price of not more than 1s. on every bookstall in this country'. However, the discussion was far more balanced; what seemed to have upset Maisky was the fact that all

speakers, and particularly Lord Halifax, were dismissive of the idea of mobilizing the League of Nations and Russia to counter Hitler's claims; *Hansard*, HL Deb 29 March 1938, vol. 108, cols 434–88.

34. Of the Non-Intervention Committee. On its agenda was Lord Plymouth's proposal to evacuate about 75 per cent of the combatants on both sides. The final decision was adopted at the end of May, but by then a separate Anglo-Italian agreement had been signed. Negotiations commenced on 8 March and the agreement, signed on 16 April, ensured the withdrawal of the Italian troops from Spain once the Civil War was over. In justifying the agreement, Chamberlain suggested that Mussolini and Hitler had sent their troops to forestall the bolshevization of Europe and were now prepared to withdraw them, as such a threat no longer existed; see Maisky, *VSD*, pp. 430–50.

35. This entry is particularly important, as no other record exists of Sun Fo's meeting with Stalin; V.V. Sokolov, 'Dve vstrechi Sun' Fo s I.V. Stalinym v 1938–1939gg', *Novaya i noveishaya istoriya*, 6 (1999).

36. Stalin's position is further elaborated in *DVP*, 1938, XXI, doc. 311.

37. This episode is covered by Steiner, *The Triumph of the Dark*, pp. 564–7, who argues that the oratory was double-edged, aimed also at relieving France of its obligations, which the chiefs of staff did not believe she could assume. This should be borne in mind when considering the accusations in the same vein levelled against the Russians, who, as the diary and related material show, were extremely well informed about the state of the Anglo-French negotiations and their aftermath.

38. *DVP*, 1938, XXI, doc. 153, 30 April 1938. Confirmed by Aleksandrovsky from Prague, see L. Bezymenskii, *Gitler i Stalin pered skhvatkoi* (Moscow, 2009), p. 141.

39. TNA FO 371 21591 C3995/13/17, 5 May 1938, and Maisky's version in *DVP*, 1938, XXI, doc. 163.

40. Maisky's report to Narkomindel, which took exception to the idea of isolation, went to great lengths to stress Wilson's vow that Chamberlain harboured no animosity towards the Soviet Union. He suggested that the hesitation in approaching the Soviet Union might reflect a concern over Soviet 'passivity' and 'scepticism' about her offensive capabilities; *DVP*, 1938, XXI, doc. 172.

41. *DVP*, 1938, XXI, doc. 176, 12 May 1938.

42. Beaverbrook papers, BBK\C\238, 20 June 1938. See also RAN f.1702 op.4 d.1532 l.3, Lloyd George and Pritt to Maisky, 29 July 1938.

43. *DVP*, 1938, XXI, doc. 174, 11 May 1938.

44. Conversations with Lloyd George and Beaverbrook on 9 and 12 May, respectively, quoted in *DVP*, 1938, XXI, p. 713, fn. 65; Webb, diary, 16 May 1938, p. 6478; Aster, 'Ivan Maisky and parliamentary anti-appeasement', pp. 323–4.

45. *DVP*, 1938, XXI, docs. 180 & 188 & fn. 70, Exchanges between Stalin and Maisky, 14, 17 & 18 May 1938.

46. RAN f.1702 op.4 d.143 ll.64–5, 26 April 1938.

47. RAN f.1702 op.4 d.143 ll.64–5, Personal letter from Maisky to Litvinov, 26 April 1938.

48. RAN f.1702 d.546. l.47, 9 May 1938.

49. Z. Sheinis, 'Sud'ba diplomata, shtrikhi k portretu Borisa Shteina', in *Arkhivy raskryvayut tainy...* (Moscow, 1991), p. 301.

50. Ada Nilsson papers, 21 July 1938.

51. Quoted in the fascinating work by Farnsworth, 'Conversing with Stalin'.

52. RAN f.1702 op.4 d.1074 l.1, Maisky to Bernard Pares, 9 Aug. 1938. Counting on their 'good personal relationship', Maisky strongly urged Beaverbrook, upon his return, to refrain from such publications, dismissing the idea of the OGPU surveillance as 'fantastic nonsense'. Likewise, he had to constantly deny rumours suggesting that Ivy Litvinov's reclusiveness in Sverdlovsk was in fact incarceration; RAN f.1702 op.4 d.854 ll.6–9, 22 Aug. 1938.

53. Bilainkin, *Maisky*, p. 204–5. Myasnikov, 'Sud'ba intelligenta v Rossii', in *Maiskii: Izbrannaya perepiska*, I, pp. 5–23; *Istoricheskii arkhiv*, 4 (1998), p. 112.

54. TNA FO 371 21731 C8433/1941/18, 17 Aug. 22289 N4317/97/38, 29 Aug. 1938; Nicolson, *Diaries*, 22 & 26 July 1938, pp. 356, 358. Maisky was enticing the British to action, but his reports to Moscow, urgently seeking instructions concerning Soviet policy towards Czechoslovakia, indicate that, like Litvinov, he was still kept in the dark; see *DVP*, 1938, XXII, doc. 318, 28 Aug. 1938.

55. Webb, diary, 7 Aug. pp. 6522–3; Lloyd George papers, LG/G/14/1/5, 24 July 1938, letter from Maisky. The first to detect this was Aster in 'Ivan Maisky and parliamentary anti-appeasement'. The diary and the recently released Soviet documents betray the wide scope of such activities.

56. RAN f.1702 op.4 d.940 l.6 & d.1357 l.2, 9 & 12 Aug. 1938. References to 'the delightful holiday' and 'our happy holiday in our country' also pervade his correspondence with Bernard Shaw and Ben Tillott; RAN f.1702 op.4 d.1184 l.12 & d.1127 l.4, 22 & 29 Aug. 1938.

57. *DVP*, 1938, XXI, doc. 319, 29 Aug. 1938. Indeed, the young De La Warr, the lord privy seal, impressed upon Halifax that a 'demonstration' of consultation with the Soviet and French ambassadors 'would do good with the Russians whose help after all we may need in the last resort'; quoted in Aster, 'Ivan Maisky and parliamentary anti-appeasement', p. 325.

58. In a Cabinet meeting preceding the talks, Halifax insisted that Britain should not take any military obligations upon itself. To discourage the Germans from embarking on hostilities, he suggested that the Germans be told that they could obtain close to 60 per cent of their demands through negotiations; TNA CAB 23/93, 27 April 1938.

59. The source was Surits, who had been briefed in detail by Bonnet; *DVP*, 1938, XXI, doc. 269.

60. The published declaration on Lake Tana (addendum No. 5 to the agreement of 16 April 1938) bore out only previous (1936) Italian commitments to Britain (M. Curtis (ed.), *Documents on International Affairs. 1938*, I (London, 1939), p. 147).

61. The démarche was prompted by erroneous information which had led the Czechoslovak government to partially mobilize in order to counter a reported concentration of German troops on the country's border; Steiner, *The Triumph of the Dark*, pp. 571-2.

62. The Nuremberg National Party Convention took place annually in early autumn in the years 1923–38.

63. Assuming the premiership in April 1938, Daladier confirmed France's obligations towards Czechoslovakia; but behind the scenes, his foreign minister, Bonnet, exerted pressure on the Czechs to make concessions, making it absolutely clear that neither France nor Britain intended to enter into a war. Informing the French of the decision to send Runciman (an elderly industrialist and former minister in Baldwin's government) to Czechoslovakia, Halifax expected them to exert pressure on the Czechs to receive his 'good services', hardly concealing the intention of giving Germany a free hand in South-East Europe; *DDF*, 2 Serie, X, Doc. 238; J.B. Duroselle, *Politique etrangere de la France. La decadence 1932–1939* (Paris, 1979), pp. 334–40. Runciman stayed in Prague between 3 August and 15 September 1938.

64. On 15 July, Franco launched an offensive aimed at capturing Valencia, the seat of the Spanish government at that time. He met a 60,000-strong Republican army under the command of Colonel Modesto, who crossed the Ebro and pushed Franco's troops some 50 kilometres back. The Republicans, however, were forced into defensive positions, having no reserves at hand.

65. Maisky told Oliphant that 'His Majesty's Government were bludgeoning M. Benes and Co. and were not being sufficiently firm with Germany'; TNA FO 371 21731 C8218/1941/18. The Soviet government's disillusionment with the West is also discernible in Suritss's failed efforts to draw a more active French response to the events in Czechoslovakia; see Carley, *1939*, pp. 48–9.

66. Maisky is referring to the Battle of Lake Khasan, which took place between 29 July and 11 August 1938, when Soviet troops encountered an attempted military incursion by Manzhouguo (the puppet Japanese government) into a territory claimed by the Soviet Union.

67. The poorly marked border of the USSR, Korea and Manzhouguo led to the Hunchun Border Pact, following the Zhanggufeng incident; see M.T. Kikuoka, *The Changkufeng Incident: A study in Soviet-Japanese conflict, 1938* (Lanham, MD, 1988).

68. The Kremlin was critical of the 'undue weakness of the Western democracies' and their failure to be 'firm enough with Germany, in whose policy there was at least 50% bluff'. In his reports home, Maisky admitted that he expected Halifax to 'forcefully deny it', but he was pleasantly surprised when Halifax preferred not to defend British policy. In reality, Maisky was rebuffed by Halifax, who bluntly informed him that there was 'no question' of Britain shifting its policy. To facilitate Litvinov's attendance in Geneva, which could no longer be taken for granted, Maisky further manoeuvred Halifax into expressing his great wish to meet Litvinov and exchange views on current affairs at the Assembly. Moreover, while he insisted in his report to Moscow that he had complied with the instructions given to him by Litvinov not to initiate any move, the British records suggest that Maisky asserted that if Germany attacked Czechoslovakia, the Soviet government would 'certainly do their bit'; TNA FO 371 21731 C8433/1941/18 and *DVP*, 1938, XXI, doc. 300, 17 Aug. 1938.

69. Article 16, the teeth of the Covenant of the League, stated that if any member of the League resorted to war in disregard of the Covenant, it would be deemed to have committed an act of war against all other Members of the League, which would immediately implement a complex set of sanctions.

70. Chamberlain announced that Britain had no obligations towards the region, where she did not have such vital interests as she had in France and Belgium; *Hansard*, HC Deb 24 March 1938, vol. 333, cols 1399–1407.

71. Franco, fully re-equipped with German and Italian weaponry, launched a counteroffensive which led the Republican prime minister, Juan Negrín, to announce on 21 September the unilateral unconditional withdrawal of the International Brigades from Spain. By 16 November, the battle was lost. Any hope of Western help had vanished after the Munich Agreement. Barcelona fell to the Nationalist troops on 26 January 1939; A. Beevor, *The Battle for Spain: The Spanish Civil War, 1936-1939* (London, 2006), pp. 352–4.

72. Self, *Chamberlain Diary Letters*, IV, pp. 342, 344–5, Chamberlain to Ida, 3 & 11 Sep. 1938.

73. Z. Steiner, 'The Soviet Commissariat of Foreign Affairs and the Czechoslovakian crisis in 1938: New material from the Soviet archives', *The Historical Journal*, 42/3 (1999), p. 764–5.

74. See Maisky's retrospective claim in *Who Helped Hitler?*, p. 79. Maisky continued to maintain correct relations with Lady Astor, inviting her to events in the embassy even after the Munich Agreement. See for instance, Astor papers, 1416/1/2/188, 28 Nov. 1938.

75. Detailed accounts of Maisky's approaches are in Amery's diary entry of 15 February 1939 (Barnes and Nicholson, *The Empire at Bay*, p. 543), and in H. Dalton, *The Fateful Years* (London, 1957), pp. 184–5. See also Haslam, *The Soviet Union and the Struggle for Collective Security*, pp. 179–81; Carley, *1939*, pp. 54–7; and Aster, 'Ivan Maisky and parliamentary anti-appeasement', pp. 326–7. Relying mostly on a couple of speeches by Zhdanov and the evaluation of Rossi, the Italian ambassador in Moscow, Silvio Pons maintains that the Russians, having become reconciled to the inevitability of war, pinned their hopes on the revolutionary potential of such a war, see *The Inevitable War*, pp. 128–46.

76. Hitherto no such meeting was known about; this sheds fresh light on their meeting on 4 September.

77. The official seat of Franco's government during the Civil War.

78. Article 11 established that 'any war or threat of war' which affected any member of the League was considered to be of concern to the whole League and required the organization to convene and discuss proper measures to safeguard the peace.

79. This is vital information, confirming a clear decision taken in support of fulfilling the commitments to Czechoslovakia under the Franco-Soviet pact. It was indeed confirmed in Litvinov's report to Aleksandrovsky about his conversations with Payart; V. Mal'tsev et al. (eds), *Dokumenty po istorii myunkhenskogo sgovora 1937-1939* (Moscow, 1979), No. 108; see also Nos. 148 & 163. The decision was sufficiently unequivocal and decisive for Maisky to feel confident in pursuing unauthorized initiatives. The approach to Payart was most certainly sanctioned by Stalin, vacationing in the Caucasus, who had been sounded out by Litvinov a day earlier; see Steiner, 'Soviet Commissariat', p. 763. Indeed, in J. Haslam, 'The Soviet Union and the Czechoslovakian crisis of 1938', *Journal of Contemporary History*, 14/3 (1979), p. 452, the author acutely observes that an article in *Pravda* during the crisis, which affirmed that Litvinov's policy represented 'the unanimous opinion of the whole Soviet people', hinted that the opinion might not have been 'unanimous' earlier.

80. Churchill, *The Second World War: The Gathering Storm* (London, 1948), pp. 229–30; Maisky, *Who Helped Hitler?*, pp. 78–80; Maisky, *Munich*, p. 38; Reynolds, 'Churchill's writing of history', p. 239. See also letter to Churchill, 22 December 1947, reproduced in M. Gilbert (ed.), *Winston Churchill and Emery Reves, Correspondence, 1937–1964* (London, 1997), pp. 279–80.

81. R. Cocket, *Twilight of Truth: Chamberlain, appeasement, and the manipulation of the press* (New York, 1989), p. 71.

82. Referring to the leader in *The Times* of 7 September, quoted above.

83. On Article 16 see note 69 above. Article 19 allowed the League to abrogate treaties which 'might endanger the peace of the world'.

84. This is misleading, as the meeting had been engineered by Maisky and failed to produce the anticipated results. As could be gleaned from Maisky's semi-clandestine meetings with Churchill of the previous days, the ambassador had been using him to impress on Halifax the seriousness of Litvinov's stance and to galvanize him into action. Considering, as he wrote in the diary on 3 September, that 'Unfortunately, we have very little time, and we must act quickly', he clearly expected his conversations with Churchill to lead to his meeting with Halifax.

85. P. Kennedy, *Strategy and Diplomacy, 1870–1945* (London, 1983), p. 19.

86. A most exhaustive and comprehensive review of the debate on appeasement is to be found in S. Aster, 'Appeasement: Before and after revisionism', *Diplomacy and Statecraft*, 19/3 (2008).

87. See R.J. Beck, 'Munich's lessons reconsidered', *International Security*, 14/2 (1989); and D. Hucker, 'The unending debate: Appeasement, Chamberlain and the origins of the Second World', *Intelligence and National Security*, 23/4 (2008), pp. 542–3.

88. Carley, *1939*; M. Carley, '"Only the USSR has... clean hands": The Soviet perspective on the failure of collective security and the collapse of Czechoslovakia, 1934–1938', *Diplomacy and Statecraft*, 21/3 (2010); Aster, 'Ivan Maisky and parliamentary anti-appeasement', pp. 326–35. See also L.G. Shaw, *The British Political Elite and the Soviet Union, 1937–1939* (London, 2003). Russia, typically, hardly figures in the pivotal work of R.A.C. Parker, *Chamberlain and Appeasement: British policy and the coming of the Second World War* (London, 1993).

89. Named after the guillotined French revolutionary whose ideas were precursors of communism.

90. The Landolt was the favourite brasserie of Lenin and Trotsky, and a meeting place of revolutionaries during the First World War.

91. 'The Prisoner of Chillon'.

92. 'I fear', Lloyd George warned Maisky from London, 'that the Czechs are being betrayed by Neville and Daladier'; Lloyd George papers, LG/G/14/1/5, 14 Sept. 1938.

93. Butler, *The Art of the Possible*, pp. 70–1 elicited a furious response from Maisky in *The Times*, 8 June 1971. For a tarnishing revision of Butler's image as a respected elder statesman, see P. Stafford, 'Political autobiography and the art of the possible: R.A. Butler at the Foreign Office, 1938–1939', *The Historical Journal*, 28/4 (1985).

94. Steiner, 'Soviet Commissariat', has done admirable work, reconstructing brick by brick the Soviet policy, unearthing many hitherto unknown documents. Her verdict that 'it is hard to believe that an offer of unilateral Soviet support, even if it had been made, would have changed the outcome of the Czech deliberations' can be confidently accepted. She is equally right to refute retrospective Soviet claims (as well as Maisky's own) that the Soviet Union would have considered rendering unilateral support to Czechoslovakia. Her narrative is only marred by an uncritical adaptation of Igor Lukes's claims that the Soviet demise in Munich led the country's leaders back 'to their revolutionary roots' (pp. 755, 759, 762). In his otherwise engaging work, *Czechoslovakia between Stalin and Hitler: The diplomacy of Edvard Beneš in the 1930s* (Oxford, 1996), as well as in 'Stalin and Czechoslovakia in 1938–39: An autopsy of a myth', *Diplomacy and Statecraft*, 10/2–3 (1999), p. 38, Lukes developed a fanciful theory that Stalin expected Hitler's offensive to be 'but a prelude to a wave of socialist revolutions in Europe'. Such ideas have been effectively refuted by Ragsdale in *The Soviets* and in his 'Soviet military preparations and policy in the Munich Crisis: New evidence', *Jahrbücher für Geschichte Osteuropas*, 47/2 (1999).

95. Maisky's account of events is in Amery papers, diary, AMEL 7/33, 15 Feb. 1939. See also P. Beck, 'Searching for peace in Munich, not Geneva: The British government, the League of Nations, and the Sudetenland question', *Diplomacy and Statecraft*, 10/2–3 (1999); D. Dunn, 'Maksim Litvinov: Commissar of contradiction', *Journal of Contemporary History*, 23/2 (1988), pp. 239–40; and P. Stegnii and V. Sokolov, 'Eyewitness testimony (Ivan Maiskii on the origins of World War II)', *International Affairs*, 154 (1999). J. Hochman's misleading *The Soviet Union and the Failure of Collective Security, 1934–1938* (Ithaca, NY, 1984), pp. 156–60, exculpates the French in a highly distorted account of the handling of the negotiations by Payart and Bonnet.

96. Kollontay, *Diplomaticheskie dnevniki*, II, pp. 396–8. A most convincing examination of the French attempts to shift responsibility onto the Russians is in M. Thomas, 'France and the Czechoslovak Crisis', *Diplomacy and Statecraft*, 10/2–3 (1999).

97. M.G. Fry, 'Agents and structures: The dominions and the Czechoslovak Crisis, September 1938', *Diplomacy and Statecraft*, 10/2–3 (1999), p. 301; Carley, *1939*, pp. 61–2.

98. Text of the speech provided by Maisky to Noel-Baker, in the Noel-Baker papers, NBKR 4/639. Litvinov was overheard telling Negrín that 'If we do not have a world war, you are damned'; R. Rhodes (ed.), *Chips, the Diaries of Sir Henry Channon* (London, 1967), p. 165.

99. Lloyd George papers, LG/G/14/1/9, 4 Oct. 1938, Maisky to Lloyd George; Aster, 'Ivan Maisky and parliamentary anti-appeasement', pp. 330–1. See also Maisky's account of the meeting in Bilainkin, *Maisky*, p. 254.

100. TNA FO 371 21777 C10585/5302/18, record of the Geneva meeting and minutes, 24 Sep. 1938. For an excellent (though somewhat overlooked) survey of the military measures taken by the Russians in anticipation of war, see G. Jukes, 'The Red Army and the Munich Crisis', *Journal of Contemporary History*, 26/2 (1991).

101. The first encounter between Chamberlain and Hitler took place in Berchtesgaden on 15 and 16 September.

102. The British delegation's take on the Russian presence is well mirrored in Rhodes, *Chips*, pp. 164–5: 'The bars and lobbies of the League's building are full of Russians and Jews who intrigue with the dominant press, and spreading rumours of approaching war … I saw Litvinoff, the dread intriguer, for the first time. He looked older and more like a Socialist MP than I had expected, and neither so smiling or so evil as Maisky.'

103. At their second meeting at Bad Godesberg, on 22 September, Hitler ruled out further negotiations and threatened an invasion of the Sudetenland on 28 September.

104. Soviet troops were indeed deployed on the border and the French gleaned through their own sources the information on the preventive measures undertaken by the Red Army general staff; see V.Ya. Sipols, *Vneshnaya politika Sovetskogo Soyuza 1936–1939* (Moscow, 1987), pp. 187–9 and O.A. Rzheshevsky (ed.), *1939. Uroki istorii* (Moscow, 1990), pp. 105–6.

105. Typically, in his programmatic memoirs Maisky somewhat misleads the reader by continuing the narrative, giving the reader the impression that he was still quoting from his diary, while reinforcing the prevailing Soviet historiography: 'As the People's Commissar for Foreign Affairs and I were returning to the Hotel Richmond, I said: "What you have just proposed to the British means war … Back in Moscow, has all that been well considered and decided in all seriousness?" Maksim Litvinov said firmly: "Yes, it has been decided in all seriousness … When I was leaving Moscow for Geneva Soviet troops were concentrating on the borders with Rumania and Poland." … I asked: "And if France lets us down and does not act? What then?" Litvinov waved his hand in irritation and snapped: "That's of secondary importance!" He was silent for a moment and then said: "The most important thing is how the Czechs will behave … If they are going to fight we shall help them with armed force"'; *VSD*, pp. 351–2.

106. Although several ministers, including Halifax, questioned Chamberlain's policies, the Cabinet avoided a decision on whether to embark on war with Germany were Beneš to reject Hitler's demands; I. Colvin, *The Chamberlain Cabinet: How the meetings in 10 Downing Street, 1937–1939, led to the Second World War* (London, 1971), pp. 162–5.

107. Litvinov had told Andrew Rothstein the previous evening that 'the English would sell the Czechs down the river'; Sheinis, *Litvinov*, p. 291.

108. Gamelin did not think much of the Maginot Line either, warning Hore-Belisha that it might still take quite a while to complete the fortification of its northern and southern sections; R.J. Minney (ed.), *The Private Papers of Hore-Belisha* (New York, 1961), p. 168.

109. He was referring to Chamberlain's infamous radio statement of 27 September, in the wake of the war scare, which led to trenches being dug in London's parks while anti-aircraft guns were mounted: 'How horrible, fantastic, incredible it is, that we should be digging trenches and trying on gas-masks here, because of a quarrel in a faraway country between people of whom we know nothing…'; quoted in E.R. May, *Strange Victory: Hitler's conquest of France* (New York, 2000), p. 165.

110. Sylvester, Lloyd George's secretary, candidly describes in his diary the reaction to the news of Hitler's invitation to a summit in Munich which reached Chamberlain as he was speaking: 'For at least 60 seconds the Prime Minister, looking away from the table, perused these documents. Meantime, the whole House was so silent that one could hear a pin drop … I shall never forget the demonstration which followed [once Chamberlain announced his

intentions of flying to Germany], unexampled in my experience or in that of anybody else I have met. Every Government supporter rose and waving handkerchiefs and order papers cheered and cheered and cheered to the echo for several minutes.' Chamberlain himself confessed that the time of the delivery of the invitation 'was a piece of drama that no work of fiction ever surpassed'. In his rather succinct diary, nonetheless, Dawson exalted 'the most dramatic occasion – the House & galleries absolutely packed', hanging on Chamberlain's account of his 'last last effort ... the house was unmistakably with him all through'. Though Maisky had just missed the drama, he could not but be aware of the effusive support for Chamberlain; Sylvester papers, diary, A45, 28 Sept. 1938; Self, *Chamberlain Diary Letters*, IV, p. 349, 2 Oct. 1938; and Dawson papers, diary, Box 42, 28 Sep. 1938.

111. 'We all had to face facts,' Halifax apologized, 'and one of these facts was, as he very well knew, that the heads of the German Government and of the Italian Government would not be willing ... to sit in conference with Soviet representative'; TNA FO 371 21743 C11100/1941/18; and Maisky's report in *DVP*, 1938, XXI, doc. 390. See also Carley, *1939*, pp. 72–3.

112. Maisky was at pains to convince Narkomindel that Halifax still displayed an interest in the proposal made by Litvinov to De La Warr in Geneva, entertaining the rather fanciful idea that Czechoslovakia would sign a non-aggression pact with Germany, while Britain, France and the Soviet Union would guarantee her borders. Moreover, Churchill, whom he met on the same day, not only praised the Soviet stand during the crisis, but elaborated on the growing opposition to Chamberlain's policies within the Cabinet. Likewise, the Labour leaders seemed to be united in their opposition to a settlement. A few days later, Maisky highlighted the press's criticism of the Munich Agreement. After being briefed by Cadogan about the Munich Agreement, he had to concede, though, that when it came to the guarantees 'there was no mention of the USSR'; *DVP*, 1938, XXI, doc. 391; and Russian Foreign Ministry, *God Krizisa: 1938–1939: dokumenty i materialy* (Moscow, 1990) (hereafter *God Krizisa*), I, nos. 13 & 14, 29 & 30 Sept. 1938, respectively. He did little to convey the exuberant welcome which awaited Chamberlain on his way from Heston aerodrome to Buckingham Palace. D. Dilks (ed.), *The Diaries of Sir Alexander Cadogan 1938–1945* (London, 1971), pp. 110–11.

113. TNA FO 371 N5164/97/38, Chilston to Halifax, 18 Oct. 1938.

114. A. Gromyko et al. (eds), *Soviet Peace Efforts on the Eve of World War II (September 1938–August 1939)* (Moscow, 1973) (hereafter *SPE*), doc. 10, 1 Oct. 1938.

115. *DVP*, 1938, XXI, doc. 408, 3 Oct. 1938. See also Haslam, *The Soviet Union and the Struggle for Collective Security*, pp. 195–7.

116. Lloyd George papers, LG/G/14/1/9, 4 Oct. 1938, Maisky to Lloyd George; Maisky to Churchill, reproduced in M. Gilbert, *Winston S. Churchill: The prophet of truth, 1922–1939* (London, 2009). *SPE*, pp. 1199–1200, 4 Oct. 1938. RAN f.1702 op.4 d.1357 l.4 & d.940 l.9 & d.1357 l.5, 5, 10 & 11 Oct. 1938, Eden to Maisky. See also, *Izvestiya*, 11 Oct. 1938, quoted in *SPE*, doc. 15. On the Winterton affair, see Maisky's report to Moscow, *God Krizisa*, I, no. 21. Maisky further reported to Moscow that his refutations received due attention in the British press, *DVP*, 1938, XXI, doc. 419.

117. *Hansard*, HC Deb 14 November 1938, vol. 341, cols 648–54.

118. Report by Te Water, the South African high commissioner, from London, quoted in Fry, 'Agents and structures', p. 310. See also McDonald, *A Man of the Times*, p. 44. When he

met Cadogan on 30 September, Maisky was 'disgruntled and complaining'; Dilks, *Diaries of Sir Alexander Cadogan*, p. 110.

119. Webb, diary, 31 Oct. 1938, p. 6567.

120. Webb, diary, 31 Oct. 1938, pp. 6566–7 (emphasis in original). In retrospect, Maisky indeed maintained that, in the wake of the Munich Agreement, the Soviet government decided 'to have done with Geneva and retire into a well-protected isolation'; Dalton papers, II, 5/2, record of a meeting between Boothby and Maisky, 15 Sept. 1939. For a similar impression that was gained, see B.H. Liddell Hart, *The Liddell Hart Memoirs* (London, 1965), pp. 167, 194–5.

121. RAN f.1702 op.4 d.1115 l.1, 10 Oct. 1938; and Dalton, *Fateful Years*, p. 185; see also Aster, 'Ivan Maisky and parliamentary anti-appeasement', p. 336. Maisky told B. Pares, *A Wandering Student: The Story of a purpose* (London, 1948), p. 360, that the Russians would wait for another six months or so to see whether the British government would 'stick' to the Munich policy, and if they did, he warned, 'we shall lock our own doors and see to our own defence'.

122. The hopes Maisky had pinned on Lloyd George were dashed when the latter, who felt he 'had bossed the whole world for years, and had unrivalled knowledge', was entirely ignored by the prime minister. He further followed the counsel of his family and fobbed off the demands of the Liberals to participate in the parliamentary debate on the Munich Agreement. Two weeks later he relented somewhat, delivering a highly critical but ultimately ineffectual broadcast speech, which ended with the words: 'history will ask but one question: Is incompetence a justification for bad faith?'; Sylvester papers, diary, A45, 9 Sep., 3 & 26 Oct. 1938. Lloyd George's views on international affairs were erratic, though throughout his political career he was consistently in favour of harmonious Anglo-German relations. The Munich Agreement, however, turned him firmly against Germany, and he castigated Chamberlain for his surrender to Hitler. He increasingly became the object of Maisky's anti-appeasement efforts in England; see K.O. Morgan, 'Lloyd George and Germany', *The Historical Journal*, 39/3 (1996).

123. Maisky's ironic comments were later adopted almost verbatim by Stalin in his famous 'Chestnuts' speech of March 1939, see commentary following the diary entry for 12 March 1939.

124. Maisky's dismissal of Halifax's ideologized outlook on Soviet foreign policy is confirmed and further elaborated in Halifax's own report; TNA FO 371 21745 C12100/1941/18.

125. Maisky's predictions proved right once again. Stafford Cripps's attempts to create a united front of the communists, the Social League (which he founded in 1937) and the Independent Labour Party were frustrated by Labour. Cripps was in fact expelled from the Labour Party in 1939; Clarke, *The Cripps Version*, pp. 65–7.

126. 'Your conversations with the Labourites,' responded Litvinov, 'produce the impression that the latter are quite helpless. The immediate future evidently belongs to Chamberlain.' Litvinov had become sceptical of the ability of the British 'to oppose the onslaught of the aggressors even if they want to'; *SPE*, p. 65; G. Roberts, 'The fall of Litvinov: A revisionist view', *Journal of Contemporary History*, 27/4 (1992), p. 646.

127. On 13 October, TASS published Maisky's statement: 'As reported by the British press, Lord Winterton said in his speech that the Soviet Union allegedly did not render assistance during the crisis over Czechoslovakia and in consequence of its military weakness confined itself to vague promises. Winterton's allegation completely distorts the actual stand of the Soviet government on the Czechoslovak question. The USSR's stand on this question had been formulated clearly and definitely, leaving no room for vagueness, by People's Commissar for Foreign Affairs M.M. Litvinov in his speech at the plenum session of the League of Nations in Geneva on 21 September. Summing up his talk with the French chargé d'affaires in Moscow on 8 September 1938, Litvinov said in his speech that the USSR intended to fulfil all its obligations under the Soviet–Czechoslovak pact and render the necessary assistance to Czechoslovakia together with France by all available means. Litvinov further added that the USSR military department was ready to commence talks with representatives of the general staffs of France and Czechoslovakia in order to outline concrete measures for joint action.'

128. Printed in *Izvestiya*, 14 October 1938 and referred to also in the following cuttings attached to the diary which appeared in the British press: *Manchester Guardian* of 13 and 14 October, and 4 November, and *The Times* of 4 November 1938.

129. The full title was 'minister for coordination of defence'.

130. On the context of those meetings, see Carley, *1939*, pp. 78–9.

131. Hitler indeed issued a secret directive on 21 October 1938, ordering the Wehrmacht to rout the remaining part of Czechoslovakia, as well as to capture Memel. A month later, similar instructions were handed down for the capture of Danzig.

132. During the Nazi period, the popular 'Die Lorelei', written by Maisky's favourite poet, Heinrich Heine – a Jew – was attributed to 'an unknown poet'.

133. Maisky's extra-parliamentary activities had become so pronounced that they were reported by the French ambassador to Paris, *DDF*, 2 Serie, XIII, Doc. 313.

134. See, for instance, RAN f.1702 op.4 d.1325 l.1, Dalton to Maisky; d.1367 ll.7–8, Cummings, editor of *News Chronicle*, to Maisky, 27 Dec.; d.1357 l.6, Eden to Maisky, 30 Dec. 1938.

135. Exchange of letters between Maisky and Litvinov, *God Krizisa*, I, nos. 42, 60 & 71, 25 Oct., 25 Nov. & 4 Dec. 1938.

136. N.J. Crowson, *Facing Fascism: The Conservative Party and the European dictators, 1935–1940* (London, 1997), pp. 331–2.

137. Quoted in I. Ivanov et al. (eds), *Essays on the History of the Russian Ministry of Foreign Affairs* (Moscow, 2002), II, p. 201; RAN f.1702 op.4 d.143 l.62, Maisky to Litvinov, 10 Nov. 1937.

138. Mikhail Ksenofontovich Sokolov started his career as a prolific innovative suprematist painter and ended up painting in a socialist realist fashion as a member of the Moscow Institute of Painters and Graphic Artists (1936–38). It was during this time that Stalin commissioned from him the portrait, as well as a painting of Lenin's arrival at the Finland Station to take charge of the revolution in Russia in 1917. Stalin is depicted disembarking from the train, following Lenin, although he had actually not been present. In 1938, Sokolov was arrested and banished, imprisoned for seven years in Siberia.

139. AVP RF f.017 op.1 pop.15 p.3 ll.16–18.